Max Horkheimer and the Foundations of the Frankfurt School

This book is the first comprehensive intellectual biography of Max Horkheimer during the early and middle phases of his life (1895–1941). Drawing on unexamined new sources, John Abromeit describes the critical details of Horkheimer's intellectual development. This study recovers and reconstructs the model of early Critical Theory that guided the work of the Institute for Social Research in the 1930s. Horkheimer is remembered primarily as the coauthor of *Dialectic of Enlightenment*, which he wrote with Theodor W. Adorno in the early 1940s. Yet few people realize that Horkheimer and Adorno did not begin working together seriously until the late 1930s, or that the model of Critical Theory developed by Horkheimer and Erich Fromm in the late 1920s and early 1930s differs in crucial ways from *Dialectic of Enlightenment*. Abromeit highlights the ways in which Horkheimer's early Critical Theory remains relevant to contemporary theoretical discussions in a wide variety of fields.

John Abromeit is an assistant professor in the Department of History and Social Studies Education at State University of New York, Buffalo State. He is the coeditor of *Herbert Marcuse: Heideggerian Marxism* (2005) and *Herbert Marcuse: A Critical Reader* (2004), and his articles and book reviews have appeared in *Theory and Society, Theory, Culture and Society, Radical Philosophy*, and *Constellations*. Professor Abromeit previously held a Harper-Schmidt postdoctoral position in the social sciences in the University of Chicago Society of Fellows.

Max Horkheimer and the Foundations of the Frankfurt School

JOHN ABROMEIT

State University of New York, Buffalo State

CAMBRIDGE
UNIVERSITY PRESS

CAMBRIDGE UNIVERSITY PRESS
Cambridge, New York, Melbourne, Madrid, Cape Town,
Singapore, São Paulo, Delhi, Mexico City

Cambridge University Press
The Edinburgh Building, Cambridge CB2 8RU, UK

Published in the United States of America by Cambridge University Press, New York

www.cambridge.org
Information on this title: www.cambridge.org/9781107660656

First published 2011
First paperback edition 2013

A catalogue record for this publication is available from the British Library

Library of Congress Cataloguing in Publication Data
Abromeit, John, 1970–
Max Horkheimer and the foundations of the Frankfurt School / John Abromeit.
p.   cm.
Includes bibliographical references and index.
ISBN 978-1-107-00695-9 (hardback)
1. Horkheimer, Max, 1895–1973.   2. Frankfurt school of sociology.
3. Critical theory.   I. Title.
B3279.H8474A825   2011
193–dc22   2010043680

ISBN 978-1-107-00695-9 Hardback
ISBN 978-1-107-66065-6 Paperback

Contents

Acknowledgments

This project has been a long time in the making and I have incurred many debts along the way. I would like to thank first the organizations that have given me financial assistance, especially the German Academic Exchange Service and the Department of History at the University of California, Berkeley, which both provided me with generous research and writing grants. I have benefited in less tangible but certainly no less valuable ways from five different intellectual communities in which I have had the privilege and pleasure to participate since the early 1990s. I first encountered Critical Theory as an undergraduate at Stanford University in the stimulating seminars of Russell Berman. Barry Kātz first made me aware of the Critical Theory archives in Frankfurt and provided excellent guidance for my undergraduate honors thesis on Marcuse and Heidegger. During my first extended stay in Frankfurt, from 1993 to 1995, I encountered Critical Theory as a living tradition in the lectures of Jürgen Habermas and the seminars of Alfred Schmidt. I would like to thank Professor Schmidt in particular for drawing my attention to the centrality of philosophical materialism to the Critical Theoretical tradition from Horkheimer's early essays to Adorno's late *magna opera*. To my delight, I discovered that the tradition of Critical Theory was also still very much alive outside the academy in Frankfurt. I owe a particular debt to the members of the international political quarterly *PERSPEKTIVEN*, whose impressive work in the mid-1990s demonstrated that Critical Theory could still illuminate political conflicts around the world and, in some cases, even suggest ways to productively intervene. I would like to thank the cofounders of the newspaper, Michael Werz and Helga Flores Trejo, as well as the other members of the editorial board – including Bagher Afshani, Harry Bauer, Jochen Freyberg, Said Hosseini, Sven Jahn, Thomas Kimmig, Heike Litzinger, Christian Meidert, Rafael Mrowczynski, Jana Müller-Gerber, Achim Seifert, and, most of all, Nenad Stefanov – not just for all the engaging discussions, but also for making me feel so at home in Frankfurt. I am also grateful to Stephan Bundschuh – whom I first met in the Herbert Marcuse Archive in 1992 and whose high intellectual and political standards have always impressed me – for his generosity and friendship over the years. When I returned to Frankfurt in 1999, Matthias Lutz-Bachmann and Axel Honneth kindly invited me to participate in their graduate philosophy colloquia. I would like to thank both of them for this opportunity and also for the helpful advice and support they gave me on my project. Detlev Claussen provided me with many valuable insights into Critical Theory as well as a much-appreciated opportunity to teach and participate in discussions in the Sociology Department at the University of Hannover. I am grateful to Helmut Reinicke and Annette Ohme for inviting me to present some of my early research at the University of Flensburg and also for hosting a workshop for our Frankfurt Marx reading group. Other friends and colleagues in Frankfurt who provided valuable intellectual and/or personal support include Odette Barbosa, Alex Demirovic, Thorsten Fath, Graeme Gilloch,, Iris Harnischmacher, Katharina Hartmann, Peter-Erwin Jansen, Jaeho Kang, Andreas Niederberger, Soraya Nour, José Manuel Romero, Olivier Voirol, and Ersin Yildiz. Finally, I owe a special thanks to the successive directors of the Max Horkheimer Archive in Frankfurt. Although Gunzelin Schmid Noerr was just completing his tenure as director when I began working in the archive, my research was facilitated greatly by the remarkable care and conscientiousness with which he carried out his duties as the principal editor of the nineteen-volume *Gesammelte Schriften* edition of Horkheimer's writings. I am, as all future scholars of Horkheimer will be, in his debt for this exemplary work. The next two directors of the Horkheimer Archive, Jochen Stollberg and Stefan Roeper, both donated their time and expertise generously to me at various stages in the project.

During my graduate studies at UC Berkeley I benefited greatly from the lively intellectual life in the History Department and throughout the campus as a whole. I owe a tremendous debt to my dissertation advisor, Martin Jay, who has generously provided me with extremely valuable support and guidance throughout the entire course of this project. It has been a true privilege to work with the historian who has done more than anyone to introduce and establish the tradition of Critical Theory in the English-speaking world. I also thank Martin Jay for introducing me to Samir Gandesha in Berkeley in 1997. It didn't take me long to realize that Samir is not just an outstanding Adorno scholar, but also an accomplished practitioner of the difficult art of negative dialectics. I have benefited immensely from his careful reading of and astute comments on the manuscript from the earliest stages to the very end. Other friends and colleagues in the Bay Area who provided me with valuable intellectual and/or personal support include Rakesh Bandari, Matt Erlin, Tina Gerhardt, David Hollinger, Robert Holub, Donna Jones, Ben Lazier, Sam Moyn, Donna Murch, Scott Murtishaw, Noah Shusterman, Ania Wertz, and, of course, Randall Wright.

During my four years of postdoctoral work at the University of Chicago, when I transformed my dissertation into a book, I was privileged to participate in two different groups of impressive scholars: the Society of Fellows and the Social Theory Workshop. I benefited greatly from my affiliation with both. I owe a particular debt to Moishe Postone – in whose thought and writing the best traditions of Critical Theory are alive and well – for his intellectual example and his comments on the chapters I presented in the Social Theory workshop. I would also like to thank William Sewell and Gary Herrigel for many stimulating and challenging discussions. I owe much to Richard Westerman, whose impressive knowledge of Kierkegaard, Husserl, and Lukács was a great help as we worked through Adorno's early writings together. I would also like to thank the following friends and colleagues from Chicago: Janet Afary, Kevin Anderson, Jason Dawsey, Parker Everett, Joe Feinberg, Deborah Gould, Chris Hayden, David Ingram, Reha Kadakal, Loren Langman, Mark Loeffler, Pierre-François Noppen, Danny Postel, Andrew Sartori, and Joe Sexauer.

Since moving to Buffalo in January 2009, I have become part of another lively intellectual community. I would like to thank my colleagues in the History and Social Studies Education Department at SUNY, Buffalo State, for welcoming me so warmly and for allowing me to delay my appointment one semester in order to finish this book. I would like to extend a special thanks to the chair of our department, David Carson, for his support, and also to my colleagues Gary Marotta and York Norman, for their intellectual camaraderie. Georg Iggers, professor emeritus of history at the University at Buffalo, has generously shared his knowledge and time with me. Becoming better acquainted with him and his wife, Wilma Iggers, and learning more about their impressive scholarly and political work as well as their remarkable lives has been a real inspiration for me.

In addition to the aforementioned communities of scholars and intellectuals in which I have had the good fortune to participate, there are a number of other individuals I would like to thank. Few people know the entire Frankfurt School tradition as well as Marcos Nobre, and I have learned much from the many conversations I have had with him over the past decade. I would like to thank him and his colleagues, especially Ricardo Terra and José Rodrigo Rodriguez, for introducing me to the remarkable group of scholars working in São Paulo on the Frankfurt School and for giving me the opportunity to present my work there on two separate occasions. I thank Mark Cobb for inviting me to give a talk on Horkheimer at Pensacola State College and for all the stimulating discussions we have had on Critical Theory, philosophy, and progressive politics since we organized the Herbert Marcuse conference together in 1998. Richard Wolin, whom I first met at the Berkeley Marcuse conference, has read and provided helpful comments on several of the chapters. I would like to thank him, Jerrold Siegel, and the other members of the New York City–area intellectual historians group for giving me an opportunity to present my work there. I am indebted to Thomas Wheatland for sharing his insider's knowledge of the academic publishing world and giving me valuable advice about how to navigate within it. I have always looked forward to and benefited from the discussions I have had over the past fifteen years with Lars Rensmann, whose profound knowledge of the *traurige Wissenschaft* of Critical Theory has, thankfully, not yet led him into the clutches of *l'esprit de sérieux*. I am grateful to Stefano Giachetti for the invitation to present my work at one of the remarkable conferences on Critical Theory he has organized in Rome over the past decade. Others who have read and provided helpful comments on various chapters include Vance Bell, Gad Horowitz, Paul Robinson, and Joel Whitebook.

Finally, I would like to thank the individuals who have made the actual production of this book possible. I am grateful in particular to my editor at Cambridge University Press, Eric Crahan, and the head of the production team at Newgen Publishing, Rajashri Ravindranathan, for their patience and professionalism. I am also very grateful to David Ingram, John McCole, and Kevin Anderson for their careful reading of the manuscript and the many helpful comments they provided.

I would like to dedicate this book with gratitude to the members of my immediate family: my parents, Shannon and Duane Abromeit; my grandmother, Betty Abromeit; my sister, Erin Bass; and my partner, Deirdra Bishop. Without their ongoing encouragement and support this project, and most of the other good things in my life, would not have been possible.

A Note on References and Permissions

Throughout the footnotes "GS" refers to the nineteen-volume *Collected Writings* edition of Horkheimer's works: Max Horkheimer, *Gesammelte Schriften*, eds. Alfred Schmidt and Gunzelin Schmid Noerr (Frankfurt a.M.: Fischer Verlag, 1985–1996).

"**MHA**" refers to the Max Horkheimer Archive in the Stadt- und Universitätsbibliothek, J. W. Goethe University, Frankfurt a.M.

Unpublished manuscripts, letters, and photos from the Max Horkheimer Archive have been used with permission of the Archive Center of the Stadt- und Universitätsbibliothek, Frankfurt a.M.

Unpublished manuscripts from the following sources have also been cited with permission:

Germaine Krull Papers; used with permission from the Museum Folkwang, Essen, Germany.

Theodor Adorno, "Kant's Critique of Rational Psychology"; used with permission of Theodor Adorno Archive, Frankfurt a.M.

Felix Weil's "Lebenserinnerungen"; used with permission from Institut für Stadtgeschichte Frankfurt a.M.

Max Horkheimer, "Bemerkung in Sachen der Habilitation Dr. Wiesengrund"; used with permission of the Archiv des Dekanats der Philosophischen Fakultät of the J. W. Goethe University.

Introduction

To judge something that has substance and solid worth is quite easy; to comprehend it is much harder; producing an adequate representation of it, which unifies
judgment and comprehension, is the most difficult of all.

Hegel, Preface to the *Phenomenology of Spirit*

WHY A NEW STUDY OF HORKHEIMER
AND EARLY CRITICAL THEORY?

This study has two main purposes, which overlap but are not identical. First,
it is intended as a comprehensive intellectual biography of Max Horkheimer
from 1895, when he was born, to 1941, which marks the threshold of a new
phase in Horkheimer's life and thought.[1] Several excellent general studies of
the development of Critical Theory[2] as a whole have been written.[3] However,
the publication of Horkheimer's *Collected Writings* and the opening of the
Max Horkheimer Archives have made available much previously unknown or
unavailable material, which has made a reassessment of Horkheimer's work

[1] Nineteen forty-one marks a logical place to end a study of the early and middle phases of his
intellectual biography for several reasons. In that year, Horkheimer reduced to a bare minimum
the activities of the New York branch of the Institute for Social Research and discontinued the
publication of the Institute's journal so he could move to Los Angeles, where he could dedicate
himself to his theoretical work unencumbered by any practical or administrative responsibilities. Nineteen forty-one also marked the culmination of a rather dramatic shift in Horkheimer's
thought. The beginnings of this shift are best symbolized by Theodor Adorno's arrival in New
York and his appointment as a full member of the Institute in 1938 on the one hand, and the
departure of Erich Fromm from the Institute the following year on the other. Although not the
only factor in the transformation of Horkheimer's thought during this time, his closer working
relationship with Adorno in the period 1938–41 did much to push Horkheimer away from some
of the key theoretical positions he had developed in the early and mid-1930s. For a more detailed
examination of this shift see Excursuses I and II and Chapter 9.

[2] Although the concept of "critical theory" is normally much more diffuse in the Anglo-American
world, I shall follow the German convention here by using it to refer specifically to Horkheimer
and the Frankfurt School tradition. In order to distinguish my use of the term in this specific way,
I will capitalize it throughout.

[3] Most notably, Martin Jay, *The Dialectical Imagination: A History of the Frankfurt School and
the Institute of Social Research, 1923–1950* (Boston, Toronto, and London: Little Brown, 1973),
and Rolf Wiggershaus, *The Frankfurt School: Its History, Theories and Political Significance*,
trans. Michael Robertson (Cambridge MA, MIT Press, 1994). See also David Held, *Introduction
to Critical Theory: Horkheimer to Habermas* (Berkeley and Los Angeles: University of California
Press, 1980) and Douglas Kellner, *Critical Theory, Marxism and Modernity* (Baltimore: The
Johns Hopkins Press, 1989).

possible. This study draws on this material as well as the extensive secondary literature on Horkheimer in German and the much less extensive literature in English. In general, the focus is directed primarily – and unapologetically – to Horkheimer's thought. Examination of the biographical details of Horkheimer's life or the lives of those who influenced him is in most cases limited to what is necessary to explain the development of his ideas. In the first two chapters, which treat Horkheimer's childhood, youth, and student years, more attention is devoted to biographical context. Beginning with the third chapter, Horkheimer's theoretical work and those writings of his colleagues, which contribute to an understanding of his own writings, become the central concern. Although I have sought to refer to and build on earlier scholarship rather than repeat it, some repetition has been unavoidable in order to present a coherent narrative. To be sure, I have drawn on previous, general treatments of the history of Critical Theory, such Martin Jay's still unsurpassed *Dialectical Imagination* and Rolf Wiggershaus's *The Frankfurt School*, but I have also sought to revise and deepen their accounts, when necessary. In addition, the principal and subsidiary arguments presented here have been developed in dialogue with a number of other authors who have written studies that either focus primarily on Horkheimer or present particularly incisive or influential interpretations of his work.[4]

The second main purpose of this study is to recover and reconstruct the model of "early Critical Theory" that largely coincides but is not identical with Horkheimer's own thought from the late 1920s to the mid-1930s. I have chosen to focus on Horkheimer's early Critical Theory here for a number of reasons. As will become apparent in the remaining pages of this introduction, I believe that Horkheimer's early work was not only his best, but also that which has the potential to contribute most to contemporary discussions and attempts to renew Critical Theory. Horkheimer's early Critical Theory is much less familiar today than *Dialectic of Enlightenment* or even *Eclipse of Reason*. Horkheimer's commitment in the 1930s to expressing himself primarily in essays (and aphorisms) rather than books has contributed to the neglect of his early writings. Yet taken together, the essays (and aphorisms) Horkheimer wrote during this time constitute a very substantial body of work that is eminently worthy of reconsideration. Of these essays, only Horkheimer's 1931

---

[4] Among the former group of authors, I have engaged most with the following studies: Helmut Dubiel, *Theory and Politics: Studies in the Development of Critical Theory*, trans. Benjamin Gregg (Cambridge, MA: MIT Press, 1985); Gerd-Walter Küsters, *Der Kritikbegriff in der Kritischen Theorie Max Horkheimers* (Frankfurt and New York: Campus, 1980); Peter Stirk, *Max Horkheimer: A New Interpretation*, (Hemel Hempstead: Harvester Wheatsheaf, 1992); Olaf Asbach, *Von der Erkenntnistheorie zur Kritischen Theorie des Gesellschaft: Eine Untersuchung zur Vor- und Entstehungsgeschichte der Kritischen Theorie Max Horkheimers 1920–27*, (Opladen, Germany: Leske und Budrich, 1997) and *Kritische Gesellschaftstheorie und historische Praxis: Entwicklungen der Kritischen Theorie bei Max Horkheimer 1930–1942/43* (Frankfurt and New York: Peter Lang, 1997). Among the latter group of authors, I have engaged most with the following: Alfred Schmidt, Jürgen Habermas, Axel Honneth, Gunzelin Schmid Noerr, Moishe Postone, and Hauke Brunkhorst. For references to their numerous works on Horkheimer, please consult the bibliography or the various discussions of them in the main text.

inaugural address as the new director of the Institute for Social Research, "The Present Situation of Social Philosophy and the Tasks of an Institute for Social Research," and his 1937 programmatic essay, "Traditional and Critical Theory," remain somewhat familiar today. However, this focus on what are interpreted as Horkheimer's "methodological" essays from the 1930s has contributed to a misleading view of the overall aims – and accomplishments – of his early Critical Theory.[5] The systematic interpretation and overview presented here of Horkheimer's work in the 1920s and 1930s will enable these aims and accomplishments to emerge more clearly and, hopefully, will also spark a renewed engagement with this remarkable body of work.

Recovering the model of early Critical Theory also requires a reexamination of Horkheimer's personal and, more importantly, theoretical relationships with Erich Fromm and Theodor Adorno in the late 1920s and 1930s. The acrimonious debates that marked Fromm's departure from the Institute in 1939 and continued with other members of the Institute – most notably Adorno and Herbert Marcuse – have obscured the important contributions Fromm made to the formation of early Critical Theory, so significant attention will be paid here to Fromm's own intellectual development and the strong affinities between his and Horkheimer's work during this time. Because Horkheimer is often remembered today primarily as the coauthor (with Adorno) of *Dialectic of Enlightenment*, I will also devote much attention here to working out the important theoretical differences that existed between him and Adorno from the late 1920s through the late 1930s. When Horkheimer and Adorno met in the mid-1920s, they had many common interests and even a shared academic advisor in Hans Cornelius. So why did the two of them part ways theoretically in the late 1920s, and why did these differences persist through the 1930s? In order fully to grasp the distinctiveness of the model of early Critical Theory and, in particular, the important ways in which it differs from *Dialectic of Enlightenment*, it is necessary to reconstruct Horkheimer's shifting attitude toward Adorno's theoretical writings in the 1920s and 1930s.

To further elaborate the main aims of this study, it would be helpful to say a few words about the title and the concept of "foundations," in particular. On the one hand, the foundations of Horkheimer's early Critical Theory were antifoundational insofar as they were thoroughly historical and not ontological or metaphysical. On the other hand, it was essential to Horkheimer to recognize that all of the theoretical concepts he developed were related in more or less mediated ways to the historical epoch in which he was living – what he called the "bourgeois epoch." Perhaps the most important way in which Critical Theory differed from its "traditional" counterparts was its refusal to naturalize modern bourgeois capitalist society and its attempt to identify the contradictions and tendencies that could possibly – if by no means necessarily – lead to a qualitatively new postcapitalist and postbourgeois historical epoch. This presupposition of a historically discrete, but still incomplete bourgeois epoch forms the basis of Horkheimer's work through the late 1930s. However, one can and must speak of the historical foundations of Horkheimer's early

[5] See discussion in Chapter 7, pp. 258–9.

Critical Theory in a more precise sense, for it is the historical transformation and antagonistic dynamic of modern bourgeois society or, in other words, the *dialectic of bourgeois society* that structured his thought at the most general level during this time. The meaning of this concept will become fully apparent in the further course of this study, but a preliminary determination of it can be found in Horkheimer's 1937 essay, "Traditional and Critical Theory":

> To put it in broad terms, the theory says that the basic form of the historically given commodity economy on which modern history rests contains in itself the internal and external contradictions of the modern era; it generates these contradictions over and over again in an increasingly heightened form; and after a period of progress, development of human powers, and emancipation of the individual, after an enormous extension of human control over nature, it finally hinders further development and drives humanity into a new barbarism.[6]

This dialectic first moved to the center of Horkheimer's work in his lectures on the history of philosophy in the late 1920s. There, and in many other essays he wrote in the 1930s, the concept was formulated in less economistic terms than in the previously quoted passage. As we shall see, the philosophical dimensions of the dialectic of bourgeois society were crucial for Horkheimer. He took very seriously the critical philosophical ideals that were articulated during the ascent of the European bourgeoisie during the early modern period, but he also came to believe that these ideals were increasingly hollowed out with the consolidation of capitalism and the gradual transformation of the bourgeoisie from an oppositional to a hegemonic social formation in the eighteenth and nineteenth centuries.

The title of this study also implies that the tradition of "Frankfurt School" Critical Theory has its foundations in Horkheimer's early work. This implication is intended, but it must be qualified in certain ways. The "Frankfurt School" label is useful to designate in a general way a tradition of critical social theory that has certain important continuities; but the label is problematic insofar as it obscures the qualitative shifts and transformations this tradition has undergone. Although there is little question that the "Frankfurt School" tradition first took shape in Horkheimer's early writings, *Dialectic of Enlightenment* represents a qualitatively different model that fits seamlessly into the larger trajectory of Adorno's work, but represents a break with Horkheimer's early Critical Theory. Habermas's early work – especially his *Structural Transformation of the Public Sphere*[7] – bears strong affinities to the model of early Critical Theory in general, and to the idea of a dialectic of bourgeois society in particular. Yet in the following years, Habermas would develop a theory of communicative action that, despite his continuing gestures to the relevance of Horkheimer's early work, represented another qualitatively new paradigm within Frankfurt School Critical Theory. My intention here is not to uphold Horkheimer's early work as a rigid orthodoxy that disavows or precludes any further innovations

---

[6] "Traditional and Critical Theory," in *Max Horkheimer, Critical Theory: Selected Essays*, trans. Matthew J. O'Connell (New York: Continuum, 1972), p. 227 (translation amended).

[7] Jürgen Habermas, *The Structural Transformation of the Public Sphere: An Inquiry into a Category of Bourgeois Society*, trans. Thomas Burger (Cambridge, MA: MIT Press, 1989).

in the tradition. Such dogmatic foundationalism would be antithetical to the fundamental openness of Horkheimer's early Critical Theory, according to which theoretical concepts must be constantly revised in light of new historical and empirical social research. I do believe, however, that Horkheimer's early work represents a distinct model that has been unjustly forgotten and could still contribute much to current attempts to develop a Critical Theory adequate to early twenty-first-century social and political conditions.

HORKHEIMER'S ECLIPSE IN THE ANGLO-AMERICAN RECEPTION OF CRITICAL THEORY

In the remainder of this introduction and in the epilogue, I will put forth my case for revisiting the model of early Critical Theory developed by Horkheimer (and Fromm). First, however, let us examine the reasons why Horkheimer's work has fared so poorly in the reception of Critical Theory in the Anglo-American world compared to that of the other members of the Frankfurt School tradition. One important cause of the eclipse of Horkheimer's work can be found already in his response to the changed political and historical conditions in Europe and the United States after World War II. After seventeen years in exile in the United States, Horkheimer returned to Frankfurt in 1950 to rebuild the Institute for Social Research and to play a role in the education of the first generation of German students after the catastrophic events of the war and the civilizational rupture of Auschwitz. Habermas's well-known anecdote, that Horkheimer kept his writings from the 1930s under lock and key in the basement of the rebuilt Institute for Social Research, is symptomatic of the dramatic shift in his thought that occurred after his return to Germany. Horkheimer became rector of the J.W. Goethe University in Frankfurt and was on friendly terms with many of the most important German and American figures in the postwar reconstruction of the Federal Republic, including Theodor Heuss and John J. McCloy.[8] Horkheimer's theoretical production came to a virtual halt and his public political pronouncements became increasingly conservative in the 1950s and 1960s. When his writings from the 1930s began to circulate once again in pirate editions during the tumultuous political climate of the 1960s, Horkheimer was reluctant to republish them. He finally did so only after distancing himself from them and arguing that the qualitatively different historical and political situation defied any unmediated application of his earlier work to present conditions. Horkheimer had, in other words, done much himself in the 1950s and 1960s to create the impression that his earlier work was no longer relevant to contemporary concerns. Anyone who takes seriously the "temporal core of truth," which was an essential characteristic of his Critical Theory throughout his life, is obligated to heed his warnings about appropriating his theoretical concepts in an ahistorical fashion. Yet

---

[8] McCloy was president of the World Bank from 1947 to 1949 and the High Commissioner for Germany, 1949–52. Heuss was the *Bundespräsident* of the Federal Republic from 1949 to 1959. For samples of Horkheimer's correspondence with these men, see GS 18, pp. 223–5, 460–2, and 525–7.

one must also recognize that social, political, and historical conditions have changed dramatically since the 1960s. If one rejects the static, positivist view of history – as Horkheimer did – and recognizes that any interpretation of historical events contains an essential subjective moment and that changed conditions in the present create new possibilities for interpreting and appropriating the past, then one need not view Horkheimer's warnings in the 1960s about the dated character of his earlier work as an absolute prohibition.

In Germany, Horkheimer and Adorno had already been prominent figures in scholarly and broader public discussions in the 1950s and early 1960s, even though the New Left and protest movements were important in the late 1960s in drawing further attention to their work.[9] With the exception of the reception of the Institute's *Studies in Prejudice* among American sociologists, Critical Theory remained relatively unknown in the United States prior to Herbert Marcuse's appearance in public debates in the late 1960s.[10] However, Marcuse's sudden rise to prominence proved to be a mixed blessing for the American reception of Critical Theory in the following decades.[11] As one commentator put it, "Unwonted media celebrity first 'gurufied' Marcuse ... then stamped his thoughts with the killing censorship of a fad whose time had passed."[12] Martin Jay's pioneering study of the history of the Frankfurt School and the Institute of Social Research, along with several other monographs, translations, edited anthologies, and journal articles in the 1970s on Critical Theory and/or particular Critical Theorists, left no doubt that their work deserved more serious attention.[13] Yet the academic reception of Critical Theory in the United States

[9] Horkheimer became head of the philosophy department and then rector of the J.W. Goethe University as a whole in the early 1950s. Although he played a crucial role in rebuilding the Institute for Social Research after the war and gave frequent public speeches and radio addresses, his intellectual production was limited, particularly compared to that of Adorno, who really found an audience for the first time in the Federal Republic in the 1950s and 1960s. On Horkheimer and Adorno's roles as public intellectuals in the postwar period, see Detlev Claussen, *Theodor Adorno: Ein Letztes Genie* (Frankfurt: Fischer, 2004), pp. 265ff. and Stephan Müller-Doohm, *Theodor Adorno: Eine Biographie* (Frankfurt: Suhrkamp, 2004), pp. 554–679.

[10] The best examination of the American reception of the work of Horkheimer and the other members of the Institute is Thomas Wheatland's recent study, *The Frankfurt School in Exile* (Minneapolis and London: University of Minnesota Press, 2009). Wheatland demonstrates that a few members of the New York intellectual community did take a serious interest in Horkheimer and his colleagues in the 1930s and 1940s. He also describes the positive reception among American sociologists not only of the *Studies in Prejudice*, but also the Institute's earlier empirical project, *the Studies on Authority and Family*. Yet he also points out that this early reception was much more limited than it could have been and that the Americans' reception of the Institute's empirical work failed fully to grasp the theoretical principles that had guided them. Thus, overall, his study confirms that a serious and comprehensive American reception of their work did not begin until the 1970s. For a more detailed discussion of Wheatland's study, see my review, "Reconsidering the History of the Frankfurt School in America," in *Reviews in American History*, vol. 39, No. 2 (June 2011).

[11] For an overview of the Anglo-American reception of Marcuse, see *Herbert Marcuse: A Critical Reader*, eds. John Abromeit and W. Mark Cobb (London and New York: Routledge, 2004), pp. 1–6, as well as the piece by W. Mark Cobb in the same volume, "Diatribes and Distortions: Marcuse's Academic Reception," pp. 163–87.

[12] Mike Davis, *City of Quartz: Excavating the Future in Los Angeles* (New York, 1992), p. 54.

[13] Martin Jay, *The Dialectical Imagination op. cit.* Other important monographs include Susan Buck-Morss, *The Origin of Negative Dialectics: Theodor W. Adorno, Walter Benjamin, and the*

remained uneven at best. Despite several first-rate studies of his life and work, Marcuse's theoretical and philosophical work had been largely forgotten by the mid-1980s.[14] A selection of some of Horkheimer's most important essays from the 1930s appeared in English translation in 1972. The first and only monograph dedicated to Horkheimer appeared in 1992, but it was written by a young British scholar and went largely unnoticed in the United States.[15] The next significant collection of Horkheimer's essays in English translation did not appear until 1993.[16]

By this time, however, the intellectual field had shifted decisively. French "poststructuralist" theory had become a dominant force in the Anglo-American academy.[17] With their thoroughgoing skepticism of "grand narratives" of progress in history and science and their efforts to reorient Critical Theory toward the concrete particular, Adorno and Benjamin's work resonated in some – if certainly not all – ways with the "postmodernism" and/or "poststructuralism" of Lyotard, Derrida, and Foucault.[18] Furthermore, because Adorno and Benjamin had devoted more attention to aesthetics and cultural theory than Horkheimer, their work was still of interest in language and literature departments, as well as interdisciplinary humanities and cultural studies programs, in which postmodern and poststructuralist theory established itself most successfully. Jürgen Habermas also established himself in the American academy in the 1980s and 1990s, but in different fields: in philosophy, and to a lesser extent, sociology and political science departments.[19] At least through the mid-1980s,

Frankfurt Institute (New York: Free Press, 1977); anthologies include *The Essential Frankfurt School Reader*, eds. Andrew Arato and Eike Gephardt (New York: Urizen, 1978); translations include Max Horkheimer and Theodor Adorno, *Dialectic of Enlightenment*, trans. John Cumming (New York: Continuum, 1972), Max Horkheimer, *Critical Theory* op. cit.; the journals that played the important role in introducing Critical Theory to an American audience in the 1970s were *Telos* and *New German Critique*.

[14] Morton Schoolman, *The Imaginary Witness: The Critical Theory of Herbert Marcuse* (New York: Free Press, 1980); Barry Kätz, *Herbert Marcuse and the Art of Liberation* (London: Verso, 1982); and Douglas Kellner, *Herbert Marcuse and the Crisis of Marxism* (London, 1984).

[15] Peter Stirk, *Max Horkheimer: A New Interpretation* (Hemel Hempstead, UK: Harvester Wheatsheaf, 1992).

[16] Max Horkheimer, *Between Philosophy and Social Science: Selected Early Essays*, trans. G. Frederick Hunter, Matthew S. Kramer, and John Torpey (Cambridge, MA: MIT Press, 1993).

[17] "Poststructuralism" was the term coined in the United States that referred in a very imprecise way to the diverse bodies of work of theorists such as Lyotard, Foucault, and Derrida. None of these theorists accepted the leveling of the differences between their work that the concept arguably implied.

[18] See, for example, Lyotard's essay "Adorno as the Devil," *Telos*, no. 19 (Spring, 1974); Derrida's appreciative discussion of Benjamin's controversial discussion of law and violence in "Force of Law: The Mystical Foundation of Authority," trans. Mary Quaintance, *Acts of Religion*. Ed. Gil Anidjar (New York: Routledge, 2002), pp. 228–98; and Derrida's discussion of Adorno and Benjamin in the speech he gave upon accepting the Theodor Adorno Prize from the city of Frankfurt in 2001: "Fichus," in Jacques Derrida, *Paper Machine*, trans. Rachel Bowlby (Stanford University Press, 2005), pp. 164–82. In a late interview, Foucault also emphasized the commonalities that existed between his own work and that of the Frankfurt School. See *Critique and Power: Recasting the Foucault/Habermas Debate*, ed. Michael Kelly (Cambridge MA: MIT Press, 1994), p. 117.

[19] Habermas's first work, *The Structural Transformation of the Public Sphere: An Enquiry into a Category of Bourgeois Society*, op. cit., which was originally published in 1962, but did

Habermas continued to present his own work as a critical reformulation of the theoretical project developed at the Institute for Social Research in the 1930s. Yet, since Habermas became increasingly focused on questions of liberal-democratic political philosophy and legal theory in the late 1980s and 1990s, few people doubt any longer that his work represented a profound break with the Critical Theory of Horkheimer, Adorno, and Marcuse. This break was illustrated by Habermas's reception in the United States, which – like his reception in Germany – expressed a need to move beyond what was perceived as obsolete in Critical Theory more than a need to draw on it in order to address contemporary problems.[20] Horkheimer's work, in which the philosophical, sociological, and historical moments all outweighed the aesthetic, did not find a place in American discussions of literature, humanities, and cultural studies, as had Adorno's and Benjamin's. By the 1980s, Horkheimer had also been eclipsed by Habermas in the reception of the Frankfurt School in American philosophy and sociology departments.

By the 1990s, those scholars and intellectuals still interested in Critical Theory had been split, for the most part, into three camps.[21] There were those who believed Jürgen Habermas had overcome the weaknesses of the first generation of Critical Theory and reformulated it in terms adequate to the changed historical conditions. Habermas's principal works were translated

not appear in English translation until 1989, stimulated much discussion among historians in the United States, as the following collection of essays makes clear: *Habermas and the Public Sphere*, ed. Craig Calhoun (Cambridge, MA: MIT Press, 1992). Since Habermas's move away in the mid-1960s from an understanding of modern European history as a "dialectic of bourgeois society" – which was indebted to Horkheimer's early Critical Theory – toward a more systematic and normative understanding of "modernity" as the differentiation of value spheres, his work has not resonated as much with historians. For a perceptive examination of this crucial shift in Habermas's theory of history, see John McCormick, *Weber, Habermas and the Transformations of the European State: Constitutional, Social and Supra-National Democracy* (Cambridge, UK and New York: Cambridge University Press, 2007).

[20] See, for example, Thomas McCarthy's "Translator's Introduction" to Jürgen Habermas, *The Theory of Communicative Action*, vol. 1: *Reason and Rationalization of Society* (Boston: Beacon, 1984), pp. v–xxxvii. Furthermore, as Russell Jacoby has pointed out – in "Das Veralten der Frankfurter Schule," in *Keine Kritische Theorie Ohne Amerika*, eds. O. Negt, D. Claussen and M. Werz (Frankfurt: Neue Kritik, 1999), p. 147 – the American reception of Habermas focused more on his strictly theoretical work, rather than the political interventions that have made him such an important figure in the German public sphere. A noteworthy exception to this trend was Robert Holub's study, *Jürgen Habermas: Critic in the Public Sphere* (New York and London, 1991) as well as the more recent study by Martin J. Matustik, *Jürgen Habermas: A Philosophical-Political Profile* (Lanham, MD: Rowman & Littlefield, 2001).

[21] Presenting the American reception of Critical Theory in this way is admittedly schematic and misleading in many ways, but it would go beyond my primary concern here – illustrating the general neglect of Horkheimer – to provide a more nuanced account. Thus, the three main tendencies in the American reception of Critical Theory in the 1980s and 1990s that I have named here are not intended as strict classifications, but simply as a preliminary means of orientation. For more detailed treatments of the American reception of Critical Theory in the 1980s and 1990s, which largely overlap with my account here, see Peter Hohendahl, *Reappraisals: Shifting Alignments in Postwar Critical Theory* (Ithaca NY: Cornell University Press, 1991), pp. 198–228, and Russell Jacoby, "Das Veralten der Frankfurter Schule," op. cit., pp. 132–49.

into English in the 1980s,[22] and his *Philosophical Discourse of Modernity* was seen by many sympathetic to Critical Theory as a compelling critique of French poststructuralism.[23] There were those who were less skeptical than Habermas about reconciling the traditions of Critical Theory and poststructuralism, either on philosophical or aesthetic grounds.[24] Finally, there were a few who were critical of both poststructuralism and Habermas's reformulation of Critical Theory.[25] Common to all three general positions, however, was a surprising lack of reflection on the origins of Critical Theory in Horkheimer's early work and the relevance it might still have for contemporary discussions. Although Jürgen Habermas stressed the ongoing importance of Horkheimer's original program, his American followers made little effort to reassess that legacy themselves.[26] They seemed to assume that the task had already been accomplished with Habermas's reformulation of Horkheimer's early interdisciplinary project in terms of a *Theory of Communicative Action*.[27] Those who sought some sort of reconciliation between poststructuralism and Critical Theory looked to the work of Walter Benjamin and, to a lesser degree, Theodor Adorno, often stressing their critiques of totalizing reason and their work on aesthetics and

[22] To name only the most important, *The Theory of Communicative Action*, vol. 1, *Reason and the Rationalization of Society*, and vol. 2, *Lifeworld and System: A Critique of Functionalist Reason*, trans. Thomas McCarthy (Boston, 1984 and 1987, respectively); *The Structural Transformation of the Public Sphere: An Inquiry into a Category of Bourgeois Society*, trans. Thomas Burger (Cambridge, MA: MIT Press, 1989) and *The Philosophical Discourse of Modernity*, trans. Frederick G. Lawrence (Cambridge, MA: MIT Press, 1987).

[23] Members of the first group, sympathetic to Habermas and generally hostile to poststructuralism, include Thomas McCarthy, Andrew Arato, Jean Cohen, Seyla Benhabib, and Richard Wolin.

[24] Members of this group include Martin Jay, Richard Bernstein, Nancy Fraser, Andreas Huyssen, Mark Poster, David Hoy, and Douglas Kellner.

[25] This group included some of the key members of the journal *Telos* – such as Paul Piccone and Russell Berman. The journal was sympathetic to Habermas in its early years, but turned increasingly to Adorno in the 1980s. See, for example, Robert Hullot-Kentor, "Back to Adorno," *Telos* 81 (Fall, 1989); other participants in discussions of Critical Theory in the United States who remained critical of both Habermas and French poststructuralism and sympathetic to Adorno and/or Walter Benjamin included Peter Hohendahl, Susan Buck-Morss, Fredric Jameson, and Jay Bernstein.

[26] One important exception was the volume *On Max Horkheimer: New Perspectives*, eds. Seyla Benhabib, Wolfgang Bonß, and John McCole, (Cambridge MA: MIT Press, 1993). This volume contains essays by some of the most important philosophers, sociologists, and intellectual historians working in the field of Critical Theory. Yet the majority of the contributions were written by German scholars, which reflects the more profound reception of Horkheimer's Critical Theory in Germany. The "emerging reevaluation of Horkheimer's work," of which the editors speak in their introduction (p. 12), still has not arrived on the other side of the Atlantic. It is perhaps not surprising that this volume, despite the impressive intellectual stature of its contributors, seems to have left few traces in American discussions of Critical Theory. The editors frame Horkheimer's work largely in terms of a theoretical inspiration for Habermas in his efforts to move beyond the putative aporias of Adorno's mature work (pp. 10–12). Furthermore, many of the contributors represented in the volume make a strong case, either in their essays in the volume or elsewhere, that a reevaluation of Horkheimer's work is no longer necessary, that it no longer speaks to present concerns.

[27] This is reflected, for example, in the introduction to *On Max Horkheimer: New Perspectives*, as mentioned in the previous footnote.

cultural theory. Those who remained steadfastly critical of both Habermas and poststructuralism called for a renewed assessment not of Horkheimer, but of Adorno's work, which they viewed as the most sophisticated formulation of Critical Theory and more relevant to present concerns.[28] Horkheimer had, in other words, been largely forgotten across the entire spectrum of discussions about Critical Theory in the United States. In the past decade, the reception of Critical Theory has expanded and diversified in ways that are too complex to recount here. One can say, however, that interest in Benjamin, Adorno, and Habermas has remained strong, while Horkheimer's work has continued to be neglected.

THE RELEVANCE OF HORKHEIMER'S EARLY CRITICAL THEORY TO CONTEMPORARY DISCUSSIONS

Horkheimer's early Critical Theory could contribute to contemporary discussions in a number of different fields. First, Horkheimer's early work provides an excellent model for a materialist intellectual history of modern Europe. At first glance, "materialist intellectual history" may appear to be a *contradictio in adjecto*, but revisiting Horkheimer's early lectures and essays makes clear why this is not the case. Horkheimer's concept of materialism is thoroughly historical, not ontological, metaphysical, mechanical, or physiological. He explicitly criticized attempts by Lenin and others to define materialism as the ahistorical primacy of "matter" over "mind." Surveying and bringing up to date the long history of philosophical materialism, Horkheimer argues that this anti-traditional tradition has manifested itself most consistently in a critique of ideas that justify socially and historically constructed forms of domination as eternal or necessary. Philosophical materialism has consistently deflated pretensions to "absolute truth," and allied itself with concrete political and social movements in the name of the more "modest" goal of improving the lives of concrete individuals living under historically specific forms of social domination. Yet materialism for Horkheimer – as for Marx – also constitutes a method of interpreting history and intellectual history. It expresses the conviction that even the most recondite ideas have a specific social content that binds them in more or less mediated ways to the struggles of concrete individuals and groups, which reproduce or alter historically specific social conditions and institutions. Taken together, Horkheimer's lectures from the late 1920s and his essays from the 1930s provide a remarkably rich materialist interpretation of the intellectual history of modern European philosophy – from the Renaissance all the way through to early-twentieth-century tendencies such as phenomenology and vitalism. Horkheimer consistently provides penetrating and original interpretations of the philosophical movements, authors, and works he examines, while at the same time demonstrating how their ideas are a mediated expression of the larger dialectic of bourgeois society that characterizes the history of modern Europe. One important example of how Horkheimer's early work

---

[28] Indeed, for some, such as Fredric Jameson, the import and relevance of Adorno's work did not become fully apparent until in the 1990s. See his *Late Marxism: Adorno, or the Persistence of the Dialectic* (London and New York: Verso, 1990).

could contribute to contemporary discussions in intellectual history is his distinctive interpretation of the Enlightenment, which identifies the critical and sensualist currents of the French Enlightenment as paradigmatic for the movement as a whole and rejects the tired, yet remarkably stubborn romantic myth that the Enlightenment was the apotheosis of abstract reason.[29] The historically specific and socially grounded interpretation of the Enlightenment found in Horkheimer's early work provides a corrective not only to recent Heideggerian- and poststructuralist-inspired interpretations – which tend to see the critical, emancipatory, and antiauthoritarian tendencies of Enlightenment philosophy as a mere façade concealing a deeper, unacknowledged drive for "truth" and "power" – but also to the more pessimistic interpretation Horkheimer and Adorno themselves put forth in the 1940s, which viewed the historical Enlightenment primarily as an episode in a much larger process of the progressive domination of internal and external nature by instrumental reason.[30]

Second, one finds in Horkheimer's (and Erich Fromm's) early Critical Theory a model of historical social-psychology that has been neglected, but which could still serve as an important point of reference in the much larger ongoing discussion of the transformation of character structures, sensibilities, and everyday life in early modern Europe. In essays such as "Beginnings of the Bourgeois Philosophy of History," "Egoism and Freedom Movements," and "Montaigne and the Function of Skepticism," Horkheimer articulates a distinctive interpretation not only of the intellectual, but also the social and social-psychological transformations of Europe during the dawn of the "bourgeois epoch." Horkheimer's essays could be read profitably alongside older and newer "classical" accounts of the transformation of sensibilities and everyday life in the early modern Europe, such as Max Weber's *Protestant Ethic*, Norbert Elias's *The Civilizing Process*, and Michel Foucault's *Madness and Civilization*. Furthermore, in a number of essays in the early 1930s, Horkheimer and Fromm present an innovative theoretical synthesis of historical materialism and psychoanalysis, which guided their interpretations of early modern Europe, and which could still provide historians with insights today. Whereas much more recent historical scholarship on the transformations of sensibilities and everyday life at the dawn of the modern era has been influenced by Foucault's model of "discipline,"[31] Horkheimer and Fromm's alternative theoretical approach

---

[29] Horkheimer would certainly have agreed with Peter Gay's argument, that "The *philosophes'* glorification of criticism and their qualified repudiation of metaphysics make it obvious that the Enlightenment was not an Age of Reason, but a revolt against rationalism." *The Enlightenment: An Interpretation*, vol. 1, *The Rise of Modern Paganism*, (London: Weidenfeld and Nicholsen, 1966). p. 41.

[30] See the more detailed discussion of these issues in Chapter 9 and the Epilogue.

[31] For example, John Bossy's *Christianity and Europe 1400–1700* (Oxford and New York: Oxford University Press, 1985) and Philip Gorski's more recent *The Disciplinary Revolution: Calvinism and the Rise of the State in Early Modern Europe* (Chicago: University of Chicago Press, 2003) both rely heavily – implicitly, in Bossy's case, and explicitly in Gorski's – on Foucault. Both draw on Foucault's insights and concepts to make a convincing case for the necessity of paying close attention to religion and its transformation in the Reformation and counter-Reformation in order to grasp the parallel transformation of character structures and patterns of everyday life in early modern Europe. With Foucault (and against Elias), both authors want to take our attention away from the centralized state and to argue that the transformation of character

could provide new insights into many of the same problems. In contrast to Foucault and the majority of historians, who have remained suspicious of psychoanalysis, some leading historians have been arguing for some time that the profession could benefit from a serious engagement with Freud's work.[32] Horkheimer's early essays provide one sophisticated model for how such an engagement could productively take place.

Third, revisiting Horkheimer's (and Fromm's) early work is also crucial to recovering the historical and theoretical foundations of the Institute's later analyses of prejudice. In the 1940s, the Institute sponsored the five-volume *Studies in Prejudice*, of which Horkheimer served as the general editor. Of the five volumes, the two coauthored by members of the Institute – *Prophets of Deceit*, by Leo Lowenthal and *The Authoritarian Personality*, by Theodor Adorno – built theoretically on Horkheimer's (and Fromm's) analyses in the 1930s of the *anthropology of the bourgeois epoch*. However, as Thomas Wheatland has recently shown, the theoretical principles that had guided the Institute's original formulation of the project disappeared into the background as the Institute was forced to adapt to the standards of mainstream American empirical social research and to the expectations of the American Jewish Committee, which generously funded the project.[33] Although these principles played a crucial role in the execution of the volumes coauthored by Lowenthal and Adorno, even here the empirical data and psychological explanations were foregrounded in a manner that rendered the underlying social and historical dimensions of the Institute's theory of prejudice practically invisible.[34] Recovering these foundations of the Critical Theorists' analyses of prejudice could provide new insights into the dominant forms of prejudice that exist in modern capitalist societies and the specific social constellations – such as fascism and conservative populism – in which these forms find their most virulent expression. Such a reconsideration would reveal striking parallels between older and more recent work on the history of prejudice in the United States.[35]

structures, sensibilities, and everyday practices among the middle and lower classes was every bit as dramatic and had equally far-reaching historical consequences. Horkheimer and Fromm's analyses also focus on the emergence of qualitatively new character structures among the middle and lower classes in early modern Europe. In contrast to Foucault, however, Horkheimer and Fromm are able to move beyond a merely descriptive account, which eschews causal explanations. To be sure, Marx's account of the rise of modern capitalism provides their primary explanatory model, yet Horkheimer and Fromm's rejection of a reductionist economism, their insistence on the "relative autonomy" of psychological structures and culture lead to questions and conclusions very similar those of Bossy and Gorski.

[32] See, for example, H. Stuart Hughes, "History and Psychoanalysis: The Explanation of a Motive," *History as Art and Science* (Chicago: University of Chicago Press, 1975), pp. 42–67; Peter Gay, *Freud for Historians* (New York: Oxford University Press, 1985).

[33] *The Frankfurt School in Exile*, op. cit., pp. 227–63.

[34] Paul Massing's contribution to the *Studies in Prejudice*, *Rehearsal for Destruction* could be seen as the exception here, insofar as it was an explicitly historical study of anti-Semitism in Wilhelmine Germany, but Massing paid little attention to psychological factors. He did not begin to work with the Institute until 1942, and his study is not indebted to its theoretical principles in the way that the volumes coauthored by Lowenthal and Adorno were.

[35] Interesting parallels to the Institute's theory and studies of prejudice could be found – to name just two examples – in Richard Hofstadter's analyses of conservative populism or David

Fourth, Horkheimer's early Critical Theory could help reestablish a truly interdisciplinary approach to Critical Theory. The sketch above of the Anglo-American reception of Critical Theory demonstrates just how uneven this reception has been. Whereas scholars in the humanities deserve much credit for preserving and extending the rich cultural and aesthetic theories of Walter Benjamin and Theodor Adorno, and scholars in philosophy and political theory also deserve credit for doing the same for the work of Jürgen Habermas, Anglo-American sociologists and historians have demonstrated less interest in Critical Theory. Revisiting Horkheimer's early work would reveal a model of Critical Theory that would appeal much more to critical, theoretically minded historians and sociologists. Furthermore, the early Horkheimer's stress on interdisciplinary collaboration and his openness to incorporating new methods and research from other fields could also provide an important theoretical model for contemporary research in the humanities and social sciences, which has increasingly blurred the boundaries between these disciplines in recent years.

Finally, revisiting his work could help move beyond the limitations of the "linguistic" and/or "cultural turn," which have become the subject of much discussion in the past two decades. During the heated philosophical debates that occurred in the 1980s and 1990s between Habermas and the poststructuralists and their respective adherents, it was often forgotten that both camps presupposed a "linguistic turn" of one sort or another. Although the main point of reference for Habermas's linguistic turn were not structural linguistics or anthropology – as was the case in France – but rather in the philosophical traditions of hermeneutics, phenomenology, and pragmatism, he too viewed the linguistic turn as a necessary condition of "post-metaphysical" philosophy in the late twentieth century, including analytic philosophy.[36] Despite path-breaking work in a variety of areas, an unmistakable disenchantment with or recognition of the limitations of the linguistic turn had become apparent by the end of the 1990s at the latest. Even Habermas himself reintroduced a concept

Roediger's more recent analyses of working-class racism in the early nineteenth century. In his analyses, Hofstadter drew explicitly on Adorno's concept of "pseudo-conservativism," which in turn relied heavily on Horkheimer's earlier work. See his *The Paranoid Style in American Politics and Other Essays* (New York: Vintage, 2008). Like *The Authoritarian Personality*, Hofstadter's analysis of the "paranoid style" in politics suffers from an overreliance on psychological methods of explanation, but his analysis in *The Age of Reform* (New York, 1955) of the *historical* origins of pseudo-conservatism in the United States demonstrates many parallels with Horkheimer's analysis of bourgeois anthropology. Similarly, David Roediger's analysis of the "*herrenvolk* republicanism" that developed among the white working class in the United States in the nineteenth century bears a striking resemblance to Horkheimer and Fromm's analysis of the sadomasochistic character in the 1930s. David Roediger, *The Wages of Whiteness* (New York and London: Verso, 1992).

[36] See, for example, "Hermeneutische und analytische Philosophie. Zwei komplementäre Spielarten der linguistischen Wende, " in Jürgen Habermas, *Wahrheit und Rechtfertigung: Philosophische Aufsätze* (Frankfurt: Suhrkamp, 1999), pp. 65–101. As the title of the essay suggests, Habermas makes a case for considering the hermeneutic and "formal pragmatic" traditions, which were so crucial for his own theory, and analytic philosophy as two complementary versions of the linguistic turn. Thus, in his view, the linguistic turn also reaches beyond structuralism and post-structuralism to encompass the dominant philosophical school in the Anglo-American world in the twentieth century: analytic philosophy.

of "weak naturalism" in order to diffuse the dangers of "linguistic idealism" he diagnosed in his own earlier work;[37] and he reconsidered the merits of "mindfulness of nature in the subject" with respect to debates about stem-cell research and genetic modification of human embryos.[38] Yet Habermas continues to defend the linguistic turn as the best – indeed, the only – possible path beyond the dead end of "consciousness philosophy" in which the main currents of Western philosophy had culminated in the early twentieth century. Although Habermas argues that Horkheimer's Critical Theory failed to recognize the necessity of taking a linguistic turn and remained beholden to an anachronistic paradigm of "consciousness philosophy," my study attempts to demonstrate why that is not the case; on the contrary, Horkheimer's early Critical Theory offers an alternative path beyond not only consciousness philosophy, but also the limitations of the linguistic turn. More recently, William Sewell, who was one of the pioneers of the "linguistic and cultural turn" in the discipline of history in the 1970s, has also pointed to its limitations and has made a case for a return to a new form of social history, which preserves the best insights of the linguistic and cultural turn while at the same time reintroducing a theory of modern capitalism that can do justice to macro-causal factors.[39] Horkheimer's early Critical Theory provides just such a model insofar as it rests on a Marxist theory of modern society as *capitalist* while at the same time moving beyond economistic determinism and recognizing the "relative autonomy" of culture and psychic structures.[40]

Although Horkheimer's early Critical Theory does have the potential to contribute to contemporary discussions in the ways just mentioned – and others – there are, not surprisingly, many ways in which it would need to be supplemented and/or updated in light of more recent historical developments. To mention only what is perhaps the most important of these ways, Horkheimer's early Critical Theory suffered from a liberal-democratic political deficit, which was already

---

[37] *Wahrheit und Rechtfertigung*, op. cit., pp. 32ff. and 286ff.

[38] The phrase "mindfulness of nature in the subject" comes from Horkheimer and Adorno (*Dialectic of Enlightenment*, op. cit., p. 40, translation amended), but could well be used to characterize one important aspect of Habermas's arguments in *The Future of Human Nature*, trans. Hella Beister (Cambridge, UK: Polity, 2003). Anxious to distance himself from what he considered the utopian implication of arguments against the domination of nature in Critical Theory, Habermas had – until his most recent work – always maintained that humans could interact with nature only in a purely instrumental way. The debate on stem-cell research and genetic modification seems to have convinced him that this argument has its limits in relation to human nature. For Habermas defends a concept of *species ethics* – the allusion to the young Marx's Feuerbachian arguments about species being is unmistakable – which defends a notion of common human nature as a necessary condition of any further moral reflection. To be sure, species ethics are only the first step in a larger argument that rests primarily on the extension of Habermas's discourse ethics to the unborn fetus – as a potential participant in an ideal speech situation. The concept does, nonetheless, represent an important shift vis-à-vis his earlier positions. See *The Future of Human Nature*, pp. 37ff.

[39] William Sewell Jr., *Logics of History: Social Theory and Social Transformation* (Chicago and London: University of Chicago Press, 2005), pp. 40–80.

[40] See, for example, Horkheimer's contribution to the introduction of the *Institute's Studies on Authority and Family*: "Authority and Family," in Max Horkheimer, *Critical Theory* op. cit., pp. 47–68.

apparent in his lectures on the history of philosophy in the late 1920s, which persisted through the 1930s, and which became even more apparent after his adoption of the "state capitalism" thesis around 1940. One manifestation of this deficit can be found – as I argue in Chapter 4[41] – in Horkheimer's interpretation of certain key Enlightenment philosophers. In his lectures and writings from the late 1920s and 1930s, Horkheimer found much more to admire in the historical Enlightenment in general and the French Enlightenment in particular than he and Adorno would in *Dialectic of Enlightenment*. Yet unlike his Institute colleague, Franz Neumann, Horkheimer was not willing to apply this interpretation of the Enlightenment to those political philosophers of the Enlightenment who articulated liberal-democratic political ideals. Whereas Neumann recognized that Marx's theory needed to recover and reintegrate the best aspects of the liberal-democratic political tradition and highlighted the ways in which Montesquieu and Rousseau's political ideals anticipated and were compatible with Marx's vision of socialism, Horkheimer's negation of this tradition and these ideals was abstract rather than determinate. This deficit in Horkheimer's thought became more apparent after 1940, when he expressed extreme skepticism about the historical substance and staying power of liberal-democratic political traditions in the West, arguing that the Western powers would be more likely to collaborate with fascism or to become fascist themselves than actively to combat fascism.[42] Nonetheless, Horkheimer's overall interpretation of the Enlightenment in his early work leaves open the possibility of a reconsideration of the liberal-democratic political tradition in a way that *Dialectic of Enlightenment* does not. So, despite this deficit, Horkheimer's arguments about the emancipatory philosophical ideals of the ascendant bourgeoisie could be extended to liberal-democratic politics in a way that he himself did not do at the time. After 1950, Horkheimer began defending the liberal-democratic political traditions of the West in a manner that was often as one-sided as his earlier critique of those traditions had been. A Critical Theory adequate to present conditions must avoid either extreme. It would need to preserve those aspects of Marx's critique of modern capitalism that are still relevant while at the same time preserving the best aspects of the liberal-democratic political tradition – such as individual rights, the rule of law, and the division of powers – that would make it impossible to repeat the catastrophic experiences in the twentieth century of so-called real-existing socialism. Yet twenty-first-century Critical Theory must refuse the complacent claims that liberal-democratic political institutions represent the end of history, and must also continue to identify and help combat the ways in which social domination reproduces itself within societies with liberal-democratic political institutions.

OVERVIEW OF THE BOOK'S STRUCTURE AND CONTENT

Let us now take a look at the structure of the book as a whole, which is divided into four main sections. Chapters 1 and 2 comprise the first section.

[41] See pp. 174–5.
[42] See Chapter 9 and the Epilogue

They examine Horkheimer's childhood and youth – which were spent mainly in Zuffenhausen, a suburb of Stuttgart, Germany – and his student years in Frankfurt. The first chapter focuses on Horkheimer's early friendship with Friedrich Pollock; his relationships with his parents and his future wife, Rosa Riekher; his reaction to and involvement in World War I; and his brief participation in a bohemian circle in Munich that was frequented by several artists and revolutionaries who would play a prominent role in the abortive council republic there in 1919. The first chapter also presents and analyzes a series of short plays and novellas that Horkheimer wrote during this time, which provide important insights into his early intellectual development. The second chapter turns to Horkheimer's studies at the J.W. Goethe University in Frankfurt, where he completed his doctorate and his *Habilitation* in philosophy in 1923 and 1925, respectively.[43] During this time, Horkheimer met Felix Weil, with whom he and Friedrich Pollock would hatch the plans for the Institute for Social Research, and Hans Cornelius, who would become not only Horkheimer's most important academic mentor, but also a close personal friend. Horkheimer wrote his Ph.D. and *Habilitationsschrift* – which both focused on Kant's *Critique of Judgment* – under Cornelius's direction. As I argue in Chapter 2, these early academic writings testify more to Horkheimer's loyalty to Cornelius at this time than to his own nascent Critical Theory.

In the second section of the book, which consists of Chapters 3, 4, and 5, I analyze how Horkheimer's early Critical Theory took shape during the period 1925–31. I argue, in particular, that Horkheimer's break with Cornelius in 1925 was at the same time a break with consciousness philosophy as whole, a break which proceeded along two interrelated yet distinct axes: a diachronic, historical axis and a synchronic, social axis.[44] In Chapter 3, I examine Horkheimer's materialist interpretation of the history of modern European philosophy, which leaves no doubt that he did not view consciousness as the absolute beginning point of philosophy. Instead, Horkheimer interpreted modern European philosophy as the mediated expression of the uneven development of bourgeois society. In Chapters 4 and 5, I turn my attention to the origins and development of Horkheimer's theory of *contemporary* society. The former chapter focuses primarily on Horkheimer's critical appropriation Marx's theory, which I reconstruct through an examination of his critique of Lenin's *Materialism and Empiriocriticism* and Karl Mannheim's *Ideology and Utopia*, and through an analysis of the collection of aphorisms Horkheimer wrote between 1926 and 1931, which were published pseudonymously in 1934 as *Dämmerung*.[45]

---

[43] The *Habilitation* is the highest qualification one can receive in the German university system. It is necessary to obtain the *venia legendi* (the right to teach) and thus a prerequisite for an academic career. To successfully complete the *Habilitation*, one must submit a second dissertation, or *Habilitationsschrift*, which demonstrates original research at a higher level than the Ph.D., and which is approved by an independent committee of professors in one's chosen field.

[44] My argument here is intended as a critique of Jürgen Habermas's influential interpretation of Horkheimer and Adorno, which maintains that their work remained trapped with the paradigm of consciousness philosophy. See, for example, Jürgen Habermas, *Theory of Communicative Action*, vol. 1, trans. Thomas McCarthy (Boston, 1984), p. 386.

[45] An incomplete and unsatisfactory English translation of *Dämmerung* has been published, which also includes notes Horkheimer wrote much later in his life: *Dawn and Decline: Notes 1926–1931 and 1950–1969*, trans. Michael Shaw (New York: Seabury Press, 1978).

Chapter 5 examines Horkheimer's integration of psychoanalysis into his Critical Theory of contemporary society, and the important contributions made to this process by his friend and analyst, Karl Landauer, and by his future Institute colleague, Erich Fromm. Here again, in Chapters 4 and 5, it is apparent that Horkheimer sees consciousness as always already mediated by society, not as an absolute point of departure. In both chapters, we see Horkheimer stress, for example, the ways in which consciousness is shaped by unconscious *character structures* that in turn are shaped by historically specific social conditions.

In the third section of the book, which is comprised by Chapters 6, 7, and 8, I turn to the "mature" formulation of Horkheimer's early Critical Theory in the period 1931–7. In terms of the development of Horkheimer's Critical Theory, the continuities between the periods before and after his assumption of the directorship of the Institute for Social Research in January 1931 are more important than the differences. In contrast to studies of Horkheimer's work that begin in 1931, the second section of this study is intended to demonstrate how Horkheimer's early Critical Theory took shape already in the late 1920s. His basic theoretical assumptions were already in place when Horkheimer became director, but he now had an opportunity to put these ideas to work within an institutional setting – to test, develop, and refine them. The 1930s were Horkheimer's most productive period theoretically and – in the opinion of this author and others – the period in which he produced his highest quality work.[46] The plethora of philosophically dense, theoretically nuanced, and historically self-reflexive essays Horkheimer wrote during this time defy synopsis. Yet a careful examination of his work does reveal four concepts that were the most crucial for the development of his thought in the 1930s: materialism, the anthropology of the bourgeois epoch, dialectical logic, and state capitalism. Chapters 6, 7, and 8 examine how the first three of these concepts, and with them Horkheimer's Critical Theory as a whole, unfold in the 1930s. Chapter 6 focuses, in particular, on the essays "Materialism and Metaphysics" and "Materialism and Morality," in which Horkheimer presents a highly suggestive, antifoundational concept of materialism. Horkheimer engages deeply with the tradition of philosophical materialism while at the same time insisting on a determination of the concept adequate to the twentieth-century social, historical, and intellectual conditions. Chapter 7 focuses on his attempts to develop a historically and social-psychologically informed theory of the character structure that became dominant in modern capitalist societies – that of bourgeois man. The chapter begins with Horkheimer's methodological reflections on this problem in essays such as "History and Psychology" and "Remarks on Philosophical Anthropology"; continues with his attempt to flesh it out historically in "Egoism and Freedom Movements: On the Anthropology of the Bourgeois Epoch"; and concludes with an examination of the Institute's collective empirical project, *The Studies on Authority and Family*, which is interpreted as an attempt to apply and test Horkheimer's concept of bourgeois anthropology in contemporary societies. In Chapter 7, considerable attention is also paid to Erich Fromm's contributions to Horkheimer's conceptualization

---

[46] Jürgen Habermas, "Remarks on the Development of Horkheimer's Work," *On Max Horkheimer: New Perspectives*, op. cit., p. 51.

of the "anthropology of the bourgeois epoch." Horkheimer considered all of the essays he wrote in the 1930s as preliminary studies for a larger, more comprehensive project on the "logic of the social sciences," or simply "dialectical logic," as he put it. Eventually, some aspects of this project would be realized in *Dialectic of Enlightenment*. However, Chapter 8 is intended to demonstrate that Horkheimer's dialectical logic had a very different form in the mid- and late 1930s than it would later assume after he began working more closely with Adorno. The contours of the project at that time – which is very much worth reconsidering today – emerge through an examination of the essays "On the Rationality Debate in Contemporary Philosophy," "On the Problem of Truth," "The Latest Attack on Metaphysics," and "Traditional and Critical Theory."

The fourth and final section of the book examines the causes and theoretical consequences of Horkheimer's move beyond his "early Critical Theory" at the end of the 1930s and the beginning of the 1940s. Put schematically, one could say that this major shift in Horkheimer's thought had three main causes: his theoretical split with Erich Fromm, his closer working relationship with Theodor Adorno, and his adoption of a modified version of Friedrich Pollock's "state capitalism" thesis. Chapter 9 continues the methodological approach of the previous section insofar as it uses the concept of "state capitalism" to demonstrate the changes that occurred in Horkheimer's thought between 1938 and 1941. It focuses, in particular, on the essays "Montaigne and the Function of Skepticism," "The Jews and Europe," "Authoritarian State," and "The End of Reason." Chapter 9 is preceded by two excursuses dedicated to Horkheimer's changing relationships at this time with Fromm and Adorno. The first, shorter excursus draws primarily on a lengthy unpublished text Fromm wrote in the fall and winter of 1936–7, which sheds new light on the theoretical foundations of his split with Horkheimer and the Institute as a whole. The second, lengthier excursus examines the development of Horkheimer's theoretical relationship with Theodor Adorno in the 1930s. As mentioned, one consequence of Horkheimer's eclipse in the Anglo-American reception of Critical Theory has been a tendency to see Horkheimer primarily as the coauthor of *Dialectic of Enlightenment* and to overlook the fact that the development of Horkheimer's and Adorno's Critical Theories followed very different trajectories. Whereas the second and third sections of this study reconstruct the development of Horkheimer's early Critical Theory, this excursus provides an overview of Adorno's trajectory in the late 1920s and 1930s, but with an emphasis on the ways in which his thought diverged from Horkheimer's. Although Adorno did move closer to some of Horkheimer's positions in the late 1930s, it was ultimately Horkheimer's abandonment of some of the basic assumptions that had guided his early Critical Theory that set the stage for their collaboration on *Dialectic of Enlightenment*. However, as I argue in the epilogue, some of the basic theoretical assumptions that guided *Dialectic of Enlightenment* appear dated and/or problematic from our perspective today. I would like to suggest that Horkheimer's early Critical Theory could serve as a more promising point of departure for a renewal of Critical Theory today than *Dialectic of Enlightenment*.

Coming of Age in Wilhelmine Germany

There is nothing a philistine hates more than the dreams of his youth.
Walter Benjamin

CHILDHOOD AND YOUTH

Max Horkheimer was born on February 14, 1895, in Zuffenhausen, a small town on the outskirts of Stuttgart, in southern Germany. Horkheimer's parents were part of Stuttgart's Jewish community that had grown steadily in the course of the nineteenth century and had succeeded in establishing itself as an integral part of the city's economic, political, and cultural life.[1] When King Charles of Württemberg approved the passage of a law in 1864 that guaranteed equal citizenship for Stuttgart's Jews, the road was opened for fifty years of prosperity and relatively harmonious coexistence. Horkheimer's father, Moritz, who was born in neighboring Baden in 1858, was able to take advantage of the economic opportunities available in Stuttgart during this period of rapid industrialization in Germany as a whole. Although Moritz Horkheimer's father had been an unsuccessful businessman from whom he had inherited substantial debts, he was able steadily to work his way up in the Stuttgart textile industry. By the beginning of World War I, Moritz Horkheimer had firmly established himself among the ranks of the city's millionaires, an elite that numbered no more than 250 at the time. In 1892, however, when Moritz Horkheimer married Babette Lauchheimer, he was still far from being an established figure. Lauchheimer's parents, who were very well-to-do and of strict orthodox faith, agreed to the marriage with considerable reluctance. Only gradually, with his mounting business success, was Moritz Horkheimer able to overcome the suspicion and condescension of his in-laws.

Moritz Horkheimer thus came to embody the promise of the liberal capitalism that was transforming the economy, if not the political institutions, of Imperial Germany in the last decades of the nineteenth century. He attributed his success in large part to the country and the region that he believed had made

---

[1] The Jewish community in Stuttgart was officially founded on August 3, 1832. At that time, it consisted of fifteen families with 124 members altogether. It grew steadily in the next few decades. By 1856, it had 547 members. In 1859, the first synagogue was opened. By 1875, it had 1100 members; in 1895, 2700; in 1905, 3900; and on the eve of World War I, 4300. *Weg und Schicksal der Stuttgarter Juden*, ed. Maria Zelzer (Stuttgart, 1964), p. 32.

it possible. He was a patriotic citizen of Germany and proud of his regional affiliation with Stuttgart and the greater region of Württemberg as well. When the Second International met in Stuttgart in 1907, Max Horkheimer recalls his father castigating the Social Democrats in general and "bloody" Rosa Luxemburg in particular for their lack of loyalty to the fatherland. Moritz Horkheimer joined in the wave of enthusiasm that swept through Germany with the beginning of World War I. In the following years, he placed his factory in the service of the war effort, producing badly needed textiles. His devotion did not go unrecognized either. In 1916, he was awarded the *Charlottenkreuz* and the *Ritterkreuz I. Klasse* by the king of Württemberg. In 1917, he was given the honorary title of *Kommerzienrat*, once again by the king of Württemberg. In 1918, he was made a citizen of honor of Zuffenhausen;[2] he was the last Jew in the Stuttgart area to receive the title. Moritz Horkheimer's patriotism was so ardent that he refused to leave Germany until 1939. He defended his choice to stay in Germany by saying that his family had been living there longer than Adolf Hitler.

Moritz Horkheimer's loyalty to Germany and Württemberg was also reflected in his cultural preferences. He was an admirer of classical German literature, particularly Goethe, Schiller, and Hölderlin. His favorite cultural pursuit, however, was collecting Württembergian painting. Yet his cultural interests should be seen more as hobbies than as passions. Moritz Horkheimer had not attended a *Gymnasium*[3] or a university, and the relatively superficial character of his cultural interests became apparent later in his consternation at his son's choice to pursue an academic career. Politically and religiously, Moritz Horkheimer was of liberal persuasion. He was a member of the Progressive People's Party, in which the relatively small number of left-liberals in Imperial Germany found a political home.[4] He attended synagogue only on important Jewish holidays and had nothing against working on the Sabbath otherwise. He was critical of Zionism and never polemicized against other religions. He saw himself first and foremost as a German citizen, and he firmly subscribed to the liberal belief that he was doing what was best for his community and his country by developing his business as rapidly as possible. Max Horkheimer recalls that his father had a good relationship with, and took a genuine interest in, his workers, although he was adamantly opposed to unionization, which eventually led to strikes in his factory near the end of World War I.[5]

---

[2] The original documents are located in MHA XX.1

[3] A *Gymnasium* was an elite public high school in Germany specializing in humanistic education. All students were required to take Greek and Latin and study classical literature and philosophy.

[4] The Progressive People's Party (*Die Fortschrittspartei*) had opposed Bismarck's autocratic politics from the beginning, in favor of genuine parliamentary government and the rule of law. After Bismarck's success in the debate to reform the military with the Prussian Indemnity Law of 1866, and more important, Prussia's defeat of Austria in that same year, many of their original constituents fled to the newly formed National Liberal Party, which would staunchly support Bismarck in the following years. The Progressive Party remained the home for the remaining constitutional liberals.

[5] Interview with Matthias Becker, (MHA, X 183a) pp. 125–6.

Max Horkheimer's mother played the role of a traditional bourgeois house-wife. She devoted herself not to cultural or intellectual pursuits, but primarily to her husband and her son, and secondarily to religion. She seems to have been an exceptionally protective mother. She would always accompany Max to school on the first day to make sure that his new teacher took especially good care of her sensitive son. She was religious and insisted that the family remain kosher, but when Max became sick and the doctor recommended that he eat ham on buttered bread to regain his health, his mother was willing to break the religious dietary laws for the good of her son.[6] The extreme protectiveness of Horkheimer's mother was also apparent later in her resistance to his relation-ship with the woman he would eventually marry, Rosa Riekher. She believed that Riekher was interested only in Horkheimer's money and took several years to become convinced of the sincerity of Riekher's love.[7] In his recollections of his mother, Max Horkheimer stressed time and again her boundless love for him. If Horkheimer's father embodied liberal economic rationality, to which necessarily belonged bourgeois coldness, as Horkheimer would argue later, his mother embodied the warmth of selfless love. Horkheimer stressed that his mother was fearful of the outside world and that he largely inherited this fear from her. The warmth of his mother's love and her fear of the outside world certainly did not ease Horkheimer's transition out of the familial sphere into bourgeois society. As Horkheimer himself stressed repeatedly in later inter-views, he sought to recapture the warmth and stability he had experienced with his mother in other relationships as he grew older. The formation of Horkheimer's relationship with his lifelong friend Friedrich Pollock provides ample evidence for this claim.

Horkheimer's friendship with Pollock played an extremely important role in his personal and intellectual development. Prior to his friendship with Pollock, which began in 1911, Horkheimer seems to have had a fairly unremarkable childhood. His mother's solicitude and his early interest in expressing his internal emotional conflicts in the form of dramas or novellas indicated that Horkheimer was an exceptionally sensitive child from the beginning. However, he does not seem to have suffered from the same extreme feelings of alienation as did his future friend and colleague Theodor Adorno, who was wounded deeply by the persecution he suffered at the hands of other children.[8] In later recollections, Horkheimer stressed that he was relatively happy and well inte-grated as a child. He spent many enjoyable hours playing with tin German soldiers with his friends. He did not recall any of his teachers being anti-Semitic, and the occasional prejudiced remarks he heard from his schoolmates he dismissed as a sign of their envy.[9] According to him, their remarks did not

---

[6] Horkheimer tells this story in a conversation with Gerhard Rein in 1972. See GS 7, p. 443.

[7] Interview with Matthias Becker, p. 186.

[8] See, for example, "The Bad Comrade," in Theodor Adorno, *Minima Moralia*, trans. Edmund Jephcott (New York and London, 1974), pp. 192–3.

[9] The situation in Horkheimer's *Gymasium* may not have been representative, because the founder and principal of the *Realgymnasium* he attended was a member of the "*Verein zur Abwehr des Antisemitismus*" ("Organization to Combat Anti-Semitism") that had been founded in 1890 to combat anti-Semitism in Stuttgart. *Weg und Schicksal der Stuttgarter Juden*, p. 67.

leave any lasting scars.[10] He did not attend the *Gymnasium*, the humanistically oriented elite German high school, but rather the *Realgymnasium*, which prepared its students for more practical careers. Horkheimer recalls that he viewed doing well in school primarily as a means of pleasing his parents, not as an end in itself. He was usually among the top five students in his school, although never the best. He left school when he was fifteen years old to work in his father's factory and prepare himself for a career as an industrialist.

It was at this time that he first made Pollock's acquaintance. Horkheimer had had one other earlier friend who was important to him. The way Horkheimer described it in an interview near the end of his life, his first meaningful friendship demonstrates how much he longed for an intimate companion, a desire that would be realized later with his friendship to Pollock:

Already in my childhood, before I left school ... I had an ideal of having a friend, with whom I could share everything that was important to me. This thought, this wish certainly resulted from the way in which I was raised to love and to long for sincerity and community, and to do good. For all this I needed a friend and that was my deepest desire. I had at that time a friend whose name was Kurt Rosenfeld but he died before I left the [middle] school. After him came Fritz Pollock and we remained friends until his death, that is from 1910/11 until 1970, for 60 years. But this was exactly what had already begun with Kurt Rosenfeld and was the direct result of the way in which I was raised.[11]

An opportunity to get to know Pollock better presented itself to Horkheimer in the fall of 1911, when a space became available in a social dancing class in which he was participating at the time. The dance class was a part of the socialization process for young persons from bourgeois families who were preparing to play their allotted role within the rigidly structured social system of Wilhelmine Germany. The formal language of Horkheimer's invitation to Pollock, which he wrote when he was just sixteen years old, reflects the stiff decorum of the dance class:

When we began to organize our dance classes, we had hoped that you [Sie] too would participate in our pleasant little winter gathering; but our hopes proved to be in vain, since you believed then, as I heard, that you would be away from our beautiful home town during this time. A few days ago Mr. [illegible] told me that you will spend the winter here after all and that you would perhaps not be averse to spending one night a week learning to dance with us.... With this hope and also the hope that I will be able to greet you tomorrow evening at 8:45, I remain, yours truly, Max Horkheimer.[12]

Pollock came to the next meeting of the dance class, but did not appear again after that. Impressed by Pollock's willingness to flout social convention, Horkheimer revealed to Pollock that he too hated playing the role expected of him, and that beneath the mask lay a miserable young man who desperately needed a friend in whom he could confide his true feelings. "Please, let it be you!" implored Horkheimer, to which Pollock responded coolly, "I'll have to

[10] Biographical interviews with Matthias Becker, p. 15.

[11] Ibid., pp. 37–8.

[12] MHA, VI.30. "Sie" is the second-person formal in German and is usually reserved for adults.

think about it," and left.[13] Soon thereafter, however, Pollock let Horkheimer know that he was willing to accept his offer. They soon went to work on a friendship contract that went into great detail about their commitment to one another and to creating a more humane world.[14] The contract sealed a friendship that would remain a pillar of both men's lives for the next sixty years.

Pollock, who was nine months older than Horkheimer, was also the son of a successful industrialist. His father owned a factory that produced leather goods in Freiburg, where Pollock spent most of his youth. In Freiburg, Pollock had attended the humanistic *Gymnasium*, and when he moved to Stuttgart he wanted to continue in the *Gymnasium* there; but he was not admitted due to the higher standards in Württemberg that had been handed down in the prestigious tradition of the *Tübinger Stift*.[15] Pollock decided to begin to prepare himself for a career as an industrialist instead, which would soon entail traveling abroad with Horkheimer in order to learn French and English, and to familiarize himself with production methods in other countries. Pollock's family was extremely assimilated. His father had renounced his Judaism and raised Pollock to hold Judaism in disdain. As Horkheimer said in a later interview, "His father belonged to those assimilated Jews, who transformed their unease into a certain negative attitude toward Jews."[16] Although Pollock had literary, philosophical, and musical interests, by temperament he was more practical than Horkheimer. As Horkheimer put it later, "He was by nature, and in accord with his entire family background, actually drawn more to positivism, and his interests were almost always related to facts."[17] It was probably this aspect of Pollock's personality that contributed most to the elective affinity between himself and Horkheimer. In letters, they began referring to each other jokingly as the "ministre de l'interieur" and "ministre de l'exterieur," which meant that Pollock took care of external details so Horkheimer could devote himself fully to his intellectual pursuits. This symbiosis between Horkheimer and Pollock remained a constant throughout their long friendship, and became one of the cornerstones of the Institute for Social Research in later years.

Pollock facilitated Horkheimer's development not only by protecting him from the harsh outside world, but also by helping Horkheimer emancipate himself from the patriarchal authority of his father. When he and Pollock became friends at the end of 1911, Horkheimer had already left school and was preparing himself to become his father's partner and eventual successor. At the behest of this father, who wanted his son to familiarize himself with the financial world, Horkheimer completed a six-month internship at the *Württembergsche*

---

[13] Ernst von Schenk, unpublished biographical manuscript on Max Horkheimer (MHA XIII 112a), p. 9–10.

[14] The contract itself has unfortunately not been preserved. See Gunzelin Schmid Noerr's remarks on the friendship contract in his afterword to Horkheimer's correspondence, GS 19, pp. 826–7.

[15] The *Tübinger Stift* was a prestigious private Lutheran school founded in 1536, which worked closely with the university of Tübingen and the principality of Württemburg to train intellectual and spiritual leaders. Its alumni included Schelling, Hegel, and Hölderlin.

[16] Interview with Matthias Becker, p. 321.

[17] Ibid., p. 154.

Vereinsbank. After he finished this internship, Horkheimer went to work in his father's factory, where he was expected to learn everything from accounting and production methods to supervising the workers. During this time, Horkheimer also strengthened his friendship with Pollock. In a lengthy letter Horkheimer wrote to Pollock on September 9, 1912, while recovering from illness at a spa-hotel on Lake Constance, Horkheimer searched for reasons for the malaise that had been plaguing him since the past winter.[18] His caustic remarks about the philistines in the hotel and Stuttgart's "jeunesse dorée"[19] expressed his general dissatisfaction with the social world of the bourgeoisie. He told Pollock that his spirits were nonetheless high, because his father recently revealed his plans to send him abroad to see how business was done in other countries and to learn French. Because Pollock's father also wanted to send him abroad for the same reasons, the two of them would work together during the next few months to convince their fathers to let them travel to Brussels together. It was here that the two of them had their first taste of liberating independence.

One term that appears repeatedly in Horkheimer's early letters is *interieur*. It was clear that Horkheimer was looking for someone to share his rich internal world, in which he sought refuge from the stifling conditions of everyday life in Stuttgart. In Pollock, he found someone who could not only empathize with his disaffection, but who also shared his intellectual interests. His personal and intellectual companionship with Pollock provided Horkheimer with much needed affirmation, as well as the opportunity to explore this interior world in greater depth. With Pollock's help, Horkheimer began to develop a vast reserve of internal resources that would enable him to withstand the extreme pressures of the external world to which he would be subjected in the coming years. As the earliest letters make clear, intellectual exploration, particularly in the areas of literature and music, were central to Horkheimer and Pollock's friendship from the beginning. Although Horkheimer displayed a superior mastery of language and facility of expression – one remarkable for his age – Pollock was the better read of the two at this time. He introduced Horkheimer to many of the classical works of literature he had studied at the humanistic *Gymnasium* in Freiburg.[20] Shortly after they arrived in Brussels, Pollock recommended a book to Horkheimer that proved decisive for his further intellectual development, namely Schopenhauer's *Aphorismen zur Lebensweisheit*.[21]

On May 12, 1913, Horkheimer's father left him alone in Brussels, after making certain that his living and working arrangements were in order. The next day, Horkheimer wrote a letter to Pollock, who would not join him there for another two weeks, that clearly expressed his joy at the prospect of beginning a new, more independent phase of his life with his best friend at his side.

[18] MHA VI.30.
[19] Gilded youth.
[20] Biographical manuscript of Ernst von Schenk, p. 8.
[21] An older English translation of Schopenhauer's aphorisms does exist: *The Wisdom of Life, being the first part of Arthur Schopenhauer's* Aphorismen zur Lebensweisheit, trans. T. Bailey Saunders (London: S. Sonnenschein, 1890) and *Counsels and Maxims, being the second part of Arthur Schopenhauer's* Aphorismen zur Lebensweisheit, trans. T. Bailey Saunders (London: S. Sonnenschein, 1890).

Horkheimer describes his departure from Stuttgart as the beginning of the end of a long illness: "You, what do you say to us walking together, hand in hand … alone, far away from the people who know us, that would be splendid, if we could live only for ourselves and then I felt softly, slowly, that I too was regaining my health."[22] In Brussels, the two of them worked as unpaid interns in two different factories, took private French lessons, and continued to pursue their intellectual interests. Horkheimer must have been taken immediately by Schopenhauer's *Aphorisms*, for when he discovered a copy of Schopenhauer's collected writings in a second-hand bookstore a few weeks later, he bought it right away and proceeded to deepen his knowledge of the philosopher to whom he would refer a few years later as his "exalted spiritual [*geistig*] father."[23] Horkheimer's high expectations for his stay in Brussels seem to have been fulfilled completely. The detailed plans he and Pollock had resolutely adopted to escape the rigid and stifling bourgeois lifestyle of Wilhelmine Germany seemed to be coming true.[24] In a letter from September to another friend, who was apparently suffering from similar feelings of alienation, Horkheimer writes, "We have escaped from the world, in which you suffer, and our memory of it is a constant joy of being rid of it."[25] The friend to whom Horkheimer addressed this letter, Suze Neumeier, would soon join Horkheimer and Pollock, if only briefly, in their *interieur* explorations.

Horkheimer had been acquainted with Neumeier for some time because she was a distant cousin who came with her parents from Paris to visit Horkheimer's family on a semiregular basis – usually at least once a year. A more serious relationship developed between the two of them in September 1912, when Neumeier spent an extended period of time with Horkheimer and Pollock during one of her periodic visits to Stuttgart. She must have caught a draft of the heady air of Horkheimer and Pollock's friendship, for she decided to turn down a marriage proposal and instead cultivated her friendship with them through regular correspondence.[26] After Horkheimer's internship in Brussels came to an end in December, Horkheimer returned to Stuttgart. His father decided to send him next to Manchester, England, where he could familiarize himself with the latest production methods there and learn English. On his way from Stuttgart to Manchester at the end of December, Horkheimer stopped in Paris to visit Neumeier, with whom he had fallen in love in the meantime.[27] At this time,

[22] GS 15, p. 10.

[23] Ibid., p. 25.

[24] Just how serious these plans were, and the tenacity with which these two young men would cling to them, is demonstrated by a private note that Horkheimer wrote to Pollock nearly four decades later: "Our life should be a testament; utopia realized on the smallest scale. We want something different, new, absolute. Our life is serious. The laws governing society should not apply to us. " Quoted by Gunzelin Schmid Noerr, GS 11, p. 290.

[25] Ibid., p. 12.

[26] Biographical manuscript of Ernst von Schenk, p. 17.

[27] The following events are described by Horkheimer in "L'ile heureuse," GS 11, pp. 292–328. In contrast to the other fictional novellas Horkheimer wrote during this time, "L'ile heureuse" is directly autobiographical. In it, Horkheimer simply attempts to record what happened between himself, Neumeier, and Pollock. This is demonstrated not only by Horkheimer's use of the persons' real names, but also by the manuscript itself, which contains exact dates in the margins

Neumeier declared her wish to become a full member of their intimate circle by committing herself to the ideals they had established in their friendship contract. When Horkheimer met with Pollock the next day in Calais, France to continue their trip to Manchester together, he explained jubilantly to Pollock that they now had a third member in their coterie. Pollock reacted skeptically at first, which led Horkheimer to write Neumeier a letter to confirm that she still stood behind her recent declarations. In a long letter, which she signed in blood, Neumeier replied, "Je suis à vous corps et âme."[28]

Over the next six months, the three of them exchanged letters "almost daily," and they met in person three times as well: on March 27 in Paris, when Horkheimer and Pollock were traveling to Stuttgart; on May 1 in Fort-Mahon,[29] on their way back to London; and finally in Fort-Mahon on May 22 and 23. All three meetings were highly charged intellectually, emotionally, and erotically. As Horkheimer puts it, "Oh sorry species of words, you are incapable of bringing to life even a shadow of the emotions which burned within us at that time."[30] After their third rendezvous, the three of them could no longer stand being apart. By the end of June, Neumeier decided to leave her family and friends in Paris behind and to join Horkheimer and Pollock in London, where the three of them would try to make their dream, the *isle heureuse*, a reality. On July 2, Horkheimer picked Neumeier up in Folkestone and brought her back to the small apartment in London that he and Pollock had rented for the three of them. Their *bateau ivre*, however, would soon run aground on the reality principle of bourgeois society, which they mistakenly believed they had left behind. Neumeier's parents notified both Scotland Yard and Horkheimer's parents right away. Two days later, Neumeier's father packed his pistol and traveled to London to find that Pollock had already been taken into custody by Scotland Yard. Horkheimer's parents had arrived in London in the meantime as well. Horkheimer and Pollock were to return immediately to Stuttgart, and Neumeier to Paris. The arrival of the adults jolted Neumeier completely out of the parallel world in which she had been living with Horkheimer and Pollock. As Horkheimer put it:

When she ... looked into the eyes of all these people living in another world, she too was in that world once again. She had found her way back to reality perfectly, she no longer understood that which had been, she herself and both of us had suddenly become foreign to her.[31]

Among the last words that Neumeier spoke to Horkheimer as they parted ways then were "Je n'ai plus d'interieur."[32] When they returned to their apartment the next day, they found that Neumeier had burned all the letters she had written before she left.

---

corresponding to the events described. Further evidence of the straightforward autobiographical character of this text was Horkheimer's refusal to publish it with the rest of his early novellas in the early 1970s. See Gunzelin Schmid Noerr's forward to "L'ile heureuse," GS 11, pp. 289–91.

[28] Ibid., p. 304. "I am yours in body and soul."

[29] A small French resort town on the English Channel.

[30] "L'ile heureuse," p. 314.

[31] Ibid., p. 325.

[32] Ibid. "I no longer have any interior."

Horkheimer felt deeply betrayed by Neumeier's choice to leave their *isle heureuse* behind. In fact, the incident precipitated what he would describe later as the only major "religious" crisis of his life.[33] However, the incident did not lead Horkheimer to abandon his and Pollock's lofty ideals; on the contrary, it led him to dig in his heels more resolutely, as is demonstrated by the semificitonalized account of the events he wrote in the following weeks. In the story, which provides a clear view of Horkheimer's worldview at this formative stage in his life, he writes passionately about the ideals that had driven the three of them to try to create an *isle heureuse*. He describes their hatred of bourgeois society and depicts it as a system of needs that prevents the upper classes from pursuing any ideals beyond material wealth or dubious fame, and forces the lower classes into a brutal struggle for existence. At a time long before he had read Hegel or Marx, Horkheimer argues that the existing society constantly reproduces "false fences" between people that can be torn down only through a firm commitment to the higher ideals of spiritual development and love. He interprets his and Pollock's relationship with Neumeier, in terms reminiscent of Plato, as the realization of ideal love:

For the first time I fully understood that the three of us formed *one* person, that even the most insignificant trait of one was agreeable to the other, that there could be no misunderstandings between us. Our love was perfect, reality had attained the truth.[34]

Horkheimer sublimates the sensual aspect of their relationship into an act of resistance against alienation: "Loving means breaking through the barbed wire fence that they have raised between me and everyone else.... Where they govern, one can at most take off one's clothes, but never tear down the fence."[35] Although tempered by Schopenhauer's ethics of compassion, Horkheimer's attitude toward others at this point was characterized primarily by Nietzschean contempt: "I feel compassion for the living, but not with their folly, for that is precisely what pains and makes suffer the part of me that I share with them."[36] By the time Horkheimer had finished the story, all his worst fears seemed to have been confirmed. World War I had begun and was greeted with enthusiasm by many Europeans. He closes his story with a universalist plea to his countrymen: "Are you not first human and then German and do you not feel as a human that a civilization, which brings forth such consequences, is still barbaric, still immature?"[37]

THE WAR YEARS

In Manchester and London, Horkheimer and Pollock were able to find internship positions, which gave them plenty of time to pursue their intellectual interests and their efforts to realize the *isle heureuse*. With the outbreak of

---

[33] Pollock confirmed this in an interview later: "That was when Horkheimer lost his faith in religion." Quoted by Gunzelin Schmid Noerr, GS 15, p. 88.

[34] "L'ile heureuse," p. 310.

[35] Ibid.

[36] Ibid., p. 311.

[37] Ibid., p. 328.

the war, however, both were forced to return to Stuttgart to work in their fathers' respective factories. One can imagine Horkheimer's consternation at being forced prematurely to interrupt his stay in London and return to work in Stuttgart. He had also just undergone what he would later describe as the only truly "religious" crisis in his life. Furthermore, this personal crisis that had occurred at the same time as the Europe-wide crisis that led to World War I, which he unequivocally rejected from the beginning. "L'isle heureuse" was the first of a series of novellas, short plays, letters, and journal entries Horkheimer would write over the next four years, in which he would give vivid expression to the manifold personal and social problems that occupied him during this time.[38] Although he continued to read Schopenhauer, his primary interest lay in literature, particularly contemporary expressionist literature and drama. This interest was clearly reflected in the content and style of his own writings from this period. During this time, Horkheimer began to consider himself as a writer and an artist.[39] Horkheimer's primary concern, however, remained throughout to express his own thoughts and feelings as clearly as possible.[40] This concern was evident in the next literary piece Horkheimer wrote after "L'isle heureuse," entitled "War: A Correspondence," which clearly demonstrates Horkheimer's early opposition to World War I.[41]

The story is a fictitious exchange of letters that takes place between Walter, a young law student with literary aspirations who is adamantly opposed to the war, and Luise, his girlfriend, a naïve young woman who enthusiastically supports the war. Walter, who almost certainly expresses Horkheimer's own views, argues that the war is not about *Kultur*, but rather the naked desire for property and power. Walter defends genuine *Kultur* as a "drive for knowledge" that "does not spring from any practical intention," and that raises one above the "lust for possession" that he believes is responsible for the war.[42] Walter excoriates the blind patriotism of the masses, the capitulation of the Social Democrats, and the hypocrisy of the religious leaders. Yet Walter is in love with Luise and would like to marry her someday soon, and he realizes that her parents see him as a good-for-nothing dreamer. So he decides to volunteer for the war to prove to Luise and her parents that he is a worthy suitor, even if it means acting against his own deepest convictions. Luise praises Walter's resolve and tells how both her brothers have recently volunteered for the war as well. As Walter slowly approaches the front, he continues to write Luise letters in

---

[38] These early unpublished writings comprise the first volume of Horkheimer's *Gesammelte Schriften*, "'Aus der Pubertät. Novellen und Tagebuchblätter' 1914–18," ed. Alfred Schmidt, (Frankfurt, 1988).

[39] GS 15, p. 45.

[40] At the time, Horkheimer claimed, "My most basic principle, my most noble character trait, is clarity." GS 11, p. 308. Alfred Schmidt also emphasizes the "monographic, indeed didactic element" of Horkheimer's early novels, which "anticipates the essayistic form of the mature work." See his "Nachwort des Herausgebers" in GS 1, p. 368.

[41] Horkheimer was opposed to the war before it even began; this is demonstrated clearly by a letter he wrote to Pollock, who initially supported the war, on July 27, 1914, the day before the Austro-Hungarian Empire declared war on Serbia. GS 15, pp. 13–14.

[42] GS 1, pp. 24 and 31.

which he rails against the war and his military companions and superiors. He describes the military as "systematic education to murder" and says, "I cannot believe that what is a crime for an individual is noble for the nation."[43] He tells how he participated in the execution of a sixteen-year-old French girl who had helped her parents kill some German soldiers staying in their village. After just a few horrific battles on the front lines, Walter is fatally wounded. In his last letter to Luise, which he dictates to the nurse tending to him shortly before his death, he renounces his love to her, saying that she never understood him in the least and that he had been driven by the desire for possession just like everyone else, namely the desire to possess her. In the meantime, Luise has also received the news that one of her brothers has fallen and the other is missing.

Although Horkheimer's deeply pessimistic story provides no solutions to the problems he describes, he does hint at a few bleak possibilities of resistance, first of all in hatred of war itself. In his last letter, Walter says, "Everyone is a criminal, just as everything that exists a sin. And therefore war will remain a necessity until the very end. But precisely for this reason it is ray of hope, a sunny solace to hate it."[44] His criticism is articulated in the Nietzschean terms of an elitist nonconformism that refuses to identify with any group whatsoever: "So long as the majority of men are idiots and boors, so long will their association, i.e. society – whether it is socialist, autocratic and anarchistic – be inferior, and I believe that this 'so long' means an eternity."[45] As he would emphasize in his later appraisals of his early literary writings, Horkheimer did not yet have the conceptual tools to analyze the complex social, historical, and psychological determinants of an event like World War I, which led him, in this particular story, to an abstract defense of individuality. Walter says, "The principle of individuation is the only thing that leads to salvation, but time is what we need – time."[46] Yet this language of "salvation" and the lofty spiritual ideals that Walter defends at the beginning of the story, and which Horkheimer had celebrated in "L'isle heureuse," are also called into question at the end of the story. One of Walter's last sentences calls abstract idealism into question and uncannily adumbrates Horkheimer's future career: "We must construct our maxims based on what *is* and not what should be; and investigating that which exists, i.e. looking inside ourselves and the world and determining accordingly what we must do, is a task that fulfills an entire existence."[47]

Yet at this point, Horkheimer was still far from devoting himself to critical social theory and research. He had recently been made junior director of his father's factory, which prevented him from being sent to the front, because it was producing materials that were badly needed for the war effort. Needless to say, Horkheimer was extremely unhappy working in his father's factory. He wanted badly to continue his artistic and intellectual pursuits, and he did so in every spare minute he could find. Horkheimer would often find hiding

---

[43] Ibid., p. 23.
[44] Ibid., p. 62.
[45] Ibid., p. 31.
[46] Ibid., p. 60.
[47] Ibid., p. 61.

spots while working in his father's factory – behind a large roll of textile or in the bathroom – so he could continue writing his novellas, plays, and journal entries. He expresses his dissatisfaction in no uncertain terms in a journal entry from July 1915:

The present day is the symbol of my current life. I have a most desirable position with an even more desirable future in my father's business. I can permit myself any pleasure I desire, immerse myself in the business of the factory, entertain myself or pursue my hobbies – and yet a flame of burning desire consumes me.... Oh, may laziness, habit, false pity, weakness, base fear and the fear of death not prevent me from fleeing from my current situation![48]

In his writings from this time, Horkheimer repeatedly explored the theme of aspiring young artists who break with their parents and the mundane world of bourgeois convention in order to devote themselves fully to their work. In most cases, however, the stories end tragically. In "Overture,"[49] which Horkheimer wrote in November 1915, he tells the story of a young man whose parents disown him because of his love for a woman from a lower social class and his insistence upon pursuing a career as a pianist. Two years later, we find the young man sitting in a concert hall, trying desperately to forget that the woman has left him and his career as a pianist has come to naught.

The conflict with his parents, which is frequently thematized in his writings at this time, had been latent at least since Horkheimer's revelation to Pollock about his disillusionment with the dancing circle, but the incident with Neumeier in London had sharpened it greatly. Both his father and his mother chastised Horkheimer severely for his affair with her, which drove Horkheimer even further into internal rebellion. Horkheimer portrayed this tension with his parents in particularly vivid colors in "The Fence,"[50] a short story he wrote in November 1915. The story opens in the front yard of a country house of a wealthy man who has just learned that his wife is mentally ill. The man implores his son not to follow through on his plans to strike out on his own and to leave behind his parents, who both love him and need him very much. After the father goes inside, a peasant girl appears on the other side of the fence that surrounds the luxurious country villa, and asks why the young man is disconsolate. She encourages him to jump the fence and join her outside. He replies that he cannot because he is too weak, so the peasant girl decides to spring over the fence to talk to him for a while. After he explains his situation to her, she urges him to lead his own life, to come with her and to do what will make him happy. They are interrupted by the house servants, who tell him that his mother is crying hysterically, wondering where her son is. After the peasant girl promises to wait for him, he goes inside and spends the entire night with his father at the bedside of his sick mother. The next morning when he comes back outside, the peasant girl is still waiting for him on the other side of the fence and still urging him to join her. But then she realizes that he does not have

[48] Ibid., p. 159.
[49] Ibid., pp. 183–91.
[50] Ibid., pp. 176–83.

the strength to resist his fate, and she leaves him behind. He watches her leave as if it were his own life walking away from him, but he also manages somehow to convince himself that he has made the right decision.

Horkheimer's conflict with his parents would soon become even sharper with his growing love for Rosa Riekher, his future wife. Riekher worked in the factory as his father's private secretary. Horkheimer first got to know her better at the company Christmas party at the end of 1914.[51] They started having lunch together regularly and two months later, on the occasion of his twentieth birthday, Riekher sent Horkheimer a bouquet of twenty roses. Horkheimer was taken by surprise and wondered how to interpret the gift. He turned to Pollock for advice, who replied laconically, "Thank her with a kiss and then you will know."[52] This was the beginning of Horkheimer's lifelong relationship with "Maidon,"[53] as he affectionately referred to Riekher. Riekher was the daughter of an English woman and a hotel owner from Stuttgart. Her father's business went bankrupt while Riekher was attending trade school, which forced her to take a job as a secretary immediately after she graduated. Not only was Riekher eight years older than Horkheimer, she was also Christian. Her humble social status, age, and religion all contributed to Horkheimer's parents' disapproval of his relationship with her. Soon after they found out that the two of them were romantically involved, Riekher lost her position in the factory.[54] However, Horkheimer did not let his parents' disfavor deter him from pursuing a relationship with her. His stories from 1915 indicate that he was probably ambivalent about the relationship initially,[55] but by 1916 his devotion to Maidon had attained nearly religious proportions.

In the story "Spring," which Horkheimer wrote in April 1916, a student has just left his wealthy parents in order to join a young woman in a nearby village, with whom he has recently fallen in love. He describes his love for her in terms of redemption, as a replacement for the religion of his parents and other authority figures whose words he can no longer believe. The young couple sets out on a walk to a chapel on a nearby hilltop. On their way, they pass by an impoverished and miserable young vagrant whom the young woman knows and fears. They continue to the chapel and try not to let him disturb their bliss. As they are sitting in the chapel, however, the vagrant appears behind the pulpit and delivers a fiery sermon on the injustice of the world. The young couple's happiness is quickly replaced by shame and pity. Yet when the vagrant sees how deeply he has shaken them, he approaches them and says:

I feel sorry for you, you now know the truth; you have taken it to heart. But it is not enough to take off the rose-tinted glasses and then to stand there confused and helpless.

[51] Biographical interviews with Matthias Becker, p. 132.

[52] Ernst von Schenk, p. 39.

[53] Horkheimer explains the name in the following way: "Maid-don. I invented this name because two things came together in it that were important to me, namely French and English. English was 'maid,' French was 'don,' or gift: 'Maid-don.'" Interview with Matthias Becker, p.127.

[54] Helmut, Gumnior, and Rudolf, Ringguth, *Max Horkheimer in Selbstzeugnissen und Bilddokumenten*, (Hamburg, 1973), p. 18.

[55] Horkheimer repeatedly explores the theme of love between persons from different social classes in his writings at this time. However, more often than not, the stories end tragically.

You have to use your eyes and learn to walk in the colder world. Intoxicate yourself and praise every minute that you spend without being conscious, for consciousness is terrible: only Gods can possess it clear and undistorted and still smile.[56]

They leave the chapel together, still in love, but no longer in a state of bliss.

In another novella, with the title "Work," which Horkheimer wrote in July 1916 and dedicated to Maidon, he tells the story of a young factory director, Franz Lehndorf, who turns against his father, the owner of the factory, and incites the workers to revolution. His conversion to the workers' cause is inspired largely by his love for a young woman, Rosa Heim, who was forced to take a job in the factory after her family went bankrupt. Franz's call for revolution is driven by his conviction that the long hours of strenuous and monotonous work in the factory robs the workers of any possibility of developing themselves spiritually and intellectually. Franz himself really wants to become a musician and has agreed to work in the factory only to please his parents. When the workers fail to respond to his passionate calls for revolution, he decides to move into a modest apartment with Rosa and devote himself fully to his music. However, he fails to gain any recognition for his compositions, and despite Rosa's inexhaustible patience and selfless support, he decides he cannot continue to force her to lead such a miserable life. He recognizes that he was being selfish and living mainly for himself, but now he wants to live for Rosa. He decides to return to the factory and work so that Rosa can have a better life. After a short period, Rosa becomes fatally ill and dies. Franz is devastated. Yet out of the horrible experience, he draws the conclusion that he will continue to live for others and not simply for himself. He decides that the best way to do this is to continue working in the factory. He rescinds his belief in revolution, saying "Revolutions are necessary to liberate oneself, but they must take place in one's own soul. General catastrophes do not help anything; this has been proven by world history."[57] When plagued by memories of his earlier ideals, he thinks of Rosa's ethic of self-sacrifice and is reinforced in his belief that he is doing what is best.

One can only speculate on whether Horkheimer's sentimental celebration of work in this story was sincere. In any case, the story alludes clearly to Horkheimer's extreme devotion to Riekher. With one small exception, which we will soon discuss, Horkheimer's love for Riekher would never waver. His letters to her during these years are a remarkable testament to Horkheimer's boundless affection and devotion to his future wife.[58] Horkheimer's parents continued to frown on their relationship, particularly when Riekher moved to Munich, and then later to Frankfurt, to live with Horkheimer. The two of them did not get married until 1926. It was only at this time, which coincided with Horkheimer's successful completion of his qualifications for an academic career, that his parents welcomed Riekher into their family. Yet by 1916, she had already become, after Pollock, the second pillar of Horkheimer's

[56] GS 1, p. 228.
[57] Ibid., p. 255.
[58] See GS 15, pp. 15–79.

emotional life: a triadic foundation that would remain unshaken until Riekher's death in 1969.

Nineteen sixteen was also the year in which Horkheimer was finally called for military service. Until then, he had been able to avoid the draft because he was working in his father's factory. In January of 1916, however, Horkheimer had to report to the recruitment office. This first time around he was not enlisted, but his second visit, in September 1916, led to his enrollment. His military training took place in Aalen, a small town approximately seventy-five kilometers east of Stuttgart. He worked as a medical aid in a regiment that traveled throughout southern Germany, but never approached the front lines. Horkheimer himself was never considered for a regiment that would see fighting because of his sickly condition, which he made no effort to hide. As we have seen, Horkheimer was opposed to the war from the beginning, and he says in his later interviews that he performed poorly on purpose during the selection and training process so he would not be sent to the front.[59] Nonetheless, Horkheimer's military service took a heavy toll on him both physically and psychologically. Even his regular trips to Stuttgart during this time were not enough to prevent his health from deteriorating. In the spring of 1918, when his regiment was in Munich, Horkheimer was sent to a doctor who decided that he was *dienstuntauglich* – unfit for further military service. The doctor recommended that Horkheimer be committed to the sanatorium Neu-Wittelsbach, in Munich, where he would remain until shortly before the end of the war.

Horkheimer's personal experiences in the military during this time only reinforced his hatred of the war. On the occasion of his first recruitment meeting in January of 1916, Horkheimer records in his journal his struggle with feelings of guilt for resisting the war. He notes how the other potential recruits accepted the process unquestioningly, even happily, and how many of them viewed him suspiciously. He writes, "It is insane to rise up against necessity. One must learn to bear it. I must relinquish my claim to personal happiness; I must no longer strive beyond the generality, I must offer myself to it and for it."[60] By the end of the recruitment process and the end of the journal entry, however, Horkheimer had overcome his dubious feelings of guilt and regained his defiance:

The war is ugly, its apologists are swindlers or swindled; they are murderers, for they are spilling blood. I hate their stupid, bloated faces with their … hard features. Compassion and love are the highest virtues; I want to spend my life in their service, want to strive for knowledge and beauty and – in spite of them – want to be proud of it![61]

As the end of the war approached, Horkheimer continued to criticize the war vehemently in his writings. In "Birth," a short story he wrote in March 1918, Horkheimer articulates – in choppy, aggressive expressionist language – the desperate thoughts running through a sensitive young man's head on the eve

---

[59] Horkheimer says: "When I was a soldier I behaved in such an unsoldierly manner that they were all happy when I was sent away later. … When I was a soldier I was undisciplined in every respect." Biographical interviews with Matthias Becker, p. 37.

[60] GS 1, p. 164.

[61] GS 1, p. 166.

of his return to his regiment after an eight-day vacation. Faced with the prospect of leaving his lover behind and returning to the infernal conditions of his regiment, the young man runs into the forest with a pistol with the intention of killing himself. He is prevented from following through with the act only by a relentless feeling of guilt, which also drives him to overcome his dread at returning to the pompous indifference of his commander, the scorn and jealousy of his fellow soldiers, and the dreary tasks that await him the next day in the hospital. When he arrives, all his worst fears and anxieties are confirmed. His colleagues make no attempt to conceal their contempt for the weakling who managed to finagle an eight-day vacation. After their regiment has lined up for morning drill, the commander rides in on his horse and delivers a stern speech about the nullity of the individual and the complete and utter dependence of every member of the nation on the state: "There is no such thing as the rights of the individual! The state alone has all rights."[62] In the end, the young man is broken. He leaves his unhappy consciousness behind and is reborn as a smoothly functioning part of the larger whole, singing heartily and marching in stride with the rest.

In "Peace," a short play Horkheimer wrote in December 1917, he tells the story of an encounter between a young Jewish painter (Claude) and a wounded soldier (Zech) in a hospital, where both are recovering. Claude does his best to ignore the war and to live solely for his aesthetic ideals. Zech's experiences on the front lines have turned him into a revolutionary; he demands that Claude take sides. In the meantime, Claude's former lover, Germaine, comes to visit him in the hospital with Norbert, a decorated lieutenant, to whom she was recently engaged. She explains to Claude that two years of working as a volunteer medical aid in the field convinced her that she could no longer love an effeminate cosmopolitan aesthete like Claude (whose real name is Siegfried; he changed it due to his love for France), and has fallen for Norbert instead, a virile embodiment of patriotic heroism. Norbert adds insult to injury by lecturing Claude about the necessity of eliminating parasitic elements, such as himself, from the body politic. In the meantime, word spreads in the hospital that the war has ended, which leads to a renewed outburst of Zech's revolutionary fervor. A fight breaks out in the hospital room between those for and against Zech. Claude observes the fray from a safe distance, refusing to join either side. After Zech's followers prevail, one of them demands that Claude be executed, not just because of his noncommittal stance, but because "The Jews cheated us the worst. They all became rich with our blood."[63] Zech protests at first, arguing that those truly responsible need to be targeted and that unnecessary cruelty must be avoided. Yet in the end, he succumbs to the pressure of the group and shoots Claude to demonstrate his loyalty to the revolutionary cause. When Norbert and Germaine reenter the scene, one of Zech's followers points out to Norbert that Germaine's father's company has declared bankruptcy, which leads Norbert promptly to abandon Germaine, who is left to mourn Claude, the only one who ever really loved her.

[62] Ibid., p. 335.
[63] Ibid., p. 317.

In addition to providing yet another depiction of the brutality and venality bred by the war, "Peace" sheds light on Horkheimer's political self-understanding at a crucial time in his development – just prior to revolutionary upheavals in Germany in late 1918 and early 1919. These events would have a radicalizing effect on him, but until then Horkheimer's attitude toward politics of any persuasion was largely negative. Although he did articulate a radical critique of society, he never believed that any particular party, movement, or group had the potential to enact positive social change. In "Peace," Horkheimer gives expression to this view with the character of Zech, who criticizes the war and social injustice in terms very similar to Horkheimer's own, but whose political principles do not prevent him from committing the barbaric act of murdering Claude. Zech's hypocritical actions illustrate Horkheimer's own deep ambivalence about politics during this time. On the one hand, Horkheimer's intense awareness of injustice and his compassion for those who suffer and are exploited fueled his desire for social change. On the other hand, his pessimistic view of politics as a base struggle for power and his fear and disgust of the lower classes made him wary of any mass-based political movement. Horkheimer gave vivid expression to this tension in the short story "Leonard Steirer,"[64] which he wrote in January 1916. The story begins with Steirer, a factory worker, confronting his former lover, Johanna, who has recently left him for the son of the owner of the factory where all three of them work. The woman insults Steirer, calls him an animal and explains to him that the son has everything that he lacks: money, leisure, education, and a future. That evening Steirer surprises her and her new lover by breaking in through their bedroom window. He demands that the son give him all his money and that Johanna come back to him. When they resist, Steirer murders the son and absconds with his money and Johanna. When they are alone, Steirer manages to convince Johanna that he is no less deserving of her love than the son was; he simply had not been born with the same privileges. They enjoy themselves for one day, spending the son's money in luxurious boutiques and restaurants, before the police arrive and arrest Steirer. Johanna tries to convince the authorities that she committed the crime in order to save Steirer, but to no avail. He's found guilty and condemned to death.

In this story and several others that Horkheimer wrote at the time, he clearly expresses his compassion for the plight of the working class and his own guilt for enjoying privileges largely dependent on their toil. In one of his journal entries from this time, he states unequivocally his desire for social change: "I want to fight to tear down the borders between the countries and the social classes, even though I know that this struggle is insane."[65] On the other hand, Horkheimer also expresses his deep fear of the potential irrationality of the lower classes. This fear is evident not only in the violent acts of Zech or Leonard Steirer, but also in numerous portrayals of anti-Semitic violence that surface in his writing beginning in 1917.[66] In the story "Jochai," which he wrote in July

[64] Ibid., p. 200–9.

[65] Ibid., p. 161.

[66] The fact that anti-Semitism did not play a role in his writing until this time suggests that Horkheimer was probably confronted with overt anti-Semitism during his period of military

1917, Horkheimer tells the story of young politicized Jew who spares the life of a general's daughter, whom he was ordered to execute. Jochai passionately believes in the necessity of a better society; he is able to convince the general's daughter to join his cause. Yet faced with the spectacle of a mob burning down the house of a Jewish industrialist, the two of them decide to flee to another country, to try to start from scratch and to create a community of solidarity of their own, rather than struggle for reform in Europe. In "Gregor," which he wrote a few months later, Horkheimer describes a large group of factory workers, poor women, and children listening to an inflammatory speech by an anti-Semitic demagogue, who declares the Jews responsible for their woes and leads them into the city where they destroy Jewish houses and property.[67] The main character of the story, Tom, has become a radical critic of society after witnessing the fate of his friend Gregor, who was thrown in prison for refusing to fire on revolting workers. He realizes that the injustice of the system has nothing to do with the Jews as such; nonetheless, he participates in the mob violence out of an irrational desire for revenge.

These unflinching portrayals of the irrational potential of mass-based politics reflect Horkheimer's own political self-understanding at this time. His vehement criticism of the war did not lead him to align himself with any particular political group. Instead, he rejected politics altogether as a base power struggle of interest only to the mediocre. He believed that true individual development could only occur in the aesthetic realm. This stance was common among German intellectuals at the time, but it usually entailed a passive acceptance or active celebration of the war.[68] In a letter he wrote in August 1917, with the title "Avowal of My Politics,"[69] Horkheimer outlines and justifies his rejection of politics. At one point, he discusses a book by a Swiss socialist who had condemned the war and called for a revolt against the governments that had made it possible in the first place. Horkheimer sees no essential difference between the antiwar appeals of the socialist and the war propaganda of the governments. Both are nothing more than instruments in a more general struggle for power. Neither has any greater claim to truth than the other:

Spurious reasons, and the clever embellishment of one's own interests with the law and moral purity are transformed into finished products that can be easily consumed by

---

service. This conjecture is supported by a letter Horkeimer wrote in August 1917 in which he describes his return to military service after a vacation. He writes, "I was regarded with spiteful apprehension because I am Jewish." GS 1, p. 277. Horkheimer's future colleague, Leo Lowenthal, also discusses his shocking encounter with anti-Semitism during his military service in 1918: "I was a constant object of ridicule. Already at that time I experienced the potential anti-Semitism and anti-intellectualism of the German proletariat and peasants." *Mitmachen wollte ich nie* (Frankfurt, 1980), p. 53.

[67] GS 1, p. 295.

[68] One thinks of here of the young Thomas Mann, who believed that culture existed above the sordid realm of politics. His experiences with National Socialism and exile would change his views considerably on this topic. This aesthetic disdain for politics, which one also finds in Horkheimer's early writings, can be attributed in part to the profound influence of Nietzsche – who also proudly referred to himself as "non-political" – on this generation of German intellectuals. On Nietzsche's reception in Germany in the period leading up to World War I, see Steven Aschheim, *The Nietzsche Legacy in Germany 1890–1990* (Berkeley, 1992).

[69] GS 1, pp. 273–85.

large groups of followers, run like a religion, and believed like a religion: that is party and popular politics.[70]

Horkheimer defines his own politics in opposition to that of the masses:

I felt that my own nature was valuable based on its distance from the people surrounding me.... Challenged by the literature of the socialists, I sought my *own* weapons, 'my *own* politics, but I did not find anything that could have been called similar, even in form, to any of the programs existing then. It was not the lust for power ... nor for money whose satisfaction I longed for – one may perhaps, for lack of a better term, call my goal enjoyment, but it is different from the pleasures of these animals! They are all striving to fulfill the same wishes, the same desires bind them together, one wants to acquire goods, the other to take them by force: all are related. Different my nature, different my goal, my path foreign to them.[71]

In his later interviews, Horkheimer stressed his disappointment with the Social Democratic support of the war in 1914 as the decisive event in the development of his political skepticism.[72] However, Horkheimer's political disillusionment cannot be reduced to any one cause. As we have seen, a wide variety of experiences during World War I strengthened his resolve to pursue a course of consistent political nonconformism. Horkheimer did not cling to a strictly consistent form of this position for long. Horkheimer's experiences with the revolutionary events in Germany in the next year would lead him to a reception of Marx in the early twenties, which would result in, among other things, his rejection of the possibility of maintaining a disinterested position above the political fray. On the other hand, Horkheimer's deep distrust of party politics would also remain an essential moment of his thought. As he would put it twenty years later in his programmatic essay, "Traditional and Critical Theory," Critical Theory was not "free floating," but neither was it "rooted" in an unreflective way in any particular political group, even those with which it sympathized.

By 1918, there was no trace whatsoever remaining of the enthusiasm that had accompanied the outbreak of the war. Most people had believed that the conflict would be decided quickly, and although the Brest-Litovsk Treaty had resolved the conflict on the Eastern front, the lines of battle on the Western front had hardly changed, despite the massive loss of life on both sides. In this context, the politicians and generals, who called for renewed sacrifice on the part of civilians, workers, and soldiers, began to lose their credibility. In 1917, massive strikes broke out in both Germany and France, and the morale of soldiers on both sides was deteriorating rapidly. Horkheimer's writings from this period, during his stay at the Neu-Wittelsbach sanatorium in Munich, articulate in the most extreme and uncompromising of terms the growing awareness of the utter insanity of the war and the profoundly pessimistic implications it

---

[70] GS 1, p. 284.

[71] Ibid., pp. 278–9.

[72] He said, "In 1914, when the war broke out and the *Reichstag* had to take a stand, not a single member of the Social Democrats voted against it. This was a momentous experience for me, because from that time onward I was able to see through politics in general, whether left or right." Biographical interviews with Matthias Becker, p. 99.

FIGURE 1. Horkheimer attending a dance social in 1910 or 1911.

FIGURE 2. Horkheimer together with workers in his father's factory in 1915.

FIGURE 3. Horkheimer with his future wife, Rosa Riekhehr, in 1916.

FIGURE 4. Horkheimer and Friedrich Pollock in military uniform in 1917.

FIGURE 5. Germaine Krull's photographic portrait of Pollock in 1923.

had for Western European civilization. In a journal entry from September 3, 1918, two months before the end of the war, Horkheimer writes:

War demonstrates what I have known all along: my life is murder. The state protects from wild animals and men. Others perform coarse labor, wither away in factories, are poisoned by cyanide, plague victims are tormented by fever, lie in their own defecation, a boy shot in the kidney writhes in barbed wire – hundreds of boys, millions of boys. Millions of boys writhe in barbed wire so people protected by the state can kiss and be happy, and cultivate themselves. The state protects from wild animals and men. War demonstrates what I have known all along: life is murder.[73]

However, the arrival of the darkest hour also signaled the coming of the dawn. During the last months of the war, in the politically volatile final days of Wilhelmine Germany, Horkheimer also began to entertain the possibility of radical social change. In a letter to Riekher and Pollock on October 28, 1918, Horkheimer mentions "Zottel" for the first time,[74] which was the nickname of Germaine Krull,[75] a young photographer he had recently met. Krull's atelier in Schwabing[76] had become a focal point for some of the most important members of the political and artistic opposition in Munich in the period leading up to and following the revolution and the Munich council

[73] GS 1, p. 359–60.
[74] GS 15, p. 45.
[75] For a survey of Krull's remarkable life and work, see Kim Sichel, *Germaine Krull: Photographer of Modernity* (Cambridge, MA, 1999).
[76] A section of Munich that was traditionally the center of bohemian life.

republic. It was with Krull that Horkheimer would have his first brush with oppositional politics.

HORKHEIMER'S BRIEF STAY IN BOHEMIA: MUNICH 1918–19

Horkheimer was introduced to Krull by one of her friends, Katja Lüx, whom Horkheimer had met in the fall of 1918 while browsing in a bookstore in Schwabing. Horkheimer soon became an active participant in their circle, which met regularly in Krull's atelier. Krull, who was two years younger than Horkheimer, had already made somewhat of a name for herself as the portrait-ist of Kurt Eisner, a journalist and theater critic who had recently become the leader of the Independent Social Democratic Party (USPD), and who would play the leading role in the revolutionary events in Munich, until his assassina-tion on February 21, 1919. Krull's parents introduced her to Eisner, and after his assassination she remained friends with his widow. Krull's friend Katja Lüx, whom she had met in photography school, was friends with Ernst Toller, a young poet and playwright. Toller would take over the helm of the USPD after Eisner's death and play a leading role in the Munich council republic the follow-ing April. In addition to the Eisners and Toller, Krull was in contact with several of the most respected poets and writers living in Munich at the time, including Stefan Zweig and Rainer Maria Rilke. All of these figures, and many other less prominent members of bohemian Munich, made more or less frequent appear-ances in Krull's atelier. Horkheimer began coming regularly to Krull's circle in September or October of 1918 to participate in the artistic and political discus-sions, and to present his own literary work. Horkheimer seems to have made quite an impression on Krull and her friends. In his letter to Riekher and Pollock, Horkheimer describes his interaction with the group in the following way:

These people understand themselves as artists and when we share with them even a small part, a mere taste of our wealth, they are astonished.... They are all exceptionally attentive to me.... They have taken me in as one of their own ... that simply means, they have the greatest possible respect.[77]

In her unpublished memoirs, Krull confirms Horkheimer's impression. She describes Horkheimer as a "uniquely ironic and precise spirit, very sharp as well," and says of his role in their circle that "Max was in his element. The dis-cussions were always very interesting and [Ernst] Toller was not always the most convincing. Max was a supporter of Rosa Luxemburg and [Karl] Liebknecht; Toller defended either [Kurt] Eisner or himself."[78] In short, Horkheimer had

---

[77] GS 15, p. 46.
[78] *La Vie Mène La Danse*, p. 48. The original version of this autobiographical manuscript has not been published. It is located in the Germaine Krull Archive in Museum Folkwang, in Essen, Germany. The manuscript has, however, been translated and published in Italian as *La Vita Conduce La Danza* (Florenz: Giunti Gruppo Editoriale, 1992). Krull actually wrote six autobio-graphical works altogether. In what follows, I will also draw upon *Chien Fou*, an unpublished autobiographical manuscript in the Germaine Krull Archive. *Chien Fou* was written in the form of a novel and describes Krull's life until 1919, when she left Munich for the Soviet Union. For a brief discussion of Krull's autobiographical writings, see Kim Sichel, *Germain Krull: Avantgarde als Abenteuer* (Essen, 1999), p. 301.

become involved in the bohemian circles of Munich and had begun to stake out a socialist political position well before the collapse of Wilhelmine Germany in early November 1918.

On the other hand, the next few months would prove that Horkheimer was unwilling to translate his radical theoretical convictions directly into praxis. He continued to maintain his distance from the explosive political events of the time and to devote himself primarily to his own personal concerns. He and Pollock had, in the meantime, made the decision to attend the university after the war. However, in order to do so they needed to make up their *Abitur* – a comprehensive exam given to students of the elite German *Gymnasium* – which was the prerequisite for university studies. In the period immediately following the war, young persons who had served in any capacity in the military had the opportunity to take an abbreviated version of the *Abitur*, even if they had not completed the normal course of studies at a *Gymnasium*, as was the case with Horkheimer and Pollock. On the same day when Philipp Scheidemann and Karl Liebknecht opened the contest for Germany's political future in Berlin – November 9th, 1918 – Pollock arrived in Munich to begin looking for a place to live for himself, Horkheimer, and Riekher, and to start studying with Horkheimer for their *Abitur*. Pollock and Horkheimer passed the *Abitur* in the spring of 1919. Horkheimer would remain in the sanatorium until mid-February, at which point he and Pollock moved into a large apartment in one of Munich's affluent quarters. Horkheimer's parents were still supporting him financially, even though their relationship with their son was more tense than ever, due to his decision to attend the university and his ongoing relationship with Riekher.[79] Riekher was unable to move to Munich right away, but they continued to exchange letters regularly, and she visited Horkheimer occasionally as well.

On one of her visits to Munich during this time, Horkheimer forgot to pick Riekher up at the train station. Apparently he had made plans with Germaine Krull and her friends on the same evening. Riekher had to spend the night alone in a hotel in Munich, where apparently she was propositioned by a charming Swedish man. She was so angry with Horkheimer that she very nearly accepted this strange man's offer to travel to Sweden with him. It was only with great difficulty that Pollock and Horkheimer were able to appease her the next day. The incident indicates the depth of Horkheimer's fascination with Krull and her circle of friends. As Horkheimer put it an interview at the end of his life, "I was so bohemian and so preoccupied that I forgot her."[80] Pollock also recalls that Horkheimer was infatuated with Krull at this time. The incident proved to be the most serious test of Horkheimer's relationship with Riekher. Although Horkheimer would remain in contact with Krull for

[79] At this point, Horkheimer had also come to view his father as a *Kriegsprofiteur*, someone who had benefited financially from the war. In the radical circles in which Horkheimer began to move at this time, the *Kriegsprofiteur* were one of the most hated symbols of the injustice of the Wilhelmine Germany. See *Chien Fou*, p. 46. Later Horkheimer would revise his opinion. In interviews at the end of his life, Horkheimer stressed the great sacrifices his father made during the war and the fact that his father lost a good portion of his fortune during this time.

[80] Biographical interviews with Ernst Schenk, (Max Horkheimer Archive, X 132b) p. 36.

the rest of his life, he assumed the role of a big brother in their relationship, giving her advice and helping her out of difficult situations on several different occasions.[81] Horkheimer's loyalty to Riekher may have wavered at this point, but his letters and Krull's memoirs indicate clearly that it never broke.[82]

During the first few months of 1919, the struggle for the political future of Germany reached its high point. On January 8, the self-proclaimed "bloodhound" of the nascent republic, the Social Democratic minister of defense, Gustav Noske, called in the Imperial Army and the *Freikorps*[83] to put down massive worker demonstrations spearheaded by the Sparticists in Berlin. A week later, Karl Liebknecht and Rosa Luxemburg were brutally murdered by the *Freikorps* while being transferred from one prison to another.[84] On February 21, Kurt Eisner was assassinated by a young royalist in Munich, which lead to an intensification of the political conflict in Bavaria. During the second week of March, more than one thousand people were killed when Noske had a second, even larger, revolt in Berlin put down. On March 21, a council republic seized power in Hungary under the leadership of Bela Kun. The Hungarian example set an important precedent for the burgeoning revolutionary movement in Bavaria, and on April 7, a council republic was declared in Munich and several other Bavarian cities.[85] During its first phase, the Munich council republic was led mainly by artists and intellectuals, such as Gustav Landauer, Erich Mühsam, Ernst Toller and Sylvio Gesell. In the second phase of the Munich council republic, which lasted from April 13 to 27, the Communists played the decisive role; of the four men in the central council – Ernst Toller, Eugene Leviné, Max Levine, and Tobias Axelrod – only Toller, who had taken over Eisner's position as the head of the Bavarian USPD, was not a Communist. The short third and final phase of the council republic began when the Communists stepped down after the majority of central council members voted to accept Toller and his faction's demands for reinstatement of freedom of the press and the reconstitution of the local police force. However, by the end of April, the counterrevolutionary troops had already surrounded Munich, and despite their tenacious efforts, the revolutionary troops were able to resist the combined force of the Imperial Army and *Freikorps* only for a few days. By May 3, Munich was firmly in the hands of the white troops who proceeded to wreak horrible vengeance against supporters of the council republic.

---

[81] On Horkheimer's relationship to Krull, see Sichel, *Germaine Krull: Avantgarde als Abenteuer*, pp. 23–4.

[82] GS 15, pp. 54–6. *La Vie Mène La Danse*, pp. 59–60.

[83] A group of counterrevolutionary soldiers who never really demobilized after the war. They applied the brutal methods of fighting they had become accustomed to in the war to the workers at home. Many members of the *Freikorps* would become zealous Nazis later. See Robert G.L. Waite, *Vanguard of Nazism: The Free Corps Movement in Post-war Germany, 1918–23* (Cambridge, MA, 1952) and Klaus Theweleit, *Male Fantasies*, trans. Stephan Conway (Minneapolis, 1987).

[84] Detlev J. K. Peukert, *The Weimar Republic*, trans. R. Deveson (New York, 1989), p. 32.

[85] On the Munich council republic, see Allan Mitchell, *Revolution in Bavaria, 1918–1919: The Eisner Regime and the Soviet Republic* (Princeton, 1965), and Ralf Höller, *Der Anfang der ein Ende war: Die Revolution in Bayern 1918/19* (Berlin, 1999).

In her memoirs, Krull describes how she, Horkheimer, and Pollock watched the white troops enter Munich from the balcony of Horkheimer and Pollock's apartment. During the previous few months, their apartment in an affluent section of Munich had become a place of refuge for Krull, where she could periodically escape from the increasingly tense political atmosphere that had engulfed her atelier in Schwabing. Although he clearly sympathized to some extent with the council republic,[86] Horkheimer maintained a safe distance from the turbulent political events, and Pollock seems to have been even more skeptical.[87] Although Horkheimer in particular identified with the lofty artistic and intellectual ideals that animated the first phase of the council republic, he felt that the conditions were not yet ripe for radical social change. Nevertheless, after the council republic was brutally suppressed, Horkheimer and Pollock became actively involved in aiding several persons who had participated directly, and who were now fleeing from the white terror. It seems, however, that their political engagement was inspired largely by Krull. Horkheimer and Pollock agreed to hide Tobias Axelrod – a Russian emissary who had played a leading role in the second phase of the council republic – in their apartment for several days. After a close call with a police inspection, Krull decided to help Axelrod and another partisan of the council republic, Willy Budich, flee to Austria. She convinced Pollock to give Axelrod his personal documents to conceal his identity. Krull, Axelrod, and Budich made it across the border, but were arrested just a few days later, on May 12, in Tirol. The Austrian police delivered them to the German authorities in Garmisch, a small town near the Austrian border.

When Horkheimer and Pollock found out that Krull had been arrested, they traveled to Garmisch to visit her. By the time they arrived, she had already been set free. The authorities apparently did not consider her as dangerous as Axelrod and Budich, who were kept in custody. On the way back from Garmisch, Horkheimer was arrested on the train, not just once, but twice, by local citizen patrols that had formed since the repression of the council republic. The patrols mistook Horkheimer for Ernst Toller, who was in hiding at the time, and for whose recovery the police were offering a substantial reward. The second time around, Horkheimer was taken by the patrol to the military headquarters, near the central train station in Munich. A young officer arrived, who was also convinced that Horkheimer was Toller, and ordered the men to beat Horkheimer. It was only with great difficulty that he was able to convince them that they had the wrong man and to let him leave later that evening.[88] When he and Pollock returned to their apartment, Krull was waiting for them there. Horkheimer explained to both of them that he no longer had any desire to risk his life by staying in Munich. As he explained in later interviews, it was

---

[86] In a letter to Riekher on April 19, 1919, Horkheimer wrote, "The liars want to murder – to murder for money; anarchy and injustice are *not* ruling here." GS 15, p. 55.

[87] Pollock believed that the conditions were not yet ripe for the formation of a council republic in Munich. According to Krull, when Pollock found out that the council republic had been established, he said that "This proclamation is completely idiotic; one should arrest Toller immediately." *La Vie Mène La Danse*, p. 50.

[88] Biographical interviews with Matthias Becker, pp. 49–50.

at this point that he decided to leave Munich for good.[89] In the next few weeks, he and Pollock would decide that Frankfurt was the best place for them to continue their studies.

However, before Horkheimer and Pollock moved to Frankfurt, they did what they could to ameliorate the condition of those who had participated in the council republic. Pollock help set up a committee that provided legal and material aid for workers who had been thrown in prison and their families.[90] Horkheimer traveled extensively with Krull in Germany during the next few weeks in an attempt to draw attention to the plight of Tobias Axelrod. Several leaders of council republic, including Gustav Landauer, had already been summarily executed by the white troops. When Eugene Leviné was condemned to death on June 3 and executed two days later, Krull's fears were heightened that Axelrod would soon meet a similar fate. In order to find help for Axelrod, Horkheimer first took Krull to Stuttgart to meet with a friend of Pollock's mother, who had since become a member of the German Communist Party. She suggested that the two of them travel to Berlin to see if Paul Levi, the head of the German Communist Party, would be willing to help them. When Levi proved unresponsive, Horkheimer made one final attempt to seek help for Axelrod. He went to the office of the Berlin journal, *Die Aktion*, in hopes that its publisher, Franz Pfemfert, would be willing to help Axelrod.

Pfemfert, who was an early and uncompromising critic of the war, had established *Die Aktion* as the most important forum in Germany for literary expressionism. Horkheimer had been an admirer of Pfemfert and avid reader of *Die Aktion* since the beginning of the war. After the November Revolution, *Die Aktion* became even more explicit in its commitment to radical democratic socialism, in the spirit of Rosa Luxemburg and Karl Liebknecht. It was Pfemfert's political position with which Horkheimer identified most during this time.[91] However, due to his harsh criticism of the new regime's repression of working-class revolts in Berlin in early 1919, and his call for the formation of a new revolutionary socialist party, Pfemfert had been arrested twice and *Die Aktion* temporarily censored.[92] When Horkheimer and Krull showed up in the office of *Die Aktion* in the summer of 1919, they learned that Pfemfert had decided it was best for him to leave Berlin until the political situation had settled. They traveled to Pfemfert's refuge in a small village in the Harz mountains in central Germany. Pfemfert and his wife were sympathetic to Axelrod's plight, but they were unable or unwilling to do anything concretely to help him. While there, Krull met another political refugee, Samuel Levit, who was staying with the Pfemferts at the time, and who was much more willing to take action on behalf of Axelrod. Krull, whose recent experiences had strengthened her radical political convictions, was taken by the fiery rhetoric of Levit, and the two of them soon became inseparable. He joined Krull in Munich for

---

[89] Ibid.

[90] *Chien Fou*, pp. 291–2.

[91] See page 50.

[92] Ursula Walburga Baumeister, *Die Aktion 1911–1932: Publizistische Opposition und literarischer Aktivismus der Zeitschrift im restriktiven Kontext* (Erlangen und Jena, 1996), pp. 261–2.

a short period, and then the two of them migrated to Russia to continue
the political struggle there. It was at this point that Horkheimer parted ways
with Krull. They would meet occasionally in Munich during the next couple
months, but Pollock's open animosity for Levit made relations among them
extremely difficult. They would not see each other again until 1922, when
Krull returned from her harrowing experience in Russia, completely disillusioned with Bolshevism.[93]

BETWEEN CONTEMPT AND COMPASSION: HORKHEIMER'S EARLY INTELLECTUAL DEVELOPMENT

Before continuing with Horkheimer's university studies in Frankfurt, let us
cast a glance back on his intellectual development through 1919. With the
beginning of his friendship with Pollock in 1911, Horkheimer entered a phase
of latent rebellion against his parents and the well-ordered bourgeois world
they represented. Horkheimer was too fearful of the consequences to rebel
openly. In Pollock's friendship, he had found a refuge from the external world,
but when the two of them attempted to give concrete form to their utopian
ideals, in their experiment with Neumeier and the *isle heureuse*, they were
quickly checked. Horkheimer's novellas about young artists who attempt
directly to live out their ideals but who quickly find themselves in desperation,
reflect his ambivalent state of disaffection, longing, and resignation. At the
time of the outbreak of World War I, Horkheimer's dominant attitude is one
of Nietzschean contempt for the norms of bourgeois society and the compact
majority that uncritically adhere to them.[94] With the outbreak of World War I,
Horkheimer's worst fears were confirmed. Contempt for the rampant conformity of the time remained an important element of this thought, but during the
next few years it was increasingly tempered by a more tragic view of the world,
which demanded not just contempt, but also compassion and love.

The most important intellectual factor in this shift in Horkheimer's worldview was without doubt his serious study of Schopenhauer, a philosopher
whose own youth resembled that of Horkheimer in many respects.[95] In 1831,
Schopenhauer wrote:

In my seventeenth year, without any formal education, I was seized by the anguish of
life, like Buddha in his youth when he saw sickness, old age, pain and death. The truth,
which spoke loudly and clearly out of the world, soon overcame the Jewish doctrines I
had been taught and, as a result, I concluded that this world could not be the creation

[93] See Krull's letter to Horkheimer and Pollock from January 12, 1922 in GS 15, p. 80. See
also Kim Sichel's description of Krull misadventures in Russia in *Avantgarde als Abenteuer*,
pp. 24–30.

[94] In later interviews, Horkheimer confirms that Nietzsche was one of the first philosophers he
read. Interview with Ernst Schenk, p. 34.

[95] Schopenhauer's father was also a wealthy businessman who wanted his son to follow in his
footsteps. Schopenhauer's mother was even more opposed to his becoming a philosopher. On
Schopenhauer's youth, see Eberhard Fromm, *Arthur Schopenhauer: Vordenker des Pessimus*
(Berlin, 1991), pp. 11–38, and Rudiger Safranski, *Schopenhauer und Die Wilden Jahre der
Philosophie: Eine Biographie* (Munich and Vienna, 1987), pp. 17–130.

of a supremely benevolent being, but indeed that of a devil, who had called beings into existence, in order to take pleasure in their suffering.[96]

Schopenhauer's pessimism increasingly captured Horkheimer's imagination during World War I. The theme of the world as a living hell recurred again and again in Horkheimer's writings at this time. Yet Horkheimer's pessimism did not lead to resignation. He concurred with Schopenhauer's criticisms of metaphysical systems or philosophies of history, such as that of Leibniz or Hegel, that justified the status quo as desirable, rational, or necessary. On the other hand, Horkheimer did not follow Schopenhauer in hypostatizing the negativity of the world by granting it the status of a metaphysical principle. The following imaginary confrontation with Buddha, which Horkheimer penned in 1918, demonstrates that he did not esteem the Buddhist otherworldly rejection of the world as highly as did Schopenhauer[97]: "Your salvation, Buddha, my hands push away disdainfully. I am more familiar than you with the infernal world, from which you would liberate me. But I do not have to flee like you, 'forgetting' of sins does not have to take me out of the world."[98] In other words, Horkheimer transformed the philosophically founded rejection of the world, which he discovered in Schopenhauer's writings, into a critique of the world *as it is*. He never despaired entirely of the possibility of change.

At first, his resistance to the *Weltlauf* took the relatively modest and personal form of an ethics of compassion and love.[99] Compassion, which is the central principle of Schopenhauer's ethics, was for Horkheimer at this time the key to overcoming the desire to flee the world or to view it purely in terms of contempt. In the novella "Longing," for example, Horkheimer tells the story of a young man who believes he is above the petty concerns of practically everyone else, and who remains dissatisfied regardless of where he goes or what he does. He finally meets another man who tells him, "You must learn … compassion, only then will you be human, otherwise your soul will remain empty, you will be filled only with vague longing and boredom."[100] The young man takes his new friend's advice and is able to find purpose in a life devoted to fighting injustice and helping those in need. It is in this gradual embrace of Schopenhauer's ethics of compassion that one can most clearly see Horkheimer's increasingly critical view of Nietzsche at this time. In several of Horkheimer's novellas

---

[96] Quoted by Alfred Schmidt in his "Nachwort des Herausgebers," GS 1, p. 369.

[97] On Schopenhauer's understanding and appropriation of Buddhism, see Peter Abelsen, "Schopenhauer and Buddhism," *Philosophy East and West*, vol. 43, pp. 255–78 (1993) and B.V. Kishan, "Schopenhauer and Buddhism," *Schopenhauer: His Philosophical Achievement*, ed. Michael Fox (Sussex, 1980), pp. 255–61.

[98] GS 1, p. 348. Horkheimer's critique of Schopenhauer's flirtation with Buddhism here – and later, in *Dämmerung* – demonstrates the baselessness of Rolf Wiggerhaus's claim that Horkheimer was interested in a "Schopenhauerian-Bhuddistic inspired modification of Marxian and Freudian thought." Rolf Wiggershaus, *Die Frankfurter Schule: Geschichte, Theoretische Entwicklung, Politische Bedeutung* (Munich: DTV, 1988), p. 300. For Horkheimer's critique of Bhuddism in *Dämmerung*, see GS 2, p. 360.

[99] *Weltlauf* can be translated as "The way of the world." See G.W.F. Hegel, "Virtue and the Way of the World," *Phenomenology of Spirit*, trans. A.V. Miller (Oxford: Oxford University Press, 1977), pp. 228–35.

[100] GS 1, p. 140. Emphasis Horkheimer's.

from this time, such as "Irene: Tale of the Night" and "The Insurrectionist," one finds negative portrayals of characters who believe themselves to be "Über-menschen," and who feel no compassion in the face of the suffering of others. In Horkheimer's journal entries from this time, one can also find passages, such as the following, that demonstrate his critical view of Nietzsche:

Is it not a beautiful hotel, this world! I am just a simple guest and cannot believe this; but I have heard that there are supposed to be *Übermenschen* who know the truth and can still dance and laugh. I am too weak to comprehend this, and I have a suspicion that they are swindlers, for the truly divine have never danced![101]

Horkheimer would continue to wrestle with the problem of compassion and the divergent views of Schopenhauer and Nietzsche on the subject in his later work, particularly in *Dämmerung* and *Dialectic of Enlightenment*.[102]

Horkheimer viewed not just compassion, but also love, as a means of resisting cynicism and despair in a tragic world. In this belief, Horkheimer went beyond Schopenhauer, who viewed romantic relations between the sexes as another negative expression of the blind, originary will.[103] Although Horkheimer's celebration of love may have been influenced by his early encounter with Tolstoy, his own experiences with Rosa Riekher and his previously documented intense desire for deeply committed and stable relationships were certainly more important than any literary or philosophical text. Horkheimer's letters to Riekher during this time demonstrate most clearly his faith in steadfast love, and the theme also appears repeatedly in his novellas and journal entries. Horkheimer often portrays the fragility and negative consequences of relationships based on utilitarian or narcissistic concerns. In any case, Horkheimer already possessed at this time the intuition, which he would develop in more detail later, that the decline of long-term love relationships was not a sign of increasing freedom, but rather of heightened alienation and helplessness vis-à-vis objective social forces.

Horkheimer's growing commitment to the ethical principles of compassion and love did not, however, lead him to abandon a fundamentally pessimistic view of the world. His pessimism did not, as we have seen, take the form of a Schopenhauerian rejection of the world; instead, it assumed the form of critical realism, of a refusal to entertain illusions of any kind. Horkheimer makes this clear in several passages in his journal entries from 1918, such as the following: "I can do without the self-deception of a happy ending; your stars have all burned out, but the night is clear. My love illuminates my path like a sun, so I will not waver and will continue assuredly and will be able to bear the knowledge of living in hell."[104] Horkheimer's sober temperament also comes through clearly in a long letter from August 1918, in which he describes and recommends his favorite works of literature to Riekher. Three of his favorite novels are *Don Quixote*, *Candide*, and *Madame Bovary*. About Voltaire's classic, Horkheimer says the following: "The external form of *Candide* is contempt for optimism. Optimism is so wildly wrong, so absolutely dishonest, that one

[101] GS 1, p. 169.
[102] On Horkheimer's later reevaluation of Nietzsche, see Chapter 7, p. 281.
[103] Eberhard Fromm, *Schopenhauer: Vordenker des Pessimismus* (Berlin: Dietz, 1991), p. 119.
[104] GS 1, p. 340.

does not need any proofs in order to respond to it, but simply contempt."[105] Horkheimer is not so hard-headed that he does not sympathize to a certain extent with characters such as Bovary or Quixote who retreat into a world of illusion when faced with a miserable reality. Yet he praises Flaubert in particular for his sober depiction of the hopelessness of Bovary's situation:

> In no other work of art have I seen the odious aspects of everyday life described with such unrelenting hatred and stylistic superiority as it is here. Madame Bovary's intelligence is certainly not above average, but Madame Bovary does not lose her youthfulness. And in their youth almost everyone longs for something better. She does not lose this longing. And this is why she is so brutally martyred.... Humans are always forced to make a choice between getting old or being martyred.... Flaubert portrays this tragedy.[106]

Like the numerous failed artists Horkheimer described in his own short stories, Madame Bovary's desperate attempt to escape into the aesthetic dimension from the banality and brutality of the everyday life of the philistine majority ends tragically. Horkheimer himself was determined not to fall into the same trap. Although he still considered himself an artist at this time, he would not do so for much longer. As his letters and writings from this period demonstrate, Horkheimer was searching for more substantial explanations to the social crises of the time than those he found in the artistic-bohemian circles of Schwabing. This search would soon lead him to Frankfurt, where he would thoroughly familiarize himself with the most advanced contemporary theoretical tendencies in philosophy, psychology, and sociology. Before opting for a theoretical education in Frankfurt, however, Horkheimer briefly considered the path many other artists at that time had chosen, namely from aesthetics to radical politics.

One of the most important products of the revolutionary consciousness that arose during and after World War I were the various theoretical and practical attempts to redefine the relationship between art and radical politics – in Dada, surrealism, futurism, constructivism, and expressionism, to name only the most significant examples. Of these avant-garde movements, the young Horkheimer was most drawn to expressionism. This was apparent in his own writings, which were replete with expressionist themes and stylistic experimentation. His affinity for expressionism was also apparent in his taste in contemporary literature. He considered Alfred Döblin's *Die Drei Sprünge des Wang-lun*, which was seen by many at the time as the first masterpiece of expressionist literature, "by far the best contemporary German novel."[107] As we have seen, Horkheimer was also an early and avid reader of *Die Aktion*, which was the most important forum for expressionist literature and poetry in Germany at

---

[105] GS 15, p. 34.

[106] GS 15, p. 33.

[107] GS 15, p. 35. The content of the book is political, and parallels in some ways Horkheimer's own development at the time. It tells the story of a young man in eighteenth-century China who, after witnessing an act of injustice, overcomes his antisocial tendencies and goes on to become the leader of a social movement of the "truly weak." Döblin's novel is also available in English: *The Three Leaps of Wang Lun: A Chinese Novel*, trans. C.D. Godwin (Hong Kong, 1991).

the time. However, Horkheimer's loyalty to *Die Aktion* was not just a question of aesthetics. The journal's editor, Franz Pfemfert, like Horkheimer, had been adamantly opposed to the war from the beginning. Toward the end of the war, he steered *Die Aktion* in an increasingly radical political direction. Horkheimer's own development at this time closely paralleled that of his favorite journal. The focus of the journal began to shift from aesthetics to politics in 1918, with a special issue dedicated to the one hundredth anniversary of Marx's birthday in May. By the beginning of 1919, the content of the journal had become nearly exclusively political. After the murder of Rosa Luxemburg and Karl Liebknecht on January 15, 1919, Pfemfert dedicated an entire issue to their memory, which was also intended to keep their political legacy alive.[108] In a letter to Riekher in February 1919, he refers to this issue of *Die Aktion*, telling her to read it "from beginning to end, without leaving out a single line; it provides an outline of our political views."[109] Horkheimer's admiration for Pfemfert was also apparent is his attempts to solicit his help later that summer in the case of Tobias Axelrod.

However, in contrast to Pfemfert, who would continue in the pages of *Die Aktion* to agitate for an international council communist revolution, Horkheimer was convinced by his observations of the October Revolution in Russia, the November Revolution in Germany, and the council republic in Munich that the possibility of a genuine socialist revolution had been foreclosed for the time being. In her memoirs, Germaine Krull recalls Horkheimer depicting the political situation in Germany in the Summer of 1919 in the following way:

There are two types of revolution, not just one type.... There was a revolution in the streets, and it was inspiring, but the streets now mean death. All the great leaders are dead – Rosa Luxemburg, Karl Liebknecht, Kurt Eisner, etc. The reaction is strong now, associated with the socialist government. The reaction is always well-organized, because it has money and weapons. The second way of making revolution consists in entering into the government and sabotaging it. This type of revolution is not bad and can in the long run be better. Karl Marx says, when the revolution in the streets is over, it is necessary to enter into the government and sabotage it. Thus there are two methods, but conflicts can also arise, because some might say that the revolution in the streets is over, and others might say that it is still alive.... I am afraid that Lenin, as a good Marxist, realizes that the revolution in the streets is over.[110]

Krull disagreed with Horkheimer's appraisal of the situation and would soon leave for Russia with Samuel Levit to continue the fight for a genuine soviet republic there. However, after two harrowing years in Russia, she too would realize that Horkheimer's diagnosis was correct. When she returned to Germany early in 1922, she no longer harbored any hopes for socialism of any kind. Horkheimer for his part moved to Frankfurt where he remained true to his long-term strategy of working for substantial social change within and on the margins of the institutions of Weimar Germany.

---

[108] *Die Aktion*, IX. Jahrgang, Nr. 2–5, February 1, 1919.
[109] GS 15, p. 54.
[110] Quoted by Kim Sichel in *Germaine Krull: Avantgarde als Abenteuer*, p. 25.

2

Student Years in Frankfurt

After his near escape in May 1919 from the Munich police, who had mistaken him for Ernst Toller, and his parting of ways with Germaine Krull at the end of the summer, Horkheimer was ready to move to Frankfurt with Friedrich Pollock, where the two of them would continue their university studies. During the spring and summer of 1919, Horkheimer and Pollock attended lectures sporadically at the university in Munich, but they were too preoccupied with the volatile political situation and with preparations for their *Abitur* to take their studies seriously at this time.[1] No longer enamored of the life of a bohemian artist and convinced that the "the revolution in the streets is over," Horkheimer had decided that the best way to pursue his political ideals was to gain a rigorous understanding of the social, psychological, and economic factors that had made a catastrophe like World War I possible. The experience of the war was central to Horkheimer's decision to attend the university. As he put it in a later interview,

The idea to study at the university did not come to me until near the end of the war, when I fully realized just how insane this war actually was.... What seemed absurd to me is that in a society like the one we live in, just like the others, one wages war instead of making each others' lives more pleasant.... That in a common culture and among cultures ... which should have respect for one another, people do not work together to make each other greater, more beautiful and more significant ... but instead attempted to destroy one another, for any old silly reason that has not even been clarified. This is why I decided after the war to get my *Abitur* and to study at the university.[2]

Horkheimer stresses repeatedly in his later recollections that he was not interested in an academic career at this point. He simply wanted to familiarize himself with the most advanced research in the social and human sciences in order to gain the best possible understanding of the chaotic world around

[1] In a later interview Horkheimer stated, "We went occasionally to this or that lecture in Munich.... then came the first lecture course by Cornelius, the first one we pursued seriously." Ernst von Schenk Interviews [MHA X 132b], p. 124.

[2] Biographical interviews with Matthias Becker, p. 38, 61. The *Abitur* is a final examination at the elite German high schools, or *Gymnasium*. It is also the prerequisite for studying at the university.

him.[3] Although he never gives any explicit reasons for his decision to attend the university in Frankfurt as opposed to another German university, after Horkheimer's harrowing experiences in Munich, the relative political calm of Frankfurt certainly played a role. The innovative character of the university, the liberal tradition of the city, and its large Jewish community may have also played a role in Horkheimer's decision.[4]

Free from the need to specialize in order to tailor his studies toward an academic career, Horkheimer opted for psychology as his major discipline, and philosophy and economics as his minor disciplines. Horkheimer would later recall:

I went to the university primarily of course for purely philosophical reasons, but since I had already read some philosophy myself – especially Schopenhauer – I thought it would perhaps be good to take psychology rather than philosophy as my major field, for in this way I would learn what one knows today about man.[5]

Although psychoanalysis was beginning to shed its marginal status in Germany at this time, it had by no means been accepted at the conservative universities yet, where psychology was still considered a natural scientific discipline. Nonetheless, the newly founded, privately funded university in Frankfurt distinguished itself from the beginning with its openness to scientific and scholarly innovation, and its psychology department was no exception in this regard.[6] It had established itself as one of the most important centers in Europe for research in Gestalt psychology, which can be seen as an attempt to overcome the mechanical methodology that had dominated psychology since its inception as a scientific and academic discipline in the second half of the nineteenth century.[7] The Gestaltists – who were well represented in Frankfurt by Max Wertheimer,[8] Wolfgang Köhler, Kurt Goldstein, and Adhémar Gelb – rejected the mechanical application to the psyche of quantitative methods derived from the natural sciences. Instead, they argued that consciousness, experience, and perception are structured by subjective and objective totalities that cannot be reduced to a mere aggregate of their parts. To defend this thesis, the Gestaltists

---

[3] For example, in a later interview, he stated, "I wanted to study at the university to learn more about condition of man. An academic career was furthest from my mind." Matthias Becker interviews, p. 61.

[4] As we shall see, Horkheimer did not, unlike some of his future Institute colleagues, get involved in any Jewish cultural organizations in Frankfurt in the 1920s; nevertheless, his fears about anti-Semitism, which were expressed clearly in his writings during the war, may have still been a factor in his choice of city such as Frankfurt, with its large Jewish community and a tradition of tolerance. Frankfurt was not only the city in Germany with the largest percentage of Jewish residents, it was also the only city in Germany before World War I in which it was possible to erect a memorial to Heinrich Heine. See Detlev Claussen, *Theodor Adorno: Ein Letztes Genie* (Frankfurt, 2003), p. 36–8.

[5] GS 7, p. 447.

[6] For the history of the foundation and first decade of the J.W. Goethe University in Frankfurt, see Paul Kluke, *Die Stiftungsuniversität Frankfurt am Main 1914–1932*, (Frankfurt, 1972).

[7] For an overview of the origins and history of Gestalt psychology, see Wolfgang Rechtien, "Gestalttheorie," *Geschichte der Psychologie: Ein Handbuch in Schlüsselbegriffen* (München, 1984), pp. 88–95.

[8] Until 1918 and then once again after 1929.

continued to rely almost exclusively on traditional empirical research; in this respect they were not as bold as Freud and his followers. However, their efforts to win more methodological independence for psychology were still innovative within the German academic context. As we shall see, Gestalt psychology would play an important role in Horkheimer's university studies in Frankfurt.

Despite his desire to explore new areas, Horkheimer's interest in philosophy remained strong. At the beginning of the winter semester in 1919,[9] soon after he had familiarized himself with the course offerings in other departments, Horkheimer decided that he would also like to sit in on a philosophy lecture. He went, more or less fortuitously, to a lecture by Hans Cornelius, who would become his most important mentor during this period. Horkheimer describes their first meeting in the following way:

> [Cornelius] was lecturing on Kant, on the transcendental aesthetic. I could repeat exactly what he was saying. He was, namely, critical of Kant's transcendental aesthetic. Then he stopped and said, "Are there any questions?" I raised my hand and said I didn't have a question, but rather an objection, because I agreed with the transcendental aesthetic, just as Schopenhauer had agreed with it, and I explained to him what I thought right there in the lecture hall. Then he said, loud enough so that everyone could hear it, "Yes, I think we will need to discuss this in more detail. Please come to my office afterwards." I did, and that point actually marked the beginning of my academic path, for I had won his lasting affection.[10]

Horkheimer speaks here of the beginning of his academic path, but this was a judgment made much later, in retrospect, for at this time Horkheimer was still anything but certain about pursuing an academic career. He had a deeply ambivalent attitude toward the university, which was characterized, on the one hand, by curiosity about modern research and, on the other hand, by contempt for the professors who carried it out. By his own admission, Horkheimer's distrust of philosophy professors was influenced by Arthur Schopenhauer, who was almost completely ignored by the philosophical establishment of his day, and who got revenge for his shabby treatment with a never-ending stream of polemics and invectives against the profession.[11]

Horkheimer's ambivalent attitude was reflected from the beginning in his relationship to Cornelius. He may have won Cornelius's respect and affection right away, but Horkheimer was slow to return this recognition. In a letter to Riekher in the summer of the following year, Horkheimer mentions that he had been meeting with Cornelius every week to discuss problems in moral philosophy. About Cornelius he says, "Our views diverge greatly. I owe him more than I can say, but precisely for that reason I refuse to make any compromises just to be polite."[12] Soon thereafter, he alludes to Schopenhauer to

---

[9] The academic calendar of German universities was and is divided into two semesters: a winter semester, which begins in October and continues into March, and a summer semester which begins in April and continues through July.

[10] GS 7, p. 448–9.

[11] See, for example, "Über die Universitäts-Philosophie," *Parerga und Paralipomena: Kleine philosophische Schriften*, Volume 7, *Arthur Schopenhauer Werke in zehn Bänden*, (Zürich, 1977).

[12] GS 15, p. 58.

express his skepticism about Cornelius's position: "Only professors fail to recognize that reason is a slave of the will."[13] In the following years, the severity
of Horkheimer's criticisms of Cornelius would increase before it decreased. In
1921, Horkheimer was particularly annoyed by Cornelius's attempt to intervene in the Weimar parliamentary debates on the financial crisis in Germany at
the time. Cornelius composed a proposal for economic reforms that he sent to
several prominent political, industrial, and intellectual figures, including Hugo
Stinnes, a big industrialist and parliamentary representative for the conservative *Deutsche Volkspartei* (German People's Party). Horkheimer and Pollock
apparently wrote a letter to Cornelius criticizing his proposal, which may have
played a role in his abandoning of the plan a few weeks later. In this context,
Horkheimer writes to Riekher about Cornelius: "In principle he is as far as
is possible from our own political and moral views."[14] Horkheimer's increasingly skeptical view of Cornelius at this time was not merely a product of
political differences; it extended to his philosophy as well. Just a week later,
Horkheimer made the following remarks about a manuscript Cornelius had
recently given him to read: "My own work is better. His thoughts are for the
most part extremely vulnerable and, above all, the work as a whole is much
too long."[15] Until 1923, when Horkheimer would finish his dissertation and
become Cornelius's assistant, his attitude toward him continued to be characterized by the audacious confidence and skepticism of authority – bordering
on downright arrogance – that permitted the twenty-four-year-old Horkheimer
during his first semester in Frankfurt to challenge Cornelius in front of a full
lecture hall.

Cornelius was by no means the only professor to incur Horkheimer's
wrath. Friedrich Schumann, a full professor in psychology who would become
Horkheimer's first dissertation advisor, was also the target of many disparag-
ing remarks. During their first meeting in 1921, Horkheimer reports getting
into a heated argument with Schumann, in which he criticized his "idiotic and
dogmatic claims that were outdated long ago."[16] During their next meeting
a week later, Horkheimer writes to Riekher that Schumann was more con-
ciliatory, but Horkheimer himself seemed even less impressed than the first
time: "We spoke for an hour, or, more precisely, I gave him detailed instruction
for an hour on some basic philosophical problems."[17] Horkheimer's attitude at
this time toward Cornelius and Schumann reflect his acute distrust of academic
philosophy in particular and contemporary German universities in general.
Horkheimer, like many of his future friends and colleagues, was trying desperately to get a critical theoretical education in a university system that was deeply
conservative.[18] As he put it in 1921, "I didn't come here with the intention to

---

[13] Ibid., p. 59.
[14] Ibid., p. 68.
[15] Ibid., p. 73.
[16] GS 15, p. 72.
[17] Ibid., p. 75.
[18] On the conservative character of the German university system, especially as it developed in the
     Wilhelmian period, see Fritz Ringer's classic study *The Decline of the German Mandarins: The
     German Academic Community 1890–1933* (Cambridge, MA, 1969). Ringer argues that German

learn much from this or that professor.... The more fascinated I become with philosophy, the further I distance myself from the way it is understood at this university."[19] Horkheimer's attitude toward Cornelius would change after he completed his dissertation and became his assistant at the beginning of 1923, but he would remain critical of the university system.

Hans Cornelius was not the only person Horkheimer met shortly after his arrival in Frankfurt in the fall of 1919 who would have a decisive influence on his further development. In an interview near the end of his life, Horkheimer described his meeting with Felix Weil as follows:

When we came from Munich to Frankfurt we first lived in a pension in one of the side streets that intersected with the Bockenheimer Landstrasse. Late one evening we looked out our window and saw three young people walking our way. I knew one of them, it was Konstantin Zetkin, the son of Clara Zetkin.... One of the others was Felix Weil, whom I did not yet know at that time, and I don't remember who the third one was. I waved and either we walked down or they came up, in any case that was the beginning or our relationship with Felix Weil.[20]

This fortuitous encounter between the future initiators of the Institute for Social Research occurred sometime in November or December of 1919. At the end of October, Weil had been forced to leave Tübingen, where he had been studying, and return to Frankfurt, where he had spent a large portion of his youth. Weil had been arrested in Tübingen along with fourteen other students for harassing a chauvinistically nationalist professor. A public protest in Tübingen by local Independent Socialist (USPD) and Communist Party (KPD) members, led by Clara Zetkin, was enough to secure the release of most of the students, but it was not enough to keep the province of Württemberg (in which Tübingen is located) from expelling Weil – who was born in Argentina – and another student from Poland.[21] From Tübingen, Weil returned to Frankfurt, where he had originally begun his studies in 1916.

Weil had left Frankfurt for Tübingen in February 1919. In the months prior to his departure for Tübingen, he had been politicized – in an even more dramatic way than Horkheimer and Pollock – by the revolutionary events in Germany at the end of 1918. The two most important events in his conversion to socialism at this time were his active participation in a workers' and soldiers' council in Frankfurt and his reading of the program from the Social

professors attained a particular Mandarin status in the Wilhelmian period, which was threatened by rapid modernization in the decades before the War and even more so by the rise of a mass democratic society afterwards.

[19] GS 15, p. 69, p. 77.

[20] Interview with Matthias Becker p. 47–8. This passage also confirms Helmut Eisenbach's suspicion that Ulrike Migdal was mistaken in her claim that Horkheimer and Pollock had met Weil already during their stay in Munich. See Eisenbach (reference in next footnote below), p. 185, and Migdal, *Die Frühgeschichte des Frankfurter Instituts für Sozialforschung* (Frankfurt, 1981), p. 34.

[21] For a detailed account of Weil's brief stay in Tübingen, as well as a brief overview of Felix Weil's life as a whole, see Helmut Robert Eisenbach, "Millionär, Agitator und Doktorand: Die Tübinger Studienzeit des Felix Weil," *Bausteine zur Tübinger Universitätsgeschichte*, Folge 3, (Tübingen, 1987).

Democratic Party congress in Erfurt in 1890.[22] Although Leo Lowenthal, Franz
Neumann, Ernst Fränkel, and other left-wing students had formed a socialist
student group in Frankfurt, Weil did not think it would be possible to pursue
his newfound interest in socialism there. He was particularly frustrated by the
complete absence of any courses on socialism or the history of the labor movement at the university in Frankfurt. So in February of 1919, Weil began to
make arrangements to move to Tübingen, where he would study political economy with Robert Wilbrandt, one of the very few professors in Germany at the
time with whom it was possible to study socialism in any form. In March, Weil
started a socialist student group of his own in Tübingen. In April, he went as
its representative to the first and only national meeting of the German Socialist
Students' group in Jena, where he met his lifelong friend Karl Korsch. At the
beginning of May, Weil finally settled down in Tübingen, where he attended
lectures with Wilbrandt and continued his political activities with the socialist
student group. During this time, Weil also went to Stuttgart on a regular basis
to visit Clara Zetkin.

Through these various activities in Tübingen, Weil was drawn increasingly to
the political left. As he put it in his memoirs, "In Frankfurt I was still close to the
Social Democratic Party. But studying Marx in greater depth in Tübingen and the
discussions I had with Clara Zetkin radicalized me."[23] So when Weil was introduced to Pollock and Horkheimer by Konstantin Zetkin, shortly after he had
returned to Frankfurt in the fall of 1919, he was thrilled to discover two students
with whom he could pursue his newfound passion for socialist theory. The fact
that these two students were also deserters from the bourgeois camp strengthened the elective affinity for Weil, who was the son of Hermann Weil, the spec-
tacularly wealthy grain merchant who had served as a political advisor to Kaiser
Wilhelm II during the war and who would soon finance the Institute for Social
Research.[24] Like many others who met Horkheimer for the first time, Weil was
very impressed. According to Pollock's later recollections, during their ensuing
relationship he would often consult the two of them for advice.[25] Horkheimer
recalls that Weil was interested "because we had the reputation of knowing a
lot about Marx and because we defended Marxist theory in our seminars."[26] In
any case, the three of them quickly became friends.[27] In fact, Weil would soon
make it possible for the two of them to move from the pension in Bockenheim

[22] Eisenbach, p. 185.

[23] Quoted by Eisenbach, p. 189.

[24] The best account of Hermann Weil's life, his political activities during the war and his role in
the foundation of the Institute for Social Research is in Ulrike Migdal's *Die Frühgeschichte
des Frankfurter Instituts für Sozialforschung* (Frankfurt, 1981), pp. 10–29. On the importance
of their shared social background for their friendship, see Ernst Herhaus's article "Institut für
Sozialforschung," which is based on a later interview with Pollock, in *Notizen während der
Abschaffung des Denkens* (Zurich, 1984), p. 42.

[25] Herhaus, p. 42.

[26] Ernst von Schenk Interviews, p. 57.

[27] In his memoirs, Weil refers to Horkheimer and Pollock as his "two closest friends" during this
time. Felix Weil, *Lebenserinnerungen*, p. 85 (the page numbers listed here and elsewhere from
Weil's *Lebenserinnerungen* are from the "Zweite Fassung" of the manuscript located in Institut
für Stadtgeschichte, Frankfurt am Main (Section: "Chroniken"; Catalogue Number: S5/421).

by providing them with the money to build a spacious house in Kronberg im Taunus, a wealthy suburb northwest of Frankfurt.[28] It was here that the three of them would hatch the plan for the Institute for Social Research in 1922.

However, before Horkheimer, Pollock, and Weil would begin seriously to discuss how to establish an institutional forum to further the study of socialist theory in Germany, their ways would briefly part. In the fall of 1920, Weil left with his new wife, Katherina Bachert, whom he had also met through Zetkin, for a one-year stay in Argentina.[29] He had promised his ailing father that he would look after the business there after he was finished with his dissertation, which had been accepted by the liberal professor of political economy Adolph Weber in Frankfurt in April.[30] Horkheimer and Pollock also left Frankfurt in the fall of 1920 to study in Freiburg for two semesters. Horkheimer went primarily to study with Edmund Husserl. Although Husserl had some important theoretical differences with Cornelius, the two of them were on good personal terms; with Cornelius's recommendation, Horkheimer was well received in Freiburg by Husserl. Horkheimer seems to have been impressed with Husserl and by the high level of discussion in his seminar, but he does not seem to have had any lasting influence on Horkheimer's intellectual development.[31]

In a paper on Husserl he presented a few years later, in February 1925, on the occasion of the successful completion of his *Habilitation*,[32] Horkheimer criticized Husserl roundly for separating phenomenology from the empirical sciences.[33] Just as Hegel had criticized the pseudo-profundity of Schelling's notion of intuition in the preface to the *Phenomenology of Spirit*, so Horkheimer rejected Husserl's nondiscursive notion of *Wesenschau*, because "it did not provide any criteria [of truth] other than one's own insight into essences."[34] In his critique of Husserl's strict division between epistemology, which was based on the putatively rigorous methods of phenomenology, and psychology, which was based on mere empirical research, Horkheimer was clearly defending Cornelius's position. However, Horkheimer's critique of Husserl went beyond that of his philosophical mentor. Horkheimer was wary of the ahistorical character of Husserl's phenomenology, which was an ambitious attempt to move beyond positivism, psychologism, and relativism, and to reestablish philosophy as the *Königin der Wissenschaften*[35] by working out its logical and ontological foundations. Anticipating Husserl's own later writings,[36] Horkheimer

---

[28] Matthias Becker interviews, p. 134.

[29] *Lebenserinnerungen*, p. 68.

[30] Weber was opposed to socialism, but was willing to accept the manuscript – which Weil had "translated into Aesopian" – based on its scholarly merits. The dissertation, *Sozialisierung. Versuch einer begrifflichen Grundlegung nebst einer Kritik Sozializierungspläne*, was published the following year as the seventh volume of series on "practical socialism" edited by Karl Korsch.

[31] See, for example, GS 15, p. 72.

[32] For an explanation of the *Habilitation*, see the Introduction, footnote 40.

[33] Husserl's erkenntnistheoretische Fundierung der Wesensschau, GS 11, pp. 82–99.

[34] GS 11, p. 92.

[35] Queen of the sciences.

[36] Edmund Husserl, *The Crisis of European Sciences and Transcendental Philosophy: An Introduction to Phenomenological Philosophy*. Trans. David Carr (Evanston, 1970).

interpreted the desire to place philosophy on an unshakeable foundation as an expression of a crisis of European science and society, and as a desperate but ultimately ineffective antidote to the spread of nihilism in Europe that Nietzsche and others had diagnosed.[37] Furthermore, Horkheimer's critique of Husserl did not change in the next few years, when he broke significantly with Cornelius's position. In the lectures on contemporary philosophy that Horkheimer gave in 1926, he expanded his criticisms of Husserl. Although his deep respect for Husserl is plainly evident in his discussion of the *Logical Investigations*, it is also apparent that Horkheimer was not ultimately convinced by his arguments. Horkheimer portrays Husserl's project as an important step in philosophy's emancipation from the natural sciences, but one that went too far in the opposite direction.[38] Even after he had broken with Cornelius, Horkheimer remained more sympathetic to his efforts to link philosophy to the natural and human sciences than to Husserl's attempt to purify it completely of their influence. For Horkheimer at this time and later, all attempts to establish absolute, timeless standards, be they ontological, logical, or metaphysical, were doomed to fail.

Upon Husserl's recommendation, Horkheimer also attended Martin Heidegger's lectures in Freiburg. Like so many others at this time, including his later Institute colleague Herbert Marcuse, Horkheimer was taken by Heidegger's anti-academic habitus, as the following letter, which he wrote to Riekher shortly after returning to Frankfurt from Freiburg, makes clear:

> I know today that Heidegger is one of the most significant personalities who spoke to me. Whether or not I agree with him? How should I, since the only thing I know for certain about him is that his motive for philosophizing is not intellectual ambition or a preconceived theory, but springs instead each day from his own experience.[39]

Yet Horkheimer's more skeptical view of the widespread "hunger for wholeness"[40] in Weimar Germany, which Heidegger's philosophy seemed to satisfy so well, made him less susceptible to Heidegger's charismatic teachings than some commentators have realized.[41] As the passage from the letter

---

[37] GS 11, p. 83. GS 10, pp. 300–2.

[38] For example, in a paper that Horkheimer gave in July 1921, probably in Husserl's seminar, he defended Cornelius's philosophical reception of Gestalt psychology: "Gegenstand der Psychologie nach Cornelius," MHA VII.1.12.

[39] GS 15, p. 77.

[40] To borrow one of Peter Gay's characterizations of Weimar culture. See his *Weimar Culture: The Outsider as Insider* (New York, 1968), pp. 70 f.

[41] Helmut Gumnior and Rudolf Ringguth, for example, claim that Heidegger's strong impression on Horkheimer helps explain his subsequent criticisms of his professors in Frankfurt, whereas in reality Horkheimer was critical of university philosophy from the beginning. See their biography, *Max Horkheimer* (Reinbeck bei Hamburg, 1973), pp. 22, 24. In their introduction to *On Max Horkheimer: New Perspectives* (Cambridge, MA, 1993), Seyla Benhabib, Wolfgang Bonß, and John McCole write: "The encounter with Heidegger provided an early impetus to the process by which Horkheimer gradually began distancing himself from the sort of neo-Kantianism represented by Cornelius" (p. 4). This interpretation also gives Heidegger too much credit for alerting Horkheimer to the shortcomings of Cornelius's philosophy, of which he was already aware. It also overlooks the fact that it was precisely in the period *after* his encounter with Heidegger that Horkheimer vigorously defended Cornelius's philosophical standpoint, in his dissertation and *Habilitationsschrift*.

indicates, Horkheimer was unsure of how exactly to appraise Heidegger's work, which in any case left no traces in Horkheimer's own philosophical writings at this time. In a later interview, Horkheimer recalls attending a lecture of Heidegger's on the topic of "Introduction to the Phenomenology of Religion," in which Heidegger spent the first three weeks talking about the concept of "introduction." He and Pollock left derogatory notes on Heidegger's lectern to express their dissatisfaction with this procedure.[42] In another interview, Horkheimer states unequivocally, "I did go to Heidegger's lectures for a year, but I was more impressed by Husserl."[43] As we shall see, Horkheimer was too concerned about the irrationalistic implications of the putatively more concrete versions of phenomenology, which were becoming increasingly popular in the 1920s, to fall under Heidegger's sway.[44]

Horkheimer also continued to pursue his practical and theoretical interest in socialism while he was in Freiburg. When he was in Munich, Horkheimer was directly exposed to Marxist ideas for the first time in the pages of the increasingly politicized *Die Aktion*, in his discussions in the bohemian circles of Schwabing, and in the speeches and actions of many of the protagonists of the revolution and council republic. In later interviews, Horkheimer states that he and Pollock started reading explicitly Marxist literature first when they arrived in Frankfurt, including the official journal of the German Communist Party, *Die rote Fahne*.[45] However, the first concrete evidence that Horkheimer was seriously studying Marxist theory dates from his stay in Freiburg: Several notebooks from the spring of 1921 are preserved in the Horkheimer Archive.[46] They contain Horkheimer's reading notes from Gustav Landauer's *Aufruf zum Sozialismus*,[47] A.W. Cohn's *Kann das Geld abgeschafft werden?*,[48] Karl Vorländer's *Marx, Engels und Lasalle als Philosophen*, Friedrich Engels's *Ludwig Feuerbach, und der Ausgang der Klassischen Deutschen Philosophie*,[49] and Karl Kautsky's *Ethik und materialistische Geschichtsauffassung*.[50] From his notes it is clear that he had read all these works in their entirety. Even more detailed notes exist for both L.B. Boudin's *Das Theoretische System von Karl Marx*[51] and Karl Marx's *Zur Kritik der politischen Ökonomie*.[52] The former work provides a comprehensive account of Marx's mature theory as well as the objections that had been raised against it until then. In the latter work, Marx published the first fruits of his extensive research on political economy in the

---

[42] Interviews with Matthias Becker, p. 51.

[43] GS 7, p. 429.

[44] See Chapter 3, pp. 134–40.

[45] Ernst von Schenk Interviews, p. 44 [MHA X 132b].

[46] MHA VII.2.

[47] *For Socialism*, trans. D.J. Parent (St. Louis, 1978).

[48] "Can Money be Eliminated?" Cohn's study has not been translated into English. Arthur Wolfgang Cohn, *Kann das Geld abgeschafft werden?* (Jena, 1920).

[49] *Ludwig Feuerbach and the Roots of the Socialist Philosophy*, trans. A. Lewis (Chicago, 1903).

[50] *Ethics and the Materialist Understanding of History*, trans. J.B. Askew (Chicago, 1918).

[51] Horkheimer had a copy of this work, which had been translated into German in 1909 by Luise Kautsky. The original was published in 1907: Louis B. Boudin, *The Theoretical System of Karl Marx in the Light of Recent Criticism* (Chicago, 1907).

[52] Karl Marx, *A Contribution to the Critique of Political Economy*, trans. S.W. Ryazanskaya (New York, 1970).

1850s, including his theory of money, which would be the subject of Friedrich Pollock's dissertation two years later. The notes make clear that Horkheimer had studied these last two works with particular care. Horkheimer's newfound interest in Marxist theory, however, by no means took the form of an abrupt conversion that entailed casting aside all he had believed until then; this is demonstrated by another notebook that documents Horkheimer's continued interest in Schopenhauer. The notebook contains extensive notes from the entirety of both volumes of *The World as Will and Representation*, which Horkheimer reread completely at this time.[53]

Horkheimer and Pollock were also members of a socialist student group in Freiburg at this time.[54] It does not seem to have been a particularly noteworthy part of their stay in Freiburg, for they do not talk about it in either their letters or in later interviews. However, Horkheimer's father apparently heard about it, for this was one of the reasons he decided to pay Horkheimer a visit in Freiburg at this time.[55] Although Moritz Horkheimer grudgingly accepted his son's decision to attend the university and provided him with enough financial support to do so, relations between the two of them remained extremely tense at this time, not only because of Horkheimer's decision to pursue a degree in a field that must have seemed useless to his father, but also because of Horkheimer's ongoing relationship with Riekher, who had in the meantime returned to work as his father's secretary. While in Freiburg, Moritz Horkheimer had an extended discussion with Husserl about his son's future. Husserl, too, seems to have been impressed by Horkheimer, for after emerging from the two-hour discussion, Moritz Horkheimer laconically reported the results to Max: "You have potential in philosophy; furthermore," the industrialist said to his rebellious son, "we also talked about politics." Husserl's social background was quite similar to that of Moritz Horkheimer; in fact, Husserl's brother had once done business with him.[56] Husserl was an upper-middle-class Jew who had converted to Christianity to become a professor. His politics were moderately conservative. All of his sons had fought in World War I, and one of them was killed. In other words, he must have seemed respectable to Horkheimer's father. Furthermore, it is very unlikely that Husserl was aware of Max Horkheimer's political sympathies, so his conversation with Moritz Horkheimer regarding his son's future probably assuaged his fears.

For his part, Max Horkheimer was careful to avoid any overt expressions of his political convictions, which might have jeopardized the support of his father or the trust of his professors. Horkheimer had learned long before to cultivate a rich interiority in which he could safely pursue his genuine concerns. The ambivalent legacy of bourgeois interiority, which the Institute would carefully analyze later, continued to play a crucial role in his life.[57] When he

[53] MHA VII.2.

[54] Ernst von Schenk biography, pp. 91–2. Gumnior/Ringhuth, p. 22.

[55] Gumnionr/Ringhuth, p. 22.

[56] Ernst von Schenk biography, p. 92.

[57] See, for example, Herbert Marcuse's discussion of the bourgeois concept of freedom that links internal autonomy with external authority in his philosophical introduction to the *Studien über Autorität und Familie*, Herbert Marcuse, *Schriften*, Band 3 (Frankfurt, 1979), pp. 85–185. See

returned to Frankfurt, Horkheimer continued to lead a double life. On the one hand, he deepened his knowledge of socialist theory and engaged in numerous lengthy discussions with Friedrich Pollock and Felix Weil on how best to institutionalize a more general theoretical discussion of socialism in Germany. These discussions would lead to the founding of the Institute for Social Research in 1923. On the other hand, he vigorously pursued his academic studies, completing his dissertation in the fall of 1922, and his *Habilitationsschrift* just two years later. Both studies were devoted to *Kant's Critique of Judgment* and were related to Horkheimer's political interests at best in only a highly mediated way.

Felix Weil returned from Argentina at approximately the same time that Horkheimer and Pollock returned from Freiburg – in the fall of 1921. Running his father's business in Argentina for nearly a year confirmed many of Weil's worst suspicions about contemporary capitalism. In his memoirs, Weil describes at length the different unethical and exploitative methods used by huge companies such as his father's to maintain their trade monopoly and increase their profits.[58] Once Weil was finally relieved of his responsibilities in his father's company after an incident with the Soviet Union around Christmas 1921,[59] he was free to pursue his interest in socialism full time. One of the ways he did this was by meeting regularly with Max Horkheimer and Friedrich Pollock in Kronberg. It was during these meetings that Weil first revealed his plans to Horkheimer and Pollock to found an institute for the study of socialist theory and the history of the workers' movement. As Weil recalls:

We had soon agreed that if the Institute wanted to maintain its independence from the department of economics and social science, which was still reactionary at base, the Institute could not be subsumed within it. It had to become an Institute at the university but not belonging to the university. It was also clear to us that the name "Institute for Researching Marxism," would incite too much resistance. Like my dissertation, the title of the Institute had to be clothed in Aesopian terms. Then Pollock recalled that an Institute for Social Research had been founded in Japan a few years before, with the new concept of "social research," which could mean something different for everyone. Thus we decided to take over this concept for our own purposes and also that I should write an article in a prominent publication about the necessity of founding an Institute for Social Research.[60]

By June of 1922, Weil had already taken the first concrete steps toward making their plans to found an Institute for Social Research a reality.[61] After

---

also Theodor Adorno's discussion of interiority in *Kierkegaard: Konstruktion des Ästhetischen*, (Frankfurt, 1962) pp. 38–98.

[58] *Lebenserinnerungen*, pp. 74ff.

[59] At this time there were rumors that the Soviet Union was suffering from an acute grain shortage, and that many people were on the brink of starvation. Weil wanted to make them a just offer for grain, rather than taking advantage of their desperation, like other Western companies were doing. He traveled to Berlin to meet with the Bolshevik representative there, Karl Radek, who informed him that the Soviet Union was not going to need the grain after all. Because he was so relieved that the threat of starvation had been averted, he didn't think to convey this information to the company headquarters in Amsterdam, which would have enabled them to dump their grain and make hundreds of thousands of dollars. After this incident his father no longer tried to talk him into following in his footsteps. *Lebenserinnerungen*, pp. 83–4.

[60] *Lebenserinnerungen*, pp. 87–8.

[61] Ulrike Migdal, op. cit., p. 120.

overcoming some initial objections from the faculty of economics and sociology and the president of the university, the Minister of Culture in Berlin
officially approved the project in January 1923. Construction of the building
began just a few months later.[62]

The details of the founding of the Institute for Social Research have been
recounted elsewhere[63] so they need not concern us here, but it is worth mentioning again that Horkheimer was instrumental in the planning of the Institute
from the very beginning, a fact that is often overlooked due to his lack of direct
involvement in the Institute's affairs under its first director, Carl Grünberg. It
was not a mere formality that Horkheimer was listed as one of the nine original
members of the Society for Social Research, the organization formed to found
the Institute.[64] Pollock was not among those on the list, but he would soon
become much more involved in Institute affairs than Horkheimer. When Kurt
Gerlach, a socialist professor of economics from the *Technische Hochschule*
(Technical University) in Aachen who was supposed to become the first director of the Institute, died suddenly in October 1922, Pollock became the provisional director of Institute affairs.[65] Later on, he would become the assistant
to the Institute's first director, Carl Grünberg, and would actively partake in a
variety of Institute projects. So although Horkheimer was not directly involved
with the Institute under Grünberg, he remained closely tied to it through his
close friendships with Pollock and Weil. The same can be said for the First
Marxist Work Week, which Weil, following a suggestion by Karl Korsch, organized and financed in Ilmenau, Thuringia in May of 1923. The Work Week
represented the first extensive meeting of some of the most important younger critical Marxist theorists in Germany at the time, including several – such
as Georg Lukács, Karl Korsch, Karl August Wittfogel, Julian Gumperz, and
Richard Sorge – who would play important roles later in the Institute for Social
Research and/or the development of so-called Western Marxism.[66] Horkheimer
could not attend for unknown reasons, but he was certainly well informed by
Weil and Pollock about the discussions that took place there, including the one
between Korsch and Lukács about the latter's recently published *History and
Class Consciousness*, which, according to Weil's later recollections, was the
highlight of the meeting.[67]

In addition to their discussions and practical cooperation with Weil on
establishing an institutional basis for research on the workers' movement and
socialist theory, Horkheimer and Pollock also continued to pursue their studies
in Marxist theory after returning to Frankfurt from Freiburg in the fall of 1921.

[62] Ibid., pp. 41–52.
[63] In most detail by Migdal. See also Martin Jay, *The Dialectical Imagination*, pp. 3–40, and Rolf
Wiggershaus, *Die Frankfurter Schule*, pp. 19–49.
[64] Migdal, p. 51.
[65] Felix Weil, *Lebenserinnerungen*, p. 93.
[66] On the "First Marxist Working Week," see Michael Buckmiller, "Die 'Marxistische Arbeitswoche'
1923 und die Gründung des 'Instituts für Sozialforschung," *Grand Hotel Abgrund*, ed.
W. van Reijen and G. Schmid Noerr (Hamburg, 1990), pp. 145–77. On the concept of "Western
Marxism," see Martin Jay, *Marxism and Totality* and Perry Anderson, *Considerations on
Western Marxism* (London, 1976).
[67] Felix Weil, *Lebenserinnerungen*, p. 85.

In November of 1922, Horkheimer gave a paper on the topic of "historical materialism" in a seminar on political economy, which he had chosen as one of his two minor disciplines.[68] During this time, Pollock was also working on his dissertation on "Marx's Theory of Money," which he would finish at the beginning of 1923.[69] In the introduction, Pollock justifies his choice of the topic by arguing that neither Marx himself nor anyone else had systematically presented his scattered thoughts on the theory of money. After outlining the location of Marx's theory of money within his work as a whole, Pollock recapitulates Marx's discussion of the different functions and the evolution of money in *Contribution to the Critique of Political Economy*. Drawing on the second and third volumes of *Capital*, he also briefly examines the function of money in capitalist economies. Pollock closes the dissertation by demonstrating Marx's position on a series of technical problems, such the relationship of the quantity of circulating money to commodity prices, the value of money and its ability to represent value, and the functioning of credit and rates of exchange. Although Pollock focuses primarily on *Contribution to the Critique of Political Economy* and the first two volumes of *Capital*, he displays familiarity with the entirety of Marx's mature work, including his extensive studies on the history of political economy published in the three-volume *Theories of Surplus Value*. Methodologically, with very few exceptions, he proceeds descriptively; he refrains from criticizing or affirming the arguments he presents. Like Horkheimer a few months earlier, Pollock was also awarded *summa cum laude* for his dissertation.

It was also during this time that Horkheimer and Pollock became friends with several other young critical intellectuals who would either play decisive roles in the future of the Institute, such as Theodor Adorno and Leo Lowenthal, or who would remain important intellectual interlocutors for some of its members, as was the case with Siegfried Kracauer and Ernst Bloch. Lowenthal and Adorno were both born – in 1900 and 1903 respectively – and raised in Frankfurt, and both were befriended and mentored by Siegfried Kracauer, who was also born in Frankfurt, in 1889.[70] Lowenthal met Bloch personally for the first time while he was studying in Heidelberg during the academic year 1920–1.[71] Horkheimer probably met Lowenthal either through Weil (because the two of them had gone to the same middle school together in Frankfurt) or in one of the lectures by Cornelius that Lowenthal attended.[72] There is no evidence that Horkheimer and Pollock were ever involved with the Frankfurt Socialist Student Group, which Lowenthal cofounded with Franz Neumann and Ernst Fränkel in 1918–19.[73] Nor were Horkheimer or Pollock drawn to the circle surrounding Rabbi Nobel, in which Lowenthal was also actively involved at

[68] Ernst von Schenk biography, p. 98. One can only speculate about its contents, because the seminar paper has not been preserved in the Horkheimer Archive.

[69] Pollock's dissertation, "Zur Geldtheorie von Karl Marx," was never published.

[70] Wiggershaus, pp. 80–3.

[71] Ibid., p. 81. See also *An Unmastered Past: The Autobiographical Reflections of Leo Lowenthal*, ed. Martin Jay (Berkeley, 1986), p. 47.

[72] *An Unmastered Past*, p. 46.

[73] Ibid., p. 35.

this time, and out of which the remarkable Frankfurt *Freies Jüdisches Lehrhaus* emerged in the early 1920s.[74] As Horkheimer put it in a later interview:

> During our university studies in Frankfurt, and not only at this time but also after I had completed my Ph.D. and became a lecturer, we were friends with Felix Weil, on the one hand, and, particularly myself, with a group of people including Ernst Bloch, Leo Lowenthal and Siegfried Kracauer, on the other hand. I did not meet Erich Fromm until later. In any case, a group which in one way or another had something to do with Judaism, for there was a Rabbi, I can't remember his name, ... a very great man, who had already passed away. All of these people had some sort of relationship to him and I was friends with them and they with me, also in part in relation to Cornelius and the Institute that would come into being later.[75]

Conspicuously absent from the names Horkheimer mentions here is that of his future friend and colleague Theodor Adorno. But Horkheimer did meet Adorno during this time, in 1922 or 1923 in a seminar with Hans Cornelius.[76] In a seminar on Kant led by Horkheimer in the winter semester of 1923–4, Adorno gave a paper on the topic "Kant's critique of rationalist psychology."[77] In July 1924, Horkheimer and Pollock invited Adorno to their house in Kronberg to help him prepare for an exam. Shortly thereafter, Adorno wrote a letter to Lowenthal in which he described his meeting with Horkheimer and Pollock as follows:

> In order to learn the material that I had heard in Schumann's lectures ... I spent ten days in Kronberg, where Max Horkheimer and his friend Friedrich Pollock, both very exceptional people, took me in most kindly and rigorously quizzed me in Schumann's psychology. Both are, by the way, communists and we had long and passionate conversations about the materialist theory of history, in which we disclosed much to one another.[78]

This letter demonstrates clearly that Horkheimer and Pollock were not as close to Adorno and Lowenthal at this time as they were to Felix Weil, with whom they had laid the foundations for the Institute for Social Research, which was

---

74 For an insightful look at the circle surrounding Rabbi Nobel and the Frankfurt Free Jewish *Lehrhaus*, see Wolfgang Schivelbusch, "Auf der Suche nach dem verlorenen Judentum: Das Freie Jüdische Lehrhaus," *Intellektuellendämmerung: Zur Lage der Frankfurter Intelligenz in den zwanziger Jahren* (Frankfurt 1982), pp. 27–41.

75 Ernst von Schenk interviews, p. 61–2. Horkheimer goes on to explain his lack of interest in the circle around Rabbi Nobel in the following way: "I must say emphatically that I did not belong to that circle, I did not know the Rabbi, I had never seen him [...] I didn't belong already for the reason that this Rabbi was the complete opposite of liberal Judaism, he represented a most conservative Judaism." Ibid., p. 63.

76 Theodor Adorno, "Offener Brief an Max Horkheimer," *Gesammelte Schriften*, vol. 20/1 (Frankfurt, 1986), p. 156. Cornelius held seminars in both the winter semester 1922–3 and in the summer semester 1923, so one can only speculate about the exact date of Horkheimer and Adorno's original meeting.

77 MHA VII.6.1. The paper, which presents many of the arguments that Adorno would flesh out in his first *Habilitationsschrift*, "Der Begriff des Unbewussten in der transzendentalen Seelenlehre," has been preserved in the Theodor Adorno Archive, Ts 21335–21348.

78 Leo Lowenthal, *Mitmachen wollte ich nie: Ein Autobiographisches Gespräch mit Helmut Dubiel* (Frankfurt, 1980), p. 248–9.

officially opened three weeks before Adorno wrote this letter. It also shows that Horkheimer's interest in Marxist theory remained strong at this time, even though there are very few traces of it in his academic writings, to which we now turn.

HORKHEIMER'S ACADEMIC STUDIES

Even though Horkheimer's interest in socialism by no means ebbed after he returned to Frankfurt, his primary concern was to finish his doctoral degree. Although he had studied philosophy with Husserl and Heidegger in Freiburg, Horkheimer was still intent upon writing his dissertation in the major field he had chosen, namely psychology. Despite their inauspicious first meeting, the psychology professor Friedrich Schumann agreed to act as Horkheimer's advisor on a dissertation in Gestalt theory bearing the title: "Gestaltveränderungen in der farbenblinden Zone des blinden Flecks im Auge."[79] The topic was indeed a technical one that involved substantial empirical research, but Horkheimer was primarily interested in the philosophical implications of the research.[80] Horkheimer worked intensely on the dissertation through the winter semester 1921–2. When he had nearly completed his work in the summer semester of 1922, Schumann informed him that he would not be able to accept the dissertation after all, because a Danish researcher had just published a study on the same topic with the same results. At this point, Horkheimer recalls seriously considering returning to work in his father's factory,[81] but fortunately for him, Hans Cornelius had also heard about Horkheimer's failed dissertation plans. Cornelius proposed that Horkheimer switch his major from psychology to philosophy and use a paper he had recently given in one of Cornelius's seminars, on Kant's *Critique of Judgment*, as the basis for a new dissertation.[82]

Horkheimer gladly accepted Cornelius's offer. It was the first time in his twenty-five years of teaching that Cornelius had accepted a Ph.D. student. Horkheimer revised and expanded his seminar paper that fall and gave the finished dissertation the title: "Zur Antinomie der teleologischen Urteilskraft."[83] On January 10, 1923, Horkheimer was awarded the doctor title; he was the first at the young university in Frankfurt to receive *summa cum laude* in philosophy.

---

[79] "Form Changes in the Color Blind Zone of the Blind Spot of the Eye."

[80] In defense of his choice of this dissertation topic Horkheimer would say later: "I found this material very interesting and it had a certain relation to Cornelius, because he had developed Ehrenhels' theory of Gestalt qualities.... These are extremely interesting things, for around the blind spot in the eye there is a color blind zone and when you place certain figures there ... they go through certain transformations of form. I worked on this topic for a long time, and there was a good reason for this ... Many fascinating philosophical problems can be discussed with respect to Gestalt theory." Ernst von Schenk interview p. 15 and 23, respectively.

[81] Zvi Rosen, *Max Horkheimer* (München, 1995), p. 23. Also, GS 7, p. 448.

[82] GS 7, pp. 323–4. Horkheimer described this as "one of the most important moments in my entire life." GS 7, p. 448.

[83] "On the Antimony of Teleological Judgment."

On the same day, Cornelius also offered to make Horkheimer his assistant.[84] Horkheimer recalls their meeting that day in the following way:

> On the day I received my Ph.D. Cornelius called me into his office and said: "I wanted to tell you myself that your Ph.D. has been awarded *summa cum laude*. Would you like to become my assistant?" Elated, I said yes. He opened up his arms and declared: "Well, then, my friend, we can also say 'Du' to each other." This is how my academic career began.[85]

It was only at this point that Horkheimer, who just a few months before had entertained the prospect of returning to his father's factory, began seriously to consider the possibility of an academic career. Horkheimer's attitude toward Cornelius changed significantly at this point as well. Although Horkheimer had already worked closely with Cornelius for several years, up to this point he had carefully maintained his critical distance. However, once he became Cornelius's assistant, the two of them rapidly developed a close personal and professional relationship. This is not to say that Horkheimer became any less critical of the German mandarin university system or of professors in general, or that he accepted all aspects of Cornelius's philosophy. After he finished his *Habilitationsschrift* in 1925, which was still heavily indebted to Cornelius, Horkheimer took leave once and for all from the tradition of neo-Kantianism that had dominated German academic philosophy for several decades, and out of which Cornelius's philosophy had also developed.[86] Nonetheless, as Horkheimer became better acquainted with Cornelius, he realized that he did not match his preconceptions about philosophy professors, and that he had much more in common with him than he thought.

Hans Cornelius was born in Munich in 1863 into a family with a long tradition of artistic and intellectual achievement, particularly on the side of his father, who was a professor of history at Munich University.[87] From his youth onward, Cornelius displayed a wide range of interests in the arts and sciences. In 1886, he received a Ph.D. in chemistry, and in 1894 he finished his *Habilitation* in philosophy, both in Munich. During his studies, Cornelius dedicated himself constantly to the arts, first with musical theory and praxis – he studied composition and played the piano as well as several different wind and string instruments – and later with sculpture, painting, and drawing. His passion for the plastic and visual arts was fueled by his frequent visits to Italy, which became a "zweite Heimat"[88] for him. In 1897, his first substantial philosophical work

---

[84] In the German university system, a professor has one or more assistants who help with research and teaching. Assistants also occasionally get to teach courses of their own, under the professor's supervision. The positions are highly coveted, because they are the best way to begin an academic career.

[85] GS 7, p. 324.

[86] Cornelius's philosophy certainly drew on other philosophical traditions beside neo-Kantianism, most importantly the positivism of Ernst Mach, but insofar as he developed the central tenets of his work as a critical response to Kant's *Critique of Pure Reason*, he too was very much within the dominant neo-Kantian paradigm.

[87] For more details on Cornelius's life, see "Hans Cornelius: Leben und Lehre," *Die Philosophie der Gegenwart in Selbstdarstellungen*, ed. Raymund Schmidt (Leipzig, 1921), pp. 81–99.

[88] "Second home." Ibid., p. 82.

appeared, *Psychologie als Erfahrungswissenschaft*,[89] in which he attempted to develop a non-metaphysical psychology that could serve as a foundation for both philosophy and the natural sciences. In 1903, he published his next major work, *Einleitung in die Philosophie*,[90] which presented the results of his intense study of the history of philosophy with a view to epistemological problems. At this time, Cornelius began a more intense occupation with the history and theory of the plastic arts – architecture in particular – which culminated in his third book, *Elementargesetze der bildenden Kunst*.[91] In 1910, Cornelius moved to Frankfurt, where he began meeting regularly with other scholars, such as Max Wertheimer, who were interested in Gestalt theory and its philosophical implications. In 1916, Cornelius published *Transzendentale Systematik*, which presented the fruits not only of these discussions, but also of a more thorough-going critique of Kant and neo-Kantianism. The last book Cornelius published before Horkheimer began working with him, *Kunstpädagogik*,[92] systematized experiences he had recently had teaching a variety of artistic subjects during the war in Munich and Frankfurt.

Cornelius had been influenced heavily by positivism, in particular by Mach and Avenarius, and his own work was positivist itself insofar as his central concern was to free philosophy from all metaphysical concepts. His critique of Kant in *Transzendentale Systematik* focused on the illegitimate nature of Kant's concept of the "thing-in-itself," which allegedly undermined the foundations of empirical research and even experience itself.[93] Cornelius drew on recent empirical research in chemistry and psychology in his attempt to refute, or at least reformulate, some of Kant's central arguments in the *Critique of Pure Reason*.[94] However, Cornelius, as he himself was quick to point out to critics such as Husserl,[95] had also moved beyond Mach and Avenarius, and the positivist tradition in general, with his philosophical reception of Gestalt theory, which was present in his work from the beginning.[96] In other words, as intent as Cornelius was to free philosophy from all metaphysical concepts and presuppositions, his awareness of Gestalt theory prevented him from succumbing completely to the inherent nominalist tendencies of positivism. The immediate experiences [*unmittelbar Erlebnisse*] of consciousness that serve as the foundation of his philosophy are not merely an arbitrary collection of sensory and mental data, but are always already located within the structured totalities of subjective consciousness, apart from which they cannot be understood. So it was that Cornelius came to be known as an important philosophical interpreter of Gestalt theory, and it was this aspect of his philosophy that most interested Horkheimer.

[89] *Psychology as an Experiential Science.*
[90] *Introduction to Philosophy.*
[91] (Leipzig, 1908). "Elementary Laws of the Plastic and Graphic Arts."
[92] *Transcendental Systematic* and *Art Pedagogy.* The original version of the latter was published in Zürich in 1921.
[93] *Transzendentale Systematik*, pp. 28–41.
[94] Ibid., pp. 28–48.
[95] "Hans Cornelius: Leben und Lehre," p. 86.
[96] *Psychologie als Erfahrungswissenschaft*, pp. 70ff., 154ff.; *Einleitung in die Philosophie*, p. 231ff.

However, Cornelius's influence on Horkheimer extended far beyond his philosophical interpretation of Gestalt theory, which Horkheimer would soon abandon. In Cornelius, Horkheimer found not only a willing mentor, but also an intellectual role model of sorts and a friend. As his mentor, Cornelius had not only held numerous philosophical discussions with Horkheimer and encouraged him to spend a year in Freiburg studying with Husserl, but he also made sure that Horkheimer familiarized himself thoroughly with the natural sciences and the arts. Regarding the former, Horkheimer's research in psychology was not enough to satisfy Cornelius; he also insisted that Horkheimer attend lectures on physics and chemistry, which he did.[97] Regarding the latter, Cornelius dedicated himself personally to making sure Horkheimer had a solid grounding in the arts, particularly the plastic and visual arts, which were his own specialty. Horkheimer's first lesson in the arts from Cornelius was a crash course, conducted according the principle "learn-by-doing." Sometime in 1922, when Cornelius was stricken by one of the periodic, severe arthritis attacks (he suffered from gout) that left him bedridden for weeks at a time, he asked Horkheimer to take over a drawing course he was teaching. Horkheimer protested that he knew nothing about drawing; Cornelius told him he would give him two weeks to prepare. Horkheimer obliged. He ended up enjoying the course immensely, which he ran cooperatively with the other students, and also learning the basics of drawing in the process.[98] To ensure that Horkheimer had an understanding of the principles of music, Cornelius would also give Horkheimer composition lessons. Even more important, though, were the trips to Italy Cornelius undertook with Horkheimer and Riekher during the next few years. They traveled to many different Italian cities so Cornelius could give them concrete and comprehensive instruction on the history of art and architecture.[99]

Cornelius was not just a mentor, but also a role model of sorts for Horkheimer, because he stood in opposition to the dominant conservative structures of the university and society in his own way. His diverse interests placed him at odds with the trend toward specialization that had become increasingly dominant in German universities in the second half of the nineteenth century.[100] Few scholars embodied the principle of interdisciplinarity, which would play such an important role in Horkheimer's later work, as well as Cornelius.[101] Furthermore, Cornelius always attempted to maintain a balance between theory and practice, in the sense that he actively engaged in the arts and sciences he taught at the university. That Horkheimer was impressed by his example is

---

[97] GS 7, p. 450.

[98] Ibid., p. 449–50.

[99] Ibid., p. 450.

[100] Herbert Schnädelbach, for example, describes this trend as a shift from "Bildung durch Wissenschaft" (education through science) to "Wissenschaft als Beruf" (science as a vocation). See his *Philosophie in Deutschland 1831–1933* (Frankfurt, 1983), pp. 35–48.

[101] As Horkheimer put it later, "Cornelius explained to me: philosophy is way of thinking that presupposes knowledge, solid knowledge of the natural sciences and the arts. Cornelius was, namely, not at all in favor of the dominant rules. He said of the university in the condition it was in then practically the same thing that people like Herwegh said in the early 19th century and what a large section of students are saying about it today." GS 7, pp. 450–1.

made clear by the following remarks he made many years later: "He trusted himself to do things for which one would normally hire professionals; for example, he designed and built his own house, he also painted and sculpted.... He was a Renaissance man."[102] Cornelius did not fit the stereotype of the conservative or apolitical German mandarin professor either. Although his attempt to intervene in the inflation debate had irritated Horkheimer, he later realized that he shared many of Cornelius's political principles. Cornelius had also been opposed to the war, which had led him briefly to study social and political philosophy.[103] Near the end of the war, he wrote an article calling for a European "federal state with a unified market, unified diplomacy and military" that could limit the possibility of future nationalist conflicts.[104] Cornelius's pro-European, antinationalist political convictions also made him sensitive early on to the threat of National Socialism. After finishing his professorial duties in 1929, rather than retiring comfortably to the house he had built for himself in Oberursel, an affluent suburb of Frankfurt, Cornelius left for Sweden so his children would not be poisoned by National Socialism in the schools.[105]

In addition to serving as a mentor and a role model for Horkheimer, Cornelius was also his friend. After Horkheimer finished his Ph.D. and became Cornelius's assistant, the two of them became quite close. Cornelius provided Horkheimer with much needed financial and emotional support. As relations became increasingly tense with his parents due to his ongoing relationship with Riekher, Horkheimer became more and more reluctant to turn to his father for financial support. Cornelius provided Horkheimer with financial support on numerous occasions.[106] In addition, Cornelius did not have any difficulties with Horkheimer's relationship to Riekher, who would soon join Pollock and Horkheimer in Frankfurt. Cornelius and his wife befriended Riekher right away.[107] Riekher also joined them on their trips to Italy. In 1926, the year after Horkheimer finished his *Habilitation* and began working as a *Privatdozent*,[108] he married Riekher. At this point, his parents finally accepted her as a part of the family, but until then Horkheimer certainly appreciated Cornelius and his wife's warm acceptance of Riekher.

Horkheimer's philosophical writings from this period – most significantly, his dissertation and *Habilitationsschrift* on Kant's *Critique of Judgment* – raise a number of difficult questions. Foremost among these, for our concerns here, are the following: How did Horkheimer's philosophical writings at this time relate to his personal and intellectual development up to that point? Were they

---

[102] Ernst von Schenk interviews, p. 16 [MHA X 132b].

[103] Cornelius wrote, "I could see in the insanity of the war nothing else but the results of the general confusion about the fundamental conditions of social existence." *Philosophie der Gegenwart in Selbstdarstellungen*, p. 10.

[104] Ibid.

[105] Horkheimer said later, "Already at that time he, like myself, saw National Socialism coming." GS 7, p. 451.

[106] Ibid., p. 26.

[107] Ernst von Schenk interviews, p. 12.

[108] A *Privatdozent* at a German university is similar to a lecturer in the Anglo-American university system. He is officially qualified to teach, i.e. he has finished his second dissertation (*Habilitation*), but he has not yet received an official position as a professor.

merely empty exercises completed to fulfill academic requirements, or did they represent a vital continuation of his incipient theoretical and philosophical interests? In 1925, when Horkheimer emerged from Cornelius's philosophical mentorship and began overtly to develop and defend an independent theoretical position, did he simply disregard what he had written under Cornelius's auspices? In other words, what lasting influence, if any, did these writings have on Horkheimer's further development? Interpreters of Horkheimer's work have differed widely on these questions. At one end of the spectrum, are those who view Horkheimer's philosophical writings from this period as "purely academic" or "docile fulfillment of an academic requirement."[109] At the other end, are those who see an essential continuity between Horkheimer's academic writings and his later work, at least in regard to certain key issues.[110] Whereas the second set of questions, regarding the lasting effects of this period on Horkheimer's later thought, can only truly be answered in the further course of this study, a few preliminary remarks can be made after we examine these writings more closely. But let us turn now to the first set of questions – which we can answer right away – regarding the relationship of Horkheimer's academic writings to his intellectual development at the time.

Horkheimer's relationship to the university was deeply ambivalent. We have already seen how skeptical he was from the very beginning about the contemporary German university in general, and its professors in particular. Theodor Adorno's first impression of Horkheimer provides further evidence of this:

When I saw you for the first time in Adhémar Gelb's psychology seminar, you, eight years older than I, hardly seemed like a student to me, more like a young gentleman from an established family who granted science a certain distanced interest. You were not affected by the professional deformity of the academic, who all-too-easily confuses the occupation with scholarly things with reality. But what you said was so perceptive, incisive and, above all, independent, that I recognized soon enough your superiority to the [academic] sphere, from which you unpretentiously maintained your distance.[111]

As Adorno immediately recognized, Horkheimer had come to the university not to pursue an academic career, but in hopes of understanding the real-existing irrationality and injustice of the society in which he lived. In this

---

[109] Gumnior/Ringhuth, p. 27 and Heidrun Hesse, *Vernunft und Selbstbehauptung: Kritische Theorie als Kritik der neuzeitlichen Rationalität* (Frankfurt, 1984), p. 16.

[110] Frank Hartmann views his dissertation and *Habilitationsschrift* as an "implicit preparation of the 'materialist phase' of Critical Theory in the thirties," and even makes the bold (and unsubstantiated) claim that one can find in them "the idea of universally binding social planning" op. cit. p. 134. Dieter Sattler follows Hartmann in seeing essential continuity between his later work and his early academic writings, in which Horkheimer allegedly "already attempted to lay the foundation for the transformation of epistemological reflection 'into the question of knowledge of society'" (Hartmann, 124). *Max Horkheimer als Moralphilosoph: Studie zur Kritischen Theorie* (Frankfurt, 1996), p. 46. Peter Stirk also claims that "the seeds of Horkheimer's later idea about the reunification of will and reason in a planned society" are present in his *Habilitationsschrift. Max Horkheimer: A New Interpretation* (Hemel Hempstead, UK, 1992), p. 112.

[111] Theodor Adorno, "Offener Brief an Max Horkheimer," *Gesammelte Schriften*, vol. 20, part 1 (Frankfurt, 1986), p. 156.

respect, Horkheimer's interest in the university was entirely genuine. Although Horkheimer had attended a few lectures in Munich, the university milieu was largely foreign to him when he came to Frankfurt in the fall of 1919. It was not until the end of the war that Horkheimer decided – much to the chagrin of his father – to pursue university studies; no one in Horkheimer's family had ever attended the university. Horkheimer's "distanced interest" was certainly also a sign of guarded, but genuine curiosity. Horkheimer wanted to familiarize himself with the most advanced research in the social, human, and natural sciences, and there was no better place to do so than the newly founded university in Frankfurt, whose progressive and innovative character was already well known. His academic writings from this period are best understood as an attempt to gain an overview of the most important theoretical debates of the day.

Horkheimer's avid interest in Gestalt psychology is the best example of his efforts to assimilate contemporary scientific debates. It would be difficult indeed to argue plausibly that Horkheimer's first dissertation, on the technical topic of "Form Changes in the Color Blind Zone of the Blind Spot of the Eye," was directly related to his own most vital concerns at that time. Nonetheless, Horkheimer carried out the project with enthusiasm and interest, and looked back fondly on it in later interviews.[112] On Cornelius's recommendation, Horkheimer attended lectures in the natural sciences, which also captured his interest. Horkheimer repeatedly stated later that Frankfurt was an avant-garde university at the time, where one was encouraged to gain an overview of the latest research in many different fields, not just to specialize in one.[113] It was at this time that Horkheimer first gained his respect for empirical research, which would remain important in his later thought. At this point, Horkheimer already recognized that philosophy had to build on the ongoing research in other disciplines, not reject it out of hand in the name of grandiose schemes to recapture logical, ontological, or metaphysical absolutes.[114] In this respect, Horkheimer consciously placed himself in the Enlightenment tradition, at a time when empiricism and "shallow" rationalism were increasingly seen in Germany as enemies of authentic *Kultur*.

However, Horkheimer's initial lively interest in contemporary discussions at the university would soon give way to disappointment. After returning from his studies with Husserl and Heidegger in Freiburg, Horkheimer remarked, "The more fascinated I become with philosophy, the further I distance myself from the way it is understood at this university."[115] As we have seen, after his first dissertation was rejected, Horkheimer seriously considered giving up his studies altogether and returning to his father's factory. It was at this point, however, that Cornelius intervened and opened the door for Horkheimer to pursue an academic career, something he had not seriously considered up to that point. Cornelius and Horkheimer soon developed a close personal relationship. Thus,

---

[112] Ernst von Schenk interviews, p. 15.
[113] GS 7, p. 450. Ernst von Schenk interviews, p. 14.
[114] GS 11, p. 91.
[115] GS 15, p. 69, p. 77.

when evaluating Horkheimer's dissertation and *Habilitationsschrift*, Cornelius's personal influence should not be underestimated. In a paper he wrote in 1921 or 1922 on Kant's mechanistic epistemology, Horkheimer viewed Cornelius's position in terms of "radical opposition" and "fundamental objection."[116] Yet after Cornelius came to Horkheimer's aid by offering to accept an expanded and revised version of this paper as a dissertation, Horkheimer became more receptive to his arguments. In both his dissertation and his *Habilitationsschrift*, Horkheimer loyally defended Cornelius's position. Although Horkheimer did genuinely agree with Cornelius on some points, his writings at this time clearly represented a tactical truce with Cornelius in many respects. In any case, Horkheimer did not spend a lot of time working on either the dissertation or the *Habilitationsschrift*. The former was hurriedly conceived and executed to get him out of a difficult situation, and the latter he completed rapidly as well, in order to finish before Cornelius retired.[117] Neither the dissertation nor the *Habilitationsschrift* exceeded seventy-five pages in length. In short, Horkheimer did not invest a tremendous amount in either the dissertation or the *Habilitationsschrift*.

Nonetheless, it would be mistaken to claim that the dissertation and *Habilitationsschrift* were nothing more than a "docile fulfillment of an academic requirement."[118] Horkheimer's own interest in coming to terms with the dominant trends in academic philosophy at the time is still clearly apparent in both works. His choice to work on Kant's *Critique of Judgment* was not determined by a desire to rethink the relationship between practical and theoretical reason, which would serve as a basis for his later critical theory, as some commentators have implied.[119] Horkheimer would begin seriously to work out the philosophical foundations of his later critical theory only *after* he had emerged from Cornelius's influence. The *Critique of Judgment* provided Horkheimer with direct access to the fundamental issues underlying contemporary academic debates in philosophy, which had been dominated by neo-Kantianism since the last decades of the nineteenth century. Furthermore, the *Critique of Judgment* was an excellent vantage point from which to reassess a debate that was of particular significance to Horkheimer, namely the controversy between his mentor Cornelius and Edmund Husserl – the most influential philosopher in Germany at the time – on the relationship between epistemology and psychology.[120] Although Horkheimer's excursion into academic philosophy was ultimately a

---

[116] "Das unmittelbar Gegebene als Urgrund der Erkenntnis. Zur Kritik der Kantischen mechanistischen Erkenntistheorie," GS 11, p. 29. Already at this point Horkheimer was eager to move beyond the entire tradition of transcendental philosophy as the passage immediately following this one just quoted illustrates: "It will soon become clear, that this objection [to Cornelius's philosophy J.A.] ... is leveled against the entire historical development of the concept of consciousness, including, in particular, all transcendental philosophy that has been influenced by Kant." This move was delayed for a couple of years, however, by the tactical truce Horkheimer made with Cornelius until he completed his *Habilitationsschrift*.

[117] GS 7, p. 324.

[118] Heidrun Hesse, *Vernunft und Selbstbehauptung: Kritische Theorie als Kritik der neuzeitlichen Rationalität* (Frankfurt, 1984), p. 16.

[119] See footnote 112.

[120] For Husserl's critique of Cornelius, see *Logical Investigations*, trans. J.N. Findlay, vol. 1 (Amherst, NY, 2000) pp. 197–207 and 419–25. For Cornelius's response, see "Leben und Lehre," op. cit. p. 86.

dead end, he did learn some important lessons along the way that would stay with him. In order to understand exactly what these lessons were, we must turn briefly to the works themselves.

Horkheimer's dissertation, "On the Antinomy of Teleological Judgment,"[121] analyzes Kant's attempt in the *Critique of Judgment* to account for the appearance of teleological causality in nature. In the *Critique of Pure Reason*, Kant responded to David Hume's skepticism about causality in nature by arguing that its source was subjective, not objective; for Kant, causality exists as a constitutive element of the transcendental subject, or, in other words, as one of the universal categories of human understanding. Through these categories, man is able to understand the laws of nature that were laid bare in the pathbreaking research of early modern science, which achieved its crowning synthesis in Newton's mechanical physics. One of the defining characteristics of the early modern scientific revolution was the rejection of teleological principles, or final causes, as explanations for natural phenomena.[122] Kant followed early modern science in this regard. He did not reject teleological causation altogether, but he did limit it strictly to the sphere of human free will and practical reason, for only intelligent beings could, according to him, act based on final causes. So although Kant insisted that natural phenomena be explained solely in terms of mechanical causation, he also recognized that the natural sciences could not do without teleological principles in certain cases. For example, Kant realized that organic beings could not possibly be understood solely in terms of mechanical causation, which is based upon the methodological principle of dividing the phenomenon in question into an aggregate of discrete parts. This atomistic form of explanation is insufficient for organic beings, because the parts themselves are fully explicable only in reference to the role they play within the larger whole. Yet if the categories of understanding that underlie the laws of nature strictly prohibit teleological causality, how can science understand organic beings? This antinomy, which Kant attempts to resolve in his third *Critique* with the concept of teleological judgment, is the subject of Horkheimer's dissertation.[123]

After describing the antinomy, Horkheimer shows how Kant tried to resolve it. The field of scientific research in general, and empirical research in particular, falls under the cognitive faculty of judgment in Kant's philosophy. In contrast to the understanding [*Verstand*], which establishes the universal laws of nature, it is the function of judgment in general – what Kant calls *determining* judgment [*bestimmende Urteilskraft*] – to apply these laws to particular phenomena. Yet because not all natural phenomena can be subsumed under the mechanical laws of the categories of understanding – such as organic beings, which seem to be governed by teleological causality – Kant posits the existence of a second

[121] "Zur Antinomie der teleologischen Urteilskraft," GS 2, pp. 13–72.

[122] In Aristotelian physics, which enjoyed a partial revival in the late Middle Ages and which served as one of the foils for early modern science, final causes are considered as one of the four basic natural forces. See, for example, *Introduction to Aristotle*, second edition revised and enlarged, ed. Richard McKeon (Chicago, 1973), pp. 138–42.

[123] For Kant's own description of this antinomy, see *Kritik der Urteilskraft, Immanuel Kant Werksausgabe*, vol. 10 (Frankfurt, 1968), pp. 334–8.

type of judgment, *reflective* judgment [*reflektierende Urteilskraft*], which fulfills the function of researching and ordering natural phenomena that defy mechanical explanation. Although the explanatory function of reflective judgment is necessary, according to Kant, he stresses emphatically that it does not possess the same explanatory power as determining judgment. Whereas the latter cognitive faculty applies the quasi-objective, transcendental categories of the understanding to particular phenomena, the former has validity merely as a heuristic principle, or, in other words, "only subjectively, for us."[124] By defining teleological causality in this way, Kant believes he has demonstrated that the antinomy between it and mechanical explanations of nature is merely an illusion, because they exist at different cognitive levels. Teleological explanations are useful, even necessary as subjective, heuristic aids in constructing unified experience at the empirical level, but mechanical explanations alone are binding at the quasi-objective, transcendental level of understanding, at which the laws of nature exist.

Next, Horkheimer shows how Kant's resolution of this antimony reveals some of the fundamental assumptions of his philosophy as a whole. In particular, Horkheimer wants to show that the mechanical principles whose primacy Kant reasserted in his resolution of the problem of teleological causality also underlie his theory of knowledge. Although Kant said in several places that transcendental subjectivity should be understood as a totality,[125] he carried out his analysis of it in the *Critique of Pure Reason* using a mechanistic methodology. As Horkheimer puts it, "even if the detailed investigation of this topic was first carried out in the *Critique of Judgment*, one may still claim that the results merely confirm the presuppositions that underlie, more or less consciously, the *Critique of Pure Reason*."[126] Horkheimer buttresses this claim by examining the relationship between sensation [*Sinnlichkeit*] and understanding in Kant's epistemology. He shows that the mechanistic division between formal and material components of knowledge determines the relationship between the senses and understanding. Horkheimer writes:

Kant assumes that every form of cognition, every "content" can be divided into given sensual elements, which are, in and of themselves, completely disparate and chaotic, and "that which actually brings these elements together as cognition and provides them with a unified content."[127]

Horkheimer shows that this strict division between the chaos of sense impressions on the one hand, and the synthesizing and ordering power of the understanding on the other, leads to problems that are even more difficult to resolve than the teleological causality of organic beings. For in the case of organic beings one could, at least, analyze their various component parts empirically, but such analysis is not possible in the sphere of cognition. Nowhere could one observe the component elements of objects of knowledge – the categories of understanding and the chaotic data of the senses – in their pure form.

[124] Quoted by Horkheimer, GS 2, p. 38.
[125] See Horkheimer's examples, GS 2, p. 49.
[126] Ibid., p. 50.
[127] Ibid., p. 54.

In the final chapter of his dissertation, Horkheimer raises two fundamental objections to Kant's arguments. First, he claims that Kant made the false assumption that teleological causality always implied conscious agency. It was this assumption that led Kant to limit teleological causality strictly to the sphere of practical reason, for if one accepted teleological causation in nature, one would have to assume the existence of an intelligent being that had created nature, which for Kant was tantamount to relapsing into dogmatic metaphysics. Horkheimer insisted that teleological causation and holistic explanation were not the same thing. One could have totalities in nature, which could not be explained in mechanistic terms, but which also in no way implied or necessitated the existence of conscious creation or guidance. Horkheimer buttressed this argument with examples from the natural sciences. Not only had this insight been confirmed long ago in the biological sciences, more recently it had been accepted in physics as well, as Horkheimer demonstrated with a lengthy quote from Max Planck.[128]

The second main objection that Horkheimer leveled against Kant was also based on empirical research from a discipline that was still considered a natural science at this time: psychology. Horkheimer argued that Kant was mistaken in assuming that the human mind, at the most fundamental level – for Kant, the categories of the understanding – always perceived isolated units first, which it subsequently synthesized into larger wholes. Horkheimer maintained that the mind could also proceed in the opposite direction: from the whole to the part. For this reason, the mind could also – so he argued – perceive totalities that were present in the "unmittelbar Gegebene"[129] sense impressions themselves. In other words, it was not the case, as Kant had believed, that matter was nothing more than a chaos of sense impressions that received whatever structure it might have solely from human understanding. To substantiate these claims, Horkheimer drew on the central thesis of Gestalt psychology, which asserted the primacy of the whole over the parts in fundamental areas of human consciousness: perception, memory, and experience. In addition to citing recent empirical research in Gestalt theory conducted by the Frankfurt psychologist Wolfgang Köhler,[130] Horkheimer also drew liberally throughout the dissertation on Hans Cornelius's *philosophical* interpretation of Gestalt theory, as following passage illustrates, in which Horkheimer quotes Cornelius to refute Kant:

Not just an imaginary divine understanding is able to move "from the whole to the parts," this movement refers instead to a fundamental characteristic of our consciousness.

---

[128] GS 2, p. 61.

[129] "Immediately given." This was a crucial concept in Cornelius's philosophy, insofar as the sense impressions immediately given to consciousness were the only instance in which a mental representation of an object was identical with the object itself. For this reason, Cornelius made the sense impressions immediately given to consciousness the cornerstone of his epistemology. It is important to note that Cornelius did not confuse the sense impressions with their source; for this reason he could still claim that his epistemology was still transcendental, and represented a continuation of Kant's philosophy in certain ways. See his *Transzendentale Systematik*, pp. 44–9.

[130] GS 2, p. 70.

Holistic qualities are the primary givens everywhere, such "that in our development the knowledge of the holistic aspects of entities always precedes the knowledge of the composition of their individual parts."[131]

Horkheimer stopped short, however, of claiming that he or anyone else had already discovered an alternative solution to the problem, for "The philosopher can learn this only by attentively observing the path that research in the natural sciences takes in the future."[132]

In his _Habilitationsschrift_, "On Kant's _Critique of Judgment_ as the Link between Theoretical and Practical Philosophy,"[133] the problem of teleological causality also plays a crucial role, although this time Horkheimer addresses it within a broader framework. The point of departure for the _Habilitationsschrift_ is not merely the concept of teleological judgment, but the systematic location of the _Critique of Judgment_ within Kant's work as a whole. Horkheimer shows that Kant's philosophy rests upon a psychological assumption he inherited from the rationalist tradition of Leibniz and Wolff, namely that theoretical and practical reason are two fundamentally different faculties. In the _Critique of Pure Reason_, Kant explicated the former in terms of the categories of understanding that underlie human perception and the laws of nature. In the _Critique of Practical Reason_, Kant explicated the latter in terms of the human will, which realizes its inherent freedom and dignity by acting according to ethical laws. Thus, theoretical reason is limited to the realm of necessity, which is governed by mechanical principles, and practical reason is limited to the realm of freedom, which is governed by teleological principles: the realization of rational ends. However, by dividing these two spheres so strictly from one another, Kant was faced with the problem of how they were interrelated. How, for example, is it possible to realize rational ends in nature? It was problems such as this, which resulted from the split of theoretical and practical reason, that Kant attempted to solve in the _Critique of Judgment_. Horkheimer shows that Kant agonized over this problem until his death. He experimented with different solutions, such as asserting the primacy of practical reason, before seriously addressing the problem in the _Critique of Judgment_, and even then he seems to have been dissatisfied with his results.[134]

In order to provide an alternative solution to this problem, Horkheimer undertakes in his _Habilitationsschrift_ a thorough investigation of Kant's assumption that theoretical and practical reason are two completely different faculties. He does this by examining three different cases in which purposefulness [_Zweckmässigkeit_] appear outside the realm of practical reason, thereby calling its rigid separation from theoretical reason into question. The first of these three cases is the seemingly nonmechanical, nonchaotic structure of the natural world that one sees, for example, in the natural division of organic life into more or less clearly defined categories, such as species. The second case is

---

[131] Ibid., p. 68. The first quote in this passage in from Kant; the second is from Cornelius.

[132] Ibid., p. 70.

[133] "Über Kants _Kritik der Urteilskraft_ als Bindeglied zwischen theoretischer und praktischer Philosophie," GS 2, pp. 73–146.

[134] As Horkheimer claims, based on unpublished material from the end of Kant's life. GS 2, p. 81.

the appearance of purposefulness in the aesthetic sphere, in both nature and works of art. The third and final case of purposefulness Horkheimer examines is the same example he used in his dissertation, namely the holistic structure of organic beings. Horkheimer's choice of these three examples was by no means fortuitous. All three examples of purposefulness play prominent roles in the *Critique of Judgment*. At first glance, it may seem strange that Kant subsumed aesthetic and biological phenomena under the same cognitive faculty in the *Critique of Judgment*, but his reasons for doing so point directly to the problem Horkheimer investigates in his *Habilitationsschrift*. As Horkheimer puts it: "The analysis of those perceptible entities [*erfahrbare Einheiten*], whose formation cannot be attributed solely to the unifying function of the faculty of cognition [*Erkenntnisvermögens*], is the central concern of the entire work."[135] In other words, Kant must be able to explain these examples of purposefulness, of "perceptible entities," if he wants to preserve his sharp distinction between theoretical and practical reason. The goal of Horkheimer's *Habilitationsschrift* is to see if he succeeds.

Horkheimer concludes that Kant's attempts to create a viable link between theoretical and practical reason fail on all three counts. The third example Horkheimer uses in his *Habilitationsschrift*, the purposefulness of organic beings, we have just examined in his dissertation. In his *Habilitationsschrift*, he makes very similar arguments. He shows once again that Kant made a distinction between determining and reflective judgment in order to highlight the merely subjective and heuristic nature not only of the purposefulness of organic beings, but also of formal purposefulness in nature in general – the first example he explores in the *Habilitationsschrift*. In both cases, Horkheimer highlights once again the denigration of empirical research that results from Kant's arguments:

The task of reflective judgment is not (as that of the understanding) determining knowledge [*bestimmende Erkenntnis*], but instead discovery, reflection, research, in other words, preliminary work for determining knowledge…. Thus the analysis of empirical facts is not even considered scientific knowledge according to this theory.[136]

In both cases of purposefulness in nature, Horkheimer concludes that the problem cannot be resolved without abandoning Kant's rigid distinction between theoretical and practical reason.

In the other example of purposefulness Horkheimer examines, namely that of aesthetic objects, Horkheimer comes to a similar conclusion. Although Horkheimer's explication of Kant's aesthetic theory takes its subtle complexities very seriously, he ultimately comes to the conclusion that Kant made the problem more difficult than he needed to. Horkheimer shows how the imagination [*Einbildungskraft*] plays a role in the aesthetic sphere similar to that of the understanding in the cognitive sphere. Whereas the understanding has the function of bringing order to the chaotic sense impressions, the imagination has the function of creating an image [*Bild*] out of the chaotic

---

[135] Ibid., p. 110.
[136] Ibid., pp. 96–7 and 102–3 respectively. Emphasis Horkheimer's own.

sense impressions of aesthetic intuition [*Anschauung*]. Kant maintains that the purposefulness of an aesthetic object consists precisely in the fortuitous corre-spondence of this image with its presentation [*Darstellung*] by the concepts of the understanding, such that it lends itself particularly well to being grasped by the understanding. However, for Horkheimer, Kant's solution begs the original question of the relationship between the senses and the understanding. Kant stressed the importance of the imagination in order to differentiate aesthetic judgment from theoretical reason, but many of the same problems he had with the relationship of the understanding to sense impressions reappear in the rela-tionship of the imagination to aesthetic intuitions. Most importantly, the rigid distinction remains between an active, ordering faculty (imagination) and the passive, chaotic raw material upon which it works (the impressions of aesthetic intuition). Rather than adequately addressing the original problem of the rela-tionship between the understanding and the senses, Kant located the origins of aesthetic purposefulness in the imagination, but the same problems reappeared. Imagination was supposed to provide a link between the understanding and the senses. Yet even with this supposed link provided by the imagination, the relationship between the understanding and the senses, which Kant himself described as "fortuitous,"[137] remained "artificial and external" according to Horkheimer.[138] Thus for Horkheimer, Kant's attempt to account for aesthetic purposefulness also ultimately fails, and his detailed discussion of the imagina-tion proves to be "superfluous."[139]

What Horkheimer concludes in regard to Kant's explication of aesthetic purposefulness holds true for natural purposefulness as well, namely that the root of the problem lies in the artificial distinction between understanding and the senses:

The relationship between sensation and understanding could have been properly deter-mined only if Kant had overcome the prejudice of their heterogeneity and carried out an unbiased investigation of the genesis of the concept in what is immediate sense impressions.[140]

As in his dissertation, Horkheimer draws upon Cornelius's theory of "immediate sense impressions" – as the epistemological archimedian point at which sub-ject and object merge, and in which the holistic structures of knowledge reveal themselves – to call certain aspects of Kant's philosophy into question. However, in the *Habilitationsschrift* the stakes are higher than in the disserta-tion, which was concerned primarily with the comparatively minor problem of the antinomy of teleological judgment. In the *Habilitationsschrift*, Horkheimer disputes the central distinction in Kant's philosophical system, namely that between theoretical and practical reason. By showing that Kant was unable successfully to account for the three main cases of purposefulness that appear independently of practical reason, he believes he has demonstrated the fallacy

---

[137] Quoted by Horkheimer, Ibid., p. 115.
[138] Ibid., p. 121.
[139] Ibid., p. 120.
[140] Ibid., p. 122.

of the distinction as a whole. For if, as Horkheimer believes, it can be proven that purposefulness exists both in the cognitive structures of the transcendental subject and in the real world, then the distinction between an essentially mechanical theoretical reason and an essentially teleological practical reason is no longer tenable. Horkheimer writes:

The specific character of these objects which, according to Kant, bear the mark of both theoretical and practical reason, can be comprehended epistemologically without recourse to practical reason, i.e. to a will. In this regard, therefore, the *Critique of Judgment* is not a "link" [between theoretical and practical reason].[141]

Furthermore, if purposefulness can be understood epistemologically, without reference to practical reason, it also follows, according to Horkheimer, that the real world is not in and of itself inimical to the realization of teleological aims. As Horkheimer puts it, "at least we may now say that – when the intention to realize an idea exists – this realization should not from the very beginning be considered possible only in a limited sense, because the essence of reality would contradict an adequate realization of this intention."[142] This conclusion, which Horkheimer adds almost as an afterthought to his *Habilitationsschrift*, could easily be interpreted as an important step toward a more Hegelian position, and Horkheimer was in fact beginning seriously to study Hegel at this time. Yet he was quick to qualify his statement, showing that he was still closer to Schopenhauer than Hegel on the question of the relationship between rationality and reality:

Based on this insight one can, however, by no means draw the Hegelian conclusion that reason in general is identical with reality. For just because reality can be in accord with reason and in certain places actually is, does not yet mean that there is *general* agreement between them.[143]

With these concluding sentences of his *Habilitationsschrift*, Horkheimer opened the door that would lead him beyond the academic philosophy of the type represented by Hans Cornelius. In the following year, he would step through it.

THE THEORETICAL LESSONS HORKHEIMER LEARNED FROM HIS ACADEMIC STUDIES

Before turning to his philosophical break with Cornelius, let us briefly return to the question of the theoretical lessons of lasting value that Horkheimer learned during his university studies in Frankfurt in the early 1920s. The important points fall under the headings of empirical research, the concept of totality, and the unity of practical and theoretical reason. Regarding the first, we have seen how important empirical research in the sciences was during this time for Horkheimer, from the courses he attended to the research he conducted himself on his first, unfinished dissertation project, and to his reliance on research in

[141] GS 2, p. 145.
[142] Ibid.
[143] Ibid., p. 146. Horkheimer's emphasis.

Gestalt psychology at crucial points in his dissertation and *Habilitationsschrift*. This interest in empirical research was by no means limited to any one specific discipline. Cornelius encouraged Horkheimer in word and deed to familiarize himself with the latest research in a broad range of disciplines, and Horkheimer did so enthusiastically. Horkheimer's interest in interdisciplinary research would remain one of the cornerstones of his thought throughout his life. His interest in empirical research would also remain central to his thinking, although the emphasis would of course shift in the late 1920s from empirical research in the natural sciences to empirical *social* research. Horkheimer would of course never adopt or implement the methods of empirical research – natural, social, or otherwise – in a naïve way, uninformed by a critical theory of society, but empirical social research provided him at this time and later with a potent weapon against ahistorical metaphysical and rationalist theories. In this regard, Horkheimer was consciously placing himself in the Enlightenment tradition, which was not an apotheosis of abstract reason, as the myth that has held tenaciously from the romantics to the poststructuralists would have it, but rather an attempt to ground reason in the senses, society, and history.[144]

Hans Cornelius's work represented a continuation of this main current of the Enlightenment tradition, insofar as he tried to free philosophy of metaphysical presuppositions and to secure a rigorous foundation for empirical research in the natural sciences.[145] Although Horkheimer's abiding interest in empirical research was sparked by Cornelius, it is not the case, as Frank Hartmann claims, that he appropriated a naïve epistemological realism from Cornelius that would remain with him for the rest of his life. Hartmann argues that Cornelius's philosophy remained beholden to the neo-Kantian "naturalization of the a priori,"[146] which eliminated the transcendental, reflexive elements of Kant's philosophy, and led willy-nilly to a precritical, "ontological"[147] position. He asserts that Horkheimer "moves hardly a step beyond [Cornelius's] analyses," and that "this influence can be found practically uninterrupted in Horkheimer's later theory."[148] Horkheimer allegedly defended a "correspondence theory of truth, whose traces can be found in his later writings."[149] Yet Hartmann overlooks the fact that Cornelius, despite his rehabilitation of empirical research, never abandoned Kant's basic presupposition that philosophy must build

---

[144] In his magisterial survey of the Enlightenment, Peter Gay writes, "The philosophers' glorification of criticism and their qualified repudiation of metaphysics make it obvious that the Enlightenment was not an age of Reason but a revolt against Rationalism." Peter Gay, *The Enlightenment: An Interpretation*, vol. 1, *The Rise of Modern Paganism* (New York, 1966), p. 141. On the tenacious myths about the Enlightenment introduced by the romantic reaction against it in the first decades of the nineteenth century, see Ernst Cassirer, *The Philosophy of Enlightenment*, trans. F.C.A. Koelln and J.P. Pettegrove (Boston, 1955), p. xi and 197.

[145] On this point, see also Susan Buck-Morss's discussion of Cornelius, whom she characterizes as an "*Aufklärer* of the old sort." *The Origins of Negative Dialectics* (Sussex, 1977), pp. 7ff.

[146] Frank Hartmann, *Max Horkheimers materialistischer Skeptizismus: Frühe Motive der Kritischen Theorie* (Frankfurt, 1990), p. 130.

[147] Ibid., p. 128.

[148] Ibid., pp. 139–40.

[149] Ibid., p. 145. For proof of the absurdity of this claim, see Horkheimer's critique of Lenin's correspondence theory of truth in chapter 4, pp. 150–56.

upon a transcendental foundation.[150] Far from being naïve "sense certainty,"[151] Cornelius's "immediate sensual givens" were always already subjectively mediated, insofar as they could be found only in human consciousness. As Olaf Asbach has convincingly demonstrated,[152] Horkheimer also remained within this transcendental horizon in his academic writings from this time. In his dissertation and *Habilitationsschrift*, Horkheimer did indeed loyally defend Cornelius's transcendental philosophy, and even his references at key points to empirical research drew from fields – Gestalt psychology and the new nonmechanical physics – in which the subjective factors of knowledge were of central concern. The speciousness of the claim that Horkheimer remained beholden to an "ontological" position or a "correspondence theory of truth" in his later writings will be become readily apparent in due course, for example, when we examine Horkheimer's critique of positivism, his appropriation of psychoanalysis, or his analysis of the social determinants of perception.

Horkheimer's university studies provided him with his first sustained exposure not only to empirical research, but also to the concept of totality, which would play an important role in his later work.[153] The concept of totality was widely discussed in a variety of different contexts in Germany in the 1920s, so it cannot be ruled out that Horkheimer first encountered it elsewhere, particularly because he had already read *A Contribution to the Critique of Political Economy*, in which Marx outlined the importance of the concept for his own method.[154] Nevertheless, it was a specific version of the concept, which Horkheimer borrowed from Gestalt psychology, that first appeared in his dissertation and *Habilitationsschrift*. In both works, the concept played a crucial role in his critique of the mechanical presuppositions of Kant's epistemology. Horkheimer's use of the concept at this time anticipated his later use of it in some important ways. In his dissertation, for example, Horkheimer criticized Kant's assumption that the appearance of totalities in nature pointed necessarily to an intelligent creator. Horkheimer maintained that objective totalities could exist that had not been consciously created nor were consciously guided. He would draw on this insight later to criticize both

---

[150] As Cornelius himself put it in his *Transzendentale Systematik*: "Despite the fundamental contradiction of methods mentioned here, the result of the investigation remains in the most important point in agreement with that of Kant. As with Kant, it has also been shown here that the concept of *nature* is conditioned by *factors of our knowing*. What we refer to with the terms of nature and its laws are only conceptualizations, through which we organize – in accordance with the conditions determined by the unity of our consciousness – the multiplicity of appearances within this unity." (Munich, 1916), p. 47.

[151] In the sense criticized by Hegel in the *Phenomenology of Spirit*, op. cit., pp. 58–66.

[152] *Von der Erkenntnistheorie zur Kritischen Theorie des Gesellschaft: Eine Untersuchung zur Vor- und Entstehungsgeschichte der Kritischen Theorie Max Horkheimers 1920–27* (Opladen, Germany, 1997), pp. 61–76.

[153] For an overview of the vicissitudes of the concept of totality in Horkheimer's work as a whole, see Martin Jay, "Max Horkheimer and the Retreat from Hegelian Marxism," *Marxism and Totality* (Berkeley, 1984), pp. 196–219.

[154] In the foreword, Karl Marx, Friedrich Engels, *Werke* (Berlin: Dietz, 1957). This edition of Marx and Engels' writings is commonly referred to as the "MEW", which is how I will refer to it in subsequent references.

Hegel's teleological philosophy of history and reified social relations in capitalist societies.[155] On the other hand, Horkheimer had by no means applied the concept of totality to history or society at this point. Although Horkheimer was aware of Georg Lukács' *History and Class Consciousness*, one finds no traces of it or its central methodological category of the concrete social totality in Horkheimer's writings at this time.[156] As Michiel Korthals and Ferio Cerruti have shown, Horkheimer did not appropriate Lukács concept of totality at this time or later.[157] The concept of totality on which Horkheimer relied in his dissertation and *Habilitationsschrift* had been drawn from scientific psychology, which Lukács rejected, along with the methodology of the natural sciences in general, as symptoms of the capitalist fragmentation of life.[158] After his break with Cornelius, Horkheimer would use the concept of totality both methodologically and substantively in his social theory, but important differences from Lukács remained, such as his more positive relationship to empirical research, or his more skeptical view of the working class's willingness to become the self-conscious subject-object of history.

In addition to empirical research and the concept of totality, Horkheimer's critique of Kant's separation of practical and theoretical reason also remained prominent in his later thought. Already in the period immediately following the completion of his *Habilitationsschrift*, Horkheimer would focus on this topic in his critical appropriation of Hegel, which took him beyond Cornelius's idiosyncratic version of neo-Kantianism once and for all. Following Hegel, Horkheimer focused on the abstract, ahistorical character of Kant's concept of practical reason and his failure adequately to mediate it with external reality. In a critical portrayal of Kant's ethics during a lecture in the fall of 1925, Horkheimer says:

In this normative insight, in the judgment of the categorical imperative, we understand ourselves as integral parts of an intelligible world, as free beings. But precisely because this certainty is given only insofar as we act, in the form of a maxim for our actions, and does not represent a theoretical insight; precisely because this certainty is not related to

---

[155] See, for example, the discussion in chapter 8 of "Traditional and Critical Theory" in which Horkheimer discusses society as an "active" but "non-conscious subject," pp. 317ff.

[156] Lukács had attended the "Erste Marxistische Arbeitswoche" along with Pollock and Weil, and Weil was financing the publishing house in Berlin, *Malik Verlag*, that published the first edition of Lukács's book in 1923.

[157] Michiel Korthals, "Die kritische Gesellschaftstheorie des frühen Horkheimer. Mißverständnisse über das Verhältnis von Horkheimer, Lukács und dem Positivismus," *Zeitschrift für Soziologie*, Jahrgang 14, Heft 4 (August, 1985), pp. 315–29. Ferio Cerruti, "Georg Lukács und die Kritische Theorie," *Links*, Nr. 195 (June, 1986), pp. 29–31. Korthals points out correctly that Horkheimer rejected a strong positive concept of totality that hubristically claimed to grasp the whole (p. 316). Horkheimer's greater openness to empirical research ensured that if social facts did not correspond to his theory, he would not simply dismiss them à la Fichte or Lukács ("so much the worse for the facts"), but reexamine his theory in light of the unexpected historical and social circumstances. Yet Korthals goes too far when he claims that Horkheimer "never used the concept of totality for his own purposes until approximately 1935" (316). Not only does the concept play an important role in his dissertation and *Habilitationsschrift* – albeit in natural scientific form – it also plays an important role implicitly or explicitly in many of his other writings from the late 1920s and early 1930s.

[158] Jay, *Marxism and Totality*, pp. 88–9.

anything real in the world, but its meaning merely reminds us normatively that we are not mere citizens of the natural world, but also integral parts of an intelligible world [... for these reasons] Kant refers to knowledge of the existence of freedom as merely practical, not theoretical certainty.[159]

In the late 1920s, Horkheimer would draw upon Hegel's efforts to overcome this dichotomy in Kant's philosophy in several different ways. He would insist, for example, that philosophy abandon the attempt to establish a priori – what Horkheimer referred to as "metaphysical" – ethical standards and dedicate itself instead to historically and socially specific problems.[160] Horkheimer also began to develop during this time, once again following Hegel's example, a unified concept of theory based on interdisciplinary research and dedicated to the concrete realization of human rationality and freedom. Yet because Horkheimer rejected the idealist concept of freedom – he insisted that free-dom was inextricably bound to particular historical and social conditions – he viewed theory's primary task as thoroughly researching the historical and social factors shaping the present in order to determine the objective possi-bilities available for the further realization of rationality and freedom.[161] For Horkheimer had concluded in his *Habilitationsschrift* that external reality was by no means inherently rational, but that it was not *eo ipso* hostile to the real-ization of rational human aims either. Only an interdisciplinary theory that had moved beyond the ahistorical realm of Kantian practical reason could pro-vide concrete answers. This critique of the idealist concept of freedom would remain a central concern of Horkheimer's well beyond the late 1920s.

As important as Horkheimer's critique of the separation of practical and theoretical reason may have been for his later thought, it would be a mistake to assume that he carried it out in his academic writings with the conscious inten-tion of laying a foundation for his subsequent work, as some commentators have claimed. This interpretation overlooks the fact that Horkheimer's primary concern in this dissertation and *Habilitationsschrift* was not the possibility of concretely realizing practical aims, the unification of reason and will, or a rationally planned society, but the inability of mechanical theoretical reason to account for objective totalities. The question of practical reason and its rela-tionship to the objective world plays only a very marginal role in his academic writings: Horkheimer does not address it at all in his dissertation, and in his *Habilitationsschrift* he touches on it only briefly at the end, as an afterthought, as it were.[162] Horkheimer's nearly exclusive focus on the *epistemological*

---

[159] GS 10, p. 53.

[160] GS 9, p. 479.

[161] Herein also lies the source Horkheimer's rejection during this time of the similarly dualistic notion of a separation of the human (*Geistes-*) und natural sciences (*Naturwissenschaften*). In "The Beginning of the Bourgeois Philosophy of History," (1930) Horkheimer writes: "Empirical [social] research is oriented epistemologically toward description that is as accurate as possible and, in the final instance, toward laws and tendencies, just like research in the areas of non-hu-man nature." Quoted by Michiel Korthals, op. cit., p. 320. Horkheimer would, however, modify his position on this issue in the mid 1930s. For a discussion of how, see chapter 8, pp. 426ff.

[162] See also Olaf Asbach's thorough discussion of the marginal status of practical reason in Horkheimer's writings at this time, op. cit. pp. 119–27.

implications of the separation of theoretical and practical reason indicates clearly that his dissertation and *Habilitationsschrift* did not transcend the transcendental horizon of academic neo-Kantianism. Horkheimer's argument that Kant's philosophy could not possibly serve as the epistemological foundation for the natural sciences was without question a radical critique of one of the fundamental premises of neo-Kantianism, particularly of Marburg persuasion. Horkheimer's critique of Kant was without doubt a critique of the predominant neo-Kantian interpretation of Kant[163] and an attempt to settle his accounts with a school of thought that had dominated German academic philosophy for nearly four decades. Nonetheless, the critique was articulated in the terms of Hans Cornelius's philosophy, which, despite opening the door for empirical research, remained firmly within the paradigm of consciousness philosophy. Thus the attempt to read Horkheimer's later concerns with practical reason into his academic writings from this time fails to note the qualitative shift in Horkheimer's thought with his abandoning of Cornelius's position in 1925. It is to that shift that we now turn.

---

[163] Horkheimer's quotation of Hermann Cohen in key places in both his dissertation and *Habilitationsschrift* to demonstrate what he was trying to refute, leaves no doubt that his critique was aimed at neo-Kantianism. See GS 2, pp. 41, 68, and 137. In his dissertation and *Habilitationsschrift*, Horkheimer also makes clear on several occasions that he is aware of the narrowness of the neo-Kantians' interpretation of Kant. See GS 2, pp. 58–9 and 81.

3

A Materialist Interpretation of the History of Modern Philosophy

Having examined Horkheimer's childhood, youth, and student years in the first two chapters, we turn now in the following three chapters to the development of his Critical Theory in the period 1925–31. In contrast to studies of Horkheimer's work that begin with his assumption of the directorship of the Institute for Social Research in 1931,[1] I would like to argue in the following three chapters that his Critical Theory took shape in the period following his break with Hans Cornelius in 1925. Although Horkheimer continued to test, refine, and develop his Critical Theory through his collaborative work at the Institute, its basic contours were already in place when he became the director in 1931. In contrast to arguments that maintain that Horkheimer's Critical Theory remained beholden to the tradition of "consciousness philosophy,"[2] a closer examination of his work during this time reveals that it developed precisely as a critique of consciousness philosophy along two interrelated yet distinct axes: one diachronic and historical, the other synchronic and social. In his move beyond the consciousness philosophy of both his philosophical mentor, Hans Cornelius, and almost the entirety of contemporary German academic philosophy, Horkheimer placed consciousness firmly within the larger objective and dynamic structures of history and society – without, however, eliminating the active role of subjective consciousness in reproducing and transforming these structures. This chapter examines how Horkheimer moved beyond consciousness philosophy along the diachronic, historical axis in his lectures and writings on the history of modern philosophy in the late 1920s. The following two chapters address the ways in which Horkheimer moved beyond consciousness philosophy along the synchronic, social axis: through an examination of his theory of contemporary society (Chapter four) and his integration of psychoanalysis into that theory (Chapter five).

HORKHEIMER'S BREAK WITH CONSCIOUSNESS PHILOSOPHY AND HIS TURN TOWARD HISTORY AND SOCIETY

Horkheimer's dissertation and *Habilitationsschrift* marked the culmination of his exploration of the debates on neo-Kantianism and phenomenology

---

[1] See, for example, Helmut Dubiel, *Theory and Politics: Studies in the Development of Critical Theory*, trans. Benjamin Gregg (Cambridge: MIT Press, 1985).

[2] Most notably, Jürgen Habermas. See footnote 7.

that dominated German academic philosophy in the mid-1920s. Although Horkheimer was skeptical of these debates from early on, he delayed explicitly developing his own position until he had completed his *Habilitationsschrift* in 1925, due to the tacit tactical truce he made with Cornelius.[3] However, with the completion of his academic requirements and his attainment of the status of *Privatdozent*,[4] Horkheimer no longer felt obliged to play the role of Cornelius's disciple. He continued to teach with Cornelius until the latter retired in 1929, and relations between the two of them remained cordial until Cornelius's death in 1948. Yet after 1925, Horkheimer was definitely ready to return to the incipient critique of consciousness philosophy he had begun to develop several years before.[5] Evidence of this readiness can be found in a passage from Horkheimer's philosophical diary from September 16, 1925, which is worth quoting at length because it so clearly illustrates this crucial juncture in Horkheimer's intellectual development.

Immanence philosophy, any type of "world" view, which equates the "world" with phenomena of consciousness, with relations or functions of phenomena of consciousness, has to have the courage for solipsism.... Separately and privately our philosopher senses of course that he is not at all a world creator, but rather a simple human being *in* the world. He imputes this idea of his essence to a construction that he calls transcendental consciousness; without this presupposition a logical analogy or any related operations would be inconceivable. One has to have experienced oneself as a human among humans before that conception of one's own individuality can arise, which make it possible to infer the existence of another "similar" individual.... A philosopher of immanence will never understand this. His entire way of thinking prevents him from doing so, in particular the odd fallacy that the world, since I must be able to analyze it down to its empirical components, is nothing more than their formation, a structure made out of elements of consciousness. But, first of all, the word consciousness loses all concrete meaning, when it no longer signifies the perception, the knowledge of a given world by a being living in it, but is instead blown up to be this world itself and then also its creator. Secondly, the fact that rational analysis penetrates or descends to the knowledge we gain from sense impressions, tells us absolutely nothing about the construction of the real world! An analysis of consciousness, or any type of phenomenology will always remain within the limits of the discipline of psychology. It will, at best, teach us something about the composition of a miniscule portion of the world, namely of a

[3] In his meticulous study of Horkheimer's development during this time, Olaf Asbach argues that Horkheimer's loyalty to Cornelius's positions in his dissertation and *Habilitationsschrift* can best be understood in terms of Horkheimer consciously choosing, from the various theories to which he had been exposed at this time, Cornelius's as the most convincing theoretically and the most closely related to his own position. Asbach particularly emphasizes Horkheimer's choice of Cornelius's position over that of Heidegger. See, for example, *Von der Erkenntnistheorie zur Kritischen Theorie des Gesellschaft*, op. cit., p. 136. Yet attempting to explain Cornelius's influence on Horkheimer in this way, from a purely theoretically immanent standpoint (for Asbach's defense of his theoretically immanent approach to Horkheimer's work, see his introduction, pp. 11–30), fails to do justice to the important *personal* influence Cornelius had on Horkheimer. Asbach makes no effort to examine the dynamics of their personal relations or the dynamics of institutional power relations, which go a lot further toward explaining Horkheimer's willingness temporarily to adopt Cornelius's position, than a choice motivated purely by theoretical concerns. See Chapter 2, pp. 65–69.

[4] See Chapter 2, footnote 108.

[5] See Chapter 2, pp. 57–65.

part of our psyche, and cannot, in particular, determine anything about the existence, the meaning or the content of reality. Everywhere where immanence philosophy has philosophical aspirations, wherever it makes even the most minor judgments about existence or non-existence, about our relationship to reality, they are always casuistic. If it does not have the courage to declare reality, the world – with the exception of itself – a phenomenon of consciousness, then the courage for solipsism![6]

Horkheimer's critical remarks about the reduction of the world to the mere phenomena of consciousness, to a "construct made out of elements of consciousness," represent an unambiguous rejection of the cornerstone of Cornelius's transcendental phenomenology, namely the claim that philosophy must take the immediate experiences of consciousness as its foundation. Yet the target of Horkheimer's critique of "immanence philosophy" extended far beyond Cornelius's philosophy. His insistence here that the philosopher of immanence is constitutionally incapable of recognizing that consciousness is not transcendental, but is instead always consciousness of concrete individuals *in* the world, and his argument that immanence philosophy, when thought through to the end, inevitably leads to solipsism, point in the direction of a radical *detranscendentalization*[7] of the knowing subject that would lead Horkheimer beyond the entire tradition of consciousness philosophy.

On May 2, 1925 – a few months before he penned this journal entry – Horkheimer officially entered the ranks of Frankfurt University's *Privatdozenten* with a talk on Kant and Hegel, in which he introduced for the first time in public the rudiments of his critique of consciousness philosophy and his efforts to move beyond it.[8] Horkheimer's reasons for choosing the topic "Kant and Hegel" are not hard to discern; the movement of German idealist philosophy from Kant to Hegel – which would also be the subject of the first lecture course Horkheimer would deliver that fall[9] – represented the most important

---

[6] GS 11, pp. 241–2.

[7] In *Wahrheit und Rechtfertigung* (Frankfurt, 1999), Jürgen Habermas returns to the problem of the detranscendentalization of the claims of consciousness philosophy (see, in particular, "Wege der Detranzendentalisierung: Von Kant zu Hegel und Zurück," pp. 186–229). This problem has occupied Habermas for many years, particularly insofar as he places his own discourse ethics within the Kantian tradition. Habermas has attempted on several different occasions to refute the claim that Hegel's critique of Kant can be applied to discourse ethics. One can debate whether or not Habermas is completely successful in this undertaking: See, for example, Gordon Finlayson, "Does Hegel's Critique of Kant's Moral Theory Apply to Discourse Ethics?" in *Habermas: A Critical Reader*, ed. Peter Dews (Oxford and Malden, MA, 1999), pp. 29–52. Habermas argues that discourse ethics represents a detranscendentalization of Kant's project. At the same time, he has claimed that Horkheimer's version of critical theory remained trapped in the paradigm of consciousness philosophy. See, for example, Jürgen Habermas, *Theory of Communicative Action*, vol. 1, trans. Thomas McCarthy (Boston, 1984), p. 386. However, the development of Horkheimer's version of critical theory in the late 1920s occurs, as I will show in what follows, was a self-conscious break with consciousness philosophy. One of the points I would like to make in what follows is that Habermas's pragmatic-linguistic turn is not the only way beyond the paradigm of consciousness philosophy. Horkheimer had clearly recognized this problem in the 1920s and offered an alternative.

[8] "Kant und Hegel," GS 11, pp. 102–18.

[9] These lectures, which were delivered during the winter semester 1925–6, have been published as "Vorlesung über die Geschichte der deutschen idealistischen Philosophie von Kant bis Hegel," GS 10, pp. 12–165. We will examine them more closely later in this chapter.

attempt so far to burst the boundaries of consciousness philosophy from within. Horkheimer realized that learning from the successes and failures of this attempt – from Hegel's critique of Kant and Fichte, in particular – was crucial for any effort to move beyond the forms of consciousness philosophy that had resurfaced more recently. Already during his immersion in the debates surrounding neo-Kantianism and phenomenology in the early 1920s, Horkheimer had begun studying Hegel's philosophy seriously;[10] this intensive critical reception of Hegel would remain one of the defining characteristics of his thought throughout the late 1920s and into the early 1930s.

In his talk, Horkheimer first briefly outlines the Copernican turn carried out by Kant, which placed philosophy firmly on the foundation of transcendental subjectivity. He stresses that this turn resulted in a strict limitation of philosophy to the sphere of subjective consciousness:

The application of our mechanism of understanding is always related solely to elements of our consciousness; knowledge *is exhausted* in its classification within the conceptual forms of the cognizing subject.... We can in principle never know anything about the origins of the elements of consciousness.[11]

Horkheimer goes on to show how Hegel rejected Kant's purist transcendentalism and insisted that subjective consciousness can only be understood in relation to the dynamic historical context out of which it has emerged. For Hegel, "The analyzing, criticizing consciousness is itself as such nothing absolutely final, but has instead its own logical and historical determinants."[12] In other words, subjective consciousness cannot be understood in isolation from the objective factors that precondition it:

Hegel's philosophy attempts to demonstrate how the intellectual factors, the forms of understanding and intuition [*Verstandes- und Anschauungsformen*], as well as all determinations and relations in general, can only be as they are and can only be known as they are, because *this* content, *this* real world has developed in nature and history in this and not in any other way. Kant's abstract forms of understanding are the product of an analysis of the concrete objective world.... we can make ourselves conscious of them *as* abstractions and as *these* abstractions only by genuinely revealing how they are necessarily related to the original totality, from which the abstraction was carried out.[13]

Horkheimer is clearly sympathetic to Hegel's critique of Kant, insofar as Hegel firmly placed the transcendental subject back into an objective context, but he also criticizes Hegel for not carrying out the process of detranscendentalization to its end. He shows how Hegel was able to overcome the limitations to knowledge set by Kant only by invoking a concept of absolute knowledge, which ultimately led to a rehabilitation of metaphysics. Horkheimer argues that this promise of a positive metaphysics explains the Hegel renaissance in Germany in the 1920s. In contrast to the early nineteenth century, when

---

[10] Horkheimer's familiarity with Hegel is demonstrated in a detailed discussion of Hegel's critique of Kant in notes from a seminar Horkheimer taught in the winter semester of 1923–24 [MHA VII 6.2].

[11] GS 11, p. 110 (emphasis his own).

[12] Ibid., p. 116.

[13] Ibid., p. 115.

Hegel's philosophy represented a mediated expression of the vital efforts of the German bourgeoisie to unify and emancipate itself, the contemporary rediscovery of Hegel's metaphysics was, according to Horkheimer, part of a widespread, frantic search for foundations, which was ultimately the product of the social contradictions of contemporary capitalism, and that could not be satisfied by consciousness philosophy.[14]

According to Horkheimer, Hegel had started down the correct path, but his attempt to overcome Kantian transcendentalism remained trapped within the paradigm of consciousness philosophy in significant ways: most significantly, in his retention of an all-embracing concept of philosophy that culminated in the metaphysical notion of absolute knowledge. Horkheimer's own attempts to move beyond consciousness philosophy at this time would soon lead him beyond the traditional disciplinary boundaries of philosophy altogether. In a thinly veiled allusion to Marx in his talk on Kant and Hegel, Horkheimer noted, in reference to the development of German Idealism, that "The most consequential continuation of this philosophical process no longer belongs to the history of philosophy."[15] Horkheimer also noted, in what could be seen as an anticipation of the interdisciplinary research methods he would develop later, that even German Idealism cannot be understood purely from an immanent philosophical standpoint:

It is not possible to understand the content of philosophical ideas that have emerged historically without painstakingly immersing oneself in the concrete intellectual climate as a whole, in which these ideas originated.... The resources that would provide the basis for this type of approach to German Idealism should be sought at least as much from those working in the disciplines of history, philology and sociology, as those in philosophy.[16]

Methodologically, Horkheimer had thus in 1925 already taken the first decisive steps beyond not only consciousness philosophy, but the traditional disciplinary boundaries of philosophy in general. These steps would, of course, eventually lead him to the program of interdisciplinary materialism that he would introduce in 1931 in his inaugural address as the director of the Institute for Social Research; but at this point, his new methodology was not much more than a set of abstract ideas.

In his lectures and writings in the following years, however, Horkheimer would make a sustained attempt to flesh out his new methodology, to develop it into a comprehensive social theory. True to his conviction that philosophy can only be understood as a moment in the larger movement of history and society, Horkheimer developed a nuanced materialist interpretation of the history of modern philosophy, which viewed it as the mediated expression of the rise and subsequent transformation of bourgeois society. This new interpretation of modern philosophy – as a product of and an active force in the development of bourgeois society – forms one pillar of Horkheimer's work during this time. It is articulated in his lectures on the history of philosophy

[14] Ibid., p. 114.
[15] Ibid., p. 103.
[16] Ibid., p. 105.

and several published and unpublished essays, including "Beginnings of the Bourgeois Philosophy of History."[17] Yet Horkheimer was not content to work out his new method in a purely historical manner. He also devoted himself during this time to a careful analysis of the contemporary state of bourgeois society in a series of mainly unpublished writings, including the collection of aphorisms bearing the title *Dämmerung*, which would appear only later – in 1934 – under the pseudonym of Heinrich Regius. In his lectures and published writings from this time, Horkheimer develops his critical theory of society at an exoteric level, within the institutional boundaries of Frankfurt University. *Dämmerung*, on the other hand, represents a continuation of the private, anti-systematic, and more authentic form of expression that had characterized his early novellas and diary entries.[18] The analysis of contemporary society that one finds in these writings forms the second pillar of his thought during this period. We will return to these writings in Chapter 4 after our examination here of Horkheimer's interpretation of modern philosophy.

HORKHEIMER'S MATERIALIST INTERPRETATION OF THE HISTORY OF MODERN PHILOSOPHY

In his lectures and essays between 1925 and 1930, Horkheimer developed an original interpretation of the history of modern philosophy – from the Renaissance all the way through to the present – as the mediated expression of the history of bourgeois society. This interpretation would provide a crucial reference point for his work well into the 1930s and beyond.[19] Although Horkheimer received important impulses from other theorists such as Hegel, whose writings he was studying intensely at the time, and Marx, whose *German Ideology* was available to Pollock and his colleagues at the Institute as early as 1925, Horkheimer's materialist interpretation of modern philosophy was not derivative in any significant way. He developed it through a painstaking analysis of a very broad range of primary and secondary texts, rather than an overreliance on any particular theoretical model. The outlines of his new materialist interpretation of the history of philosophy emerge clearly in the overarching structure within which his lectures and essays from this time are embedded, but his discussions of individual philosophers, works, and problems often differ little from a traditional history of ideas approach. However, Horkheimer's theoretical sophistication and his thorough and nuanced understanding of the history of modern philosophy ruled out the possibility of any form of simplistic materialist or sociological

---

[17] Max Horkheimer, *Between Philosophy and Social Science: Selected Early Writings*, trans. G.F. Hunter, M.S. Kramer and J. Torpey (Cambridge, MA and London, 1993), pp. 313–88.

[18] On this point, see also Gunzelin Schmid Noerr, "Nachwort des Herausgebers," GS 2, p. 466.

[19] As Peter Stirk puts it, "By 1930 he [Horkheimer] had developed a history of bourgeois society, which was to structure the rest of his life's work" op. cit. p. 7. Stirk is correct to emphasize the central importance of the history of bourgeois society, although he does not pay close enough attention to the way in which Horkheimer's understanding of the concept emerged in the period prior to 1930. He provides only a cursory examination of Horkheimer's lectures on the history of early modern philosophy. See the first chapter of his study, "The History of Bourgeois Society," op. cit., pp. 14–36.

reductionism from the beginning. In short, Horkheimer combines, on the one hand, systematic insights into the relations of modern philosophy to the historical development of bourgeois society with, on the other hand, analyses of individual philosophers, works, and problems at least as meticulous as any one would find in more traditional histories of philosophy. Horkheimer developed his new interpretation of the history of modern philosophy in a series of lectures and essays between 1925 and 1930. The most important of these, and the ones on which the following sketch of Horkheimer's interpretation will be based, are the following: "The History of German Idealist Philosophy from Kant to Hegel,"[20] a one-hour lecture course Horkheimer held during the winter semester of 1925–6; "Introduction to Contemporary Philosophy,"[21] a one-hour lecture course he held during the summer semester of 1926; "Introduction to Modern Philosophy,"[22] a three-hour lecture course he held during the summer semester of 1927; "The Emancipation of Philosophy from the Natural Sciences,"[23] an essay Horkheimer prepared in 1928, but never published, that was based on but diverged in significant respects from his lectures on contemporary philosophy; and finally, "Beginnings of the Bourgeois Philosophy of History,"[24] a lengthy essay Horkheimer published in 1930 that was based on his lectures on modern philosophy, as well as a second series of lectures on the philosophy of history he held during the summer semester of 1928. Taken together, these lectures and essays provide a comprehensive view of the materialist interpretation of the history of modern philosophy that Horkheimer worked out during this time. In order to understand the further course of Horkheimer's intellectual development, it is necessary to examine his interpretation of modern philosophy in some detail. In what follows, we will be particularly attentive to the model of the development of bourgeois society that emerges in Horkheimer's work at this time, for it is only within this underlying context that Horkheimer's interpretations of individual philosophers, works, and problems become clear.[25]

[20] "Vorlesung über die Geschichte der deutschen idealistischen Philosophie von Kant bis Hegel," GS 10, pp. 12–165.

[21] "Einführung in die Philosophie der Gegenwart," GS 10, pp. 170–333. These lectures treat the history of European philosophy (with a concentration on Germany) from approximately 1850 to the present. For a full list of Horkheimer's lectures during the late 1920s and early 1930s, see GS 19, pp. 218–20.

[22] "Einführung in die Geschichte der neueren Philosophie," GS 9, pp. 13–480. These lectures treat the history of European philosophy from the Renaissance through the Enlightenment, up to, but not including, Kant.

[23] "Zur Emanzipation der Philosophie von der Wissenschaft," GS 10, pp. 335–419. This essay treats the empiriocriticism of Ernst Mach, the neo-Kantianism of Hermann Cohen, the phenomenology of Edmund Husserl and Max Scheler, and the *Lebensphilosophie* of Henri Bergson as progressive stages in a narrative of the "emancipation of philosophy from science" that occurred the late nineteenth and early twentieth centuries.

[24] *Between Philosophy and Social Science: Selected Early Writings*, op. cit., pp. 313–88. The essay explores the "history of the philosophy history" (as the essay was originally subtitled) through an examination of Machiavelli, Hobbes, Thomas More, and Giambattista Vico.

[25] In several places in his lectures, Horkheimer makes this point explicitly, telling his students that the history of philosophy cannot be understood in isolation from the social history of the period, and that he views as one of the most important goals of his own lectures to encourage his students to study this social history in greater depth. See GS 9, p. 20.

At the most abstract level, Horkheimer's understanding of the history of bourgeois society is relatively simple: It consists in the bourgeoisie's struggle to emancipate itself from the reins of feudalism and absolutism, and its eventual victory and subsequent transformation. Yet this most cursory summation of the historical dynamic underlying Horkheimer's interpretation attains shape and color only when one considers its manifestations in the intellectual realm. At the level of the history of modern philosophy, the structure of Horkheimer's narrative is much more complex. He divides the early modern period roughly into three main stages: a defiant and youthful first stage, in which the first attempts were made to attack the intellectual hegemony of the church and to establish new, immanent sources of intellectual authority; a more hesitant second stage, in which the desire to find a stable compromise between the new and old sources of authority was expressed in the metaphysical systems of the seventeenth century; and finally, a revolutionary phase, in which the bourgeoisie reappropriated the rebellious ideas of its youth to liquidate the metaphysical remnants of the *ancien regime*, and to establish its own supremacy in the name of lofty universalist ideals. Horkheimer divides the late modern period into two main phases: a confident first phase, in which the bourgeoisie's illusion of still representing the interests of humanity finds intellectual expression in the dominance of affirmative positivist ideas; and a desperate, often cynical second phase, in which new forms of metaphysics as well as irrational and authoritarian ideologies were called upon to compensate the failed progressive promise of positivism, and to justify the bourgeoisie's particularist domination in the face of the new challenge of the workers' movement. This schematic and linear account of Horkheimer's understanding of the history of bourgeois society and the concomitant course of modern philosophy by no means does justice to the complexity of his presentation, not least of which because it fails to address his repeated emphasis on the uneven development of bourgeois society in different national contexts. In order to illustrate this point, and to gain a more concrete understanding of Horkheimer's interpretation of the history of bourgeois society and modern philosophy, let us turn now to a more detailed examination of his lectures and writings.

The Early Modern Period

The Robust Beginnings of Bourgeois Philosophy in Italy and England

At the dawn of what Horkheimer would later refer to as the "bourgeois epoch," Machiavelli postulated famously that man no longer needed to suffer the slings and arrows of *fortuna* in a completely passive way: that by cultivating his *virtu*, he could, if not fully, at least partially take his fate into his own hands.[26] One cannot, of course, overlook the ideological dimensions of the humanist concept of "man,"[27] particularly because Machiavelli's advice was directed only to the most powerful members of nascent bourgeois society, and

---

[26] *The Prince*, trans. R.M. Adams (New York, 1977), p. 70.

[27] See, for example, Joan Kelly, "Did Women Have a Renaissance?" in *Women, History and Theory* (Chicago: University of Chicago Press, 1984), pp. 19–50.

because the self-determination promised by *virtu* would prove elusive even for them – as the imminent defeat of the Italian city-states at the hands of the new Spanish and French monarchies would demonstrate. Nonetheless, Horkheimer was fascinated by the Renaissance's newfound belief in the possibility of at least partially controlling the course of history, of not simply being a plaything of higher powers. Horkheimer viewed the development of early modern science and politics primarily in terms of the attempt to realize this belief in the possibility of self-determination by developing the tools necessary to control nature and other humans. For example, he writes:

In its origins, bourgeois science is inextricably linked to the development of technology and industry, and cannot be understood apart from bourgeois society's domination of nature. But society is not just based on the domination of nature in the narrower sense, nor merely on the invention of new methods of production … it is equally based on the domination of human beings by other human beings. The aggregate of the means designed for this end and of the measures which serve to maintain this domination, goes under the name of politics.[28]

Horkheimer illustrates this interpretation of early modern science and politics, as the domination of nature and other humans, by examining those who contributed most to developing these new disciplines. We will limit ourselves here to a brief look at his discussion of Machiavelli and Hobbes in the sphere of politics, and to the Italian natural philosophers and Francis Bacon in the sphere of natural science.

Machiavelli plays a key role at the beginning of Horkheimer's presentation of the history of modern philosophy, because he was the first to formulate a coherent theory of the modern centralized state, which would replace the church as the highest authority during the subsequent early stages of the development of bourgeois society. Horkheimer writes:

The basic intention of all of Machiavelli's writings lies in the propagation of the view that a stabile, undisturbed, completely centralized government, which provides continuity in all public relations and in the administration of law in particular, is the first demand and precondition of cultural life.[29]

Horkheimer argues that the importance of the state for Machiavelli is not based on speculation about the ideal form of government, but rather on the real need to protect and further the incipient capitalist form of production: "It is not the form of government that is of primary interest for him … but rather external defense and the maintenance of domestic order, both in order to allow the free development of production and commerce."[30] Horkheimer also shows how Machiavelli has a thoroughly disillusioned, instrumental view of religion, subordinating it as he does, along with all other aspects of life, to the central authority of the state. The prince should decide which form of religion to support based solely on considerations of its efficacy for maintaining state power. Finally, Horkheimer also points out that Machiavelli's belief in the possibility

[28] "Beginnings of the Bourgeois Philosophy of History," p. 316 (translation amended).
[29] GS 9, p. 33.
[30] Ibid., p. 36.

of a science of statecraft rests on an assumption that human psychology is historically constant. Although Machiavelli does not pursue the consequences of this assumption in any detail, his arguments anticipate a long bourgeois theoretical tradition that engages in the systematic analysis of human interests and drives in order to develop better methods of control.[31]

Among the Italian natural philosophers, dramatic new methods of prediction and control were being developed at this time as well. Horkheimer points to Giordano Bruno's heretical claim – for which he was burned at the stake by the Inquisition in 1600 – that the universe is infinite and governed everywhere by the same natural laws, as a particularly important step in this direction. Horkheimer writes:

> The great astronomers just mentioned [Copernicus and Kepler, J.A.] still believed that the area in which the stars were located was a stabile surrounding that defined the limits of our solar system. But Giordano Bruno went beyond this view by declaring not only that space is infinite, but also that it is has the same composition in all places, that, in other words, the same laws of nature must be valid everywhere.[32]

According to Horkheimer, Bruno's pantheistic belief in the strict immanence and lawful harmony of the universe anticipates another important bourgeois tradition that extends through the metaphysical systems of the seventeenth century – in Spinoza's concept of substance or Leibniz's concept of *harmonie préétablie* – into the eighteenth-century English political economists' belief in the harmonious functioning of the laws governing bourgeois society. Of Bruno's contemporaries, however, it was Galileo who made the most decisive practical and theoretical contributions to the development of the concept of law in the natural sciences. With his pathbreaking discoveries in astronomy and mechanics, Galileo was the first to combine successfully the new experimental method with mathematics.[33] Horkheimer identifies Galileo as the first to state explicitly the overarching goal of all modern natural science, namely "The establishment of exactly formulated laws that possess general validity, that is, laws that can be applied at any time in the future."[34] Horkheimer also emphasizes the crucial importance of Galileo's arguments regarding the criteria and validity of truth claims in the natural sciences. Galileo insisted that the validity of scientific arguments be judged based on their ability to explain natural phenomena in the simplest and most elegant manner, not on their compatibility with tradition of any sort. Furthermore, Galileo insisted – to the great consternation of the Jesuits and the church – that arguments validated in this manner were not simply feasible hypotheses, but could legitimately claim the status of genuine knowledge.[35] This antitraditional moment in early modern natural science was articulated in an even more radical way in the work of Francis Bacon, who plays a decisive role indeed in Horkheimer's understanding of the history of modern philosophy. Like the Italian natural philosophers,

---

[31] "Beginnings of the Bourgeois Philosophy of History," p. 327–8.
[32] GS 9, p. 49.
[33] Ibid., p. 61.
[34] Ibid., p. 63.
[35] Ibid., p. 65.

Bacon insisted that scientific knowledge be based strictly on the experience gained through empirical research and experimentation, not on the tradition of the church or even the ancients. However, Bacon went beyond the pantheism of the Italians in his introduction of a new, pragmatic standard of validity for scientific knowledge, and in his unabashed insistence that the purpose of science is not merely to understand objectively but rather actively to control nature.[36] Horkheimer also singles out Bacon's defense of the inherently historical nature of knowledge, that "the truth is the daughter of time, not authority,"[37] as an additional major contribution to the development of early modern scientific thought. Taken together, Bacon's contributions – establishing scientific method firmly upon experience, judging its validity from the standpoint of practical results and potential applicability, and denying it any claim to transhistorical truth – establish him as the founding father of empiricism, one of the two major traditions whose transformations Horkheimer traces throughout the history of modern philosophy.[38] However, the great historical significance of empiricism in Horkheimer's eyes, and its link to the history of bourgeois society, lies in its thoroughly secular conception of knowledge as temporally bound and open-ended. As Horkheimer puts it, for the first time in Bacon's thought

the ground is torn out from underneath all scholastic discussions and metaphysical speculations about a transcendent realm and eternity. Knowledge is secularized, integrated into the metabolic interaction [*Stoffwechsel*] of human society with the natural world, and stripped of its absolute character.[39]

Finally, Horkheimer emphasizes that not only knowledge, but perception as well is drawn into the material reproduction of society in Bacon's thought. Horkheimer views Bacon's critique of naïve sense certainty and his reflections on the various factors that distort perception and hinder the attainment of useful knowledge – his theory of the "idols" – as the first step in the development of a theory of ideology. The next steps in this process – which, in the early modern period, run through the epistemological reflections of Spinoza, Leibniz, and Locke to the Enlightenment's critique of metaphysics and religion – figure prominently in the further course of Horkheimer's narrative.

With its defeat of the Spanish Armada in 1588, England began to move to the forefront in the struggle for European hegemony, a struggle that would be largely determined by the strength of the nation's bourgeoisie. This was also the year of the birth of Thomas Hobbes, who witnessed, gave expression to, and sought to influence the fitful, but ultimately triumphant development of bourgeois society in England in the seventeenth century. Whereas Bacon's thought still expressed the "youth" of bourgeois society in England, Hobbes's philosophy expressed the maturity and strength of the English bourgeoisie, which it amply demonstrated in the course of the seventeenth century by establishing its supremacy not only over its main European rival, the Dutch, but also over the tenacious

---

[36] Ibid, p. 80–1.
[37] *The Works of Francis Bacon*, vol. IV (London, 1858), p. 82. Quoted by Horkheimer, GS 9, p. 82.
[38] The other major tradition is, of course, rationalism.
[39] GS 9, p. 81.

remnants of feudalism at home. Hobbes built on the secular, empirical scientific foundations Bacon had established, although he was much more interested in the domination of humans than nature.[40] Horkheimer emphasizes that Hobbes's thoroughly mechanical view of politics, his conception of the state as an aggregate of isolated individuals bound together by their fear for their lives and property, was the first systematic attempt to apply the new conceptions of natural law to the study of human society.[41] On the one hand, Hobbes's basic assumptions are pragmatic and secular, like Bacon's. With his introduction of a limited notion of popular sovereignty and contract theory, he undermines divine rights, although like Machiavelli, he subordinates all aspects of life to the authority of a strong state, whose form is less important than its duty to protect foreign and domestic commerce.[42] On the other hand, Hobbes's recourse to natural law is also an attempt to establish an even firmer foundation for knowledge than Bacon's notion of experience. Horkheimer writes:

The objective reason … why Hobbes … does not base his demands directly on real needs, but deduces them instead from a contract theory, i.e. more or less from pure reason, or in any case with logical stringency from eternal laws … lies in the general situation, in which reason is counterposed as authority, as the new anti-traditional God, to the old tradition.[43]

In this respect, Hobbes's theory anticipates the rationalist metaphysics of his colleagues on the Continent. However, Horkheimer insists that the attempt to found transhistorical foundations for theoretical claims is always deceptive: "In truth, Hobbes' demands result from particular deficiencies, restrictions and needs in the real world."[44] So before turning to the second stage of Horkheimer's history of early modern philosophy – rationalist metaphysics – let us take a quick look at his treatment of the desperate reactions of the peasants and workers, for whom the development of bourgeois society often meant tremendous sacrifices without any real compensation.

Horkheimer describes the development of bourgeois society in early modern Europe as a battle on two fronts. Although the struggle against the church, aristocracy, and absolute monarchy comes first, he by no means overlooks the bourgeoisie's repression of peasants and workers that accompanied its rise to power from the very beginning. For Machiavelli and the other philosophers who expressed the robust confidence of nascent bourgeois society, brutal means were completely justified to prepare the way for a freer, more rational future, whereas those who became the objects of this instrumental logic expressed their suffering and their protest in the form of utopian ideas and actions. Horkheimer writes:

The philosophy of Hobbes, like that of Spinoza and the Enlightenment, expresses unabashed trust in the way in which bourgeois society is organized. This society and its

---

[40] As Horkheimer points out, "the science of politics is the highest and most fundamental science" for Hobbes. Ibid., p. 121.

[41] "Beginnings of the Bourgeois Philosophy of History," p. 350.

[42] GS 9, p. 121.

[43] Ibid., p. 131.

[44] Ibid.

development is the purpose of history, its fundamental laws are eternal laws of nature, whose observation is not merely the supreme moral doctrine, but also the guarantee of worldly happiness. The great utopias of the Renaissance, on the other hand, are the expression of the desperate classes, who had to bear the hardships that accompanied the transition from one economic form to another.[45]

In this context, Horkheimer discusses, among others things, Thomas More's *Utopia* and Thomas Münzer's and the radical Anabaptists' failed efforts to realize their utopian ideals concretely. He walks a very fine line between expressing understanding for the suffering of the victims of bourgeois primitive accumulation, while at the same time criticizing the means they employed to remedy that suffering. Whereas the utopians' analysis of the social conditions is more advanced than that of the bourgeois philosophers insofar as they recognized property relations as the root of injustice in bourgeois society,[46] they failed to see that the conditions were not yet ripe for establishing a new society based on transformed property relations. As Horkheimer puts it:

The economic prerequisites for a rational organization of society based on collective property ownership were by no means present during their time … collective ownership of property, egalitarian conditions of life, as demanded by the utopians, would have meant the death of civilization.[47]

Horkheimer clearly demonstrates his characteristic sober realism when he argues in this context that the cold calculations of Machiavelli and Hobbes were objectively more progressive than the utopians' fantasies of a just society, because the former were firmly grounded in the objective tendencies of the time, whereas the latter were either attempts to restore outdated conditions or to impose abstract models upon reality through persuasion or force.[48] Nonetheless, Horkheimer explicitly rejects any attempts to justify or give meaning to suffering or oppression in the name of lofty historical goals. He insists that the duty of the theorist is not to bestow history with metaphysical meaning, but to understand the real reasons why it has been a "slaughter bench" until now.[49]

The Tentative Consolidation of Bourgeois Philosophy on the Continent: Rationalism and Rationalist Metaphysics

In his account of the history of modern philosophy, Horkheimer pays particularly close attention to the development of the empiricist and rationalist traditions. Along with his outline of the history of bourgeois society, his examination of the origins and transformation of these two central philosophical traditions serve as the guiding thread throughout his narrative. As we have seen, Horkheimer considered Francis Bacon the founder of the modern empiricist tradition because of his historical, secularized, pragmatic, and

---

[45] "Beginning of the Bourgeois Philosophy of History," p. 363 (translation amended).
[46] Ibid., p. 370.
[47] Ibid, p. 369.
[48] Ibid, pp. 367, 370, and 367.
[49] Ibid., p. 373.

experience-based concept of knowledge. In the early modern period, he traces the further development of this tradition through the work of Hobbes and Locke into Hume and the French Enlightenment. Horkheimer views René Descartes as the founder of the modern rationalist tradition, even though his ahistorical, nonpragmatic, and nonexperiential concept of knowledge did not, in his eyes, represent nearly as abrupt a break with medieval philosophy as did empiricism. He follows the further course of early modern rationalism in the metaphysical systems of Spinoza, Leibniz, and Christian Wolff into Kant and German Idealism. Yet what exactly characterizes rationalism, according to Horkheimer, and why does he see Descartes as its modern founder?

The most important dividing line between rationalism and empiricism consists in their differing responses to the question of whether reason or the senses are the source of valid knowledge. Descartes' response leaves no doubt about his position on this matter. As Horkheimer puts it:

In Descartes' philosophy this question is decided completely in favor of reason. For him reason is identical with the natural light, on which we can depend due to the goodness and truthfulness of God.... Empirical knowledge, that part of the *cogitationes*, to which we normally refer as our sensual experiences and conditions ... is completely shoved aside in the development of [Descartes'] system as merely confused and unclear knowledge.[50]

Horkheimer shows how this privileging of reason over the senses finds further expression in Descartes' philosophy in his deductive method and his doctrine of innate ideas. Yet even more important for Horkheimer's interpretation of Descartes is the fact that he attempted to separate philosophy from practical experience and experimentation in order to establish an unshakeable foundation for knowledge. Whereas Bacon was interested primarily in the concrete implications of knowledge, Descartes was concerned, as Horkheimer writes,

about secure knowledge as such, about the final, unconditional, incontrovertible, absolute truth – solely for the sake of itself.... Under no conditions whatsoever can practice be a secure criteria of truth. For ... if changeable practice decides – be it as scientific experiment, or as accordance with natural law or whatever else – then this eternal and unassailable certainty, which is his primary concern, will never be possible ... there is no eternal truth – and there is no longer any reason at all to pursue science.[51]

Horkheimer stresses that this attempt to establish unshakeable foundations, based solely on reason, represented a continuation of a long scholastic tradition, and that Descartes – who was a pious Catholic his entire life – was driven primarily by his desire to reconcile the new mechanical worldview with the church. For these reasons, the widespread understanding of Descartes as the founding father of modern philosophy must be reconsidered according to Horkheimer.[52] Nonetheless, Horkheimer also emphasizes that

---

[50] GS 9, p. 150–1.

[51] Ibid, p. 139.

[52] Horkheimer shows that Descartes was not considered the founder of modern philosophy by the *lumières* either: "If you run across the name of René Descartes in the writings of the French Enlightenment ... he by no means appears as the father of modern philosophy, but instead as a

Descartes was indeed the founder of the modern tradition of consciousness philosophy, and that this is why his work played such an important role in the more recent, epistemologically oriented discussions of neo-Kantianism and phenomenology.[53] Yet for Horkheimer, the attempt, initiated by Descartes, to locate the foundations of philosophy within consciousness did not represent a breakthrough, but rather an impoverishment of philosophy – one whose consequences Horkheimer was still trying to overcome in the 1920s.

The next major philosopher Horkheimer discusses is Spinoza, whose work he views as the first full-fledged articulation of metaphysics in the modern period. As with Descartes' rationalism, Horkheimer stresses the formal continuities between Spinoza's rationalist metaphysics and medieval scholasticism. But modern metaphysics goes beyond methodological rationalism – which had searched primarily for unshakeable founding principles – in its attempt to create, solely on the basis of reason, a systematic, all-inclusive, and completely closed worldview. As Horkheimer puts it:

What the metaphysics of the Middle Ages, scholasticism, achieved based on revelation – by attempting to explicate the worldview of the church using the means of rational thought – Spinoza wanted to develop without any foundation whatsoever ... solely with reason. The difference between modern epistemology ... and modern metaphysics consists solely in the fact that the latter is certain that it is possible to locate the content of the sciences within a larger system of absolute knowledge, while the former rests content with demonstrating or proving that the sciences in their existing form are valid knowledge.[54]

However, Horkheimer does not treat rationalism and metaphysics purely from the standpoint of the history of ideas. He stresses that the need for certainty and stability that characterizes rationalism, and which reached its apotheosis in the metaphysical systems of the seventeenth century, has clearly discernible historical as well as social-psychological roots in the development of bourgeois society. He writes:

Spinoza's philosophy, like all modern epistemology and metaphysics, was born of the situation of the bourgeois individual cast back upon himself, who cannot and does not want to believe in anything except that which must appear certain to him through natural means.... Modern metaphysics springs from the need to restore the lost paradise of faith in an eternal realm ... through the means of science, through secure methods that are beyond all doubt.... The collapse of medieval metaphysics brought with it as a necessary consequence – in precise proportion to the extent of science's liberation from traditional authority – the search for a new metaphysics, and for a new standpoint that could claim absolute validity.[55]

    philosopher who achieved certain important things in the development of modern mechanics, which, of course, are not seen as being superior to the accomplishments of Galileo or Hobbes. Voltaire was of the opinion that it was Descartes' great misfortune to have failed to seek the counsel of Galileo during his travels in Italy, but conferred instead with the Jesuit Scheiner, the plagiarizer and enemy of Galileo, who brought Galileo before the Inquisition and thereby brought shame upon all of Italy." Ibid., p. 133.

53 Ibid., pp. 154–8.
54 Ibid., pp. 196–7.
55 Ibid., pp. 196, 197, and 199, respectively.

Horkheimer pays particularly close attention to the socio-historical conditions that determined the rise of modern metaphysics because – as we shall see shortly – he was deeply concerned about a widespread rehabilitation of metaphysics in his own day. However, Horkheimer was always extremely careful to distinguish the determinants and implications of seemingly similar philosophical tendencies in different historical periods. Thus, despite the elements of continuity with the Middle Ages that exist in Spinoza's philosophy, Horkheimer interprets it primarily as an expression of the ascending bourgeoisie. This interpretation is apparent not only in his discussion of Spinoza's political philosophy, in which he demonstrates his continuity with Bacon and Hobbes on the question of a strong, secularized central state, his defense of tolerance and bourgeois economic interests, and his insistence that the fourth estate be ruled with an iron hand. It is also apparent in his discussion of Spinoza's theory of knowledge, which demonstrates the bourgeoisie's strong desire to establish an unshakeable intellectual foundation of its own, independent of the authority of the church. Spinoza expressed this desire powerfully with his defense of a static mathematical-mechanical, deterministic monism that postulates clear and distinct perception of the basic, logical axioms that rule the universe as its highest goal, and counsels the subordination of all other human impulses to this lofty drive for pure knowledge.

Leibniz is the second important representative of the rationalist metaphysics of the seventeenth century. Like Spinoza, Leibniz was a natural scientist and mathematician who engaged in metaphysics in an attempt to create an all-encompassing, systematic worldview. As Horkheimer says:

> The essential reason that Leibniz is still treated, and rightfully so, as an outstanding figure in the history of philosophy is that all the decisive scientific problems of the time are unified in his thought, that his thought reflects all of these difficulties and the efforts to solve them, that, in other words, he was not a "pure" metaphysician.[56]

Metaphysics was, in other words, for both Leibniz and Spinoza, not only a search for stable foundations, but also a means of addressing the most important theoretical problems of the day in a wide variety of fields. In contrast to the later development of what Horkheimer calls here "pure" metaphysics – whose sole remaining function after the increased differentiation of knowledge in the eighteenth and nineteenth century was to satisfy diffuse needs for stability and meaning – the metaphysics of the seventeenth century was the most advanced expression of knowledge at this time, at least in continental Europe, where the development of bourgeois society lagged behind that in England. Horkheimer argues that Leibniz's philosophy, more so than Spinoza's, built on and developed many of the basic presuppositions of Descartes' rationalism. Whereas Spinoza's monism did not preclude pantheist, even materialist interpretations, Leibniz's appropriation of Descartes' concept of innate ideas, and his placement of individual consciousness at the center of his philosophy – in the form of discrete, dynamic monads – represented a clear continuation of the tradition of consciousness philosophy initiated by Descartes. In fact, Leibniz's

---

[56] Ibid., p. 245.

understanding of space as a function of individual consciousness signaled a significant step beyond Descartes' mechanical dualism, toward Kant's derivation of all the categories of understanding from transcendental subjectivity. Leibniz also moved beyond the mathematical-mechanical worldview with his reintroduction of the concept of teleology, not only in his theory of knowledge, which posits a continuous development of consciousness from primitive forms of sense certainty through self-consciousness and finally to the lofty heights of quasi-divine reason, but also in his ethics, which introduces the optimistic doctrines of the perfectibility of man, or the belief that rational insight leads automatically to the best of all possible worlds. Of even greater consequence for Horkheimer is the fact that Leibniz was the first to counter the latent tendencies toward nihilism in the mechanical worldview. As he puts it: "Here for the first time the coldness and sobriety of the physical-mechanical worldview is recognized and the attempt is made to move beyond it through a scientifically sound integration of the concept of teleology, taken from theology."[57] In short, Horkheimer attempts, as he had done in his discussion of Descartes and Spinoza, to demonstrate both the progressive impulses in Leibniz's thought, as well as its important continuities with the medieval worldview.[58]

Bourgeois Philosophy Comes of Age: The Enlightenment

If Leibniz was the first modern philosopher to recognize that the new mathematical-mechanical worldview contained latent tendencies toward nihilism, which he sought to counter by drawing upon the theological tradition in order to justify the status quo as the best of all possible worlds, or as a "harmonie préétablie," then Pierre Bayle was the first modern philosopher to refuse to attribute any meaning whatsoever to the world in and of itself. Bayle plays an important role in Horkheimer's narrative of the history of modern philosophy, because his refusal to bestow meaning upon the world in an affirmative manner struck at the heart of the attempts to reconcile science and religion in seventeenth-century rationalism and rationalist metaphysics, and in so doing, set the stage for the antireligious, antimetaphysical, and antiauthoritarian critiques of the Enlightenment. Horkheimer writes:

According to Bayle, the world has no reasonable purpose. For him it is completely impossible to apply the religious concept of a benevolent God, who is concerned about the redemption of man ... to nature or even to place this concept in relation to nature in any meaningful way.... According to him, the exercise of our reason never gives rise to insights that are in harmony with religious teachings, and insofar as metaphysics, including natural theology, lives precisely from the attempt somehow to create such harmony ... [it] is a completely misguided undertaking.[59]

Although Horkheimer does not overlook the fact that Bayle's insistence on a strict separation of science from religion, on the grounds that the latter was fundamentally irrational, was carried out ostensibly in the name of rescuing religion, he stresses the devastating consequences that Bayle's arguments had

[57] Ibid., p. 248.
[58] Ibid., p. 243.
[59] Ibid., pp. 294–5.

for religion. Regardless of his subjective convictions, whose sincerity was open to question,[60] Bayle's writings did indeed have a tremendous objective effect. His magnum opus, *Dictionnaire historique et critique*, was one of the most widely read and influential works among intellectuals throughout Europe at the beginning the eighteenth century. Throughout his writings, he expressed objective historical tendencies and pointedly articulated insights that were often far ahead of his time.[61] Bayle was, for example, the first to reject the pragmatic argument so popular among early modern bourgeois philosophers – even the most disenchanted, such as Machiavelli and Hobbes – that religion was necessary in order to keep the fourth estate in its proper place. He was also the first to defend openly the thesis that atheists could be every bit as ethical as the religious. Yet Bayle's thoroughgoing separation of religion from science remained his most important contribution, according to Horkheimer, insofar as it paved the way not only for Enlightenment critiques of religion,[62] but also for later, more sophisticated analyses of the social-psychological origins of religion.[63]

In Horkheimer's narrative of the history of modern philosophy, John Locke plays an even more important role in overcoming the rationalist metaphysics of the seventeenth century and preparing the way for the heroic phase of bourgeois society, which found its fullest expression in the philosophy of the French Enlightenment. Horkheimer's description of the impact Locke's philosophy had in Europe at the beginning of the eighteenth century is worth quoting at length:

We have already seen the great extent to which rationalism, in all its sprawling systems, was permeated by metaphysical and theological elements. We have also seen how rationalism presented itself precisely as the conscious reconciliation of theology and modern science. The reactions against it from Gassendi to Bayle were weak, since the grandeur of the rationalist systems, replete with material knowledge and appearing securely complete, gave them a philosophical monopoly on the continent – due also in no small part to the strength of feudal elements that were still present there. Then there appeared, at the same time as the conscious seizure of political power by the most advanced section of the bourgeoisie, Locke's *Essay on Human Understanding*, as a complete system in four volumes, a work in which all the arguments against rationalism were, at the same time, combined with the development of a new empirical epistemology and presented in brilliant, clear and convincing prose. Although it may not have been Locke's intention, his work appeared not only as a declaration of war of empiricism against rationalism, of experience against pure thought, but just as much as an attack of materialism against rationalism, science against theology, the society of free competition against the world of the meaningful *Ordo*.[64]

---

[60] Horkheimer writes: "a defense of religion, as Bayle carried it out, could hardly be surpassed by the most effective attack." Ibid., p. 303.

[61] With respect to his rejection of deism, for example, Horkheimer considered Bayle "even more advanced than his great student Voltaire." Ibid., p. 304.

[62] Ibid., p. 295.

[63] Horkheimer mentions Feuerbach, who published a full-length study of Bayle in 1838, and Freud in this context. He writes: "[Bayle's] reference to the possibility of unbiased investigations of the instinctual [*triebmässigen*] foundations of religion is an illuminating insight, which only the most advanced representative of modern psychology have developed further with concrete studies." Ibid., p. 300.

[64] Ibid., pp. 308–9.

Horkheimer goes on to describe in more detail Locke's critique of rationalism and the relationship of his philosophy to the triumphant English bourgeoisie. He views Locke's philosophy as a continuation of the practically oriented empirical legacy of Hobbes and, even more so, of Bacon. Locke did move beyond both of them with his sophisticated epistemological analyses, but Horkheimer repeatedly emphasizes that his philosophy did not represent a continuation of the tradition of consciousness philosophy begun by Descartes. To defend this thesis, Horkheimer outlines Locke's critique of innate ideas and stresses that consciousness and reason are never primary – not to mention ends in themselves – for Locke. The basis of knowledge for Locke is not reason or revelation, but *experience*, which comes into being only through contact with a world external to consciousness, mediated by our senses.[65] Horkheimer links Locke's philosophy to the English bourgeoisie in the period following the Glorious Revolution by showing how it was the first expression of a national bourgeoisie that had demonstrated that it no longer needed to make any compromises with the *ancien regime*. By the end of the eighteenth century, the English bourgeoisie's economic strength was so great that it no longer needed the paternalistic protection of the absolutist state to further the development of commerce. Horkheimer presents Locke's liberal political philosophy as an expression of this new constellation: his defense of a separation of the legislative from the executive branch of government, which consolidated the hegemony of the bourgeois-controlled parliament over the crown; his ardent defense of property and his insistence that the primary role of government lies not in guiding the economy, à la mercantilism, but in maintaining the preconditions for its smooth functioning; finally, his defense of individual interests in ethics and his belief that what is best for the individual is also best for society.

Before continuing with an explication of Horkheimer's understanding of the French Enlightenment, it is worth briefly recalling why it plays such an important role in his narrative of the history of modern philosophy. First, from his contemporary standpoint, Horkheimer was deeply concerned about the revival of metaphysical, irrationalist, and authoritarian ideas in Germany in the 1920s, and he viewed the critical, antiauthoritarian legacy of the French Enlightenment as an important source to draw upon in the fight against such tendencies. Horkheimer was reinforced in this belief by the widespread neglect of, and outright hostility to, the Enlightenment in general and the French Enlightenment in particular that was so widespread in Weimar Germany. We will explore these tendencies in more detail in the next chapter in our examination of *Dämmerung*. Second, from a historical standpoint, the French Enlightenment illustrated very clearly the principles underlying Horkheimer's interpretation of modern philosophy. The philosophy of the French Enlightenment represented the most advanced and uncompromising expression of the ideals of bourgeois society to date. The reasons for this are to be sought, according to Horkheimer, in the specific development of the bourgeoisie in France in the eighteenth century. Horkheimer explicitly rejects the thesis that there was a unified European Enlightenment that can be understood purely from the standpoint of the history

[65] Ibid., p. 335.

of ideas.[66] He stresses instead the uneven development of bourgeois society in different national contexts, which gave the Enlightenment a qualitatively different character in each place. As Horkheimer puts it:

> There was, in other words, no such thing as *the* Enlightenment in Western and Central Europe, there was instead the political movement of the French bourgeoisie, in which a group of brilliant, philosophically and aesthetically inclined writers used the medium of knowledge to undermine the remnants of feudal life in absolutism and thereby prepared the way for the great revolution.[67]

Thus, in the genuine sense of the term – or at least in the sense that Horkheimer interpreted the concept at this time – the Enlightenment existed only in France. Horkheimer does speak of the Enlightenment in the British and German contexts as well,[68] but it is clear that neither of them exemplify the concept as well as eighteenth-century France. The concrete reasons for this lie in the differing trajectories of bourgeois society in these three areas. The unique historical constellation in France produced what was for Horkheimer one of the most important defining characteristics of the French Enlightenment, namely the *lumières'* articulation of universalist principles that pointed beyond bourgeois society, principles that would remain relevant even after the bourgeoisie's becoming conscious of itself as a new particularist power in the course of the nineteenth century. Yet equally important for Horkheimer was what he identified as the basic *materialist* tendency of the *philosophes'* work, which not only pointed toward the later development of socialist theory, but also provided Horkheimer with an important historical alternative to consciousness philosophy. As we shall see, this alternative would figure prominently in his own attempts in the early 1930s to develop a new concept of materialism adequate to the transformed social conditions of the twentieth century.

In his actual presentation of the French Enlightenment, Horkheimer insists on its basic thematic unity. Although he makes no effort to conceal his exceptionally high estimation of certain of the *philosophes* – most notably Voltaire and Helvetius – Horkheimer does not portray the French Enlightenment in the manner of Nietzschean monumental history.[69] Horkheimer's narrative does not retrace the passage of *Geist* from one towering individual to the next; instead, it reconstructs a number of particular problems, to whose solution many different individual thinkers contributed. These problems can perhaps best be summed up under the broad and interrelated headings of the Enlightenment's concept of reason and its discovery of society and history.

---

[66] For a defense of the Enlightenment as a unified European project, see Peter Gay, *The Enlightenment: An Interpretation*, vol. 1, *The Rise of Modern Paganism* (New York, 1966), and vol. 2, *The Science of Freedom*, (New York, 1969).

[67] GS 9, p. 349.

[68] Although he does discuss Vico at length and enthusiastically in "The Beginnings of the Bourgeois Philosophy of History," Horkheimer does not devote any attention to other important figures in the Italian Enlightenment, such as Cesare Beccaria, in his lectures or writings at this time.

[69] Friedrich Nietzsche, *On the Advantage and Disadvantage of History for Life* (Indianapolis, 1980), pp. 14f.

Regarding the former, Horkheimer places the *lumieres'* concept of reason squarely within the empiricist tradition – critical of rationalism while at the same time making no concessions to irrationalist tendencies. As he puts it:

In the Enlightenment, reason is nothing other than correct thinking in contrast to incorrect thinking, or error. Reasonable is someone who makes proper use of his experiences, and who, based upon them, makes useful judgments and acts accordingly. If one understands rationalism merely as the opposite of the idea that we should let ourselves be driven by "elementary" forces and we should act without reflecting, then the Enlightenment is certainly opposed to this irrationalism. But if one uses the expression – as I have up to now – in relation to the philosophy that stands opposed to empiricism, then the Enlightenment was certainly not rationalistic; for it always attacked and dismissed thinking that moved independently of experience.[70]

Horkheimer also stresses, however, that the Enlightenment concept of reason moved beyond Locke and the rest of the empiricist tradition in its determination to change existing conditions in order to realize, to the greatest extent possible, human happiness in this world. Horkheimer characterizes what he considers the fundamental principle of the Enlightenment in the following way:

It is the principle that human knowledge, without any transcendent aid or revelation, is competent and responsible in all areas ... It is the rejection of all transcendence and otherworldliness ... We encounter things through our senses and science discerns the relations and regularities that exists among things. The process of knowledge is also a purely natural happening, which proceeds in us, as natural beings, through the relationships that exist between us and things. But as such, it is also the necessary condition for changing and improving conditions. We are able to act as human beings only when we act on the basis of knowledge. The object and aim of all activity is neither heaven nor our own interiority, but rather the real relations in the world. Thus ignorance is one of the greatest dangers for society and its elimination, the expansion of knowledge, "Enlightenment," is always the precondition for happiness.[71]

This desire to create a rational society, in which happiness for all is realized to the greatest extent possible – "the conscious organization of reality" as Horkheimer puts it[72] – could not of course be realized without a critical attitude toward existing conditions. Horkheimer returns time and again to this critical, antiauthoritarian stance, which he views as one of the defining characteristics of the French Enlightenment.[73] Closely related to the antiauthoritarianism of the French Enlightenment is also the critique of prejudice, which plays a particularly important role in the work of materialists like Holbach and Helvetius. Horkheimer demonstrates how the Enlightenment critique of prejudice represents a continuation of a certain tradition of critical epistemological reflection – expressed, for example, in Bacon's theory of the idols, Hobbes's mechanical materialism, and Leibniz's individualistic idealism – which it

---

[70] GS 9, p. 353.

[71] Ibid., pp. 351–2.

[72] Ibid., p. 356.

[73] He states, for example: "The French Enlightenment is mercilessly anti-authoritarian vis-à-vis the ruling powers. For precisely this reason it is by no means identical with contemporary English and German philosophy – even if it relies on quite similar theoretical ideas." Ibid., p. 348.

then transforms into full-fledged ideology critique. The critical nature of the Enlightenment concept of reason pushes the critical reflections of its early modern predecessors beyond a mere theory of knowledge – even a practically oriented one, such as Bacon's – to social criticism. Horkheimer quotes a passage from Holbach's *Système da la Nature* to make this point: "The rulers believe it lies in their interest to maintain the prevailing views; the prejudices and errors, which they consider necessary to secure their power, are maintained with violence that is never reasonable."[74] For Horkheimer, this passage exemplifies the critical impulse of Enlightenment materialism, which he sums up as the "struggle against the bad status quo and the effort to change it."[75]

In addition to the *philosophes'* critical concept of reason, Horkheimer also devotes a significant amount of attention to the closely related topic of their discovery of society and history. Regarding the former, he first examines the *lumieres'* sensualist theory of knowledge, which takes Locke's empiricism as its point of departure, and is progressively developed in the philosophical writings of Voltaire, Condillac, Diderot, Holbach, and Helvetius. Horkheimer interprets the increasing reliance on the senses as the sole source of knowledge, which characterizes the development of sensualism, primarily as an example of the Enlightenment's belief that consciousness is always dependent upon its other, that it can only be understood in relation to the concrete conditions in which it exists.[76] Yet Horkheimer also points out that this sensualist epistemology does not imply a reductionist or determinist position – the rejection of the totalizing, metaphysical *l'esprit du systeme* does not rule out the productive application of discursive *l'esprit systematique*, to draw on a distinction made by d'Alembert. Horkheimer writes:

Materialism does not, of course, deny in any way the fact that humans think, but it is convinced that their thoughts can be explained in terms of material conditions and that with the change of these material conditions – be it the physical constitution of the individual or the living conditions of society as a whole – their thoughts will change as well.[77]

In his interpretation of the *philosophes'* concept of education, Horkheimer also focuses on the social and material factors that determine an individual's "character." Horkheimer argues that the Enlightenment concept of education is extremely broad, even broader than the standard sense of the French *éducation* or the German *Erziehung*. For the *lumières*, education means "the totality of real life conditions in which a person develops, by no means merely what one is told in school or by other educators."[78] With this interpretation, Horkheimer is able not only to refute the claim that Helvetius or any of the other *philosophes* advocated an educational dictatorship, but also to demonstrate that Rousseau's ideas on education and the social origins of inequality are very much within the main current of Enlightenment thought.[79]

[74] Ibid., p. 374.
[75] Ibid.
[76] Ibid., pp. 356–8.
[77] Ibid., p. 377.
[78] Ibid., p. 367.
[79] Ibid., pp. 381–2.

Horkheimer argues that the very concept of "character" is relativized, once one recognizes the social and material conditions that largely determine it: "the material relations, one's position within society as a whole, particularly one's economic standing, determine the actions and so-called character of men."[80] Horkheimer's remarks here also illustrate the link between his investigations in the history of philosophy and his parallel efforts to develop a theory of contemporary society and ideology.[81]

In the Enlightenment theory of knowledge and its ideas on education, Horkheimer attempted to illustrate the *philosophes'* discovery of society. According to him, it was clear to them that "experience and knowledge are not merely individual, but also social matters.... The law-like progression of knowledge cannot be described solely with the concepts of physics and the individual subject, it also always requires social and sociological categories."[82] Nevertheless, Horkheimer also insists that despite the *lumières'* awareness of its importance, they did not succeed in developing the concepts necessary to comprehend the explosive development of bourgeois society. Horkheimer illustrates this point in his discussion of the *philosophes'* understanding of ethics and history. He places the *philosophes'* views on ethics within a long tradition of psychological writings in France that extends back to Montaigne and La Rochefoucauld. What Helvetius and other astute psychological observers among the *philosophes* took from this tradition was the fundamentally interest-driven nature of human motivation and behavior. Horkheimer views this insight as a decisive step beyond the rationalist ethics of the seventeenth century, which maintained that ethical behavior must always be guided by abstract principles. Horkheimer writes:

The point of this French theory, that *amour-propre* forms the basis of human actions, is essentially the rejection of the rationalist theory that moral principles of reason, coming from above, could be the decisive impulse for any conduct. For these psychologists it is, on the contrary, always a drive-based interest alone that can motivate action, and providing a rational justification does not suffice to reveal the true motivation. Whenever such a rational justification is given, particularly one that is considered commendable and noble, the question is appropriate: what is the real interest that stands behind this façade?[83]

So whereas the *lumières* viewed concrete individual interests as the proper basis of human behavior, they did not hypostatize a *harmonie préétablie* between the interests of the individual and society as did Leibniz in the seventeenth century and the English political economists in the eighteenth century. They were fully aware that social institutions could come into conflict with the interests of the individuals who make up society. However, they did not make any attempt to conceptualize society abstractly – as a structural entity that followed laws of its own, laws that transcended the interests of individuals. For the *lumières,*

---

[80] Ibid.

[81] Horkheimer would examine in rich detail the social determinants of character in contemporary, industrial capitalist societies in his pseudonymously written collection of aphorisms, *Dämmerung*, to which we will turn in the following chapter.

[82] GS 9, p. 368.

[83] Ibid., p. 359.

society does not exist as an independent entity apart from its individual members, and if its institutions came into conflict with their interests, society must be transformed based on the principle of "Adaption to the natural interests of the largest possible number of its members."[84] The *philosophes* did not, in other words, develop a sophisticated understanding of the mechanisms that drive bourgeois society or how to change them.

This individualistic understanding of society was also apparent in their understanding of history. Like his contemporary Ernst Cassirer, with whom he agreed on little else, Horkheimer goes out of his way to refute the romantic myth that the Enlightenment had no understanding of history.[85] As Horkheimer bluntly puts it: "The constantly repeated objection that the Enlightenment was unhistorical just shows that it really applies to those who say and stupidly repeat it."[86] To illustrate this point, Horkheimer focuses on Voltaire and the great progress that his historically oriented works, such as the *Essai sur les moeurs*, represented in comparison to what was considered the most advanced historiography at the time, such as Bossuet's thoroughly theological *Discours l'histoire universelle*. Yet Horkheimer also points out that the Enlightenment's failure to develop the concepts necessary to understand the dynamic development of bourgeois society was also readily apparent in its historiography. He writes:

Individuals dominated by love of themselves are what Voltaire attempts to examine behind historical legends, people who pursue their individual, drive-based aims.... He does not yet know that society itself follows different laws than the individual and that one cannot study the former based on the isolated individual.[87]

Society and history had, in other words, been raised to the level of conceptual consciousness in the *philosophes*' work, but that concept remained abstract, insofar as it was still determined in individualistic terms. With regard to bourgeois society, the Owl of Minerva did indeed first take flight at dusk. To find the first sophisticated concepts that were developed to understand bourgeois society, one had to leave eighteenth-century France, where the bourgeoisie was still struggling to establish its hegemony, and return to Britain, where the bourgeoisie had already triumphed, and where its intellectual spokesmen had already developed a theory to explain and justify the principles of its functioning – the theories of civil society and classical political economy.[88]

Horkheimer traces the development of theories of civil society and classical political economy in eighteenth-century Britain in the work of Bernard Mandeville, Adam Ferguson, and Adam Smith. Horkheimer places Mandeville in the tradition of other disillusioned bourgeois political theorists such as Machiavelli and Hobbes, who – like the "dark" authors of the bourgeoisie

---

[84] Ibid., p. 365.
[85] Ernst Cassirer, *Philosophy of the Enlightenment*, trans. C.A. Koelln and J.P. Pettegrove (Boston, 1955), pp. 197f.
[86] GS 9, p. 361.
[87] Ibid., pp. 361–2.
[88] Horkheimer writes, "the actual theory of society attained its most advanced form not in France, but in England, which had progressed much further." Ibid., p. 392.

he would praise later in the *Dialectic of Enlightenment* – viewed politics as a science of human domination, and did not shy away from expressing the brutality and cynicism necessary to ensure the proper functioning of bourgeois society. Horkheimer emphasizes that Mandeville's *Fable of the Bees* was not only one of the first clear articulations of the differentiation of bourgeois society from the state, but also an unflinching and perceptive description of its *modus operandi*:

According to Mandeville, it is not the state or the laws, but completely other forces that determine the course of history.... Mandeville relies upon the insight that society is in fact completely unharmonious, so that – in its current form – vices are indispensable and useful.... He declares that the government is a business that can only be run properly if one knows, based on a thorough understanding of human instincts and means of deception, how to manipulate the drives of the masses so that they do not become a threat to maintenance of order.[89]

Among those who productively developed Mandeville's insights, Horkheimer singles out Adam Ferguson, whose *Essay on the History of Civil Society* (1767), moved decisively beyond contract theory not only by outlining a plausible historical explanation of the origins of bourgeois society and the state, but also by refuting the assumption – held also by the *philosophes* – that the naturalized individual was the proper point of departure for political and social theory.[90] Horkheimer praises Ferguson's account of the origins of inequality as being much more realistic and convincing than that of John Locke. Whereas Locke had argued that inequality could be traced back to the greater prudence and frugality of the wealthy, Ferguson insisted that it was primarily a result of the plunder seized by those with political power.[91] When portrayed against this backdrop of Mandeville's and Ferguson's sober analyses of bourgeois society, the political economy of Adam Smith takes on an unfamiliar, far less impressive appearance. In fact, Horkheimer devotes little attention to Smith's political economy itself; he focuses instead on the moral and psychological assumptions that guided his work, which actually fell behind the insights attained by Mandeville and Ferguson. Whereas Ferguson recognized that human interests were thoroughly historical, Smith hypostatizes the desire for material gain as the quasi-anthropological force that drives individuals and, in turn, society. He assumes that if this force is given free reign – in the sense of the motto *laissez faire* that he had adopted from his friends and colleagues in France, the physiocrats – the *harmonie préétablie* inherent in bourgeois society would unfold naturally. Thus, in contrast to the *lumières*, or even Mandeville and Ferguson, Smith's theory ends on an apologetic note, which expressed the confidence and quietism of the triumphant English bourgeoisie.

In his examination of Berkeley and Hume, Horkheimer also highlights the essentially apologetic and quietistic character of their philosophy, and this provides him with further evidence for his argument that nothing comparable

[89] Ibid., pp. 396 and 395, respectively.
[90] Ibid., pp. 396–7.
[91] Ibid., p. 397.

to the French Enlightenment existed in England in the eighteenth century. He maintains that "English philosophy no longer had a revolutionary function in the eighteenth century; its most important representatives – Berkeley and Hume – consciously pursued accommodation to the status quo."[92] This is not to say, of course, that Horkheimer paid no attention to the fundamental differences between Berkeley and Hume. He goes out of his way to discredit the standard interpretation of eighteenth-century British empiricism, which posits an unbroken line of development from Locke through Berkeley to Hume. Berkeley cannot be considered a legitimate heir of Locke's empiricism, according to Horkheimer, because he defended an antisensualist consciousness philosophy that abandoned the foundations of empirical and natural scientific research, and which was guided throughout by conservative theological interests. Horkheimer writes:

The original appropriation of Locke's sensualism ... was not at all in the sense of a pure empiricism.... Berkeley never "rests content" with a demonstration of sensual appearances; instead, he always delves further into the primary causes. These primary causes are explicitly not, for example, the laws discovered by the positive sciences, but rather theological, religious essences.[93]

Horkheimer argues that Hume, on the other hand, was much closer to the *philosophes* than to Berkeley, insofar as he developed the sensualist moment in Locke's philosophy. He illustrates this point using the example of Hume's famous critiques of causality and personal identity. Horkheimer also stresses the affinity between Hume and the *philosophes* regarding their religious skepticism. However, Hume's atheism did not lead him to a critique of ideology or society, as was the case with the *philosophes*. As Horkheimer puts it: "The fact that the earth corresponds so poorly with the idea of a wise and benevolent God does not lead Hume to the demand that these conditions be changed, as would have been self-evident for a Helvetius or Holbach, but instead to skeptical resignation."[94] Horkheimer interprets Hume's skeptical resignation as an expression of the quietism of the British bourgeoisie, who were convinced that the social order they had established was natural and eternal. More broadly, Horkheimer viewed Hume's nominalist skepticism as the first full expression of the thoroughly disenchanted, indeed nihilistic, tendencies that had been latent in the bourgeois understanding of the world from the beginning. He writes:

There are neither material nor spiritual [*geistige*] substances, there are only experiences and a certain regularity, which allows us to make certain predictions with sufficient probability.... With this, we have arrived at the furthest consequences of philosophy that are reached in England. Skeptical epistemology and liberal economics, utilitarian ethics ... the deduction of science and religion from anonymous regularities of experience – this is the most extreme secularization and disenchantment of the world.[95]

---

[92] Ibid., p. 349.
[93] Ibid., p. 421.
[94] Ibid., p. 445.
[95] Ibid., pp. 439 and 456–7, respectively.

In this respect, Hume's philosophy expressed not only a preliminary culmination of certain tendencies latent in bourgeois society, but also a preview of what was to come with the spread of bourgeois hegemony throughout Europe and the rest of the world in the nineteenth century. Hume's nominalism – if not always his skepticism – anticipated the triumph of positivism in the nineteenth century, which would accompany the consolidation of bourgeois society on the European continent. But before turning to Horkheimer's interpretation of positivism and other important philosophical developments in the nineteenth century, let us first examine his interpretation of German Idealism.

German Idealism

Horkheimer's Interpretation of the History of German Idealism

Horkheimer's interpretation of German Idealism in the late 1920s is more difficult to present than his reading of many of the other chapters of modern philosophy, because his interest in German Idealism – Kant and Hegel in particular – at this time was by no means only historical, but also contained a strong systematic component. In other words, Horkheimer approached German Idealism – as he had also done with the French Enlightenment – not only from the standpoint of the history of bourgeois society, but also with a view to its relevance for contemporary philosophical discussions and for his own efforts to develop a critical theory of society. Only by addressing both of these dimensions – the historical and the systematic – can one understand Horkheimer's interpretation of German Idealism and its significance for his own thought at this time.

As we have already seen in our brief examination of the paper on Kant and Hegel that Horkheimer delivered in 1925 on the occasion of his becoming a *Privatdozent*, Horkheimer interpreted Kant's philosophy historically as a crucial step in the transformation of modern philosophy into consciousness philosophy. Although there were other powerful counter-tendencies in modern philosophy, most importantly those issuing from the empiricist tradition, Kant's famous Copernican turn firmly placed philosophy upon the foundation of subjective consciousness. This epistemological turn initiated by Kant would continue to dominate philosophy – at least the main stream of German academic philosophy from which Horkheimer was still struggling to free himself at this time – into the 1920s. In his lectures on German Idealism, which he delivered in the winter semester of 1925–6, Horkheimer fleshed out the argument he had made a few months earlier by showing the place Kant's philosophy occupied within the larger trajectory of the development of consciousness philosophy. Picking up the thread where he would leave it at the end of his lectures on modern philosophy in 1927, Horkheimer showed how Kant continued the rationalist and metaphysical traditions that had been established in Germany by Leibniz and popularized by Christian Wolff. Yet Kant's continuation of these traditions was by no means unbroken; his primary concern, according to Horkheimer, was to rescue the most fundamental assumptions of the rationalist and metaphysical traditions from the challenge posed to them by modern science and empiricism, which had attained their most advanced form in Newton's mechanics and Hume's skepticism, respectively.

Horkheimer singles out Kant's distinction between theoretical and practical reason as his most important means of rescuing rationalism and metaphysics. By reducing the natural world to the level of phenomena conditioned by transcendental subjectivity and separating these phenomena from the noumenal world of "things-in-themselves," Kant created a space for freedom, God, and the immortal soul without in any way detracting from the validity of the laws of Newtonian physics. Furthermore, he had done so without making any claims about the "external" world, in a manner that Hume would have considered dogmatic; for if basic scientific principles such as causality related only to the natural, phenomenal world, one could and must leave the question of the way things "really" are "in-themselves" unanswered. The order humans perceive in the phenomenal realm of their experience comes from the transcendental and subjective faculties of theoretical reason (understanding), not the objective world. Kant insists nonetheless that another realm that transcends time, space, nature, the senses, and human experience does exist. This realm is governed by metaphysical principles that are deducible from reason and reason alone. As Horkheimer puts it:

> Kant by no means claimed that, just because the objects of metaphysics are not perceptible by means of the natural sciences, we cannot *know* anything about them.... On the contrary, precisely the idea that the objects of traditional metaphysics correspond to a function of reason different from natural scientific knowledge, was Kant's most characteristic achievement. Although it is not at all possible for theoretical philosophy to demonstrate the reality of metaphysical objects, as dogmatic philosophy had believed, it can indeed demonstrate their intellectual necessity. The ideas of God, freedom and immortality are not concepts derived from experience, they are inherent in our reason.[96]

It is these metaphysical principles that serve as regulative ideas for practical reason, which in Kant's system has primacy over theoretical reason. In other words, all forms of theoretical reason, including the sciences, are always ultimately subordinated to practical human ends, and these ends are reasonable only insofar as they are regulated by, and have their proper place within, the kingdom of ends based on the metaphysical principles of God, freedom, and immortality. In contrast to everything within the phenomenal realm of human experience, these regulative ideas are *unconditional*, that is, they possess the substantial character of a rationalist axiom, whose existence is not dependent upon anything else. Regulative ideas are also *infinite*, which does not mean that they cannot serve as a guide for practical human ends, but only that they will never be perfectly realized in the finite, natural world.

Whereas Kant's Copernican turn had unmistakably placed philosophy on subjective foundations, his idealism was not absolute insofar as he maintained a split, which could never be perfectly overcome, between theoretical and practical reason, and between phenomenal appearance and the noumenal "thing-in-itself." It was precisely this crucial moment of nonidentity

---

[96] GS 10, p. 48.

in Kant's philosophy that Fichte criticized most vehemently and sought most energetically to overcome.[97] He did so by posing the question of the *origins* of both transcendental apperception, whose basic categories Kant had posited as unconditional and constant, and the "thing-in-itself," which Kant had attributed to an objective realm. Yet if one carries the principles of idealism to their logical end, as Fichte was determined to do, then both the categories of transcendental apperception and "things-in-themselves" must also be subjective in origin. Fichte attempted to prove this by transforming Kant's static concept of transcendental apperception into his own dynamic concept of self-consciousness, whose self-positing could purportedly explain, in subjective terms, the genesis of both transcendental apperception and the "thing-in-itself." Furthermore, the predicates of unconditionality and infinity, which Kant had reserved for the transcendent metaphysical realm, Fichte could now attribute to self-consciousness, whose boundaries were determined solely by itself, not by any objective transcendent or transcendental conditions. For this reason, Horkheimer refers to Fichte's philosophy as *absolute* subjective idealism.[98] He interprets it not just as another step in the development of consciousness philosophy, but as the most consequential form it can and must take when its premises are thought through to their logical end. As Horkheimer puts it:

[Fichte] had the courage to emphasize that idealistic philosophy, in its theoretical part, was not able to produce a legitimate reason for assuming the existence of a living being outside myself. He had the courage to admit that idealistic philosophy, as long as it remains epistemology, must necessarily be solipsistic.[99]

In other words, Fichte's robust and uncompromising *espirit du system* confirmed the suspicions that Horkheimer had recently expressed in his philosophical diary about the solipsistic tendencies inherent in all consciousness philosophy.[100]

Whereas Fichte had pushed consciousness philosophy to its logical end, Schelling took the first decisive steps to move beyond it. In his early Nature Philosophy, which Horkheimer – like Marx – considers his most important philosophical contribution, Schelling moves beyond the absolute subjectivism of Fichte by arguing that the ego develops only through a long process that has the non-ego as its necessary prerequisite, and that nature cannot be reduced to the categories of transcendental subjectivity or self-consciousness. Horkheimer argues that the most basic principle of Schelling's Nature Philosophy is "that nature has its own essence,"[101] and that Schelling "rejects Kant's and Fichte's limitation of theoretical truth to the realm of reflecting consciousness,"[102] and that it was his intention "to eliminate the phenomenalistic, solipsistic character

---

[97] Horkheimer writes, "Compared to Kant, Fichte's system is in fact much more consistent; the breaks that runs throughout Kant's critical philosophy and mark it as, in truth, a dualist worldview, are completely removed by Fichte." Ibid., p. 99.

[98] Ibid., p. 112.

[99] Ibid., p. 118.

[100] See passage cited earlier, pp. 86–7.

[101] GS 10, p. 138.

[102] Ibid., p. 158.

of Fichte's version of idealism."[103] However, Horkheimer also stresses that even Schelling's Nature Philosophy remains firmly within the idealist tradition inso-far as it posits an absolute identity that underlies all manifestations of subject and object. Whereas Fichte had grounded this identity principle in an absolute meta-subject, Schelling posited it as a metaphysical principle that remains neu-tral vis-à-vis the subject-object dichotomy. As Horkheimer says:

> One no longer moves from the facts of consciousness *toward* unconditional truth and the absolute, but rather, as Schelling puts it, one philosophizes from the standpoint within the absolute itself. In other words, the absolute and the identity of the ideal and the real, or nature and spirit, must simply be presupposed.[104]

In order to illustrate this point, Horkheimer turns from Schelling's Nature Philosophy to his later Identity Philosophy and his aesthetics. He shows how in his later work Schelling develops one of the central theses that Kant had advanced in the *Critique of Judgment* by locating this crucial moment of unconditioned and infinite identity not in the realm of theoretical or practical reason, but in the realm of art, in which it could attain at least symbolic repre-sentation. Horkheimer states:

> In order to understand this conclusive and systematic, highest function of art for Schelling, we need to recall one of the essential ideas of German Idealism, which has characterized it since Kant. It states, ... that human beings can fully realize their essence and potential only in the realm of the *infinite*.... But Kant had already ... demon-strated in the *Critique of Judgment* that art is the only way that sensual beings could be capable of really producing, if not the idea itself, at least something that corresponds and "symbolizes" it. Schelling adopts this idea and places it ... at the highest point of philosophy.[105]

However, Horkheimer also stresses that the absolute moment of identity that Schelling reserves for autonomous works of art remains unmediated. For exam-ple, Schelling subscribes to the romantic belief that the artistic genius produces largely unconsciously, that he serves as a vessel through which the absolute manifests itself. He also insisted, much to Hegel's chagrin, that one could get access to the absolute in art not discursively through conceptual analysis or rational reflection, but only directly, through intuition. For Horkheimer, this turn away from discursive rationality in Schelling's later philosophy signals a significant decline in his thought and also marks the point at which Hegel parted ways with him.[106]

Horkheimer shows how Hegel goes beyond Schelling by returning, at a higher level, to the rationalist assumptions that had guided German Idealism from the beginning and that Schelling had abandoned, at least in his later phi-losophy. Hegel agrees with Fichte's and Schelling's claims, against Kant, that absolute identity does exist, but he also insists that it is not merely posited by self-consciousness, nor is it accessible directly through intuition. Hegel

---

[103] Ibid., p. 157.
[104] Ibid., pp. 153–4.
[105] Ibid., pp. 147–8 (emphasis mine).
[106] Ibid., p. 155.

preserves the objective moment that Schelling had introduced in his Nature Philosophy as a critique of Fichte's absolute subjectivism. On the one hand, self-consciousness is, according to Hegel, always confronted with a contingent natural and an objective historical world that are essentially other than self-consciousness. On the other hand, Hegel also moves beyond Schelling by preserving the subjective moment that Fichte had introduced, albeit at a higher level. Through the labor of the concept, self-consciousness is able to retrace the complex steps in the development of objective spirit, become fully aware of its contemporary form, and thus partake consciously in the process of its further development and the ongoing historical transformation of the contingent natural world. For Hegel, however, the historical process of the transformation of the objective natural world by subjective self-consciousness is unified at a higher level of absolute identity, namely that of absolute spirit. History is the self-externalization and the becoming self-conscious of absolute spirit; finite, conditioned human beings are merely the means, not the ends of this larger process. Horkheimer argues that Hegel posits the existence of absolute identity in this way in order to rescue the fundamental metaphysical assumption of idealism, namely the possibility of unconditioned and infinite knowledge, while at the same time preserving an essential role for discursive rationality and a differentiated understanding of history and the empirical world. In his lectures Horkheimer describes this positing of absolute identity as self-conscious spirit as the "quintessence of Hegel's metaphysics."[107] In short, Horkheimer was convinced that some of the basic principles of rationalism and metaphysics, which first emerged in Descartes and were further developed by Spinoza, Leibniz, and Wolff, remained intact throughout the complex development of German Idealism. Crucial for Horkheimer's concept of metaphysics is that these principles were unconditioned, ahistorical, and that they provided "knowledge of reality that could serve as the foundation for the scientific exploration of factual conditions and that was, therefore, independent of science."[108] As was the case with earlier forms of rationalism and metaphysics, Horkheimer viewed this need for the absolute, that was also articulated in German Idealism, as a product of the development of bourgeois society.

In his attempt to develop a materialist history of modern philosophy, Horkheimer is always very careful to avoid interpretations that reduce the ideas to nothing more than functions or reflexes of the historical base.[109] Horkheimer stresses that this care is particularly important when interpreting German Idealism, which is – to an even greater extent than any of its philosophical predecessors – impossible to understand without extensive philosophical training.[110] Nonetheless, Horkheimer argues that even in its loftiest flights, German Idealism is "kein ausser der Welt hockendes Wesen."[111] True

---

[107] GS 10, p. 160.

[108] Ibid. p. 299.

[109] See, for example, Horkheimer's critical remarks on Dilthey's historicism: GS 10, pp. 16–17.

[110] See his introductory remarks to his lectures on German idealism, GS 10, pp. 12–13.

[111] "Not an abstract being, squatting outside the world," as Marx once said of human beings. "Introduction," Contribution to the Critique of Hegel's Philosophy of Right, in *The Marx-Engels Reader*, ed. R. Tucker (New York: Norton, 1978), p. 53.

to his interpretation of philosophy as "a certain type of intellectual pursuit of real historical human beings,"[112] Horkheimer also insists that German Idealism must be understood within its concrete historical context, whose essence in the early modern period, he maintains, was the development of bourgeois society. In order at least provisionally to illustrate its mediated links to the development of bourgeois society, Horkheimer discusses the close and crucial relationship of German Idealism to the French Revolution. Following Hegel, Horkheimer interprets the French Revolution as an attempt to realize the bourgeois concept of reason in reality. The dominant tendency of the French Revolution was to reject all that was merely given, to reconstruct society from scratch based on the principles of reason, which all persons, as rational human beings, have the capacity to grasp. In the politically fragmented Holy Roman Empire, out of which the German nation-state would emerge some eighty years later, social and political conditions were not yet ripe for the ideals of the French Revolution to be carried out in reality, so they found expression in the cultural realm, especially in philosophy.[113] German Idealism also demanded that reality be subordinated to the laws of reason, which all humans, as rational beings, had the capacity to understand in equal measure.

These were the ideals that Horkheimer had traced in the development of bourgeois society throughout the early modern period since its break with the authority of the church and the attempts of its representative philosophers to establish reason as a new and more powerful authority. However, the bourgeoisie was still much weaker in Germany than in France, not to mention England. In the eighteenth century, the French bourgeoisie won its first spectacular victory with the revolution, and in England, it already had a successful revolution behind it and was entering a more conservative phase. But in eighteenth-century Germany, where bourgeois society was still fragmented and the Enlightenment was still mired in metaphysical and theological discussions,[114] the powerful political impulse that issued from the French Revolution "had of necessity a much more internalized, ideal, theoretical character," as Horkheimer put it.[115] In other words, in German Idealism the philosophical ideals of bourgeois society were expressed in highly sublimated form; in fact, Horkheimer views German Idealism – at least in its early stages – as the final, spectacular articulation of the utopian ideals of the ascending bourgeoisie.[116] The consolidation of bourgeois hegemony on the Continent in the nineteenth century would be accompanied by very different philosophical tendencies, which had already been anticipated by the quietistic skepticism of Hume in England.

[112] GS 10, p. 16.
[113] Horkheimer's interpretation here runs parallel not only to Marx, but also to Norbert Elias's interpretation of German bourgeois culture. See his *The Civilizing Process*, trans. Edmund Jephcott (Maldam, MA: Basil Blackwell, 1994), pp. 5–43.
[114] GS 9, p. 349.
[115] GS 10, p. 20. Here again Horkheimer's analysis parallels closely that of Norbert Elias.
[116] Herbert Marcuse would develop this interpretation of Hegel's thought, in particular, in his 1941 study *Reason and Revolution: Hegel and Origins of Social Theory* (Boston, 1960), pp. 3–16.

Horkheimer argues that this crucial shift in the self-understanding of the bourgeoisie – that first appeared in England in the eighteenth century and that would spread to the Continent in the nineteenth century – is also already apparent in the development of German Idealism itself, which was marked not only by tremendous initial enthusiasm about the French Revolution, but also by painful disappointment in its subsequent development into terror, despotism, and restoration.[117] Whereas the first phase of German Idealism was marked by a complex reaffirmation of the *verités eternelles* of rationalism, which had its basis in the cognitive capacities of each individual, the second phase was marked by the growing awareness of the relativity and contingency of bourgeois ideals. Horkheimer illustrates this point in his detailed analysis of the shift beyond the subjectively based consciousness philosophy of Kant and Fichte, which was initiated by Schelling and carried to its completion by Hegel. He summarizes this development in the following words:

From the Enlightenment's apologetic portrayal of the social demands of the bourgeoisie as eternal truths of reason, [idealist philosophy] had progressed to the conceptualization of the historical development and transitory validity not only of these truths, but of all the ideals of the Enlightenment, particularly the absolute significance of the individual. The individual as motivation and goal, the highest value in the entire liberation struggle of the Enlightenment, is granted only relative reality in Hegel's philosophy.[118]

Horkheimer also provides other, more concrete examples of this shift in German Idealism, with an examination of Fichte's abandonment – around 1800 – of the universal principles of the Enlightenment for the particularist concept of the nation, or the later Schelling's turn toward aestheticism and mysticism.[119]

Nonetheless, Horkheimer also insists that the unprecedented prestige that philosophy enjoyed in Germany, well into the *Vormärz* period,[120] rested largely on the fact that it expressed the aspirations of the German bourgeoisie, which was still struggling to emancipate itself at this time. Paraphrasing Schelling, Horkheimer states that "in Germany philosophy was a general concern, something of national import" during this time.[121] The highly prestigious position philosophy occupied in Germany at this time would not, however, outlive the *Vormärz* period. The process of the "decomposition" of Hegel's philosophy, which was already well under way in the 1840s, would be followed in Germany by a period of deep distrust of philosophy. Philosophy as an academic discipline would reestablish itself only slowly and with much difficulty in the late nineteenth century. During this period, the critical, universal elements of German Idealism were, as Horkheimer put it, "not advanced by pure philosophy, but were instead taken up by movements, whose portrayal goes beyond the scope of our concerns here."[122] Before turning to Horkheimer's portrayal of the further development of philosophy in the nineteenth century, however, let us first

---

[117] See *Reason and Revolution*, op. cit., p. 3.
[118] GS 10, p. 22.
[119] Ibid. pp. 120ff. and 155, respectively.
[120] The period leading up to the revolutions of 1848.
[121] Ibid. p. 172.
[122] Ibid. p. 165.

briefly examine the *systematic* importance Kant and Hegel had for him in his attempts during this time to develop a critical theory of society.

The Systematic Importance of German Idealism for Horkheimer

We have already seen how in his dissertation and especially in his *Habilitationsschrift* Horkheimer developed a fundamental critique of Kant that disputed the viability of his central distinction between pure and practical reason, and which asserted that his philosophy as a whole had been rendered obsolete by more recent developments in the natural sciences. One of the most notable changes in Horkheimer's thought after 1925 was a more favorable reinterpretation of Kant's philosophy. Before 1925, Horkheimer's prime target was the dominant neo-Kantian interpretation of Kant – represented most prominently by Hermann Cohen – which claimed that Kant's theoretical philosophy could provide the natural sciences with an epistemological foundation. Horkheimer appropriated key arguments from his mentor Hans Cornelius – such as his philosophical interpretation of Gestalt psychology – and turned them against Kant himself in order to undermine the dominant neo-Kantian position. After 1925, however, Horkheimer was much more careful to distinguish between the neo-Kantian interpretation of Kant and Kant's own philosophy. He did this primarily by stressing the neo-Kantians' overemphasis on Kant's theoretical philosophy and their almost complete neglect of his practical philosophy. Although this stress on Kant's theory of knowledge may have been understandable in the positivist-dominated intellectual climate of the mid-nineteenth century in which neo-Kantianism first established itself, it by no means did justice to Kant's own philosophy, in which theoretical reason is ultimately subordinated to practical reason.[123] As Horkheimer puts it:

> Whoever is familiar with contemporary epistemological philosophy, particularly so-called neo-Kantianism, knows that the modern affirmation of Kant represents in many respects the affirmation of this particular interpretation of Kant.... Modern philosophy's inability to move beyond the limits of epistemology ... was deeply necessary ... but it was not for this reason Kantian.... For Kant the exact natural sciences were one branch of human activity among others.... The ideas, which he believed he had deduced with just as much certainty as the categories, are in truth volitional aims, ends. Reason is at base always practical, its actual concepts, the ideas, are guidelines for our actions. In the final analysis, science too is an attempt to realize these ideas.[124]

Horkheimer stressed that this primacy of practical reason, which he rediscovered in Kant's philosophy during this time, demonstrated Kant's affinity with the larger Enlightenment tendency to root reason firmly within the world and to conceptualize it as a means of realizing human ends, not an absolute end in itself. As we shall see, Horkheimer would integrate this aspect of Kant's concept of practical reason as a moment in his own critical theory of society.

---

[123] For a richly detailed interpretation of the origins of neo-Kantianism and the social and intellectual factors that contributed to its subsequent domination of German academic philosophy, see Klaus Christian Köhnke, *Entstehung und Aufstieg des Neukantianismus: Die deutsche Universitätsphilosophie zwischen Idealismus und Positivismus* (Frankfurt, 1986).

[124] GS 10, pp. 40, 47.

During this time, he would also defend Kant, and even the neo-Kantians to a certain degree, against the irrationalist broadsides against the Enlightenment and "shallow reason" that were becoming ever more popular in Germany in the 1920s.[125]

However, as we have seen, Horkheimer also argued that the concept of practical reason was Kant's way of smuggling metaphysics back into philosophy, and that he had fallen behind the most advanced Enlightenment positions in this regard. Horkheimer did, however, hold fast to one of the most important consequences of Kant's defense of the metaphysical character of practical reason, albeit for different reasons. If regulative ideas were indeed infinite and unconditioned, as Kant claimed, then they could never be perfectly realized in the finite and conditioned world of human experience. In other words, something like absolute knowledge or a perfect identity of reason and reality – as defended, for example, by Hegel – could never be attained. Knowledge and the realization of its aims in the phenomenal world would always be an ongoing, open-ended process. However, according to Horkheimer, the best defense of this claim could be found not in Kant's metaphysically oriented practical philosophy, but rather in the Copernican, critical turn he initiated with his theoretical philosophy. For it was actually in his theoretical philosophy that Kant demonstrated that knowledge is always subjectively conditioned. Thus, Kant's theoretical philosophy was critical insofar as it insisted that genuine knowledge must always be aware of its own conditions, that is, it must always be self-reflexive. Kant's recognition of this active, subjective moment inherent in knowledge was the most advanced aspect of his philosophy. Not only did it point beyond the materialism of the eighteenth century – as Horkheimer pointed out, by reminding his students of Marx's first thesis on Feuerbach –[126] it also retained its relevance to the present day. Horkheimer writes:

Having said all of this, the question remains, why is Kant's philosophy still important in the present? ... The answer can be found by recalling the basic intention of Kant's philosophy, which he himself always considered its essential moment: the critique of knowledge. Kant's insight that the entire content of our knowledge always rests upon intellectual presuppositions, which are not simply extracted from the things themselves, but which instead make the particular natural worldview possible in the first place, that knowledge, in other words, is not an undistorted reflection of an objective world, but is instead a product of our reason and the experience delivered to us by our senses, this insight is certainly still relevant in the present.[127]

Yet Horkheimer's efforts to integrate this moment of self-reflexivity into his own critical theory of society would push him far beyond Kant's abstract transcendentalism. In *Dämmerung*, for example, Horkheimer examines how concrete individuals' knowledge is conditioned by social, historical, and psychological factors. *Dämmerung* – to which we will turn shortly – provides an excellent example of his efforts to reinterpret the "critical" moment in Kant's theoretical

---

[125] As will be discussed below.
[126] GS 9, pp. 479–80.
[127] GS 11, p. 207.

philosophy in a manner relevant for contemporary societies.[128] To sum up, Horkheimer's positive reinterpretation of Kant in the late 1920s did lead him to integrate certain key concepts from Kant's philosophy – the primacy of practical reason, the open-ended character of knowledge and its self-reflexivity – but even in regard to these concepts, Horkheimer always pushed beyond Kant's philosophy, which he still believed was motivated at the most basic level by his desire to rescue metaphysics.[129]

Horkheimer also integrated certain key aspects of Hegel's philosophy into his own thought in the late 1920s. Horkheimer viewed Hegel's critique of consciousness philosophy and his insistence that philosophy can only be understood historically not only as his most important contribution to German Idealism, but also as that aspect of his work that was most relevant to contemporary debates. Horkheimer was by no means the only theorist in the 1920s who was convinced that the dominant neo-Kantian and positivist paradigms were exhausted and that Hegel's philosophy could still point the way beyond them. Horkheimer was also careful, however, to distinguish his own interpretation and appropriation of Hegel from other theorists involved in the "Hegel Renaissance" in the 1920s. Horkheimer argued that the renewed interest in Hegel was driven by an open or concealed need for metaphysical foundations that neo-Kantianism and positivism had been unable to satisfy. The general move from Kant to Hegel in the 1920s was – as Horkheimer argued already in 1925 – from epistemology to metaphysics:

What makes Hegel appear today as a salvation from Kant ... is the circumstance that ... his thought contains a positive doctrine of metaphysics. Contemporary consciousness, which has worked its way through critical epistemology, remains unsatisfied and reaches out to Hegel.[130]

As we have seen, Horkheimer believed that the core of Hegel's metaphysics lied in his positing of an absolute identity between subject and object. Horkheimer recognized this tendency not only among attempts by conservatives such as

---

[128] Gunzelin Schmid Noerr also points this out. At this time, Horkheimer's interpretation of Kant was, according to him, "characterized by the combination of critical, transcendental epistemology with an analysis of the empirical (historical, social and psychological) conditions of knowledge." GS 11, p. 202.

[129] Although Olaf Asbach is correct to emphasize the importance of Horkheimer's materialist reappropriation of Kant's concept of practical reason during this time, he is mistaken to claim that it provided the context for, and played a more important role than, his interpretation of Marx. Although Horkheimer was indeed critical of the dominant, mechanical, and metaphysical interpretations of Marx at this time, as Asbach correctly points out, he did not, as Asbach suggests, confuse them with Marx's own writings, as little as he confused Kant with the interpretations of the neo-Kantians. See Asbach, op. cit., pp. 203–28 and 298–302. On the contrary, it was Horkheimer's interpretation of Marx that provided the context for his rereading of Kant, as his reference to Marx's First Feuerbach Thesis – quoted earlier – illustrates, and his more general understanding of the history of philosophy as a moment in the development of bourgeois society. Despite his appropriation of certain elements of Kant's philosophy at this time, he remained critical of the basic metaphysical tendency of Kant's work. For one example of Horkheimer's continued criticism of Kant see GS 9, p. 479.

[130] GS 11, p. 114.

Max Scheler to reappropriate Hegel at this time, but also among Marxists such as Georg Lukács. In an unpublished manuscript from this time, Horkheimer criticizes Lukács's neo-Hegelian interpretation of the proletariat as a mythical unity, as the "subject-object" of history:

Lukács as well ties the knowledge of the "totality" to a "subject-object," not, of course, the absolute spirit, but rather the "practical class consciousness of the proletariat." In other words, he too retains identity as the condition of the possibility of "truth" and, at the same time, posits this supra-individual unified entity as the bearer of knowledge and agent of history.[131]

Yet it was precisely this assumption of an absolute unity between subject and object that Horkheimer rejected as metaphysical. If one strongly affirmed, as Horkheimer did, that Hegel's entire system was held together and determined by this assumption, was there anything left in Hegel's philosophy that could still contribute to contemporary discussions?

Horkheimer answered this question affirmatively, primarily by contrasting his own "empirical" appropriation of Hegel to the dominant "metaphysical interpretations." If Kant's continuing relevance lay in his emphasis on the self-reflexivity of philosophy, Hegel's contemporary importance rested on his stress on its historical determinateness. According to Horkheimer, however, the strength of Hegel's historical interpretations rested on their firm grounding in and understanding of the empirical determinants of history, not abstractions such as "reason" or "absolute spirit" that were posited *ex post facto* as the true subjects of "world history." Horkheimer refers to Hegel as one of the "greatest researchers in the eighteenth and nineteenth centuries of history and society"[132] and as a "great empiricist, whose insights in historical, sociological and psychological matters anticipated in several places important results of the organized labors of an entire century and whose work could still point the way for research today."[133] He also quotes Hegel himself to highlight the importance of empirical research for his own work: "without the development of the experiential sciences in and of themselves, philosophy would not have been able to progress any further than it did in antiquity."[134] As we have seen, Horkheimer places the concept of bourgeois society, which plays such a crucial role in Hegel's own theory of modern society, at the center of his attempt in the late 1920s to develop a materialist history of modern philosophy. Hegel's insistence that modern philosophy must integrate empirical research from a

---

[131] Quoted by Gunzelin Schmid Noerr, GS 11, p. 223. Lukács himself would later confirm the correctness of Horkheimer's criticism of his concept of the proletariat as the "subject-object" of history. For example, in the preface to the new edition of *History and Class Consciousness* from 1967, he wrote: "Thus the proletariat seen as the identical subject-object of the real history of mankind is no materialist consummation that overcomes the constructions of idealism. It is rather an attempt to out-Hegel Hegel, it is an edifice boldly erected above every possible reality and thus attempts objectively to surpass the Master himself." Trans. Rodney Livingstone (Cambridge, MA, 2002), p. xxiii.

[132] GS 11, p. 299.

[133] Ibid., p. 296.

[134] Quoted by Horkheimer, Ibid., p. 306.

wide variety of disciplines served as an important methodological model for Horkheimer's efforts to develop a comprehensive critical theory of society.[135]

From a methodological standpoint, Horkheimer was also interested in Hegel's modern reformulation of the dialectic as well as his concept of totality. Here once again though, his appropriation of Hegel was more selective than that of Lukács or Herbert Marcuse, for example, who were also searching at this time for the origins of the Marx's dialectical method in Hegel's thought.[136] Although Horkheimer believed that both Hegel's dialectical method and his concept of totality were still necessary for contemporary critical theory, he was also aware of the potential of both to be abused and appropriated in a manner that defeated their original purpose. On the one hand, Horkheimer praises Hegel's dialectic in a lecture from 1926 as

a powerful method that finds and shows the way ... from the most ethereal heights of the seemingly most isolated intellectual realms to the most concrete forces of contemporary historical life; a method that discloses the historical origins of seemingly timeless essences and images of gods, and at the same time discovers within these entities themselves the real forces that lead to their passing away.[137]

On the other hand, Horkheimer emphatically denies that "history" or "reality" itself is governed by dialectical laws or that the dialectical method is a magic formula that can exist apart from empirical research and the conscientious formation of concepts. The same is true for the concept of totality. On the one hand, around 1930, Horkheimer says that "in response to the question of what the truth is, one can still say, with Hegel, the totality," but only with the important qualification that

this totality does not form a system, a unified order, a "cosmos," but is composed instead of the provisional ordering of phenomena and events in the most diverse fields, as it presents itself, for example, in our understanding of humans and animals, of society and nature, but also of the process of cognition and the logical structure of its content.[138]

Horkheimer is particularly careful to reject the concept of totality when applied to abstract universals, such as "thought," "being," or "history":

The *thinking* of different people may concur, but it cannot therefore be seen as independent, unified process ... It is also meaningless to speak of self-thinking *being*. Being [*Sein*] in this sense is not some sort of existing unity, but instead a mere reference to a multiplicity of entities [*Seiendem*].... The same is true for *history*, as for *thinking* and *being*. No essence or unified force exists which could bear the name history.... All these totalities, upon which the great totality of the "subject-object" is based, are all completely meaningless abstractions and by no means the soul of reality, as Hegel believed.[139]

---

[135] As will become apparent in more detail in our further investigations: see Chapter 8.

[136] See, for example, Marcuse's essay "On the Problem of the Dialectic," in *Herbert Marcuse: Heideggerian Marcuse*, eds. R. Wolin and J. Abromeit (University of Nebraska Press, 2005).

[137] GS 10, p. 165.

[138] GS 11, p. 227.

[139] GS 2, p. 301–2.

How and why, then, does Horkheimer propose to salvage Hegel's dialectical method and his concept of totality at all?

Although Horkheimer rejects the idea that dialectical laws govern the development of history or reality, or that abstract totalities of any type can exist apart from the empirical world, he does not fall back into a nominalist position. Horkheimer accepts Hegel's argument that "at base the dialectic always consists in relating a particular, and as such necessarily abstract judgment to the totality of the truth, in other words, in recognizing and thereby comprehending its one-sidedness." Yet what exactly is this totality, if not "thought," "being," or "history"? For Horkheimer at this time, it consisted in the totality of conscious and unconscious forces exercised upon concrete individuals under particular historical and social conditions. As Horkheimer put it in "Hegel and the Problem of Metaphysics:" "There is no such thing as 'thinking' in and of itself, but always only the determinate thinking of a determinate person, which is without doubt co-determined by the conditions of society as a whole."[140] Here and elsewhere, Hegel's concept of totality continues to play an important role in Horkheimer's thought, as the "conditions of society as a whole." However, as this quote also illustrates, and as Martin Jay has pointed out,[141] Horkheimer's interpretation of the dialectical method at this time does not reduce the individual to a mere function of the larger totality: The individual is "co-determined" not "determined" by the "conditions of society as a whole." So although Horkheimer praised Hegel – as we have seen – for moving beyond the general Enlightenment tendency to posit the individual as the *ultima ratio* of social and historical analysis, he also insisted that the reproduction of the social totality is always mediated by the needs, desires, and knowledge of concrete individuals, who cannot – *pace* Hegel – be reduced to the "cunning of reason" or the "becoming self-conscious of absolute spirit." Horkheimer also emphatically denies the possibility of determining abstractly, once and for all, the particular form that the dialectic between social totality and concrete individual should take. He continues:

Research does not permit any final decisions regarding an individual or holistic dynamic of historical events, as one could perhaps demand from a metaphysically oriented philosophy; instead, concrete analyses are always necessary in order to determine the relative influence of individual versus supra-individual factors.[142]

Horkheimer's denial of the possibility of establishing ahistorical laws in the field of social research, however, does not lead him to abandon the concept of law altogether. The overarching goal of the concrete analyses of critical theory remains the determination of historically bound and empirically grounded laws, which can anticipate, explain, and help guide the future development of the social totality, but which can also be refuted by new research or historical changes. Horkheimer viewed the Marxian concept of "tendency" as a good example of this methodological principle. He writes: "The aim of

---

[140] Ibid., p. 301.
[141] *Marxism and Totality*, op. cit., p. 211.
[142] GS 2, pp. 301–2.

empirical investigation of historical events is – just like research in the fields of non-human nature – description that is as accurate as possible and, in the final analysis, recognition of laws and tendencies."[143] Although Horkheimer attempted to realize some of these methodological principles already in the late 1920s, he did not have a chance to put them fully into practice until the early 1930s, after he had become the director of the Institute of Social Research.

The Emancipation of Philosophy from Science: The Development of Bourgeois Philosophy in the Late Nineteenth and Early Twentieth Centuries

Horkheimer presented his interpretation of the history of contemporary philosophy – that is, the period extending from the dissolution of German Idealism to the time he was writing – on two different occasions in the late 1920s. The first was a series of lectures he delivered at the University of Frankfurt during the summer semester of 1926.[144] The second was a lengthy manuscript entitled "On the Emancipation of Philosophy from Science" that he composed in 1928 but never published.[145] The manuscript is based largely on his lectures from two years before, but it also differs from them in significant respects. In the lectures, the continuing influence of his mentor Cornelius is still evident, particularly in Horkheimer's detailed examination of the origins of scientific psychology in the late nineteenth century. In the manuscript, Horkheimer focuses on the relationship between philosophy and the sciences more generally and makes no mention whatsoever of the origins of scientific psychology. In the lectures, in other words, Horkheimer was still deeply concerned with coming to terms with and moving beyond the traditions to which Cornelius was most indebted – scientific psychology in particular and the tradition of consciousness philosophy more generally – whereas in the manuscript, Horkheimer was more concerned with working out the relationship between philosophy and the sciences as a whole, which was a crucial methodological issue in his own efforts at that time to develop a critical theory of society. In what follows, I will focus primarily, if not exclusively, on the manuscript, because it represents a more mature formulation of Horkheimer's interpretation of the history of contemporary philosophy.

In his manuscript "On the Emancipation of Philosophy from Science," Horkheimer examines the development of contemporary philosophy from

---

[143] GS 2, p. 307. Horkheimer's belief in the possibility of determining social tendencies and "laws" in this way illustrates that he still believed that there was a significant overlap in the methodological principles of the natural and social sciences. In this respect, he also differed significantly from many of his contemporaries, such as Lukács and Heidegger, who followed Dilthey's lead in demanding a strict separation of the "human" and "natural" sciences. Horkheimer would change his position on this issue, at least to a certain degree, after his confrontation with logical empiricism and behaviorism in the mid-1930s. See the discussion in Chapter 8.

[144] These lectures have been published in their entirety. "Einführung in die Philosophie der Gegenwart," GS 10, pp. 169–333.

[145] The manuscript has been published in Horkheimer's *Collected Writings*: "Zur Emanzipation der Philosophie von der Wissenschaft," GS 10, pp. 334–419.

its precipitous decline in the 1850s to its dramatic renaissance in the 1920s. Horkheimer conceptualizes this development as a transformation, from one extreme to the other, of the relationship of philosophy to the sciences.[146] Following the disintegration of German Idealism in the *Vormärz* period, the positivist subordination of philosophy to the natural sciences, which had already been well established in England and France, established its unquestioned supremacy in Germany as well.[147] The birth of scientific psychology, which proposed to solve "spiritual" problems by applying the methods of the natural sciences to the study of the mind, was a striking example of the complete delegitimation of philosophy. Only slowly, in the work of Ernst Mach and neo-Kantians like Hermann Cohen, for example, did questions about the limitations of scientific method and the need to reflect upon them philosophically reemerge. Edmund Husserl's *Logical Investigations* (1900–1) represented a watershed insofar as he no longer believed that philosophy's role was merely to address the epistemological questions left unanswered by science, as had Mach and Cohen. He insisted that philosophy can and must be reestablished as a discipline completely independent from, and superior to, science; for only philosophy could, when based on the immutable foundations of pure logic, make absolute claims to truth. Finally, with the emergence and rapid popularization of *Lebensphilosophie* around the turn of the century, the opposite extreme had been reached, according to Horkheimer. In the work of Henri Bergson, for example, science was no longer even granted an auxiliary status in obtaining the truth, as was still the case with Husserl. Scientific reason and rational concepts were seen as shackles to be thrown off in the quest for authentic experience and pure intuition.

Horkheimer's interpretation of the history of contemporary philosophy was not, however, simply a narrative about the dramatic shift in the relationship between science and philosophy. It also represents a continuation of the methods and themes he had pursued in his other lectures and essays during this time: the attempt to develop a materialist history of philosophy that focused on the transformation of bourgeois society. As was the case in his portrayal of early modern philosophy, Horkheimer devotes himself primarily to presenting the work of the theorists he analyzes in a nuanced way, while at the same time suggesting how their ideas are indicative of more general social developments. He argues that the rise of positivism cannot be separated from the parallel consolidation of bourgeois hegemony on the Continent in the nineteenth century.[148] In contrast to the eighteenth century in France or the early nineteenth century in Germany, when the bourgeoisie was still in the process of overthrowing the dominant feudal and absolutist institutions, after

---

[146] With "sciences," I am translating Horkheimer's concept of *Einzelwissenschaften*, by which he means both the natural and the social sciences. The German term *Wissenschaft* is not restricted to the natural sciences, as is the English "science"; it includes psychology, sociology, as well as *Literatur* or *Theaterwissenschaft* not just physics, chemistry, biology, etc.

[147] As Horkheimer put it, "In other countries the expression 'German metaphysics' had become a term of derision that referred to unclear, vain and useless intellectual endeavors, and even in Germany itself most were inclined to accept this formula." GS 10, p. 170.

[148] GS 10, pp. 317–8.

the revolutions of 1848, the continental bourgeoisie took a decidedly conservative turn, which manifested itself philosophically in two main ways, according
to Horkheimer. First, it abandoned of the universal regulative ideals that had
guided it during its heroic phase. The positivist attack on metaphysics was
directed not only against religious concepts such as God or the eternal soul, but
against transcendent ideals of any type, even progressive ones such as universal rights, human dignity or a just society. Second, it entailed a corresponding
loss of self-reflexivity. The Copernican, critical turn in philosophy initiated and
developed in German Idealism, which thematized the subjective conditions of
knowledge, was also eliminated by the positivists. The positivists believed they
could dispense with abstract universals and self-reflexivity because they were
convinced that scientific rationality and its concrete application would lead not
only to ever-increasing control of nature, but also to constant improvement
of the conditions of human life. They believed, as one of the early defenders
of modern positivism, Saint-Simon, put it, "the state of affairs which is most
favorable to industry is ... the most favorable to society," and that, therefore,
science should be primarily the "science of production."[149] When it became
increasingly apparent that bourgeois society would not automatically realize
this promise of creating a more just and humane society – that the interests of
large industry and its bourgeois proprietors might not be identical with the
interests of society as a whole – philosophy was called on to justify the aims
of science. Horkheimer also shows how, at a later stage, when disillusionment
with social developments and positivist promises of progress increased even
more, repressed metaphysics returned with a vengeance, dovetailing with the
irrationalist currents of *Lebensphilosophie*. In what can certainly be seen as an
anticipation of one of the central arguments from *Dialectic of Enlightenment*,
Horkheimer demonstrates how the positivist hypostatization of a truncated
version of Enlightenment reason terminated in the recrudescence of metaphysics
and myth.

Before turning to a closer examination of Horkheimer's interpretation of
late-nineteenth- and early-twentieth-century philosophy, it is also important
to note what he chose to exclude from this narrative and his reasons for doing
so. As we saw at the end of our examination of Horkheimer's interpretation
of German Idealism, he argued that the critical impulses from the French
Enlightenment, German Idealism, and the young Hegelians – whom he referred
to as the "philosophy of the belated Enlightenment in Germany"[150] – were not
preserved in the further development of philosophy in the nineteenth century.
As he put it, they were "not advanced historically by pure philosophy, but were
instead taken up by movements, whose portrayal goes beyond the scope of our
concerns here."[151] Horkheimer is, of course, referring to the development of
Marxism and the European workers' movement, which played a crucial role

---

[149] Quoted by Herbert Marcuse in *Reason and Revolution*, p. 330. For an overview of Simon-
Simon and the origins of positivism more generally, see *Reason and Revolution*, pp. 323–74.

[150] GS 2, p. 154. Horkheimer refers, in particular, to Bruno and Edgar Bauer, David Friedrich
Strauss and Ludwig Feuerbach.

[151] GS 10, p. 165.

in his thought at this time, even though he did not treat either topic in any great length in his lectures or published writings from this period. If one examines his unpublished writings from this period – which we will do in the next chapter – the theoretical importance of Marx for Horkheimer becomes much clearer. However, as was the case both earlier and later in his life, Horkheimer approached his exoteric, published pronouncements differently than his private, unpublished reflections. To be sure, during this period the distance between the two did diminish compared to the straightforward academic style of his dissertation and *Habilitationsschrift*. In his lectures and published essays in the late 1920s, Horkheimer was, after all, attempting to develop a materialist interpretation of the history of philosophy. Nonetheless, this attempt remained tentative and incomplete. The lectures, in particular, remained largely within the academic parameters set for the time. He always provided his students with rich and nuanced presentations of philosophical ideas, while his remarks on the ways in which these ideas where socially and historically mediated often remained more suggestive in character. In any case, Horkheimer clearly took his duties as a university lecturer in philosophy extremely seriously, and could not be accused of presenting ideas to his students in a tendentious manner. In his unpublished writings, on the other hand, Horkheimer continued to analyze and express the matters that were most dear to him with the same passion and intellectual independence that characterized his early novellas or his first encounter with Hans Cornelius.

In his lectures and the manuscript on contemporary philosophy, however, Horkheimer focused on the development of the dominant currents of "pure" philosophy in the late nineteenth and early twentieth century. He began his account with a discussion of positivism, using metaphysical materialism, scientific psychology, and Ernst Mach's empiriocriticism as his examples. The metaphysical materialism of Ludwig Büchner, Karl Vogt, and Jacob Moleschott – which completely rejected philosophy and psychology, and dogmatically insisted upon the absolute materiality of everything and the ability of the natural sciences to solve all human problems – represents the positivism in its most reductionist form for Horkheimer. Anticipating his more detailed discussions of materialism in the early 1930s, Horkheimer is very careful here to distinguish the metaphysical materialism of the mid-nineteenth century from its philosophical predecessors, which had a qualitatively different social function. He writes:

This materialism, which has its intellectual origins in the dissolution of the Hegelian School, is completely unworthy of its ancestors in the French and English Enlightenment and in classical antiquity, primarily for the reason that it was no longer permissible, after the appearance of Hegel's dialectical idealism and at the level of knowledge attained at that time, to understand material reality simply as reality in the sense of the physical and natural sciences.... Thus one can say that philosophical ideas that were relevant and served an important purpose in the writings of a La Mettrie or Cabanis, displayed an impoverished and reactionary character in the language of someone like Vogt.[152]

---

[152] Ibid., p. 195.

Horkheimer explains the social function of metaphysical materialism on the Continent in the mid-nineteenth century in the following way:

> The tendentious defense of all forms of science that could potentially benefit industry and the attempt to raise the general level of education to a point that would enable active participation in this seemingly absolute process of rapid growth, these were the underlying causes of the popularity of the materialism of Vogt, Büchner and Moleschott, particularly among young people.[153]

The first important breakthrough beyond the monolithic worldview of metaphysical materialism occurred in 1872, according to Horkheimer, with the famous paper "On the Limits of the Knowledge of Nature" that Emil Du Bois-Reymond delivered at an important scientific congress in Leipzig. Du Bois-Reymond argued that human consciousness could not be explained solely in terms of physical or physiological processes in the brain. With this argument, Du Bois-Reymond opened the door for the subsequent development of scientific psychology which, however, remained largely beholden to the prevailing positivist paradigm. Although the new science no longer subscribed to a monism of matter, it remained positivist methodologically. It bridged the Cartesian gap between mind and matter, which du Bois-Reymond had just reopened, by applying the methods of the natural sciences to *res cogitans*: Through observation and experiment it sought to discern the laws that governed both the operations of mental life and its relations to the physical world.

Like his contemporaries in the new field of scientific psychology, Ernst Mach recognized the limits of metaphysical materialism. However, he also believed that they could be overcome using natural scientific methods. Horkheimer describes the basic assumptions of scientific psychology in the following way:

> Whereas physics investigates ... the regularities of physical objects, psychology is left with the investigation of the laws governing all the elements that make up our conscious life, in other words, all the facts that we normally call appearances of consciousness [*Bewusstseinserscheinungen*].[154]

Although Mach was concerned with a different basic problem than the psychologists – he was interested in securing the epistemological foundations of natural science, not explaining consciousness – he came to very similar conclusions. He too insisted that science is always ultimately based on describing and ordering the sense impressions that register in our consciousness. In contrast to the psychologists, Mach did not feel obligated to specify whether the origins of these impressions were psychic or physical; this question was ultimately meaningless for him, insofar as he considered sense impressions the epistemological foundation of all knowledge.[155] Mach's rejection of anything that transcends immediate sense impressions as "metaphysical" places him squarely in the "tradition of English positivism," as Horkheimer notes.[156] As was the case with Hume's philosophy, Mach's empiriocriticism was also based on "the deduction

---

[153] Ibid., pp. 194–5.
[154] Ibid., p. 193.
[155] Ibid., p. 260 and 258, respectively.
[156] Ibid., p. 258.

of science from anonymous regularities of experience," and also represented "the most extreme secularization and disenchantment of the world."[157] For Horkheimer, the appearance of Mach's empiriocriticism also signaled that the social relations that had already been established in England a century earlier had now been attained on the Continent as well. Just as Hume's philosophy expressed the quintessential bourgeois belief that the laws that governed its particular form of society were natural and eternal, Mach's philosophy was, according to Horkheimer, "The expression of a societal situation, in which the natural sciences still appear to lead directly to the general, unbroken progress of humanity. They do not need to be 'logically' justified, for they depend primarily upon 'practical' justification in reality."[158] In other words, even though Mach had taken a step beyond the crude positivism of the metaphysical materialists, by explicitly addressing epistemological problems, he did so purely from the standpoint of his own scientific research, not yet from a separate philosophical standpoint. Thus, his justification of science was still, as Horkheimer put it, "practical" and not yet "logical."

In his lectures and manuscript on contemporary philosophy, Horkheimer devoted so much time to Mach not only because he was such an important representative of positivism in Europe at the time, but also because he had decisively influenced Horkheimer's own mentor, Hans Cornelius.[159] As we have seen, Cornelius accepted Mach's central argument that sense impressions were the basis of all theoretical inquiry, even though his reception of Gestalt psychology made him more sensitive to the subjective determinants of perception. The differences in his treatment of Mach in his 1926 lectures and his manuscript from 1928 reflect Horkheimer's shifting relationship to Cornelius and to the positivist tradition in general. Although Horkheimer expresses some reservations about Mach in his lectures,[160] he treats him in a generally favorable way. He praises Mach as a "great thinker" who made "important contributions to philosophy and psychology" and who worked out problems in the English positivist tradition with "remarkable rigor and clarity."[161] He also discussed the important continuities between Mach and Cornelius. In the manuscript, on the other hand, Horkheimer is generally critical of Mach and says nothing about Cornelius. He criticizes Mach not only for his dismissal of universals, but also for the loss of self-reflexivity that resulted from his characteristically positivist faith in power of the natural sciences.[162] Horkheimer's criticisms of Mach and his insistence on the importance of philosophy for critical theory – in the form of universals like "the good of the whole" or "humanity," or his insistence that science loses its self-reflexivity when separated from a theory of the laws governing the social totality in which it is conducted – demonstrate clearly that Horkheimer's position at this time was not nearly as "positivist"

[157] GS 9, p. 457.

[158] GS 10, p. 350.

[159] At this time, Horkheimer was also interested in Lenin's critique of empiriocriticism, as we shall see in Chapter 4.

[160] He rejects Mach's complete liquidation of the ego, for example. See GS 10, p. 263.

[161] Ibid., pp. 257, 258, and 264.

[162] Ibid., pp. 350–1.

as several commentators have claimed.[163] For within Horkheimer's larger narrative of the history of contemporary philosophy, positivism represented an abstract negation of philosophy, a negation that Horkheimer rejected just as emphatically as the abstract negation of science by *Lebensphilosophie*, which we will examine shortly. Even within the positivist context, Horkheimer interprets Mach's epistemological reflections upon the foundations of science as the first tentative step beyond the vulgar positivism of the metaphysical materialists, and the beginning of a trend toward the rehabilitation of philosophy that would continue with neo-Kantianism and phenomenology.

Although Horkheimer discusses several different representatives of neo-Kantianism in his lectures, including members of the so-called Southwest or Baden school such as Wilhelm Windelband and Heinrich Rickert, in the manuscript his analysis of neo-Kantianism is based on the work of the central figure of the so-called Marburg school, Hermann Cohen.[164] Within Horkheimer's larger narrative in the manuscript, neo-Kantianism represents a step beyond empiriocriticism insofar as Cohen attempted to secure the epistemological foundations of the natural sciences, not through the use of its own methods, as Mach had done, but rather through recourse to philosophy, and in particular, to Kant's theoretical philosophy. In the *Critique of Pure Reason*, Kant too had attempted to establish the epistemological foundations of the modern mathematical-mechanical sciences by posing the famous question of how synthetic a priori judgments are possible. So when similar problems arose in a different historical context, it was not surprising that Cohen and many others of his generation returned to Kant to see if his solutions were still viable. However, as Horkheimer attempts to demonstrate, the changed socio-historical conditions manifested themselves clearly in the rather selective interpretation of Kant by Cohen and other neo-Kantians. Whereas Kant was deeply concerned with the threats posed to human freedom and dignity, as well as to metaphysical notions such as God and the immortal soul, by the new mathematical-mechanical worldview and the philosophical skepticism it had spawned, the neo-Kantians were, according to Horkheimer, responding to an increasingly widespread delegitimation of the sciences in the late nineteenth century, which resulted from their apparent inability to fulfill the liberal promise of prosperity for all. Horkheimer writes:

Insofar as the general belief disappeared that the natural sciences and technology were a direct guarantee for general happiness ... reflection upon their constitution and

---

[163] See Michiel Korthals, "Die kritische Gesellschaftstheorie des frühen Horkheimer: Missverständnisse über das Verhältnis von Horkheimer, Lukács und dem Positivismus," op. cit. Korthals is correct to emphasize Horkheimer's differences from Lukács, but his portrayal of Horkheimer's reception of Hegel is too one-sided. Although Horkheimer criticized Hegel's identity theory as metaphysical, he clung to certain version of Hegel's concept of totality, a modified materialist concept of the *social* totality influenced by his reception of Marx. It is no coincidence that Horkheimer uses precisely this concept to criticize Mach at this time. For other equally unconvincing attempts to portray Horkheimer as a positivist during this time see Hauke Brunkhorst, "Dialektischer Positivismus des Glücks," *Zeitschrift für philosophische Forschung*, vol. 39, no. 3 (1985), pp. 353–81 and Hans-Joachim Dahms, *Positivismusstreit* (Frankfurt, 1994).

[164] For Horkheimer's critical discussion of the Southwest School of neo-Kantianism, see GS 10 pp. 241–57.

purpose – if only at first merely in the form of an apologetic justification – gained increasing social recognition.[165]

Furthermore, whereas Kant's theoretical philosophy was only the first part of a larger project, which ultimately subordinated the natural sciences to the primacy of practical reason and the transcendent regulative ideals that guide it, Cohen made no systematic effort to address the factors that lie beyond theoretical reason. His attempt to work out a purely *logical* foundation for the natural sciences – in contrast to Mach's *practical* epistemological reflections – eliminated the central contradictions in Kant's philosophy by hypostatizing the spontaneity of understanding and the categories of transcendental subjectivity. In terms that echo his original philosophical mentor, Arthur Schopenhauer, who interpreted Kant's noumenal thing-in-itself as an expression of irrational will, Horkheimer says:

Cohen and his school carried out the unification of Kantian philosophy through the theoretical negation of an irrational factor of cognition [*Erkenntnis*] that was simply given and had to be accepted as such; in so doing they also negated the existence of any and all forms of transcendent reality.... It belongs to the very core of the neo-Kantian doctrine that there is no room in philosophy for Kant's dualisms.... There is no receptivity in science.[166]

Thus, it is not surprising that Horkheimer stresses the similarities between Cohen's philosophy and that of Fichte, who also sought to overcome Kant's dualisms with a purely consistent theory of subjective reason.[167]

In contrast to the arguments in his dissertation and *Habilitationsschrift*, Horkheimer now stressed the differences between Kant and the neo-Kantians' interpretation of him, arguing that the dualisms in Kant's system were not simply logical inconsistencies, but a testimony to the depth of his insight and his intellectual probity. As Horkheimer put it:

For all his trust in the power of subjectivity, in the productive force of transcendental consciousness, Kant never abandoned his belief in the difference between actual being and finite knowledge. This insight is no longer present in the neo-Kantian system.[168]

The neo-Kantians' abandonment of Kant's insistence upon the finitude and non-identity of scientific knowledge has several important consequences, according to Horkheimer. First, it reproduces the positivist loss of self-reflexivity, albeit at a higher level. For even though Cohen recognizes the necessity of philosophy, he limits its task to providing a logically consistent explanation of the epistemological foundations of science. In this way, he not only reproduces the positivist subordination of philosophy to the natural sciences, he also makes it impossible for science to reflect upon the external factors that influence its development. In other words, by liquidating the empirical moment in Kant's philosophy, Cohen also eliminated one of the most important redeeming qualities of the empiricist tradition out of which positivism emerged, namely its

[165] GS 10, p. 354.
[166] Ibid., pp. 363–4.
[167] Ibid., pp. 363, 372–3.
[168] Ibid., p. 364.

orientation to the external world.[169] Thus, even though Cohen wanted to place philosophy in the service of the natural sciences, he began the baleful process of separating philosophy entirely from the empirical sciences, which would continue with Husserl and *Lebensphilosophie*.

In his discussion of phenomenology, Horkheimer addresses both Husserl and Max Scheler, although he focuses primarily on the pathbreaking work Husserl published at the turn of the century, the *Logical Investigations*.[170] In that work, Husserl made the first sustained and widely acknowledged attempt to emancipate philosophy from the natural sciences and to reestablish it as an autonomous discipline. He argued that all forms of positivism, including psychology and other natural and social sciences, were relativistic insofar as their findings were always ultimately based on empirical evidence. Philosophy, on the other hand, could make justified claims to absolute truth insofar as it is based on the immutable foundation of pure logic. Thus, the most important problem facing contemporary philosophy, according to Husserl, was to determine more precisely just what those logical foundations are. In the *Logical Investigations*, Husserl attempted – self-consciously in the rationalist tradition of Plato, Descartes, and Leibniz – to lay the foundations for the solution to this problem. Horkheimer notes that Husserl's definition of the basic problem that phenomenology must address represents a qualitatively new relationship between philosophy and the sciences:

It is precisely the opposite of what epistemological positivism had believed: logic cannot be grounded in any form of empirical science.... Not only the empirical sciences find themselves in a relation of dependence vis-à-vis logic, but also all forms of exact, rigorous science.[171]

Yet Horkheimer believed that Husserl's attempt in his *Logical Investigations* to reestablish the logical foundations of philosophy deductively was beset with many of the same problems that had riddled his rationalist predecessors. Whereas the positivists had relied too exclusively on sense impressions, Husserl was too quick to sever philosophy from empirical considerations in general and the sciences in particular. The consequences that followed from this undialectical separation were practically the same for Husserl as they had been for Cohen. Phenomenology was no longer able to reflect upon on the historical, social, and psychological conditions of knowledge. For Husserl, knowledge is no longer the "finite insights of finite beings," but rather an "absolutely independent discipline ... which is completely self-sufficient," a "formal ontology

---

[169] Ibid., pp. 374–5.

[170] Horkheimer addresses Heidegger's philosophy only briefly, in two different footnotes in the manuscript. Although the manuscript was written only a year after *Being and Time* was published in 1927, Horkheimer's brief, critical remarks testify to a solid understanding of the text. He writes, for example: "In this ontology there is a lot of talk about history, but in truth only to demonstrate that Dasein does not 'stand in history,' but that all historicity comes from Dasein itself. Here as well the philosophical attempt is made to articulate once and for all the structure of genuine being. Even though this genuine being is understood as 'temporal,' its description presents itself as supra-temporal, as genuine ontology" GS 10, pp. 396–7.

[171] Ibid., pp. 306–7.

in the strict sense of the word," which is "independent of the knowledge of any real subjects."[172] However, throughout his history of modern philosophy, Horkheimer was always extremely skeptical of claims to absolute truth. Also, in Husserl's case, he endeavored to show how these claims had their origin not in some ahistorical, ideal realm, but in the concrete needs of real individuals living in specific social relations and historical conditions.

Horkheimer argues that Husserl's subordination of science to philosophy is a mediated expression of a more widespread decline in the positivist faith in science. Despite continuing progress in the sciences, social contradictions had not decreased, as the economic crises of 1873 and 1891, the continuing growth of the workers' movement, and the nationalist and imperialist economic competition that would eventually lead to World War I all made clear. Yet if science could not solve human problems, what could? During this time, the timeless truths of metaphysics became more appealing to many who had lost their faith in science in the face of the volatile dynamics and undiminished contradictions of capitalist society. Although it was not his intention, Husserl contributed to the widespread rehabilitation of formerly discredited metaphysics at the beginning of the twentieth century. Husserl did insist with great emphasis, even pathos, that phenomenology could provide answers to what was increasingly perceived as a crisis situation, but only if it remained a rigorous science – not in the narrow sense of the natural sciences, but in the sense of theory, in the strictest sense of the word.[173] So even if Husserl himself was opposed to returning to metaphysics, his attempt to reestablish timeless theoretical truths lent itself easily to metaphysical interpretations, as the ensuing popularization of phenomenology would make clear.[174] Horkheimer's rich description of this dynamic and the social context in which it occurred is worth quoting at length:

The task of the [phenomenologically oriented] philosopher is always to intuit the pure meaning of essences, completely independent of factual explanations; his task is to investigate being completely independently from becoming … Precisely for this reason he is able to rehabilitate … all the religious and metaphysical conceptions that had been declining steadily since the Enlightenment…. The cultural situation in the period immediately preceding the war could be characterized in the following way: the dismal material situation of the greater part of humanity in the most developed countries was combined with a paucity of ideas that could have rationalized this dismal material situation. To the same degree to which the ideology of progress from the mid-nineteenth century had disappeared, the medium of this ideology, namely the natural sciences, had disenchanted the world. Thus this last, paltry remainder of a unifying belief relating to the future improvement of the most basic material conditions was also in the process of disappearing…. After the war this situation was by no means any better; instead, the material exigency, combined with the absence of any general, binding norms or a satisfying worldview, had actually become even worse. Now one should consider that this was a philosophy that claimed to inaugurate an absolute and universally valid science … of the absolute reality, which earlier epochs believed they had captured in

---

[172] Ibid., p. 358, 306, 313, and 312, respectively.
[173] Husserl spoke openly of a "spiritual [*geistig*] crisis of our time … the most radical *life crisis* we are suffering." Quoted by Horkheimer, Ibid., p. 377.
[174] Ibid., p. 316.

their religions, which had been declared dead by the natural sciences and which Bergson had reintroduced merely through intuition and as life, and, in any case, in an unscientific manner. Thus the demonstration of the possibility of a reality that does not consist of the facts of natural reality, but instead atemporal, unconditional being, marks the essential beginning of phenomenological philosophy.[175]

This formulation from one of Horkheimer's lectures in 1926 describes not only the structural affinities between phenomenology and metaphysics, it also provides insight into the social, historical, and psychological factors determining the larger process of the dialectic of Enlightenment that was already at the center of Horkheimer's interpretation of contemporary philosophy. When the truncated version of Enlightenment reason preserved in the positivist tradition proved helpless in the face of continuing social contradictions, the conditions became ripe for a radical negation of what was perceived as Enlightenment reason. For Horkheimer at this time, *Lebensphilosophie* represented the next step, beyond phenomenology, in this dialectic.

As was the case with phenomenology, Horkheimer discusses several different representatives of *Lebensphilosophie*, and he is careful to distinguish between the theoretical articulations and the popularizations of the doctrine. Horkheimer does address Wilhelm Dilthey and Georg Simmel, but in the end he chooses to focus on Henri Bergson, because the latter best exemplified the shifting relationship between science and philosophy that interested him.[176] Husserl had subordinated science to philosophy, but he still considered philosophy to be a logically rigorous and strictly theoretical undertaking. Bergson, in contrast, rejected all forms of conceptual knowledge as inadequate for the purpose of understanding reality. For Bergson, all forms of conceptual knowledge, including science, do not reveal to us the way things are "in themselves," but are instead useful devices for manipulating reality, particularly "lesser" forms of reality, such as nature or inert matter. Bergson argues that reality in its highest and most authentic form is the unceasingly active, inexhaustible creative will of life.[177] The further one distances oneself from this *élan vital* – as one must when one applies the reifying concepts of the natural sciences – the less relevant one's findings become as a form of knowledge. If one hopes to access life directly, rather than disfigure it with rational concepts, one must rely on *intuition*. For Bergson this means, first and foremost, turning inward and becoming aware of the creative will in ourselves: the never ending activity that registers in our consciousness as *durée* – a flow of constantly new and qualitatively different

---

[175] Ibid., p. 301–2.

[176] For Horkheimer's brief treatment of Simmel and Dilthey, see GS 10, pp. 287–99. Horkheimer also makes explicit his reasons for not discussing the other obvious representative of *Lebensphilosophie*, Friedrich Nietzsche: "We won't discuss Friedrich Nietzsche here, because I do not presume to say something about him simply in passing, since it would necessarily be distorted, indeed misleading." Ibid., p. 183.

[177] The similarity of Bergson's argument to the philosophy of Schopenhauer did not escape Horkheimer. He is, however, quick to come to Schopenhauer's defense. He argues that for Schopenhauer the irrationality of the will was something negative, which unfortunately could never be overcome, whereas for Bergson it was something positive. GS 10, p. 277.

elements. *Durée* represents the most authentic form of human experience for Bergson, and it can be accessed only through intuition, and never through conceptual knowledge, let alone science. Horkheimer summarizes the significance of Bergson's position within the larger trajectory of contemporary philosophy in the following way:

> Scientific knowledge, understood in the traditional theoretical sense, was given a philosophical foundation by neo-Kantianism, demoted to the position of a subordinate and particular type of knowledge by phenomenology, and completely rejected as a means of finding truth in the vitalistic philosophy of Bergson.[178]

Despite his grave criticisms of the irrationalist tendencies in Bergson's philosophy, Horkheimer also praises him for making important contributions in certain areas. He viewed Bergson's rejection of the application of the mechanical methods of the natural sciences to the human psyche, for example, as an important step beyond the scientific psychology of the nineteenth century. Bergson's critique of science also pointed to the necessity of not separating conceptual knowledge from the social and historical contexts in which it is produced.[179] As was the case with Husserl and phenomenology, Horkheimer was ultimately more concerned about the popularizations of Bergson and *Lebensphilosophie* and the fateful social dynamic that they obscured and thereby reinforced, than with the philosophical doctrines themselves, which contained moments of truth.

As an example of the worst sort of popularizations of *Lebensphilosophie*, Horkheimer discusses Oswald Spengler's *Decline of the West*. Horkheimer dismisses Spengler's study – which enjoyed wide popularity in Germany in the 1920s, especially among culturally conservative circles – as an eclectic and superficial synthesis of poorly understood material from a wide variety of fields. He is particularly vehement in his rejection of Spengler's facile comparison of the development of human culture with that of plants. For Horkheimer, there is no comparison between genuine *Lebensphilosophie* and popularizers like Spengler:

> Whereas Bergson and, to a much greater degree, Simmel were very much aware of the internal difficulties associated with *Lebensphilosophie* in all its forms, insofar as it calls the absolute validity of thought and science into question, without, however, diminishing the emphatic claim to truth for its own arguments – whereas, in other words, these ... thinkers take this logical problem squarely upon themselves, Spengler blithely and pathetically presents his sweeping views about the relativity and transience of all types of science, indeed, of culture in general, while at the same time drawing on every page upon claims that he has appropriated – without, of course, investigating them himself – from this same science.[180]

---

[178] GS 10, p. 400–1.

[179] On this point, Horkheimer compares Bergson to Hegel, but argues that Hegel's insight into this problem was superior insofar as he preserved it as a moment in a larger process of self-reflexivity, and did not absolutize it, as did Bergson. GS 10, p. 418. Horkheimer would develop this critique of Bergson in the mid-1930s. See the discussion in Chapter 8.

[180] GS 10, pp. 295–6.

In other words, *Decline of the West* provided simple and spurious explanations for very real problems. Herein lies both its popularity and its ideological character, according to Horkheimer:

Spengler's efforts are a perfect example of the numerous attempts in the present, now that all stable values are wavering, to provide a convenient replacement or an easy escape. What Simmel referred to as the crisis of the present, namely the transformation of cultural forms, is reduced to a source of increased book sales and ever new quasi-philosophical products addressing the problems of the day.[181]

Yet Spengler and other popularizers of *Lebensphilosophie* were not the only ones providing chimerical answers to genuine problems.

Horkheimer also accuses Husserl's students of reducing phenomenology to a false panacea for the contemporary cultural crisis. He focuses on Max Scheler in particular, whose work – in contrast to that of Spengler – he still takes seriously philosophically, while at the same identifying the mystifying elements in it that were unreflectively adopted among the much broader phenomenological movement. Horkheimer points, for example, to Scheler's appropriation of Husserl's concept of the intuition of essences [*Wesensschau*]. Whereas for Husserl, *Wesenschau* could provide access to essences only insofar as they existed *logically*, Scheler claimed it could unlock the *metaphysical* essences of objects, to their being as such. In this way, as Horkheimer put it, "Phenomenology came increasingly to resemble a characterization made of it by Max Scheler in one of his recent works: the renewal of an intuitive Platonism."[182] Scheler believed, at this time, that the *Wesenschau* might even provide the key to liberating Western civilization from the stifling iron cage into which it had haplessly maneuvered itself. Displaying once again his penchant for Platonic metaphors, Scheler describes the reenchantment of the world, which could be brought about by phenomenology as he understands it, in the following way:

It will be like the first step into a garden in full bloom of someone who has been living in a dark prison for many years. And this prison will be our milieu, which has been restricted by an understanding directed merely toward the mechanical and mechanizable [*Mechanisierbare*], with its "civilization." And this garden will be the colorful world of God, which we will see – if only in the distance – opening itself up and greeting us warmly. And this prisoner will be the European man of today and yesterday, who enters sighing and groaning under the burden of his own mechanisms and who, with nothing but the earth in view and with heaviness in his limbs, has forgotten his God and his world.[183]

However, this tantalizing reenchantment of the world could not be brought about by just anyone; politically and pedagogically, Scheler adhered to a Platonic model as well. As he puts it, "From a sociological point of view, metaphysics is … among the other forms of knowledge, the one reserved for a *spiritual* elite."[184] As Horkheimer points out, Scheler was like the late Schelling

[181] Ibid., pp. 296–7.
[182] Ibid., p. 326.
[183] Quoted by Horkheimer, GS 10, p. 324.
[184] Quoted by Horkheimer, Ibid., p. 329.

in this regard. Essence perception and intuition were not something that could be learned discursively or disputed rationally. One is either born with a sense for it or not.

The attempt to rehabilitate metaphysics, which spread quickly from Scheler and other students of Husserl to the influential phenomenological movement as a whole, and the rejection of conceptual knowledge in favor of intuition, which characterized the popularized versions of both phenomenology and *Lebensphilosophie*, were part of a much larger cultural current in Europe during the first decades of twentieth century. Horkheimer characterizes this current in the following way:

At this point phenomenology merges with the widespread contemporary trend toward a new romanticism which has as its motto, to genuine reality, to the concrete and primordial, away from decadent, Western European, intellectualized man, and which is fascinated with primitive cultures, foreign cultures in general, classical antiquity and the Middle Ages.[185]

Not surprisingly, another defining characteristic of this current was its rejection of the Enlightenment.[186] In fact, many of its adherents viewed the Enlightenment, which had mounted the first concerted attack on metaphysics and rejected appeals to legitimacy based on authority or intuition, as the source of their problem. Horkheimer was deeply concerned about this widespread sentiment and he took it very seriously, as our examination of his interpretation of the history of modern philosophy has demonstrated.[187] Horkheimer devoted an inordinate amount of time to the Enlightenment in his lectures on modern philosophy, for he believed that "an acceptable presentation of this philosophy does not exist,"[188] and thus many myths had to be dispelled and many prejudices overcome. Furthermore, his interpretation of the history of contemporary philosophy was structured largely as a dialectic of Enlightenment that played itself out in the nineteenth and early twentieth centuries. The dialectic began with the collapse of the original, ethically driven Enlightenment project into a monolithic scientific worldview whose nihilistic implications soon became apparent.[189] The dialectic continued as a backlash against this disenchantment of the world, as a sweeping return of all that positivism had repressed. The increasingly irrational forms in which this backlash against positivism manifested itself deeply troubled Horkheimer, as did its rejection of the legacy of the Enlightenment *tout court*. For Horkheimer was convinced that the only way

[185] Ibid., p. 331.
[186] Horkheimer notes, for example, "In the last decades in Germany one has become accustomed to seeing the two words, Enlightenment and superficiality, as belonging together, even as meaning the same thing." GS 11, p. 205.
[187] Horkheimer's palpable concern for the potential of neo-Romanticism to be abused politically comes through clearly in the following passage from the end of his lectures in 1926: "Wherever the absolutization and hypostatization of expressions like 'race,' 'culture,' 'spirit of the people,' and other such things is supposed to lead beyond relativity and reveal true meaning ... there one can find the project of violently, impermissibly and prematurely – perhaps also with radically misguided intentions – seeking stability." GS 10, p. 332.
[188] GS 9, p. 346.
[189] GS 10, pp. 319–20.

beyond the contemporary crisis was through discriminating reappropriation of the Enlightenment legacy.

Horkheimer's interpretation of contemporary philosophy in terms of the shifting relationship between science and philosophy was part of his attempt to determine how such a reappropriation of the Enlightenment legacy could be possible. Horkheimer too was convinced that the traditional model of science was in crisis, but he was not prepared to abandon science altogether. As he put it:

> In response to the question of where, in my opinion, those elements are to be found that point beyond the present situation, I would say first, wherever intellectual inquiry is pursued in an upright and rigorous manner.... In contrast to most all of the previously mentioned philosophers, I still believe that scientific understanding and its labors will contribute more to moving beyond the current intellectual situation than those schools of thought that believe we should do without it. I do not, of course, think that traditional natural science or even a psychology from the last century can guide us today. But there is a modern physics, there are new and relevant psychological theories, there is sociology and related pursuits, all of which only need to be liberated from superstition and from an absolutizing and hubristic self-importance.[190]

At this time, Horkheimer was still laying the methodological foundations of his own critical theory of society – he would present them for the first time in his inaugural address as director of the Institute for Social Research in 1931. However, his examination of the *history* of the relationship between science and philosophy in contemporary philosophy was a crucial step along the way. It convinced him that the relationship between scientific "correctness" and philosophical "truth" had to be rethought in a manner that did not entail simply subordinating one to the other or separating them entirely. He writes:

> Scientific "correctness" and philosophical "truth" are not related to one another as opposites. Insofar as new possibilities of knowledge have become apparent in philosophy – and this is indeed the case – they require application, demonstration, and ongoing verification in concrete research projects.... Insofar, on the other hand, as science contains metaphysical prejudices ... it requires a philosophical perspective in order to recognize and move beyond its dogmatic limitations.[191]

Yet Horkheimer is also convinced that the proper relationship between scientific research and philosophical reflection cannot be determined abstractly, isolated from the social and historical context in which they occur. For both are moments within a larger social totality – what Horkheimer calls the life process of human society. Thus, the crucial duty of maintaining the self-reflexivity of critical theory as a whole, at least for the foreseeable future, falls to "science of society itself." Horkheimer writes:

> The difference between scientific correctness and philosophical truth and, accordingly, the difference between philosophy and science cannot itself be verified or declared invalid by philosophical theories, for this difference undergoes substantial changes within the life process of human society. The theory of society itself appears at present as an important theoretical factor in this process. It not only has the advantage that its

---

[190] Ibid., pp. 332–3.
[191] Ibid., pp. 338–9.

very subject requires it attentively to follow this process, due to its tradition it has also remained freer from dogmatic methodological restrictions than other disciplines. In this respect it has preserved what it inherited from dialectical idealism. But which aspects of this inheritance will prove fruitful, depends as much upon movements in other areas as upon its own advances.[192]

Thus, the shifting relationship between science and philosophy, the dialectic of Enlightenment that Horkheimer described in his interpretation of contemporary philosophy, were also mediated expressions – not simple reflections – of the development of bourgeois society. In his lectures and manuscript, Horkheimer attempted to explain more precisely how these mediations functioned, just as he had in his materialist interpretation of the history of modern philosophy.

Looking back, one can see how Horkheimer's central concerns in the late 1920s – his "dual front ... against ... dogmatic metaphysics ... and anti-conceptual positivism," as Alfred Schmidt puts it – informed his materialist interpretation of the history of modern and contemporary philosophy.[193] Horkheimer's concern about the contemporary revival of metaphysics was reflected in his positive reading of the empiricist tradition in early modern philosophy. Horkheimer interpreted the French Enlightenment – which he viewed as the paradigmatic tendency within the Enlightenment as a whole – as a continuation and culmination of the empiricist tradition, not a rationalist apotheosis of abstract reason. In Horkheimer's account, German Idealism played the important role of making the Enlightenment self-reflexive, but this crucial philosophical moment was lost with the rise of positivism. By transforming empiricism into a dogmatic monism of matter, positivism eliminated the critical, progressive moments that had characterized its development in the early modern period: its firm grounding of reason in history and the external world, not in ahistorical principles or human consciousness. Positivism transformed the methods of the natural sciences themselves into metaphysical principles, which were subsequently grounded – by Mach and the neo-Kantians – in either sense impressions or the categories of the transcendental apperception, both of which could only be found in human consciousness. Thus, the trend toward consciousness philosophy, which Horkheimer had associated with the rationalist currents in early modern philosophy, also continued in the positivist-dominated climate of the nineteenth century, as was also demonstrated by the work of his own mentor, Hans Cornelius. As Horkheimer notes in several places, the critical moments of the empiricist tradition and the French Enlightenment, as well as the crucial moment of self-reflexivity introduced by German Idealism, were preserved outside the realm of pure philosophy, in the theoretical tradition of Marxism and the political tradition of the international workers' movement. In his capacity as a lecturer in the philosophy department at Frankfurt University, Horkheimer did not explicitly address Marx or the workers' movement, but a glance at his unpublished writings reveals that both were central to his concerns at this time. Far from accepting either uncritically,

---

[192] Ibid., p. 339.
[193] Alfred Schmidt, "Max Horkheimer's Intellectual Physiognomy," *On Max Horkheimer: New Perspectives*, op. cit. p. 27 (translation amended).

however, Horkheimer was convinced that both were threatened by a variety of dangerous tendencies that had become particularly apparent during and after the Great War. Renewed theoretical reflection was necessary, according to Horkheimer, to diagnose and counter these trends. It is Horkheimer's unpublished writings during the late 1920s to which we now turn.

4

The Beginnings of a Critical Theory
of Contemporary Society

As we have seen, Horkheimer was deeply dissatisfied with the philosophical schools that dominated German universities in the 1920s. One of the central tasks he pursued in the lectures on the history of modern and contemporary philosophy that he gave after becoming a *Privatdozent* in 1925 was to provide a socio-historical explanation of the origins of the dominant philosophical tendencies at that time, such as neo-Kantianism, positivism, phenomenology, metaphysics, and *Lebensphilosophie*. These lectures occupied much of Horkheimer's time during this period, and they reflected his interests in important ways, but they did not represent his primary concern, particularly after 1928. Skeptical about the prospects of imminent political change and no longer satisfied with a purely aesthetic refusal, Horkheimer had originally come to Frankfurt in hopes of gaining a rigorous, scientific understanding of modern capitalist society, whose exploitative underpinnings and volatile irrational potential he had witnessed first hand during World War I. In 1928, when it became clear that he would most likely become the next director of the newly founded Institute for Social Research, Horkheimer's latent desire to develop a critical theory of contemporary society was given new impetus. It suddenly became more important that he work out explicitly the principles that would guide him as the new director. As Horkheimer would soon make clear, under his direction the Institute would not be dedicated primarily to the *history* of the workers' movement and socialist theory, as it had been under Carl Grünberg, but rather to developing a theory of *contemporary* society.[1] There are no detailed statements of Horkheimer's plans for the Institute prior to the inaugural address he delivered in 1931, "The Present Situation of Social Philosophy and the Tasks of an Institute for Social Research,"[2] but an examination of his writings from the late 1920s goes a long way toward clarifying the evolution of the theory of society that he would outline in his inaugural address. In our examination of his lectures, we have already touched on the historical sources of some of the ideas he presents there – in the French Enlightenment and German Idealism,

---

[1] Horkheimer stresses this difference between himself and Grünberg also in his retrospective assessment of his becoming director of the Institute. In a letter from 1964, he writes, "In contrast to Grünberg, I was not concerned primarily with the history of the workers' movement and socialism, but rather with an appropriate sociological theory of society at that time and research that would contribute to it." GS 18, p. 571.

[2] Max Horkheimer, *Between Philosophy and Social Science: Selected Early Writings*, trans. G. Frederick Hunter, Matthew S. Kramer, and John Torpey (Cambridge, MA, 1993), pp. 1–15.

for example – but we have not yet explicitly examined Horkheimer's appropriation of Marx at this time, because it took place largely in writings that were
published only later, if at all. In what follows, we will examine Horkheimer's
writings from the late 1920s that illustrate most clearly his efforts to develop
a Critical Theory of contemporary society. We will focus particularly, if by no
means exclusively, on his interpretation and appropriation of Marx, because of
their central importance to these efforts.

Horkheimer first offered a seminar on Marx at the university during the summer semester of 1928, shortly after learning that he would probably become
the next director of the Institute. Friederich Pollock's notes from this seminar
make clear, however, that it was a rather rudimentary academic undertaking,
intended for those with no previous knowledge of the topic.[3] Sometime during
the following semester (winter semester 1928–9) Horkheimer wrote a more
theoretically substantial critique of Lenin's *Materialism und Empiriocriticism*,
which he originally intended to publish pseudonymously, but never actually
did.[4] This essay provides important insights into Horkheimer's critique of the
type of Marxism that the Bolsheviks had established as the official ideology
not only of the Soviet state, but also, after 1920, of the Communist Third
International and its various national branches – including the substantial
German Communist Party (KPD). In 1930, Horkheimer's first and only publication during this time relating directly to Marx appeared in what was still
the official organ of the Institute, Carl Grünberg's *Archiv für die Geschichte
des Sozialismus und Arbeiterbewegung*. The article, "A New Concept of
Ideology?",[5] was a critique of Karl Mannheim's *Ideology und Utopia*. In it,
Horkheimer defended Marx's concept of ideology against Mannheim's attempt
to transform it into the methodological basis of a sociology of knowledge.
Most important of all for an understanding of Horkheimer's appropriation of
Marx and his efforts to develop a Critical Theory of contemporary society at
this time, however, are the collection of aphorisms he wrote between 1926 and
1931. *Dämmerung: Notizen aus Deutschland* was finally published in Zürich
in 1934 – that is, only after Horkheimer had already been forced to flee from
Germany – and even then under the pseudonym of Heinrich Regius.[6] After
examining Horkheimer's critique of Mannheim and Lenin and his understanding of contemporary society as it emerges in *Dämmerung*, we will continue, in
following chapter, with an examination of Horkheimer's integration of psychoanalysis, which was also an essential aspect of the formation of his Critical
Theory of contemporary society. Chapters 3, 4, and 5 belong together thematically, insofar as they all address the development of Horkheimer's Critical

---

[3] Pollock's notes have been preserved in the Max Horkheimer Archive, MHA VIII 10.
[4] See Gunzelin Schmid Noerr's editorial remarks, GS 11, p. 171.
[5] Max Horkheimer, *Between Philosophy and Social Science*, trans. G.F. Hunter, Matthew S.
Kramer, and John Torpey (Cambridge, Mass.: MIT Press, 1995), pp. 129–50.
[6] An English translation of *Dämmerung* has been published (together with some of the
notes Horkheimer wrote in the postwar period), but it is incomplete and unreliable. *Dawn and
Decline: Notes 1926–1931 and 1950–1969*, trans. Michael Shaw (New York: Seabury Press,
1978).

Theory in the late 1920s; the former examines its *historical* dimensions, and the latter two address its relationship to *contemporary* society.

NEITHER "FREE FLOATING"...: HORKHEIMER'S CRITIQUE
OF KARL MANNHEIM'S SOCIOLOGY OF KNOWLEDGE

At first glance, it seems that Karl Mannheim and Max Horkheimer had much in common around 1930. In *Ideology and Utopia* – whose publication in 1929 consolidated Mannheim's reputation as one of the leading sociologists in Europe and secured him a professorship at Frankfurt University in 1930 – Mannheim presented an interpretation of the history of modern philosophy as the rise of consciousness philosophy, and argued that this narrowly subjective approach was inadequate for understanding ideas insofar as it separated them from the social and historical context out of which they had emerged.[7] The proliferation of mechanical models in the sciences that had accompanied the rise of positivism in the nineteenth century also deeply concerned Mannheim.[8] Like Horkheimer, he believed that positivism had undermined not only meta-physics, but all objective and universal ideals, and had also contributed greatly to the current situation of fragmentation and crisis in the sciences and in knowledge in general.[9] Mannheim was also deeply interested in the problem of ideology; he had already distinguished himself as a perceptive critic of conser-vative ideology in Germany[10] – in both its traditional and modern bureaucratic forms. In *Ideology and Utopia*, he supplemented this early work with incisive critiques of both the abstract rationalism of the bourgeois liberal-democratic tradition and the irrational voluntarism of the fascists.[11] Furthermore, when Mannheim moved to Frankfurt from Heidelberg in 1930 to take over Franz Oppenheimer's sociology professorship, he took up residence in the first floor of the Institute for Social Research.[12] He also participated in a regular discussion group with Horkheimer, Adorno, Pollock, Leo Lowenthal, and several other non-Institute members, including Paul Tillich and the curator of Frankfurt University, Kurt Riezler.[13] Despite all these seeming similarities, Horkheimer's critical reaction to *Ideology and Utopia* demonstrated that he found very lit-tle to agree with in Mannheim's study. However, Horkheimer's sharp critique of Mannheim is not just an example of the narcissism of small differences; it illustrates the significant and real theoretical differences that existed at this

---

[7] See, for example, part 3 of the first chapter of *Ideology and Utopia*, trans. L. Wirth and E. Shils (New York, 1936), pp. 13–33.

[8] Ibid., pp. 43ff.

[9] Ibid., p. 42.

[10] In his *Conservatism: A Contribution to the Sociology of Knowledge*, eds. D. Kettler, V. Meja and N. Stehr, trans. D. Kettler and V. Meja (New York: Routledge & Kegan Paul, 1986), which was originally written as his *Habilitationsschrift* at the University of Heidelberg and published in 1925.

[11] For Mannheim's analysis of the ideological nature of liberal-democratic rationalism, see *Ideology and Utopia*, pp. 122–25 and 219–29. For his analysis of fascist ideology, see pp. 134–46.

[12] Although there appears to have been very little contact at the Institute between Mannheim and its members. See Wiggershaus, *Die Frankfurter Schule*, op. cit. p. 129.

[13] *The Dialectical Imagination*, op. cit., p. 24.

time between his incipient Critical Theory of society and Karl Mannheim's sociology of knowledge.

In *Ideology and Utopia*, Mannheim suggested that it would be possible to ameliorate the fragmentation of Weimar intellectual and political life by fostering the development of a group of "free-floating" intellectuals who would be in a position to pursue scientific truth in a disinterested way. In contrast to his former friend and interlocutor Georg Lukács, Mannheim did not believe that only the proletariat, or intellectuals who identified completely with it, could overcome the "epistemological limits" of the bourgeoisie and recover the universalist political principles they had abandoned.[14] Although Mannheim recognized Marx as the first to introduce the concept of *total* ideology,[15] he argued that Marx had neglected to apply this insight to his own theory, which therefore remained particularistic, non-self-reflexive, and ideological.[16] The privileged ability to discern universal truth that Marx and Lukács had ascribed to the standpoint of the proletariat could only be recovered through a collectivity of "free-floating" intellectuals, according to Mannheim.[17] However, Horkheimer defended Marx (if not Lukács) against Mannheim's criticisms, and maintained that Mannheim's arguments represented yet another attempt to rehabilitate what Horkheimer would later call "traditional" theory. Marx's theory was "critical," not "traditional," insofar as his underlying intention was to change society, not to interpret it in the most objective way possible. By turning the concept of total ideology against Marx's own theory and placing it in the service of generalized sociology of knowledge, Mannheim had destroyed – not expanded – its original meaning, according to Horkheimer: "The concept has become so generalized that it has gained the authority to deal with questions of totality, in Mannheim's sense, but at the same time it has forfeited its concrete content."[18] By transforming Marx's concept of ideology in this way, Mannheim had regressed behind Marx's insight that there is no transcendent truth that exists above and beyond the interests and needs of concrete human beings. Horkheimer criticized Mannheim's attempt to attain greater objectivity in this way as an "idealistic attempt to conceive intellectual processes as unsullied by the raw power struggles of real human beings."[19] For Horkheimer, in other words, Mannheim's argument that free-floating intellectuals were cognitively

---

[14] For Lukács' argument, see "The Standpoint of the Proletariat," the third section of his seminal essay on "Reification and the Consciousness of the Proletariat," in *History and Class Consciousness*, trans. R. Livingstone (Cambridge, Mass: MIT Press, 1971), pp. 149–222.

[15] Mannheim distinguishes between *particular* and *total* ideology. The former refers to the more or less conscious adherence to certain ideas because they are advantageous to one's own particular interests. The latter refers to an unconscious standpoint or worldview that is a function of one's social or historical location; one has no real control over it or ability to see through it. See *Ideology and Utopia*, pp. 55–9.

[16] Ibid., pp. 124–34.

[17] Martin Jay, "The Frankfurt School's Critique of Karl Mannheim's Sociology of Knowledge," *Permanent Exiles* (New York, 1986), p. 66.

[18] "A New Concept of Ideology?" in Max Horkheimer, *Between Philosophy and Social Science: Selected Early Writings*, trans. G.F. Hunter, M. S. Kramer and J. Torpey (Cambridge, MA, 1993), p. 141.

[19] Ibid., pp. 144–5 (translation amended).

privileged or were able to grasp the "totality," was tantamount to restoring philosophy in the metaphysical form that Marx had overcome.[20]

Horkheimer's criticisms of Mannheim demonstrate his conviction that Marx's theory was not just one standpoint among many that had to be considered as a more or less significant element in a larger synthesis, but was instead the foundation upon which any attempt to grasp and transform contemporary societies must build. Horkheimer states this clearly in some notes from this time on an unpublished project that was to illustrate in more detail Marx's supersession of philosophy:[21] "Marxism [is] not just the only sociology, it is also the only philosophy. Marxism has taken the place of philosophy and Mannheim wants to undo this."[22] Yet even if Horkheimer did see Marx's work as the foundation of his own efforts at this time to develop a Critical Theory of contemporary society, important questions remain. How did Horkheimer interpret Marx, and what role did he play in Horkheimer's own theory? Horkheimer's firm conviction that the truth was always historically and socially mediated obviously precluded any dogmatic understanding of Marx's theory as a set of static principles that could be applied abstractly to any concrete situation. We can begin to answer these questions by examining Horkheimer's critique of Mannheim's concept of ideology in more detail. At first glance, Mannheim's attempt to explain ideas in terms of the social and historical context out of which they emerged does indeed seem similar to Horkheimer's own approach to ideology.[23] A closer look at his critique of Mannheim's method of analyzing the socially determined nature of ideas, however, reveals significant differences. These differences also shed important light on Horkheimer's appropriation and modification of Marx at this time for his own theory of society.

For Mannheim, the transition from Marx's concept of total ideology to his own sociology of knowledge is brought about by making Marx's concept self-reflexive. This occurs, in his own terminology, by transforming it from *special* ideology, which is reserved only for one's opponent, to *general* ideology, which is also applied to oneself.[24] This new concept of total, general ideology, which forms the methodological basis of Mannheim's sociology of knowledge, comes in two different variations. Mannheim stresses that the border between the

---

[20] Martin Jay aptly describes Horkheimer's position in the following way: "Neither the proletariat in its imputed role as the subject and object of history, nor the free-floating intelligentsia with their symphony of partial viewpoints could really attain a total view of truth, for truth did not reside in the totality, at least not yet." *Permanent Exiles*, op. cit., p. 71.

[21] Horkheimer's article, "Hegel and the Problem of Metaphysics" (GS 2, pp. 295–308), was originally planned as one part of this larger project, which, however, was never completed. See Gunzelin Schmid Noerr's brief remarks on the project in GS 11, pp. 221–4.

[22] GS 11, p. 222.

[23] Following the publication of his *Habilitationsschrift* in 1925, which examined the social roots of conservative ideology in Germany, Mannheim was in fact attacked as a "historical materialist" by his former academic teachers at Heidelberg, Alfred Weber and Carl Brinkmann. "Karl Mannheim," David Kettler and Volker Meja, *Klassiker der Soziologie 1: Von Auguste Comte bis Norbert Elias*, ed. Dirk Kaesler (Munich, 2000), p. 300.

[24] Mannheim writes, "With the emergence of the general formulation of the total conception of ideology, the simple theory of ideology develops into the sociology of knowledge." *Ideology and Utopia*, op. cit., pp. 77–8.

two of them is not absolute; nonetheless, the first is tendentially value-free und useful primarily in historical research. He stresses that its value-free nature does not lead to relativism, but rather to what he calls a *relational* approach to intellectual history, which seeks to understand ideas in terms of their historical location and sociological bearers.[25] The second variation of the total, general concept of ideology is *valuing* and *dynamic*, according to Mannheim, and is primarily useful as a sociological diagnosis of the present.[26] He argues not only for the primacy of this second version of the concept over the first, but he also maintains that the transition from the latter to the former is necessitated by a certain understanding of history that all sociological research must ultimately presuppose.[27] History must be understood as a meaningful totality in which man gradually reveals his essence – a process that Mannheim refers to as the "development of the essence of 'man.'"[28] If history is simply a series of random coincidences, then it would be pointless to conduct historical or sociological research at all, or least impossible to do so in a scientifically rigorous and justifiable manner. Yet once one has accepted that history is a meaningful process, in which man's essence is gradually revealed, one has to define the criteria one uses to orient oneself and one's research at the present stage of history. Like the young Lukács,[29] Mannheim believed that man had become transcendentally homeless in the modern world: Meaning no longer exists for him in a unified, self-evident way. Most people respond to this predicament by adhering to one of the many ideologies that attempt to give meaning to the world and offer guidelines for orienting oneself in it. Yet this is not enough for Mannheim. Rather than attempting to choose the best among the various ideologies dominant at the present – such as liberal democracy, conservatism, socialism, or fascism, at the time Mannheim was writing – the sociologist of knowledge must analyze all of them as expressions of particular social groups. For ideologies never exist in a vacuum, independent of the socio-historical context in which they emerge; they are, as Mannheim puts it, "ontologically rooted" [*Seinsgebunden*]. Mannheim's sociology of knowledge is, in other words, a "science of the social ascription of ideas," as Horkheimer puts it.[30]

However, Mannheim also tries to provide a criterion that can be used to judge the truth content of ideologies. This criterion is whether or not the ideology is up to date; that is, whether or not it is still adequate to the current historical stage of the society that it purports to explain. Thus, the criterion that Mannheim presents as the foundation of his valuing concept of total,

[25] Ibid., pp. 78ff.

[26] Ibid., p. 93.

[27] Ibid., p. 93.

[28] Ibid., p. 92 (translation amended).

[29] *The Theory of the Novel*, trans. Anna Bostock (Cambridge, MA, 1971). Mannheim participated in Lukács's and Bela Belazs's "Sunday Circle" discussion group in Budapest during World War I. It was during this time that Lukács wrote *The Theory of the Novel*.

[30] "A New Concept of Ideology?" p. 130. Mannheim himself describes one the two main goals of *Ideology and Utopia* as "the elaboration of a method which will enable us, on the basis of increasingly precise criteria, to distinguish and isolate diverse styles of thinking and to relate them to the groups from which they spring." p. 45.

general ideology is not absolute, but rather "perspectival," as he himself says.[31] The sociologist of knowledge must analyze all of the dominant ideologies with a view to their relevance to the present empirical reality. He redefines false consciousness as an ideology that lags behind the present stage of reality and is determined by categories that no longer have any empirical relation to it.[32] Only after the researcher has become aware of the limitations of all the particular ideologies can he or she begin to formulate a more objective position that transcends and synthesizes all of them. Yet Mannheim expressly denies the possibility of ever achieving a genuinely objective position. The sociologist of knowledge can transcend the particularities of ideology only in a relative – not absolute – way. In the end, all ideologies remain more or less false, and there can be no overarching criteria, beyond their relevance to the present, by which they can be judged. Mannheim argues that the perspectival approach of the sociology of knowledge is not a weakness, but its great strength. He writes:

Only when we are thoroughly aware of the limited scope of every point of view are we on the road to the sought-for comprehension of the whole. The crisis in thought is not a crisis affecting merely a single intellectual position, but a crisis of a whole world which has reached a certain stage in its intellectual development. To see more clearly the confusion into which our social and intellectual life has fallen represents an enrichment rather than a loss.[33]

In short, the task of the sociologist of knowledge, and the concept of total ideology upon which it is based, is not only *valuing*, insofar as he or she must also seek to judge whether or not an ideology is up to date, but also *dynamic*, insofar as it can never be satisfied with one single standpoint nor ever attain absolute objectivity.

But how is Mannheim able to reconcile his assertion of the essentially limited nature of all particular ideologies (including the "more objective" syntheses of the sociologist of knowledge) with the allegedly necessary assumption that history is a meaningful totality in which "man" gradually reveals himself? Are not these assumptions also the mediated product of determinate social and historical conditions and thus limited, like any other particular standpoint? Horkheimer recognizes this contradiction and uses it as the basis of an immanent critique of Mannheim's theory. He accuses Mannheim of smuggling a version of absolute truth back into his theory, and in so doing, not applying consistently the principles he sets forth with his concept of total, general ideology. Comparing Mannheim's position to Dilthey, Horkheimer writes:

If we take Mannheim's theory of ideology seriously, then there is no adequate justification for claiming that, in a thoroughly conditioned and mutable reality, the "realization of humanity" alone should occupy this exceptional position. Nor is it convincing to argue that, of all kinds of knowledge, the anthropological is not ideological. From a standpoint which claims "to discover the ideological element in all thinking," Dilthey's

---

[31] Ibid., p. 103 (the concept of "Perspektivität" is lost in the translation. The translators render it as "ambiguity").

[32] Ibid., pp. 94–5.

[33] Ibid., p. 105.

belief in a "humanity" which unfolds in the course of history … must appear as the mere "absolutization" of a single situationally determined perception.[34]

Thus, according to Horkheimer, Mannheim's and Dilthey's anthropological notions of the realization of humanity are spurious not only historically, but also sociologically. Whereas Horkheimer's critique of Mannheim's "free-floating" intellectuals paralleled Marx's critique of the false universality of civil servants and the state in Hegel's *Philosophy of Right*, his critique of Mannheim's concept of "man" echoed Marx's critique of Feuerbach's anthropological materialism.[35] Like Marx, Horkheimer insisted that the abstract concept of "man" realizing itself in history did not overcome, but rather merely inverted the idealist concept of an absolute spirit realizing itself in history. "Man," as something which exists above and beyond real historical individuals, has no more substance than absolute spirit, according to Horkheimer. He writes: "Only human beings themselves – not the 'essence' of humanity, but the real human beings in a definite historical moment, dependent upon each other and upon outer and inner nature – are the acting and suffering subjects of history."[36] This stress on the centrality of the concrete individual – not any abstract group or collective unconscious – as the site where ideology is reproduced played a crucial role in Horkheimer's incipient theory of society at this time, as we shall see in more detail in our examination of *Dämmerung* and the empirical study of German workers' attitudes.

Mannheim's concept of the "realization of man" is what gives history meaning, and one must, according to him, assume that history is a meaningful totality in order to conduct any sort of productive historical or sociological research. However, Horkheimer had already rejected the thesis of the meaningfulness of history – the identity of reason and history – in Hegel's philosophy of history, and he did so again when he encountered it, albeit in a weaker form, in Mannheim's sociology of knowledge. In his critique of Mannheim's faith in the inherent meaningfulness of history, Horkheimer draws explicitly on arguments from Schopenhauer and Marx, arguments that also underlay some of his own most important assumptions about history and society at this time. Building on Kant's first Critique, Schopenhauer had argued that any rational order that exists in the world comes from human beings, not from the world in and of itself, which could only be seen as a blind, irrational willing. For Marx, too, the capitalist phase of the prehistory of mankind was ultimately governed by the law of value, which was determined by the blind imperatives of capital accumulation, not a consciously willed organization of human society. In his critique of Mannheim, Horkheimer explicitly synthesized these arguments of Schopenhauer and Marx. He writes:

But given Mannheim's sociology, can unity have a greater ontological probability than multiplicity – indeed, than chaos? Can the divine be more likely than the diabolical

---

[34] "A New Concept of Ideology?" p. 136.
[35] For Marx's critique of Feuerbach, see the first section of *The German Ideology*, in *The Marx-Engels Reader*, ed. R. Tucker (New York, 1978), pp. 147–200.
[36] "A New Concept of Ideology?" p. 139.

(such as the blind will Schopenhauer believes underlies the world?) ... Indeed, history as a whole cannot possibly be the expression of some meaningful whole. For history is the recapitulation of processes that arise from the contradictory relationships of human society. These processes reveal no spiritual or intellectual unity; they are not the effect of struggles between mere attitudes, positions, styles of thought, and systems. Instead, completely unequal human and extrahuman forces influence their development. Insofar as history does not emerge from the conscious purposefulness of human beings determining it according to a plan, it has no meaning [*Sinn*]. One can attempt to comprehend the various driving forces of a certain epoch under laws, but the assertion of a comprehensible meaning behind these facticities is founded upon philosophical fantasy ... It is central to Marxian materialism to give expression to the unsatisfactory condition of earthly reality as true being, and not to permit vague ideas of humanity to be hypostatized as Being in a higher sense.... According to Marx, we are forbidden any such consolation about the world.[37]

Horkheimer's refusal to accept that any overarching meaning could be discerned in the progression of "history" and his insistence that this baleful situation could only be overcome by creating a socialist society that is governed not by the law of value, but by conscious planning, were both important principles that informed his nascent Critical Theory of society at this time.

As we shall see shortly in our examination of *Dämmerung* and the Institute's empirical study of workers' attitudes in Germany in 1929, Horkheimer was, like Mannheim, very much interested in the specific sense of the relationship between ideas and their social agents. However, Mannheim's sociology of knowledge did not, according to Horkheimer, provide the means to explain this relationship adequately. Horkheimer argued that Mannheim's sole criterion for judging the truth content of ideas – whether or not they were adequate to the present social and historical situation – was much too vague and did not really answer the question he had posed. For how is one supposed to determine if an ideology is up to date without having some other standards of judgment? For Horkheimer, these standards must be based on an explicitly articulated theory of society, which, as we have seen, has its roots in the Marxist tradition:

The question of the correctness or falsity of equally situationally determined ideologies can only be put in terms of a judgment of their appropriateness for their time.... The sociology of knowledge must remain arbitrary and unreliable because the determination of what is appropriate for the time and what is obsolete is not made on the basis of an explicit, scientific theory of society.[38]

Yet a theory of society that can explain ideology more adequately cannot simply apply Marx's conception of it in a mechanical way; in order to come to terms with the qualitatively new socio-historical situation in post–World War I Europe, it must also have an *empirical* and a *psychological* dimension. Mannheim's sociology of knowledge fails on both counts according to Horkheimer, for he rests content with simply identifying a correspondence between certain groups and certain ideas without providing an explanation of

[37] Ibid., pp. 138–9.
[38] Ibid., p. 147.

why someone belongs to a certain group or *why* they defend a certain ideology. Horkheimer writes:

Neither interest nor any empirical facts whatsoever are supposed to serve as an explanation for the emergence and consolidation of a person's overall perspective; instead an unadorned, unmediated "correspondence" is asserted. The fact that such a perspective represents a false consciousness must thus appear as fateful providence, as mystical destiny. In this regard Mannheim must reject not merely the old-style psychology of interest, but contemporary psychology as well, insofar as the latter inherits the attempt to explain intellectual processes ultimately in terms of the external exigencies of life. He wants to replace psychological findings with "an analysis of the correspondence between the situation to be known and the forms of knowledge." What he means by this is never clearly expressed.[39]

Like Mannheim, Horkheimer was highly attuned to the problem of ideologies becoming rigid, losing contact with empirical reality, and lagging behind current social and historical developments. He was particularly interested in the failure of the German working class to fulfill the role that Marx had attributed to it, namely to overthrow capitalist relations of production when the conditions were ripe, which they seemed to have been during the period of crisis following World War I. The questions of why German workers did not live up to their revolutionary ideology at that time, and the extent to which they still adhered to it ten years later, were what motivated the Institute's empirical study of workers' attitudes in 1929. As we shall see, however, Horkheimer believed that the question of the relationship between the social situation of the various segments of the working class and their conscious and unconscious attitudes could only be answered using the most advanced methods of empirical social research and psychology, not just an abstract notion of "correspondence."

... NOR "FIRMLY ROOTED": HORKHEIMER'S CRITIQUE OF LENIN'S *MATERIALISM AND EMPIRIOCRITICISM*

If Horkheimer's critique of Karl Mannheim's sociology of knowledge demonstrated his conviction that Marx's theory must serve as the foundation of any attempt to develop a Critical Theory of contemporary society, his critique of Lenin's principal philosophical work, *Materialism and Empiriocriticism*, made it clear that Horkheimer was not satisfied with this particular interpretation of Marx, which had come to dominate not only the Soviet Union, but also the Communist Third International. Whereas Horkheimer had argued against Mannheim that "free-floating" intellectuals, whose loyalties always transcended any and all particular standpoints, could not develop a genuinely critical theory of contemporary society, he also rejected the position of Lenin, Lukács, and the Bolsheviks that critical theory must be "rooted" in the "a priori" universal position of the working class or the party that claimed to represent it.[40] Thus, already at this time, Horkheimer's incipient Critical

---

[39] Ibid., pp. 142–3.

[40] In his seminal essay on "Traditional and Critical Theory," Horkheimer would also emphasize that Critical Theory is neither "rooted" nor "free-floating." *Critical Theory: Selected Essays Max Horkheimer*, trans. Matthew O'Connell et al. (New York, 1972), pp. 223–4.

Theory demanded the seemingly paradoxical commitment not only actively to change society, but also constantly to maintain one's independence of judgment vis-à-vis real-existing political movements, for which "theory" often serves merely a legitimatory function.[41] Horkheimer's critique of Lenin illustrates that he never would have willingly subordinated the independence of theory to any party line, as had Lukács – beginning with Zinoviev's censure of his early work at the Fifth Congress of the Third International in 1924. Despite his criticisms of Mannheim's attempts to separate social theory from concrete political movements and worldviews, the distinction between theory and praxis remained crucial for Horkheimer at this time. This distinction was based, however, not on a dualistic separation of theory from praxis, but rather on a dialectical understanding of both as moments in the larger process of the reproduction of society.[42] Theory did not, in other words, float above society, looking back on it from a transcendent and more or less neutral standpoint, as Mannheim would have it, but played a crucial role in the ongoing, dynamic process of reproducing a historically specific form of social relations. Horkheimer illustrates concretely the active role that theory, and knowledge more generally, play in reproducing society in *Dämmerung*, to which we will turn shortly.

Horkheimer's critical analysis of *Materialism and Empiriocriticism* is important not only because it is his only detailed engagement with Lenin; it also represents an attempt to come to terms with a school of thought that had played a significant role in his own intellectual development, insofar as the work of his philosophical mentor, Hans Cornelius, was heavily indebted to Ernst Mach's empiriocriticism. Mach and his followers in Russia were, of course, the main target of Lenin's polemical ire, but in *Materialism and Empiriocriticism*, Lenin also explicitly criticizes Cornelius as one of Mach's most important adherents in Germany. Lenin notes that Mach himself approvingly cited Cornelius as an example of someone who was continuing his own work.[43] As we have seen, Horkheimer was more critical of Mach's (and Cornelius's) theoretical position in 1928 than he had been a few years earlier.[44] It is possible that his encounter with Lenin's critique of Mach, which also occurred in 1928, may have dampened his sympathies for empiriocriticism. Lenin may, in other words, have drawn Horkheimer's attention to certain problems in empiriocriticism, but he certainly did not provide Horkheimer with any new theoretical arguments against Mach. Although Horkheimer did recognize the correctness of several of Lenin's basic conclusions, he rejected most of the arguments that Lenin used

---

[41] For a critique of the subordination of theory to politics, which voices some of the concerns about politics that Horkheimer had articulated in his early novellas, see the entry from his philosophical diary from December 10, 1926. GS 11, pp. 257–8.

[42] Horkheimer would develop this argument in his 1937 essay, "Traditional and Critical Theory." See Chapter 8, pp. 326ff.

[43] *Materialism and Empirio-Criticism: Critical Comments on a Reactionary Philosophy*, trans. A Fineberg (Moscow, 1947), p. 221.

[44] On Horkheimer's interpretation of Mach, see Chapter 3, pp. 128–30. It is worth reiterating, as the following discussion of Horkheimer's critique of Lenin will also make clear, that Horkheimer was already very critical of Mach's empiriocriticism at this time, not just later, as Michiel Korthals and Hauke Brunkhorst have claimed (see the discussion of their argument in Chapter 3, p. 130).

to reach them, and he defended Mach against Lenin's criticisms on several key points as well.

In his unpublished article on Lenin, Horkheimer recognizes the *historical* importance of *Materialism and Empiriocriticism*. The book did in fact succeed in breaking the influence of empiriocriticism on Russian social democracy after its publication in 1908, and in the 1920s it was canonized by the Bolsheviks and used to legitimate the party line of the Third International as well.[45] Horkheimer, however, also stresses that his own interest in *Materialism and Empiriocriticism* is based primarily on the main *theoretical* problem it addresses, namely the relationship of historical materialism to epistemology. Horkheimer's numerous reflections on this problem during this time demonstrated his belief that this relationship was still one of the most important problems facing a Critical Theory of contemporary society. His rejection of Lenin's treatment of this problem is important not only because it illustrates the reasons for Horkheimer's dissatisfaction with Lenin's interpretation of Marx, but also because it provides insight into the importance of a specific type of materialist epistemology for Horkheimer's own thought at this time. In his critique of *Materialism and Empiriocriticism*, Horkheimer accuses Lenin of falling behind not only the subtle discussions of epistemology by neo-Kantians, Gestalt psychologists, and other contemporary "bourgeois" theorists, but also Marx's own theoretical treatment of epistemological problems.[46] In other words, Horkheimer recognized epistemological reflection as an important moment in Marx's theory, a moment that he wanted to preserve, develop, and refine for his own Critical Theory of society.

In his critique of Mach, Lenin relies heavily on Engels's study of Feuerbach, and in particular, on the central distinction Engels makes between materialism and idealism. According to Engels: "Those who claim that spirit is more primordial than nature, i.e. accept in the final instance some sort of creation of the world ... are part of the idealist camp. The others, who view nature as primordial, belong to the different schools of materialism."[47] Based on this distinction, Lenin discusses a number of characteristics of Mach's empiriocriticism that – he believes – distinguish it clearly as a "reactionary" idealist philosophy. Lenin claims that empiriocriticism represents nothing more than a new version of Berkeley's subjective idealism, with the same solipsistic implications. As we have seen, Mach (and Cornelius) argue that the world and all knowledge of it are based on sense impressions that register in human consciousness. Lenin interprets this argument as idealist, because Mach asserts the epistemological priority of sense impressions over the existence of the external, natural world. Sense impressions are not mere subjective reflections of an external, objective

[45] As Gunzelin Schmid Noerr points out in his editorial remarks on Horkheimer's text on Lenin, GS 11, p. 173.

[46] On this point, see Alfred Schmidt's afterward to volume 11 of Horkheimer's *Collected Writings*: "Unter welchen Aspekten Horkheimer Lenins Streitschrift gegen den 'machistischen' Revisionismus beurteilt," GS 11, p. 421.

[47] Friedrich Engels, *Ludwig Feuerbach und der Ausgang der klassischen deutschen Philosophie*, in *Marx/Engels Werke*, vol. 21 (Berlin, 1962), p. 275. Quoted by Horkheimer, GS 11, p. 176.

world, they are themselves the most basic *elements* of that world, according to Mach. As Lenin asserts, this position leads willy-nilly to solipsism:

We have seen that the starting point and most fundamental premise of the philosophy of empirio-criticism is subjective idealism. The world is our sense impressions ... The absurdity of this philosophy lies in the fact that it leads to solipsism, to the recognition only of the existence of the philosophizing individual.[48]

Lenin claims that Mach's arguments also throw the door wide open for a return of metaphysics and religion: "[If] natural scientific theories do not describe objective reality, but instead only metaphors, symbols, forms of human experience, etc. then humanity is without question justified in creating no less 'real concepts' for other areas, such as God, etc."[49] Thus, according to Lenin's categorical argument, as soon as one has departed from the fundamental assumption of materialism – that sense impressions, or any other phenomena of consciousness, merely *reflect* the external, natural world – one must accept *all* the consequences of idealism, including solipsism and metaphysics.

Horkheimer agrees with Lenin's conclusion that Mach's empiriocriticism is not materialist and therefore not directly reconcilable with theoretical views of Marx or Engels. He writes:

Engels's definition of idealism can without doubt be applied to this philosophy [Mach]. It considers sense impressions, not nature primary, and the world of material things as a product of the conceptual order of what exists, in a certain sense as a creation of the ordering process. Mach's thoughts correspond exactly to the idealistic thesis, which Engels combats, of the primordial identity of thinking and being. Thus empiriocriticism does in fact run contrary to the philosophical views of Marx and Engels.[50]

As we have seen, Horkheimer had already criticized Mach for failing adequately to address social and historical factors in his philosophy, and he went even further in his criticism of Hans Cornelius's philosophy, which he saw as a form of consciousness philosophy that actually did lead to solipsism.[51] Horkheimer does not, however, agree with Lenin's argument that Mach's own position is solipsistic or metaphysical. Solipsism is, by definition, an absolutization of the ego, more particularly, of one's own spontaneous consciousness, such that the entire world and other people as well are seen merely as its creations. Horkheimer shows that Mach does not adhere to this position, insofar as he conceives of the ego, like the external world, as being composed of and therefore ultimately derivative to sense impressions. Horkheimer quotes Mach himself to make this point:

Thing and *ego* are provisional fictions of the same type.... The ego is not primary, but instead the elements (sense impressions).... The elements *form* the ego. *I* sense green; this means that the element green appears in a certain context with other elements (sense impressions, memories). If *I* stop sensing green, if I die, the elements no longer

---

[48] *Materialism and Empirio-Criticism*, p. 90 (translation amended).
[49] Quoted by Horkheimer, GS 11, p. 181.
[50] Ibid., p. 178.
[51] See Chapter 3, pp. 86–7.

appear in the society in the habitual, familiar way. There is nothing else to be said.... The ego cannot be rescued.[52]

Horkheimer also takes issue with Lenin's claim that Mach's subordination of the external world to subjective sense impressions was tantamount to recognizing the existence of immaterial entities, including metaphysical and religious entities. For Mach always insisted, as Horkheimer points out, that sense impressions were *neutral* vis-à-vis mind and matter, psychic and physical reality. Not unlike Spinoza, who had subordinated Descartes' *res cogito* and *res extensa* to attributes of a single immanent substance, Mach reduced the psychic and the physical to "provisional fictions" necessary to make sense of monistic world of sense impressions. In short, Horkheimer demonstrates that Mach's epistemology was hardly crypto-metaphysical; he also notes that Mach showed little patience for religion elsewhere in his writings – with his claim, for example, that "fear of ghosts [is] the real mother of religion."[53]

For Horkheimer, Lenin's verdict of "reactionary idealism" was not, in other words, the full story on Mach. Horkheimer even viewed empiriocriticism as a continuation of the Enlightenment tradition of materialism in the specific sense that Mach maintained the primacy of science and conceptual thought over the allegedly independent or transcendent realms of religion and culture. In the European intellectual climate of the late 1920s – which was characterized by a return to metaphysics, a proliferation of vulgarized versions of *Lebensphilosophie*, and a preference for culturally based methods in the human and social sciences – Mach's insistence on science's right to refuse religious and cultural categories, and to interpret these "higher" phenomena in terms of their "lower" origins, remained progressive. This aspect of empiriocriticism was fully reconcilable with Horkheimer's own theory, as the following passage indicates:

[Mach] belongs to a category of bourgeois scholars that is in the process of disappearing: those whose scientific endeavors refuses to resign in the face of sacred objects. In contrast to today, when one attempts to interpret the methods and results of physics with higher, organic categories, as an heir of the Enlightenment Mach retained for himself the freedom to apply natural scientific methods also to "higher" realms; thus he was able, for example, to repeatedly demonstrate the dependence of cultural upon economic development in several concrete cases.[54]

Yet Horkheimer also recognized many problems with Mach's theory. He may have seen the theory as a continuation, in certain respects, of the Enlightenment tradition of materialism, but he also agreed with Lenin's conclusion that it was not reconcilable with Marx's more sophisticated concept of *historical* materialism. Lenin was right for the wrong reasons, according to Horkheimer. Mach's problem lay not in his departure from the reflection theory of knowledge, but rather in his problematic relationship to time and history. Horkheimer sharply criticized Lenin's defense of an epistemology based on reflection. He characterizes Lenin's claim that "objective reality is copied, photographed

---

[52] GS 11, pp. 178–9 (Mach's own emphasis).
[53] Quoted by Horkheimer, ibid., p. 182.
[54] Ibid.

and reflected by our sense impressions" as "the reflection theory of knowledge in its most naive form."[55] Horkheimer pointed to the familiar and widely accepted refutation of epistemological naturalism, that it is never possible to determine the relationship between a "reflection" and "reality" insofar as we never have a pure, subjectively unmediated view of "objective" reality.

Furthermore, and more important, Horkheimer maintained that Lenin's attempt to criticize Mach based on the principle of the absolute primacy of the objective, material world caused him to fall behind Marx's *dialectical* understanding of epistemology. Despite his insistence on the importance of praxis in proving truth claims, Lenin's absolute and ultimately naturalistic concept of epistemology cannot be reconciled with Marx's concept of praxis, which – as Alfred Schmidt points out – recognizes that all epistemological dualisms are *historically* mediated.[56] As Horkheimer puts it, "[Lenin posits] the relationship between subject and object, consciousness and object as something that remains constant for all time and [he fails] to comprehend it as part of human praxis."[57] In his inadequate attention to the temporal and historical dimension of knowledge, Lenin reveals himself to be at one with Mach, despite all his criticisms. Whereas Lenin granted the absolute primacy of the material world an ahistorical status, Mach's insistence on the absolute primacy of sense impressions does not make an exception when it comes to time either. Horkheimer identifies this as the "weakest point in Mach's philosophy." He writes:

Is time just like things merely a complex of elements, or are the elements located within time? How can Mach concede the reality of human and natural history, when, according to him, "the passage of time is bound only to conditions of our senses [*Sinnlichkeit*]?" The theory that the elements of the world are neutral and identical with sense impressions was not, despite detailed investigations, able to solve the difficulties that arose with the problem of time.[58]

In short, neither Mach nor Lenin is able to solve the epistemological problems they address because both ultimately rely on theoretical absolutes. This theoretical shortcoming manifests itself concretely in both men's work, according to Horkheimer, in a "deficit in clear relations to the present."[59]

As an alternative to both Mach and Lenin, Horkheimer develops an immanent critique of Lenin that draws, in particular, on his later references to Hegel's dialectical logic. Lenin had argued, in Hegelian terms, that "there is no such thing as abstract truth, the truth is always concrete,"[60] and that "human praxis in its entirety ... [must] enter into the complete 'definition' of an object."[61] But as we have seen, Horkheimer insists that a fully concrete and genuinely

[55] Ibid., p. 183.
[56] Alfred Schmidt, "Unter welchen Aspekten Horkheimer Lenins Streitschrift gegen den 'machistischen' Revisionismus beurteilt," GS 11, p. 422.
[57] This passage is from a manuscript that Horkheimer prepared in conjunction with the essay on Lenin, but which was not included in it. The manuscript is located in the Horkheimer Archive (MHA VIII 15) and is quoted here by Alfred Schmidt, ibid.
[58] GS 11, pp. 180–1.
[59] Ibid., p. 184.
[60] Quoted by Horkheimer, ibid., p. 184.
[61] Quoted by Horkheimer, ibid., p. 187.

dialectical concept of praxis – within which the relationship of historical materialism to epistemology could also be addressed – can only be developed in conjunction with a theory of the social totality, in its contemporary form. In his critique of Lenin, Horkheimer emphasizes this point once again:

It is a very timely impulse to remove philosophy from the realm of validity, in which each pretends to the other that its methods and results have no relation to society, and to comprehend it in the context of the social totality in which it develops, from which its content is derived and in which it takes effect.[62]

Critical social theory cannot, in other words, rely on any absolute philosophical standpoint, in the sense criticized by both Hegel and Marx. For as Horkheimer would illustrate in *Dämmerung*, all aspects of individuals' lives, including of course their knowledge and actions, are largely determined, in subtle and not-so-subtle ways, by the antagonistic and therefore false social totality of capitalist society. It is to Horkheimer's *Dämmerung*[63] that we now turn.

THE TWILIGHT OF BOURGEOIS SOCIETY: *DÄMMERUNG*

The Place of *Dämmerung* in Horkheimer's Thought

In the third chapter, we focused primarily on Horkheimer's published writings or public lectures in the period 1925–30. In these lectures and writings, Horkheimer displayed more willingness to depart from the academic guidelines to which he had faithfully adhered in his writings during his philosophical apprenticeship with Hans Cornelius. After 1925, he did not hesitate, for example, to structure his lectures on the history of modern philosophy on an innovative material-ist interpretation that represented a qualitative break with the consciousness philosophy of Cornelius. Nonetheless, Horkheimer's lectures during this time remained confined in many respects to the traditional academic form in which they were presented. His materialist methodology often lapsed into the more traditional history of ideas approach, which he was trying to overcome. His efforts to illustrate the social and historical content of the ideas he treated were often overshadowed by his richly detailed description of the ideas he presented and their immanent relations to other philosophical systems. The same cannot be said, however, for the collection of aphorisms that Horkheimer wrote between 1926 and 1931 and published in 1934 under the pseudonym of Heinrich Regius.[64] In *Dämmerung*, Horkheimer gives free expression to his

---

[62] Ibid.

[63] In German, *Dämmerung* means both twilight and dawn. Although the overall tone of *Dämmerung* has much more to do with twilight than dawn, Horkheimer was not yet willing at this time to completely abandon the hopeful connotations of the second meaning of the term, as the aphorism bearing the title "Dämmerung" that opens the collection makes clear. See *Dawn and Decline*, op. cit., p. 17. I have chosen to leave the title of the book untranslated, to capture both meanings.

[64] Henricus Regius (1598–1679) was a materialistically inclined student of Descartes and a doctor of medicine. In a brief discussion of Regius in a lecture course on "Materialism and Idealism in the History of Modern Philosophy," Horkheimer mentioned that Regius believed only in *res extensa*, not *res cogitans*, which led Descartes, who feared the atheistic implications of his

passionate and revolutionary critique of contemporary monopoly capitalism.[65] Although Horkheimer fulfilled his academic duties in an extremely conscientious manner, these aphorisms demonstrated his unbroken determination to maintain some critical distance from the conservative German academy. Even in Frankfurt, which was certainly Germany's most open and innovative university at the time, Horkheimer continued to need an outlet to express ideas that were too radical for the contemporary German academic milieu. *Dämmerung* served this function for Horkheimer,[66] and in this regard represented a return to the "vie intérieur" of his earlier novellas, dramas, and diary entries that had provided him with a means of expressing his vehement rejection of his social surroundings during the war. As Gunzelin Schmid Noerr points out, *Dämmerung* also anticipates the aphorisms at the end of the *Dialectic of Enlightenment* as well as the voluminous notes Horkheimer penned after the war.[67] This dichotomy between *extérieur* and *intérieur* takes different forms in Horkheimer's writings throughout his life, and is certainly one of the keys to understanding his work as a whole.

On the one hand, the aphorisms collected in *Dämmerung* represented a continuation of Horkheimer's earliest writings, not only in their function – by providing him with means of expressing his most authentic thoughts – but also in their form and, to a lesser extent, their content as well.[68] On the other hand, they also represent a qualitative step beyond his early dramas, novellas, and diary entries insofar as Horkheimer's great refusal of contemporary capitalist society is no longer framed primarily in moral and moralizing terms. Although the aphorisms still occasionally display the pathos that characterized Horkheimer's earliest writings, they move decisively beyond it insofar as they are informed by an incipient theory of society that builds on some of the most advanced tendencies in contemporary sociological and psychological research.[69] This is not to

argument, to write a polemical pamphlet against him. Horkheimer views Regius as one of first of a series of prominent medical doctors who played an important role in the development of materialist tradition in France, a tradition that was continued in the eighteenth century by La Mettrie and Cabanis, for example. See MHA VIII.14.

[65] As Gunzelin Schmid Noerr puts it, "At no other time, in none of his other writings, did Horkheimer commit himself so emphatically to socialism as in *Dämmerung*; nowhere else did he place his theoretical efforts so unconditionally in the service of this goal." "Editor's Afterword," GS 2, p. 467. It is thus no coincidence that Horkheimer's *Dämmerung* was also one of the most popular and most quoted writings during the militant phase of the student movement in Germany in the late 1960s. *Dämmerung* circulated in numerous illegal pirate editions, particularly in Frankfurt, during this time.

[66] In the introduction to *Dämmerung*, Horkheimer notes that the aphorisms were written "during breaks from strenuous work, and without taking time to polish them." GS 2, p. 312 (these prefatory remarks were not included in *Dawn and Decline*).

[67] "Editor's Afterword," GS 2, p. 466.

[68] The continuities in content, which I will not address here, are apparent, for example, in Horkheimer's ongoing preoccupation with World War I and its consequences (in *Dawn and Decline*, see the aphorisms "Bourgeois Morality" p. 54, or "Responsibility" p. 86), his caustic remarks about the social forms of the upper classes ("The Sociability of the Rich" GS 11, p. 271), or the very personal remarks for his own motivation to rebel against the injustices of capitalism ("Bad Superiors," p. 82).

[69] Horkheimer's passionate denunciation of contemporary society continued to be driven by moral impulses, but by this time he had already begun to work on a materialist appropriation of

say, however, that Horkheimer's reflections in *Dämmerung* remain at the level of abstract theoretical discourse. The opposite is the case. Based on his theoretical insights, Horkheimer is able to attain a new level of concreteness in his description of the mechanisms at work in the reproduction of capitalist social domination. As Marx pointed out, these mechanisms are abstract and real at the same time. They operate, in other words, not only behind the backs of individuals; they are also – and this is crucial for Horkheimer – reproduced by concrete individuals themselves in all aspects of their lives, even the seemingly most insignificant. The central, if by no means only, problem that Horkheimer addresses in *Dämmerung* is the various ways in which the historically unique dynamic of capitalist society reproduces itself through the knowledge and ignorance, actions and inaction, behavior, attitudes, and feelings of concrete individuals. Horkheimer's focus on the finite, socially and historically conditioned individual is crucial for the development of his own Critical Theory for several reasons. It provides him with an alternative to the infinite and unconditional nature of knowledge, which he identified as the common denominator of German idealism. It also allows him to apply Marx's insights not just at the general level of society, but also at the particular level of its individual members. This attempt to extend and update Marx's theory through closer scrutiny of the subjective determinants of society would also lead Horkheimer to psychoanalysis.

Horkheimer's primary method in *Dämmerung* is interpretive description. *Dämmerung* can justifiably be seen as an *empirical* analysis of contemporary society. However, Horkheimer's aphorisms do not merely describe what he sees around him in a passive or arbitrary way. In both form and content, Horkheimer moves beyond a purely empirical approach. Formalistically, Horkheimer draws particularly on the rich psychological tradition in French literature in the early modern period, from Montaigne to La Rochefoucauld to Voltaire and his friend Vauvenargues.[70] Like them, Horkheimer uses aphorisms, anecdotes, metaphors, and concrete examples to describe and reflect on more general social tendencies and psychological mechanisms. Horkheimer's choice of these specific formal and stylistic means – as opposed to a more systematic approach – also reflects the extra-, even antiacademic nature of *Dämmerung*. The content of *Dämmerung* consists in large part in Horkheimer's attempt to highlight and make visible these mechanisms, which can also be understood as mores, in the anthropological sense: as the norms that govern the everyday lives of individuals in an unspoken and largely unconscious way. He describes and analyzes, in other words, the concrete manifestations of reified social relations

---

Hegel's critique of Kant's moral philosophy, which he would carry out in more detail in his essay "Materialism and Morality" in 1933. Horkheimer already recognized at this time that it was impossible to explain why lofty moral ideals are not realized without a critical theory of the social totality. GS 3, p. 126.

[70] Horkheimer refers explicitly to this tradition in his lectures on the French Enlightenment: GS 9, pp. 358–62. This was the same tradition that influenced other renowned modern masters of the aphorism, such as Nietzsche or Baudelaire, whose dark reflections on everyday life in modern society in *Paris Spleen* anticipate many of Horkheimer's concerns in *Dämmerung*.

that have become second nature in modern capitalism. Horkheimer's treatment of this problem can be called empirical insofar as he moves beyond a merely abstract description of the laws that govern society, such as one finds in Marx's law of value, his theory of the tendential decline of the rate of profit, or even his description of commodity fetishism. Whereas Marx certainly could not be accused of failing to provide empirical evidence for his most general theses, Horkheimer moves a step beyond him in the specific sense that he describes in more subtle detail the social and psychological manifestations in the concrete individual of the "laws" that govern monopoly capitalism.

This procedure of Horkheimer is illustrated clearly, for example, in an aphorism entitled "The Little Man and the Philosophy of Freedom," in which he offers a suggestive reformulation of Marx's theory of commodity fetishism. Horkheimer writes:

The businessman is subject to laws which neither he nor any power with such a mandate created with purpose and deliberation. They are laws which the big capitalists and perhaps he himself skillfully makes use of but whose existence must be accepted as a fact. Boom, bust, inflation, wars and even the qualities of things and human beings the present society demands are a function of such laws, of the anonymous social reality, just as the rotation of the earth expresses the laws of dead nature. No single individual can do anything about them.[71]

But like Marx, Horkheimer refuses any hypostatization of this state of affairs as eternal or necessary. He continues:

Bourgeois thought views this reality as superhuman. It fetishizes the social process. It speaks of fate and either calls it blind, or attempts a mystical interpretation. It deplores the meaninglessness of the whole, or submits to the inscrutability of God's ways. But in actuality, all those phenomena which are either experienced as accidental or given a mystical interpretation depend on men and the way they arrange their social existence. They can therefore also be changed.[72]

Dämmerung as a whole can be seen as, among other things, an attempt to demystify the mechanisms of social domination in capitalism by describing the social and psychological "laws" that govern its operation. In the spirit of the Enlightenment, Horkheimer clearly believed that the first step toward overcoming these reified mechanisms was to raise them to consciousness and to make them visible. Horkheimer's commitment to the Enlightenment ideals of transparency and a rationally organized society also come through clearly in this aphorism. He continues:

If men consciously took their life in society in hand and replaced the struggle of capitalist enterprises by a classless and planned economy, the effects the process of production has on human beings and their relationships could also be understood and regulated. What today appears as a fact of nature in the private and business dealings of individuals are the effects of social life as a whole. They are human, not divine products.[73]

[71] *Dawn and Decline*, p. 50.
[72] Ibid., pp. 50–1.
[73] Ibid.

As long as this rationally planned society is not realized, according to Horkheimer, individual freedom will suffer greatly. He continues:

> Because these effects of life in society are present but not conscious, willed or controlled, and are the results of an equal number of individual wills that grasp neither their dependence nor their power, the limitation on individual freedom in our time is immeasurably greater than would be necessary, given the available means.[74]

However, as Horkheimer illustrates in many different aphorisms in *Dämmerung*, it is not just a question of the unnecessary limitation of individual freedom. The present social system is also based on high levels of surplus suffering, that is, suffering that could be eliminated in a more rational society. By describing this unnecessary suffering, Horkheimer returns to the motif of compassion, which he had taken over from Schopenhauer, and which had played such an important role in his own earliest writings. Thus, the unnecessary suffering of concrete individuals and the solidarity with "finite beings" that it evokes continues to be an important impulse for Horkheimer's passionate plea for a transition from an antagonistic capitalist society, which places a premium on ruthlessness,[75] to a rationally planned socialist society, based on the principles of compassion and solidarity.

Although Horkheimer's primary concern in *Dämmerung* is the concrete, empirical manifestations of the social and psychological "laws" that govern the reproduction of monopoly capitalist society, the aphorisms also provide many implicit and explicit references to his nascent Critical Theory of society. In fact, all of Horkheimer's remarks and observations in *Dämmerung* can be seen as attempts to develop and apply his theoretical insights through his observations of contemporary European society. Thus, in what follows, Horkheimer's aphorisms will be examined not only as examples of theoretically informed observations; an attempt will also be made to determine at a more abstract level the ways in which they illustrate certain key aspects of his theory of society. We will focus in particular on his discussions of epistemology, ideology, the Enlightenment, psychology, and Marxist theory.

Dämmerung as an Expression of Horkheimer's Nascent Critical Theory

The problems of epistemology and ideology are, not surprisingly, inextricably intertwined in *Dämmerung*. Let us, nonetheless, separate them provisionally and address the former before turning to the latter. After the opening aphorism – which is also called "Dämmerung," and which illustrates the title of the collection as a whole – follows an aphorism bearing the title "Monadology" that treats the problem of epistemology. The prominent location of this aphorism highlights the centrality of the topic of the socially mediated character of knowledge that runs throughout the book as a whole. As we have already seen, Horkheimer rejects Leibniz's appropriation of the doctrine of innate ideas, but he finds his notion of monadology useful nonetheless as a

---

[74] Ibid.
[75] See the aphorism "A Premium Placed on Vileness," ibid., pp. 28f.

metaphor to describe the status of knowledge and the difficulties of mutual understanding in contemporary society. Horkheimer adopts Leibniz's metaphor to describe the mechanical and largely blind interaction of individuals, but he does not go so far as to claim that these "monads" have no windows whatsoever. They have small windows that grant them a narrow and distorted view of the external world. Yet distorted perceptions and systematically distorted communication with others are not to blame on the senses; they are, rather, rooted in the subjective dispositions of each individual that are largely socially determined. As Horkheimer puts it:

It is not my impression that man's knowledge of others comes from God. Instead, I would say that those houses do have windows but that they let in only a small and distorted segment of events in the outside world. But this distorting effect is not so much a consequence of the peculiarities of the sense organs as of the worried or joyful, anxious or aggressive, slavish or superior, sated or yearning, dull or alert psychic attitudes which constitute that ground of our life against which all other experiences stand out, and which gives them their specific qualities. In addition to the direct force of one's external fate, the possibility of understanding among men is dependent on these factors.[76]

In this aphorism, Horkheimer suggests only one possibility of overcoming the socially determined limitations on knowledge and communication: "I know of only one kind of gust that can open the windows of the house wider: shared suffering."[77]

As we have seen, Horkheimer was highly critical of the claim that knowledge is absolute, infinite, or unconditioned. He viewed this claim as a remnant of medieval scholasticism that was continued in the rationalist and metaphysical currents of early modern philosophy, and which reached its pinnacle in German Idealism.[78] In an aphorism entitled "Sky Scraper," Horkheimer continues his reflections on epistemology and his critique of philosophical attempts to deny the socially determined character of knowledge. He uses the multiple stories of the skyscraper as a metaphor for the various levels of power and privilege in the world, from the corporate magnates to the workers and the unemployed in the industrialized nations all the way down to the destitute masses in the colonialized countries, and even to the animals below them. With this image in mind, he problematizes the abstractly universal and essentialist claims made by contemporary phenomenologists:

We hear a great deal these days about the "intuition of essence" [*Wesensschau*]. Anyone who once "intuited" the "essence" of the skyscraper on whose highest floor our philosophers are allowed to pursue their discussion will no longer be surprised that they know so little about the real height at which they find themselves, and that they always talk only about an imaginary one. Such a person knows, and they may suspect, that otherwise they might become dizzy. He is no longer surprised that they would rather set up a system of values than one of disvalues, that they rather talk about "man in general" than about the concrete individual, about being generally rather than their own. For if

---

[76] Ibid., pp. 17–18 (the translator omitted the last entire sentence of this quote in the English version).

[77] Ibid.

[78] See Chapter 3, pp. 111ff.

they did, they might be punished by being sent to a lower floor. The observer will no longer be surprised that they prattle about the "eternal," for as does the mortar, that prattle holds together this present-day house of mankind. The basement of that house is a slaughterhouse, its roof a cathedral, but from the windows of the upper floors, it affords a really beautiful view of the starry heavens.[79]

Horkheimer highlights not only the social structures that underlie the production of philosophical knowledge, he also emphasizes the role that this knowledge plays in reinforcing these structures. He points to the very real punishments that exist for those who violate the laws concerning the reproduction of this knowledge.

In two other aphorisms entitled "Social Space" and "Time is Money," Horkheimer expands his reflections on epistemology to what are normally considered its two most basic categories, namely space and time. Far from existing as abstract, universal categories – in the natural world or a universal transcendental subject – space and time are also inextricably linked to concrete individuals who live in particular socio-historical conditions. Like the guileless philosophers in the top of the skyscraper, those fortunate enough to exist in the power centers of society assume that their conceptions of space are universal. Yet Horkheimer argues that real borders and divisions that define space in capitalist society are only apparent from its margins and periphery. He writes:

To recognize the space in which one finds oneself, one must discover its limits.... As long as someone stays in the center of society, i.e. as long as he occupies a respected position and does not come into conflict with society, he does not discover what it really is. The further he moves away from that secure center ... he finds that this society is based on the total negation of all human values. The way the police occasionally treat the workers during an uprising or beat the imprisoned unemployed with the butts of their rifles, the tone the factory porter uses with the man looking for work, the workhouse and the penitentiary, all these function as the limits that disclose the space in which we live. The more central positions must be understood through the more peripheral ones.[80]

In "Time is Money" Horkheimer shows that time cannot be determined abstractly either.[81] A concept of time unmediated by concrete individuals is unthinkable according to him. He writes:

As if it were a matter of indifference whom we are talking about! Whether my time or yours, the time of Mr. Krupp or an unemployed, it is money. Nor are we told whose money it is, or how much of it, although it is clear, for example, that when Mr. Krupp wastes his time, it costs him his own money. And when the worker wastes time, it also costs him his own, Mr. Krupp's own money.... "Time is money." There seems to be a need to find a criterion by which to judge how much money a certain span of time is worth. The following observation may be useful in the search for it: A worker who leases a car to get to his place of work in time in the morning is stupid (just compare the cost of daily transportation with his wage). An unemployed person with a few dollars in his pocket who uses a car to save time is crazy. But a middle level administrator who

---

[79] Ibid.
[80] Ibid.
[81] See also the aphorism, "Time and Truth." GS 11, pp. 283–4.

does not use a car to transact his business may already be called untalented. A minute in the life of an unemployed person does not have the same value as the administrator's minute. One should figure out how many hundreds of lives of workers would have to be added up to equal the value of a moderately well-off banker's day. Time is money – but what is the value of the lifetime of most people.[82]

In short, Horkheimer repeatedly attempts to show how all types of knowledge, even the seemingly most abstract, such as the perception of space and time, are always mediated by concrete individuals who occupy radically different positions within the antagonistic capitalist social totality.

We have already seen how Horkheimer viewed the transition from abstract examinations of epistemology to an active critique of ideology in the history of modern philosophy. Whereas Bacon, Hobbes, Leibniz, and other early modern philosophers had explored the factors that prevented one from properly grasping the truth or, in other words, the causes of impure, distorted, and false forms of knowledge, it was only in the French Enlightenment that the social and historical determinants of knowledge were explicitly thematized. The early modern philosophers had viewed the epistemological distortions caused by idols or closed monadological windows as anthropological or historical constants. Yet the thematization by the *philosophes* of the socially determined character of knowledge and its role in reproducing historically specific relations of domination leads beyond abstract epistemological reflections to an active attempt to use knowledge to create a more rational society.[83] In *Dämmerung*, as in his critique of Karl Mannheim, Horkheimer rejects any attempt to define knowledge in a passive, disinterested, or ahistorical manner. In an aphorism with the title "Disinterested Striving for the Truth," Horkheimer conducts a thought experiment in which he asks what would be left if one expunged all possible interests, desires, and wishes, as well as love, hate, anxiety, vanity, and compassion from the process of obtaining knowledge. This would reduce knowledge to a mere ghost, and a very odd one at that: one with no relationship to the present and the past, and thus no real reason to even haunt the living. Based on this thought experiment, Horkheimer concludes:

The claim that there is a disinterested striving for truth ... is a philosophical delusion, which has been made ideologically effective. Originally, the bourgeois doctrine of the pure striving for truth may have been proclaimed as the opposite of thought in the service of religious ends. Nowadays, capitalist professors deny that any human impulses enter their work. They do not want anyone to find out that they pursue wisdom for the sake of their career. Although there is no disinterested striving for truth, there is such a thing as thinking for thinking's sake, a ritualized thinking which has lost its purpose, namely as a means to improve people's lives. It should not be confused with the pleasure that lies in the activity of thinking which enlightening and intensely interested minds feel when contributing to progressive historical tendencies.[84]

---

[82] Ibid., pp. 22–3 (translation amended).

[83] See Chapter 3, pp. 103ff. See also Adorno's discussion of this historical transition in his article "Ideologie," in *Frankfurter Beiträge zur Soziologie*, vol. 4, *Soziologische Exkurse*, ed. T.W. Adorno and Walter Dirks (Frankfurt, 1956), p. 164.

[84] *Dawn and Decline*, pp. 53–4.

In other words, Horkheimer follows the *philosophes* in assuming that knowledge is always bound to passions and interests, including putatively objective knowledge.

Yet Horkheimer also moves beyond the *philosophes* in insisting that particular ideology is not the only form of ideology. Ideology is not merely manipulation, and it is not possible to expose and eliminate it with the purely rational methods of critique. In this regard, Horkheimer follows Marx, who also went beyond the Enlightenment in stressing the *necessity* of false consciousness in capitalist society, in the sense that ideology is not merely a question of subjective convictions or insight. As Karl Mannheim pointed out, Marx was the originator of the modern concept of total ideology, which stresses its social origins. In *Dämmerung*, Horkheimer incorporates Marx's insight by showing how ideology is rooted in the quasi-objective social structures and institutions of contemporary monopoly capitalism; but he also pushes Marx's dialectical logic one step further by pursuing the mediation of ideology not only from the particular to the general, but also back to the concrete individual. Horkheimer pursues the theme of the reproduction of socially determined ideology at the level of the concrete individual in other aphorisms in *Dämmerung*. He shows time and again the material rewards and punishments that go hand in hand with the acceptance or rejection of hegemonic ideology. He illustrates how these mechanisms operate mostly at an extremely subtle, even unconscious level. In an aphorism entitled "Rules of the Game," for example, he shows how dissimulation is necessary to ensure peaceful social interaction between members of different classes:

If the man who merely makes a living is to associate with members of the upper classes, it is essential that what is most important, the class difference between the two, not be mentioned. Good manners require not only that nothing be said about this but that the difference be skillfully masked by expression and behavior. The pretense that both move on the same social plane must be maintained. The millionaire does his part. When he goes to Trouville for his summer vacation and his impecunious acquaintance into some wretched Black Forest hamlet, the millionaire is not going to say, "That's all you can afford?" but rather, "We'd like to go back to that beautiful Black Forest some time." ... Now his poor acquaintance must answer, "It's true, I am really looking forward to the Black Forest." Should he say, "I'd also rather go to Trouville but I can't afford it," the first thing he will be told is, "You must be joking." Should he insist, not only as regards his summer vacation but whenever this answer is relevant, he would appear vulgar, and the association would terminate.[85]

This example also illustrates Horkheimer's belief that ideology cannot be explained merely in terms of subjective illusions or convictions that can be changed at will. Ideology is not only deeply anchored in the objective structure of society, but also actively reproduced by concrete individuals in their everyday lives through a system of subtle and not-so-subtle incentives and punishments.

Horkheimer's remarks on religion in *Dämmerung* provide an excellent example of his efforts to analyze the roots and function of ideology in contemporary capitalist society. Horkheimer's critique of the ideological aspects of

[85] Ibid., p.33.

religion illustrates once again his debt to the French Enlightenment and Marx, while moving beyond them in important ways as well. Marx's continuity with the French Enlightenment was readily apparent in his critique of religion (and morality) as quintessential forms of ideology. Yet Marx also went beyond the French Enlightenment in his appropriation of Feuerbach's anthropological critique of religion, which recognized the deep psychological roots and the mechanisms of alienation that underlie religion. Drawing on Feuerbach, Marx interpreted religion as a veiled form of protest against inhumane social conditions.[86] For Marx, religion was ideological not because it was merely a particular ideology propagated by priests in order to further their own selfish interests – a belief that was widespread in prerevolutionary France, and not only among the *philosophes* – but rather because it mystified the real relations of domination that existed in capitalism, and provided people with spiritual compensation for their suffering, rather than helping them to understand and change its material causes. Like Marx, Horkheimer insists that religion is not merely an illusion or a form of deception, but also a mystified form of protest. Horkheimer writes:

In its symbols, religion places an apparatus at the disposal of tortured men through which they express their suffering and their hope. This is one of its most important functions. A respectable psychology of religion would have to distinguish between its positive and negative aspects, it would have to separate proper human feelings and ideas from an ideological form which falsifies them but is also partly their product.[87]

Horkheimer also moves beyond Marx, because he had also learned from Schopenhauer that the psychological energies invested in religion – what Schopenhauer called man's "metaphysical needs" – are thoroughly labile and can be placed in the service of many different ends.[88] As with all forms of knowledge and ideology, Horkheimer insists on the historical specificity of religion and its function in modern capitalist society.

Horkheimer illustrates this point in the continuation of the aphorism just quoted, "A Different Kind of Criticism." In this extremely dense and rich aphorism, Horkheimer shows how religion has been reduced to one form of ideology among others in contemporary society. It is not simply the case that Europe had become more secular and rational in the course of the nineteenth century. The psychological energies that had previously been invested in religion have, according to Horkheimer, now found other forms of articulation: in the ideologies of unlimited economic and scientific progress or nationalism, for

---

[86] *The Marx-Engels Reader*, op. cit., p. 54.

[87] *Dawn and Decline*, p. 58.

[88] See chapter 17 of the second volume of Schopenhauer's, *The World as Will and Representation*, trans. E.F.J. Payne, "On Man's Need for Metaphysics," (New York, 1958), pp. 160–87, in which Schopenhauer describes the different concrete forms in which specifically human metaphysical needs have manifested themselves and also been manipulated. This chapter clearly made a lasting impression on Horkheimer early in his life, as is made clear in a letter he wrote to his future wife, Rosa Riekher, in 1920, in which he places the chapter at the top of his list of recommendations for her to read. See GS 15, p. 60. On Schopenhauer's philosophy of religion, see also Alfred Schmidt, *Die Wahrheit im Gewande der Lüge: Schopenhauer's Religionsphilosophie* (Munich, 1986).

example. Whereas religious ideals, when taken seriously, had often been the basis of progressive social change in the past,[89] the transcendent moment in religion – the moment of protest that Marx had still taken seriously, and which would play an important role in Horkheimer's late work – had virtually disappeared in advanced capitalist societies in the twentieth century. As Adorno would document empirically later,[90] in the twentieth century, religion had, with few exceptions, been reduced to a conformist and affirmative ideology whose function differed little from other forms of contemporary ideology such as nationalism. Horkheimer writes:

The criticism of religion as mere ideology is justified if it reveals that what were previously impulses in religious disguise, such as dissatisfaction with the order on earth, may become effective today in a different form…. These days, Christianity is not primarily used as a religion but as a crude transfiguration [*Verklärung*] of existing conditions. The genius of political, military and industry leaders, and especially the nation, compete with God for the first place.[91]

In another aphorism, entitled "Europe and Christianity," Horkheimer argues that the transcendent, critical moment in religion suffers the same fate as the universal ideals that guided the bourgeoisie in its struggle against the feudal world. In the course of the nineteenth century, the realization of these ideals was dismissed as a utopian fantasy, but one was not willing to part with them entirely either. Horkheimer describes the lazy compromise that resulted in the following unflattering terms:

It is not part of life in this civilization to take religion seriously. Non-religious values such as justice, freedom or truth are not taken seriously either. Acknowledging them is no more than a *façon de parler*…. Acknowledging the gulf between the moral criteria of Christians, and their actual conduct therefore impresses one as an unrealistic, odd, sentimental, superfluous observation. You may call it a lie or say that it is old hat, just as you please, but you should not trouble a reasonable European with it. In this regard Jews and Christians are of one mind. The compromise between the implementation of religion and its inexpedient abolition is the reconciliation with God via the all-encompassing lie.[92]

Despite his diagnosis of the virtual disappearance of the transcendent moment in contemporary religion, Horkheimer also insists that it remains, like other forms of contemporary ideology, not merely an illusion or deception, but rather an objective form of fetishism produced in contemporary capitalist society that has a firm basis in the psychic economies of its individual members.[93] The

---

[89] *Dawn and Decline*, pp. 58f.
[90] See *The Authoritarian Personality* (New York, 1950), pp. 727–43.
[91] *Dawn and Decline*, pp. 58–9.
[92] Ibid., p. 91.
[93] This analysis of the transformation and diffusion of "religious" ideology in modern mass societies, which Horkheimer and Adorno would work out in greater detail in their later work, has been developed by the sociologist Detlev Claussen. He analyzes the development and persistent virulence, into the present, of ideologies such as anti-Semitism and ethnonationalism, as forms of what he calls "everyday religion." See, for example, *Grenzen der Aufklärung: Zur Gesellschaftlichen Genese des Modernen Antisemitismus* (Frankfurt, 1994) and

power of these social-psychological mechanisms is illustrated by the fact that in contemporary society, even the rejection of religion often assumes an ideological form. Horkheimer writes, "There is no logically compelling reason for replacing the toppled absolute by some other absolute, the toppled gods by others, devotion by denial. Even today, men could forget irreligion. But they are too weak for that."[94] In short, the material conditions for a more rational and humane orientation toward the world and other individuals are present, but the ongoing dynamic of capitalism prevents its realization and reinforces the illusions that are "necessary" to function within it.

Despite his pessimistic diagnosis of the deeply rooted material power of ideology in contemporary monopoly capitalism, Horkheimer does not rule out the efficacy of ideology critique entirely. In the opening title aphorism of *Dämmerung*, Horkheimer implies that ideology critique has actually become more threatening than ever to those with a vested interest in the status quo because of the development of critical consciousness among the general population in Europe. Horkheimer writes:

The less stable necessary ideologies are, the more cruel the methods by which they are protected. The degree of zeal and terror with which tottering idols are defended shows how far dusk has already advanced. With the development of large-scale industry, the intelligence of the European masses has grown so greatly that the most sacred possessions must be protected from them. Whoever does this well is ensured a good career.[95]

Horkheimer's ongoing efforts during this time, in *Dämmerung* and elsewhere, to analyze and criticize these new forms of ideology testify to his unbroken belief in the necessity and importance of ideology critique. Horkheimer did not subscribe to either the determinist philosophy of history of Karl Kautsky, nor to the vanguardism of the Bolsheviks, for both assign to the wide majority of the population, in whose interest the transition to socialism should take place, a merely passive role. Horkheimer clung to the egalitarian Enlightenment ideal, which also formed the basis of German Idealism from Kant to Hegel, that all individuals have the capability to exercise their reason, to step out of the condition of self-incurred immaturity, and to develop a critical understanding of the society in which they live. As Adorno would also repeatedly stress in his later writings, it is not the complexity of society in and of itself that makes it impossible for a normal person to understand the mechanisms of capitalist domination, but rather the overwhelming presence and material power of ideology.[96] Horkheimer states this clearly in an aphorism entitled "Platitudes":

If it were really generally recognized that the continuation of exploitation which benefits only a small number of men is the source of present day social wretchedness; if

Aspekte der Alltagsreligion: Ideologiekritik unter Veränderten Gesellschaftlichen Verhältnissen (Frankfurt, 2000).

[94] "Atheism and Religion," *Dawn and Decline*, p. 66.

[95] Ibid., p. 17 (translation amended).

[96] For example, Adorno would later write: "In many respects society ... is more transparent than ever before. If knowledge were dependent solely on the functional composition of society, the proverbial house maid could probably understand the system very well today." Theodor Adorno, "Theorie der Halbbildung," in *Gesammelte Schriften*, vol. 8 (Frankfurt, 1997), p. 117.

every newspaper reader grasped that the preservation of the present order is the cause of all the wars, crimes, poverty, misery and murder he reads about; if these platitudes which not even people with an average knowledge of the world, let alone our learned men, understand because we have a marvelously functioning brainwashing apparatus, if these platitudes, I say, were even to penetrate the understanding of the lowest guardian of this order, mankind could be spared a terrible future.[97]

Thus, the role of the critical intellectual for Horkheimer is not simply to study the laws that govern capitalism nor to impose with force correct conscious-ness upon the "ignorant masses," but rather that of a gadfly – that is, as one who never ceases to point to the unrealized potential for a more rational and humane society and to the forces hindering the realization of this potential.[98] For a better society can only be brought about through the *conscious* efforts of its members, not behind their backs. As Horkheimer puts it: "The socialist order of society is not prevented by world history; it is historically possible. But it will not be realized by a logic that is immanent in history but by men trained in theory and determined to make things better. Otherwise, it will not be realized at all."[99] This makes it understandable why ideology critique con-tinued to play such an important role in Horkheimer's own theoretical work during this time.

Nonetheless, Horkheimer entertained no illusions about the virtually insur-mountable barriers facing ideology critique in the present. In the continuation of the title aphorism quoted earlier, Horkheimer leaves no doubt about this:

Woe to the man who tells the truth in simple terms. There is not only the general, sys-tematically engineered brainwashing but the general threat of economic ruin, social ostracism, the penitentiary and death to deter reason from attacking the key conceptual techniques of domination.[100]

However, he also realized that any attempt to carry on the tradition of ideology critique must reflect upon those barriers – make them visible – in order to main-tain its self-reflexivity and contemporary relevance. First and foremost among these is that the potential addressees of the critique are, for the most part, deeply dependent on the status quo and on those who benefit disproportion-ately from it. As we shall see in more detail shortly in our examination of the study of the attitudes of workers in Germany in 1929, this dependence existed not just at the material, but also at a deep psychological level. Horkheimer describes this situation in *Dämmerung* in the following way:

The dependence of the oppressed classes stems not just from not being given enough to eat, but that they are also kept in a wretched intellectual and psychological state. They are the apes of their wardens, worship the symbols of their prison and, far from

---

[97] *Dawn and Decline*, p. 48.
[98] In this respect, Horkheimer's views were similar to Herbert Marcuse's understanding of the role of the critical intellectual at this time to "make the truth visible," not to impose it with force or to reject the possibility of the "masses" being able to comprehend it all. See "On Concrete Philosophy," *Herbert Marcuse: Heideggerian Marxism*, eds. J. Abromeit and R. Wolin (Lincoln: University of Nebraska Press, 2005).
[99] "Skepsis and Morality," *Dawn and Decline*, p. 37.
[100] Ibid., p. 17.

attacking their guardians, stand ready to tear to pieces the person that undertakes to free them from their tutelage.[101]

This situation also has consequences for ideology critique, according to Horkheimer. It is the reason why critique often evokes such a negative response, and not just among the most powerful. As he puts it an aphorism entitled "Thankfulness," "Progressive action, publicly attacking and criticizing the dominant form of society, appears not only harmful, but in most cases also morally repugnant."[102] This ideologically mystified and justified situation of dependence also explains why critique is particularly suspect if it comes from the ranks of the less privileged. For then, it often appears as base envy or *ressentiment*. Horkheimer writes:

A neat trick: the criticism of the system is to be the prerogative of those that have an interest in it. The others, who have the opportunity of getting to know its underside, are disarmed by the contemptuous remark that they are annoyed, vengeful, envious. They harbor resentment.... To restrict testimony about this society which is largely a penitentiary to those who do not experience it as such almost seems like a tacit agreement among the fortunate ones.[103]

Horkheimer was, in other words, well aware of the many obstacles that ideology critique faced under the conditions of contemporary capitalism.

It is, however, worth mentioning one final obstacle to ideology critique that Horkheimer identifies, not only because it provides a transition to our next topic – Horkheimer's interpretation of the Enlightenment in *Dämmerung* – but also because it provides some important clues on how to approach Horkheimer's intellectual biography as a whole in a manner that does justice to the spirit of his work. The analysis of authoritarian attitudes and their perpetuation and reinforcement within the cultural edifice of capitalist society would play an important role in the work of the Frankfurt School as a whole. Horkheimer anticipates these concerns in *Dämmerung* in an aphorism entitled "Categories of Burial." He shows how revolutionary ideas or revolutionary theory is routinized, and thus robbed of its critical potential, through its popularization and personalization. He writes:

The most popular way of making a theory innocuous these days is not really orthodoxy but the blithe transportation of its categories into a context which is totally at odds with the author's intentions. In contrast to the author, who will always enjoy a formal respect, especially after his death, his orthodox followers, who are at least attempting to carefully preserve his ideas, are despised as pitiful, barren intellects. The person of the creator is thus shown greater respect than the substance of this thought. The attitude toward the revolutionary pioneers of bourgeois thought is a particularly striking instance. The names of those who became known as forerunners of the bourgeois order ... have become too glorious to be passed over in silence. From Voltaire, Rousseau, Lessing, Kant on down to their successors in modern literature and science, all are acknowledged as great men, profound thinkers and fiery spirits. But wherever they are

---

[101] "Europe and Christianity," ibid., pp. 88–9.
[102] GS 2, p. 417 (My translation. This was one of the aphorisms that the editors of *Dawn and Decline* chose to omit).
[103] *Dawn and Decline*, "Concerning Resentment," p. 31.

actually encountered, their beliefs, drives and motives, the meaning of their teaching, their uncompromising rejection of the prevailing injustice, are spurned and mocked, called pathetic, superficial and onesided, and even persecuted and exterminated when conditions warrant. The Middle Ages banished the dead authors of heretical views to hell. In its heyday, capitalism is more tolerant. It apotheosizes greatness, productivity, personality, potency itself, but rejects what they bring forth.[104]

Ideology critique is, in other words, also in danger of losing its critical potential by the dubious respect paid to the person, rather than his or her work. Horkheimer highlights this tendency with respect to the critical thinkers of the Enlightenment in particular. As we have seen, Horkheimer rejected a monumental historiography of the Enlightenment and stressed the collective nature of the critical discourse developed in prerevolutionary France.[105] In his lectures on the history of philosophy, Horkheimer does not create a pantheon of "great thinkers;" he is, instead, at pains to preserve the critical core of their ideas by showing, for example, the ways in which they contributed to the development of the tradition of ideology critique. But as Horkheimer makes clear time and again in *Dämmerung*, the critical tradition of the Enlightenment is relevant to contemporary problems in many other ways as well.

However, before turning to Horkheimer's recourse to the Enlightenment in *Dämmerung*, it should also be noted that Horkheimer's analysis of the recuperation of ideology critique through popularization and personalization also provides important guidelines for an appropriate approach to his own work. An uncritical celebration of Horkheimer's life and work, particularly one that focuses more on his life than his work, would be precisely the type of recuperation that he criticizes here. Although it would take us too far afield to reflect on the inherent strengths and weaknesses of the genre of intellectual biography here, it is clear from Horkheimer's remarks that to do justice to the spirit of his life and work as a whole – which has been aptly characterized by one qualified commentator as "consistent non-conformism" and "the capacity for incorruptible criticism, even of his own ideas"[106] – no mere uncritical celebration of his work, and much less his person, will do. An intellectual biography that aspires to remain true to Horkheimer's critical spirit – as this one does – must not only attempt to present his ideas in all their complexity and radicalness, and thereby to wrest them from the wave of amnesia and conformism that is threatening to overwhelm in the present. It must also attempt to identify the social and historical factors that conditioned his Critical Theory at the various stages of its development. For only then will it be possible to address the final important task of determining which aspects of Horkheimer's Critical Theory are still relevant in the present and which must be revised or abandoned.

We have just seen how Horkheimer defends the Enlightenment tradition by insisting on the contemporary relevance of ideology critique – albeit in a radicalized form suitable to the changed socio-historical conditions of the

---

[104] Ibid., p. 25.
[105] See Chapter 3, p. 104.
[106] Alfred Schmidt, "Max Horkheimer's Intellectual Physiognomy," op. cit., p. 42.

early twentieth century. The passage quoted earlier about the recuperation of the "great thinkers" of the Enlightenment also illustrates that their critical potential may have been defused, but has by no means been exhausted. The Enlightenment is still relevant, according to Horkheimer, because the ideas formulated by the *philosophes* in the eighteenth century pointed not only beyond feudal society, but also beyond its historical successor, capitalist society. In *Dämmerung* and other writings from this time, Horkheimer stresses time and again that "in the writings of the philosophes" there are "impulses which point not only beyond feudal society but class society generally."[107] For Horkheimer, this is also the reason why the Enlightenment was so hated in Germany at that time. Horkheimer believed, as we have seen, that the revival of metaphysics and the spread of popularized versions of *Lebensphilosophie* represented the most dangerous ideological tendencies in Europe in the 1920s. It was against these neoromantic tendencies in particular that Horkheimer sought to preserve the progressive core of the Enlightenment tradition. He states this clearly in an unpublished lecture manuscript on Kant from 1930:

Hatred of the Enlightenment began around the turn of the nineteenth century and has, in one section of the leading literature of today, advanced to a methodical rejection of rational thought.... The élan of the *Übermenschen* has driven even the last traces of Enlightenment and French Revolution out of the heads of philosophers, and what Nietzsche, in naive candor, proclaimed only about himself, has in the meantime been strongly echoed in a thousand books in philosophy and the humanities: "We have emancipated ourselves from the fear of *raison*, the spectre of the eighteenth century; we dare once again to be absurd, childish, lyrical – in a word, 'We are musicians.'" Occasionally in recent years it has indeed seemed that music has taken the place of philosophy, that confusion is more in demand than clarity, and that the task of thinking is not to penetrate but to produce obscurity in the world.[108]

His defense of Ernst Mach's scientific methodology against Lenin's criticisms illustrated Horkheimer's belief that Marxism too can and must continue to utilize the intellectual tools forged during the Enlightenment. The following passage from an unpublished aphorism from *Dämmerung*, which contains an unmistakable allusion to Lukács's early romantic anticapitalism, also makes this clear: "The proletariat has nothing against the 'rational-calculating' mode of thought, which is seen as the cardinal sin of capitalism by philosophizing socialists today."[109]

In another aphorism in *Dämmerung*, entitled "The Struggle Against the Bourgeois," Horkheimer demonstrates that the contemporary hatred of the Enlightenment also expresses itself in certain forms of criticism of the bourgeoisie. Horkheimer distinguishes between the progressive Marxist critique of the bourgeoisie, which was developed in the course of the nineteenth century in the context of the European workers' movement, and a reactionary critique

---

[107] "Two Elements of the French Revolution," *Dawn and Decline*, p. 105.
[108] "Über Kants Philosophie," GS 11, p. 204–5. The passage from Nietzsche that Horkheimer quotes here is located in *Der Wille zur Macht*, *Gesammelte Schriften* (Musarionausgabe), vol. 19, (Munich, 1926), p. 341.
[109] "Metaphysische Verklärung der Revolution," GS 11, p. 265.

of the bourgeoisie that originated during the romantic period, primarily in aristocratic circles. Horkheimer remarks that scornful criticism of the bourgeois personality type is mostly fed by the latter, reactionary tradition, because with the transition from liberal to monopoly capitalism, typical "bourgeois" characteristics have been largely separated from most powerful members of the capitalist elite. Anticipating arguments that he and his colleagues at the Institute would develop in more detail later, Horkheimer notes that monopoly capitalism has resulted in a far-reaching destruction of the middle class and the relatively small scale enterprises upon which it was based.[110] As a result of this development, typical "bourgeois" character traits have shifted down to this dispossessed middle class and even the working class, who are forced to struggle harder than ever to maintain their modest standard of living. Thus, it makes little sense in the present to vilify the typical bourgeois personality of the nineteenth century, for the critique is directed at the wrong target. Horkheimer writes:

In the class struggles of the nineteenth century, the term bourgeois took on the quality of a deadly declaration of war. Bourgeois meant exploiter, bloodsucker, and it was meant to characterize all those who were interested in maintaining the bad social order. Marx has clarified this meaning in all its detail. But following a tradition stemming from romanticism, the profoundly reactionary feudal enemies of capitalism gave the term bourgeois a contemptuous meaning. What has survived of this ideology was absorbed by the nationalist movements in all countries. Much like the pre-war "bohème," they paint the bourgeois as a bugaboo, they contrast the bad bourgeois as a human type of the past epoch, particularly the nineteenth century, with the new man of the future and point out how the biological core, the race, the mode of thought of the one is the diametric opposite of the other.[111]

Horkheimer goes on to show how this reactionary critique of the bourgeois personality type plays directly into the hands of the powers that be, not only because it misses its target, but also because it discredits the bourgeois tradition as a whole, which also includes the critical heritage of the Enlightenment. Horkheimer writes:

When modern metaphysicians attempt a sociological critique of the history of philosophy as the development of "bourgeois" thought, they are not concerned with those aspects of that class which the proletariat has to overcome. These ideologues only want to stigmatize and eradicate the theoretical vestiges of the revolutionary epoch of the bourgeoisie.[112]

Thus, Horkheimer's careful and conditional defense of the bourgeois legacy here is part of his larger attempt to rescue the progressive elements of the Enlightenment tradition from an abstract negation by the increasingly influential metaphysical and irrationalist currents in Germany in the late 1920s.

In contrast to some of his and Adorno's later arguments in *Dialectic of Enlightenment*, at this time Horkheimer was hardly concerned about locating

---

[110] See Chapter 7.
[111] *Dawn and Decline*, pp. 67–8.
[112] Ibid., pp. 68–9.

the roots of a totalizing form of reason in the Enlightenment tradition. In our examination of his lectures on the history of modern philosophy, we have already seen that Horkheimer stressed the antitotalizing, antiauthoritarian, and materialist character of the Enlightenment concept of reason.[113] This interpretation is also present in *Dämmerung*. Horkheimer continues to draw upon philosophical arguments from the Enlightenment to reject absolute claims of all types: epistemological, metaphysical, or political. He writes, "Along with Lessing, he leaves the 'pure' truth with God alone";[114] or "Absolute justice is just as unfathomable as absolute truth. The revolution does not need to concern itself with either."[115] Those, like Ernst Bloch, who turn socialism into a quasi-religious undertaking, are treated with caustic irony by Horkheimer. He writes:

> Due to the limitlessness of their expectations, the metaphysicians of the revolution are not taken very seriously by the bourgeoisie and in relatively stable periods they are even seen gladly.... I do not by any means want to contradict these philosophical transfigurations [*Verklärungen*] of the revolution. Perhaps they are justified, perhaps socialism really will mark the beginning of the golden millennium and all the prophecies of the Old Testament will be fulfilled. But it seems more correct to me that we do not worry about such things. More urgent today is not that men become something different, but that their lives are improved.[116]

This passage also demonstrates that another important legacy of the Enlightenment – and the French Enlightenment in particular – for Horkheimer at this time was its defense of the needs, interests, and happiness of the concrete individual. Throughout *Dämmerung* and in his other writings at this time, Horkheimer insists on the priority of the concrete individual – who has a legitimate claim not only to fulfillment of his needs and to freedom from unnecessary fear and suffering, but also to pursue interests, pleasure, and happiness – over abstract principles or the demands of abstract collectivities.[117] It was, in other words, not any abstract belief in the iron laws of history or utopian longings for a "new socialist man," but rather the widespread violation of these legitimate claims and the impossibility for large sections of the population to fulfill them within capitalist society that was the most important motivation of Horkheimer's Critical Theory at this time.[118] Horkheimer's criticism of ideological attempts to provide individuals with symbolic compensation for real suffering or sacrifice is part of his attempt to rescue the progressive aspects of bourgeois legacy – its defense of the material interests of real individuals and their right to pursue happiness – and would remain a cornerstone of his Critical Theory into the 1930s and beyond.

---

[113] For a more detailed examination of the Enlightenment's non-absolutist concept of truth, see David W. Bates, *Enlightenment Aberrations: Error and Revolution in France* (Ithaca and London: Cornell UP, 2002), pp. 18ff.

[114] GS 11, p. 285.

[115] *Dawn and Decline*, p. 32.

[116] GS 11, pp. 265–6.

[117] See, for example, the aphorism "Heroic Worldview," *Dawn and Decline*, pp. 37–8.

[118] See, for example, the unpublished aphorism from *Dämmerung* entitled "Lust und Unlust," GS 11, p. 272.

One consequence of Horkheimer's emphasis on the materialist character of the Enlightenment and his defense of the concrete individual was his skeptical and critical appraisal of the abstract political liberties that were so crucial for many of the philosophers of the Enlightenment. In his lectures on the history of philosophy, Horkheimer pays relatively little attention to the development of democratic and liberal political principles, and when he does address them, it is usually to expose their "ideological" character. In his discussion of John Locke, for example, Horkheimer views his political philosophy reductively as a direct expression of the interests of "those strata of the bourgeoisie that supported the government of William of Orange."[119] Thus, Locke's argument for the division of the executive from the legislative branch of government has, according to Horkheimer, "no other purpose than the possibility for the bourgeoisie represented in parliament to control the executive powers."[120] Horkheimer devotes virtually no attention to the defense of subjective rights in Locke's philosophy. Similarly, in his very brief discussion of Montesquieu, Horkheimer emphasizes that his political theory was "a purely bourgeois theory that was very dependent on Locke."[121] Montesquieu's further development of the division of powers through his defense of an independent judiciary also has a simple socio-historical explanation. Horkheimer writes:

In France at that time the court used completely arbitrary means – the famous "lettres de cachet" – to throw anyone in prison that displeased it, while such things had already been made impossible in England with the Habeas Corpus Act (1679). Thus Montesquieu must have viewed not only control of the court by parliament, but also a completely independent judiciary as especially desirable, in order to put an end to the arbitrary acts of absolutism.[122]

Unlike his future Institute colleague, Franz Neumann, Horkheimer failed to detect any radical potential in Montesquieu's discussion of the rule of law;[123] instead, he interprets Montesquieu's concept of the "esprit général" as a precursor of Herder and romantic nationalism. Horkheimer has nothing positive to say about the development of democratic political principles in Rousseau's thought either. He stresses instead their abstract and ideological nature:

Rousseau's political theory became a utopia that no longer had anything to do with reality.... Its deficiencies, its naiveté soon became apparent in the French Revolution, for it provided the *Declaration of the Rights of Man* and the constitution of the French Republic with material that was used as an ideological justification of the social relations that were being established at that time.... When it was proclaimed, with reference to Rousseau, that the philosophical idea of freedom had been realized in the new order ... the real meaning of this freedom soon became apparent. Shortly thereafter, the wealthy members of the third estate were free to purchase, for a modest price, the confiscated property of the aristocrats and to expand their manufacturing operations. On the other hand, the emancipated serfs and the masses who had carried the revolution

---

[119] GS 9, p. 339.
[120] Ibid.
[121] Ibid., p. 369.
[122] Ibid.
[123] See Franz Neumann, "Montesquieu," in *The Democratic and the Authoritarian State*, ed. Herbert Marcuse (New York: The Free Press, 1957), pp. 96–148.

in the cities were free to sell themselves, their wives and their children to these estates and manufactures – if they did not want to die of hunger right away. Constructing the republic upon an imaginary contract instead of an empirical investigation of its real origins, the proclamation of abstract freedom, Rousseau's immense mistake of not separating society clearly from the state, all made it possible that in the ensuing period precisely those interests were able to make use of his theory, which he himself had hated the most and believed he had fought for his entire life.... As it developed, the philosophical pathos and the increasing lack of precision made Rousseau's theory ideal as the official ideology of democracy in the French Republic.[124]

It may come as a surprise to see that Horkheimer, who in other respects was so eager to preserve the progressive elements of the Enlightenment tradition, had virtually nothing to say about the progressive potential of bourgeois liberal and democratic political principles. Despite the positive references to the Enlightenment throughout *Dämmerung*, none of them addresses the liberal or democratic political tradition. In this respect, Horkheimer's Marxism was, at this time, more orthodox than Marx himself, as it were.[125] It was not until the early 1950s that Horkheimer would develop a more positive attitude toward the liberal and, to a lesser extent, democratic political traditions. It would take us too far afield to explore all the reasons for Horkheimer's extreme skepticism about abstract liberal and democratic political principles here, but they will become more apparent in the course of this study.

As we have seen, Horkheimer also praised the *philosophes* for being the first to recognize and analyze the socially mediated nature of character and personality.[126] Horkheimer develops this idea in great detail in *Dämmerung*, which is crucial for understanding the role that psychology plays at this time in his nascent theory of society. One of the most important themes that Horkheimer addresses throughout *Dämmerung* is the ways in which almost all aspects of an individual's life are shaped by his or her position within the monopoly capitalist hierarchy. Horkheimer argues that everything from education,[127] to the value of one's person,[128] to the quality of one's marriage,[129] to one's health,[130] to one's erotic life,[131] to the seriousness of one's responsibility,[132] to how long one has to wait,[133] and even the way one ages[134] and dies[135] are all dependent on social

---

[124] GS 9, pp. 386–7.
[125] One could plausibly make this claim not only because Marx himself denied that he was a Marxist, but also, and more important, because the early Marx, at least, viewed the abstract political principles established by the bourgeois revolutions as a necessary, if by no means sufficient, condition for the establishment of a truly just, socialist society. See, for example, "On the Jewish Question," *Marx-Engels Reader*, op. cit., pp. 26–52.
[126] See Chapter 3, pp. 106ff.
[127] "Grade der Bildung," GS 2, p. 387.
[128] "Value of the Human Being," *Dawn and Decline*, op. cit., p. 70.
[129] "Conversations about the Wealthy," ibid., p. 91.
[130] "Health and Society," ibid., p. 48.
[131] "Die Hand, die Samstags ihren Besen führt, wird sonntags dich am besten karessieren," ibid. p. 329.
[132] "Responsibility," ibid., p. 86.
[133] "Warten," ibid., p. 450.
[134] "Vom Unterschied der Lebensalter," ibid., p. 442.
[135] "Everyone Must Die," ibid., p. 38.

standing. The thoroughgoing social mediation of individuals' experience, not only of the decisive but also of even relatively inconsequential aspects of their lives, is at the same time Horkheimer's most emphatic argument against the premature positing of the existence of universals or objective criteria of truth in a society that is still rigidly stratified and antagonistic. In what follows, we will focus on Horkheimer's examination of the manner in which character and personality are socially determined in contemporary capitalist societies, which will reveal once again just how important it is for Horkheimer to decipher the effects of quasi-objective social structures on the knowledge and actions of individual members of society. For as he puts it, "It is difficult to predict the course of the capitalist economy by following the stock market. Its effects on the human psyche can calculated precisely."[136]

In the aphorism "Character and Social Structure," Horkheimer conducts a thought experiment that could be seen as a test of this hypothesis. He isolates two representatives of the extreme poles of the capitalist power spectrum – a long-term prison inmate and the director of a large corporation – and examines the effects that their social position has on their character. The inmate leads an extremely limited, miserable existence in which even the most insignificant events can evoke powerful emotional responses. The trust director, on the other hand, responds to events – that for those lower in the social hierarchy would incite powerful emotions or significant changes in their lives – with equanimity or even indifference, because he has become accustomed to their regular occurrence. Based on these extreme examples, Horkheimer draws some more general conclusions that illustrate not only his understanding of the links between character and contemporary capitalist society, but also his view of what a socialist alternative might look like. He writes:

In the case of these extremes, the magnate and the prison inmate ... it will be largely admitted that psychic reactions and the formation of character depend on material conditions. But the difference in character between a minor union official and a factory director, a big landowner and a mailman, are just as tied to their situation as are those between the prisoner and the powerful man. We certainly cannot maintain that men are born equal, and who can say how many behavioral nuances we inherit. But the horizon defined for each of us by his function in society, the structure of those fundamental interests which fate inculcates in us from childhood on, is such that a relatively smooth development of those individual dispositions is probably extremely rare. The higher the social stratum in which a person is born, however, the better the chance for such a development becomes. In spite of the isolation inside the cells, the psychological typology of the inmate is easily sketched: prison is a leveler! And that is generally true of poverty and misery. Most people are born into a prison, which is precisely why the present form of society, so-called individualism, is actually a society of standardization and mass culture. So called collectivism, i.e. socialism, on the other hand, is the development of individual talents and differences.[137]

In several other aphorisms in *Dämmerung*, Horkheimer moves beyond this insight to demonstrate that capitalism not only hinders true individuality, it

---

[136] "Der Hotelportier," ibid., p. 325 (My translation. This is another aphorism that was not included in *Dawn and Decline*).

[137] *Dawn and Decline*, op. cit., pp. 46–7 (trans. modified).

also actively encourages the development of antisocial and inhumane character traits. These traits are, as Horkheimer notes with his typical lack of sentimentality, by no means limited to the powerful either. He writes:

Many will recognize that those on top in this society are horrible.... It is tacitly assumed that with decreasing wealth, the moral worth of those that fight for it increases or that their viciousness becomes more moderate, at least. But the capitalist economy is organized in such a way that greater affinity with the psychological makeup of the men at the top actually insures better chances on all levels.... A millionaire and especially his wife, can afford to be very honest, noble people. They can develop all sorts of admirable qualities. The larger the enterprise, the more it permits a certain latitude in the adoption of measures that will "benefit" the worker and be humane ... without becoming unprofitable. Here also, the smaller manufacturer is at a disadvantage. He has to be exploitative as a person if he wants to survive.... A person that does well on the lower echelons shows his competence in the same moral order in which the more fortunate magnates operate.... There can be no doubt that getting ahead is a poor index of moral scruples.[138]

In several other aphorisms in *Dämmerung*, Horkheimer develops his insight – that the intense competition within capitalist societies usually rewards those with the fewest scruples – into a scathing critique of Social Darwinism, the ideology that had accompanied the rise of imperialism and monopoly capitalism, and that was so congenial to the fascist movements in Europe as well.[139]

For Horkheimer, the most important theoretical reference point for a theory of the objective social and historical factors at work in contemporary society was still Marx's work, as his critique of Mannheim's sociology of knowledge made clear. We have already examined several key aspects of Horkheimer's critical appropriation of Marx in the late 1920s: from his innovative attempt to develop a materialist interpretation of the history of modern philosophy; to his defense of the need to incorporate epistemological reflection as part of a critique of ideology adequate to the changed socio-historical conditions of the early twentieth century; to his rejection of economist or deterministic interpretations of Marx that lead to political quietism and theoretical stagnation. We have also already touched on Horkheimer's positive vision of socialism at this time, as a society in which individual freedom flourishes and surplus suffering is eliminated by replacing the blind dynamic of capital accumulation and the accompanying class antagonisms with a rationally planned economy. However, *Dämmerung* also provides several other important insights into Horkheimer's appropriation of Marx in the late 1920s – at both the general theoretical and the particular empirical level. Of particular importance, at the general theoretical level, is not only his critique of the current forms of utopian socialism, but also his rejection of reformist, or what one commentator has described as "traditional," socialism.[140] If traditional socialism is understood as a critique of capitalism "from the standpoint of labor," a critique that focuses on the way

---

[138] Ibid., pp. 21–2.

[139] See, for example, the aphorism "A Premium Placed on Vileness," ibid., pp. 30–1.

[140] See Moishe Postone, *Time, Labor and Social Domination: A Reinterpretation of Marx's Critical Theory* (Cambridge, UK, 1993), pp. 43–83.

in which the fruits of labor are distributed,[141] rather than on the way in which production and, with it, social labor itself is organized in capitalist society, then Horkheimer can definitely be considered one of its most ardent critics at this time. Not only does Horkheimer emphatically reject any celebration of labor in and of itself,[142] he insists throughout *Dämmerung* that socialism must break qualitatively with the forms of production and labor in capitalism, not simply distribute social wealth more justly and/or organize social labor in a more efficient or productive manner. He writes, for example: "Justifying the abolition of capitalism with the necessity of principle of selection that would raise productivity is wrong, because it accepts the categories of the dominant economic system as the norm. It assumes that repairs alone would suffice."[143] Horkheimer also insists that "socialists are not interested in distribution, but in the socialization and the restructuring of the process of production,"[144] and that "in a rational society the concept of labor will have a different meaning."[145] The critique of reformist, or "traditional" Marxism was, in other words, an important general principle guiding Horkheimer's appropriation of Marx at this time.

However, Horkheimer's understanding of Marxist theory at this time cannot be understood merely in terms of the various general assumptions mentioned here, for at this time the "temporal core of truth"[146] was already a cornerstone of Horkheimer's thought. Marx's theory too was, according to Horkheimer, a historically specific critique of capitalist society, and his concepts must be constantly updated in order to remain self-reflexive and adequate to changed socio-historical conditions. As we shall see shortly in our examination of the Institute's study of workers' attitudes in Germany in 1929, Horkheimer viewed empirical social research as one of the most important ways of testing and updating a critical theory of capitalist society. Yet several aphorisms in *Dämmerung* also offer crucial insights into Horkheimer's diagnosis of the socio-historical situation in Europe in the late 1920s. Horkheimer's understanding of the relevance of Marxist theory and the most important problems it needed to address cannot be separated from this diagnosis. Two aphorisms in *Dämmerung* are particularly important in this regard. The first, "Indications," addresses the situation in the Soviet Union, and the second, "The Impotence of the German Working Class," analyzes the situation in Weimar in the late 1920s. The latter aphorism in particular, which is the longest and one of the richest aphorisms in *Dämmerung*, represents an excellent example of the methodological approach of *Dämmerung* as a whole, namely Horkheimer's

---

[141] Ibid., pp. 8f.

[142] He writes, for example: "In a socialist society, pleasure will not derive from the nature of the work to be done. That is a reactionary aim," or "To make work the most important human activity is an ascetic ideology.... The proletariat demand is that work be reduced." *Dawn and Decline*, pp. 88 and 83 respectively.

[143] "Freie Bahn dem Tüchtigen," GS 2, p. 438 (My translation. This is another aphorism that was not included in *Dawn and Decline*).

[144] "Socialism and Resentment," *Dawn and Decline*, op. cit., p. 74.

[145] "Whoever Doesn't Want to Work Shouldn't Eat," *Dawn and Decline*, p. 84 (translation amended).

[146] *Dialectic of Enlightenment*, op. cit., p. ix.

use of subtle empirical observation and description of concrete particulars to illustrate larger, objective socio-historical tendencies.

Horkheimer's point of departure in "The Impotence of the German Working Class" is the problem of technological development in capitalist societies and its effects on production and the composition of the working class – a problem that Marx had analyzed in detail for the first time in the *Grundrisse* and that remains central to capitalist societies to the present day.[147] Continuing the skeptical analysis of the social role of technology that he developed in lectures and writings on contemporary philosophy,[148] Horkheimer argues that the development of capitalism since Marx's death warrants far more pessimistic conclusions than Marx himself had drawn. Whereas the tendency of technological innovations to diminish the proportion of "variable capital" in the process of production – that is, through constant layoffs and an increase in the size of the standing reserve army of unemployed – had not seriously effected the solidarity of the working class in the nineteenth century, this was no longer the case in the early twentieth century, according to Horkheimer. More recent technological developments had made the border between employment and unemployment much more rigid, and this new rift was reflected in the organization and consciousness of workers in Weimar Germany. On the one side were the workers, most of them trade union members, with relatively well-paid and stable long-term positions who had more to lose than simply their chains and who were thus more moderate in their political demands. These workers formed the basis of the Social Democratic electorate. On the other side were the workers with poorly paid, unstable positions and the increasing number of unemployed, who had the most direct interest in a fundamental restructuring of society. They formed the basis of the Communist Party electorate.

It was this new divide in the working class that was at the root of its current powerlessness, according to Horkheimer. The interests and consciousness on both sides of the divide had diverged so much that it was no longer possible to brush it aside with wishful talk of the proletariat as the unified "subject-object" of history. Horkheimer takes the divide seriously and addresses the particular political and theoretical problems presented by both camps. Although the Social Democrats were better organized and more theoretically sophisticated, they lacked the fundamental experience of the necessity of social change. As a result, their politics had become reformist and increasingly opportunistic, and their theory positivist and increasingly relativistic.[149] The communists, on the other hand, were all too aware of the necessity of fundamental change, but their electorate was much more difficult to organize and educate. Thus

[147] See, for example, *Karl Marx's* Grundrisse: *Foundations of the Critique of Political Economy One Hundred and Fifty Years Later*, ed. Marcello Musto (London and New York: Routledge, 2008).

[148] See Chapter 3, pp. 126ff. On Horkheimer's analysis of the social implications of technology at this time see also the important remarks in the aphorism "Unlimited Possibilities," *Dawn and Decline*, op. cit., p. 19.

[149] Ibid., pp. 63–4 (translation altered).

their leaders simplified matters and took shortcuts that made their politics unimaginative and authoritarian, and their theory rigid and dogmatic.[150] In other words, Horkheimer diagnosed a dissolution of the dialectical unity of the rational and empirical moments in Marxist theory, which also had deleterious effects on the praxis of the two wings of the workers' movement in Weimar. Horkheimer saw it as his task to try to overcome this chasm, at least at the theoretical level. For although emancipatory praxis seemed to be precluded by this division in the working class, Horkheimer was still convinced that theory had to continue to try to understand the root causes of this impasse and to reflect on the possibility of moving beyond it. It was precisely this lack of a critical theory of society that Horkheimer diagnosed on both sides of the divide of the working class and its representatives in Weimar.

HORKHEIMER'S (AND POLLOCK'S) UNDERSTANDING OF THE SOVIET UNION IN THE LATE 1920S

Based on Horkheimer's critique of the German Communist Party, which had moved away in the early 1920s from a position determined by Luxemburg and the workers' council movement toward a greater submission to Moscow by gradually accepting the Bolsheviks' strict criteria for membership in the Third International,[151] one could surmise that he did not look to the Soviet Union as a model for a theoretical or practical renewal of socialism in the West. This is true to a large extent. Horkheimer rarely mentions the Soviet Union in any of his writings or lectures throughout the 1920s. Yet Horkheimer did not belong to those who simply rejected the Soviet experiment out of hand, at least not in the 1920s. Horkheimer's sole mention of the Soviet Union in *Dämmerung* comes in the aphorism "Indications," which he penned in 1930. By this time, Stalin had solidly established himself at the head of the Soviet state, but his first five-year plan and the forced collectivization of agriculture, which would put an end to the "relatively open mid-1920s"[152] and cost hundreds of thousands of peasants their lives, were still in the beginning stages. The world economic crash in 1929 also made the Soviet Union's "planned" economy, which was not seriously affected by the crisis, seem more appealing to many. Nonetheless,

---

[150] Ibid., pp. 63 (translation altered).

[151] The German Communist Party (KPD), which emerged out the Luxemburg's and Karl Liebknecht's Sparticist movement, was founded on January 1, 1919. The Weimar government's ongoing suppression and final defeat of the workers' council movement in 1920 led many of its members to join the KPD. It was these workers who originally formed the mass basis of the party. However, by 1923 at the latest, the KPD, under the influence of leaders such as Ruth Fischer, pushed the party away from its democratic socialist origins into the orbit of the Bolsheviks' hierarchical centralism. The subordination of the KPD to Moscow and the Third International became even more pronounced in the late 1920s. On the origins of the KPD and their relationship to the Bolsheviks and the Third International, see Detlev K. Peukert, *The Weimar Republic*, trans. Richard Deveson (New York, 1992), pp. 28–35, and 66–72, and William David Jones, *The Lost Debate: German Socialist Intellectuals and Totalitarianism* (Urbana and Chicago, 1999), pp. 22–42.

[152] Robert O. Paxton, *Europe in the 20th Century* (New York, 1985), p. 346.

Horkheimer expresses his support for the Soviet Union at this time with much caution and reserve. He writes:

In 1930, the attitude toward Russia casts light on people's thinking. It is extremely difficult to say what conditions are like there. I do not claim to know where the country is going; there is undoubtedly much misery. But those among the educated who do not even perceive a hint of the effort being made there, adopt a cavalier attitude and dismiss the need to reflect, are pathetic comrades, whose company is unprofitable. The senseless injustice of the imperialist world can certainly not be explained by technological inadequacy. Anyone who has the eyes to see will view events in Russia as the continuing painful attempt to overcome this terrible social injustice. At the very least, he will ask with a throbbing heart whether it is still underway. If appearances were to be against it, he would cling to his hope like the cancer patient to the questionable report that a cure for his illness may have been found.[153]

In other words, neither the critique by Rosa Luxemburg – for whom the young Horkheimer had had so much respect – of the undemocratic methods of the Bolsheviks,[154] nor the brutal repression of the workers' uprising in Kronstadt in 1921 by the Red Army (still under Trotsky's command),[155] nor Stalin's ascension to power in 1925 and his subsequent suppression of the old Bolshevik vanguard were enough to make Horkheimer abandon all hope in the Soviet experiment.[156] But in 1930, the most violent period of repression in the Soviet Union was still to come. Horkheimer would abandon what little hope he still had invested in the Soviet Union in 1930 in the further course of the decade.[157]

---

[153] *Dawn and Decline*, op. cit., p. 72–3 (translation modified).

[154] Rosa Luxemburg, *The Russian Revolution and Leninism or Marxism?*, trans. Bertram Wolfe (Ann Arbor, 1961).

[155] See, for example, Paul Avrich, *Kronstadt 1921* (Princeton, 1970).

[156] In interviews in the 1960s, Horkheimer, whose political sympathies had in the meantime become very solidly pro-Western, stated clearly that he was "very enthusiastic" in 1917 about the Russian revolution, but that also that "The first thing that actually led me to dislike these Russians was the news that Lenin had the Csar's entire family executed." Biographical Interviews with Ernst von Schenk (MHA, XIII 112a), p. 51. Horkheimer may have been disillusioned by Lenin's actions, but they were by no means enough to cause him to reject the Soviet experiment *tout court*, as was illustrated by his reaction to a letter from his friend Germaine Krull in January 1922, who had just been expelled from Russia after spending two harrowing years there, and who had become, in her own words, an "emphatic anti-Bolshevik." GS 15, p. 80. In letters to Rosa Riekher shortly afterward, Horkheimer insists that they must continue to support Krull as a friend – he and Krull would remain friends for the rest of their lives – but he also strongly rejects her anti-Bolshevik position. He writes: "There are principled reasons against social revolutions that I respect, but I have always hated the excuse of 'becoming wise through experience' – and even if it were the experience of one's physical death! – of which this letter [from Krull] rottenly stinks." GS 15, p. 82. This passage illustrates clearly that not all of Horkheimer's "enthusiasm" for the Bolshevik revolution in 1917 had dissipated by 1922. The aphorism from *Dämmerung* quoted earlier illustrated that Horkheimer had become much more careful in his support by 1930, but also that he observed the development of the Soviet experiment in the 1920s with sympathy and cautious support.

[157] Horkheimer's attitude toward the Soviet Union at this time was not unusual for leftist intellectuals in Weimar Germany. As William David Jones has shown, a serious critique of the Soviet Union did not begin to emerge on the German left – Arthur Rosenberg's book, *The History of Bolshevism* (1932) being perhaps the most important example – until the end of the Weimar Republic. See William David Jones's study, *The Lost Debate*, op. cit., pp. 21–63. On

Before concluding our discussion of *Dämmerung*, it is worth mentioning that Horkheimer's understanding of and relationship to the Soviet Union during the 1920s was also influenced by projects being carried out at the Institute for Social Research at the time. Horkheimer would not, of course, become the official director of the Institute until July 1930, but he was, as we have seen, intimately involved with the Institute from the very beginning. There can be no doubt that Horkheimer closely followed the happenings of the Institute in the mid-1920s, because his best friend and housemate, Friedrich Pollock, was employed there as one of Carl Grünberg's assistants. Horkheimer's involvement with the Institute became more direct after Grünberg's stroke in January 1928, as it became clear that he would become the Institute's next director. In any case, the Institute had cordial relations with the Marx-Engels Institute in Moscow in the mid-1920s. Its director, David Ryazanov, had met and studied with Grünberg during his exile in Vienna from 1909 to 1915, and the two of them remained friends after Ryazanov returned to Russia.[158] In 1921, Ryazanov became the director of the newly founded Marx-Engels Institute (MEI) and in 1924 the Communist International entrusted the MEI with the task of publishing a complete edition of Marx and Engel's works (the "MEGA" edition).[159] Once Grünberg became the director of the newly founded Institute for Social Research in Frankfurt in 1924, Ryazanov succeeded in enlisting his and the Frankfurt Institute's aid in this project. A special organization was founded – the Marx-Engels Archive Publishing Society (MEAV) – with Felix Weil and Pollock as its directors, which served as an intermediary between the MEI and the German Social Democratic Party (SPD), in whose archives the vast majority of Marx and Engels's unpublished writings were located.[160] This cooperation between the MEI and the Institute for Social Research on the MEGA continued for four years, until the SPD withdrew access to its archives in November 1928 and the MEAV was disbanded in 1929.[161]

In 1927, Ryazanov invited Pollock to come to the Soviet Union to participate in the celebrations of the ten-year anniversary of the revolution and

Horkheimer's shifting relationship to the Soviet Union during the period 1930–45, see Helmut Dubiel, *Theory and Politics: Studies in the Development of Critical Theory*, trans. Benjamin Gregg (Cambridge, MA, 1985).

[158] *Erfolgreiche Kooperation: Das Frankfurter Institut für Sozialforschung und das Moskauer Marx-Engels Institut (1924–1928)*, eds. Rolf Hecker, Carl-Erich Vollgraf and Richard Sperl (Berlin: Argument, 2000), p. 19. Ryazanov had, with the permission of August Bebel, already made public several of Marx and Engels's unpublished texts in a journal he founded before the war. He would also become the "heart and the head" of the MEGA project as a whole. He was also well known as a dissident among the Bolsheviks who was not afraid to criticize Lenin or Stalin publicly. In 1931, Stalin himself had him deported to Siberia. Ibid., pp. 14 and 118. For more information on Ryazanov, see *David Rjasonow: Marx-Engels-Forscher, Humanist, Dissident*, ed. Volker Külow and André Jaroslawski (Berlin, 1993).

[159] Ibid., pp. 26–32.

[160] *Erfolgreiche Kooperation…*, pp. 40–50. For the most detailed description of the founding of the MEAV and the problems it caused Pollock and the Institute as a whole with the University of Frankfurt and German political authorities, see Migdal, op. cit., pp. 98–111.

[161] *Erfolgreiche Kooperation…*, pp. 92–116.

to gather material for a study he was preparing on the development of the planned economy there in the past decade. Pollock's study, *Experiments in Economic Planning in the Soviet Union 1917–1927*,[162] was published as the second volume of the Institute's own series of writings.[163] Although it would take us too far afield to discuss Pollock's pathbreaking study in detail here, it is important to note that it was characterized by the same reserve and cautious support for the Soviet experiment that we saw in Horkheimer's aphorism "Indications" from 1930. Pollock's approach was empirical and his aim was not to judge the Soviet Union politically, but rather to describe to his readers, in extensive detail, the methods it had used and the difficulties it had encountered in its ongoing attempt to establish a planned economy. Pollock was perfectly willing to criticize the mistakes that had been made so far[164] and to offer suggestions for future improvement.[165] However, he was also always quick to point out the virtually insurmountable difficulties facing the Soviet Union, such as the low state of technological development in Russia and its lack of skilled workers, technicians, and administrators – not to mention the disorientation and destruction resulting from war, revolution, and civil war; the ongoing resistance of many within the country, especially the wealthier peasants; and its isolation from largely hostile international community. For these reasons, Pollock could safely suggest that the inability of the Soviet Union to establish a fully operational planned economy did not disprove the possibility of establishing one under more optimal conditions, such as in a more highly developed Western country.[166] Pollock's repeated stress on the benefits of a planned economy – immunity from the periodic crises of capitalism and the ability to replace its "anarchic" mode of production with one that was more transparent and thus subject to conscious control – made it clear that he still deemed it a defensible ideal. Pollock demonstrated, with guarded optimism,

---

[162] *Planwirtschaftliche Versuche in der Sowjetunion 1917–1927* (Leipzig, 1929).

[163] The first volume was Henryk Grossmann's *The Law of Accumulation and Collapse in the Capitalist System* (Leipzig, 1929).

[164] Pollock was, for example, particularly critical of the total mobilization and "militarization" of labor as well as the dangerous overexpansion of the state bureaucracy that occurred during "War Communism." Friedrich Pollock, *Planwirtschaftliche Versuche in der Sowjetunion 1917–1927* (Leipzig: C.L. Hirschfeld, 1929), p. 99.

[165] Toward the end of his study, for example, Pollock devoted a lot of attention to the development of different empirical means of obtaining information about the progress and functioning of the economy. He stresses that one of the great advantages of a planned economy is its ability to consciously regulate itself based on comprehensive knowledge of its own state of affairs, but that this advantage had not yet been fully exploited in the Soviet Union due in large part to the inadequacy of its methods of gathering information. Without this information, it would be impossible not only to run the economy efficiently, but also to obtain a more theoretically rigorous understanding of its development, which would, in turn, also make it possible to avoid many mistakes in the future. Pollock's study of the fitful development of the planned economy in Russia alerted him to the importance of rigorous methods of empirical social research, a lesson that dovetailed with and probably reinforced Horkheimer's own interest in empirical social research at this time. See *Planwirtschaftliche Versuche...*, pp. 291–329.

[166] On this point, see also Rolf Wiggershaus's discussion of Pollock's study, *Die Frankfurter Schule*, op. cit., pp. 78–9.

that the Soviet Union had, despite unfavorable conditions and numerous mistakes, been able to make some progress toward attaining this ideal.[167] Yet like Horkheimer, he refrained from making any hasty judgments, arguing that the experiments with socialism in the Soviet Union were still only in their beginning stages and more research needed to be done.[168]

[167] In the study, Pollock portrays the transition from "War Communism" to the "New Economic Policy," as well as the various phases within each that were in themselves often characterized by radical policy shifts, as a gradual learning process, one that was in 1927 still in its beginning stages.

[168] *Planwirtschaftliche Versuche...*, p. 380.

5

Horkheimer's Integration of Psychoanalysis into His Theory of Contemporary Society

As the final step in our examination of the development of Critical Theory in Horkheimer's thought in the late 1920s, we turn now to his appropriation of psychoanalysis. In order to understand this process, it is necessary to reconstruct, at least briefly, the historical and biographical, as well as the theoretical, context in which it occurred. This will entail an examination not only of the principal protagonists, Horkheimer and Erich Fromm, but also the important supporting roles played by Leo Lowenthal, Frieda Fromm-Reichmann, and Karl Landauer. It will also be necessary to retrace certain key developments at the Institute for Social Research in late 1920s as well as the founding of the Frankfurt Psychoanalytic Institute in February 1929. One should be forewarned, however, that it is no longer possible to reconstruct the biographical and historical context in any great detail or with absolute certainty, because the vast majority of sources upon which such a reconstruction would be based have been lost or destroyed.[1] One cannot, in other words, avoid a certain amount of conjecture at the biographical and historical level. However, when combined with an analysis of Horkheimer's and Fromm's *theoretical* development from this time, a relatively clear picture emerges of the integration of psychoanalysis into Critical Theory. Toward this end, we will cast a quick glance back at Horkheimer's move

---

[1] There is relatively little material in the Max Horkheimer Archive from the period 1925–30. For example, almost all of Horkheimer's letters from this time were destroyed by the National Socialists, who seized control of the Institute for Social Research, in which Horkheimer's correspondence was located, on March 13, 1933. On the fate of the letters and other materials from the Institute from the late 1920s and early 1930s, see Gunzelin Schmid Noerr, "Nachwort des Herausgebers zu den Bänden 15–18: Eine Geschichte der 'Frankfurter Schule' in Briefen," GS 18, pp. 826–32. Rainer Funk, the director of the Erich Fromm Archive, in Tübingen, Germany, has also informed me that there are no letters, or any other documents from Fromm's life during the late 1920s, there either. In her recent biography of Frieda Fromm-Reichmann, Gail A. Hornstein also confirms that virtually no traces remain of the details surrounding her relationship with Erich Fromm in the 1920s: *To Redeem One Person Is To Redeem the World: The Life of Frieda Fromm-Reichmann* (New York, 2000), p. 58. The same can also be said for the Leo Lowenthal Archive, also located in the *Stadts- und Universitätsbibliothek* in Frankfurt. The Frankfurt Sigmund Freud Institut, which was reestablished in 1959 in the tradition of the original Frankfurt Psychoanalytic Institute, which was housed in the same building as Institute for Social Research and also closed by the National Socialists in 1933, also has no archival material from the period before 1933. As Heinrich Meng, one of the leading figures of the Frankfurt Psychoanalytic Institute in its first years, put it: "Everything from our old Institute was destroyed." Quoted by Michael Laier, in his *Materialien aus dem Sigmund-Freud-Institut*, No. 9, *Das Frankfurter Psychoanalytische Institut 1929–33* (Münster and Hamburg, 1994), p. 2.

from Gestalt psychology to psychoanalysis in the late 1920s, and also answer the question of why Theodor Adorno's interpretation of psychoanalysis in his first *Habilitationsschrift* (submitted in 1927) failed to capture Horkheimer's attention at that time. We will then proceed to an examination of Fromm's theoretical trajectory in the late 1920s, including the influence of his colleagues, such as Siegfried Bernfeld, from the Berlin Psychoanalytic Institute. Finally, we will examine the empirical study of the attitudes of German workers that Horkheimer and Erich Fromm began in 1929. The study represents a decisive moment, not only in Horkheimer's integration of psychoanalysis, but also in the development of Critical Theory as a whole, insofar as it was the first time that both were applied to a concrete social problem. Although Fromm officially directed the study, a closer examination of the conditions in which it was conceptualized and carried out leaves no doubt that it was the first concrete attempt to put Horkheimer's nascent program of Critical Theory to the test. The undogmatic Marxist theoretical hypotheses and the emphasis on empirical research that informed the study as a whole were largely attributable to Horkheimer, whereas the implementation of psychoanalytic methods in the formulation of survey questions and the analysis of responses to them were Fromm's primary contribution. The study was the first product of a fruitful collaboration between Fromm and Horkheimer and would play a crucial role in the further development of both Horkheimer's own thought and Critical Theory as a whole.

THE BIOGRAPHICAL AND HISTORICAL CONTEXT

Fromm and Lowenthal were both born in 1900 into Jewish families in Frankfurt's bourgeois West End.[2] The two of them were friends already as teenagers, and the paths of their lives would remain closely intertwined well into the 1930s and beyond. After studying law unhappily for two semesters in Frankfurt, Fromm left for Heidelberg in 1919 to study sociology, psychology, and philosophy. He received his doctorate in sociology in 1922 with a dissertation on "The Jewish Law: A Contribution to the Sociology of the Jewish Diaspora," supervised by Alfred Weber.[3] In the summer semester of 1920, Leo Lowenthal also went to Heidelberg to study philosophy, sociology, literature, and history. In 1923, he received his doctorate in philosophy with a dissertation on "The Social Philosophy of Franz von Baader: Example and Problem of a 'Religious Philosophy.'"[4] As the topics of their dissertations indicate, Fromm

---

[2] Since Lowenthal and Fromm's biographies have been treated elsewhere, the following remarks will be reduced to the minimum necessary to understanding their connections with Horkheimer. On Lowenthal, see his own autobiographical remarks in *An Unmastered Past: The Autobiographical Writings of Leo Lowenthal*, ed. Martin Jay (Berkeley, Los Angeles and London, 1987) and Rolf Wiggershaus, *Die Frankfurter Schule*, op. cit., pp. 80–2. On Fromm see Rainer Funk, *Erich Fromm* (Frankfurt, 1980) and *Erich Fromm: Liebe zum Leben* (Stuttgart, 1999).

[3] Alfred Weber was Max Weber's younger brother. He continued to teach sociology in Heidelberg after his brother's death in 1920.

[4] Only the German original has been published: "Die Sozietätsphilosophie Franz von Baaders Beispiel und Problem einer 'religiösen Soziologie,'" Leo Lowenthal, *Philosophische Frühschriften, Schriften*, vol. 5, ed. Helmut Dubiel (Frankfurt, 1987), pp. 99–168.

and Lowenthal were both very much interested in religion at this time. Around 1920, Fromm introduced Lowenthal to the circle around the charismatic Rabbi Nobel, who would, following the lead of Franz Rosenzweig, found the renowned *Freies Jüdisches Lehrhaus* (Free Jewish House of Learning) that same year.[5] Fromm and Lowenthal would, during shorter and longer stays in Frankfurt between 1920 and 1926, actively participate as teachers and students at the *Lehrhaus*. Lowenthal and Fromm's interest in Judaism at this time was also reflected in their romantic relationships. In 1920 or 1921, Fromm became friends with Golde Ginsburg, an orthodox Jew from Königsberg, East Prussia. Fromm introduced Ginsburg to Lowenthal, who fell in love with her; the two of them got married in 1923. It was through Ginsburg that Fromm met his future wife as well, Frieda Reichmann, a longtime friend of Ginsburg's who was also from an orthodox Jewish family in Königsberg. After receiving her doctorate in psychology in Frankfurt in 1918, Reichmann – who was eleven years older than Fromm and Lowenthal – underwent training in Freudian psychoanalysis for three years in Dresden.[6] Not long after completing her training in 1923, Reichmann moved to Heidelberg, where she opened a sanatorium that was "a kind of Jewish-psychoanalytic boarding school and hotel" with an "almost cultlike atmosphere."[7] Almost everyone in the clinic underwent analysis with Reichmann, including Lowenthal and Ginsburg, who had moved to Heidelberg in 1924 to help Reichmann with the sanatorium. Fromm was also a frequent visitor at the clinic, and he too underwent an analysis: one that would have a profound effect on the further course of his life.

This analysis with Reichmann was Fromm's first serious exposure to psychoanalysis. By the end of it, Fromm had not only decided to marry Reichmann and to become a psychoanalyst himself, he had also become disillusioned with the rituals of orthodox Judaism. This latter effect of the analysis was not limited to him alone.[8] Several others involved with the clinic, including Lowenthal and Reichmann herself, had lost interest in practicing their religion by 1926. Reichmann's clinic soon acquired the ironic nickname of the "Torah-peutikum," because of the numerous orthodox Jews who were "healed" of their faith

[5] On Nobel, Rosenzweig and the Free Jewish House of Learning see Wolfgang Schivelbusch, "Auf der Suche nach dem dem verlorenen Judentum: Das Freie Jüdische Lehrhaus," in *Intellektuellendämmerung: Zur Lage der Frankfurter Intelligenz in den zwanziger Jahren* (Frankfurt, 1982), pp. 27–41, and Martin Jay, "1920: The Free Jewish School is Founded in Frankfurt am Main under the Leadership of Franz Rosenzweig," *Yale Companion to Jewish Writing and Thought in German Culture, 1096–1996*, eds. Sander L. Gilman and Jack Zipes (New Haven, 1997).

[6] On Reichmann's life see, Gail A. Hornstein, *To Redeem One Person Is To Redeem the World: The Life of Frieda Fromm-Reichmann* (New York, 2000).

[7] As Lowenthal characterized it, *An Unmastered Past*, p. 26.

[8] It would be an exaggeration to attribute Fromm's turn away from orthodox Judaism solely to his analysis. As Rainer Funk has shown, Fromm's subsequent attempt to rethink some of the ideals he had discovered in Judaism in secularized, humanistic terms was also prepared by his intense studies with Rabbi Salman Baruch Rabinkov, who defended a humanistic and politically radical version of Chassidic Judaism, which had also influenced Ernst Bloch and Walter Benjamin. On Fromm's important relationship to Rabinkov, see Funk, *Erich Fromm*, op. cit., pp. 37–45. On Rabinkov, see *Sages and Saints*, *The Jewish Library*, vol. 10, ed. Leo Jung (Hoboken, 1987).

there.[9] In 1926, Fromm moved back to Frankfurt, where he underwent psychoanalytic training himself with Karl Landauer. In the following years, Fromm would divide his time between Frankfurt and Berlin, which had a psychoanalytic institute of its own that rivaled the significance of Vienna in the burgeoning psychoanalytic movement. Fromm gave lectures at the Berlin Institute in June of 1927 and then again in March of 1928. He went on to complete his psychoanalytic training there in 1930, and shortly thereafter opened a private practice in Berlin as well.[10] Like Fromm, Lowenthal returned in 1926 from Heidelberg to Frankfurt, where he worked both as a teacher at a local secondary school and as a research assistant at the Institute for Social Research, which had given him a fellowship. Lowenthal would attest later that he "was in close intellectual contact with Max Horkheimer and Friedrich Pollock" already in 1926, and that their "collaboration became more intense in 1928 and 1929."[11] Although it is impossible to determine exactly when Lowenthal introduced Fromm to Horkheimer, it was most likely during this time, in 1926 or 1927. In his autobiographical recollections, Lowenthal mentions that he was responsible for bringing Fromm into contact with the Institute, but he does not say exactly when.[12] During his studies in the early 1920s, Horkheimer knew Lowenthal, but he did not meet Fromm until later.[13] It is likely that Horkheimer and Fromm drew closer at this time through their mutual contact with Karl Landauer as well. In 1926, Fromm became a student of Landauer's and, beginning in 1927, Horkheimer pursued his growing interest in psychoanalysis by undergoing an intense analysis with Landauer.

Landauer was born in Munich in 1887 into a family of Jewish bankers that had, since the middle of the eighteenth century, helped the Bavarian royal family finance various projects in the development of Munich as its capital city.[14] In 1912, Landauer, who was studying medicine in Munich at the time, traveled

---

[9] See, for example, Gerschom Scholem's remarks on the clinic in *Von Berlin nach Jerusalem: Jugenderrinerungen* (Frankfurt, 1977), p. 197.

[10] Funk, *Erich Fromm*, p. 54.

[11] *An Unmastered Past*, pp. 52–3.

[12] Ibid., p. 51.

[13] Ernst Schenk Interviews, MHA 132a, pp. 60–1. The reason that Horkheimer knew Lowenthal but not Fromm at this time is perhaps due to the fact that Lowenthal had, through their mutual mentor Siegfried Kracauer, become friends very early on with Adorno, who was in contact with Horkheimer and Pollock already in the early 1920s. Furthermore, Lowenthal moved in the same radical political circles in Frankfurt as Horkheimer and Pollock's friend Felix Weil. Lowenthal belonged to the founding members of the Frankfurt branch of the "German Socialist Student Group." Weil was not active in the group at this time, but after moving from Frankfurt to Tübingen in the spring of 1919, he soon founded a branch of the " German Socialist Student Group" there, and was actively involved in their meetings throughout the country. After moving to Heidelberg in late spring of 1920, Lowenthal also remained active in the "German Socialist Student Group" (*An Unmastered Past*, pp. 36–7, 40–1). Fromm, on the other hand, sympathized with Zionism for a while in the early 1920s, but he does not seem to have been politically active in any socialist groups in the early 1920s. On Fromm's politics and his relationship to socialism and Marxist theory in the 1920s see footnote 83.

[14] The following biographical sketch is based largely on Hans-Joachim Rothe's short description of Landauer's life in his introduction to *Karl Landauer: Theorie der Affekte und andere Schriften zur Ich-Organisation*, ed. Hans-Joachim Rothe (Frankfurt, 1991), pp. 7–23.

to Vienna to receive psychoanalytic training with Freud. During his first year in Vienna, Landauer was analyzed by Freud himself, and he attended the public lectures that Freud delivered at the Psychiatric Clinic at the University of Vienna. In the fall of 1913, Landauer became at the age of twenty-six a full member of the Vienna Psychoanalytical Society. He also became a regular participant in its weekly meetings, which were held on Wednesday evenings in Freud's practice until the outbreak of the war. After the war, Landauer moved to Frankfurt, where he continued his psychiatric training at the University Psychiatric Clinic. In 1923, he opened his own private psychoanalytic practice in Frankfurt. Alongside his practice, Landauer became a key contributor to the German Psychoanalytic Society, which had recently emerged out of the Berlin Psychoanalytic Society. In October 1924, Landauer organized, along with Karl Abraham, the first German Congress for Psychoanalysis in Würzberg, and in the following year he played a key role in organizing the Ninth International Psychoanalytic Congress in Bad Homburg.[15] After this conference, Landauer was given the opportunity to introduce psychoanalysis to the University Psychiatric Clinic in Frankfurt. The invitation was initiated by, among others, the director of the clinic, Kurt Goldstein, with whom both Frieda Reichmann and Horkheimer had studied in the late 1910s and early 1920s, respectively.[16] Reichmann came from Heidelberg to attend these first lectures on psychoanalysis at the clinic,[17] which continued for three months, and which were greeted with great interest.[18] Out of these first lectures and discussions developed a working group that met once a month under Landauer's guidance. In 1928, the group renamed itself the Southwest German Psychoanalytic Working Group and began meeting twice a month. At this point, if not earlier, Erich Fromm joined his wife Frieda as a regular participant in the group.[19] They were also joined at this time by the fourth key member of the future Frankfurt Psychoanalytic Institute, Heinrich Meng – a doctor whom Landauer had met during the war and convinced to undergo psychoanalytic training.[20]

As we have seen, Horkheimer himself had been seriously interested in psychology from the beginning of his studies in Frankfurt. In the early 1920s, however, psychoanalysis had not yet become a "respectable" science within the conservative German university system. Even Gestalt psychology, to which

---

[15] *Deutsche Zusammenkunft für Psychoanalyse.*

[16] Reichmann had studied much more intensely with Goldstein than Horkheimer. She wrote her 1914 dissertation in Königsberg under Goldstein's guidance, and she accompanied him when he came to Frankfurt in 1918. Funk, *Erich Fromm*, p. 51. In the course of his studies in psychology in the early 1920s, Horkheimer also attended Goldstein's seminars on the psychology of brain damage. Gerald Kreft, "Zur Archäologie der Psychoanalyse in Frankfurt am Main: Fundstücke und Perspektiven um Ludwig Edinger," *Psychoanalyse in Frankfurt am Main: Zerstörte Anfänge, Wiederannäherung, Entwicklungen*, ed. Tomas Plänker, Michael Laier, Hans-Heinrich Otto, Hans-Joachim Rothe, and Helmut Siefert (Tübingen, 1996), p. 199.

[17] Reichmann and Fromm were already friends with Landauer at this point. In 1925, they discussed with him the potential dangers of an analyst marrying her patient before going through with their marriage plans. Funk, *Erich Fromm*, p. 51.

[18] Ibid., p. 16. See also Kreft, op. cit., p. 195.

[19] Funk, *Erich Fromm*, p. 53.

[20] On Meng, see his autobiography, *Leben als Begegnung* (Stuttgart, 1971).

Horkheimer had been exposed through Cornelius and several of his other professors, had a quasi avant-garde status at this time, and thus was represented only at the most liberal German universities, such as Frankfurt. Although it had played an important role in his critique of Kant and the neo-Kantians in his dissertation and *Habilitationsschrift*, Horkheimer moved decisively beyond Gestalt psychology and its philosophical appropriation by Hans Cornelius in his transition beyond consciousness philosophy around 1925. Despite his shift at this time to more objective forms of theoretical analysis grounded in history and society, Horkheimer did not simply eliminate the subjective or psychological moment in his nascent critical theory. He turned to psychoanalysis to theorize this crucial moment, because he realized that it represented something qualitatively new vis-à-vis traditional and Gestalt psychology, and that it also had far reaching social and philosophical implications.[21]

Before returning to Horkheimer's theoretical integration of psychoanalysis, let us first finish our brief sketch of the biographical and historical context out of which it emerged. Horkheimer's growing interest in psychoanalysis at this time expressed itself most palpably in his decision to ask Karl Landauer to analyze him in the summer or fall of 1927. Horkheimer was not suffering from any acute neuroses at the time; he simply wanted to gain a better understanding of psychoanalysis, and thought that undergoing analysis with Landauer would be one good way to do this.[22] Landauer refused at first, insisting that Horkheimer present him with a symptom to be cured. A few days later, Horkheimer returned to Landauer and told him that he was unable to give lectures without reading directly from a prepared manuscript. Landauer now agreed to an analysis, and thereafter they met for an hour every day, six days a week, for an entire year,[23] even though Horkheimer had been cured of his "symptom" after six weeks.[24] In a later interview, Horkheimer would say the following about his analysis with Landauer: "My analysis never really became psychoanalysis in the strict

---

[21] Ernst von Schenk interviews, MHA 132a, p. 5.

[22] Horkheimer recounts this episode in an interview with Gerhard Rein in 1972. See GS 7, p. 453.

[23] Ernst von Schenk interviews, p. 5.

[24] About this symptom, Horkheimer writes the following: "[In the course of the analysis] I returned to the topic of my symptom and said: 'If I don't write everything out, then the students will just think I'm stupid,' to which Landauer replied, 'Well then they will just have to think you are stupid then.' This made such an impression on me, and it seemed so clear and natural, that from then on I really did only need fifteen minutes to prepare the notes I needed to say what was essential in my lectures." GS 7, p. 454. This incident in the analysis, which helped Horkheimer overcome his fear of what his students thought of him, left a lasting impression on both men. Not long after afterward, Landauer published one of his most important articles "On the Psychosexual Genesis of Stupidity," in which he drew on his experiences with Horkheimer to defend the thesis that stupidity, as an "acquired inability to experience," is ingrained and reinforced by fear. Horkheimer would himself elaborate on this idea in one of the aphorisms at the end of the *Dialectic of Enlightenment*, entitled "The Genesis of Stupidity." For Landauer's article see *Theorie der Affekte*, op. cit., pp. 86–109. For Horkheimer's note, see *Dialectic of Enlightenment*, trans. John Cumming (New York, 1972), p. 256. On this incident and its relationship to both men's theoretical work, see also Hans-Joachim Rothe, *Materialien aus dem Sigmund Freud Institut Frankfurt*, No. 4. "Zur Erinnerung an Karl Landauer," (Frankfurt, 1987).

sense. For a year I told Karl Landauer everything I was concerned with, every day, six days a week. Afterwards he knew a lot about philosophy, but in reality it never developed into a proper analysis."[25] Landauer agreed with Horkheimer that he was too content at the time for the analysis to be genuinely product- ive. He suggested that if Horkheimer were, for example, separated from his recently wedded wife, Rosa Riekher, they might have grounds for continuing the analysis; because this was not the case, they stopped after one year.[26] In any case, both men viewed the analysis from the beginning primarily as a learn- ing, not a therapeutic, exercise.[27] After the analysis was over, Landauer and Horkheimer continued to meet regularly, not only in the context of their work at the Institute for Social Research – the newly founded Frankfurt Psychoanalytic Institute was housed in the same building – but also for long evenings of discus- sion at Landauer's house, which were attended by other Institute members as well.[28] Horkheimer's analysis with Landauer was, in other words, not only the beginning of a productive working relationship, but also a warm friendship, which lasted until Landauer was captured by the Gestapo in Amsterdam and deported to Bergen-Belsen, where he died in January 1945.[29] This friendship was one of the most important prerequisites for the founding of the Frankfurt Psychoanalytic Institute (FPI) in February 1929.[30]

The other crucial prerequisite for the founding of the FPI and the larger integration of psychoanalysis into Critical Theory was Horkheimer's increased influence in the planning of Institute affairs in the late 1920s, which came about following the unexpected stroke – in January 1928 – suffered by the director of the Institute at this time, Carl Grünberg.[31] Grünberg would live for another twelve years, but the stroke left him in a mental and physical state that prevented him from working productively. By the time he officially stepped down as dir- ector the following year, it had become nearly certain that Horkheimer would become the next director of the Institute. To be sure, a few important institu- tional hurdles still stood in the way of Horkheimer's assumption of Grünberg's position – these would be removed by October 1930 at the latest[32] – but for our purposes here, it is important to note that Horkheimer's influence on the further course of the Institute was already evident at the beginning of 1929. The founding of the FPI on February 16, 1929, would not have taken place without Horkheimer's active support. Just a few months later, the empirical

[25] Ernst von Schenk interviews, MHA 132a, p. 5.

[26] GS 7, p. 454.

[27] *Theorie der Affekte*, op. cit., p. 18.

[28] Ibid.

[29] Ibid., pp. 21–3. See also Horkheimer's extensive correspondence with Landauer in GS 15 and 16.

[30] Laier, *Das Frankfurter Psychoanalytische Institut 1929–1933* op. cit., p. 33. Hans-Joachim Rothe, "Ein Exemplarisches Beispiel: Karl Landauer 1887–1945," in Plänker et. al., op. cit., p. 94.

[31] Although he had played an important role in the original planning of the Institute (see Chapter 2), Horkheimer was – unlike Pollock, who was working as Grünberg's assistant at this time – not directly involved with the Institute before 1928.

[32] For a more detailed account of Horkheimer's accession to the directorship of the Institute, see *The Dialectical Imagination*, pp. 24–5, and *Die Frankfurter Schule*, op. cit., pp. 46–50.

study on German workers' attitudes, in which psychoanalytic methods would play a prominent role, was begun under the guidance of Erich Fromm.[33] It is highly unlikely that the Institute would have initiated these projects under the leadership of Grünberg, who displayed little interest in psychoanalysis.[34] In later interviews, Pollock and Horkheimer recounted the significance of this transition. Pollock stated:

In 1928 Grünberg had a stroke and when it became apparent that he was not going to recover from it, the question of his successor arose. At that time we asked ourselves, primarily due to Horkheimer's initiative, why wouldn't it be possible to make something entirely different out of the Institute? ... An Institute, in which one could make a serious effort to further the development of theory and the development of theory meant for us at that time the development of Marx's theory by integrating everything that we had learned in the meantime about psychoanalysis, modern philosophy, modern economics and similar things.... Although we had the rights to continue the publication of the *Grünbergsche Archiv*, we made no effort whatsoever to do so.[35]

In another interview a few years later, Horkheimer stated:

Sociology was not adequately supported in the German universities at that time, nor was psychoanalysis, which was flatly rejected in German universities at the time. For this reason I invited a group of psychoanalysts to give lectures and seminars at our Institute. To this group belonged, among others, Karl Landauer, Heinrich Meng and Erich Fromm. They were, as Freud confirmed in a wonderful letter to me, the first group to bring psychoanalysis into contact with a German university.[36]

In short, the practical and theoretical integration of psychoanalysis into the Institute began as soon as it became likely that Horkheimer would become its next director. This development was due primarily to Horkheimer's initiative and testified to his commitment at this time to grant psychoanalysis an important role in his nascent Critical Theory of society.

Although Horkheimer also played an important role in the founding of the FPI, the primary initiative for the project did not come from him. Although it is difficult to say with certainty who was responsible for the original idea,[37] Karl Landauer, Frieda-Fromm Reichmann, and Erich Fromm, who were meeting

[33] Wolfgang Bonss, "Kritische Theorie und empirische Sozialforschung: Anmerkung zu einem Fallbeispiel," introduction to Erich Fromm, *Arbeiter und Angestellte am Vorabend des dritten Reiches: Eine Sozialpsychologische Untersuchung* (Munich, 1983), p. 7.

[34] *The Dialectical Imagination*, p. 87.

[35] Ernst von Schenk Interviews, MHA 132a, p. 87.

[36] GS 7, pp. 365–6. Like almost all of Horkheimer's letters during this time, the letters from Freud, of which he was particularly proud, have not been preserved. For a brief discussion of the fate of these letters from Freud, see the editor's afterward by Gunzelin Schmid Noerr, "Eine Geschichte der 'Frankfurter Schule' in Briefen," GS 18, pp. 831–2.

[37] There seems to be some disagreement in the secondary literature on who deserves credit for the idea to found a psychoanalytic institute in Frankfurt. Rainer Funk and Rolf Wiggershaus claim that the idea originated in the Heidelberg group around Frieda Fromm-Reichmann. See Rainer Funk, *Erich Fromm*, p. 59 and *Die Frankfurter Schule*, p. 69. However, in more recent scholarship there seems to be a consensus that Landauer was the original and primary initiator of the Frankfurt Psychoanalytic Institute. "Ein Exemplarisches Schicksal: Karl Landauer 1887–1945," op. cit., p. 94. See also Michael Laier, *Das Frankfurter Psychoanalytisches Institut 1929–1933*, op. cit., pp. 13–14.

regularly in his Southwest German Psychoanalytic Working Group at the time, were primarily responsible for the establishment of the FPI. At its official opening on February 16th, 1929, Fromm gave a talk on "Psychoanalysis and Sociology," to which we will return shortly. In contrast to the Berlin Psychoanalytic Institute, to which Fromm also belonged at the time, the FPI did not see its primary duty in training analysts, but rather in introducing psychoanalysis to a broader public and exploring its implications for other fields of theoretical inquiry.[38] As Horkheimer would say later of the FPI:

We were of the common opinion that the significance of Freud's theory went far beyond the realm of psychology or psychiatry and that what mattered was to preserve and develop not only the techniques and therapeutic skills, but more importantly the spirit and letter of Freud's thought.[39]

Landauer also defined one of the most important tasks of the FPI at the time as making "Freud's ideas accessible to a broader public through lectures and introductory courses."[40] The FPI was, in other words, conceived in the spirit of Enlightenment that was so important for Horkheimer at this time. Just a few months after its founding, the FPI began offering lectures and seminars at the Institute for Social Research. The topics included not only the fundamentals of psychoanalysis, but also its application to social and pedagogical problems.[41] Already in its first semester, the courses taught by Landauer, Meng, and Fromm-Reichmann were attended by thirty to eighty students.[42] The FPI also organized a lecture series featuring some of the most prominent members of the psychoanalytic movement at the time, which also drew large audiences.[43] Lectures were also given at other institutions in Frankfurt – such as community colleges and workers' organizations.[44] A branch of the FPI was also soon established in Heidelberg, at which seminars and lectures were also held.[45] In short, the FPI played an important role in introducing psychoanalysis not only in university circles – which, with notable exceptions such as Kurt Goldstein, remained stubbornly resistant[46] – but also to a broader audience and thereby contributing to an environment in which it would soon be possible, for example, for

[38] Michael Laier, *Das Frankfurter Psychoanalytische Institut 1929–1933*, p. 59.

[39] *Materialien aus dem Sigmund Freud Institut Frankfurt* #4, op. cit., p. 38.

[40] Quoted by Michael Laier, in "'Sie wissen, dass alles von unserem Institut vernichtet wurde': *Das Frankfurter Psychoanalytisches Institut 1929–1933*," in Plänker et. al., op. cit., p. 49.

[41] For a full list of the course offerings, see Laier, *Das Frankfurter Institut für Sozialforschung 1929–1933*, op. cit., pp. 59–69.

[42] Funk, *Erich Fromm*, p. 58. Erich Fromm, who was also occupied with his practice in Berlin and the empirical study on workers' attitudes, would not offer courses at the FPI as regularly as Landauer, Meng, and Fromm-Reichmann.

[43] Lectures were given by, among others, Siegried Bernfeld, Anna Freud, Paul Federn, and Sandor Rado. *The Dialectical Imagination*, p. 88 and *Theorie der Affekte*, p. 18.

[44] Michael Laier, "Sie wissen…" op. cit., p. 60.

[45] Funk, *Erich Fromm*, p. 59.

[46] Michael Laier argues that the connection of the FPI to the university through the Institute for Social Research remained merely "spatial" and that "no reception of psychoanalysis took place at that time." *Das Frankfurter Psychoanalytische Institut 1929–1933*, p. 59. On the resistance to psychoanalysis in university circles see also Wolfgang Schivelbusch, "Der Goethe-Preis und Sigmund Freud," *Intellektuellendämmerung*, op. cit., pp. 77–93.

Sigmund Freud to receive the highest distinction of the city of Frankfurt, the Goethe Prize.[47]

It is impossible to say with certainty when the working relationship between Horkheimer and Fromm began, but it was certainly no later than 1928, at which time the constellation that existed between Horkheimer, Lowenthal, Fromm, Fromm-Reichmann, and Landauer was firmly in place. It seems that Landauer also played a role in encouraging Horkheimer to integrate Fromm more closely into the Institute.[48] In any case, a strong theoretical elective affinity drew Horkheimer and Fromm together during the late 1920s that would have decisive effects on the further development of Critical Theory. With a view to Fromm's separation from the Institute in the late 1930s, and the scathing critiques of his position by Adorno and Marcuse in the 1940s and 1950s, there has been a tendency to overlook Fromm's importance for the formation of Critical Theory – particularly for Horkheimer – during the late 1920s and early 1930s.[49] In more recent scholarship, however, it is generally agreed that Fromm became Horkheimer's most important theoretical interlocutor during this time.[50] In his later autobiographical reflections, Leo Lowenthal testified to the importance of Fromm for the Institute in the late 1920s in the following way:

The systematic interest that must have spawned this fascination with psychoanalysis for me and many of my intellectual fellow travelers was very likely the idea of "marrying" historical materialism with psychoanalysis. One of the fundamental problems in Marxist theory is, after all, the absence of mediating elements between the base and superstructure, which psychological theory might supply. And for us, psychoanalysis came to fill this gap. I probably foresaw this already in the early 1920s. It became consciously apparent to me and to all of us starting around 1930, perhaps already in 1927–1928…. Later, in the circle of my colleagues in the Institute, when we jested about the quality of my contributions, I would say, "I did, in any case, bring Fromm to the Institute." In those days he was certainly one of the most important influences. Particularly during the Frankfurt years the connection with Fromm was extraordinarily stimulating, even though at first he was not a formal member of the Institute and was usually not in Frankfurt.[51]

[47] Freud was awarded the Goethe prize in August 1930. See Schivelbusch, ibid.
[48] In a letter from Landauer to Horkheimer from January 28, 1940, Landauer says: "I had to struggle with myself, when, during your analysis, I emphatically recommended Fromm. I would have rather suggested that I work with you myself. That's how it occurred that I never really became part of your working group." GS 16, p. 698.
[49] See, for example, Zoltan Tar's presentation of Horkheimer's early development, which fails to mention Fromm at all. *The Frankfurt School: The Critical Theories of Max Horkheimer and Theodor W. Adorno* (New York, 1977), pp. 15–72.
[50] See, for example, Wolfgang Bonss, who emphasizes, indeed, overemphasizes Fromm's contribution. "Kritische Theorie und empirische Sozialforschung," op. cit., p. 27. Martin Jay also recognized Fromm's importance already in 1973. See *The Dialectical Imagination*, where he writes, "It was thus primarily through Fromm's work that the Institute first attempted to reconcile Freud and Marx." Op. cit., p. 88. See also, *Erich Fromm und die Frankfurter Schule*, eds. R. Funk and M. Kessler (Tübingen: Francke, 1992).
[51] *An Unmastered Past: The Autobiographical Reflections of Leo Lowenthal*, ed. Martin Jay, trans. D. Berger, B. Gregg, D.J. Parent, D.J. Ward, S. Wilke, and T.R. Weeks (Berkeley and Los Angeles: University of California Press, 1987), pp. 50–1 (trans. modified).

A closer examination of Horkheimer's integration of psychoanalysis into his Critical Theory in the late 1920s – to which we will turn shortly – fully corroborates Lowenthal's statements.

However, Fromm's importance for Horkheimer was also expressed in his personal relationship with Fromm at the time, which he described in interviews toward the end of his life. Horkheimer had a high estimation of Fromm at the time not only because of his psychoanalytic training, but also because he had studied sociology and was able to mediate his psychoanalytic insights with social theory. Horkheimer says, for example:

> Fromm became part of our group when I said that it is also very important for us now to tend to psychoanalysis, which is neglected in an irresponsible way in German universities.... Thus we founded a small working group at the Institute.... The members of this working group were Landauer, Meng, Fromm, his wife and another young man, who is now in England.... At that time I got along very well with Fromm, because he also had an understanding of social theory.[52]

In the interviews, Horkheimer stresses that his respect for Fromm at the time was also based on the fact that his understanding of psychoanalysis and sociology made him sensitive very early to the threat of a National Socialist victory and the necessity for the Institute to flee not only from Germany, but from Europe as a whole. In contrast to Pollock, for example, who was skeptical about the urgency to flee and very skeptical about going to the United States,[53] Horkheimer began to think seriously about arrangements for relocating the Institute as early as 1929. Fromm agreed with Horkheimer on this move from the beginning. Fromm helped Horkheimer with his efforts to set up a branch office of the Institute in Geneva in 1930, and he was the first to travel to the United States to explore the possibility of relocating the Institute there. Horkheimer says:

> I did, in any case, get along with Fromm very well and he was among those who fully approved that I had, already before 1933, founded a refuge for the Institute in Switzerland.... And Fromm really shared with me, and this is crucial, my views on the developments in Germany, which were beginning to take shape at that time; we were among the few who actually knew what was happening. In contrast to the others, Fromm sensed, just as I did, that we would not be able to stay in Europe. Contrary to the views of the others [Pollock, e.g., JA], Fromm went, on my request, to America and looked around a bit.... When he returned he spoke very positively about America and that [was what made me decide] to leave myself with my wife for America.[54]

There is, in other words, no question that Horkheimer esteemed Fromm highly at this time, both personally and theoretically. Nonetheless, important theoretical differences also existed between the two of them from the very beginning.

---

[52] Ernst von Schenk interviews, MHA 132a, p. 131. The young therapist, whose name Horkheimer does not remember here, was Sigmund Foulkes, a former student of Kurt Goldstein who, after completing his psychoanalytic training in Vienna, joined Landauer, Meng, Fromm-Reichmann, and Fromm as the fifth permanent member of the FPI in 1930. On Foulkes, see Sabine Rothe, "Psychoanalyse im Netzwerk der Gruppe. S.H. Foulkes in Frankfurt a.M.," in *Psychoanalyse in Frankfurt am Main*, op. cit., pp. 161–79.

[53] Pollock himself admits, "I was very opposed to going to the U.S. at that time." Ernst von Schenk interviews, p. 83.

[54] Ibid., pp. 82 and 131–2.

As Horkheimer put it, "I learned very much from him about psychoanalysis, but I did not share his opinion that one had to explain everything first and foremost psychoanalytically. History, in particular, could not only be explained psychoanalytically."[55] This important theoretical difference would, however, remain latent during the first few years of their highly productive collaboration. It became, as we shall see, increasingly manifest in the mid-1930s and would lead to Fromm's departure from the Institute in 1939.[56]

THE THEORETICAL PLACE OF PSYCHOANALYSIS IN
HORKHEIMER'S THOUGHT IN THE LATE 1920S

Horkheimer: From Gestalt Psychology to Psychoanalysis

Theoretically, Horkheimer's integration of psychoanalysis into his nascent Critical Theory in the late 1920s went hand in hand with arguments he had developed at this time in his interpretation of the history of modern philosophy and his efforts to develop a Critical Theory of contemporary society. Although Horkheimer's break with consciousness philosophy firmly established the primacy of the social and historical in his thought, the subjective moment remained essential, as we have seen in our examination of *Dämmerung*. Horkheimer's Critical Theory in the late 1920s rested not only on Marx's critique of political economy, but also on Horkheimer's own materialist critique of the absolute and unconditioned concepts of knowledge and subjectivity in German Idealism.[57] Marx's appropriation and critique of Feuerbach in the *German Ideology*, his insistence that history is made neither by a transcendental or transcendent subject nor – at least not yet – by a collective "humanity," but rather by concrete, sensuous, and suffering human individuals, resonated with the strong Schopenhauerian moment in Horkheimer's thought. Like Marx, Schopenhauer was thoroughly skeptical of the lofty, but all-too-often insubstantial and affirmative abstractions of idealism.[58] In his dissertation and *Habilitationsschrift*, Horkheimer had drawn on empirical research conducted in the field of Gestalt psychology to criticize the overly abstract rationalist models of Kant and the neo-Kantians – albeit from within the dominant academic paradigm of consciousness philosophy. However, several years after he had left this discourse behind him, he was still keenly interested in the most advanced tendencies in psychology, which were at that time to be found in psychoanalysis. Horkheimer's continued interest in developing a viable theory of subjectivity and his openness to research in different disciplines led him naturally to psychoanalysis.

Another important theoretical reason for Horkheimer's interest in psychoanalysis at this time was without question his aversion to the unreflective celebrations of the unconscious that were – along with the popularizations and

---

[55] Ibid., p. 134.
[56] See Excursus 1.
[57] See Chapter 3, pp. 111ff.
[58] See Alfred Schmidt, *Idee und Wirklichkeit: Schopenhauer als Kritiker Hegels* (Munich, 1988).

vulgarizations of *Lebensphilosophie* and phenomenology – part of the larger irrationalist cultural tendencies in Germany in the late 1920s. Horkheimer's appropriation of psychoanalysis at this time was perfectly in line with the basic tendency in his writings and lectures in the late 1920s to criticize rationalism without falling into an irrationalist position himself – that is, to criticize the ahistorical and abstract foundations of rationalism with historical, sociological, and/or empirical arguments.[59] This general position had guided Horkheimer's reinterpretation of the Enlightenment, and it also informed his approach to psychoanalysis. Horkheimer's appropriation of psychoanalysis was – like his attempt to recover the critical potential of the Enlightenment – motivated in no small part by his desire to counter contemporary irrationalist tendencies. Far from simply dismissing the unconscious or subordinating it in a facile way to reason, Horkheimer – as a student of Schopenhauer – was thoroughly aware of its explosive and potentially destructive power. Horkheimer, however, recognized that psychoanalysis had begun to develop concepts to discuss the unconscious in a systematic and empirically grounded way. It was, however, not Horkheimer, but Theodor Adorno who would develop this argument most explicitly in the mid-1920s, albeit in a form that was ultimately unsatisfying for Horkheimer as well as for Adorno himself. In his first *Habilitationsschrift*, "The Concept of the Unconscious in the Transcendental Theory of the Soul,"[60] Adorno placed psychoanalysis squarely in the Enlightenment tradition in an effort to highlight its critical potential for the present and to rescue it from its uncritical admirers.[61] Adorno's first *Habilitationsschrift* is worth examining briefly here not only because it was influenced by Horkheimer, but also because it represented a serious, if ultimately unsuccessful attempt to appropriate psychoanalysis from the standpoint of Hans Cornelius's transcendental philosophy. Understanding the reasons for its failure sheds light not only on Horkheimer's interpretation of psychoanalysis at this time, but also on Adorno's further development and the orthodox interpretation of psychoanalysis that he would energetically defend in later debates within the Institute for Social Research.

Demystifying the Unconscious: Theodor Adorno's First *Habilitationsschrift*

Adorno first formulated the arguments he would develop later in his *Habilitationsschrift* in a paper entitled "Kant's Critique of Rational Psychology,"

---

[59] Horkheimer would develop this argument in more detail in 1934 in his essay "The Rationalism Debate in Current Philosophy," *Max Horkheimer. Between Philosophy and Social Science: Selected Early Writings* (Cambridge, MA, 1993), pp. 217–64.

[60] This was Adorno's "first" *Habilitationsschrift* because, after submitting it to the philosophical faculty in 1927, he decided to retract it, after learning that Hans Cornelius had read a significant portion of it and was disinclined to accept it. Adorno submitted his "second" *Habilitationsschrift*, "The Construction of the Aesthetic in Kierkegaard," to Paul Tillich in 1931, who accepted it. See Excursus II.

[61] "Der Begriff des Unbewussten in der transzendentalen Seelenlehre," *Gesammelte Schriften 1*, ed. Rolf Tiedemann (Frankfurt, 1973), p. 81.

which he gave in a seminar led by Horkheimer in the winter semester of 1923–4.[62] It is worth quoting from Adorno's early paper at length here, because it contains the argument of his first *Habilitationsschrift* in a nutshell. He writes:

One may certainly note that contrary to the dominant view, which sees Kant's logical method principally at odds with all empirical-psychological research, Kant, with his positing of indirectly given unconscious elements, stands very close to psychological *and, indeed, precisely to psychoanalytic* research. It is not the case, as it may appear at first glance, that Kant, as a rationalist fanatic of system building, excluded everything unconscious from the realm of cognition. On the contrary, precisely his critique of rationalism makes unconscious elements and the empirical ego accessible to scientific research, whereas in the metaphysical speculations of the time that were hostile to Kant, such as Hamann and Herder, these elements are removed from the purview of systematic inquiry and handed over to intuition, which defies verification. Along with the critiques of the proofs of immortality, the most important result seems to be that this critique opens up the realm of the unconscious to consciousness and in so doing eliminates the mythological notion of two modes of being, the conscious and the unconscious, that are separated from one another by an unbridgeable chasm.[63]

Adorno wants to demonstrate that Kant developed a critique of the rationalist psychology of the Leibniz-Wolff school that marked a significant step forward in the prehistory of the systematic exploration of the unconscious. In so doing, Adorno highlights the parallels that exist between the irrationalist, abstract negation of Enlightenment thought in the eighteenth and twentieth centuries. According to Adorno, Kant overcame the undialectical separation of conscious and unconscious with his insistence on sense impressions as an independent and indispensable source of knowledge, and thereby opened up the unconscious for *rational* exploration, rather than relegating it to an unfathomable, metaphysical realm, à la Hamann and Herder.[64] The parallels with Horkheimer's interpretation of the proliferation of irrationalist intellectual and cultural currents in the 1920s, and his belief in the potential of psychoanalysis to demystify them, are not hard to discern. Three years later, Adorno drew out these parallels explicitly in his first *Habilitationsschrift*, in which he describes psychoanalysis as "a potent weapon against all metaphysics of instinct and deification of mere inchoate, organic life. It is not a coincidence that the wrathful ire of all those who see the unconscious as their ideological refuge and private property is directed against psychoanalysis."[65] The parallels between Horkheimer and Adorno's positions at this time are based at least partially, if by no means exclusively, on theoretical insights Adorno had gained through discussions with Horkheimer and through reading Horkheimer's dissertation

---

[62] The title of the seminar was "Philosophische Übungen zu Kant und Hegel." There are references to the paper that Adorno gave here in Horkheimer's notes, which have been preserved in Horkheimer Archive. MHA VII. 6.1. Adorno's paper has also been preserved in its entirety, the Theodor W. Adorno Archive, Frankfurt am Main, Ts 21335–21348.

[63] T.W. Adorno Archive, Ts 21335–21348 (emphasis my own).

[64] The notion of sense impressions [*Empfindungen*] serving as an irreducibly material moment of cognition would continue to play a crucial role in Adorno's later work. See, for example, his discussion of the concept in *Negative Dialektik* (Frankfurt, 1966), pp. 193ff.

[65] "Der Begriff des Unbewussten in der transzendentalen Seelenlehre," op. cit., p. 321.

and *Habilitationsschrift*. Adorno explicitly acknowledged these debts in the preface to his *Habilitationsschrift*.[66]

However, the main arguments Adorno presents in his *Habilitationsschrift* diverge in significant ways both from Horkheimer's early academic writings on Kant and from his own position after 1925. The central task that Adorno attempted to accomplish in "The Concept of the Unconscious in the Transcendental Theory of the Soul" was to provide a *transcendental* foundation – or at least to demonstrate its possibility and necessity – for a theory of the unconscious in general and for psychoanalysis in particular.[67] Thus, despite Adorno's emphasis on the crucial empirical moment in Kant's philosophy, he ended up defending an even stronger version of consciousness philosophy than had Horkheimer in his academic writings. In his concluding remarks, Adorno writes:

The critique of the standard notions of the unconscious is fully affirmed and no reconciliation with them is possible…. With respect to them, the jurisdictional claims of transcendental philosophy are fundamentally maintained. The intention here has been to demonstrate that the concept of the unconscious, which is also understood as a philosophical concept, is not irreconcilable with transcendental idealism and its system, but has rather its proper place within this system.[68]

In his academic writings on Kant, Horkheimer had drawn more heavily on recent empirical research, in Gestalt psychology in particular, to call some of the central concepts of Kant's transcendental philosophy into question.[69] As the passage quoted above from his 1923 paper on Kant's critique of rational psychology demonstrates, Adorno was unwilling at this time to disqualify Kant's epistemological position based on more recent empirical research in the field of psychology. He was still convinced that the most advanced research in psychoanalysis could be reconciled with the transcendentalism of Kant. However, it was precisely this position that Adorno would reject soon after finishing his *Habilitationsschrift*.[70] In fact, as Rolf Tiedemann has pointed

---

[66] Adorno wrote: "I am obligated to thank … Dr. Max Horkheimer for many important suggestions. Whoever is familiar with Horkheimer's work on the border and mediating concepts in Kant's system, will see the connections between it and this study not only in the attempted resolution in of the antinomy of the unconscious – insofar as it is based on the hypostatization of Kant's border concepts – but also in the conceptualization of the unconscious as a *task*." Ibid., p. 82.

[67] In the introduction, Adorno defines his task as "achieving a transcendental theory of the unconscious" (p. 104), and in the conclusion he states clearly that "the highest aim we have for this study is the universal transcendental grounding of psychoanalysis as a science" (p. 304).

[68] Ibid., pp. 309–10.

[69] In his academic writings, Horkheimer does defend Cornelius's weak version of transcendentalism, which does not exclude the possibility that the human mind can perceive certain structural totalities – implied by teleological causality – that exist in the external world, but he is critical of Kant's stronger version of transcendentalism, which insists that, in the final analysis, structural totalities are always imposed on nature by the transcendental subject. See Chapter 2.

[70] It is interesting, and perhaps not inconsequential for the course of his subsequent development, that Adorno's emphatic defense of a concept of Enlightenment, based primarily on the *transcendental* and *epistemological* aspects of Cornelius's idiosyncratic neo-Kantianism, would soon turn into an equally emphatic rejection of this very same position, which Adorno tended

out,[71] in the conclusion of his first *Habilitationsschrift*, Adorno had already opened the door through which he would soon take leave of transcendental philosophy and academic consciousness philosophy in general. Adorno writes:

> If, nonetheless, psychoanalysis remains beholden in some respects to dogmatic presuppositions about the unconscious, the reasons for this lie not merely in the shortcomings of the theory but in social factors; namely, that changed social conditions are the presupposition of bringing many unconscious elements to light.... Based on everything that we elaborated here on the transcendental-idealistic possibility of a lawfully ordered connection between the material and psychical world, it cannot come as a surprise to us that the knowledge of not only unconscious elements but also their constitution is dependent in part on the material world, that is, on society.[72]

With these sentences from 1927, in which he acknowledges the socially mediated character of the unconscious, Adorno had unquestionably recognized the threshold of consciousness philosophy – and thus already moved beyond it – as had Horkheimer two years earlier. Both Horkheimer and Adorno would come to view the importance of psychoanalysis not as a quasi-transcendental theory of subjectivity, which could be applied universally or separated from social and historical conditions, but rather as a materialist theory of subjectivity, which could help explain the consciousness and actions of particular individuals and groups under determinate social and historical conditions. Yet the period of Adorno's intense collaboration with Horkheimer would not begin for another decade or so. Adorno would distance himself from consciousness philosophy in the following years, in large part through a critical appropriation of Walter Benjamin's writings from the 1920s, in which psychoanalysis did not figure prominently.[73] Horkheimer, on the other hand, would explore the implications

---

to see as characteristic of the Enlightenment as a whole. Horkheimer had, to be sure, also relied on Cornelius's work in his academic writings, but he had, in contrast to Adorno, drawn more heavily upon the *empirical* elements of Cornelius's thought to develop a critique of Kant's mechanistic epistemology, which was in reality intended to undermine the transcendental epistemological positions of neo-Kantians, such as Hermann Cohen. Even in his academic writings, Horkheimer was, in other words, less reluctant to criticize Kant's epistemology as a holdover from seventeenth-century rationalism rather than a break with it, and a genuine expression of the Enlightenment, as Adorno would maintain until 1927. Hence, in contrast to Adorno, Horkheimer's break with neo-Kantian epistemology and consciousness philosophy more generally was not accompanied by a radical critique of the Enlightenment. Instead, he developed in the following years the positive reinterpretation of the Enlightenment outlined earlier, which placed the Enlightenment squarely in the empirical tradition. After 1925, Horkheimer would also stress the serious limitations of neo-Kantian interpretations of Kant, such as Cohen's, that focused on the transcendental and epistemological aspects of his thought and neglected the primacy of *practical* reason in Kant's thought. Adorno, in contrast, would turn his attention increasingly to Benjamin's writings during the following years, in which a critique of an impoverished concept of experience that emerged from the neo-Kantian epistemological position was, tendentially, equated with Kant and the Enlightenment *tout court*. See Excursus II.

[71] In his afterword to the first volume of Adorno's collected writings. Ibid., p. 382. Later, in a letter to Tiedemann, Adorno would describe the principal problem of the manuscript in the following way: "It relates Freud in a one-sided way to the epistemology of, for example, Mach and Avenarius, and neglects the materialist moment present in Freud's theory from the very beginning, which in his work is represented by the fundamental concept of organ-pleasure." Ibid., p. 381.

[72] Ibid., p. 321.

[73] See Excursus II.

of psychoanalysis for his own incipient Critical Theory of society primarily through a closer working relationship to Erich Fromm.

The Beginnings of Fromm's Analytic Social Psychology and His Theoretical Elective Affinity with Horkheimer

As we have seen, Fromm received his doctorate in sociology in Heidelberg in 1922. After meeting Frieda Reichmann in 1924, Fromm soon began devoting himself full time to training as a psychoanalyst, but his interest in sociological questions remained strong. In 1927, he gave his first lecture at the Berlin Psychoanalytic Institute. The talk was on a technical topic – "Curing a Case of Lung Tuberculosis During Psychoanalytic Treatment" – that showed no signs of Fromm's sociological background.[74] However, the title of his next talk at the Berlin Institute in March of 1928 – "Psychoanalysis of the Petty Bourgeois"[75] – illustrated not only his continued interest in sociology, but also an interest in Marx, which would remain with him for the rest of his life. It is not surprising that Fromm's renewed interest in sociology and Marx coincided with the beginnings of his involvement with the Berlin Psychoanalytic Institute, for when he first came to Berlin the Institute had already for some time been exploring the social, political, and pedagogical implications of psychoanalysis as well as its potential to supplement Marxist theory.[76] Siegfried Bernfeld, who was listed as one of the discussants present at Fromm's second talk,[77] was the most responsible for advancing these particular discussions at the Berlin Institute,[78] but there were others as well, such as Otto Fenichel, Barbara Lantos, and Alfred Döblin. Wilhelm Reich, who was also actively exploring the theoretical and practical potential of synthesizing psychoanalysis and historical materialism at this time, would also become a participant in discussions at the Berlin Institute

[74] It was a technical topic that would, oddly enough, soon acquire substantial personal significance for Fromm. Four years later, at a time when his marriage with Reichmann was in a terminal crisis, Fromm came down with lung tuberculosis himself and had to leave Reichmann to go to Davos, Switzerland for a year to recover. Funk, *Erich Fromm*, op. cit., p. 54.

[75] Ibid.

[76] On the Berlin Psychoanalytic Institute, see *Psychoanalyse in Berlin: Beiträge zur Geschichte, Theorie und Praxis* (Meisenheim, 1971) and Veronika Fuechtner, *Berlin Psychoanalytic: Culture and Psychoanalysis in Weimar Republic Germany and Beyond* (Berkeley and Los Angeles: University of California Press, 2011).

[77] Funk, *Erich Fromm*, p. 54.

[78] Bernfeld's book, *Sysiphus, oder die Grenzen der Erziehung* (Sysiphus, or the Limits of Education), which was first published in 1925, was the first serious contribution in Germany to the development of a critical social psychology. Bernfeld addressed not only issues of pedagogy, but also political issues from an explicitly socialist standpoint. He clearly posed the question, which would also be central for Fromm and Horkheimer later, of how psychoanalysis might help explain the stillbirth of the German revolution after the Great War. On *Sysiphus*, see Helmut Dahmer, *Libido und Gesellschaft: Studien über Freud und die Freudsche Linke* (Frankfurt, 1982), pp. 286–9. Bernfeld also published an article in 1926 on "Sozialismus und Psychoanalyse," which represented the first explicit attempt to reflect on the theoretical possibility and potential of merging psychoanalysis and historical materialism. Bernfeld's article has been reprinted in *Marxismus, Psychoanalyse, Sexpol*, vol. 1, ed. H.P. Gente (Frankfurt, 1970), pp. 11–18. On Bernfeld, more generally, see *Siegfried Bernfeld, oder die Grenzen der Psychoanalyse*, ed. Karl Fallend und Johannes Reichmayr (Basel, 1992).

by 1930 at the latest. The Berlin Institute was, in other words, an ideal climate for Fromm to develop a theory of social psychology based on a synthesis of the theories of Marx and Freud.

Of the members of the Berlin Psychoanalytic Institute at the time, Fromm seems to have been most influenced by Bernfeld. In 1930 and 1931, Fromm wrote two articles and taught courses at the Frankfurt Psychoanalytic Institute on the topic of psychoanalysis and criminology, which drew explicitly on Bernfeld's own investigations in these areas.[79] Even before this time Fromm's writings demonstrated striking parallels with Bernfeld's work. In his seminal article from 1926, "Socialism and Psychoanalysis," Bernfeld outlined theoretical problems that Fromm would take up and develop on his own. Anticipating Fromm, Bernfeld stressed Freud's rejection of the concept of a collective unconscious or group soul.[80] The object of psychoanalysis was always the concrete individual. It was precisely this emphasis on the concrete individual by Freud that opened up a new realm to systematic exploration that had not been adequately addressed by Marx. As Bernfeld put it: "Marx did not treat the problem – which Freud did, if only, of course, in a very preliminary way – of how the psychic mechanisms operate, through which the ideology corresponding to the given relations of production is reproduced in the heads of living and working persons."[81] Bernfeld had, in other words, already recognized the potential of psychoanalysis to clarify the problem of ideology through its pathbreaking insights into the "psychic mechanisms" that mediated between the individual and society. Bernfeld insisted, however, that Freud's study of these psychic mechanisms was still in its preliminary stages and that attempts to mediate between psychoanalysis and sociology were even less developed. Bernfeld writes:

The competition between social scientific and psychological explanations of the same phenomenon can not yet be decided in favor of the one or the other because it has not

---

[79] Fromm, "Der Staat als Erzieher: Zur Psychologie der Strafjustiz," and "Zur Psychologie des Verbrechers und der strafenden Gesellschaft," in *Erich Fromm Gesamtausgabe*, ed. Rainer Funk (Munich, 1989), pp. 7–10 and 11–30. Fromm cites Bernfeld in his first article, p. 9. On Fromm's appropriation of Bernfeld's work in this context, see also *Libido and Gesellschaft*, op. cit., p. 312. Wolgang Bonss also stresses Fromm's indebtedness to Bernfeld and the theoretical discussions at the Berlin Psychoanalytic Institute in the mid-1920s. Bonss argues that the attempts to appropriate psychoanalysis for critical social theory in Weimar Germany could basically be divided into two camps, namely those such as Bernfeld and Reich who were interested in a critique of Marxist economism, and those such as Bloch and Adorno, who were interested in a philosophical interpretation of psychoanalysis that could provide an antidote to the increasingly widespread reactionary and irrationalist celebrations of the unconscious. Fromm's analytical social psychology was clearly more indebted to the first camp. See Wolfgang Bonss, "Analytische Sozialpsychologie – Anmerkungen zu einem theoretischen Konzept und seiner empirischen Praxis," in *Erich Fromm und die Frankfurter Schule*, p. 28. For the English translations and insightful commentary on these two essays, see *Erich Fromm and Critical Criminology: Beyond the Punitive Society; with two essays by Erich Fromm*; trans. Heinze D. Osterle and Kevin Anderson, eds. Kevin Anderson and Richard Quinney (Urbana, IL: University of Illinois Press, 2000).

[80] Bernfeld, "Sozialismus und Psychoanalyse," op. cit., p. 17.

[81] Ibid.

yet taken place, due to the meager development of both theories at the present time in the border area between them.[82]

In 1928, when Fromm's theory began to take a new direction, he departed precisely from this point, the intersection of psychoanalysis and sociology. Fromm set himself the task of mapping the *terra incognita* Bernfeld had identified at the boundaries between psychoanalysis and critical social theory. He was uniquely qualified for this task, for among the psychoanalysts working in Germany at the time, he was the only one who had also been trained as a sociologist. Fromm also began to display a serious interest in Marx's work at this time,[83] even though the divergence of his interpretation of Marx – and, more importantly, Freud – from Horkheimer's would soon become apparent and ultimately lead to his departure from the Institute in the late 1930s.

Fromm's first publication in 1927 was an orthodox psychoanalytic interpretation of the religious ritual of the Sabbath that made official his departure from the practice of orthodox Judaism but revealed no trace of his interest in critical social theory.[84] The fruits of Fromm's new interest in synthesizing sociology and psychoanalysis appeared for the first time in February 1929 in a talk entitled "Psychoanalysis and Sociology," which he gave on the occasion of the opening of the Frankfurt Psychoanalytic Institute. Picking up the idea advanced by Bernfeld in 1925, Fromm insisted that sociology had not yet adequately addressed the concrete individual as the genuine foundation of society. He writes: "The psychoanalyst must point out that the object of sociology, society, consists in reality of single persons, and that it is these persons, and not an abstract society as such, whose actions, thoughts and feelings is the

---

[82] Ibid.

[83] In contrast to Horkheimer, or even his close friend Leo Lowenthal, Fromm displayed less interest in the early 1920s in socialist theory and practice. Whereas Horkheimer and Pollock had been involved, at least marginally, in the Munich council republic after the war, and Lowenthal was active in student socialist groups in both Frankfurt and Freiburg, Fromm devoted himself to the *Freies Jüdisches Lehrhaus*, where he had the reputation of being particularly pious. Fromm was an active member in the Zionist youth movement centered around the *Lehrhaus*, but he became disillusioned with Zionism quite quickly in the early 1920s (see Funk, *Erich Fromm*, op. cit., p. 50). Although Fromm did attend two seminars on Marx with Emil Lederer during his studies in Heidelberg (letter from Rainer Funk to me, December 12, 2002), his main advisor in Heidelberg, Alfred Weber, was an outspoken opponent of Marx, who would in the late 1920s denounce even Karl Mannheim as being too Marxist. In any case, Fromm's interest in Marx in the early 1920s left no significant trace in his work. In the years following his studies in Heidelberg, Fromm devoted himself primarily to his psychoanalytic training and to Frieda Reichmann's clinic in Heidelberg. Fromm did spend a significant amount of time studying with Rabbi Salman Baruch Rabinkov in Heidelberg, who merged a humanist interpretation of Hassidic Judaism with the revolutionary politics he had imbibed in Russia before coming to Germany. Yet even Rabinkov seemed to have little explicit interest in Marx. Furthermore, Marx's early writings, upon which Fromm's appropriation of Marx in his later writings were based, were not published until the early 1930s. Thus, as Rainer Funk points out (*Erich Fromm*, op. cit., p. 56), in the late 1920s Fromm certainly received the most important impulses in his reception of Marx from Horkheimer and Lowenthal, although his colleagues at the Berlin Psychoanalytic Institute, such as Bernfeld, must have also played a role in his renewed, more serious interest in Marx at this time.

[84] "Der Sabbat," *Erich Fromm Gesamtausgabe*, vol. 6, op. cit., pp. 1–9.

object of sociological research."[85] The contribution that psychoanalysis can make to critical social theory lies, according to Fromm, precisely in providing it with a means of studying the psychic structures of concrete individuals, the ways in which they are shaped by society, and the ways in which they in turn affect the reproduction of society. Fromm writes:

What psychoanalysis can offer sociology is – if still only imperfectly – insight into the psychic apparatus of man, which in addition to technical, economic and social factors determines social development and deserves no less attention than those just named. It is the common problem of both sciences to investigate the extent to which and ways in which man's psychic apparatus affects the development of society as a cause or determinant.[86]

In order to emphasize the point that it is the task not only of psychoanalysis but also of sociology to analyze the psychic structure of the concrete individual, Fromm closed his talk with a quote by the social theorist whose work had, in the meantime, become one of the pillars of his own thought: Karl Marx. Fromm quoted the following passage from the *German Ideology*, the text that his future colleagues at the Institute had recently rescued from the Social Democratic Archives: "History does not do anything, it does not possess massive wealth, it does not fight any battles. It is instead human beings, real, living human beings that do everything, possess and fight."[87] Like Horkheimer, whose suspicion of supra-individual historical and anthropological categories also displayed a deep affinity with Marx's arguments in the *German Ideology*, Fromm was also interested in working out the subjective dimensions of a critical theory of society.

Fromm's talk on "Psychoanalysis and Sociology" in 1929 was nothing more than a brief outline of some of his most basic hypotheses, but he would soon have a chance to put them to the test, both practically and theoretically. At this time, he and Horkheimer had probably already begun to conceptualize the empirical study of the attitudes of German workers carried out by the Institute in 1929. But before turning to Fromm's attempt to test his new social-psychological hypotheses practically in that project, let us examine his first serious attempt to test them theoretically, which came the following year in a study of the historical development of early Christianity entitled "The Development of the Dogma of Christ."[88] This early study of Fromm's is important, because it represents, as Franz Borkenau put it in a review of the study in the first issue of the *Zeitschrift für Sozialforschung* two years later, "the first attempt to illustrate by way of a concrete example the method of a synthesis of Marxism with Freudian psychoanalysis."[89] Fromm chose the development of early

---

[85] "Psychoanalyse und Soziologie," *Erich Fromm Gesamtausgabe*, vol. 1, p. 3.

[86] Ibid.

[87] Ibid., p. 5.

[88] *Erich Fromm Gesamtausgabe*, vol. 6, pp. 13–68; in English, *The Dogma of Christ, and Other Essays on Religion, Psychology, and Culture*, trans. James Luther Adams (New York, 1963).

[89] *Zeitschrift für Sozialforschung*, vol. 1, (Leipzig, 1932), p. 174. In his preface to the publication of the first English translation of "The Dogma of Christ," Fromm also emphasized the seminal nature of the essay for his own further development. He wrote, "Whatever the merits of this interpretation, the method of the application of psychoanalysis to historical phenomena is the

Christianity as his concrete example because he wanted to offer an alternative to the strictly psychoanalytic account of the origins and psychological function of Christian dogma put forth by his former colleague and mentor in Berlin, Theodor Reik.[90] In an article published in 1927 entitled "Dogma and Compulsion,"[91] Reik had argued that early Christian dogma provided a solution to the Oedipus complex – even if only an ambivalent one – and thus proved more attractive and durable than its main historical rival, Gnosticism, in which hostility to the symbolic father was still openly expressed. Yet the Christians' victory was Pyrrhic insofar as it had been achieved by repressing the hostility to the father in a manner that gave rise to compulsive forms of behavior that were expressed in Christian beliefs and rituals. In other words, Reik viewed Christian dogma as a form of collective neurosis that could be analyzed and explained in the same way as individual neuroses.

Fromm was quick to point out that Reik's personal or individual psychological interpretation of Christian dogma entailed treating Christians as a uniform group whose beliefs and rituals, and the psychological function they fulfilled, remained constant over time. According to Fromm, this approach failed to do justice to the specific and varied socio-historical conditions in which early Christians had lived. Reik's failure to investigate these conditions led to an idealist *quid pro quo* that reduced the bearers of Christian ideas to disembodied repositories of a transcendent dogma. Thus Reik's position shared some important similarities with the official position of the Catholic Church, which he was trying to refute. Fromm writes:

> [Reik] does not attempt to investigate the masses, whose unity he assumes, in their real life situation. He assumes the masses are identical, and deals only with the ideas and ideologies produced by the masses, not concerning himself concretely with living men and their psychic situation. He does not interpret the ideologies as produced by men; he reconstructs the men from the ideologies.... By his method Reik implicitly supports the theological approach, which ... emphasizes the unity of Christian religion – indeed, Catholicism claims immutability.... The element common to the two viewpoints is fundamentally the idea that man neither changes nor develops in history.[92]

In his study, in contrast, Fromm explains the development of Christian dogma in terms of the diverse social and changing historical conditions that shaped the lives of early Christians. In this way, he comes to fundamentally different conclusions than did Reik. Fromm argues that early Christian dogma was an expression of the political radicalism of various disenfranchised groups that had begun to rebel against the repressive rule of the Roman administration and an "extreme caste spirit" that pervaded Jewish society at that time.[93] However, by the time of its adoption as the official religion of the Roman Empire in the

---

one which has been developed in my subsequent books. While it has since been refined in many ways, its nucleus is contained in 'The Dogma of Christ.'" *The Dogma of Christ*, op. cit., p. viii.

[90] Reik had established himself as one of the leading authorities on religion within the psychoanalytic movement. In the late 1920s, he came from Vienna to the Psychoanalytic Institute in Berlin to give a series of lectures on the psychology of religion, which Fromm attended.

[91] Theodor Reik, "Dogma und Zwangsidee," *Imago*, vol. 12 (Leipzig, 1927).

[92] *The Dogma of Christ*, pp. 63–4.

[93] Ibid., p. 30.

fourth century, Christianity had been widely diffused among the middle and upper echelons of Roman society, due in large part to the efforts of Paul, the first Christian leader who did not come from the lower classes. The result was a complete transformation of Christian dogma and its social-psychological function. In its original, Adoptionist form, Christian dogma was based on the idea of man being elevated to the place of God, and entailed an eschatological transformation of this world. In its later, Homoousian form, it was based on God descending voluntarily to save man, whose primary duty was now to win God's love and approval by renouncing his earthly desires and maintaining the purity of his soul, for which he would be compensated in the afterlife. Fromm argues that the material causes of this transformation of Christian dogma are to be found in a series of devastating defeats of the groups who bore the original, antiauthoritarian Adoptionist dogma. As their situation became increasingly hopeless and Christian beliefs were slowly diffused into the middle and upper social strata, the Adoptionist hostility to the father was slowly turned inward, against themselves, and their messianic hope for real, historical change was given up in favor of spiritual salvation.[94]

Fromm's arguments about the actual historical development of Christianity are less important for our concerns here than the fact that they illustrated a new theoretical approach that would have a significant impact on the development of Horkheimer's Critical Theory of contemporary society.[95] In the "Dogma of Christ," Fromm spells out the theoretical assumptions underlying this approach in much greater detail than in his talk on "Psychoanalysis and Sociology." Fromm's point of departure is a distinction, which he views as the basis of Freud's theory of human psychic development, between an individual's *inherited sexual constitution* and his or her *life experiences*. Fromm tries to show how this distinction opens the door for the development of the sociological insights contained in psychoanalysis.[96] Fromm argues that despite certain important breakthroughs, psychoanalytic research on inherited sexual constitution is still in its infancy, and not yet in a position to put forth many firm conclusions. As a consequence, psychoanalytic research and therapy has focused much more on the second factor of psychic development, namely the concrete life experiences of individuals. He writes:

For psychoanalysis, the constitutional element in the psychic structure of the healthy or ill person is a factor that must be observed in the psychological investigation of individuals, but it remains intangible. What psychoanalysis is concerned with is experience; the investigation of its influence on emotional development is its primary purpose. Psychoanalysis is aware, of course, that the emotional development of the individual is

94 Ibid., pp. 38–54. Fromm's account here of the origins of the Christian "soul" and Christian "*ressentiment*" through a long process of the internalization and redirection of aggression against oneself bears strong resemblances to Nietzsche's treatment of the same problem in the *Genealogy of Morals* and elsewhere, but there are no explicit references to Nietzsche in "The Dogma of Christ."

95 For the importance of Fromm's "Dogma of Christ" as a precursor of Horkheimer's concept of bourgeois anthropology, see also Chapter 7, pp. 252–3.

96 "The Dogma of Christ," p. 3.

determined more or less by his constitution; this insight is a presupposition of psycho-analysis, but psychoanalysis itself is concerned exclusively with the investigation of the influence of the individual's life situation on his emotional development.[97]

Downplaying the importance of sexual constitution in this way – anticipating his later abandonment of Freud's drive theory altogether – is important for Fromm insofar as it allows him, in a further step, to render more fluid the boundary between personal and social psychology. If the primary concern of psychoanalysis is understanding the life experiences of an individual patient, then social psychology can apply the same methods to groups of individuals, insofar as they have had similar life experiences that have had similar effects on their psychic development. Fromm expresses this methodological unity between personal and social psychology in the following way: "Demonstrating the influence of the course of life upon the psychic structure ... is the central analytical problem of both social and personal psychology."[98] The only remaining difference between the two, according to him, lies in the fact that personal psychology treats unhealthy, neurotic individuals who have been unable to adapt themselves to their social surroundings, whereas social psychology examines groups of normal individuals whose lives have been shaped through common historical experiences.[99]

Yet how did Fromm propose to investigate group psychological traits? Because he explicitly rejected the concept of a group soul or collective unconscious, he did not attempt to establish group characteristics, à la Reik or Jung, through recourse to universal psychological constants or unconscious dispositions. Fromm relied instead on empirical research – either on history, as he did in "The Dogma of Christ," or on contemporary society, as he would do in the study of German workers in 1929. This crucial empirical component of Fromm's social psychology was an important aspect of his theoretical elective affinity with Horkheimer at this time. Like Horkheimer, Fromm rejected all general or abstract claims about human nature or human character, because they failed to take into account the socio-historical conditions in which concrete individuals lived. In contrast to the manifold metaphysical interpretations of "man" at that time, of which Horkheimer was so skeptical, the basis of Fromm's social psychology was the concrete individual within a determinate socio-historical context. Furthermore, Fromm's emphasis on psychoanalytically informed empirical research opened up an entire new field of inquiry, which seemed to hold the key to redressing the inadequacies of Marx's theory

[97] Ibid., p. 4.

[98] Erich Fromm, *Die Entwicklung des Christusdogmas: Eine Psychoanalytische Studie zur Sozialpsychologischen Funktion der Religion* (Vienna: Internationaler Psychoanalytischer Verlag, 1931), p. 17. For some reason, this passage has been omitted from the English text.

[99] Fromm would later be heavily criticized by the members of the Institute for defining psychic "health" in terms of successful adjustment to one's social surroundings. See Martin Jay, "The Dialectical Imagination," pp. 103–5. For a more recent critique of the Fromm's analytic social psychology in terms of its subsumption of the individual under abstract sociological categories and his inability to account for nonconformity and dissent, see Dahmer, *Libido and Gesellschaft*, pp. 282–5, and Detlev Claussen, *Unterm Konformitätszwang: Zum Verhältnis von kritischer Theorie und Psychoanalyse* (Bremen: Verlag Bettina Wassman, 1988), pp. 10ff.

of ideology, which had become evident in the first decades of the twentieth century. As Fromm would put it in 1932:

In many instances, to be sure, historical materialism could provide the right answers without any psychological presuppositions. But only where ideology was the immediate expression of economic interests; or where one was trying to establish the correlation between economic substructure and ideological superstructure. Lacking a satisfactory psychology, Marx and Engels could not explain *how* the material basis was reflected in man's head and heart.[100]

Fromm's approach also offered an alternative to Mannheim's sociology of knowledge, which failed to move beyond an abstract notion of correspondence between ideas and their social carriers. With the help of psychoanalysis, Fromm would be able not merely to identify a correlation between particular groups and ideas, but also explain *why* these groups adhered to them – even if the ideas did not express their own best interests.

In order to interpret adequately the effect of life experiences on the psychic development of individuals or groups of individuals, Fromm drew on Freud's early drive theory, which posited self-preservation and libido as the dominant forces in human psychic life. Whereas self-preservation drives are relatively stable and admit satisfaction in only a limited number of ways, libidinous drives are relatively malleable and can be satisfied in many different ways. When one is hungry, one must eat, but the need for love and protection can also be satisfied in imaginary ways: through membership in an imagined community, for example, or belief in a loving God. This plasticity of libidinous drives is, according to Fromm, the reason why life experiences can have a decisive impact on psychical development. He writes:

The sex drives up to a certain and not insignificant point, permit a gratification in fantasies and with one's own body; they are therefore much more independent of external reality than are the ego drives.... This flexibility and versatility within the sexual drives are the basis for the extraordinary variability of the psychic structure and therein lies also the basis for the possibility that individual experiences can so definitely and markedly affect the libido structure.[101]

Crucial for Fromm, and later for Horkheimer, is to show how libidinal drives are formed ideologically, that is, by existing relations of social domination. Like Horkheimer, Fromm moves beyond Marx by returning from the general, social determinants of ideology, to an investigation of the ways in which it is reproduced at the level of the concrete individual. But rather than relying on theoretically inflected micrological observations of everyday life, as Horkheimer had done in *Dämmerung*, Fromm analyzes the *libidinal* forces that keep the dominated in a state of self-imposed psychic immaturity.

Adumbrating an argument he would develop in more detail two years later in the first issue of the *Zeitschrift für Sozialforschung*,[102] Fromm argues that

---

[100] Fromm, "The Method and Function of Analytic Social Psychology," in *The Essential Frankfurt School Reader*, eds. Andrew Arato and Eike Gephardt (New York, 1982), p. 491.

[101] "The Dogma of Christ," p. 8.

[102] "The Method and Function of an Analytic Social Psychology," in *The Essential Frankfurt School Reader*, eds. A. Arato and E. Gebhardt (New York, 1982), pp. 477–96.

social cohesion does not result from individuals pursuing their own interests and it is not created solely by the potential and real force of reigning institutions either; instead, it is based primarily on libidinal forces that bind individuals unconsciously to existing social relations and institutions.[103] In other words, libidinal bonds are the "cement" that holds society together, but they can, under certain circumstances, also become "explosive." In "The Dogma of Christ," Fromm reconstructed the historical circumstances under which Christianity was transformed from an explosive, revolutionary set of beliefs, into an affirmative, self-abnegating ideology that reinforced social domination. Fromm argued that the fate of Christianity illustrated certain psychic mechanisms that were also at work in modern class societies. Drawing upon Freud's early analysis of religion,[104] Fromm argued that in its affirmative form, religion is a form of psychic infantilism: the believer's relationship to God re-creates the infant's relationship to his or her father. Like Horkheimer, who argued that the ideological function of religion has been largely taken over by new secular forms such as the national "community," Fromm argues that in modern capitalist societies the libidinal ties to real or imagined religious authorities are transferred to the most powerful representatives of the current social order.[105] He writes:

> In the class structure of society the infantile situation repeats itself for the individual. He sees in the rulers the powerful, strong, wise, intimidating. He believes that they mean well for him and only want what is best for him. He knows that any rebellion against them will be punished and is satisfied when he can win their praise through compliance. These are just the same feelings that he had about his father as a child, and it goes without saying that he is every bit as inclined to believe uncritically what the rulers present to him as correct and true, as he was used to believing uncritically all his father's assertions when he was a child.[106]

Fromm also points out that self-imposed psychic infantilism entails not only a loss of autonomy, but also a willingness to undergo real privations in the name of maintaining the existing social order. However, if such sacrifices become too burdensome in intensity or duration, they can lead to the delegitimation of the rulers and/or a revolt among the ruled, as demonstrated by the origins of Christianity. However, if those who suffer such privations are compensated in other ways – with the imaginary satisfactions of religion, for example, or

---

[103] Ibid., p. 493.

[104] Fromm acknowledges that Freud developed a more complex interpretation of religion in *The Future of an Illusion*, but Fromm does not believe that the changes were significant enough to undermine his own arguments, which continued to be based primarily upon Freud's earlier position. See "The Dogma of Christ," p. 12.

[105] Fromm elaborates this argument and applies it to the contemporary judicial and penal system in the aforementioned articles, "The State as Educator: On the Pyschology of Penal Justice" and "On the Psychology of the Criminal in the Penal Society," in *Erich Fromm and Critical Criminology*, op. cit. In these essays, Fromm argues that the state, in its ability to threaten and to punish, takes over the roll of the father for the masses, and notes that "this is demonstrated most clearly by the death penalty. The ability to castrate, that is, to cause substantial bodily damage, is the core of the paternal power to punish." *Erich Fromm Gesamtausgabe*, vol. 1, p. 10.

[106] "Entwicklung des Christusdogmas," p. 21.

nationalism – they will be willing to make much greater real sacrifices, for a longer period of time, than if they were not compensated at all. This insight provides the key not only to Fromm's interpretation of the transformation of early Christianity, but also to his pathbreaking attempt to understand the changing function of ideology in twentieth-century monopoly capitalist societies.

Although Horkheimer's interpretation of the role of paternal authority in social integration would later diverge from that of Fromm, his psychoanalytic insights into the imaginary compensation of real privations would have a lasting impact on Horkheimer.[107] With the rise of nationalism as a mass ideology at the end of the nineteenth century and then the rise of mass culture in the first decades of the twentieth century, the role of imaginary compensation in ideology formation became much more important; it became a crucial object of analysis for a critical theory of society. This was one of the most important reasons why Horkheimer was initially drawn to Fromm's methods, and why he and his colleagues at the Institute would continue to rely heavily on psychoanalysis. Thus, it is worth quoting at some length Fromm's description of the ways in which these mechanisms work. He writes:

Man strives for a maximum of pleasure; social reality compels him to many instinctual renunciations, and society seeks to compensate the individual for these renunciations by other satisfactions harmless for the society – that is, for the ruling class. These satisfactions are such that they are realized essentially in fantasies, especially in collective fantasies. We can call these fantasies, shared by all, collective imaginary satisfactions. They perform an important function in social reality. In so far as society does not permit real satisfactions, fantasy satisfactions serve as a substitute and become a powerful support of social stability. The greater the renunciations people endure in reality, the stronger must be the concern for compensation. Fantasy satisfactions have the double function which is characteristic of every narcotic: they act both as an anodyne and as a deterrent to active change of reality. The common fantasy satisfactions have an essential advantage over individual daydreams: by virtue of their universality, the fantasies are perceived by the conscious mind as if they were real. An illusion shared by everyone becomes a reality.[108]

So, although Fromm is convinced that collective fantasies can and do play a decisive role in shaping both social reality and individuals' psychic structures, he has not, at this point, abandoned a materialist approach to society and individual subjectivity. For Fromm still insists not only that domination in capitalist societies is ultimately based on socio-economic structures, to which individual drives are actively and passively adapted; he also speaks of the natural foundations of subjectivity, which set the "limits of the modification" of human drives.[109] Fromm views the foremost task of analytic social psychology to examine "how the economic situation is transformed into ideology via man's drives." Finally, Fromm also argues that psychoanalysis can help explain the

[107] See the discussion of Horkheimer's essay "Egoism and Freedom Movements: On the Anthropology of the Bourgeois Epoch," in Chapter 7.

[108] "The Dogma of Christ," p. 14 (translation modified).

[109] "The Method and Function of Analytic Social Psychology," op. cit., p. 490.

new forms of ideology that have emerged in the early twentieth century, but it cannot by itself overcome them. This can only be done *politically*, that is, by changing the material social conditions that make ideological self-deception seem necessary.[110]

The Empirical Study of German Workers in 1929 as the First Attempt to Put Horkheimer's Theory of Contemporary Society into Practice

Having examined the outlines of Horkheimer's nascent Critical Theory of society in the late 1920s, including his first efforts to integrate psychoanalysis, we are now ready at last to turn to the empirical study on the German working class in 1929, which was, as Martin Jay put it, "the first real effort to apply Critical Theory to a concrete, empirically verifiable problem."[111] The study was officially directed by Fromm, and it is no longer possible to reconstruct exactly the nature of Horkheimer's role in the conceptualization and execution of the study. In an interview in 1969, Horkheimer stressed the collective nature of the project:

We had come to the conclusion that theoretical work required empirical research as an instrument. Thus we discussed a certain problem, first gathered data and thought about how to carry out the necessary empirical research. I am thinking in particular about an investigation of workers' consciousness that we had begun at that time. First a question- naire was designed, which was then constantly revised based upon the practical results, until it was sufficient for our theoretical questions. All of this research work was carried out in close cooperation between theoretical and empirical reflection.[112]

For his part, Erich Fromm claimed in a letter from 1971 that "Horkheimer participated very little in this study and did not have much interest in it."[113] Once the questionnaires had been designed and sent out, Horkheimer did in fact play a negligible role in completing the study, and by the time it had been completed he and Pollock were opposed to publishing it.[114] Nevertheless, Horkheimer probably did play an important part in conceptualizing the study in its early stages. His inaugural address as the new director of the Institute for Social Research in January 1931, in which he explicitly mentioned the study,

[110] Fromm, "Politik und Psychoanalyse," *Gesamtausgabe*, vol. 1, p. 36.

[111] Jay, *The Dialectial Imagination*, op. cit., p. 116.

[112] "Dokumente – Stationen" Interview with Otmar Hersche, GS 7, p. 327.

[113] This letter to Martin Jay has been published in *Erich Fromm und die Frankfurter Schule*, eds. Michael Kessler and Rainer Funk (Tübingen: Francke, 1992), pp. 249–56. The passage quoted here is p. 255.

[114] Other scholars helped Fromm to complete the study at various stages. Most important in the early stages, prior to the Institute's relocation to the United States, was Hilde Weiss, an associate of the Institute who was well versed in empirical research methods. On Weiss's important role in the study, see Wolfgang Bonss, "Kritische Theorie und empirische Sozialforschung: Anmerkungen zu einem Fallbeispiel," in *Erich Fromm: Arbeiter und Angestellte am Vorabend des Dritten Reiches*, ed. Wolfgang Bonss (Munich: Deutscher Taschenbuch Verlag, 1983), p. 32. After the immigration to the United States, Anna Hartock, Herta Herzog, Paul Lazarsfeld, and Ernst Schachtel all helped Fromm in his efforts to complete the study. For a discussion of the fate of the study and the reasons why it was never published, see Martin Jay, *The Dialectical Imagination*, op. cit., p. 116.

demonstrated that he still had a lively interest in the project at that time.[115] More important, however, if one examines the design and results of the study, it is unmistakably clear that it embodied the principle tenets of Horkheimer's Critical Theory at this time. One could summarize these tenets rather schematically as the primacy of a Marxist theory of history and society, supplemented by empirical social research and a critical appropriation of psychoanalysis. In what follows, we shall see how the study applied these principles to the fateful problem of the conscious and unconscious attitudes of the German working class in the period immediately preceding the National Socialist seizure of power.

As we have seen, Marxist theorists in central Europe in the 1920s were preoccupied with the question of why the German working class had failed to fulfill the role Marx had assigned it: to act as the historical subject of the transition from capitalism to socialism as soon as the historical conditions were ripe, as they seemed to have been in the period immediately following the October Revolution in Russia and the widespread delegitimation of imperial institutions in Germany at the end of the war. However, with some notable exceptions, the German working class and its leaders – particularly those in the Social Democratic Party – proved to be reluctant revolutionaries at best. Rather than viewing these historical developments as a refutation of Marx's theory, or – at the other extreme – claiming that this "factual" deviation from the theory was "so much the worse for the facts"[116] but did not have any implications for the truth value of Marx's theory, Horkheimer believed that critical theorists must analyze the reasons for this unexpected turn of events and update Marx's theory in light of their findings. The empirical study on the attitudes of German workers in 1929 was an attempt to do just this through an analysis of the conscious and unconscious political and social attitudes of German workers. But the study was also intended to provide some insight into a question that had direct practical consequences for Horkheimer, Fromm, and the other members of the Institute, namely whether or not they would live up to their political ideals if faced with an attempt by the National Socialists to seize power. By revealing just how widespread unconscious authoritarian attitudes were – even among many workers who professed to hold radical political beliefs – the study did in fact provide pathbreaking and prescient answers to these central problems of Marxist theory in the 1920s.[117] As Wolfgang Bonss, who edited and published the study for the first time in 1980, put it: "Scientifically and historically speaking, the study can be seen, essentially, as the expression of an historically specific reformulation of Marxist social theory, which in Fromm's eyes, and not only his, was to be broadened by social-psychological concepts and tested by empirical

---

[115] GS 3, p. 33.

[116] As did Georg Lukács.

[117] According to Fromm, the reason why Horkheimer refused to publish the study later, when the Institute was in exile in the United States, was because it was in fact "too Marxist" and thus ran the risk of jeopardizing the Institute's fragile position in the anti-Marxist American academic climate.

analysis."[118] However, as we have seen, Erich Fromm had become seriously interested in Marx only shortly before beginning work on the study; thus, it stands to reason that these basic questions that guided the study as a whole were a product of Horkheimer's nondogmatic Marxist Critical Theory.

The decisive importance of Horkheimer's nascent Critical Theory in the original conceptualization of the study is also apparent when one examines its empirical component. Before meeting Frieda Reichmann and beginning his psychoanalytic training, Erich Fromm had completed his Ph.D. in sociology under the direction of Alfred Weber. During his studies with Weber, who exemplified the historical and cultural approach to sociology dominant in Germany at that time,[119] Fromm learned nothing about empirical methods for researching contemporary society.[120] Thus it is not surprising that Wolfgang Bonss poses the question of why Fromm decided to embark, seemingly out of the blue, on a study of the German working class that relied so heavily on empirical field research. He says:

> If one compares Fromm's concept with the hypotheses of other representatives of the Freudian Left, it emerges that, while there are differences of content between them, the type of theory was ultimately the same, in that they were all engaged to provide relatively general explanatory models; Fromm's work, like that of Reich, for example, contained few statements which might have presented a starting point for empirical verification.... The question is how, given the connection between theory and empiricism, he arrived at the decision to undertake empirical work. This question cannot be answered on the basis of Fromm's theory alone.[121]

Bonss speculates that the answer should be sought in two different places. First, Fromm's earlier training as a sociologist made it easier for him to conduct empirical research. Second, and more important, according to Bonss, was Fromm's involvement with the Institute for Social Research, through which he came into contact with Hilde Weiss, who played an important role in carrying out the study once it was begun. Yet neither of Bonss's responses really answers the question of the source of the original impulse to conduct

---

[118] Wolfgang Bonss, "Critical Theory and Empirical Social Research: Some Observations," in Erich Fromm, *The Working Class in Weimar Germany: A Psychological and Sociological Study*, ed. Wolfgang Bonss, trans. Barbara Weinberger (Warwickshire UK: Berg Publishers, 1984), p. 3.

[119] On sociology in Germany at this time, see Jürgen Habermas, *Texte und Kontexte* (Frankfurt: Suhrkamp, 1991), pp. 184–204; Dirk in M.Rainer Lepsius, *Soziologie in Deutschland und Osterreich 1918–1945, Kölner Zeitschrift für Soziologie und Sozialpsychologie*, Sonderheft 23, (Opladen: Westdeutscher Verlag, 1981), pp. 199–245; and M. Rainer Lepsius, "Die Soziologie der Zwischenkriegszeit: Entwicklungstendenzen und Beurteilungskriterien," also in *Soziologie in Deutschland und Osterreich 1918–1945*, op. cit., pp. 7–23.

[120] Although Alfred Weber had, like his brother Max, participated in empirical research projects conducted by the Society for Social Politics (*Verein für Sozialpolitik*) before the war, in the 1920s he was, as Erhard Stölting points out, the representative of "cultural sociology" in Germany. See Stölting, *Akademische Soziologie in der Weimarer Republik* (Berlin: Duncker und Humboldt, 1986), pp. 106f. Weber emphasized empirical field research neither in his writings nor in his teaching at this time. On Weber's teaching activity at the University of Heidelberg in the 1920s, see Eberhard Demm, *Von der Weimarer Republik zur Bundesrepublik: Der politische Weg Alfred Webers 1920–1958* (Düsseldorf, 1999), pp. 78–115.

[121] Bonss, "Critical Theory and Empirical Social Research," op. cit., pp. 23–4.

a large empirical study, because Fromm's early sociological training did not include empirical field work and Weiss was only in charge of the "concrete execution" of the study.[122] The real answer should be sought in the nascent Critical Theory of Horkheimer, in which the empirical tradition in general and empirical social research in particular played such an important role. Bonss does recognize that the study of German workers reflects the fact that Horkheimer had already begun to play an important role in Institute affairs by 1929, but refrains from making any specific speculations about his influence.[123] Based on our presentation of Horkheimer's intellectual trajectory so far, and the statements he would soon make about the importance of empirical social research in his inaugural address as the next director of the Institute for Social Research,[124] it seems quite clear that Horkheimer was primarily responsible for the strong empirical dimension of the study, as he was for its basic Marxist orientation.

One of the defining characteristics of Horkheimer's thought at this time was an interest in integrating the most advanced research in a wide variety of fields and placing it in the service of an overarching critical theory of society. This is important to remember in order to understand Horkheimer's interest in empirical social research, because he certainly believed that it was lacking in German sociology at this time. Despite some contentions to contrary, the Institute's use of certain methods of empirical field research represented something qualitatively new at that time. There is no question that the psychoanalytic techniques used in the construction and evaluation of the questionnaires was unprecedented, but the use of advanced sociological techniques of empirical field research was also highly innovative within the context of German sociology in the 1920s. Wolfgang Bonss recognizes this when he states, "Appearing at a time when there was almost no empirical research in the academic field, the present study marked a first step towards the rediscovery of the proletariat as an object of empirical study."[125] Many other commentators have noted the general lack of emphasis on empirical field research in German sociological discussions in the 1920s.[126] Although there had been some emphasis on empirical field research prior to the war, early German sociology was "conceptualized primarily as a human science [*Geisteswissenschaft*]."[127] This tendency only gained momentum in the strongly anti-positivist intellectual climate in Weimar Germany, with the increasing popularity of historicism, phenomenology, vitalism, and metaphysics that also influenced the young discipline of sociology. This tendency was

[122] Ibid., p. 24.

[123] Ibid., p. 16.

[124] See, for example, "The Present Situation of Social Philosophy and the Tasks of an Institute of Social Research," in Max Horkheimer, *Between Philosophy and Social Science: Selected Early Writings*, trans. G.F. Hunter, M.S. Kramer, and J. Torpey (Cambridge, MA: MIT Press, 1995), p. 13.

[125] Bonss, "Critical Theory and Empirical Social Research," op. cit., p. 15.

[126] See, for example, Habermas, "Soziologie in der Weimarer Republik," op. cit., pp. 193–4.

[127] Helmut Vogt, "Max Weber und die deutsche Soziologie der Weimarer Republik: Aussenseiter oder Gründervater?" in M.Rainer Lepsius, *Soziologie in Deutschland und Österreich 1918– 1945*, op. cit., pp. 245–72.

called into question only at the end of the decade in the work of younger scholars such as Horkheimer and Karl Mannheim, or Paul Lazarsfeld in Austria, but their influence would be halted prematurely by the National Socialist seizure of power in 1933.[128] In short, there is no question that empirical methods used in the Institute's study on German workers in 1929 represented an important innovation in the context of German sociology at that time.

If the tradition of empirical social research was so weak in Germany in the 1920s, where did Horkheimer and Fromm turn to for instruction and ideas for this crucial aspect of their study of the German workers? Wolfgang Bonss asserts that Adolf Levenstein's empirical study of German workers in 1912 was their most important model. He writes:

> The decisive impulses for working out the empirical methods can be clearly traced to a quite specific precursor, namely to Adolf Levenstein. His ideas are noticeable in many places of the questionnaire ... so that the present study can in some respects be described as a second edition of his inquiry.[129]

However, the later testimony of Fromm, Horkheimer, and Pollock indicates that they sought to address the deficit of empirical research in German sociology at the time not by returning to prewar German models, but by turning to the more advanced methods that had been developed in the United States. In an introduction to the study that he wrote later, Fromm mentions Levenstein's study but stresses that his work lacked theoretical sophistication and that "American social science has led the way towards a comprehensive empirical approach."[130] In his inaugural address as the new director of the Institute, Horkheimer stressed that their research projects would draw on the most advanced empirical methods, which were being developed in the United States at the time.[131] In later interviews on two separate occasions, Pollock also stressed the importance of American empirical research methods for the study. In an interview with Ernst von Schenk in 1965, Pollock said:

> We were conducting at that time the first comprehensive empirical study of the attitudes of German workers, a study based on American models. At that time we had no other methods [of empirical research, JA] than the American ones. It was an intensive study. The questionnaire alone had sixteen pages and the result was the following: there is no trace of resistance present here! It is true that these workers listened to the speeches on the first of May, about the general strike and socialism, but, on the other hand, they had petty bourgeois ideals, while the Nazis were demonstrating genuine resolve to seize power.[132]

[128] See M. Rainer Lepsius, "Die Soziologie der Zwischenkriegszeit," op. cit., p. 16.

[129] Bonss, "Critical Theory and Empirical Social Research," op. cit. p. 24.

[130] *The Working Class in Weimar Germany*, op. cit., p. 41. In a later letter, Fromm stated, "I was not aware of Levenstein's having been the first to use an interpretive questionnaire." See "Ein Memorandum in eigener Sache: Erich Fromm an Martin Jay," *Erich Fromm und die Frankfurter Schule*, op. cit., p. 255.

[131] "The Present Situation of Social Philosophy and the Tasks of an Institute for Social Research," op. cit., p. 13.

[132] MHA X 132a, p. 46.

In another interview in the 1960s, Pollock mentioned Robert and Helen Merrel Lynd's *Middletown*[133] as one particularly important model for the study:

> *Middletown* was the first comprehensive study of an American city and its social structure, and it was not just statistical, but also sociological and social-psychological.... It played a role in the history of the Frankfurt Institute insofar as it made a big impression on us at the end of the 1920s and on the comprehensive investigation of the working class, which we conducted at the beginning of the 1930s. This study was interrupted by National Socialism and was never completed, but it showed that the workers were much more interested in middle-class furniture and apartments than in transforming society. This result was plainly evident in the responses to the very extensive questionnaire we made at that time, based on the experiences that had been gathered in America with such questionnaires.[134]

Pollock's testimony illustrates clearly that it was not first in exile in the United States, but rather in the late 1920s that he and Horkheimer and Fromm became interested in American sociology.

Before continuing with an examination of the crucial psychoanalytic aspects of the study of German workers in 1929, let us first briefly examine the debate on the status of sociology in Horkheimer's thought at this time. Although most commentators recognize the crucial sociological component of Horkheimer's Critical Theory, which would remain with him for the rest of his life, others maintain that even Horkheimer's early program suffered from a sociological deficit. For example, Michael Bock has argued that the received opinion of the innovative character of Horkheimer's work at this time needs to be revised in light of his limited familiarity with contemporary sociological discussions in Germany.[135] Axel Honneth also maintains that even Horkheimer's early Critical Theory suffered from a "sociological deficit."[136] Although it would take us too far afield to fully engage with these claims here, it can hardly be denied that the study of German workers' attitudes represented – regardless of how one judges the final outcome of the study – something qualitatively new for German sociology in the Weimar period in its use of both the most advanced empirical methods from American sociology and psychoanalysis. Claims that Horkheimer had not paid sufficient attention to the empirical research being done in Germany during the 1920s, such as that of Michael Bock, fail to recognize that the empirical sociological research being conducted in Germany at that time had little impact on the principal debates in which the future of the young discipline was contested.[137] Moreover, and more important, it was

[133] *Middletown: A Study in Modern American Culture* (New York, 1929).

[134] Ernst Herhaus, *Notizen während des Abschaffung des Denkens* (Frankfurt: März Verlag, 1970), pp. 121–2.

[135] See his "Lästige Verwandtschaft: Die kritische Theorie im Kontext der 20er Jahre," in C. Albrecht, G.C. Behrmann, M. Bock, H. Homann, and F.H. Tenbruck, *Die intellekuelle Gründung der Bundesrepublik: Eine Wirkungsgeschichte der Frankfurter Schule* (New York and Frankfurt: Campus, 1999), pp. 36–56.

[136] See his "Max Horkheimer and the Sociological Deficit of Critical Theory," in *On Max Horkheimer: New Perspectives*, eds. S. Benhabib, W. Bonss and J. McCole (Cambridge, MA: MIT, 1993), pp. 187–215.

[137] See Habermas, "Soziologie in der Weimarer Republik," op. cit., and Käsler, "Der Streit um die Bestimmung der Soziologie auf den deutschen Soziologentagen 1910 bis 1930," op. cit.

precisely because the establishment of the academic discipline of sociology in Germany had lagged behind that in the United States that the empirical social research conducted there in the 1920s was not as methodologically advanced as its American counterpart. So there is little question that the Institute's introduction – however tentative it may have been – of American empirical methods represented something qualitatively new in Germany at the time.

Regarding claims, such as Honneth's, that Horkheimer's reliance on a Marxist philosophy of history and, to a lesser extent, a psychoanalytic "theory of total socialization"[138] prevented him from developing an independent sociological theory of cultural action or social struggle, one must emphasize the fact that the definition of sociology as a discipline was still very much open in Weimar Germany,[139] and that branding Horkheimer's Critical Theory nonsociological based on subsequent disciplinary boundaries seems arbitrary. Honneth's critique of Horkheimer is based on one of Jürgen Habermas's central objections to Marx's theory: that his theory of history and society are based on a model of labor conceived as instrumental action, as the manipulation of nature according to rational-purposive imperatives, which obscures the fundamentally different character of symbolically mediated social interaction.[140] Honneth essentially levels Habermas's objection to Marx against Horkheimer, assuming that he had wholly adopted Marx's assumptions. Quite apart from the question of whether or not Habermas's criticism of Marx is justified,[141] or whether or not Horkheimer actually adopts the "Marxist" position attributed to him,[142] one must note that Habermas himself considers Horkheimer one of

---

[138] Honneth quotes here the term Helmut Dahmer coined in his critique of Erich Fromm's social psychology. "The Sociological Deficit of Critical Theory," op. cit., p. 205.

[139] See, for example, Lepsius, "Die Soziologie der Zwischenkriegszeit: Entwicklungstendenzen und Beurteilungskriterien," op. cit.

[140] See, for example, Jürgen Habermas, "Technology and Science as 'Ideology,'" in *Toward a Rational Society: Student Protest, Science and Politics* (Boston: Beacon, 1970), pp. 91ff.

[141] Habermas's critique of Marx attributes to him an ahistorical concept of labor as rational-purposive activity that fails to do justice to Marx's mature formulation of abstract labor as the historically specific form of labor in capitalist societies. For an incisive evaluation of the weaknesses of Habermas's critique of Marx, see Moishe Postone, *Time Labor and Social Domination: A Reinterpretation of Marx's Critical Theory* (Cambridge, UK: Cambridge University Press, 1996), pp. 226–60.

[142] Honneth writes, for example: "From the very beginning, critical theory was shaped by a peculiar inability to analyze society. It failed to treat that sphere of the social that constitutes the particular object of sociology. The difficulties that Horkheimer encountered in his attempt to ground a critical social theory are rooted in a philosophy of history that conceptually reduces the process of social development to the dimension of the domination of nature. As a result of this narrow model of history, Horkheimer was forced to exclude the whole spectrum of everyday social action from the object domain of the interdisciplinary social research he attempted to develop in his programmatic essays." "Max Horkheimer and the Sociological Deficit of Critical Theory," op. cit., p. 187. In the remainder of his essay, it becomes clear that the philosophy of history that Honneth attributes to Horkheimer is indeed the Marxian model, or at least his interpretation of it. He continues, "It is this [Marxist] interpretation of the contradiction between productive forces and productive relations that now governs Horkheimer's attempt to provide a foundation for a critical theory of society: The productive forces are seen as an emancipatory potential whose unplanned organization in capitalism is regarded only as the expression of human self-deception" p. 191. However, Horkheimer neither ignored "the spectrum of

the most important members – along with Theodor Geiger, Karl Mannheim, and Hans Freyer – of a younger generation of thinkers who provided the most important impulses for the discipline of sociology during the final years of the Weimar Republic.[143] In other words, Habermas judges neither the pluralistic discussion of sociology in Germany at the time nor Horkheimer's own position in terms of a subsequent, quasi-absolute definition of the discipline. For Habermas – who accepts Helmut Dubiel's argument on this point[144] – Horkheimer's Critical Theory does not begin to suffer from a "sociological deficit" until he begins to become more skeptical, between 1937 and 1940, of the findings of all the traditional sciences. In any case, there is no question that Horkheimer had a lively interest in sociology in the late 1920s, both in terms of sociological approaches to history and culture[145] and in terms of particular discussions within the discipline.[146] One can speak of a "sociological deficit" in his thought at this time only from a narrow, quasi-transcendental standpoint.

everyday social action," nor did he see the "productive forces" as an "emancipatory potential" that was thwarted by "human self-deception." Regarding the former point, we have already seen in our analysis of *Dämmerung* how Horkheimer moved beyond Marx's analysis of the social origins of ideology in his analysis of the ways in which concrete individuals reproduce relations of social domination in their everyday lives. With the study of German workers in 1929, he also attempted to gain a better understanding of patterns of everyday behavior and the psychological dispositions underlying them (such as one's attitudes toward women and children, one's cultural tastes, how one spends free time). Honneth has a very specific, quasi-transcendental definition of "everyday social action" in mind, and because Horkheimer's analyses do not conform to that particular model, he views them as insufficiently sociological. Horkheimer had recognized already in his lectures on the history of contemporary philosophy that the dream of the inherently emancipatory potential of the development of the productive forces – in either its positivist or Marxist form – had been widely discredited by the end of the nineteenth century. Furthermore, the persistence of historical domination that Marx addressed resulted not from the "self-deception" of the human species, but rather from the real division of society into groups with antagonistic interests, which links the self-preservation of the dominant groups to their ability to deceive the dominated groups.

[143] "Soziologie in der Weimarer Republik," op. cit., p. 186–7.

[144] See Helmut Dubiel, *Theory and Politics: Studies in the Development of Critical Theory*, trans. B. Gregg (Cambridge, MA, 1985), p. 106.

[145] Horkheimer's lectures on the philosophy of history are a good example of his "sociological" approach to history. Some texts from the Horkheimer Archive that illustrate that Horkheimer was self-consciously pursuing a sociological approach to history and culture at this time have been published in his *Collected Writings*. See, for example, "Über das Recht soziologischer Interpretation" and "Über Sinn und Grenzen einer soziologischen Behandlung der Philosophie" in GS 11, pp. 158–65 and 209–20, respectively. The eleventh volume of Horkheimer's *Collected Writings* also contains the beginning of the introduction of a study of the history of sociology that was never completed. This fragment illustrates the tendency found in much of Horkheimer's work during this time to approach sociology historically, not from a quasi-transcendental standpoint.

[146] Horkheimer's interest in the still largely inchoate discipline of sociology was evident in two unpublished texts from the late 1920s, in which he discusses Max Scheler, Gottfried Salomon, and Heinz O. Ziegler. The latter two were students of the Frankfurt sociolgist Franz Oppenheimer. See "Max Scheler (1874–1928)" and "Pareto und die 'Frankfurter' Soziologische Schule," GS 11, pp. 138–44 and 196–201, respectively. The large section devoted to sociology in the review section of the *Zeitschrift für Sozialforschung*, from the first issue onward, also testifies to the importance Horkheimer accorded to keeping abreast of developments in the field.

If the undogmatic Marxian assumptions and the important empirical research components of the Institute's study of workers' attitudes in 1929 should be seen primarily as expressions of Horkheimer's incipient Critical Theory of contemporary society, its third crucial component, psychoanalysis, should be attributed to Erich Fromm. As we have seen, Horkheimer had been interested in psychology since he came to Frankfurt in 1919, but neither of the two psychological discourses that had seriously interested him prior to his discovery of psychoanalysis was adequate to the tasks posed by his Critical Theory of contemporary society. Gestalt psychology had played an important role in his work with Hans Cornelius, but it remained firmly lodged within the paradigm of consciousness philosophy that he abandoned in 1925. In the late 1920s, Horkheimer became interested in the tradition of French interest psychology. In his lectures on the French Enlightenment, Horkheimer devoted a section to a discussion of this tradition, the influence of which could be seen in many aspects of the *lumieres'* thought.[147] Horkheimer showed, for example, how the basic principles of interest psychology informed Enlightenment historiography, and he devoted a section of his lengthy essay on "The Beginnings of the Bourgeois Philosophies of History" to the "psychological" understanding of history.[148] Interest psychology would continue to inform Horkheimer's later work, but it was not sophisticated enough to provide complex explanations of irrational behavior, that is, situations in which individuals or groups of individuals acted in contradiction to their own best interests, or situations in which their actions ran contrary to their professed beliefs. Horkheimer was attempting to come to terms with precisely such a situation in Germany in the late 1920s. Why had the vast majority of the German working class and its leaders failed to live up to their professed political ideals by succumbing to nationalist hysteria at the beginning of the war, undergoing a period of lengthy privation and sacrifice (often mortal) during the war, and proving so reluctant to pursue its own revolutionary interests in the period of crisis immediately afterward? In the face of the growing menace from the right in the late 1920s, Horkheimer was also concerned about how the German working class would react to an attempt by the National Socialists to seize power. Would they offer substantial resistance, as demanded by their political ideals, or would they capitulate once again?

These crucial questions, to which the study of German workers was devoted, could not be answered using a straightforward interest psychology. Erich Fromm's decisive contribution to Horkheimer's Critical Theory at this time was to provide him with the psychoanalytic categories he needed to obtain more nuanced answers to these questions. In *Dämmerung*, Horkheimer had explored the ways in which knowledge, perception, and everyday actions differed radically and were thoroughly conditioned based on one's location within monopoly capitalist society. Through his subtle observations, he was to demonstrate a general correspondence between one's social standing and one's knowledge, perceptions, and behavior. In this regard, Horkheimer's

---

[147] GS 9, pp. 358–60.
[148] GS 2, pp. 181–204.

analysis paralleled Mannheim's sociology of knowledge, which also addressed the socially conditioned character of knowledge. Horkheimer criticized Mannheim's inability to establish more than a "correspondence" between ideas and their social bearers, but the same criticism could be made of his own analyses in *Dämmerung*. Only with the psychoanalytic categories provided to him by Fromm was Horkheimer able to move beyond both Mannheim's sociology of knowledge and his own micrological analysis of ideology in *Dämmerung* to offer concrete explanations of *why* certain groups of individuals were the bearers of certain ideologies, even if they did not express their own best interests, or if they existed unconsciously and contradicted the person's professed political ideals.[149] Fromm's method at this time was – as we have seen in our analysis of "The Dogma of Christ" – to study carefully the life experiences that individuals shared with other members in the same group in order to understand how these experiences had helped form relatively homogenous and stable character structures that were rooted emotionally in their libidinal drives. In "The Dogma of Christ," Fromm utilized this method to analyze a historical problem. In the study of the attitudes of workers in 1929, he applied the method to several key groups and subgroups in contemporary Germany. In this way, Horkheimer's attempt in *Dämmerung* to analyze the reproduction of capitalist social relations and ideology at the level of the concrete individual could be formulated in more precise terms.[150]

It would take us too far afield to summarize the study and its results in any detail.[151] Instead, we will briefly examine the ways in which the study illustrates Fromm's psychoanalytic methods of that time. These methods were evident primarily in the construction and evaluation of the questionnaire, which they sent to approximately 3,300 people (mainly workers), and which provided the empirical foundations of their study.[152] More specifically, Fromm's psychoanalytic considerations informed the type of questions that were posed as well as the interpretation of the respondents' answers. The

[149] Mannheim's model of "relationism" could be used to analyze what he called particular ideologies, that is, when there was indeed a direct correspondence between ideologies and the interests of their bearers. When this was the case, one could, as Mannheim suggested, simply establish empirically who the bearers of the ideology were, and explain the composition of the group based on the content of their ideology. But if there was a difference between the manifest and latent content of the ideology, or if the ideology did not express the direct interests of its bearers, Mannheim's model of relationism faltered.

[150] As Wolfgang Bonss puts it: "Fromm's arguments were important for the Institute in the early 1930s insofar as they revealed a realm existing between the laws governing economic structures and the ways in which individuals reacted to them, which could become the subject of empirical research." "Analytische Sozialpsychologie – Anwendungen zu einem theoretischen Konzept und seiner empirischen Praxis," in *Erich Fromm und die Frankfurter Schule*, op. cit., p. 29.

[151] For a summary of the methods and results of the study, see Bonss, "Critical Theory and Empirical Social Research: Some Observations," op. cit.

[152] By the end of 1931, approximately 1,100 completed questionnaires had been returned to the Institute. Many of these were lost when the Institute was closed by the National Socialists in 1933, so that only 584 completed questionnaires remained in possession of the Institute in New York. See Bonss, "Critical Theory and Empirical Social Research," op. cit., pp. 1–2.

questionnaire was designed to provide answers to the basic questions guiding the study as a whole, which Fromm summarized in the following way: "The aim was to discover how meaningful political doctrines were for the respondent, and which personality types accorded with which political and economic groups."[153] Psychoanalytic methods were used to answer these questions in ways that would not have been possible using a more conventional approach. For example, Fromm correctly assumed that it was not enough just to inquire about someone's political beliefs, for this would, in most cases, simply elicit the standard responses expected of someone who supports a particular political party, that is, responses derived from the party's program or its publications. This approach would fall victim to the mistake of explaining a group's ideology based on its manifest content, rather than exploring the unconscious character structures of the group itself, which revealed themselves only indirectly through a careful empirical study guided by psychoanalytic insights. Only in this way could one determine how meaningful the manifest political beliefs of the group were, that is, whether or not they were emotionally anchored in the personalities of its members.

How exactly did Fromm use psychoanalytic methods to address these problems? In addition to the straightforward questions that were used to establish the respondents' socio-economic status, their party affiliation, and the correlations between them, the questionnaire also contained numerous questions that were used to determine the respondents' psychological character structure or "personality type." These questions focused on three mains areas: views on socio-economic and political problems, attitudes toward authority, and attitudes toward other people. The last two categories of questions were particularly important for Fromm in determining the respondents' personality types, for they provided the most conclusive evidence of unconscious character structures. Based on the respondents' answers to these three groups of questions, they were divided into three different categories of personality types: authoritarian, radical, and reformist. Authoritarian characters were those who were deeply skeptical about individual freedom, who favored the subjugation of men to higher, external powers, and who identified with the powerful rather than the weak or oppressed. They favored authoritarian solutions in the political sphere and viewed the world as a *bellum omnium contra omnes* in which each person must fend for himself or herself and is not obligated by ties of social solidarity. They saw duty and sacrifice as the most important values in personal life. The radical or revolutionary personality type, on the other hand, were those who favored the freedom of the individual and were opposed to his or her subordination to external powers while at the same time recognizing the importance of social solidarity, particularly with the weak and oppressed. Their politics were democratic and socialist, and they saw pleasure and happiness as the most important aims in life. The reformist type lay somewhere in the middle between these two. For example, this type of person "rejects authority at the point when it becomes too strict or impinges too much on the

---

[153] *The Working Class in Weimar Germany*, op. cit., p. 60.

individual; but on the other hand it wishes for authority at just those times when such qualities are absent," as Fromm put it.[154]

Let us briefly consider a few concrete examples of the type of indirect questions and examine how Fromm used the respondents' answers to classify them within one of the three main personality types. One question that he posed in the area of socio-economic and political attitudes was the following: Who, in your opinion, is responsible for the inflation? The responses "Foreign countries, peace treaty, Jews, Social Democrats, individuals," were classified as authoritarian, "capitalists or capitalism" as radical, and "monarchy" as reformist.[155] The questions included in the survey to determine unconscious attitudes toward authority included the following: "Do you think it right that married women should go out to work? Why (not)?" The respondents who replied affirmatively, without qualification, or who stressed the importance of women's independence were classified as radical; those who responded negatively, for any number of reasons (work outside the home is against female nature or it interferes with the man's occupation), were classified as authoritarian; those who applied affirmatively, but only under certain conditions, were considered reformist.[156] A second example of a question used to ascertain attitudes toward authority was the following: "Do you think one can bring up children entirely without corporal punishment?" The response "Yes, because children should grow up free and fearless," was considered radical; negative responses for a variety of reasons ("a child needs to experience authority," or "that is how I grew up," for example) were considered authoritarian; and conditional answers ("only if really necessary," or "Yes, because other punishment is more effective") were considered reformist.[157] Finally, to determine respondents' attitudes toward fellow human beings, Fromm included questions such as the following: "What is your relationship with your colleagues at work? With your immediate superiors? With those above them?" People who responded that they had better relations with their colleagues than their superiors were considered radical, and those who had better relations with their superiors were considered authoritarian.[158] Based on their responses to these questions and others, Fromm was able to classify respondents according to the aforementioned personality types, which he could in turn compare with their political affiliation and socio-economic status.

Although it is quite clear that the Institute's own political orientation played an important role in formulating these questions and determining the classificatory categories for personality types – the study has been criticized for this reason[159] – its psychoanalytic dimension lay precisely in the attempt to determine the extent to which "leftist" personality types corresponded with leftist party affiliation and/or working class socio-economic status. The questions and categories were in fact sensitive enough to determine that there was

[154] Ibid., p. 210.
[155] Ibid., p. 213.
[156] Ibid., p. 216.
[157] Ibid., p. 217.
[158] Ibid., pp. 220–1. There were no reformist responses to this question.
[159] See Bonss, "Critical Theory and Empirical Social Research," p. 27.

much less overlap than expected between leftist party affiliation and "leftist" personality types. Based on this information, Fromm was able to come to the prescient conclusion that the German working class would – despite its vast numbers, substantial parliamentary representation, and professed allegiance to antiauthoritarian political principles – not offer much resistance if the National Socialists attempted to seize power. As he put it near the end of the study:

> Without doubt, the most important result [of the study] is the small proportion of left-ists who were in agreement in both thought and feeling with the Socialist line. In critical times the courage, readiness for sacrifice and spontaneity needed to rouse the less active and to overcome the enemy could only be expected from a rather small group of 15%. Although the Left had the political loyalty and votes of the great majority of workers, it had by and large not succeeded in changing the personality structure of its adherents in such a way that they could be relied upon in critical situations.[160]

However, Fromm did not rest content with a mere diagnosis of the deep rift in the working class between explicit political ideals and unconscious character structures. He also used the psychoanalytic methods to explain how this rift had developed. He explained it primarily in terms of the fact that psychic structures change more slowly than economic structures. Due to its crucial importance for both the study as a whole and the further development of Horkheimer's Critical Theory, it is worth quoting Fromm's elaboration of this point at length:

> Just as a political doctrine is itself an expression of interests and wishes grounded in the material situation of particular social classes, so the emotional elements it contains are likewise those which have arisen on the basis of the historical development of the vanguard of these classes. The psychic structure of a class is an aspect of this object-ive situation. Its *Weltanschauung* is partly determined by those psychic characteristics and emotional drives which evolve within a class in the course of the historical pro-cess and which, at the same time, appeal to those drives and emotions. But psychic change proceeds more slowly than economic change. While a class can develop in a relatively unified manner as regards the economic aspect, psychically it may be only the most advanced elements who exhibit the psychic structure in a relatively pure form, toward which the class as a whole slowly tends. Other members of this class can be very advanced in their political views, but very reactionary in their emotional attitudes.[161]

Fromm was able to detect a significant divergence between the voters, or "rank and file" member of the parties, and the party leaders, because the respondents were also identified and classified according their roles within the party and the union (active members or merely passive voters).[162] This classification enabled Fromm to demonstrate that those who voted for the party but were not active members were generally much more authoritarian. Fromm distinguished between two different kinds of authoritarianism: conservative-authoritarian and rebellious authoritarian.[163] The former type was widespread among the bourgeois parties, the National Socialists, and the Social Democratic voters. The

---

[160] Ibid., p. 228.
[161] Ibid., p. 209 (translation modified).
[162] Ibid., pp. 74–7.
[163] Ibid., p. 226.

latter type was most prominent among the bourgeois parties and Communist voters.[164] The discovery of both types in significant numbers among the voters of the leftist parties illuminated the well- or not-so-well-concealed unconscious attitudes that would make large sections of the working class susceptible to the temptation of the authoritarian politics that would triumph in 1933.

Fromm's identification of authoritarian attitudes among the working class represented perhaps the key psychoanalytic insight of the study. In this regard, Fromm's findings in the study on German workers in 1929 provided a contemporary example of a tendency he had examined in his historical study of the origins of Christianity: a history of political defeats could create authoritarian personality types that belied explicit ideological views, be they Christian or socialist. In one other important regard, however, the study of German workers in 1929 failed to develop the psychoanalytic insights that informed the methodology of "The Dogma of Christ." Fromm did not make any sustained efforts to identify the *historical* events that had led to the formation of authoritarian personality types among the German working class.[165] At certain points in the study, Fromm takes recourse to historical interpretation to clarify the phenomena in question. For example, in his discussion of the conservative and rebellious authoritarian types, he mentions the Wilhelmine petty bourgeoisie, who thoroughly identified with the pompous nationalist symbols and public ceremonies of the *Kaiserreich*, but who, after losing their savings in the inflation of the early 1920s, often joined leftist parties, not because they suddenly agreed with socialist ideals, but because the leftists were powerful and were critical of the republican institutions that they held responsible for their own economic decline.[166] Due to their lack of fundamental agreement with socialist ideals, however, these petty bourgeois "fellow travelers" quickly jumped on the National Socialist bandwagon when it emerged as a powerful political force in the early 1930s. Fromm also mentions that the leftist parties lost legitimacy because they were well represented in parliament but were not very successful in realizing many of their political aims.[167] In any case, a mere 2 percent of all

[164] Ibid., p. 224.

[165] Authoritarian attitudes were, of course, not limited to the working class, but the discovery of their widespread existence among workers was more significant for the purposes of the study. The existence of authoritarian attitudes among the bourgeoisie was expected and was also confirmed by the study; for example, it came as little surprise that among bourgeois respondents Bismarck and Hindenburg were chosen most often as the "greatest historical personalities" (ibid., p. 124), or that they were the group that was most positively inclined to the reactionary German judiciary in the 1920s. The responses to the indirect questions also clearly demonstrated the widespread existence of conservative authoritarian attitudes among the German bourgeoisie in the 1920s. For example, bourgeois respondents responded negatively more often than even the National Socialists on the questions of whether or not it was possible to raise children without corporal punishment and whether or not married women should be allowed to work (ibid., pp. 172 and 169, respectively). Yet perhaps most revealing of all were the responses to the question, "How, in your opinion, can the world be improved?" to which a mere 3 percent of bourgeois answered "knowledge and enlightenment." This demonstrated beyond any doubt that the Enlightenment ideals of the German bourgeoisie – which had, as Horkheimer demonstrated elsewhere, taken root only weakly in the first place – had been largely abandoned by the 1920s.

[166] Ibid., p. 226.

[167] Ibid., p. 82.

the respondents believed that the locus of real power was located in the government or parliament.[168]

However, these historical observations were scattered and unsystematic, offered at key junctures in order to explain certain surprising patterns of responses. In order to explain the social-psychological origins of the "great schism"[169] in the ranks of German social democracy, and genuinely to carry out the psychoanalytic methodology he had first outlined in "The Origins of the Dogma of Christ," Fromm would have had to undertake a much more detailed historical study of the German working class. This deficit is, to be sure, due to the inherent limitations of empirical field research, which cannot accomplish the same tasks as historical research. In its next major empirical project, the 1936 *Studies on Authority and Family*, the Institute would devote more time to historical analysis, as would Horkheimer in his individual explorations of the "anthropology of the bourgeois epoch" in the 1930s. Nonetheless, the study of German workers in 1929 had clearly demonstrated that unconscious character structures played a crucial role in the reproduction of society as a whole, a role that any serious critical theory of society could not afford to ignore. The study had confirmed Fromm's arguments from "The Origins of the Dogma of Christ" that the drives of concrete individuals were bound up in and formed by larger historical and social processes, and that they in turn played a decisive role in the further development of these processes. In any case, the study of the attitudes of German workers in 1929 should be seen, despite the prescience of its results, as only the first attempt to apply Fromm's social-psychological insights to a concrete problem within the larger context of a critical theory of contemporary society. As Wolfgang Bonss points out, Fromm and his coworkers were fully aware of the *experimental* nature of the study, and saw it also as a means of testing and developing their theoretical assumptions and practical methods of research.[170] As we shall see in subsequent chapters, the attempt to test and develop Fromm's psychoanalytic insights, which was begun in this study, would continue to play a central role not only in the Institute's collective work, but also in Horkheimer's individual essays in the 1930s.

In the period between 1925 and 1930, Horkheimer broke decisively with the paradigm of consciousness philosophy that dominated his own work, the work of his mentor Hans Cornelius, and German academic philosophy as a whole in the early 1920s. He did so along two axes: history and society. Regarding the former, he developed a nuanced, materialist interpretation of the history of modern philosophy based on the rise and subsequent transformation of bourgeois society. Regarding the latter, he laid the foundations for his own Critical Theory of contemporary society through a combination of different endeavors: a critique of other theorists, such as Mannheim and Lenin; a theoretically informed exploration of the subjective and objective underpinnings of contemporary monopoly capitalist society in the aphorisms of *Dämmerung*; and,

---

[168] Ibid., p. 85.
[169] Carl Schorske, *German Social Democracy 1905–1917: The Development of the Great Schism* (Cambridge, MA: Harvard University Press, 1955).
[170] *The Working Class in Weimar Germany*, op. cit., p. 25.

finally, a critical appropriation of psychoanalysis, which drew heavily on the work of Fromm. By 1929, when it was clear that Horkheimer would become the next director of the Institute for Social Research, his theory of contemporary society had already been developed to the point that he was ready to put it into practice in the form of the empirical study on the attitudes of the German working class. Thus, Horkheimer's programmatic formulations on "The Present Situation of Social Philosophy and the Tasks of an Institute for Social Research"[171] or his important methodological remarks on the relationship between history and psychology[172] did not represent tentative formulations that he would work out only subsequently; they were, rather, based on a process of critical reflection that had been under way at least since 1925. To be sure, Horkheimer would refine and even modify his views on history and society in subsequent years, but the theoretical assumptions that would guide the Institute's work through its most fruitful period in the 1930s were largely in place before Horkheimer officially became its director in 1930. It is to the further development of Horkheimer's Critical Theory in the 1930s that we now turn.

[171] This was the title of the inaugural address that Horkheimer delivered on January 24, 1931, upon taking over the helm of the Institute for Social Research. See *Between Philosophy and Social Science*, op. cit., pp. 1–14.
[172] "History and Psychology," *Between Philosophy and Social Science*, op. cit., pp. 111–28.

6

Horkheimer's Concept of Materialism in the Early 1930s

> The standpoint of the old materialism is bourgeois society; the standpoint of the new is human society, or socialised humanity.
>
> Marx, Tenth Thesis on Feuerbach

Having completed our examination of the origins of Horkheimer's Critical Theory in the period 1925–31, we turn now to its further development during the time when Horkheimer served as the director of the Institute and editor of its journal, the *Zeitschrift für Sozialforschung*. Whereas the previous three chapters were intended to demonstrate how Horkheimer moved beyond consciousness philosophy along two interrelated yet distinct axes – one diachronic and historical, the other synchronic and social – the following four chapters adopt a different approach to Horkheimer's Critical Theory. Each chapter examines a particular concept that was essential to his Critical Theory during a particular time. Through an examination of these key concepts – materialism (Chapter 6), the anthropology of the bourgeois epoch (Chapter 7), dialectical logic (Chapter 8), and state capitalism (Chapter 9) – the overall development and transformation of Horkheimer's Critical Theory in the period between 1931 and 1941 should become clear. Despite this change of approach, the continuities in Horkheimer's work in the periods before and after 1931 are much greater than those between his work before and after approximately 1940. After becoming director of the Institute, Horkheimer tested, refined, and developed his Critical Theory. However, a qualitative shift in his Critical Theory did not occur until the late 1930s, when he broke with Erich Fromm, began working more closely with Theodor W. Adorno, and adopted a modified version of Friedrich Pollock's state capitalism thesis. Thus, while Chapter 9 pursues the same methodological approach as Chapters 6, 7, and 8, thematically it belongs to a separate section of the study that, along with the two excursuses that examine Horkheimer's changing relations with Fromm and Adorno, address the transformation of Horkheimer's early Critical Theory into something qualitatively different.

HORKHEIMER'S PHILOSOPHICAL DETERMINATION OF MATERIALISM

Materialism and Metaphysics

In the essays "Materialism and Metaphysics" and "Materialism and Morality," both published in the *Zeitschrift für Sozialforschung* in 1933, Horkheimer examined the relationship of contemporary materialism to a wide range of philosophical schools, from metaphysics and idealism to nominalism and positivism, and also to older forms of materialism itself. Horkheimer developed his own concept of materialism through a series of determinate negations of each of these various historical schools and/or philosophical concepts. He demonstrated in each case which aspects of these schools a concept of materialism adequate to contemporary socio-historical conditions should preserve and which it should negate. In what follows, we will briefly reconstruct Horkheimer's analysis of the relationship of materialism to these various schools in order to clarify his own concept of materialism, which served as the philosophical foundation of his Critical Theory at this time.

Horkheimer was fully aware that his attempt to rehabilitate materialism in the twentieth century would meet resistance. He realized that materialists have almost always been seen as pariahs by their fellow philosophers, and that in the standard narratives of the history of philosophy, materialism is treated – if at all – in a dismissive manner. In the opening pages of "Materialism and Metaphysics," Horkheimer shows how this attitude toward materialism continues to dominate contemporary philosophical discussions. He illustrates how the most common objection to materialism – that mental and/or spiritual processes or entities cannot be explained merely in terms of the movement of matter – has been repeated in different forms by many of the most influential philosophers in the past half century. As he puts it, "Materialism ... appears to the philosophers as an obvious metaphysical error which is very easily refuted."[1] Horkheimer also recognizes that this consistent reduction of materialism to a straw man is also socially determined, insofar as materialism refers not to a metaphysical system or static worldview, but to a self-reflexive theory that has had, and continues to have, certain practical political implications. He suggests that the roots of the contemporary philosophical struggle waged on two fronts in the name of consciousness philosophy against spiritualism on the one hand, and materialism on the other, may well be found in the social struggle on two fronts of the bourgeoisie in the nineteenth century against the remnants of feudalism and the increasingly self-conscious proletariat.[2] As we have already seen, Horkheimer also recognized that philosophy in general had regained its strength only very slowly in the late nineteenth century. The middle of the century, the period following the dissolution of Hegel's system in continental Europe, was characterized by a general antiphilosophical mood.[3] During this time, a vulgar form of metaphysical materialism developed as a popular correlate to the dominance of positivism in the sciences. It was precisely this notion of metaphysical materialism that provided such an easy target for academic philosophers in the following years. However, rather than exploring the social roots of these developments – as he had done in his lectures – in "Materialism and Metaphysics," Horkheimer focuses primarily

---

[1] Max Horkheimer, "Materialism and Metaphysics," in *Critical Theory: Selected Essays*, trans. Matthew J. O'Connell, (New York: Continuum, 1992), p. 16.

[2] Ibid., p. 14.

[3] See Chapter 3, pp. 124ff.

on the philosophical characteristics that materialism has displayed throughout its long history, characteristics that made it possible for Horkheimer to place Critical Theory squarely within the materialist tradition. Foremost among these characteristics was the *antimetaphysical* character of materialism.

All forms of metaphysics share the assumption that it is possible to deduce positive practical guidelines based on knowledge of timeless entities such as the idea of the good, God, axioms of reason, the kingdom of moral ends, absolute spirit, or the meaning of Being. Materialism, on the other hand, denies the existence of such timeless entities and thus negates the possibility of acting based on knowledge of them. Whereas metaphysics always attempts to construct a unified system based upon these "timeless" truths, materialism rests on the necessarily limited character of human knowledge and the never completely realizable identity of human reason and the objects it attempts to grasp. The systems of metaphysics can attain unity and closure only by being completely separated from history, or by reducing history to the realization of certain predetermined metaphysical ends or the repetition of metaphysical conditions that lay dormant in the past. Materialism, in contrast, never attains the form of a closed system, because it is historical to the very core. It views history as an open-ended process that does not preclude the possibility of qualitatively new developments. Its content is determined by current social and historical problems, not by any normative guidelines putatively derived from insight into timeless metaphysical structures. Echoing his earlier criticisms of German Idealism, Horkheimer writes:

The claim that there is an absolute order and an absolute demand made upon man always supposes a claim to know the whole, the totality of things, the infinite. But if our knowledge is in fact not yet final, if there is an irreducible tension between concept and being, then no proposition can claim the dignity of perfect knowledge. Knowledge of the infinite must itself be infinite ... Consequently metaphysics tends to regard the whole world as the product of reason, for reason knows only itself perfectly.[4]

A further consequence of the antimetaphysical, nonidentical, and open-ended character of materialism is that it considers philosophy not as an end in itself, but as a means of improving the quality of human life. Whereas metaphysics and idealism conceive reality as a product of reason, materialists view reason, particularly in the collective and systematic forms of philosophy and critical theory, as one moment within the larger socio-historical life process.[5] Far from reducing philosophy or theoretical reflection to a mere epiphenomenon or ineffectual reflex of this process, materialists view it as an essential moment in the creation of a society that would permit a greater realization of individual potential and general happiness.

[4] "Materialism and Metaphysics," p. 27.
[5] Horkheimer's Critical Theory was *systematic*, in the sense of pursuing discursive knowledge in a rational manner without succumbing to the temptation of system building, in the sense of constructing closed, ahistorical constructs that made absolute claims to truth. In this regard, Horkheimer followed, once again, the example set by the *philosophes*, in this particular case, d'Alembert, who argued that philosophy should be characterized by *l'esprit systematique*, but not *l'esprit du systeme*.

In this context, Horkheimer insists that metaphysical or idealist attempts to provide a *logical* justification of hope or the pursuit of happiness are superfluous at best, dangerous at worst. Such justifications not only get trapped within the bad infinity of moral argumentation – as Adorno would argue later as well[6] – they also usually lead to a rationalization of the status quo or of the course of history. This is so because metaphysics and idealism are based on the assumption that human actions must ultimately be grounded philosophically, whereas materialism derives its substance from general human interests and the concrete socio-historical barriers to their realization. As Horkheimer puts it:

> Materialism is not interested in a world view or in the souls of men. It is concerned with changing the concrete conditions under which men suffer and in which, of course, their development will be stunted. This concern may be comprehended historically and psychologically; it cannot be grounded in general principles.[7]

The idealist inflation of reason to an end in itself leads not only to the superfluous attempt to justify the general human interest in happiness, but also to the attempt to discover rational meaning within the course of history itself. Horkheimer recognizes that idealist systems contain many important insights, and he does not reject them *tout court* – he notes, for example, that "the dialectic itself is idealist in origin"[8] – but he does identify this apologetic, compensatory positing of an underlying meaning in history, nature, or being as an essential characteristic of idealism that is irreconcilably opposed to materialism.[9] As we have already seen, Horkheimer insists that nature and history are in and of themselves meaningless, and can be given meaning only through conscious human intervention.[10] Any attempt to claim otherwise would be tantamount to post facto justification of past and present suffering.

Although Horkheimer does not mention Voltaire explicitly in this context,[11] his merciless parody in *Candide* of Leibniz's praise of the status quo as the best of all possible worlds, is a fitting example of Horkheimer's argument. Despite its view that the pursuit of happiness requires no further philosophical justification, Horkheimer maintains that materialism is – not unlike *Candide* – essentially pessimistic, and is characterized by a profound moment of mourning at

---

[6] *Negative Dialektik*, p. 281.

[7] "Materialism and Metaphysics," p. 32 (trans. modified).

[8] Ibid., p. 34.

[9] On the importance of the refusal to attribute any inherent meaning to nature, history, or being as a decisive criteria for differentiating materialism from idealism, see also the protocol of the discussion held between Horkheimer, Adorno, Leo Lowenthal, and several other Institute members in 1931: "Differenz zwischen Idealismus und Materialismus," GS 12, pp. 373–97.

[10] For this reason, Horkheimer is – like Schopenhauer – also highly critical of pantheism or any effort to identify divine purpose in nature itself.

[11] This is not to say that Horkheimer's predilection for the French Enlightenment had diminished in the least during this time. In his discussion of materialism, it is clear that he still sees the materialism of the *philosophes* as exemplary in many respects. For example, he names Diderot as an example of the relative indifference of materialists to the "big," "eternal" questions of metaphysics, an indifference that did not, however, diminish Diderot's passionate engagement in the philosophical, aesthetic, and political discussions of his time. See "Materialism and Metaphysics," p. 20.

the senseless suffering that has characterized the course of human history so far. Yet unlike conservative theorists, who use the slaughter bench of history to justify a fundamentally pessimistic view about the future and repressive measures in the present, the materialist's melancholy is rooted firmly in the past. Horkheimer expresses this sentiment in the following way:

Materialism views every type of philosophy that seeks to justify a groundless hope, or even to obscure its groundlessness, as deception. For all the optimism it is able to muster with regard to changing present conditions, for all that it treasures the happiness which comes from solidarity among men and the effort to change society, materialism contains an essential moment of pessimism. The injustices of the past can never be rectified. The suffering of past generations will find no compensation. But while the pessimism of contemporary idealist schools is directed toward present and future life, that is, toward the impossibility of future happiness for all, and usually expresses itself in fatalistic or apocalyptic tendencies, the mourning [*Trauer*] characteristic of materialism is related to past events.[12]

Horkheimer's solemn proclamation that the dead are really dead, that suffering in the past cannot be undone was an important point of contention with his friend and colleague Walter Benjamin, who maintained that each generation inherits a weak messianic power from its predecessor, which obligates it to remember the lost struggles and needless suffering of the past and to continue to contest the ongoing continuity of historical domination.[13] If this negative continuum of history were one day to be broken, according to Benjamin, then the suffering of the past would be partially redeemed. Although Horkheimer's pessimistic materialism placed him firmly within the "cold" current of Western Marxism[14] and led him to reject Benjamin's theological assumptions, it did not carry any conservative implications[15] – as it would later in his life when his thought did acquire a pronounced theological dimension.[16] At this point, he still fully agreed with Benjamin on the desirability of a rupture in the continuity of

---

[12] Ibid., p. 28.

[13] For Benjamin's argument about the weak-messianic power of the present generation and the redemptive implication of a radical break with the "prehistory" of mankind, see his "Theses on the Philosophy of History," in Walter Benjamin, *Illuminations,* trans. Harry Zohn, ed. Hannah Arendt (New York: Schocken, 1968), pp. 253f. For a more detailed explication of this crucial aspect of Benjamin's theses, see also Michael Löwy, *Walter Benjamin: Avertissement de l'incendie, Une lecture des thèses "Sur le concept d'histoire"* (Paris, 2001), pp. 35–40.

[14] It also worth repeating here that, because of the predominance of the "cold" current in Horkheimer's Critical Theory, his politics were not redemptive in the strong sense, as were Benjamin's or Bloch's. In fact, Horkheimer was very critical of the affirmative implications of the exaggerated hopes of redemptive politics. See his unpublished aphorism, "Metaphysische Verklärung der Revolution," GS 11, pp. 264–6. On the "warm" vs. "cold" currents in Marxism, see Ernst Bloch, *Das Prinzip Hoffnung,* vol. 1 (Frankfurt: Suhrkamp, 1959), pp. 235ff.

[15] On this point, see Gérard Raulet, "Kritik der Vernunft und kritischer Gebrauch des Pessimismus," in *Max Horkheimer heute: Werk und Wirkung,* eds. A. Schmidt and N. Altzwicker (Frankfurt, 1986), pp. 31–51.

[16] See, for example, Matthias Lutz-Bachmann, "Humanität und Religion. Zu Max Horkheimers Deutung des Christentums," and Hans Günter Holl, "Religion und Metaphysik im Spätwerk Max Horkheimers," both in *Max Horkheimer heute: Werk und Wirkung,* op. cit., pp. 108–28 and 129–45, respectively.

historical domination, even if he was always more cautious about the objective conditions that would be necessary to make it possible.[17]

Horkheimer's multifaceted criticisms of metaphysics and idealism parallel in many ways similar objections that have traditionally been raised by nominalism, empiricism, and positivism. As we saw in his lectures on the philosophy of history, Horkheimer was indeed more sympathetic to the empiricist than the rationalist tradition (both broadly conceived), due to the former's greater attention to the temporal core of truth and concrete socio-historical problems. With the National Socialist seizure of power in 1933, however, one of the most important motivations for Horkheimer's sharp critique of the rationalist, metaphysical, and idealist traditions had been removed. For these criticisms were directly or indirectly related to a series of theoretical attacks on positivism that had begun around the turn of the century and that, particularly in Germany in the 1920s, spawned or reinforced a plethora of irrationalist, even mythical ideologies that helped prepare the way for the National Socialists' victory.[18] After his migration to the United States in 1934, Horkheimer quickly realized that the metaphysical and idealist traditions, which had never been particularly influential in the history of Anglo-American philosophy, had been even further discredited by the success of the National Socialists. Although the reign of positivism in the United States in particular was by no means uncontested in the first decades of the twentieth century, alternatives such as pragmatism were indeed weakened and ultimately marginalized by the ensuing dominance

[17] See the discussion in Chapter 3 (pp. 96–7), of utopian thought in early modern Europe. In regard to the objective conditions necessary for a genuinely emancipatory revolution, i.e. whether the "messiah could appear at any moment," to put it in Benjamin's theologically charged language, Horkheimer would change his position, at least for a brief period of time, to a position closer to Benjamin in his essay, "Authoritarian State," where he states, "For the revolutionary the conditions have always been ripe." GS 5, p. 305. However, this more optimistic position would soon give way to the deeply pessimistic arguments in *Dialectic of Enlightenment* against the possibility of qualitative social change at any time in the near future.

[18] The seemingly paradoxical and contradictory argument that the philosophy of the rationalists and idealists, who viewed the principles of reason as the highest form of reality, anticipated or even contributed to the rise of irrationalist tendencies in the first decades of the twentieth century should be seen primarily in the tendency, discussed in the preceding section, of rationalism and idealism to abstract from concrete socio-historical problems, to search for stability and authority in systems that make absolute claims to truth, and to provide "spiritual" compensation for real suffering by offering "meaningful" explanations and rationalizations of the course of history. This underlying affinity that concerned Horkheimer is perhaps most clear in the case of metaphysics, which, in its classical seventeenth-century form, still often contained substantial theological elements. The backlash against positivism in Germany in the 1920s was also driven by a deep desire to reenchant what was seen as a completely meaningless world. In both its left- and right-wing form, these currents were highly critical of traditional science and "*blosser Verstand*" ("mere understanding"), as one can see, for example, in the work of Georg Lukács and Martin Heidegger. In the late 1920s and well into the 1930s as well, Horkheimer continued to stress the importance of the sciences for Critical Theory and the necessity of the labors of understanding [*Verstand*] as a prerequisite for the more far-reaching syntheses of reason [*Vernunft*]. For Horkheimer's own nuanced discussion of this problem, see his 1934 essay, "The Rationalism Debate in Contemporary Philosophy," in *Max Horkheimer: Between Philosophy and Social Science*, trans. G.F. Hunter et al. (Cambridge, MA: 1993), pp. 217–64.

of positivism in a wide variety of fields.[19] Positivist-oriented scholars who had fled from Europe also contributed significantly to this trend.[20] In any case, despite his respect for certain aspects of empiricist, even positivist philosophy, Horkheimer emphatically stressed their essential differences from his own concept of materialism. The positivists' negation of metaphysics was itself based on certain unexamined metaphysical assumptions, according to Horkheimer, and its theoretical concepts were, in any case, a woefully inadequate means of coming to terms with the crises of contemporary society. One of the most striking developments of Horkheimer's thought in the 1930s – to which we will return in the further course of this study – was his increasing skepticism about the empirical tradition and its contemporary embodiment in positivist theory and various scientific disciplines. Horkheimer's fundamental critique of logical empiricism in his 1937 essay, "The Latest Attack on Metaphysics," represented a significant step in this direction. His increased collaboration with Adorno after 1938 reinforced this trend, which culminated in a sweeping dismissal of the sciences in *Dialectic of Enlightenment*.[21] In his determination of the concept of materialism in the early 1930s, Horkheimer was also critical of empiricism, positivism, and the sciences, but he went to greater lengths than he would in the following years to preserve the progressive moments of the empirical tradition for his own Critical Theory.

In "Materialism and Metaphysics," Horkheimer presents materialism not only as a determinate negation of metaphysics and idealism, but also of nominalism, sensualism, utilitarianism, positivism, and empiriocriticism. Like nominalism, materialism is critical of universal concepts, but it does not reject them altogether; instead, it interprets them in terms of concrete socio-historical conditions as an articulation of the interests of (groups of) concrete individuals. Horkheimer uses the universal concepts of the Enlightenment to illustrate this point. The demand that all men have a right to liberty, equality, and the pursuit of happiness was made within the context of the bourgeoisie's gradual overthrow of feudalism and absolutism; these universal principles were an expression of particular interests at a particular time. The fact that other groups continued, after the historic victory of the bourgeoisie, to demand that these rights be extended beyond male property owners illustrates that they were not merely abstract concepts, but could also continue to serve as the basis for concrete historical struggles against the particularist hegemony of the bourgeoisie. As Horkheimer puts it:

When the concept of justice thus changes its meaning, we glimpse the historical origins of what was originally proclaimed as an eternal principle, and we understand that that

---

[19] See, for example, *American Academic Culture in Transformation: Fifty Years, Four Disciplines*, eds. Thomas Bender and Carl E. Schorske (Princeton, 1998).

[20] For a comparative study of intellectual émigrés in a wide variety of fields, which also stresses the Viennese positivists' great success in integrating into and actively shaping American scientific culture and the American academy during and after the war, see Lewis A. Coser, *Refugee Scholars in America: Their Impact and Their Experiences* (New Haven and London, 1984).

[21] See Excursus II.

concept was an idea proposed by definite individuals and conditioned by relationships within a class society.[22]

Horkheimer's argument against nominalism, that general concepts are not ipso facto meaningless, but acquire their significance only within specific socio-historical conditions, is also reflected in his differentiation of a concept of materialism relevant to his time from earlier forms of materialism. Horkheimer quotes from Hobbes's *Leviathan* to provide an example of the pragmatic, antimetaphysical materialism of the bourgeoisie in the early stages of its development and asserts that this was also the historically appropriate form of materialism then.[23] At that time, speculative concepts were still used primarily to buttress the *ancien regime*, and the bourgeoisie needed to focus on the concrete task of developing the means of production to secure its own victory. In the present, however, materialism must, according to Horkheimer, move beyond a mere pragmatic focus on developing science and the means of production. Thus, he concludes, "in the present, knowledge of the tendencies of the development of society as a whole possesses constitutive significance for materialist theory."[24] In other words, rigorously denying the possibility of grasping general social tendencies in the present would be tantamount to blindly affirming a *necessary* correlation between the development of science and the means of production and the happiness of all. It would also be tantamount to denying that the massive productive forces unleashed by capitalism could be separated from the particularist interests of the bourgeoisie and placed in the service of the vital interests of mankind as a whole.

Just as materialism shares nominalism's skepticism toward universal concepts without dismissing them entirely, so it also shares sensualism's emphasis on the necessity of knowledge being based on sense impressions without reducing sense impressions to an ahistorical entity or the sole source of human knowledge. In order to illustrate his claim – that materialism has always contained an important sensualist moment – Horkheimer quotes the following passage from Epicure: "If you fight against all sensations, you will have no standard by which to judge even those of them which you say are false."[25] On the one hand, this theory of knowledge has served materialism throughout its history as a "critical weapon against dogmatic concepts," according to Horkheimer.[26] On the other hand, "materialism" – at least in its contemporary form – "does not absolutize sensation" either.[27] There are several reasons for this refusal, according to Horkheimer. First, the sense impressions that we receive are by no means constant, ahistorical building blocks of the external world. They have been shaped by historical events and remain within the larger flux of natural and historical change. Second, the manner in which we perceive sense impressions always contains a subjective moment. Horkheimer was still

[22] "Materialism and Metaphysics," p. 22.
[23] See Horkheimer's discussion of Hobbes in "The Beginnings of the Bourgeois Philosophy of History," in *Between Philosophy and Social Science*, op. cit., pp. 335–63.
[24] "Materialism and Metaphysics," p. 20 (translation amended).
[25] Ibid., p. 42.
[26] Ibid.
[27] Ibid.

willing at this time to cite Hans Cornelius's philosophical appropriation of Gestalt psychology to corroborate this point.[28] Finally, anticipating an important argument he would make later in "Traditional and Critical Theory," and echoing Marx's argument in the *Paris Manuscripts*, Horkheimer also insisted that our sense organs are themselves historically shaped. The way in which we see, hear, smell, taste, and touch are all historically and socially meditated.[29] Horkheimer sums up his discussion of the relationship between sensualism and contemporary materialism with the following statement, which also echoes his earlier critique of consciousness philosophy: "Sense experiences [*Erlebnisse*] are indeed the basis of knowledge, and we must constantly refer to them, but the origin and the conditions of knowledge are not identical with the origins and conditions of the world."[30]

Just as materialism accepted nominalism's skepticism about universal concepts and sensualism's reliance on sense impressions without hypostatizing either of them, so it also accepted positivism's defense of the sciences without, however, granting them absolute or ahistorical validity. Drawing on insights he had developed in his earlier lectures on the shifting relationship between science and philosophy in the late nineteenth and early twentieth centuries,[31] as well as on Marx's methodology, Horkheimer argues that materialism rests on a unification of philosophy and science, not a one-sided privileging of the former, à la metaphysics, or the latter, à la positivism. Materialism is particularly opposed to the positivists' hypostatization of science as a reflection of the eternal, natural laws governing the universe, as well as its belief that science can explain everything in terms of differing combinations of matter or – as was the case with the empiriocriticists[32] – sense impressions. Against Max Scheler, who portrayed materialism as being identical with positivism in these respects, Horkheimer argues:

[Materialism] is the exact opposite of any attempt to absolutize particular scientific doctrines. It requires instead that all knowledge be regarded, not of course as a purely arbitrary creation, but as a representation by particular men in a particular society, context, and moment of time.... Materialism is not bound to a set conception of matter.[33]

By positing the goal of science as the determination of the eternal laws of nature and its object as an equally abstract and ahistorical "matter," positivists wittingly or unwittingly place the subjective carriers of science outside of history. Because we have already examined this argument of Horkheimer's in some detail,[34] we need not recapitulate it here, but Horkheimer does reiterate that contemporary materialism preserves the active, self-reflexive moment of knowledge that, as Marx stated in the first Feuerbach thesis, was developed in modern philosophy "by idealism – but only abstractly."[35] Furthermore, Horkheimer greatly

[28] Ibid., p. 43.
[29] *Marx-Engels Reader*, op. cit., pp. 87–93.
[30] "Materialism and Metaphysics," p. 43 (translation amended).
[31] See Chapter 3, pp. 124ff.
[32] See Chapter 4, p. 154.
[33] "Materialism and Metaphysics," p. 35.
[34] See Chapter 4, pp. 154ff.
[35] *The Marx-Engels Reader*, op. cit., p. 143.

emphasizes the importance of the distinction between essence and appearance for materialism, a distinction that the positivists deny. Anticipating arguments he would pursue in greater detail in his essays "On Bergson's Metaphysics of Time" and "The Latest Attacks on Metaphysics," Horkheimer insists that the positivists' exclusive reliance on what is immediately given as the only true source of knowledge – its denial of the existence of any more essential, under-lying forces that may not be readily apparent – threw the door wide open for metaphysical, intuitive, and outright irrationalist interpretations of these forces.[36] As we shall see, Horkheimer would soon come to view the positivists' denial of the distinction between essence and appearance and the rigid dual-ism between a knowable world of appearances and an unknowable world of "things-in-themselves" as typical of the bourgeois epoch as a whole.[37]

In contrast to this skepticism, which in the work of many modern philos-ophers existed side by side with absolute metaphysical claims, Horkheimer places his concept of materialism in a tradition that extends back through Hegel to the Enlightenment, a tradition that refuses to accept any a priori limitations on the exercise of reason. Although Horkheimer already recognizes that positivism has its origins in the Enlightenment, he by no means equates the two.[38] He argues instead that what materialism has in common with Hegel and with "genuine Enlightenment" is that they "admit nothing to be fundamentally inaccessible to human knowledge and subject to surmise alone."[39] But, one may ask, how does Horkheimer reconcile this emphatic defense of material-ism's refusal to accept any fixed boundaries to its exercise of reason with his equally emphatic insistence on the open-ended character of reason, that is, its inability to ever attain absolute truth? How, in other words, can materialism ground its claims to truth, to grasping what is "essential" with any absolute standard? Or, put negatively, how can it avoid falling into a relativist position itself? To be sure, Horkheimer insists that the fact "that we do not know every-thing does not at all mean that what we do know is the nonessential and what we do not know the essential," but he does not explore this thorny problem in any great detail here, as he would two years later in his essay, "On the Problem of Truth."[40] In "Materialism and Metaphysics," he reiterates the argument he had made earlier in his critique of Karl Mannheim.[41] He writes:

Contemporary materialism is not principally characterized by the formal traits which oppose it to idealist metaphysics. It is characterized rather by its content [*Inhalt*]: the

---

[36] As Horkheimer points out here, this restriction of knowledge to the immediately given is clearly and consciously expressed in the concept of "positivism" itself, which developed historically as an alternative to the "negative" philosophy of Hegel. Positivism's epistemological taboos foreclose the possibility of exploring the "negative" forces that could potentially undermine the status quo. Herbert Marcuse would set forth these arguments more systematically in his 1940 study, *Reason and Revolution*.

[37] See Chapter 8, pp. 308ff.

[38] "Materialism and Metaphysics," p. 38.

[39] Ibid., p. 39 (translation amended).

[40] We will explore the arguments in this essay – especially Horkheimer's efforts to explain the epistemological foundations of Critical Theory and its truth claims – in greater detail in Chapter 8, pp. 330ff.

[41] See Chapter 4, p. 149.

economic theory of society.... The various materialist doctrines, therefore, are not examples of a stable and permanent idea. The economic theory of society and history arose not out of purely theoretical motives, but out of the need to comprehend contemporary society. For this society has reached the point where it excludes an ever larger number of people from the happiness made possible by the widespread abundance of economic forces.[42]

Thus, practical considerations, not absolute principles, provide the final criteria of truth for materialism. A critical theory of society, guided by, but not limited in a dogmatic way to, Marx's critique of political economy – what he refers to here as "the economic theory of society and history" – must serve as the ultimate arbiter for such questions, for such a theory is the most advanced form of reflection on the barriers to improving the condition of human life in the present.

This argument leads directly to Horkheimer's differentiation of materialism from utilitarianism and hedonism. Following once again the method of determinate negation, Horkheimer maintains that materialism preserves the utilitarian principles of self-interest and the maximization of happiness, as well as the related hedonistic pursuit of pleasure and the avoidance of pain without hypostatizing any of these notions. As we have seen, one of the most important characteristics of materialism, according to Horkheimer, is its recognition of the pursuit of happiness as a legitimate justification for human behavior, indeed, one that needs no further philosophical legitimation. However, Horkheimer also insists that materialism is not based on a trivial or one-dimensional psychology, which views human behavior as determined solely by egoistic interests or the desire to satisfy "base" material needs or sexual desires. As we shall see in the following section, one of Horkheimer's central concerns in his efforts to analyze the "anthropology of the bourgeois epoch" was to explain in historical and social-psychological terms the origins and tenacity of truculent self-interest – what Horkheimer also referred to as "property instincts" – as the dominant trait in modern character structures. At this time, however, Horkheimer rests content with a few arguments and an explicit reference to "the work of Erich Fromm"[43] to contest the equation of materialism with narrow self-interest. Horkheimer points first of all to the ideal of a better society developed through the critical analysis of contemporary conditions, an ideal that is indeed ultimately grounded in concrete human interests, but which transcends the narrow definition of interest in the present to encompass notions of compassion and solidarity. To illustrate the importance that such objectively possible ideals have always had for materialism, Horkheimer points to the struggles of the past:

The known and unknown devotees of the materialist outlook have for centuries given up their freedom and their lives in the struggle for the most varied goals, but especially

---

[42] "Materialism and Metaphysics" p. 45 (translation amended).

[43] "Materialism and Metaphysics," p. 44. In his essay, "On the Method and Function of an Analytic Social Psychology," Fromm objected to Bertrand Russell's argument that Marx's theory was based on a trivial psychology of self-interest. Fromm argued that Marx's primary concern was to demonstrate and analyze the subordination of the individual in capitalist societies to objective social mechanisms that had taken on a life of their own, thus Marx's theory did not really contain an explicit psychology of any sort. See *The Essential Frankfurt School Reader*, op. cit., pp. 486–7.

in solidarity with suffering men. They prove that a narrow concern for personal well-being is no more closely associated with this kind of thinking than with any other. In rejecting the illusions of idealist metaphysics they have surrendered every hope of an individual reward in eternity and, with it, an important selfish motive operative in other men.[44]

So although Horkheimer does stress the importance of ideals – not only of a better society, but also of compassion and solidarity – for materialism, he by no means falls into the opposite position of denigrating self-interest or "base" material desires. On the one hand, Horkheimer distinguishes between happiness and pleasure, arguing that materialism is more concerned with the former than the latter, insofar as the former cannot be separated from society as a whole. On the other hand, he refuses to sever pleasure from happiness, insofar as "the satisfaction of desire," like the pursuit of happiness, and "unlike 'higher' motives, requires no reasons, excuses or justifications."[45] Most important of all for Horkheimer, however, is the insight that needs, desires, pleasure, and conceptions of self-interest are all historically and socially determined and cannot be reduced to an ahistorical psychology or anthropology. We will return to this problem, which occupied a central place in Horkheimer's thought in the 1930s, in the following section.

Materialism and Morality

Morality is the final philosophical concept that Horkheimer critically examines in order to determine his own concept of materialism. His analysis of materialism's relationship to morality is the most complex of all; the fact that he devoted an entire essay to this problem indicates just how serious he considered it to be. Nevertheless, it would be misguided to interpret Horkheimer as a moral philosopher in the strict sense of the term, as one recent commentator has done,[46] for his reflections lead him to the conclusion that morality – at least in the form that it has assumed in modernity, or the "bourgeois epoch" as Horkheimer would say – must be overcome if the humane moments it contains are to be realized. In "Materialism and Morality," Horkheimer clarifies this argument in particular and the relationship of materialism to morality more generally in the following way. First, he demonstrates why morality is a strictly modern phenomenon, why its form and existence are inextricably linked to the structure of bourgeois society as whole. Next, he illustrates this point through a more detailed examination of Kant's moral philosophy, which he understands as the quintessential expression of modern morality. Using Kant as his representative example, Horkheimer elaborates in particular the affirmative and repressive aspects of morality, which materialism rejects, as well as its critical and humane aspects, which materialism preserves. Finally, Horkheimer argues

---

[44] "Materialism and Metaphysics," p. 44 (translation amended).

[45] Ibid., p. 45. See also Herbert Marcuse's 1938 essay, "On Hedonism," in which he develops Horkheimer's ideas here in greater depth. *Negations*, op. cit., pp. 159–200.

[46] See Dieter Sattler, *Horkheimer als Moralphilosoph: Studie zur Kritischen Theorie*, (Frankfurt, 1996).

that under the present historical conditions, the most important expressions of "moral sentiment" that materialism should preserve are compassion and politics. We shall see presently why he considers these two concepts to be so important and how he determines them.

We have already seen how Horkheimer viewed the development of modern science and politics as attempts to establish a qualitatively new form of authority that could replace the authority of the Catholic Church and that could also provide the means for dominating nature and other humans.[47] Horkheimer views morality as one aspect of this larger historical development. He writes:

> While it was important for the members of higher social strata to establish moral principles because they had constantly to make consequential decisions, which had been taken out of their hands earlier by authority, a rationally grounded morality to dominate the masses became increasingly necessary, insofar as a mode of conduct was demanded of them that diverged from their own vital interests.[48]

Thus, as a new form of self-reflexivity and authority for the dominating classes and a means of imposing their will upon the dominated classes, bourgeois morality had very little, if anything, to do with the ethical doctrines of classical antiquity or the Middle Ages. Horkheimer writes:

> A new category of virtue has emerged in philosophy since the Renaissance: moral virtue. It does not have much in common with either the ethical ideas of the Greeks, which concerned the best way to achieve happiness, or with the religious ethics of the Middle Ages.... The modern moral problematic has its roots in the basic characteristics of the bourgeois order. [49]

Horkheimer grounds this argument by examining the basic structure of bourgeois society. Following Hegel and anticipating Hans Blumenberg, Horkheimer sees the unleashing of subjective self-interest as the defining characteristic of modern society.[50] This principle of constantly seeking one's own advantage and viewing others as potential means toward this end achieves the objective status of "natural law" in bourgeois society, and comes to dominate subjective character structures as well, "even in a person's most subtle and seemingly most removed impulses."[51] Yet the pursuit of self-interest in bourgeois society does not lead automatically to a harmonious totality or to the preservation of everyone's best interests. On the contrary, it unleashes a *bellum omnium contra omnes* which, if left to follow its "natural" course, would lead to chaos, barbarism, and self-destruction. Thus, some barriers must be erected against the unbounded pursuit of self-interest to ensure that the fractured social totality is able to reproduce itself: The state plays this role in the political sphere, and morality in the subjective sphere. However, neither the state nor morality fundamentally alter the underlying conflict between particular and general interests,

---

[47] Chapter 3, pp. 92ff.
[48] GS 3, p. 112.
[49] Ibid., p. 114.
[50] For a brief discussion of the similarities and differences between Horkheimer's, Hegel's, and Blumenberg's interpretation of modern self-assertion, see footnote 60 in Chapter 7, p. 263.
[51] GS 3, p. 116.

which, according to Horkheimer, proceeds from the structure of property relations in bourgeois society. He writes:

> A rational relationship does not exist between the free competition of individuals as the medium and the existence of the society as a whole as that which is mediated. The process does not take place under the control of a conscious will, but as an act of nature instead. The life of the whole proceeds blindly, fortuitously and badly from the chaotic bustle of individuals, industries and states.... This problem, which only the society itself could solve rationally by integrating each of its members in its consciously guided labor process, appears in the bourgeois epoch as a conflict in the inside of its subjects.[52]

Horkheimer's main point, then, is that if the pursuit of self-interest did lead naturally to a nonantagonistic social totality, one in which all its members' interests were preserved, there would be no need for metaphysically grounded moral imperatives, which demand – in diametrical opposition to the governing reality principle – that other individuals not be treated merely as means, but as ends in themselves.

Yet morality is conceptualized in precisely this way in Kant's philosophy, and Horkheimer's next step is to demonstrate in greater detail why Kant's moral theory should be understood as a remarkably astute expression of the basic conflicts underlying bourgeois society. Horkheimer focuses first on the affirmative and repressive aspects of Kant's ideas. However, he also analyzes the critical and humane moments in Kant's theory that materialism must preserve. Horkheimer points to Kant's insistence that moral actions be based on duty rather than interest as one particularly repressive aspect of his theory. Anticipating arguments he would develop in "Egoism and Freedom Movements," Horkheimer views the social content of this demand as a justification of the heavy sacrifices demanded of the dominated classes during the unprecedented development of the means of production in modern capitalism. Whereas the pursuit of private self-interest by the property owners was seen as a public virtue – as in Mandeville's "Fable of the Bees"[53] – for the propertyless, it was essentially a vice: a violation of the moral imperative that they subordinate their private interests to the general will. Kant's reliance on the correctness of the volitional principle guiding an act, rather than its real consequences, as his primary moral criteria points more generally to the formalistic character of his theory, according to Horkheimer. He writes:

> The view that the good will ... is the only thing that is good, and that an action should be evaluated only on the basis of intent and not also according to its consequences at that particular historical moment, is an idealist delusion. A direct path leads this ideological side of the Kantian concept of morality to the modern mystification of sacrifice and obedience.[54]

Horkheimer discusses one by one numerous examples that Kant himself gives in order to demonstrate that even if everyone obeyed the moral law, this would

---

[52] "Materialism and Morality," p. 117.

[53] See Chapter 3.

[54] GS 3, p. 121.

not remove the basic causes of injustice in bourgeois society.[55] Morality cannot possibly grasp these causes, because it is grounded metaphysically – that is, in purely formalistic terms – and not in terms of a theoretical analysis of the concrete historical situation. Insofar as it judges all historical injustice in terms of the same absolute criteria, it is barred from grasping its specificity, thereby rendering any interventions it might make in the external world – to aid the forces attempting to remedy contemporary forms of injustice – highly tenuous.

We have already encountered several of the arguments that Horkheimer presents here as materialist responses to these repressive and affirmative aspects of bourgeois morality, such as his demand that materialism be guided by concrete analysis of socio-historical forces rather than metaphysical arguments. Horkheimer also reiterates here that interests, and thereby also the conflict between duty and interest posited by morality, are themselves historical and thus subject to change in the future. Similarly, he insists that the general interests expressed in morality not be sequestered in an imaginary metaphysical realm or within the depths of the beautiful soul, but should instead be realized concretely in society. Horkheimer recognizes that Kant himself also viewed this as the highest goal of his moral theory, and he sees this as one of the most important positive aspects of morality that materialism must preserve. Horkheimer illustrates this point with several quotes from Kant's *Perpetual Peace*:

Kant too considered possible the unification of happiness and duty in a better society. For him there is "no conflict of praxis with theory," "the pure principles of right [*Recht*] have objective reality, that is, they can be carried out." He is convinced that the proper task of politics is to bring itself into accord with the "universal end of the body politic (happiness)."[56]

Horkheimer also points to Kant's anthropology to underscore this argument. He writes:

Kant found harsh words ... for the so-called cunning men of politics, because they claimed that human nature made improvement in the name of ideals impossible.... There are not any convincing anthropological objections to overcoming bad social conditions. Kant's arguments against the psychological defense of absolutism are valid in any epoch, in which the sciences, including the science of man, is misused in the fight against progress.[57]

Horkheimer considered these beliefs of Kant's – that a condition of relative harmony between particular and general interests is really possible and that nothing in the "nature" of man opposes its realization – crucial moments of his own materialist theory. Yet he did point to other elements of Kant's theory as utopian in the bad sense, namely his belief that history is constantly and naturally approaching the ideal of a reconciled society, and also his belief that such a society could ever come about through the isolated decisions of its individual members. Horkheimer sees these ideas as prime examples of Kant's hypostatization of the categories of the status quo and thus in need of a materialist corrective,

---

[55] GS 3, pp. 119–21.
[56] Ibid., p. 124.
[57] Ibid., p. 125.

namely a critical theory that aims at the establishment of a planned economy, which "would be administered with rational necessity in the interest of all."[58] At this point, Horkheimer's belief in the desirability and possibility of a planned economy was still strong, though this would change in the late 1930s.[59]

After demonstrating the positive moments of Kant's moral theory that materialism must preserve, Horkheimer concludes with a discussion of the two most important characteristics of a contemporary materialist ethics. Both of the characteristics that Horkheimer introduces as the appropriate expression of "moral sentiment" in the present do in fact point to the supersession of bourgeois society and its particular form of morality. The first, *compassion*, results from an unflinching awareness of the condition of man in crisis-ridden capitalist society.[60] Horkheimer makes this point emphatically in the following passage, which clearly conveys his own awareness of the depth of the contemporary crisis in Europe and the rest of the world:

The world seems to be heading for a catastrophe, or, more precisely, already to be in its throes, which in the known history of mankind can only be compared to the decline of classical antiquity. The meaninglessness of individual destiny, which had earlier already been conditioned by the lack of rationality, the merely natural character of the production process, has advanced in the current phase to the dominant characteristic of existence.... Humans do not appear as subjects of their destiny, but rather as objects of a blind process of nature, and the reaction of moral sentiment to this state of affairs is compassion.[61]

Horkheimer adds that this compassion should take the form of solidarity not only with other humans, but also with animals, for they too suffer unnecessarily in the current order.[62] The second essential component of a contemporary materialist ethics for Horkheimer is *politics*. The brief discussion at the end of "Materialism and Morality" makes it clear that Horkheimer still views politics primarily in materialist terms, but also that Enlightenment ideals are still crucial for him. For example, he writes:

Today it is claimed that the bourgeois ideals of freedom, equality and justice have proven to be bad; but not the ideals of the bourgeoisie, rather conditions that do not correspond to them, have demonstrated their indefensibility. The leading ideas of the

---

[58] Ibid., p. 126.

[59] See Chapter 9. For a helpful discussion of Horkheimer's concept of the planned economy and the theoretical debates out of which it emerged, see Peter Stirk, *Max Horkheimer: A New Interpretation*, op. cit., pp. 83–107.

[60] Peter Stirk also rightfully points out that Horkheimer was convinced that the violent crises in Europe at this time could not be separated from the structure of bourgeois society as a whole. For a discussion the important concept of crisis in Horkheimer's work at this time see chapter 3, "The World Crisis, Interdisciplinary Research and Psychology," of his study *Max Horkheimer: A New Interpretation*, op. cit., pp. 62–83.

[61] Ibid., p. 135–6.

[62] Horkheimer's concern for the suffering of animals runs throughout his work. See, for example, the aphorism "The Skyscraper," in *Dämmerung*, op. cit., p. 66, or the draft at the end of *Dialectic of Enlightenment*, "Man and Animal," op. cit., pp. 245–55. Horkheimer was also an active member of the Society for the Prevention of Cruelty to Animals in New York in the 1930s. In "Materialism and Morality," Horkheimer credits Schopenhauer for drawing attention to the similarities – if, of course, not identity – between the joys and pains of humans and animals and the resulting responsibility humans have to treat animals ethically. GS 3, p.136.

Enlightenment and the French Revolution are more valid than ever.... Thus politics based upon them must realize, not abandon these demands – not, of course, by clinging in a utopian way to temporally conditioned definitions, but in accordance with their purpose.... Materialist theory is concerned with improving general conditions, not with preserving the purity of concepts.[63]

Horkheimer demonstrates how the critical thrust of the Enlightenment ideals of justice, freedom, and equality has been undermined in a "merely formal democracy,"[64] how those who benefit from contemporary relations of domination have, in reality, abandoned these ideals, and how they need to be recaptured and reformulated by those with a genuine interest in justice. In the past, inequality may have been a necessary condition for the development not only of the forces of production, but also of science, the arts, and other manifestations of higher culture. In the present, this is no longer the case, according to Horkheimer; inequality is a necessary result of the antagonistic dynamic of bourgeois society, which has itself in the meantime become the greatest barrier to the further development of mankind. For Horkheimer, in other words, the struggle for the fulfillment of Enlightenment ideals is still the defining characteristic of the "transitional epoch" in which he believed he was living.[65] The success of this transition beyond the "bourgeois epoch" depended on the "development of character structures in which property instincts are no longer dominant."[66]

THE INSTITUTE'S RESEARCH PROJECT ON THE HISTORY OF MATERIALISM

In the succeeding discussions of Horkheimer's concept of the anthropology of the bourgeois epoch and his efforts to develop a dialectical logic, we will see how he elaborates and concretizes some of the ideas related to his concept of materialism. Before continuing, though, let us first briefly examine another Institute project in the 1930s that developed out of Horkheimer's interest in materialism. On May 5, 1936, Horkheimer and Herbert Marcuse both sent brief letters to Theodor Adorno, Walter Benjamin, Ernst Bloch, Eduard Fuchs, Henryk Grossmann, Paul Honigsheim, and Hans Mayer announcing the beginning of a project to compile a "source book that contains the materialist theories in Western philosophy from classical antiquity to the end of the 19th century."[67] Although Marcuse was primarily responsible for the project, it was without question important to Horkheimer and clearly demonstrated his interest in rehabilitating the materialist tradition – if one can speak of such a thing – that had always been marginalized within the history of Western philosophy. As Horkheimer put it in his letter: "It is extremely important to us that especially those philosophical and literary authors are included who in standard historiographies have either hardly been mentioned, misinterpreted or completely

---

[63] GS 3, p. 137.
[64] Ibid., p. 142.
[65] GS 3, p. 138.
[66] Ibid., p. 144.
[67] GS 15, p. 517.

overlooked."[68] This project was, in other words, part of Horkheimer's attempt to rediscover the "underground history" of European civilization, "the fate of human instincts and passions" that it has "repressed and disfigured," as he put it in a long note at the end of *Dialectic of Enlightenment*.[69] In the 1930s, Horkheimer would pursue this project theoretically in his major essay, "Egoism and Freedom Movements"; and in the 1940s, it would continue to remain important to him, as evidenced by the second excursus in *Dialectic of Enlightenment* on "Juliette, or Enlightenment and Morality" and his essay on "The Revolt of Nature" in *Eclipse of Reason*.[70] Marcuse's efforts to compile a source book on the history of materialism in the 1930s can be seen as companion project to these theoretical efforts.

As would become apparent in one of the responses to their letters, Horkheimer and Marcuse were not the only ones interested in excavating the history of materialism at this time. In his response, Ernst Bloch informed Horkheimer and Marcuse that he had recently initiated a similar project with some acquaintances in Paris and Moscow, and that he himself had already written a long essay on the history of the concept of "matter" in Western philosophy from antiquity to the present.[71] Like Horkheimer and Marcuse, Bloch was interested primarily in the "non-mechanical materialists," and in rescuing the important materialist impulses in metaphysical and idealist systems, for he too realized that the intellectual poverty represented by mechanistic understandings of matter had often prevented materialism from being taken seriously.[72] Yet Bloch's discussion of the history of the concept of matter was not as broadly conceived as Marcuse and Horkheimer's source book. He emphasized – in accord with his own long-standing interests – Aristotle and the Aristotelian tradition in the Middle Ages, Renaissance natural philosophers such as Giordano Bruno, German Idealism, and Marx. In the preliminary bibliography for the source book that Marcuse had compiled by 1938, in contrast, Horkheimer's interests were clearly apparent: Much emphasis was placed on the positivist and nominalist traditions in antiquity and the Middle Ages, as well as libertine currents in both the Middle Ages and the early modern period. Like Bloch's, Marcuse and Horkheimer's list also included a large section on the nature philosophy of the Renaissance, but it devoted more attention the heretics of the Reformation as well as the English, German, and particularly the French Enlightenment, which Bloch had discussed only in reference to La Mettrie and Holbach, whom he dismissed as mechanical materialists. Nonetheless, the parallels between the two projects were remarkable, and their differences could be explained in part simply due to the larger scope of Horkheimer and Marcuse's source book.[73]

[68] Ibid., p. 518.

[69] "The Importance of the Body," *Dialectic of Enlightenment*, op. cit., p. 231.

[70] "Juliette, or Enlightenment and Morality," Ibid., pp. 81–119. "The Revolt of Nature," *Eclipse of Reason* (New York, 1974), pp. 92–127.

[71] GS 15, pp. 630–1. Bloch's essay was finally published in 1972 as the fifth chapter of his book, *Das Materialismusproblem, seine Geschichte und Substanz* (Frankfurt, 1972), pp. 132–315.

[72] *Das Materialismusproblem, seine Geschichte und Substanz*, pp. 126–31.

[73] It should also be noted that these two projects bore a marked theoretical affinity with Walter Benjamin's negative philosophy of history as articulated in his posthumously published "Theses

It is not entirely clear why the materialist source book was never completed, but the Institute's financial crisis at the end of the 1930s – which would eventually force Marcuse to join the struggle against fascism at more practical level by accepting a job in the research and analysis division of the newly founded intelligence branch (the Office of Strategic Studies) of the U.S. government[74] – is the most likely explanation. In a report on the history, aims, and activities of the Institute, published in 1938, Horkheimer places the source book second on the list of their current research projects. Displaying his characteristic caution about any terms that would betray the Institute's Marxist sympathies, he avoids the concept of materialism in his description of the project:

> The book … we have projected … will approach philosophical theories from social problems and their solution. Precise analysis reveals that even the most abstract theories of knowledge, reason, matter, or man can be comprehended only from the struggle of mankind for liberation from restricting social forms. Such an approach will bring to the fore philosophers and sociologists who are neglected or distorted in the traditional histories of philosophy and sociology.[75]

Horkheimer also notes in his description of the project here that it will require at least two more years and additional funding to complete. In a report on the project that Marcuse wrote at about the same time, he also stresses difficulties the project faces:

> Many of the texts have never been published in English and must be translated from the original. Frequently the sources themselves are inadequately treated in contemporary official historiography. In such cases, an attempt will be made to restore the original texts.… Two assistants with a thorough knowledge of Greek, Latin, French and German are needed. It might also be necessary to search the major European archives and libraries, since a considerable number of texts have not been published in the current editions of philosophers and theologians.[76]

Like Horkheimer, Marcuse concludes that "the project cannot be completed in less than two years."[77] Although the Institute would actively seek funding from American foundations in the coming years for projects such as this and others, it would have little success. Nonetheless, the impulses and insights that informed the project would reemerge frequently in Horkheimer and Marcuse's later work.[78]

on the Philosophy of History," insofar as Benjamin too was interested in "brushing history against the grain" and rescuing heretical artistic and intellectuals impulses that had been defeated and cast into oblivion by the triumphalist understanding of history. See Benjamin, *Illuminations*, op. cit., pp. 253–64.

[74] For this chapter in Marcuse's life, see Barry Kātz, *Herbert Marcuse and the Art of Liberation* (London, 1982), pp. 111–39.

[75] *International Institute of Social Research: A Report on its History, Aims and Activities 1933–1938*, (New York, 1938), pp. 19–20.

[76] MHA, IX 59.1, p. 3.

[77] Ibid.

[78] Herbert Marcuse's efforts in *Eros and Civilization* to rehabilitate a concept of *erotic reason* based on artistic, intellectual, and even mythical tendencies that have run counter to what he viewed as the monolithic development of *instrumental reason* in Western civilization was also based on many of the same theoretical convictions that informed the materialist source book project. See, for example, *Eros and Civilization* (Boston, 1955), pp. 96–114, 144–56.

FIGURE 6. Horkheimer in 1930.

FIGURE 7. Erich Fromm at the Institute for Social Research
in Frankfurt am Main in the early 1930s.

FIGURE 8. Horkheimer and Riekhehr on a ship to the United States in 1934.

7

The Anthropology of the Bourgeois Epoch

Although Horkheimer's reflections on materialism should not be seen as foundational in a strong or static sense, insofar as his thought was thoroughly historical and not ontological or metaphysical, they do present the most general, philosophical assumptions that informed his Critical Theory in the early 1930s. As we shall see in the following chapter, with his project on dialectical logic Horkheimer would continue throughout the 1930s to develop and refine the theoretical assumptions that guided his Critical Theory. Yet many interpretations of Horkheimer's work in the 1930s have focused on the methodological reflections he puts forth in what have become his two best-known essays, "The Present Situation of Social Philosophy and the Tasks of an Institute for Social Research"[1] and "Traditional and Critical Theory," without adequately examining the philosophical reflections that underlay them.[2] It was Horkheimer's understanding of materialism and dialectical logic that informed his methodological reflections in these two essays, not vice-versa. This general focus on methodology in the reception of Horkheimer's writings from the 1930s has led to a neglect not only of his important reconceptualization of materialism and dialectical logic, but also of his substantial contributions to fleshing out the positive content of Critical Theory. Horkheimer's writings in the 1930s can

[1] Referred to hereafter as "The Present Situation of Social Philosophy."
[2] Helmut Dubiel, for example, devotes the second half of his study, *Theory and Politics*, op. cit. to working out the methodological foundations of Horkheimer's model of interdisciplinary research. For a discussion of Dubiel's study, see pp. 258–9. In his study, *Der Kritikbegriff der Kritischen Theorie Max Horkheimers* (Frankfurt and New York, 1980), Gerd-Walter Küsters also argues that the substantive content of Horkheimer's Critical Theory was increasingly marginalized in the 1930s in favor of methodological reflections. He writes, for example, "Theoretical critique means for Horkheimer ... primarily the attempt to formulate an adequate concept of theory for social research, and not necessarily the articulation of a critique of reality, as it did for Marx," (39). Küsters goes on to argue that this tendency to move away from an immanent critique of reality toward dehistoricized reflection on methodological issues or the abstract preconditions of subjectivity in the relation between man and nature, triumphs completely in Horkheimer's work after 1939. Although Küsters is correct to emphasize the general tendency of a loss of historical specificity that is evident in some of the central arguments of *Dialectic of Enlightenment*, he fails adequately to examine the historical foundations of Horkheimer's Critical Theory in the 1930s. His critique of Horkheimer's thought after 1939 as "dialectical anthropology" is symptomatic, for he fails to examine the roots of Horkheimer's concepts of anthropology, which are closely related to the concepts of *bourgeois society* and the *bourgeois epoch*, which Küsters also overlooks. As we shall see in this chapter, Horkheimer's notion of the anthropology in the 1930s was historically specific and founded on empirical research.

by no means be reduced to abstract reflections on the methodology of critical, interdisciplinary social scientific research. With his concept of the *anthropology of the bourgeois epoch*, Horkheimer moves beyond and carries out concretely – at least in a preliminary way[3] – his more general methodological and philosophical reflections. This concept captures Horkheimer's understanding of the dominant character structure in modern capitalist societies and thus forms an essential part of the *substance* of his Critical Theory in the 1930s. In order to counter this widespread neglect of what must be seen as the core of Horkheimer's Critical Theory in the 1930s, we will reconstruct Horkheimer's concept of the anthropology of the bourgeois epoch with regard both to its historical foundations as well as its implications for a Critical Theory of European societies in the 1930s. We will begin with an examination of his methodological reflections, which are found primarily in the essays "The Present Situation of Social Philosophy," "History and Psychology," and "Remarks on Philosophical Anthropology." We will then see how he fleshes out the historical content of these reflections in the essay "Egoism and Freedom Movements." Finally, we will examine how the Institute's collective *Studies on Authority and Family* represent an attempt to test Horkheimer's working hypotheses about bourgeois anthropology in contemporary Europe and also serve as an important point of departure for his subsequent historical investigations in "Egoism and Freedom Movements."

METHODOLOGICAL AND THEORETICAL UNDERPINNINGS

In order better to understand how the concept of the anthropology of the bourgeois epoch was worked out concretely in Horkheimer's essay "Egoism and Freedom Movements" and in the Institute's collective *Studies on Authority and Family*, one should first examine the methodological and theoretical reflections underlying the concept. Taken together, Horkheimer's critique of philosophical anthropology in "Remarks on Philosophical Anthropology," as well as his discussion of the role of psychology and empirical research in a dialectical theory of history and a Critical Theory of contemporary society in "History and Psychology" and "The Present Situation of Social Philosophy," provide an outline of these reflections. In "Remarks..." Horkheimer makes it abundantly clear that his own concept of "anthropology" is significantly different from the traditional concept of philosophical anthropology as articulated, for example, in Kant's *Anthropology from a Practical Point of View* or in the work of Max Scheler in the 1920s.[4] Traditional philosophical anthropology is based

---

[3] In his letters, Horkheimer repeatedly stresses the preliminary nature of the essays he wrote in the 1930s, all of which he viewed, as we shall see in the next section, as contributions to a larger project on dialectical logic to be completed sometime in the future.

[4] Horkheimer cites Scheler's discussion of philosophical anthropology in his essay "Die Sonderstellung des Menschen," in *Die Stellung des Menschen im Cosmos* (Darmstadt, 1928), pp. 246f. On the difference between Horkheimer's concept of anthropology from that of Kant, see also Stephan Bundschuh, "The Theoretical Place of Utopia: Some Remarks on Marcuse's Dual Anthropology," in *Herbert Marcuse: A Critical Reader*, eds. John Abromeit and W. Mark Cobb (London, 2004), pp. 152–63.

on the premise that it is possible to determine essential human characteristics independent of contingent social and historical conditions. Horkheimer argues that even if notions of becoming and change are incorporated into these reflections, as they were to a certain degree in Scheler's thought, the very way the problem is posed presupposes a static conceptual hierarchy that reduces history to a predetermined process. As we have seen, Horkheimer objected to Karl Mannheim's notion of a human essence that realizes itself gradually in the course of history for the same reason.[5] He also makes a similar objection to Dilthey's historicized version of philosophical anthropology, which posits the existence of a "constant and unchanging human nature [that] functions as the foundation for an epoch."[6] In other words, Horkheimer maintains not only that it is impossible to determine the essential characteristics of "man" in an ahistorical fashion, but he also rejects any attempt to define a historical period in terms of a unique and unified anthropology that supposedly underlies and suffuses all aspects of it. Horkheimer views both of these tendencies within philosophical anthropology as another example of the search for philosophical or metaphysical absolutes that has characterized the bourgeois epoch as a whole.[7]

The similarities among certain groups of people that do exist at the same time or that persist over a lengthy period of time must be explained in social and historical terms, not in terms of a human essence that is eternal or uniformly characteristic of everyone living in a certain period. Horkheimer writes:

The social life process in which they [group similarities] emerge involves both human and suprahuman factors. This process consists not simply in the representation or expression of human nature in general, but rather in a continuous struggle of individual human beings with nature. Furthermore, the character of every individual within a group originates not only in the dynamic that pertains to him in his capacity as a representative product of human nature, but in his individual fate within society as well. The relationships among social groups arise from the changing constellations between society and nature. These relationships are determining factors in the creation of the spiritual and psychological makeup of individuals, while this resulting character in turn affects the social structure.[8]

In other words, Horkheimer rejects philosophical anthropology's positing of a unified foundation of man, even during a particular historical period. The closest thing to a foundation or an ontology that one can find in Horkheimer's Critical Theory in the 1930s is the concept of the *social* or *material life process*, which he uses in this passage and elsewhere to describe the historically mutable character of a given society's interaction with nature and the relations between different social groups that result from the way in which this interaction is organized. In this regard, Horkheimer follows Marx, for whom the social life process and the "metabolic" interaction [*Stoffwechsel*] of man and nature

---

[5] See Chapter 4.
[6] "Remarks on Philosophical Anthropology," *Between Philosophy and Social Science*, op. cit., p. 151.
[7] Ibid., pp. 153–4.
[8] Ibid., p. 152.

provide what might be called the ontological foundations of human society.[9] However, as Gerd-Walter Küsters has correctly argued, this emphasis on the "suprahuman," or natural foundations of human society is of course secondary in both Marx's thought and Horkheimer's Critical Theory in the 1930s to the historical forms of human relations *within* society.[10] In other words, all societies must appropriate nature in order to exist, but the way in which they do so differs based on specific, objective socio-historical conditions. Yet philosophical anthropology fails to take these conditions into account, according to Horkheimer. Drawing on his earlier criticisms of both metaphysics and consciousness philosophy, Horkheimer argues in "Remarks..." that philosophical anthropology is another attempt to understand human beings, history, and society in terms of the expression, manifestation, or development of certain essential *human* characteristics, which can be understood independently of history and society. Horkheimer reiterates this point near the end of "Remarks ..." with a critique of the hypostatization of the abstract individual, whose abilities and characteristics cannot, he insists, be understood apart from society as a whole.[11] Like his critique of consciousness philosophy in the late 1920s, Horkheimer's critique of philosophical anthropology also leads to an empirically founded contextualization of the abstract individual within the larger structures of history and contemporary society – with the important difference, however, that psychology plays a much more important role in Horkheimer's reflections in the 1930s.

But if Horkheimer rejects traditional philosophical anthropology, why does he retain the concept of anthropology at all, particularly to describe a phenomenon that goes to the very core of his Critical Theory in the 1930s? What does he see as the role of anthropology within Critical Theory? Horkheimer argues for the "incorporation of anthropology into a dialectical theory of history,"[12] which is possible only if anthropological studies limit their object to *particular historical periods* and *particular groups* existing within society as a whole. Horkheimer writes:

Anthropological studies ... can extend and refine the understanding of historical tendencies. They would then be concerned with historically determined human beings [*Menschen*] and groups of human beings instead of with man as such, and would seek to understand their existence and development not as isolated individuals but rather as integral parts of the life of society.[13]

At this point, Horkheimer's methodological reflections in "Remarks..." connect directly with his earlier methodological arguments in his remarkable and

---

[9] The concept of the social life process plays a crucial role in Marx's first full-length discussion of his materialist concept of history in *The German Ideology*. See, for example, *The Marx-Engels Reader*, op. cit., pp. 149ff. Marx develops the concept of labor in its abstract-universal form as the metabolic interaction [*Stoffwechsel*] of man and nature in the first volume of *Capital*. See *Capital*, trans. Ben Fowkes (New York, 1977), pp. 133f.

[10] See footnote 2.

[11] "Remarks..." op. cit, pp. 166–71.

[12] Ibid., p. 159.

[13] Ibid., p. 161.

oft-overlooked essay "History and Psychology."[14] In that essay, Horkheimer's stated purpose was "a characterization of the role of psychology in the context of a theory of history that does justice to the current state of the social sciences."[15] In "Remarks...," Horkheimer had argued that anthropological studies need to focus on particular groups at particular times. In "History and Psychology," he had already laid down the methodological guidelines for such studies. Insofar as anthropology – in the sense that Horkheimer uses the concept – is concerned with the characteristics not of "man" as a whole, but rather with particular groups in specific socio-historical contexts, it must turn to psychology in order to understand how these characteristics have been formed and how they in turn affect the further development of history and the reproduction of society. Horkheimer outlines this method in the most general terms in the following way:

In the analysis of a historical epoch it is especially important to know the psychic powers and dispositions, the character and mutability of the members of different social groups.... A differentiated group psychology – that is, inquiry into those instinctual mechanisms common to members of the important groups in the production process – takes the place of mass psychology. Above all, this group psychology must investigate the extent to which the function of the individual in the production process is determined by the individual's fate in a certain kind of family, by the effect of socialization at this point in social space, but also by the way in which the individual's own labor in the economy shapes the forms of character and consciousness.[16]

The immediately apparent affinity of these methodological remarks by Horkheimer to Erich Fromm's analytical social psychology are by no means coincidental. In fact, Horkheimer's reflections on the proper role of psychology in a dialectical theory of history and an interdisciplinary Critical Theory of society mark the first real theoretical fruits of his collaboration with Fromm. Thus, let us cast a brief look back on the development of Fromm's analytic social psychology up to this point, for one cannot understand Horkheimer's concept of the anthropology of the bourgeois epoch without understanding how he appropriated and developed Fromm's insights in the 1930s.

As we have seen, Fromm considered his early essay, "The Dogma of Christ," the "nucleus" of all his later efforts to develop a "method of the application of psychoanalysis to historical phenomena."[17] In that essay, Fromm attempted to move beyond Theodor Reik's orthodox psychoanalytic interpretation by examining the concrete socio-historical conditions that affected the bearers of Christianity in order to explain its transformation from a rebellious, politically motivated doctrine into an affirmative and passive ideology. Fromm's essay can be seen as a prototype for Horkheimer's attempt to develop an anthropology of the bourgeois epoch in the 1930s. Whereas Fromm focused on the historical development of early Christianity, Horkheimer analyzed the origins

---

[14] "History and Psychology," *Between Philosophy and Social Sciences*, op. cit., pp. 111–28. This essay was originally delivered by Horkheimer as a talk at the Frankfurt Kant Society in 1930.

[15] Ibid., p. 111.

[16] Ibid., p. 121.

[17] See Chapter 5, footnote 89.

and transformation of the character structure and ideals of the modern bourgeoisie. By the time Horkheimer had written his essay "Egoism and Freedom
Movements" in 1936 – in which he first fully elaborated his concept of the
anthropology of the bourgeois epoch – he had refined Fromm's methods to
a significant degree. Yet many of their basic methodological assumptions
remained the same. Like Fromm, Horkheimer rejected concepts such as the
"collective unconscious" or "mass soul" that posited the existence of common psychological characteristics independent of socio-historical experience.
On the one hand, Horkheimer insisted in "History and Psychology" that "'the
individual psyche always remains the foundation of social psychology.' There
exists neither a mass soul nor a mass consciousness."[18] On the other hand,
Horkheimer also recognized that in all societies concrete individuals were
divided into groups that had common experiences and thus developed common psychological traits. Horkheimer accepted Fromm's distinction between
inherited sexual constitution and life experiences, which provided the key for
historical analysis of group psychological traits.[19] Like Fromm, Horkheimer
also used Freud's early drive theory,[20] which rested on the distinction between
physiological self-preservation drives and libidinal drives in order to explain
the historical formation and persistence of specific character traits.[21] Finally,
Horkheimer agreed with Fromm's most basic assumption: that psychoanalysis
provided the concepts necessary to analyze the psychic mechanisms that mediated between the individual and society, and that modern societies could not be
adequately understood without analyzing these mechanisms.

Horkheimer drew on all of these methodological insights of Fromm, but
he also supplemented them with insights of his own in order to determine
the proper place of psychology in a "dialectical theory of history."[22] Many

---

[18] "History and Psychology," p. 121.

[19] See Chapter 5.

[20] For an overview of the three main stages of Freud's drive theory, see Herbert Marcuse, *Eros
and Civilization* (Boston, 1955), pp. 20ff, or "Instinct (or Drive)," in J. Laplanche and J.B.
Pontalis, *The Language of Psychoanalysis*, trans. Donald Nicholson-Smith (New York and
London: Norton, 1973), pp. 214–17.

[21] "History and Psychology," p. 124.

[22] After his essay on the "Dogma of Christ" in the late 1920s, Fromm's own research moved
away from concrete historical studies. In the early and mid-1930s, Fromm focused on refining
the methodological foundations of his analytical social psychology in essays such as "On the
Method and Function of an Analytic Social Psychology" and "Psychological Characterology
and its Significance for Social Psychology," which were both published in the first volume of
the *Zeitschrift für Sozialforschung* (an English translation of the former essay was published
in the *The Frankfurt School Reader*, eds. A. Arato and E. Gephardt, op. cit., pp. 477–96). His
next two essays, which appeared in the second and third volumes of the *Zeitschrift*, addressed
the maternal right theory. Although Fromm's general conclusion in these essays did reinforce
Horkheimer's central claim that the dominant, bourgeois character traits developed in the patriarchal conditions of modern capitalism were not static anthropological constants, Fromm's
argument remained at a very general, macrohistorical level. Thus, it would be fair to say that
it was Horkheimer who developed the original impulse, articulated in Fromm's "Dogma of
Christ" essay, to combine psychological categories with detailed historical research in order
to analyze and explain concrete historical developments. Fromm would, of course, play an
important role in Institute's collective *Studies on Authority and Family*, but these studies were

of these insights are articulated in his essay "History and Psychology." He begins the essay with a critique of the two dominant theories of history in German academic philosophy at the time: the neo-Kantians on the one hand, and Heidegger on the other. He criticizes the former for remaining within the bounds of a subjective, transcendental approach to history, and also for being unable to transcend the passive, uncritical methods of academic historiography at that time. Horkheimer criticizes Heidegger for the opposite reason: His ontological concept of "historicity" is severed completely from the methods of traditional historiography and from historical research. Both approaches were at one, however, in their rejection of psychology. Thus, developing a critical alternative to them entailed not only reconceptualizing the role of traditional historiographical methods within a larger dialectical theory of history, but also overcoming their psychological deficit. Horkheimer's next step is to present and criticize Hegel and Marx's dialectical theories of history. Both recognized the primacy of objective conditions, either in the hidden form of the self-realization of absolute spirit or in the law of value that asserts itself behind the backs of individuals in modern capitalism. But as a result, both Hegel and Marx also failed to do justice to the importance of psychology. Like the *lumières*, Hegel recognized human drives and passions as the driving forces of history, but he did not deem it necessary to explore these drives in any psychological detail, insofar as they are merely products of the cunning of reason, the unconscious realization of the rational telos of absolute spirit. Marx, in contrast, did not make the mistake of viewing history as a meaningful process. Although Marx did recognize the subjective origins of the objective dynamic of history, he insisted people do not make history under conditions of their own choosing; in the modern world, the imperatives of capital accumulation, not the needs of humanity, ultimately drive history. Yet rather than exploring concretely the psychological factors that perpetuated this fateful situation, Marx believed that the contradictory dynamic of capitalism contains strong tendencies that would make its own collapse – and a subsequent transition to socialism – highly likely.

It was precisely this aspect of Marx's thought – his progressive philosophy of history – that became so influential after his death, both in the metaphysical interpretations of Marx in the East, which came to be known as DiaMat, and in the evolutionist philosophy of history of the leaders of the German Social Democratic party. Thus, Horkheimer was particularly critical of this general tendency to reduce Marx's philosophy of history to a metaphysical construct. He writes:

This conception of history can be transformed into a closed, dogmatic metaphysics if concrete investigations of the contradiction between growing human capacities and the social structure – which reveals itself in this connection as the motor of history – are replaced by a universal interpretive scheme, or if that contradiction is inflated into a force that shapes the future as a matter of necessity.[23]

---

primarily concerned with the transformation of bourgeois character traits in twentieth-century European societies.

[23] "History and Psychology," p. 118.

However, it was precisely these sanguine metaphysical or evolutionary interpretations of Marx's philosophy of history that had been so thoroughly discredited, first by the failed revolution in Central Europe during and after 1918 and, even more dramatically, by the rise of fascism in Italy, Germany, and elsewhere. In view of these painful historical developments, it was clearly not enough for Marxist theorists like Lukács to console themselves with statements such as "so much worse for the facts." In order to reassess the explanatory power of Marxist theory – and Horkheimer was still convinced that even recent historical developments could not be understood without it – he put forth two main proposals. First, he insisted that "concrete investigations" be conducted, such as the Institute's empirical study of the attitudes of the German working class, that could not only provide insight into the causes of such surprising developments, but could also contribute to the reconceptualization of Marxist theory itself. Horkheimer's emphasis on empirical studies was fully in line with Marx's own theory, but it did represent a break with some of the main currents of Marxist theory in Central Europe in the 1920s and 1930s. Horkheimer's second proposal for moving beyond the ossified Marxist theory of his day was to integrate psychoanalysis into Marx's theory. This proposal was a genuinely new moment in Marxist theory, and should be seen as Horkheimer's single most significant contribution to the development of Marxist theory in the twentieth century.[24]

Thus, Horkheimer was convinced that even the most advanced theory of history, that of Marx, needed to integrate psychoanalytic insights in order to remain adequate to twentieth-century conditions. Horkheimer makes this point in "History and Psychology" in the following way:

As long as it remains unknown precisely how structural economic changes manifest themselves, through the psychic constitution present at any given time among the members of different social groups, in changes in their overall way of life, the claim that the latter depends upon the former contains dogmatic elements that seriously undermine its hypothetical value for explaining the present.[25]

Yet Horkheimer also insists that as long as the materialist theory of history reflects on these conditions, it remains "a formulation of historical experience consistent with contemporary knowledge."[26] Even with the increasing importance of psychology in his Critical Theory in the 1930s, Horkheimer continued to emphasize that it remains an auxiliary science of history, albeit an indispensable one, because reified objective – not conscious subjective – forces remain the ultimate determinants of human activity in modern capitalism. True to the radically historical nature of his own theory, Horkheimer does not rule out the possibility that this relationship between history and psychology could be

---

[24] Horkheimer's stress on the fundamental openness of Critical Theory, his insistence on the regular reassessment of its concepts based on up-to-date empirical and historical research, and his integration of psychoanalysis make it difficult to accept Jürgen Habermas's claim that Horkheimer defended a "hidden Marxist orthodoxy" in the 1930s. Jürgen Habermas, *Theory and Practice*, trans. John Viertel (London: Heineman, 1974), p. 203.

[25] History and Psychology, p. 120 (translation amended).

[26] Ibid., p. 118.

reversed in the future, but in the bourgeois epoch, which he viewed as persisting into the present, it remained intact. Horkheimer believes it is possible for him to discuss the "anthropology" of the bourgeois epoch as a whole, because it represents a form of social relations that developed in modernity, was qualitatively different from feudalism, and has remained constant in certain essential ways through the present. In other words, because the bourgeois epoch was historically discrete, even though its end was not yet in sight, Horkheimer could discuss its anthropology in psychological terms: "The theory of human Being is thus transformed into the psychology of human beings living in a definite historical epoch."[27] In "Egoism and Freedom Movements," Horkheimer attempts to identify and explain in socio-historical terms the psychological traits that have evolved and remained consistent in the bourgeois epoch.

It is nonetheless crucial to reiterate that, despite his efforts to identify certain unconscious character traits that remained relatively consistent throughout the bourgeois epoch, Horkheimer never reverted to a position similar to that of the early Dilthey, who posited the existence of uniform psychological structures among *everyone* existing during a certain historical period. One Marxist assumption that Horkheimer did not question at this time was that capitalist societies are antagonistic and necessarily divide their members into discrete groups with competing interests. Thus psychology, as an auxiliary science within a larger dialectical theory of history, must examine the *divergent* psychological traits that develop within different groups. Horkheimer writes:

Psychology must ... penetrate to these deeper psychic factors by means of which the economy conditions human beings; it must become largely the psychology of the unconscious. In this form, determined by given social relations, it cannot be applied to the action of the various social strata in the same way.[28]

This important insight represents a continuation of one the central themes of *Dämmerung*: that the manifestations of life, knowledge, and perception within capitalist society are radically divergent. Although he does not discuss the concept of ideology explicitly in his methodological reflections here, Horkheimer's move from an ahistorical anthropology to group psychology as an auxiliary science within a larger dialectical theory of history also develops a more rigorous conceptual foundation for his earlier discussions of ideology. One should view Horkheimer's brief discussion of Kant's concept of "schematism" in "History and Psychology" from this viewpoint. Kant introduced the concept of schematism to explain the way in which empirical data were "preformed" in such a way that they can be assimilated by the cognitive faculties of transcendental subjectivity. What for Kant was an anthropological constant, located in the murky depths of the human cognitive apparatus, Horkheimer explains in terms of historically and socially contingent, unconscious factors that influence the knowledge and perception of individuals and particular groups of individuals. He writes:

The adaptability of the members of a social group to their economic situation is especially important among the methodological guidelines of a psychology useful for

27 Ibid., p. 113.
28 Ibid., p. 120.

history.... Here must be included ... the capacity of human beings to see the world in such a way that the satisfaction of the interests derived from a group's economic situation is in harmony with the essence of things.... Such an orientation need not develop so rationally that distortion and lying are necessary.... In his discussion of "schematism" ... Kant spoke of a hidden art in the depths of the human soul "whose real modes of activity nature is hardly likely ever to allow us to discover" ... Psychology must explain that particular preformation, however, which has as its consequence the harmony of world views with the action demanded by the economy; it is even possible that something of the "schematism" referred to by Kant might be discerned in the process.[29]

In short, the discussions in *Dämmerung* of the radically fragmented character of knowledge, perception, and even character structures themselves are not disqualified by Horkheimer's concept of the anthropology of the bourgeois epoch.

In our discussion so far of the methodological and theoretical reflections that informed Horkheimer's concept of the anthropology of the bourgeois epoch, we have focused primarily on the role of psychology within a larger dialectical theory of history. However, in order to complete this discussion, we also need to examine the important role empirical research played in Horkheimer's reflections. This role is made most clear in his inaugural address as the new director of the Institute for Social Research, "The Present Situation of Social Philosophy and the Tasks of an Institute for Social Research." It is of course true that empirical social research was only one moment in Horkheimer's overall determination of social philosophy and his concrete program for interdisciplinary research.[30] But we shall highlight its

---

[29] Ibid., p. 123. In his study, *Max Horkheimer: A New Interpretation*, Peter Stirk downplays the importance of psychology in Horkheimer's work – a tendency that is, by the way, found in much of the secondary literature on Horkheimer. He argues, for example, that "Epistemology, not psychology, provides the key to Horkheimer's own thought" (82). However, in his discussion of his materialist epistemology in the fifth chapter of his book, which includes a lengthy discussion of Horkheimer's appropriation of Kant's concept of the "schematism," Stirk's neglect of the importance of psychology has serious negative consequences for his interpretation. Despite his correct emphasis elsewhere on the centrality for Horkheimer of the history of bourgeois society, Stirk fails to grasp the historically and socially specific character of Horkheimer's epistemology, which is expressed very clearly in his discussion of Kant's schematism. Stirk's overemphasis on the "unity of cognitive structures" (122) for Horkheimer, stems from his misguided argument that "Kant's epistemology provided the main reference point and model for Horkheimer," (122) and that his "materialist epistemology ... was dependent upon his interpretation of Kant's theories" (126). For even if Horkheimer did see Kant's schematism as a remarkable expression of socially necessary false consciousness in capitalist societies, he certainly did not see it as the final word on epistemological questions. As we have already seen in our analysis of *Dämmerung*, which Stirk – once again in unison with much of the secondary literature on Horkheimer – largely ignores, Horkheimer's materialist epistemology is based on the premise that knowledge and perception are radically fragmented in capitalist societies. His appropriation of Fromm's analytic social psychology in the late 1920s and early 1930s provides him with a more sophisticated conceptual apparatus to analyze this phenomenon. As the passage quoted above clearly illustrates, he also subordinated Kant's concept of schematism to his psychoanalytically informed theory of history.

[30] "The Present Situation of Social Philosophy..." op. cit., p. 11.

importance within his interdisciplinary program as a whole, because it represents one of Horkheimer's own most important contributions to the development of Critical Theory in the late 1920s and 1930s.[31] This contribution has often been overlooked in the secondary literature on Horkheimer and Critical Theory. Helmut Dubiel, for example, has identified Horkheimer's model of interdisciplinary research as his key contribution to the development of Critical Theory in the 1930s. In the first half of his study, Dubiel does an admirable job of relating the development of Critical Theory to concrete historical events in the 1930s and early 1940s, but in the second half he departs from this historical approach in order to work out the methodological foundations of Horkheimer's interdisciplinary model. On the one hand, Dubiel recognizes that "this project, worked out between Horkheimer and Fromm, of an analytically oriented and materialistically based social psychology was surely the chosen paradigmatic core of the Institute's theoretical orientation in the early 1930s."[32] On the other hand, Dubiel argues that "This plan ... was never expanded beyond programmatic remarks."[33] Dubiel defends this claim, for example, by pointing to the preliminary nature of the results of the empirical research in the *Studies on Authority and Family*.[34] Dubiel also downplays the importance of empirical social research in general for Horkheimer in the late 1920s and early 1930s by reading Horkheimer as a representative of the antiempirical tendencies that dominated Weimar sociology.[35] As we have seen, however, it was precisely these tendencies that were Horkheimer's main target and his main reason for stressing the importance of empirical social research. This interpretation fails to do justice to the importance for Horkheimer in the late 1920s and early 1930s of empirical social research in particular and the empirical philosophical traditions in general, which set him apart not only

[31] When one compares Horkheimer's theoretical development in the 1920s and early 1930s with other important figures in what would come to be known as "Western Marxism," such as Adorno, Marcuse, Benjamin, Bloch, and Lukács, Horkheimer was really the only one who emphasized empirical research.

[32] Helmut Dubiel, *Theory and Politics: Studies in the Development of Critical Theory*, trans. Benjamin Gregg (Cambridge, MA, 1985), p. 158 (translation amended).

[33] Ibid.

[34] Ibid., p. 189. See the discussion pp. 411f. of the place of the empirical research within both the *Studies on Authority and Family* and Horkheimer's Critical Theory as a whole.

[35] Dubiel writes: "It was only after the 1934 emigration to America that the Frankfurt Circle confronted a predominantly empirically oriented social research.... Until the outbreak of the war, the German authors of the *Zeitschrift* continued to orient themselves on the political and scientific culture of the Weimar Republic. As a consequence, they were quite isolated within the American scholarly community until the end of the 1930s. It is significant that the well-known controversy between Lazarsfeld and Adorno, which is rightly understood as a controversy between the American and German traditions of research, did not occur until the late 1930s" (139). This view of things fails to do justice not only to Horkheimer's critique of antiempirical tendencies in Weimar sociology and Weimar intellectual life more generally, it also overlooks Horkheimer's interest in American empirical social research methods, which he mentions explicitly in his inaugural address, and which, as we have seen in Chapter 4, had already played a role in the conceptualization and execution of the study on the attitude of German workers in 1929.

from Adorno, but also from other critics of positivism in Weimar, such as Georg Lukács and Martin Heidegger.[36]

In arguing that Horkheimer's program for a materialist social psychology was never fulfilled, Dubiel is forced to downplay the importance not only of the *Studies on Authority and Family*, but also some of Horkheimer's most significant and substantial essays during this time. Whereas empirical social research was central to the *Studies on Authority and Family*, historical research played a significant methodological role in both "Egoism and Freedom Movements" and "Montaigne and the Function of Skepticism." In his inaugural address, Horkheimer offers the following example of what his program for social research would look like concretely:

Which connections can be demonstrated between the economic role of a specific social group in a specific era in specific countries, the transformation of the psychic structure of its individual members, and the ideas and institutions as a whole that influence them and that they created? The possibility of the introduction of real research work comes into view, and these are to be taken up in the Institute.[37]

The Institute would indeed take up precisely this program in the *Studies on Authority and Family*. The theoretical grounding of the empirical methods used there are clearly articulated in Horkheimer's inaugural address.[38] Horkheimer assesses the development of diverse forms of questionnaires as "particularly important."[39] He notes that "American social research has made great preliminary contributions to the design of survey questionnaires, which we hope to adopt for our own further purposes."[40] It is, nonetheless, also important to reiterate that empirical social research remains, like psychology, simply one moment within a larger dialectical theory of history and society, albeit an indispensable one. This empirical moment manifests itself in the 1930s not only in the empirical social research conducted for the *Studies on Authority and Family*, but also in some of Horkheimer's historical and philosophical essays. Already in his lectures on the history of philosophy, Horkheimer expressed his hope that his students' interest in philosophy would lead them to study more carefully the historical context out of which it had emerged.[41] In his essay on "Bergson's Metaphysics of Time," Horkheimer defends the crucial role of critical, empirically based historical research against the metaphysical interpretations of history of philosophers such as Bergson and Heidegger.[42] In

---

[36] Rolf Wiggershaus makes a similar mistake when he downplays the importance the empirical tradition in Horkheimer's work in the 1930s. Like Dubiel, Wiggershaus reads Horkheimer's position in the late 1930s through the mid 1940s – during which time Horkheimer moved closer to Adorno's much more skeptical assessment of the role of empirical social research and traditional science – as characteristic of his Critical Theory as a whole. However, Horkheimer's more skeptical assessment of the sciences and empirical social research was a late development. See Excursus II.

[37] "The Present Situation..." op. cit., p. 12.

[38] Ibid., pp. 13–14.

[39] Ibid., p. 13 (translation amended).

[40] Ibid.

[41] See Chapter 3, footnote 25.

[42] GS 3, pp. 246–8.

essays such as "Egoism and Freedom Movements" and "Montaigne and the Function of Skepticism," Horkheimer would rely on both established and more recent historical research to develop his key concept of the anthropology of the bourgeois epoch.[43]

Before turning to a closer analysis of that concept, let us conclude our examination of its methodological presuppositions with a brief look at the concept of a historical epoch. Horkheimer reflects on this concept most systematically in the first part of his general introduction to the _Studies on Authority and Family_.[44] On the one hand, he recognizes that dividing history into different epochs is a subjective act that depends on the level of knowledge attained at the time. On the other hand, he insists that the concept of an epoch can be suffused with objective content, and is thus eminently defensible from a philosophical standpoint. It would, in any case, be even more fallacious, and render all systematic historical inquiry meaningless, to assume that the past was nothing more than a series of arbitrary events. Horkheimer mentions Comte's division of history into three stages – the theological, metaphysical, and positivist or scientific eras – as well as the much cruder attempt by the National Socialists to restructure history in their own image, as examples of concepts of historical epochs that were faulty, insofar as they soon proved to lack any real objective substance. Horkheimer also criticizes idealist and historicist conceptualizations of the epoch – such as Hegel and Dilthey – for viewing history as the predetermined unfolding of a spiritual or anthropological essence. He agrees in most respects with Marx's determination of historical epochs in terms of different modes of production, but also moves beyond him by placing greater stress on the relative autonomy of culture and psychological structures. As an example of the relative independence of these factors vis-à-vis economic developments, Horkheimer discusses the reverence for ancestors in China and the caste system in India. He notes that both of these cultural beliefs contributed greatly to the resistance in China and India to the penetration of European economic forms. Horkheimer also draws on Nietzsche to illustrate how cultural forms do not simply exist at the level of consciousness or belief, but are instead internalized psychically and become second nature. Because of this relative constancy of psychic structures, they can be studied as part of the foundation of a historical epoch. Horkheimer does not deny that these psychic and cultural structures can change; they can even accelerate historical change in periods of dissolution. Yet such periods are the exception rather than the rule. He views the long periods of stability as the proper object for studying historical epochs. In fact, Horkheimer is convinced, as we shall soon see, that certain psychic structures and the corresponding social constellations have persisted throughout the modern era, through such momentous events as the French Revolution

---

[43] A quick glance at the footnotes of "Egoism and Freedom Movements" and "Montaigne and the Function of Skepticism" suffices to demonstrate the broad range of historical research Horkheimer drew on while writing these essays. See Max Horkheimer, _Between Philosophy and Social Science_, op. cit., pp. 392–400 and 409–15.

[44] Max Horkheimer, "Authority and the Family," in _Critical Theory_, trans. M. J. O'Connell (New York, 1992), pp. 47–68.

or the rise of National Socialism, and that these structures cannot be explained simply in terms of external force or deception.[45]

"EGOISM AND FREEDOM MOVEMENTS": THE HISTORICAL
FOUNDATIONS OF BOURGEOIS ANTHROPOLOGY

"Egoism and Freedom Movements: On the Anthropology of the Bourgeois Epoch," was the lengthiest and – at least in his own eyes – most important essay Horkheimer wrote in the 1930s. The essay was highly praised at the time by Horkheimer's colleagues,[46] and it went on to play a crucial role in the Institute's further work.[47] It informed Herbert Marcuse's important essays "The Affirmative Character of Culture" and "On Hedonism," which were published in the *Zeitschrift* in 1937 and 1938 respectively.[48] Walter Benjamin cited "Egoism…" in his 1937 essay on Eduard Fuchs to make the point that any truly emancipatory social revolution would have to draw its poetry from the future, not look back to the bourgeois revolutions as its model.[49] In his *In Search of Wagner*, which was written in 1937–8, Adorno drew on Horkheimer's social psychological analysis of the fourteenth-century Roman populist leader Cola di Rienzo in "Egoism…" to interpret Wagner's opera on the same subject.[50] Horkheimer viewed the essay as a foundation for further historical research sponsored by the Institute. For example, he was encouraging and the Institute was supporting Ludwig Marcuse to write a study of Turnvater Jahn as a case study of a bourgeois leader of a mass movement during the German wars of liberation.[51] The Institute also had an assistant in Geneva at the time who was working on a study of the Reformation based on "Egoism…."[52] Horkheimer's own later work and his collaborative efforts with Adorno, such as the chapters

[45] Ibid., p. 65.

[46] For a discussion of Adorno's enthusiastic reception of the essay, see Excursus II, pp. 379–80. Walter Benjamin praised the essay highly and recognized its affinity with *Dämmerung*: see GS 15, p. 674. Henryk Grossmann also praised the essay (Ibid., p. 641) as did Karl Wittvogel. It seems to have convinced the latter that Horkheimer was capable of illustrating and grounding his theoretical insights in extensive historical research (Ibid., p. 657.) Another non-Marxist colleague of Horkheimer, Adolph Lowe, praised the essay for the same reason: "the felicitous connection forged here between historical research and theoretical insight" (Ibid., p. 648).

[47] For a brief overview of the ways in which "Egoism…" influenced the Institute's further work, see the "Introduction to Horkheimer" that Martin Jay wrote to the first English translation of the essay, in *Telos* #54, pp. 5–9. The following remarks about its influence are based largely on Jay's account.

[48] See, for example, Horkheimer's letter to Walter Benjamin from October 27, 1936, GS 15, p. 696–7 and Marcuse's remarks in *Negations*, trans. J. Shapiro (Boston, 1968), p. 277 and 282.

[49] Walter Benjamin, "Edward Fuchs: Collector and Historian," *The Essential Frankfurt School Reader*, eds. A. Arato and E. Gephardt (New York, 1978), pp. 360–1.

[50] See Excursus II, pp. 379–80.

[51] For Horkheimer's efforts to clarify his theoretical expectations for the study, see his letter to Marcuse from August 5, 1936, GS 15, pp. 601–6. Horkheimer's efforts were ultimately unsuccessful; Marcuse never really accepted Horkheimer's theoretical conditions for the study, thus the Institute soon decided not to support it any longer. On this episode, see also Jay, *The Dialectical Imagination*, p. 115.

[52] See Horkheimer's letter to Adorno from November 14, 1936, GS 15, p. 718.

"Juliette, or Enlightenment and Morality" and "Elements of Anti-Semitism," as well as many of the "Notes and Drafts"[53] from *Dialectic of Enlightenment* and "The Revolt of Nature" from *Eclipse of Reason*, also develop and refine ideas Horkheimer first systematized in "Egoism...." Furthermore, some of the most important theoretical insights that informed the Institute's later empirical work, both during and after the war, could also be traced back to "Egoism...."[54] For example, in the foreword to his 1948 study of protofascist agitators in the United States, Leo Lowenthal and his coauthor Norbert Gutermann note that "Egoism..." provided them with the historical framework for their research.[55] Thus, it is not surprising that Herbert Marcuse later referred to the essay as "one of the most successful elaborations and nearest to the paradigmatic ideal of early Critical Theory."[56] Martin Jay has also said of "Egoism..." that "as a seed-bed for much of the Frankfurt School's later work, it is virtually unparalleled."[57] Yet despite the fact that "Egoism..." played a crucial role in Horkheimer's own theoretical development and that of Critical Theory as a whole, it has received surprisingly little attention in the secondary literature up to now.

Horkheimer originally wanted to subtitle "Egoism and Freedom Movements" "On the Concept of Bourgeois Man," but he opted for "On the Anthropology of the Bourgeois Epoch" instead, apparently for tactical reasons.[58] The essay is in fact about the origins, proliferation, reproduction, and persistence into the present of the type of man that became dominant in the modern period, that is, bourgeois man. Horkheimer's goal, as he put it in a letter to Ludwig Marcuse on August 5, 1936, was to obtain

> precise knowledge of that questionable construct that we call the bourgeois character. Specific analyses of particularly important events in modern history should contribute to comprehending the origins of this structure and the means of its preservation (or elimination), to describing how it functions and manifests itself concretely, and to working out what is typical about it.[59]

The procedure he uses and the conclusions he reaches in his examination of the bourgeois character in "Egoism..." can be summarized fairly quickly. The essay is divided into three parts. In the shorter first and last parts, Horkheimer presents his theoretical reflections on the origins, structure, and consequences

[53] In the introduction to *Dialectic of Enlightenment*, Horkheimer and Adorno state clearly that most of the "Notes and Drafts" are "concerned with a dialectical anthropology." Op. cit., p. xvii.

[54] In his preface to the *Studies in Prejudice*, for example, Horkheimer states, "The central theme of the work is a relatively new concept – the rise of an 'anthropological' species we call the authoritarian type of man." It was this "dialectical" concept of anthropology, to which Horkheimer and Adorno referred in *Dialectic of Enlightenment*, that was worked out in preliminary form in "Egoism...."

[55] Lowenthal and Guterman, *Prophets of Deceit* (New York, 1949), p. 9.

[56] Marcuse quoted by Alfons Söllner in his *Geschichte und Herrschaft: Studien zur Materialistischen Sozialwissenschaft, 1929–1942* (Frankfurt, 1979), p. 231.

[57] "Introduction to Horkheimer," op. cit., p. 5.

[58] Horkheimer states this in a letter to Adorno on May 14, 1936. See GS 15, p. 541.

[59] GS 15, p. 602.

of the bourgeois character, which he views – as have several other important theorists before and after him – primarily in terms of individual self-assertion.[60] Building on Marx, he argues that this character must be understood in terms of the particular position of the bourgeoisie in modern capitalism. Building on Fromm and Freud – but also on Nietzsche – he introduces a series of psychoanalytic and more broadly psychological concepts to explain in a more precise way its function, persistence, and consequences. He is particularly concerned to link the bourgeois character to a specific type of cruelty and repression of both self and others, something he refers to as the "*particular* type of cruelty that has arisen historically in modernity."[61] In the lengthier middle section of the essay, Horkheimer demonstrates his argument historically by examining several bourgeois freedom movements and their leaders in the early modern period. He focuses, in particular, on the fourteenth-century Roman tribune Cola di Rienzo, the fifteenth-century Florentine populist leader Savonarola, Luther and Calvin, and Robespierre. He shows how the social-psychological structures and mechanisms that are operative at an unconscious level during normal periods became particularly visible during periods of crisis and transformation. Thus, analysis of these exceptional periods provides the key to understanding bourgeois man in his "natural" condition. In short, Horkheimer uses a complex constellation of Marxist, historical, and psychoanalytic arguments to illustrate

---

[60] Horkheimer is far from alone is identifying self-assertion as the dominant characteristic of modern man. Hans Blumenberg has also argued, albeit from a very different and essentially idealist standpoint (he views modern self-assertion as the "second overcoming of Gnosticism"), that self-assertion is the defining principle of the modern age. See his *Legitimacy of the Modern Age*, trans. Robert Wallace (Cambridge, MA, 1983), esp. pp. 125–226. Hegel identified the emergence of bourgeois society, a sphere separate from both the family and the state, as the defining characteristic of modern society. In contrast to the family and state, Hegel recognized that bourgeois society is defined by the principle of self-assertion and self-interest. Like Horkheimer, Hegel recognized the positive and desirable aspects of the development of bourgeois society, which he sees in the historical realization of the principle of subjective freedom. Yet he also recognizes the self-destructive tendencies inherent in bourgeois society, i.e. that the principle of self-assertion, if left unchecked, will also destroy the principle of subjective freedom that it originally ushered into the world. See the *Philosophy of Right*, trans. T.M. Knox (Oxford, 1967), pp. 122–55. In *The Political Theory of Possessive Individualism, Hobbes to Locke* (London, Oxford, New York, 1962), C.B. Macpherson has also identified competitive self-assertion as the dominant characteristic of modern British political theory. He traces its origins to the doctrine of "possessive individualism," i.e. a society founded on the principle that man's most basic characteristic is the ownership of his own labor power and his right to alienate that labor power. Like Horkheimer, Macpherson is interested in "the historically acquired characteristics of men" (21). He defends his main argument, that the "relation of ownership ... was read back into the nature of the individual" (3), by demonstrating how "possessive individualism" underlay such diverse political theories as those of Hobbes, the Levelers, James Harrington, and John Locke, and thus formed the unexamined *socio-historical* basis of their political theories. Like Horkheimer and Hegel, Macpherson also recognizes the transformed and increasingly deleterious function of aggressive self-assertion in the nineteenth century, after the progressive goals it originally ushered in had been realized – if only abstractly – in the bourgeois revolutions (4). One can see Horkheimer's analysis of the structural continuity and functional transformation of the bourgeois character as a highly sophisticated contribution to this long-standing theoretical and practical problem.

[61] GS 15, p. 555 (my emphasis).

and analyze the anthropology of the bourgeois epoch. In what follows, we will examine these three interrelated moments in the essay in order to present Horkheimer's most important points in more detail, examine potential objections to his arguments, and illustrate the crucial place the essay occupies within Horkheimer's Critical Theory as a whole.

Perhaps the most important Marxist argument underlying "Egoism..." is Horkheimer's grounding of the bourgeois character structure in the unique social position of the bourgeoisie during the early modern period – that is, its location between the defenders of feudalism and absolutism on the one hand, and the masses of workers and peasants on the other. The bourgeoisie was, of course, intent on overcoming the former, but it could not do so without the help of the latter. Thus, the bourgeoisie had to mobilize the most desperate sections of the population in order to realize its goals, while at the same time ensuring that the interests of the masses always remained subordinated to their own particular interests. It was precisely this social constellation that became strikingly apparent in the bourgeois freedom movements of the early modern period. Horkheimer writes:

> The bourgeoisie's efforts to push through its own demands for a more rational administration against the feudal powers with the help of the desperate popular masses, while simultaneously consolidating its own rule over the masses, combine to account for the peculiar way the struggle for the "the people" is carried on in these movements.[62]

In order to illustrate the character of the social-psychological relationship that exists between bourgeois leaders and the masses, Horkheimer subjects the two main currents in early modern philosophical anthropology to an ideology critique. He shows that not only the pessimistic view of man, but also its optimistic counterpart, are based on the negation of egoism, indeed the negation of pleasure itself, which were regarded as immoral and antisocial.[63] In the case of Machiavelli and Hobbes – and to an even greater extent with Luther and Calvin – the link between a pessimistic view of human nature and a direct interest in repressing the masses is clear to see.[64] Yet Horkheimer also stresses the less obvious, but hardly less pronounced, interest in repression represented by the idealist morality of Rousseau or Kant. Horkheimer uses Robespierre, "the orthodox student of Rousseau," to illustrate the typically bourgeois condemnation of egoism and pleasure that characterizes even those who ascribe to an optimistic view of human nature.[65] In his discussion of Robespierre and the ideological function of bourgeois morality, Horkheimer develops arguments we have already examined in "Materialism and Morality." In "Egoism...," he was also highly attentive to the pronounced contradiction between idealist moral imperatives and the reality of a society dominated by ruthless self-assertion. However, in "Egoism..." Horkheimer is able, through the use of numerous historical examples, to demonstrate more clearly how the ideological moment

---

[62] "Egoism and Freedom Movements: On the Anthropology of the Bourgeois Epoch," in *Between Philosophy and Social Science*, op. cit., pp. 61–2.

[63] Ibid., p. 54.

[64] Ibid., p. 51.

[65] Ibid., p. 53.

of idealist morality plays itself out concretely and how it is rooted in a particular socio-historical constellation. The denial of egoism and pleasure in idealist morality corresponds to the sacrifices demanded of the masses by their bourgeois leaders. Horkheimer maintains that the "The leader is just the magnified version of this [ascetic] type. His character structure corresponds to that of his followers,"[66] and that "the hostility toward pleasure contained in the modern age's optimistic and pessimistic conception of humanity stems from the social situation of the bourgeoisie."[67]

In addition to stressing the specific socio-historical preconditions of bourgeois anthropology, a second crucial Marxist moment in "Egoism..." is Horkheimer's insistence on the antagonistic structural dynamic of bourgeois society. It is worth examining this point in more detail, because some commentators have argued that Horkheimer did not fully differentiate himself from the monolithic models of philosophical anthropology he had criticized so vehemently.[68] The implication is that Horkheimer's own model of bourgeois anthropology is too unitary. However, this is not the case for several reasons. Horkheimer shows how the interests of the bourgeoisie and the masses diverged from the very beginning of the modern era. Even though they did indeed have a common, objective interest in overthrowing feudalism and absolutism, it was not the case that their conflict of interest first emerged after the bourgeoisie had come to power. Horkheimer shows how this conflict determined the ways in which the bourgeoisie treated the masses from the very beginning. He traces the demagogic methods used by bourgeois leaders to manipulate the masses all the way back to Cola di Rienzo in the fourteenth century, and he maintains that these forms remained relatively constant not only through the French Revolution, but also right down to the present. As he had in previous discussions of early modern philosophy and history, Horkheimer also displayed his Marxist convictions in "Egoism..." by arguing that the repressive methods used by the bourgeoisie were necessary, even justified, in order to overcome feudalism and establish the conditions for a future society in which such systematic repression and deception would no longer be necessary. The very fact that the bourgeois character persisted so stubbornly, even after the period in which it had played a historically progressive role had passed, lent particular urgency to Horkheimer's arguments. It was, in fact, precisely this persistence that interested Horkheimer and led him to conclude that psychic structures

---

[66] Ibid., p. 93.

[67] Ibid., p. 106

[68] Peter Stirk, for example, argues that regarding Horkheimer's objections to monolithic models of philosophical anthropology, "Horkheimer himself was not entirely free of the same vice. His own history of the bourgeois era unequivocally associates a particular type of man with a historical era." *Max Horkheimer: A New Interpretation*, op. cit., p. 44. Horkheimer does argue that the bourgeois character becomes increasingly widespread, also among the lower classes, with the development of capitalism; nonetheless, this never leads him to abandon his view of capitalism as socially antagonistic. For, as we shall in what follows, even when the bourgeois character becomes more widespread, its function continues to remain radically different for the masses than for the bourgeoisie themselves. Thus it would be a mistake to say that Horkheimer's anthropology is ever unitary or monolithic.

cannot be reduced to mere reflections of economic relations. Due to its relative autonomy from the economy and its relative independence as a moment in the overall reproduction of society, the bourgeois character structure has contributed significantly, according to Horkheimer, to prolonging the antagonistic and irrational dynamic of capitalism beyond what was historically necessary.

Thus, Horkheimer does argue that the bourgeois character structure became more widespread with the historical development of bourgeois society. With respect to the historical triumph of bourgeois society, for which the workers and peasants had also fought, Horkheimer writes: "The bourgeois revolution did not lead the masses to the lasting state of joyful existence and universal equality they longed for, but to the hard reality of an individualistic social order instead."[69] In his analysis of the Reformation, Horkheimer also stresses that the spread of the bourgeois character had already begun much earlier:

The cultural progress of the masses initiated by the Reformers was directly connected with a much more active shaping of individuals than was usual with the old clergy. In light of the new economic tasks, the bourgeoisie had to raise its members to a completely different level of self-discipline, responsibility and zeal for work than they were accustomed to in the old times.[70]

Despite this steady diffusion through inculcation of the bourgeois character, Horkheimer also constantly emphasizes its contradictions and differing functions for members of different classes. Continuing the discussion from "Materialism and Morality," Horkheimer illustrated how the bourgeoisie was in fact encouraged to pursue its own interests, whereas the masses were inculcated to sacrifice themselves for the particularist interests of the bourgeoisie, which were presented to them as the "good of society as a whole." Both pessimistic and optimistic bourgeois theories of human nature reinforced this view, and only those who Horkheimer would later call the "dark authors of the bourgeoisie" recognized and explicitly articulated this contradiction. For example, Mandeville "knew well that the open advocacy of egoism is unwelcome precisely to those who embody it most strongly."[71] In other words, if the bourgeoisie were really to encourage the masses to pursue their own best interests, they might well decide to put an end to bourgeois society. Thus, idealist morality and other forms of repression are necessary to encourage further sacrifice, rather than collective self-assertion of the lower classes.[72] As we have seen, Horkheimer recognized the ambivalent nature of bourgeois morality, that is, that it also contained a transcendent rational moment, and that even its repressive moment had a historically progressive role in overcoming feudalism and absolutism. In "Egoism...," Horkheimer argues that these two contradictory moments contained in morality are grounded in "universal social interests" on the one hand, and "class interests" on the other. Horkheimer argues that the moment of "class interest" came increasingly to dominate that of "universal

[69] "Egoism...," p. 62.
[70] Ibid., p. 83.
[71] "Egoism...," p. 56.
[72] Ibid., p. 55 (translation amended).

social interest" in the morality of the nineteenth century.[73] Hence, we see once again that the spread of the ruthless individualism of bourgeois society did not lead to the imposition of a seamlessly unified character structure, and even those elements of the bourgeois character that did take hold among the masses continued to have a different function for them. For Horkheimer, as for Marx, the foundation of modern capitalist society remains its antagonistic social relations, not any unitary anthropology, even if Horkheimer moves beyond Marx in his sophisticated analysis of how the important role the bourgeois character plays in prolonging and reinforcing these relations.

Horkheimer's discussion of bourgeois anthropology in "Egoism..." illustrates the ongoing importance of not only the Marxist but also the historical moment in his Critical Theory, which can be seen in his decisive move beyond mere methodological or formalistic reflections in "Egoism...." One of the consequences of this move is his unambiguous identification of the bourgeois character as a specifically modern phenomenon. Apart from providing an opportunity to examine the particular historical content of his argument in "Egoism..." in more detail, it is also important to reiterate and demonstrate the modernity of bourgeois anthropology in order to differentiate Horkheimer's Critical Theory in the 1930s from key arguments put forth both by Theodor Adorno at that time, and by Horkheimer and Adorno several years later in *Dialectic of Enlightenment*. Because *Dialectic of Enlightenment* is often interpreted as a critique of a form of Western rationality that remained essentially constant from Homer's time to the present, it is important to recall the reasons Horkheimer presents in the mid-1930s for grounding the bourgeois character, and the specific form of rationality that accompanies it, in the *bourgeois*, or *modern*, epoch. Before returning to this point, however, let us first examine Horkheimer's concept of bourgeois anthropology as both a crucial complement to, and decisive move beyond, his extensive methodological reflections from the 1930s.

In earlier chapters, we have traced the importance of the empirical philosophical tradition and empirical research in general for Horkheimer's Critical Theory. In his lectures on the history of philosophy, for example, Horkheimer privileged the empiricist over the rationalist tradition in modern Western philosophy, insofar as the empiricists viewed knowledge as temporally bound and open-ended. The empiricist recognition of the "temporal core of truth" served as an important safeguard against the dogmatic or merely formalistic claims of metaphysics and rationalism. We saw how he attempted to rehabilitate the Enlightenment by demonstrating how it – particularly its French variant, which he viewed as paradigmatic – developed the critical impulses of empiricism and was no by no means an apotheosis of abstract reason. We also saw that Horkheimer's lectures were not simply an abstract application of a Marxist philosophy of history to modern philosophy, but were instead based on a detailed knowledge, remarkable in its breadth and depth, of the history of modern philosophy in particular, and the history of modern Europe in general. Horkheimer's insistence that the uneven development of bourgeois society

---

[73] "Egoism...", p. 55.

should serve as the central organizing concept for understanding modern philosophy was never simply asserted dogmatically, but was always demonstrated
concretely through in-depth analysis of the particular philosophy in question.[74]
Although Horkheimer's concept of the anthropology of the bourgeois epoch
builds on insights he first developed in these lectures – in which he first laid out
his understanding of the history of bourgeois society – they also move beyond
them in their application of psychoanalytic categories. Thus, although Peter
Stirk's argument that the history of bourgeois society should be understood as
the core concept of Horkheimer's Critical Theory is not wrong, it fails to grasp
the increasing importance of psychology in Horkheimer's work in the 1930s,
and how its integration into his Critical Theory refined and modified his understanding of bourgeois society.[75] The development of Horkheimer's Critical
Theory from the 1920s to the 1930s could be summarized in the broadest
sense as a movement from the *history of bourgeois society* to the *anthropology
of the bourgeois epoch*. In both phases, he was of course also concerned with
developing a Critical Theory of bourgeois society in its contemporary form,
but his efforts are largely based on his understanding of its historical evolution. We will return to this crucial psychological dimension of Horkheimer's
concept of bourgeois anthropology shortly. The crucial point in this context is
that Horkheimer's Critical Theory cannot be reduced to the methodological
reflections he puts forth in his widely read inaugural address or his essay on
"Traditional and Critical Theory," or even to his reflections on materialism in
his much less widely read essays from the early 1930s. More than any other
concept in his work in the 1930s, the anthropology of the bourgeois epoch
represents the *content* of Horkheimer's theory: his effort to provide a positive
determination of the historical period in which he was living.

The historical moment in Horkheimer's Critical Theory is crucial for understanding his concept of bourgeois anthropology insofar as it pushes him beyond
mere methodological reflections to make concrete statements about the real
forces determining the dynamic of history and society.[76] Just as Marx's critique
of political economy was not merely a criticism of a classical liberal economics,
but at the same time an attempt to determine self-reflexively the laws governing
the movement of history and society within the historically specific era of modern capitalism, Horkheimer's concept of bourgeois anthropology takes him
beyond a critique of philosophical anthropology, metaphysics, and positivism
to analyses of the concrete forces that have determined and continue to determine the structure and development of society. Thus, it is not a coincidence that
particular historical observations and historical methods of proof play a larger
role in "Egoism…" than in any other essay of Horkheimer's in the 1930s. In
the first and last section of "Egoism…," Horkheimer presents the theoretical

---

[74] See Chapter 3.

[75] For Stirk's argument, see Chapter 3, footnote 19.

[76] Peter Stirk recognizes this fact, when he writes that Horkheimer's "critical theory is not a methodology of the social sciences but a theory of history" (*Max Horkheimer: A New Interpretation*,
op. cit., p. 91) but, as noted earlier, he does not fully explore the important role that psychology
plays in Horkheimer's theory of history.

reflections that informed the essay, but in the middle section Horkheimer turns to historical events in order to illustrate concretely these historical insights. Although Horkheimer did not conduct any original archival research for these essays, he did draw extensively on older and more recent historical secondary literature as well as numerous collections of published primary sources.[77] In addition, his encouragement of other historical research projects in conjunction with "Egoism…" illustrates that Horkheimer did not limit the importance of empirical research merely to contemporary issues. At this point, Horkheimer still believed that theoretical concepts – including those of Marx – must also be reexamined in light of empirical *historical* research. In this regard, Horkheimer saw no essential contradiction between the empiricist philosophical tradition and a Critical Theory in the Hegelian-Marxist tradition. In fact, it must be seen as one of Horkheimer's most important achievements that he illustrated just how important the empirical moment was for a critical theory of society that builds on the insights of Hegel and Marx. It was precisely the insistence on moving beyond ahistorical or merely formalistic theoretical reflection that the empirical tradition, as Horkheimer interpreted it, shared with the dialectical theories of Hegel and Marx. This is why Horkheimer had no trouble making the seemingly paradoxical claim that Hegel was a "great empiricist."[78] As Adorno would discuss at some length later in *Negative Dialectics*, through Hegel's criticism of Kant, "philosophy had regained the right and the capacity to think substantively [*inhaltlich*] instead of being put off with the analysis of cognitive forms that were empty and, in the emphatic sense, null and void."[79] Marx's critique of political economy would build on Hegel's critique of Kant insofar as his concepts were also attempts to grasp self-reflexively the historically specific dynamic of capitalist society, and not an attempt to establish ontological laws of being or history, as the purveyors of DiaMat and others would later claim. Of course, Hegel and Marx (and Horkheimer) did go beyond the empirical tradition – in this regard building on Kant's notion of critique – in their recognition of the subjective and socially mediated nature of all empirical observations. However, this does not diminish the fact that their own dialectical theories were developed through an empirically based study of history. In this particular sense, Horkheimer's concept of bourgeois anthropology should also be seen as "*begriffene Geschichte*,"[80] that is, as *substantive* claims about the forces determining social and historical reality, not mere methodological reflections or neutral observations about the past.

Let us turn now to the historical arguments themselves that Horkheimer presents in "Egoism…." He attempts to demonstrate the historical substance of his concept of bourgeois anthropology by examining four bourgeois freedom movements in the early modern period. He pays particular attention to the dynamics that existed within these movements between their leaders and

---

[77] See footnote 43.

[78] GS 11, p. 296.

[79] *Negative Dialectics*, trans. E.B. Ashton (New York, 1973), p. 7.

[80] "Conceptually grasped history." See Hegel, *Phänomenologie des Geistes*, *Werke*, vol. 3 (Frankfurt a.M.: Suhrkamp, 1970), p. 591.

the masses that followed them. Horkheimer's argument is structured in terms of a progressive realization of bourgeois society. He views Cola di Rienzo and Savonarola as precursors of Luther and Calvin, who were the first to succeed in breaking the dominance of the Catholic Church and establishing bourgeois ideals in the spiritual realm, which in turn greatly accelerated the spread of the bourgeois character structure. Horkheimer views Robespierre and the French Revolution in terms of the historical realization of bourgeois ideals as the guiding political principles of modern societies, which reinforced and facilitated the further spread of bourgeois character traits. Once these ideals became the real foundation of further historical developments, their contradictory character was plain for all to see. However, Horkheimer's main point in "Egoism..." is to demonstrate that the socio-historical and social-psychological constellation that gave rise to the bourgeois character was present from the very beginning of the modern era. In the social movements led by Cola di Rienzo, Savonarola, Luther and Calvin, and Robespierre, Horkheimer identifies some of the defining characteristics of the bourgeois character and the mechanisms that reproduce it. Most important, Horkheimer establishes that these leaders were really representatives of bourgeois interests, even though they portrayed themselves as champions of the "people." In each case, Horkheimer shows how, once the leaders had come to power, they began to oppress the masses, thereby revealing their own true character and the dominant tendencies within the movement as a whole. Because the leaders did not have any real desire to enlighten the masses about their own best interests, they used irrational means to win and keep their support. Horkheimer points in all four cases to the anti-intellectualism of the leaders of bourgeois freedom movements and to their use of bombastic symbols and pageantry to bind the masses to them emotionally and reinforce their authority as the legitimate representatives of society "as a whole." Finally, Horkheimer also pays close attention in all four movements to the use of public speech as one of the most important means of inculcating bourgeois values. In the following section, we will examine the psychoanalytic underpinnings of some of these mechanisms in more detail, but let us first take a quick look at Horkheimer's documentation of their historical existence.

Cola di Rienzo and Savonarola both came from relatively humble backgrounds: The former was a notary and the latter a Dominican monk. Horkheimer attempts to demonstrate how both came to power as representatives of the propertied classes: Rienzo in a struggle against the Roman aristocracy, and Savonarola in opposition to the Florentine aristocracy and bourgeois families that attained aristocratic status, such as the Medicis. He notes how a broad spectrum of the Roman bourgeoisie, from the lower to the upper-middle classes, participated in the revolts that brought Rienzo into power.[81] He argues that Savonarola put forth typical bourgeois political demands, that most members of the Dominicans and other brotherhoods of itinerant monks and preachers were from the middle class, and that their interests overlapped with the urban bourgeoisie.[82] Horkheimer also documents Luther and Calvin's

---

[81] "Egoism...", p. 64.
[82] Ibid., pp. 69 and 75f.

defense of propertied interests. Even though Robespierre was – like his philosophical mentor Rousseau – resentful of large property owners, he too ardently defended the bourgeois principle of private property. On the eve of his fall, he was even considering enacting the Ventôse decrees, which would have dispossessed suspected "internal enemies" and distributed their property among the *sans-culottes*. However, by this time it was too late; he had already lost the support of the Parisian masses, because he had begun to institute repressive measures – such as forbidding them to change their places of work or instituting forced labor in the countryside – that revealed the real social forces that were guiding his actions.[83] Horkheimer describes this characteristic shift from mobilization to repression of the masses in the cases of Rienzo, Savonarola, and Luther and Calvin as well. He cites the "oppressive taxes and unscrupulous financial measures"[84] that led to the uprising against Rienzo, as well as Savonarola's exclusion of the lower classes from government, his disproportionate taxation of them, and his condemnation of any resistance on their part to these measures.[85] Horkheimer points out that Luther's deep distrust, indeed virulent hatred of the masses, went so far that he condemned revolts even when they were directed against the devil incarnate, that is, the pope – not to mention his vulgar attacks of the rebellious participants in the peasant wars.[86] Despite the antiauthoritarian implications of Calvin's teachings, he too saw "obedience and suffering" as the duty and destiny of the masses, and "considered an aristocratic and oligarchic form of government to be the best one."[87]

Horkheimer also documents the irrational methods used by the bourgeois leaders to reinforce their authority and keep the masses in a state of dependence and immaturity. True to his argument that the dynamics of the leader-masses relationship are structurally similar throughout the bourgeois epoch and thus manifest themselves in structurally similar ways, Horkheimer shows how all four of the freedom movements display the same irrational moments, although in each case one particular moment may predominate over the others for contingent reasons. In the case of Rienzo, Horkheimer emphasizes his use of mythical symbols, pompous costumes, and spectacular ceremonies to captivate the masses.[88] Despite his proverbial ascetic temperament, even the "incorruptible" Robespierre was unable to forego the use of similarly bombastic methods to bolster his authority. As Horkheimer demonstrates, Robespierre was sharply critical of the revolutionary "Festival of Reason," which ran contrary to positive religion. He participated in the "Festival of the Supreme Being" instead, and burned an effigy representing atheism in the course of the events.[89] Thus, it comes as no surprise that Robespierre was also critical of the Enlightenment and the materialist tradition more generally, particularly Epicure and the Encyclopedists.[90] For his part, Savonarola relied less on pompous costumes and

[83] Ibid., pp. 89–90.
[84] Ibid., p. 65.
[85] Ibid., pp. 69–71.
[86] Ibid., pp. 73 and 81.
[87] Ibid., p. 82.
[88] Ibid., pp. 65–6.
[89] Ibid., p. 92.
[90] Ibid., pp. 94–5.

ceremony than on cultivating his own alleged mystical and magical qualities. According to Horkheimer, this aspect of Savonarola's rise to power demonstrates the broader principle that "The endowment of the leader with magical qualities was a condition for his influence on the masses."[91] This principle was also illustrated by Savonarola's fall, which began when he failed to appear for his trial by fire and thus dispelled the magical aura that surrounded him.[92] With Luther and Calvin, the antiintellectual tendencies of the ascendant bourgeoisie break into explicit and virulent irrationalism. Horkheimer does not, of course, have any difficulty finding quotes from both reformers to illustrate the antiintellectual tendency of the Reformation. In contrast to the standard understanding of modernity as the triumph of rationality over the benighted Middle Ages, Horkheimer's notes that the estimation of reason had declined steadily from the Catholic theology of Thomas Aquinas, through nominalism to the Reformation: "Luther knows no limit in his obscene denunciations of reason," and he "senses the deep connection between pleasure and intellect and persecutes both with the same hatred."[93] Horkheimer concludes his discussion of this pronounced antiintellectual tendency in bourgeois freedom movements with a critique of Max Weber, who "stressed the rationalistic trait of the bourgeois mind, but," as Horkheimer insists, "irrationalism is from the start no less associated with its history."[94]

The final aspect of Horkheimer's historical analysis of bourgeois anthropology that we shall examine here, namely his discussion of public speech, serves at the same time as a transition to our examination of the psychoanalytic moment in "Egoism...."[95] During relatively peaceful times, schools, churches, and the family perform the role of instilling bourgeois values, but during periods of tumult or revolution, public speech emerges as the main mediator between bourgeois leaders and the masses, according to Horkheimer. He distinguishes broadly between two types of public speech, namely that aimed at convincing its listeners through rational argumentation and that aimed at dominating them through unconscious or affective manipulation. He views the former as the predominant type of public speech in antiquity and the latter as characteristic of bourgeois freedom movements.[96] Horkheimer focuses primarily on the

---

[91] In addition to the more general criticisms of Max Weber's theory of rationalization that run throughout "Egoism...," Horkheimer also offers an alternative materialist explanation of the phenomena of charisma here, which was so central for Weber.

[92] Ibid., p. 72.

[93] Ibid., p. 86.

[94] Ibid., p. 87.

[95] Horkheimer considered public speech so central to understanding bourgeois anthropology that he gave a talk in October 1936 at the American Historical Association in Chicago just on this topic: "The Function of [Public] Speech in the Modern Era." The German version of this talk has since been published in Horkheimer's Collected Writings. See GS 12, pp. 24–38.

[96] Horkheimer does not deny that public speech in antiquity was also often intended to manipulate listeners through appeals to emotion, but he insists that this aspect of public speech became dominant in the modern period because of the need of the bourgeoisie to transform the peasant and working masses into active participants bourgeois society. Because slaves performed most of the necessary labor in antiquity, there did not exist a similar necessity to cajole the lower classes into active participation. Horkheimer insists that "Speech before a mass audience is a social function that takes place between free persons, not between master and slave." GS 12, p. 37.

public speeches of bourgeois leaders at mass gatherings, because they displayed most clearly the unconscious mechanisms at work. Horkheimer describes, for example, the legendary power of Savonarola's speeches, which evoked waves of religious emotion and paroxysms of sacrificial devotion among the masses.[97] However, Horkheimer also discusses the structurally similar function of speeches delivered by wandering monks in the period leading up to the Reformation and sermons delivered in churches afterward. He underscores the moment of psychological violence essential to bourgeois public speech by showing how workers, peasants, or the dispossessed were often forced to attend church or public gatherings at which sermons were delivered.[98] Horkheimer also discusses the distinction between public speech as Enlightenment versus public speech as mass deception in relation to revolutionary movements. He points out that the latter have often organized themselves in smaller groups, and even when they did use mass gatherings to further their political goals, critical discussion and rational insight still retained their primacy over unconscious manipulation.[99] As a final example of the irrational and demagogic use of public speech, which at the same time highlights the persistence of the mechanisms of bourgeois society into the present, Horkheimer even cites several passages from Hitler's *Mein Kampf* that explicitly discuss strategies for manipulating the masses with public speech.[100]

In addition to analyzing the function of public speech *within* the bourgeois epoch, Horkheimer also distinguishes broadly between its functions in modernity and antiquity. He illustrates this point, while at the same time making the distinction between rational and irrational uses of public speech more precise by introducing the psychoanalytic concept of "introversion." He writes:

In this new type of speech, which is linked very closely to the development of the urban bourgeoisie, a certain characteristic plays a key role that it did not possess in antiquity, namely, the ability of speech to change the listener's character, even at the depth dimension. He is not supposed simply to be convinced of something, he is supposed to "go into himself," improve himself, become someone else, become a new person. Instead of orienting themselves towards joy and pleasure, the sermon is intended to get people to keep their conscience clean, to lead a spotless life, always and everywhere to do one's duty.... We call this function of speech its "introverting quality," or, to use the substantive form, the "introversion" that it effects.[101]

It is important to note that Horkheimer stresses here once again the qualitatively new character of the modern epoch.[102] We shall soon see that Horkheimer also objected to Nietzsche's interpretation of "slave morality," because he linked it to Christianity as a whole, rather than identifying its specifically modern origins. Horkheimer agreed with Nietzsche that introversion played a decisive role in the spread of "slave morality" and sadomasochistic character

---

[97] "Egoism...," pp. 71–4.

[98] Ibid., pp. 47–8.

[99] Ibid., p. 79.

[100] GS 12, p. 36.

[101] Ibid., pp. 27–8.

[102] See also Horkheimer's discussion of this point in "Egoism...," pp. 21 and 43.

structures, but he linked the phenomenon in a more historically specific way to the rise of bourgeois society, and to the important role public speech played in this process. It is also important to note that Horkheimer relied here on the psychoanalytic concept of introversion to explain the modern function of public speech. In contrast to rational argumentation, the goal of the bourgeois leader is to change the very character of his audience with his public speech. The goal of the bourgeois leader is, in other words, to convince his audience to identify thoroughly with him, such that they relinquish their own interests and internalize the interests he represents.[103] His speech facilitates this task by convincing the masses of their own deeply sinful nature and worthlessness, which can be redeemed only through adherence to the doctrine of the leader. In return for this obedience, the masses are compensated with the imaginary love of the leader and, as we shall see, the permission to punish with a good conscience those whom he rejects, those who refuse to follow him, and/or those who are not willing or are simply perceived as unwilling to sacrifice themselves for him.

The concept of introversion represents one crucial aspect of Horkheimer's larger efforts to illuminate bourgeois anthropology using psychoanalysis. As we have already seen, Horkheimer was convinced by the early 1930s at the latest that modern society could not be understood without psychological concepts. He believed that Freudian psychoanalysis, in particular, had an essential role to play as an auxiliary science within a larger dialectical theory of history. Horkheimer carried out this program concretely for the first time in "Egoism...." He used psychoanalytic concepts both to analyze the historical emergence of the dominant bourgeois character type and also to explain its historical function and consequences. There is no question that Horkheimer's psychoanalytic analyses of modern history were motivated and informed by the catastrophic historical events of the twentieth century. In the first chapter, we saw how the senseless slaughter of World War I and the failure of the German working class after the war to carry out the historical role ascribed to it by Marx both played a decisive role in his decision to pursue a rigorous theoretical education. The rise of fascism in Europe in the 1920s and 1930s – which the socialist movements in the respective countries had also been unable to prevent – made the task of coming to terms with the contradictions of contemporary society all the more urgent. Just as Marx had insisted that the anatomy of the ape could only be explained in terms of the more fully evolved human anatomy, so Horkheimer attempted, in light of recent historical events, to reexamine with a fresh eye the essential historical factors that had made them possible. Psychoanalysis was crucial in this endeavor, insofar as it provided him with the conceptual tools to analyze the emergence and reproduction of character structures that were shaped by underlying economic structures, but that could not be reduced to a mere function of economic relations. Horkheimer believed that this *relative autonomy* of psychic structures provided the key to understanding the catastrophic events of the twentieth century, and that these structures must be understood in *historical* terms.

---

[103] See also "Egoism..." p. 59.

In order to understand the role psychoanalysis plays in Horkheimer's analysis of the emergence of the bourgeois character, it is important to recall his critique of philosophical anthropology, because Horkheimer criticizes Freud along very similar lines in the last section of "Egoism...." He argues that the socio-historical substance of Freud's concepts was plainly apparent in his early work, but that in his later work an ahistorical, biological approach gained the upper hand. Horkheimer shows that Freud developed a static philosophical anthropology in these later writings that transformed the basic assumptions of his bourgeois worldview into eternal natural laws.[104] Horkheimer focuses, in particular, on Freud's hypostatization of certain forms of cruelty and aggression, which found its most dramatic expression in his positing of a death drive in the third and final phase of his drive theory.[105] Horkheimer writes, "the destruction drive, 'the inborn human inclination to "evil," to aggressiveness and destructiveness, and so to cruelty as well,' was posited as a basic fact of psychic life that was directly determined by biology,"[106] and, more caustically, "like the devil in the Middle Ages, the eternal destruction drive is to be blamed for all evil."[107] However, the Marxist and empirical historical arguments that Horkheimer presents in the first two sections of "Egoism..." are intended to demonstrate that cruelty and aggression are not historically constant, as Freud assumed. They result from the specific "nature" of bourgeois society, which – despite all its moralizing self-deception – is in reality based on ruthless "self-assertion." One of the theoretical consequences of the increasing dominance of biological concepts in Freud's later thought, according to Horkheimer, was his neglect of the external, socio-historical factors in character formation. In this respect, Fromm's interpretation and critique of Freud was crucial for Horkheimer. He combined Fromm's insistence on the importance not only of inherited sexual constitution, but also of life experiences (and the shared life experiences among groups) in the formation of psychological character structures, and his emphasis on the plasticity of libidinal drives and their "passive and active adjustment"[108] to underlying socio-economic structures, with his own critique of philosophical anthropology to move beyond Freud's categories and to analyze empirically the specific socio-historical factors that led to the formation of the bourgeois character at the dawn of the modern era.

In addition to analyzing the historical emergence of the bourgeois character in "Egoism...," Horkheimer was particularly interested in examining what he saw as one of its most baleful consequences, namely the perpetuation of certain forms of cruelty and aggression that he believed Freud had wrongly

[104] See "Egoism...," pp. 103ff.

[105] On the three main stages in the development of Freud's drive theory, see Herbert Marcuse, *Eros and Civilization*, op. cit., pp. 20f.

[106] "Egoism...," p. 104 (translation amended).

[107] Ibid., p. 105.

[108] This is Fromm's formulation (see "The Method and Function of an Analytic Social Psychology," in *The Essential Frankfurt School Reader*, op. cit., p. 480), but one which Horkheimer adopted during this time. See, for example, his discussion of "adaption" in "History and Psychology," op. cit., pp. 121–2.

naturalized.[109] In accordance with the basic Marxist assumptions of the essay, Horkheimer's alternative interpretation of the particular forms of modern cruelty and aggression are class-specific. In relation to the bourgeoisie, Horkheimer stresses once again the ruthless individualism that characterizes the reality of bourgeois society. Whereas the market and the individualism to which it helped give birth ultimately played a progressive historical role in the early modern period, the continued dominance of the market as the primary means of social mediation after the historical triumph of the bourgeoisie not only hinders further progressive development, according to Horkheimer, it also threatens to throw humanity into a new form of barbarism. For Horkheimer, the market "mediates the reproduction of society only with severe losses in human life and goods, and with the advancement of the capitalist economy it is unable to save humanity, despite its growing wealth, from a reversion to barbarism."[110] This domination of the market manifests itself socially in the ruthless indifference and coldness of the bourgeois character.[111] Horkheimer also attempts to demonstrate how the alienness, coldness, and indifference characteristic of bourgeois society manifests itself among the lower classes, even though they are systematically prevented from pursuing their own interests and desires. He writes:

Since the egoism of the masses led by the bourgeois leader must not be satisfied, since their demands are repressed as inner purification, obedience, submission, and self-sacrifice, since love and recognition of the individual are deflected toward the leader, who has been magnified to superhuman dimensions, and toward lofty symbols and great concepts, and since one's own being is annihilated along with its claim to existence ... the individual as such, his pleasure and happiness is despised and denied.[112]

In this way, Horkheimer argues that one of the most important prerequisites for systematic cruelty and aggression – and its counterpart, the absence of genuinely felt compassion for one's fellow man – lies at the very heart of bourgeois society.

Yet Horkheimer also offers more precise psychoanalytic explanations for cruelty, particularly among the lower classes. Despite his critique of Freud's philosophical anthropology, he insists that Freudian psychoanalysis, particularly as articulated in his early work, is essential for understanding the phenomena in question. He writes:

The analysis of the psychic mechanisms by which hatred and cruelty are generated was begun in modern psychology mainly by Freud. The conceptual apparatus which he created in his early works can significantly aide one's understanding of these processes. His original theory shows that social prohibitions, under the given familial and general social conditions, are suited for arresting people's instinctual development at a sadistic

---

[109] The prominence of this problem in "Egoism…" is expressed clearly in a letter Horkheimer wrote to a friend on June 5, 1936, in which he describes the essay as an examination of the "specific type of cruelty that has manifested itself historically in the modern epoch." GS 15, p. 555.

[110] "Egoism…," p. 95.

[111] Ibid., pp. 95–6.

[112] Ibid., pp. 97–8.

level or reverting them back to this level.... The transformation of psychic energies that takes place in the process of introversion cannot be understood today without the psychoanalytic perspective.[113]

Horkheimer also argued, however, that Freud failed to comprehend the specific causes and the dialectical nature of modern cruelty. Whereas Freud viewed civilization as a relative constant necessary to keep the equally constant pressure of innate human aggression in check, Horkheimer maintains that the exceptionally virulent forms of modern aggression result from the exceptionally high level of repression bourgeois society imposes on individuals.[114] This exceptional level of repression may have been justified at one time, but cannot be any longer. But introversion, the "passive and active adjustment of the drives" to socio-economic conditions, never occurs seamlessly, without a "remainder," as Adorno would put it later.[115] We have already seen how the masses were cajoled and forced into relinquishing their own interests and desires, and how they were partially compensated for their sacrifice through the imaginary love of their leader and membership within his community. Yet this recognition by the leader and other members was not enough to ensure social cohesion, particularly in times of crisis. Horkheimer also illustrates how the pain and anger resulting from renunciation is usually deflected from its genuine cause – capitalist social domination and its concrete embodiment in the bourgeois leader – and projected onto a tacitly or explicitly approved object. Those who refuse or appear to refuse to follow the leader or to make the same sacrifices as the rest of his followers are in the most danger of becoming the objects of this form of pathological projection.[116]

Horkheimer illustrates this point historically with a discussion of the French Revolutionary terror. He distinguishes two primary motivations behind the terror: intimidation of one's opponents and the satisfaction of one's own followers. He views the second moment as characteristic of bourgeois society. He writes:

Insofar as this second element plays a role even in such progressive movements as the French Revolution, it corresponds to the deep contempt, the hatred of happiness itself, that is connected with the morally mediated compulsion to asceticism.... If pleasure, or even just the capacity for pleasure, which they have had to fight in themselves since their youth, is so ruinous, then those who embody this vice and remind one of it ... should also be extinguished so that the source of scandal disappears and one's own renunciation is confirmed.... Behind the hatred of the courtesan, the contempt for aristocratic existence, the rage over Jewish immorality, over Epicureanism and materialism is hidden a deep erotic resentment which demands the death of their representatives.... This brutality toward personal destiny ... is made plain for all to see by the guillotine, which

---

[113] Ibid., p. 103–4.

[114] This is an argument that Herbert Marcuse would develop in more detail some twenty years later in his *Eros and Civilization*. See *Eros and Civilization*, op. cit., pp. 31–49 and 71–80.

[115] Adorno elaborates on this point at some length in his essay "Zum Verhältnis von Soziologie und Psychologie," *Soziologische Schriften*, vol. 1, ed. Rolf Tiedemann (Frankfurt: Suhrkamp, 1972), pp. 42–85.

[116] On Horkheimer and Adorno's concept of "pathological projection," see the "Elements of Anti-Semitism," in the *Dialectic of Enlightenment*, op. cit., p. 187f.

moreover gives the masses the blissful feeling of omnipotence by virtue of their own negative principle having attained power. The guillotine symbolizes negative equality … which is identical with its opposite: utter contempt for the person.[117]

It is important to reiterate what Horkheimer saw as specifically bourgeois about this type of terror. The first is the historically specific levels of repression, which increased greatly for the masses as they were forcefully integrated into bourgeois society, but which became increasingly unnecessary after its triumph and further development. The second, and perhaps more important characteristic of bourgeois cruelty, is its systematic, instrumental nature. In a letter to a friend written while he was still conceptualizing "Egoism…," Horkheimer identified the problem of *rationalized cruelty* as one of his central concerns. He wrote: "The cruelty that has manifested itself historically, and the present provides us with new examples of it every day, has been, at least during the past half-millennium, *rationalized* cruelty; it is terror 'in the name of' God, the nation, etc."[118] Horkheimer was by no means denying the existence of cruelty and aggression as normal components of the human psyche. As we have seen, it was precisely those bourgeois thinkers that had a rosy view of human nature – such as Rousseau – who were the most energetic defenders of idealist morality. Horkheimer argued instead that cruelty and aggression become particularly destructive at both the individual and collective level, when their existence is dishonestly repressed and then yoked to the particularist interests of bourgeois leaders. If the existence of cruelty and repression were squarely acknowledged as a normal component of human psychic life, they would lose their unconscious power to seize control of individuals' lives and also – even more ominously – to be instrumentalized "in the name of" dubious collective goals.

Anyone familiar with *Dialectic of Enlightenment* will recognize the similarity of Horkheimer's arguments here about cruelty to his later analysis of the "dark authors" of the bourgeoisie in the chapter on "Juliette, or Enlightenment and Morality." His introductory essay to the *Studies on Authority and Family* and "Egoism…" does in fact represent an important shift in Horkheimer's understanding of Nietzsche in particular. Horkheimer does not mention the Marquis de Sade – the second main figure in the "Juliette…" chapter – explicitly in "Egoism…," but he does discuss him in the letter mentioned earlier.[119] Although it seems like Horkheimer would use de Sade as an example of the unconscious power that sadism comes to possess in bourgeois society – as he would argue later in the *Dialectic of Enlightenment* – Horkheimer views de Sade at this point as a precursor of Nietzsche, insofar as he also recognized cruelty – even enjoying cruelty – as a "normal" component of human psychic life. By admitting this normality, Nietzsche and de Sade were supposedly able

---

[117] "Egoism…," pp. 101–2 (emphasis Horkheimer's own). Horkheimer was by no means the first to analyze the link between ascetic morality and terror. Hegel also saw a link between the abstract morality of Rousseauian and Kantian provenance and the terror of the French Revolution. See, for example, "Die absolute Freiheit und der Schrecken," in his *Phenomenology of Spirit*.

[118] GS 15 p. 460

[119] GS 15, pp. 459–61.

to defuse the potential manifestation of more virulent or systematic forms of cruelty. The two of them made it possible, according to Horkheimer,

> To see that the elimination of repression, the non-ideological consciousness of the natural connection between cruelty and pleasure is precisely what makes it possible to break this connection in real life. It becomes possible to place this pleasure in a rational relationship to other desires and to integrate it into the overall economy of one's life. It loses the universal, overpowering energy that dominates the individual's entire being from the depths of the soul.[120]

Although this argument seems hardly to apply to de Sade, Horkheimer does point to de Sade's refusal to condone the death penalty to make his point. Horkheimer's references to Nietzsche's "harmless" life, which offered such a dramatic contrast to his epigones' pompous interpretation of the *Übermensch* in terms of the "philistine bourgeois' wildest dreams,"[121] is more convincing. In any case, Horkheimer's praise here for the "dark authors" of the bourgeoisie is not grounded in an apology of sadism, but in the psychoanalytic argument that raising sadistic impulses to the level of consciousness and accepting them as such, robs them of the destructive power they come to possess when they are repressed and then instrumentalized by bourgeois leaders.[122] Horkheimer's social-psychological interpretations of cruelty in "Egoism..." represent the first nuanced articulation of positions that would continue to inform much of his own individual work and that of other Institute members, as well as some of the collective projects of the Institute. Horkheimer's arguments were crucial, for example, for the analysis of anti-Semitism in *Dialectic of Enlightenment* as well as the theoretical foundations of the *Studies in Prejudice*. Leo Lowenthal would draw on them in his analysis of anti-Semitism among American workers, and Horkheimer would reformulate them theoretically for an English audience in his *Eclipse of Reason*.[123]

The continued importance for the Institute members' later work of Horkheimer's historical analysis of bourgeois anthropology in "Egoism..." illustrates once again that Horkheimer wrote the piece with a view to contemporary problems, such as the decline of the European workers' movement and the rise of fascism. Yet in "Egoism..." itself, Horkheimer remains rather vague about the specific implications of his analysis of the bourgeois character for analyzing these problems. One notable exception, which also provides us with a final example of Horkheimer's use of psychoanalysis in "Egoism...," is his brief examination of the "affirmative character of culture."[124] Erich Fromm had shown in the "Dogma of Christ" that a series of political defeats had led to an internalization and spiritualization of the originally militant demands of the early Christians.[125] Similarly, Horkheimer argued in "Egoism..." that the

---

[120] Ibid.

[121] "Egoism...," p. 109.

[122] Ibid.

[123] See the chapter on the "Revolt of Nature," in *Eclipse of Reason* (New York, 1974), pp. 92–127.

[124] "Egoism...," p. 99. These brief remarks on culture in "Egoism..." would serve as the point of departure for Herbert Marcuse's full-length essay "The Affirmative Character of Culture," which was published the following year in volume 6 of the *Zeitschrift*.

[125] See Chapter 5, p. 206.

development of the bourgeois institution of culture – which, as Walter Benjamin also noted,[126] lent art a fetishistic "aura" and systematically denied its connections to concrete socio-historical conditions – and its uncritical acceptance by Social Democratic leaders had also contributed to the weakening and ultimate defeat of the workers' movement in Europe. Horkheimer writes:

The necessity to move the greatest part of society by spiritual practices to a renunciation which is necessitated not by external nature but by the organization of society into classes gives the whole cultural thinking of the age an ideological character.... To the extent that other goals, satisfactions and joys would develop, these would completely lack the character of the higher, more noble and sublime, which today invests all spiritual [*geistig*] and so-called cultural endeavors in contrast to materialistic non-internalized desires.... The preservation of aesthetic, literary and philosophical elements of the past epoch does not mean the conservation of the ideological context in which they stood.... This undialectical view, which naively adopts the bourgeois notion of culture, ascetic scale of priorities, and concept of morality but remains ignorant of its great artistic achievements, has dominated the reform efforts of even the progressive nineteenth-century political parties to this very day, made thinking shallow, and ultimately contributed to defeat.[127]

Apart from these brief remarks on the compensatory function of culture as a bourgeois institution, which contributed to the weakening of the European workers' movement, Horkheimer has relatively little to say in "Egoism…" about the state of bourgeois anthropology in the present and its relation to contemporary political crises. In his discussion of early modern bourgeois freedom movements, Horkheimer's attention to demagogic public speech, pompous symbols and ceremonies, and the social-psychological mechanisms underlying virulent forms of prejudice certainly reflected the methods of domination being used by fascist groups at the time. However, Horkheimer's only explicit remarks about fascism in "Egoism…" come in the context of a discussion of the differences between mass action in revolutionary and counterrevolutionary movements. Horkheimer argues that the former are usually guided by the most conscious wing of the movement, whereas in the latter, the masses regress into an undifferentiated mob. With a view to the present Horkheimer writes:

The question of whether the uprisings that have taken place in the most recent past in some European states are to be classified more as one or the other kind of historical events … is not as easily answerable as it may appear to be from a liberal perspective. At any rate, what are involved here are not absolutist or clerical reactions but the staging of a bourgeois pseudo-revolution with radical populist trappings, wholly contrary to any possible reorganization of society. The forms they take seem to be a bad imitation of the movements previously discussed.[128]

As Herbert Marcuse had already done before him, and in accord with the Institute's overall analysis of fascism, Horkheimer refused to see fascism as a

---

[126] In his well-known essay, "The Work of Art in the Age of Mechanical Reproduction," Walter Benjamin, *Illuminations*, op. cit., pp. 217–52.

[127] "Egoism…," pp. 99–100.

[128] Ibid., p. 97.

radical break with bourgeois society.[129] Horkheimer's far-sighted analysis of the mechanisms within bourgeois society that reappear in fascism are one of the main reasons why the essay is still worth reading today. However, in order to get a more detailed picture of how Horkheimer viewed the contemporary state of bourgeois anthropology and its implications for recent political problems, one needs to turn to the Institute's collective project, *Studies on Authority and Family*.

Before continuing, however, let us briefly examine the changed significance of Nietzsche for Horkheimer that emerges in "Egoism...." Despite positive references to Nietzsche in some of his earliest writings, Horkheimer was, for the most part, hostile to Nietzsche from his youthful novellas and plays through *Dämmerung*. For example, in several of his early novellas, such as "Irene" and "The Insurrectionist," one finds negative portrayals of characters who believe themselves to be "*Übermenschen*," and who feel no compassion in the face of the suffering of others.[130] Horkheimer was clearly sympathetic to Schopenhauer's defense of compassion for the creaturely suffering of humans and all living beings as the foundation of an ethics that went beyond metaphysically grounded imperatives. Yet the critique of Schopenhauer's notion of *Mitleid*, which Nietzsche read more in terms of pity than compassion, had been central to Nietzsche's work, from his early essay on "Schopenhauer as Educator" to *Thus Spake Zarathustra*, in which overcoming the "love of man" was Zarathustra's final and most difficult obstacle to becoming an *Übermensch*. Horkheimer's continued rejection of Nietzsche's position comes through clearly in *Dämmerung*, in aphorisms such as "Concerning Resentment" or "Nietzsche and the Proletariat." As becomes clear from his letters,[131] however, Horkheimer studied Nietzsche more carefully in the following years, and the results of this study are clearly apparent in his introductory essay to the *Studies on Authority and Family* and in "Egoism...."[132] Horkheimer had since come to view Nietzsche as one of the most insightful critics of idealist morality, even though the grounds of his critique remained ultimately unsatisfactory for Horkheimer. Thus, instead of simply rejecting Nietzsche's concept of *ressentiment* as elitist ideology, Horkheimer has, through his analysis of the mechanisms underlying bourgeois anthropology, provided a materialist explanation of the same phenomenon. Horkheimer now praised Nietzsche for his own acute analysis of *ressentiment*, even though he failed to identify its socio-historical roots or the concrete possibility of diminishing its dangerous effects through political change.[133] This more appreciative – and dialectical – assessment of Nietzsche

---

[129] See Marcuse's essay, "The Struggle Against Liberalism in the Totalitarian View of the State," in *Negations*, op. cit., pp. 3–42.

[130] GS 1, pp. 141–6 and 209–17. See also the discussion of Horkheimer's attitude toward Nietzsche at this time in Chapter 1, pp. 47–8.

[131] See, for example, GS 15, p. 459.

[132] See also Horkheimer's defense of Nietzsche in his highly critical review of Karl Jasper's *Nietzsche: Einführung in das Verständnis seines Philosophierens*, which was published as "Bemerkungen zu Jaspers' *Nietzsche*," in vol. 6 of the *ZfS* (1937), pp. 407–14, and was also republished in GS 4, 226–35.

[133] "Egoism...," p. 109.

would remained unchanged through *Dialectic of Enlightenment* and into Horkheimer's postwar writings.

THE *STUDIES ON AUTHORITY AND FAMILY* AND THE CONTEMPORARY STATE OF BOURGEOIS ANTHROPOLOGY

We turn now to the *Studies on Authority and Family*, which was published in Paris in 1936 by Felix Alcan, the same house that would publish the Institute's *Zeitschrift* until the National Socialist invasion of France in 1940. Although Horkheimer and Fromm had already begun an empirical study of the German working class in 1929, and the *Studies on Authority and Family* was intended primarily as a preliminary report on a project that was still under way, it did, nonetheless, represent the first collective research project published by the Institute and thus the first realization of Horkheimer's call, in his inaugural address five years earlier, to carry out interdisciplinary, empirical research projects in which theoretical insights are tested and then reformulated or made more precise in light of the results.[134] Rather than presenting a summary of the *Studies* as a whole, which has already been done elsewhere,[135] we will examine its significance for understanding Horkheimer's concept of bourgeois anthropology. It is not a coincidence that Horkheimer began writing his essay "Egoism and Freedom Movements" directly after the *Studies* were published. As we shall see, the theoretical arguments and empirical findings presented in the *Studies* served as an important point of departure for Horkheimer's analysis of bourgeois anthropology. Although the *Studies* also contain an important historical dimension, much of the empirical research on which it was based focused on recent developments in various European societies. Erich Fromm's analysis of the sadomasochistic character structure, which was an important theoretical source of Horkheimer's concept of bourgeois anthropology, focused on what he considered the predominant psychological personality type in *contemporary* society. Like Fromm, Horkheimer believed character structures were formed historically, and one had to reconstruct the life experience of individuals or groups of individuals in order to understand their nature and function. Thus, Horkheimer's reconstruction of the historical development of bourgeois anthropology can also be seen as an attempt to extend and explain the findings first presented in the *Studies*. Therefore we will first examine Fromm's important theoretical essay,[136] because it presents the social-psychological

---

[134] "The Present Situation of Social Philosophy...," op. cit., p. 9.

[135] See Jay, *The Dialectical Imagination*, op. cit., pp. 124–33; and Wiggershaus, *Die Frankfurter Schule*, op. cit., pp. 171–8.

[136] The importance of Fromm's introductory essay in the *Studies* – called simply its "Social-Psychological Part" – was widely recognized, both at the time and later. Rolf Wiggershaus called it "the best thing that Fromm ever wrote" (*Die Frankfurter Schule*, op. cit., p. 173), and Herbert Marcuse continued to refer it as approvingly into the 1970s – i.e. even after his heated debates with Fromm in the preceding decades – as one of the most important texts of early Critical Theory. See, for example, Herbert Marcuse, *Toward a Critical Theory of Society*, ed. D. Kellner (London and New York, 2001), p. 170. Remarkably and unfortunately, this essay has not yet been published in English translation.

assumptions that not only guided the *Studies*, but also informed Horkheimer's subsequent investigations of bourgeois anthropology.[137] Next, we will turn to Horkheimer's own introductory essay for the *Studies* in order briefly to explain the role of the concepts of authority and family in his conception of bourgeois anthropology. Finally, we will cast a glance on the preliminary empirical findings of the *Studies* in order to assess the applicability of Horkheimer's concept of bourgeois anthropology to contemporary European societies.

Fromm's analysis of the sadomasochistic character begins with a discussion of the same psychological mechanism that Horkheimer placed in the center of his analysis of the bourgeois character, namely *introversion*. Fromm explains how introversion is related to the psychoanalytic concept of the superego. He shows how the superego represents in the individual's psyche the internalization of external familial and social forces. Precisely this introversion of external forces or external authority is what makes the superego an important step forward in the process of human civilization, according to Freud, insofar as it enforces necessary social prohibitions and does so from *within* each individual's psyche. Fromm points out that this internalization of authority also changes the way it functions, insofar as authority is now largely based on willing, subjective recognition rather than the threat of external force.[138] However, once authority is internalized and willingly accepted in this way, it becomes an integral part of the individual's psyche, and subject to all the other conscious and unconscious forces at work there. Fromm argues that most forms of authority, particularly the irrational forms that dominate the sadomasochistic character, have a heavy emotional component. He writes,

What is decisive in the relationship of the ego to the superego, as with the relationship of the individual to the authorities, is its emotional character. The person wants to feel loved by its superego as well as by the authorities, it fears their enmity and satisfies its self-love, when he pleases his superego or the authorities, with whom he identifies.[139]

Fromm clarifies this point by introducing a distinction between real fear and fear of authority. The former is based on a "clearly defined fear with a concrete consequence, which the forbidden action would have."[140] In other words, real fear is consciously processed, the person is aware of its object and can reflect upon its possible consequences. Fear of authority, on the other hand, operates through repression [*Verdrängung*], in the technical psychoanalytic sense,[141] and thus remains largely unconscious, because the superego censors the source of

---

[137] In "Egoism and Freedom Movements," Horkheimer explicitly cites Erich Fromm's introductory essay to the *Studies on Authority and Family* as having provided an analysis of the psychological structure produced through the interaction of the bourgeois leader with his followers. See "Egoism...," p. 67. The subsequent analysis of Fromm's will make clear just how similar Horkheimer's analysis of bourgeois anthropology was to Fromm's analysis of the sadomasochistic or authoritarian character.

[138] Thus, a prisoner who continues to despise his captor would not be a good example of authority, as Fromm points out. Fromm quotes Georg Simmel here, who also argued that authority must contain a moment of voluntary recognition. *Studien*, p. 79.

[139] *Studien*, p. 95.

[140] Ibid., p. 96.

[141] See Freud's essay "Die Verdrängung," in his *Gesammelte Werke*, vol. 10, pp. 248–61.

the fear before one can rationally reflect on it. Real fear and fear of authority represent two possible ways of coming to terms with one's drives. With
the former, the drives are more or less integrated into the ego; if the drive
is not acted upon, it is as a result of conscious reflection and judgment, or
what Freud called condemnation [*Verurteilung*].[142] With the latter, the drives
remain external to the ego; the superego protects the person from the impulse
by automatically repressing it, that is, by ensuring it never emerges from the
unconscious and never becomes an object of rational reflection. Furthermore,
because the authority represented by the superego has been internalized and
operates automatically, its legitimacy also remains exempt from rational criticism. In other words, the authority based on repression is accepted willingly,
but the reasons for doing so are unexamined and emotional, not the product
of conscious reflection.[143]

In his essay on repression, Freud had already emphasized the dangers
associated with it. He wrote:

The instinct-presentation [*Triebrepräsentanz*] develops in a more unchecked and
luxuriant fashion if it is withdrawn by repression from conscious influence. It proliferates in the dark, so to speak, and takes on extreme forms of expression, which when
translated and revealed to the neurotic are bound not merely to seem alien to him, but
to terrify him by the way in which they reflect an extraordinary and dangerous strength
of instinct. This illusory strength of instinct is the result of an uninhibited development
of it in fantasy and of the damming-up resulting from the denial of real satisfaction.[144]

Fromm takes seriously Freud's description of the potentially dangerous
consequences of repression that result when internal impulses are automatically rejected by a superego that has usurped the place of a weak ego, which is
no longer capable of acting on, deferring, or rejecting those impulses based on
conscious reflection. Fromm's argument as a whole is indeed heavily indebted
to Freud – as he himself emphasizes[145] – but he disagrees with Freud on the
crucial point of the *origins* of the pathological superego and the concomitant
weakening of the ego. For Freud, the superego is formed within the familial
constellation of the Oedipal conflict. It represents the internalization of the
authority of the father. Because Freud tended to naturalize the bourgeois family,
he viewed this intrafamilial process as an ahistorical norm that one could use
to measure various types of pathological deviation. Fromm, on the other hand,
insisted that the bourgeois family was a product of bourgeois society as a

---

[142] For this distinction, see Freud's essay, "Die Verdrängung," op. cit., p. 248.

[143] Fromm's argument here was similar, if not identical to the important distinction Horkheimer
made in his introductory essay to the *Studies* between rational and irrational authority. See
Studies, pp. 47–9.

[144] Freud, "Repression," in *A General Selection from the Works of Sigmund Freud*, ed. J. Rickmann,
trans. C.M. Baines (New York, 1957), p. 90 (translation amended).

[145] Fromm states at the beginning of the essay that Freud is the "only psychologist who can serve
as a guide," and his categories are the "only ones useful, because of their dynamic character
and because he treated the problem of authority directly and produced important and fruitful
insights." Such strong praise of Freud would become increasingly rare in Fromm's work, since
he was slowly moving away from orthodox Freudianism toward a "revisionist" position during
this time. See Excursus I.

whole, and that the internalization of paternal authority must be understood in terms of specific socio-historical conditions.[146] He writes:

> But he [Freud] overlooked the fact that … first and foremost the family represents certain social norms and that the most important social function of the family lies in conveying these norms, and not just in the sense of conveying opinions and attitudes, but in producing socially desired character structures. Freud's theory of the super-ego suffers from this deficit.[147]

Fromm criticizes Freud's overly static theory of superego formation not only by pointing to the social role played by the family. He also draws once again on Freud's distinction between inherited sexual constitution and the psychologically formative influence of life experiences in order to stress the importance of social factors in maintaining the superego, particularly beyond childhood. Freud also wrote that the structure of the superego was influenced by extra-familial factors as one grows older, but he placed much more emphasis on its formation during the early years. Fromm argues instead that, despite the importance of the early formation of the superego in the family, it by no means remains unchanged throughout one's later life. The maintenance of the superego must be overtaken to a large degree by forces outside of the family, forces in society itself. In short, Fromm argues both that the father is a representative of a specific social constellation and that society plays a direct and decisive role in determining the structure of the superego later in life. Accordingly, in his introductory essay for the *Studies on Authority and Family*, Fromm pointed to the *social conditions* that gave rise to excessive repression, weak egos, and sadomasochistic character structures.

Thus, the next logical step in Fromm's argument would clearly be a description of the specific factors in contemporary societies that play a decisive role in determining individuals' character structures. Fromm did make some important remarks about conditions in contemporary societies and their effect on character formation, but it was the purpose of the empirical part of the *Studies* to explore these factors in more detail. We will return to the preliminary results of this empirical research soon, but let us first conclude our examination of Fromm's theoretical remarks. Like Horkheimer, Fromm stressed the unequal distribution of satisfaction in capitalist societies, with the dominant class being encouraged to pursue its interests while the dominated class was forced or "encouraged" in various ways to sacrifice its own. There was no question for Fromm that in modern capitalist societies in general "the dependent class must repress its drives to a greater degree than the dominant class."[148] In fact, for the

---

[146] In the preceding years, Fromm had conducted extensive research on maternal right theory, which he also used to argue – as Engels had done fifty years before – that the specific social and legal forms of the bourgeois, patriarchal family were a creation of modern capitalism. See Erich Fromm, "Robert Briffaults Werk über das Mutterrecht," *ZfS*, vol. 2, pp. 382–7 and "Die Sozialpsychologische Bedeutung der Mutterrechtstheorie," *ZfS*, vol. 3, pp. 196–226. Friedrich Engels's, "The Origin of the Family, Private Property and the State," in *The Marx-Engels Reader*, op. cit., pp. 734–59.

[147] *Studien*, p. 87.

[148] Ibid., p. 101.

great majority of the lower classes, the level of external repression is so high, according to Fromm, that it renders impossible the development of egos strong enough to cope with their drives in a conscious and rational manner. The external demands placed upon the ego are so great, that the individual is able to satisfy his internal impulses only to a very limited extent. In order to protect himself from repeated demands of drives that must consistently be refused – so that he can meet the external demands imposed upon him – the individual is forced increasingly to repress his impulses. As a result, there is little opportunity for the conscious integration of drives. Furthermore, because these impulses are internalized automatically for the most part, even the pain caused by internalization, the knowledge of the source of the pain, and the desire to resist it are all banned from consciousness. This process results in the paradoxical situation that, in order to protect themselves from their own drives, oppressed groups often identify with the representatives of the social forces that make this surplus repression necessary in the first place. This identification buttresses the mechanisms of repression and provides alternative, socially sanctioned satisfactions for the thwarted impulses. The resulting character structure Fromm identifies as *masochistic*, and he argues that it is "prevalent to such an extent among the majority of people in our society, that for researchers who view the character of bourgeois man as 'normal,' it does not even become an object of scientific inquiry."[149] Fromm contrasts this masochistic-authoritarian character with an ideal type of the "healthy" genital character, which has a strong ego and is able to process the demands of her drives consciously.[150] Although Fromm's use of the genital character is based on Freud's teleological model of psychosexual development, which has been rightfully criticized,[151] its problematic

[149] Ibid., p. 113.

[150] Fromm does not, in other words, advocate a mere abstract negation of repression in the sense of indiscriminately freeing or affirming the drives. In this sense, he also agrees with Horkheimer, insofar as he does not posit a Rousseauian vision of positive human nature that has been enslaved by civilization and simply needs to be liberated. Fromm criticizes Wilhelm Reich along these lines, for placing too much faith in the emancipatory power of unrepressed sexuality independent of other social or psychological factors. Fromm does not advocate replacing the superego with the id as the new unquestioned master of the ego. He argues instead that only by strengthening the ego is it possible to defuse the destructive power and break the irrational compulsion that results from repression, because only a strong ego is capable of integrating the drives, which leads to greater individual autonomy. See *Studien*, p. 113.

[151] Freud assumes that the psychological development of a "healthy" individual progresses teleologically from the polymorphous perversity of the chaotic partial drives characteristic of a newborn child, through the oral and anal phases, and finally to the centrally organized concentration of the libido on the genitals, which characterizes the "mature" "genital character." Freud often explained psychic disorders in terms of a failure to adequately complete this cycle of development. Fromm follows this model quite closely in his essay, which leads him to posit a high correlation between authoritarianism and homosexuality. Fromm does point out that authoritarian behavior is often the result of *repressed* homosexual desires, which then manifest themselves unconsciously or surreptitiously. Fromm also points out that "the extent to which the sado-masochistic character is linked to homosexuality is an issue that has not been clarified in many respects" (*Studien*, p. 125). Fromm's argument was, unfortunately, fairly widespread among the German left in thirties, which often attacked the National Socialists by accusing them of being an openly or latent homosexual organization. See, for example, M. Burleigh and W. Wippermann, *The Racial State: Germany 1933–45* (Cambridge, UK, 1991), p. 188. See

aspects do not diminish the force of his main argument, namely that objective social conditions in modern capitalist society make it extremely difficult for the great majority of persons to attain psychic maturity.[152] It is this crucial aspect of Fromm's argument to which Horkheimer alludes in "Egoism…" when he describes the "socially determined sado-masochistic psychic structures" of the petty bourgeois and working masses.[153]

If the masochistic character is as widespread as Fromm would have us believe, the troubling question arises of what happens to all of the libidinal energy that is repressed in order to ensure a minimum of social cohesion and a maximum accumulation of capital. As we have already seen, Freud insisted that this energy does not simply dissipate, but "proliferates in the dark … and takes on extreme forms of expression."[154] The constant repression of his libidinal impulses causes the masochistic individual to suffer, which would normally

also Andrew Hewitt, "The Frankfurt School and the Political Pathology of Homosexuality," in his *Political Inversions: Homosexuality, Fascism and the Modernist Imaginary* (Stanford, CA, 1996), pp. 38–78. Hewitt's critique focuses primarily on Adorno, who, like Fromm, posited a link between repressed homosexual impulses and hyper-masculine behavior, even fascism. Hewitt identifies the latent and manifest homophobia in some of Adorno's arguments, but he tends to exaggerate the significance of the problem for Adorno and for Critical Theory as a whole. He writes, for example, "The confrontation with homosexuality is the definitive and destructive crisis in the Frankfurt School's whole Freudo-Marxist project" (p. 77). He himself points out that Herbert Marcuse did not make the same mistakes as Adorno. He does not examine Adorno's critique of homophobia in "Sexual Taboos and Law Today" (Theodor Adorno, *Critical Models: Interventions and Catchwords*, trans. Henry W. Pickford, New York, 1998, pp. 71–88) nor the young Adorno's own erotically charged relationship with Siegfried Kracauer: Theodor W. Adorno / Siegfried Kracauer, *Briefwechsel 1923–1966*, ed. Wolfgang Schopf (Frankfurt: Suhrkamp, 2008). Hewitt does not discuss Horkheimer either, but it seems like Horkheimer's critique of "bourgeois anthropology" anticipated and could still contribute to discussions in feminist, gender, and queer theory of the construction and consequences of the rigid bourgeois subjectivity. For my own attempt to delineate the critical from the anachronistic aspects of Freud's theory of sexuality – and Fromm's appropriation of it – see Excursus 1.

[152] Kant's demand, in his famous essay "What is Enlightenment?" that individuals free themselves from their "selbstverschuldete Unmündigkeit" (self-imposed immaturity) appears in a new light if one takes Fromm's and Horkheimer's arguments in the *Studies on Authority and Family* seriously. Kant's stress that no one is to blame but himself for his immaturity clearly illustrates the Institute's claims about the transformed function of bourgeois cultural norms in modern European history. The internalization of paternal authority, the development of a strict conscience, which found its most dramatic expression in the Protestant tradition of self-excoriation, may have served a progressive function during the early modern period, but it becomes increasingly irrational with the development of capitalist society. Horkheimer writes, "For the formation of the authority-oriented character it is especially decisive that the children should learn, under pressure from the father, not to trace every failure back to its social causes, but to remain at the level of the individual and to hypostatize the failure in religious terms as sin or in naturalistic terms as deficient endowment. The outcome of such paternal education is men who always seek fault in themselves. At times this has been a productive trait, namely as long as the fate of the individual and the common good both depended, at least in part, on the efficiency of the individual. In the present age, however, a compulsive sense of guilt … renders fruitless any criticism of the real causes of trouble" (Max Horkheimer "Authority and Family," in *Critical Theory*, op. cit., p. 109).

[153] "Egoism…," p. 79.

[154] Freud, "Repression," op. cit., p. 90.

lead to anger against the persons or institutions imposing this repression. Yet because this person is the same one upon whom the individual depends for his self-worth, he must find another object for this anger and aggression. This dynamic of displacement is the reason instances of sadism are so widespread and often so brutal in societies with high levels of repression. Sadism and masochism are inseparable, according to Fromm. He writes:

Psychoanalytic research has demonstrated that a character structure that contains masochism also necessarily contains sadism.... Since the strengthening of one side, the masochistic side, for example, strengthens the entire structure, the other drive-instantiation [*Triebinstanz*] will also and necessarily be intensified in the process. This has the important social psychological consequence that a society, which produces sado-masochism as the dominant instinctual structure, must provide possibilities for satisfying both sides of sado-masochism.[155]

Fromm points out that the authorities themselves must also pay heed to this dynamic, and must provide their followers with a means of satisfying their sadistic impulses, or else their legitimacy could begin to crumble and the impulses could be directed against the authorities themselves.[156] These impulses are satisfied in most cases by directing them against the weak and defenseless in one's own society, but if this is not enough, other "solutions" can also be found. Fromm writes:

One must repress hatred against those who are stronger, but one can enjoy being cruel to those who are weaker.... women, children and animals play an extremely important social psychological role in this regard. If they prove to be insufficient, then objects of sadism can be artificially created, by throwing slaves or captured enemies into the arena, or members of a class or racial minorities.[157]

Fromm's comments here demonstrate not only the strong affinities of his analysis of the social-psychological origins of sadism with Horkheimer's analysis of similar tendencies in the bourgeois character in "Egoism...," but they also make it clear why both essays would continue to serve as a crucial reference point for the Institute's later work on anti-Semitism and prejudice more generally. In short, there can be no doubt that Fromm's *psychoanalytic* examination of the sadomasochistic or authoritarian character,[158] which he viewed as the dominant character type in contemporary Europe, served as an important point of departure for Horkheimer's *historical* analysis of bourgeois anthropology.

---

[155] *Studien*, pp. 114–5.
[156] The link to Horkheimer's analysis of the bourgeois leader in "Egoism..." is particularly clear here. As we have seen, Horkheimer pointed to the fact that the bourgeois leader enlisted the aid of the masses by promising to serve their interests, only to discount these interests as soon as the masses had swept him into power. If the bourgeois leader was not able to provide sufficient compensation for these thwarted interests, he could soon become the victim of the masses' fury which, as we have seen, was the case with Rienzo, Savonarola, and Robespierre.
[157] Ibid., p. 117.
[158] At this point in Fromm's career, and in the development of Critical Theory more generally, the terms "sado-masochistic character" and "authoritarian character" were used more or less interchangeably. See Wiggershaus, op. cit., p. 176.

The very title of the *Studies* leads us to our next question: Why are authority and family crucial for understanding Horkheimer's concept of bourgeois anthropology? In order to answer this question, we need to turn to Horkheimer's own general introductory essay to the *Studies*. He makes it clear from the very beginning that authority and family should not be counted among the most fundamental concepts of a Critical Theory of society, but that they are crucial for understanding the mechanisms that mediate between the material and cultural spheres in modern societies.[159] Ever since his decisive break with consciousness philosophy in the mid-1920s, Horkheimer had insisted that history and society were the fundamental categories of Critical Theory; just as it was impossible to comprehend their objective substance from the subjective standpoint of individual consciousness, so authority and family must also be understood as mediating mechanisms within the larger context of the historical development of bourgeois society. An examination of authority and family held the promise of providing a more precise explanation of the "passive and active adaptation" of individuals' drives to underlying socio-economic forces, as a comparison of the *Studies* with the Institute's first empirical studies on the working class in Germany in 1929 makes clear. In the 1929 study, Horkheimer and Fromm did address the role of authority and, to a lesser degree, the family in some of their questions, but the study as a whole was based on an attempt to establish a *direct* correlation between workers' social standing and their character structures. The *Studies*, on the other hand, take more seriously Horkheimer's remarks in his inaugural address as the new head of the Institute that the *relative autonomy* of cultural and psychological factors vis-à-vis economic forces would be an important consideration in the Institute's future work.[160] To illustrate this point, Fromm includes in his social-psychological essay a quote in which Freud criticizes the "materialist conception of history" for underestimating the importance of the superego in the historical process. Freud writes:

Mankind never lives entirely in the present; in the ideologies of the super-ego the past, and the tradition of the race and the people lives on, all of which give way only slowly to the influences of the present and new developments and will continue to play a powerful role in human life – independent of economic relations – as long as these forces exercise an influence through the super-ego.[161]

Fromm does not disagree with Freud, but he does argue that his criticisms of Marx go too far in discounting the importance of socio-economic factors. Fromm argues that – at least in highly dynamic capitalist societies – these factors remain primary "in the final analysis," but that the relative autonomy of cultural and psychological factors must also be taken into account, insofar as they too can, in the short term, play a decisive role in determining historical developments. Fromm offers a precise psychoanalytic explanation of this

---

[159] *Studien*, p. xii.
[160] "The Present Situation of Social Philosophy...," op. cit., pp. 11f.
[161] *Studien*, p. 91.

"cultural lag" by tracing it back to the powerful libidinal and emotional forces invested in individual character structures.[162]

In the first section of his introductory essay to the *Studies*, Horkheimer also explicitly addressed the relative autonomy of cultural factors. He illustrated the point historically by discussing the caste system in India and the reverence of ancestors in China as two examples of cultural factors that ensure the relative stability of society and also help explain their resistance in modern times to the penetration of the dynamic economic forces coming from the West.[163] Despite these examples, Horkheimer was clearly interested in examining the implications of the relative autonomy of cultural factors for modern Western "bourgeois" society in general, and for the new forms of authoritarianism that had emerged in twentieth-century Europe in particular. Horkheimer was particularly interested in explaining the failure of the German working class to resist the authoritarian chauvinism that had led to the First World War, to carry through a socialist revolution after the war, and to resist the rise of National Socialism in the late 1920s and early 1930s. Horkheimer believed that the economic conditions for a transition to socialism were ripe, but that cultural factors played a decisive role in paralyzing the resistance of the working class. In order to explain these cultural factors and their recent consequences, Horkheimer placed them within the larger context of the bourgeois epoch as a whole. With regard to the concept of authority, for example, we have already seen how, in his lectures on the history of philosophy, Horkheimer explained the crucial role of authority in bourgeois society in terms of the bourgeoisie's desire to liberate itself from the confines of feudalism and absolutism. Philosophical defenses of natural law and reason – which were often articulated in the form of absolute metaphysical principles – provided an alternate standard of authority to which the bourgeoisie could appeal in these political struggles.[164]

In a lecture he gave in Columbia in 1937 on the topic of "Authority and Family," Horkheimer outlined once again the socio-historical specificity of authority in bourgeois society, that is, "that aspect of the category of authority ... which is unique to this entire bourgeois epoch, vis-à-vis other epochs."[165] In the lecture, as in his introductory essay to the *Studies*, Horkheimer differentiates authority in bourgeois society from *force* on the one hand, and *autonomy* on the other; the former is broadly characteristic of the direct relations of servitude (such as slavery or serfdom) found in antiquity and the Middle Ages, and the latter would be the guiding principle of rational and egalitarian social relations in a future, socialist society. Horkheimer characterizes authority in

---

[162] See, for example, "Die psychoanalytische Charakterologie und ihre Bedeutung für die Sozialpsychologie," *ZfS*, vol. 1, p. 268f.

[163] "Authority and the Family," op. cit., pp. 60–5.

[164] See Chapter 3.

[165] GS 12, p. 52. Horkheimer's lecture was part of a lecture series that the Institute was offering at Columbia University in 1937 under the title "Authority and Status in Modern Society." Other persons involved with the Institute more or less directly who gave lectures in this series included Herbert Marcuse, Friedrich Pollock, Erich Fromm, Leo Lowenthal, Franz Neumann, Paul Lazarsfeld, and Julian Gumperz. Sections from Horkheimer's lectures have been published in the twelfth volume of his *Collected Writings*. See Gunzelin Schmid Noerr's editorial remarks in GS 12, p. 39.

bourgeois society primarily in terms of its abstract, economic nature, but he also describes the concrete ways in which it manifests itself. Echoing Marx's account of primitive accumulation, Horkheimer discusses the abstract economic forces that drove landless peasants in the early modern period into the sites of manufacturing and protoindustry. Even though laws were passed later to confine them within the new sites of capitalist production, in the early phases of primitive accumulation no one forced landless peasants to work. It was, rather, a new constellation of abstract economic forces that the dispossessed had to obey in order to survive. Horkheimer writes:

> Whereas earlier the needs and wishes of society were proclaimed by privileged persons and associations, they manifest themselves today through objective economic and social forces ... Authority is no longer a direct relation between persons, but rather a relation mediated by things. Dependence upon anonymous facts has taken the place of dependence upon persons.[166]

Despite assuming the appearance of an abstract, nonpersonal force, the authority imposed on individuals by the capitalist economy remains irrational, according to Horkheimer, because that economy is still dominated by particular interests and is not guided by a rational plan based on the needs and interests of all. Because of this hidden persistence of heteronomy in bourgeois society, the potential of the bourgeois struggle against feudal and absolutist authority turning into its opposite was present from the beginning. Although it was necessary to overcome the feudal order and to establish the material conditions for a higher form of society, the long process of inculcating respect for the facts, which becomes second nature in the bourgeois character, rendered it very difficult for most to imagine an alternative to the increasingly irrational forms of social domination that emerged in the early twentieth century.

One of the most important duties of the family in bourgeois society, according to Horkheimer, is to instill in the next generation this respect for the facts demanded by the abstract form of authority operative in bourgeois society. With an eye to the authoritarian states in power in Europe at the time, Horkheimer describes this crucial role of the family in bourgeois society in the following way:

> The authority of the leader and all the other elements of the authoritarian state only seems to spring directly from the love of the leader. In reality the leader and his apparatus ... have massive means of power at their disposal. But these means of power are an expression of the fact that this dictatorial government has now become a solid and mighty fact, which will destroy the individual as soon as he calls it into question.... The authority, which these leading personalities and their apparatus enjoy, is itself built upon and really only conceivable in relation to the psychological character structures of the masses, which obey it.... It is constructed upon the sense for the authority of facts.... But people bring this sense with them already from their childhoods; in the states in question here, it is conveyed to them in their familial socialization. This is the reason why everything is done in these states to promote a strong and authoritarian family life.[167]

[166] Ibid., p. 57.
[167] Ibid., p. 62.

Horkheimer's description here of the relationship between authority and family stresses its essential continuity throughout the bourgeois epoch, and this is indeed his most basic assumption. However, against this more general backdrop of "educating authority-oriented personalities," which belongs to the "traits of the bourgeois family which are inseparable from the foundation of bourgeois society,"[168] Horkheimer also distinguishes between different phases in which the family's transmission of authority to the next generation assumes different forms and functions. For Horkheimer, in other words, "The family in the bourgeois era is no more a single and uniform reality than is, for example, man or the state."[169] Horkheimer's as well as Fromm's discussion of these different phases in the form and function of the family provide an important key to understanding the homologous shifts in the structure of the bourgeois character. Horkheimer argues that "in the bourgeois golden age," there was a more rational and propitious relationship between the authority of the father and the reproduction of bourgeois society as a whole. The father's authority, at least within the bourgeois family, was based on his economically productive role and thus had some rational basis. The father's relatively stable economic position also enabled him to maintain a certain amount of independence for his family vis-à-vis both the state and bourgeois society.[170] In contrast to some of his later essays, in which Horkheimer would differentiate clearly between liberal, monopoly, and state capitalist phases in the nineteenth and early twentieth centuries, he distinguishes here only between a bourgeois "golden age" and the authoritarian states of the present. The latter are characterized by the erosion of the authority of the bourgeois *pater familias* and an increasing, direct intervention of the state in socializing the next generation. So even though the authoritarian governments seem to advocate stronger families, in reality their policies continued to undermine its relative autonomy.[171] In short, the Institute's examination of the family was intended to provide a more precise analysis of the family as one of the key mediating institutions between the material and cultural spheres in bourgeois societies, but ironically, one of the

---

[168] "Authority and Family," op. cit., p. 127.

[169] Ibid.

[170] Horkheimer's description of the relationship between the family, bourgeois society, and the state in the "golden age of the bourgeoisie" follows quite closely Hegel's model in the *Philosophy of Right*, op. cit., pp. 105–22. For Horkheimer, as for Hegel, the family provided a sphere that was protected from the powerful disintegrative forces of bourgeois society. Whereas the latter were determined by the ruthless pursuit of self-interest, the family maintained a sphere in which the interests of the whole were placed above one's own egoistic interests. Socialization in this sphere thus fostered a concern for one's fellow human beings and for society as a whole that served as an important counterweight to the unbounded forces of self-interest that drove, and often threatened to drive apart, bourgeois society. For his part, Marx was much more skeptical about the "relative autonomy" of the family, bourgeois or otherwise. Far from offering any resistance to bourgeois society, Marx believed that the family simply reinforced its particular forms of social domination. See, for example, "The Communist Manifesto," in *The Marx-Engels Reader*, ed. R. Tucker (New York, 1978), pp. 487f. As Martin Jay points out, "The Institute's own approach … mediated between these two perspectives, although tending increasingly toward Marx's more pessimistic one." *The Dialectical Imagination*, op. cit., p. 124.

[171] "Authority and Family," pp. 127–8.

main conclusions of the *Studies* was that the relative autonomy of the family had been in decline during the past few decades.

Both Horkheimer and Fromm distinguish between different phases in the form and function of the family *within* the development of bourgeois society, but it is worth emphasizing once again that these distinctions take place on the larger and ultimately more significant backdrop of the basic characteristics of bourgeois anthropology as a whole. The myth that Horkheimer had ever or had always been an uncritical defender of the patriarchal family, which probably developed as a consequence of the more conservative positions on the family he defended in the postwar period,[172] is refuted by a close reading of his writings from the 1930s. Rolf Wiggershaus is correct to note that in his introductory essay for the *Studies*, "there appeared in Horkheimer's work a tendency to embellish the liberal bourgeois past."[173] However, in contrast to Horkheimer's later work – particularly in the postwar period – this tendency was still rather weak and overshadowed by his critique of bourgeois anthropology as a whole. The fact that Horkheimer developed the concept of bourgeois anthropology – and paid little attention to the rise and fall of a bourgeois "golden age" – in "Egoism and Freedom Movements," which he wrote immediately after the *Studies* were finished, also illustrates this fact. As we have seen, in the early 1930s Erich Fromm was reexamining the long-discussed link between capitalism and the patriarchal bourgeois family. He was convinced that Critical Theory had much to learn from maternal right theory – despite the efforts of reactionaries like Ludwig Klages to appropriate ethnological research on maternal right theory for their own purposes.[174] The most important of these lessons was the fact that the bourgeois, patriarchal family was not natural or eternal. In a letter from October 1936, Horkheimer praised Fromm's essay on maternal right theory for stressing the subordination of happiness to duty in the bourgeois family,[175] and in his introductory essay to the *Studies* his agreement with many of Fromm's other arguments emerges clearly. Horkheimer outlines the continuity of the domination of women in bourgeois society from the belief in "witches," which he describes as a "rationalization for the most frightful terror ever committed against a gender group," right up through the subordination and exploitation of women in the modern bourgeois family, as it is portrayed in the plays of Ibsen and Strindberg.[176] Horkheimer also illustrates how the repression of the mother in the bourgeois family reinforces the reified authority of bourgeois society as a whole. The dependent mother wants what is best for herself and especially her children, so she encourages the ambition

---

[172] See, for example the following notes Horkheimer wrote near the end of his life: "Ist die Pille das Ende der Liebe?" "Ehe, Prostitution, Liebe und die Pille," GS 14, pp. 495–6 and p. 537; "Zerfall der bürgerlichen Ehe," GS 6, pp. 406–7.

[173] *Die Frankfurter Schule*, p. 177.

[174] See his discussion and critique of the contemporary conservative appropriations of maternal right theory in his essay, "Die Sozialpsychologische Bedeutung der Mutterrechtstheorie," in *ZfS*, vol. 3, p. 196f.

[175] GS 15, p. 694.

[176] "Authority and Family," p. 119. See also Horkheimer's aphorism in *Dawn and Decline (Dämmerung)*, "Strindberg's Women," op. cit., pp. 70–1.

and conformity of her husband. The husband must care for his wife and children, so any thought of rebellion also entails putting their lives at risk.[177] Like Fromm, Horkheimer also offers an explanation for the sentimental celebration of the maternal by reactionaries such as Klages; he argues that the dictate of sexual monogamy and the treatment of the mother in the bourgeois family as an "immaculate" being, force the sons strictly to repress any sensual moments that may be contained in their affection for their mother or sisters, which often leads to the return of the repressed in the form of the irrational celebration of a mythical maternal ideal. In short, Horkheimer has no illusions about the deleterious effects of patriarchal dominance, which he views as one important *historical* characteristic of the bourgeois epoch as a whole.[178]

We have been examining the *Studies on Authority and Family* with a view to how it helps us understand Horkheimer's concept of bourgeois anthropology, particularly in relation to more recent historical developments. As the final part of this examination, let us turn now to the preliminary results of the empirical research presented in the *Studies*. It is worth emphasizing at the outset the obvious point that the extensive empirical research and specialized studies from many different disciplines that were conducted in conjunction with the *Studies* illustrate once again the crucial importance of the sciences in general and empirical social research in particular still had in Horkheimer's Critical Theory. Rolf Wiggershaus's claim that the *Studies* showed "how little one could still speak of an interpenetration of constructive and empirical methods" does not hold up under closer scrutiny of the *Studies* – or Horkheimer's subsequent work, for that matter. In his preface to the *Studies*, Horkheimer stresses that the theoretical reflections contained in the first part were developed "in constant interaction with the material contained in the second and third sections and on the basis of a thorough knowledge of the published literature."[179] There is little reason to doubt Horkheimer's claim here, as Wiggershaus does, simply because the theoretical essays in the first part of the *Studies* contain no explicit references to the second and third parts, in which the results of the empirical research and specialized studies are presented. The first section on the empirical results presents some preliminary findings from the study – discussed earlier – on German workers' attitudes in 1929. Members of the Institute had been aware of the most important result of this study long before they began work on the *Studies on Authority and Family*. In fact, the earlier study certainly contributed greatly to their decision to explore the problem of authority – this time with a greater emphasis on the mediating role of the family – in much greater theoretical and empirical depth. Furthermore, the reasons why the empirical results presented in the study were so preliminary and were downplayed by Horkheimer himself were largely external.[180] Some of the research had been lost during the Institute's flight to the United States, and other parts of it had

---

[177] Ibid., p. 120.
[178] For a discussion of Horkheimer's shifting view of the family and its relation to his own biography, see Chapter 9, pp. 418ff.
[179] *Studies*, p. ix.
[180] Ibid., p. x–xii.

run into unexpected difficulties.[181] However, the Institute had every intention not only of continuing the numerous empirical research projects it had initiated in conjunction with the *Studies*, but also starting several new ones in the United States.[182] One of the main reasons why many of these projects were not carried out to completion in the following years was not simply Horkheimer's loss of interest, but the financial crisis of the Institute in the late 1930s, which made it increasingly difficult to finance costly empirical projects.[183] The Institute did, however, continue to look for outside sources of funding for such projects and was eventually successful.[184]

The preliminary results of the empirical research in the *Studies in Authority and Family* itself, presented in the second section, and the short essays on specialized topics, presented in the third section, confirm and complicate Horkheimer's argument in "Egoism..." in interesting ways. Although one should not exaggerate their importance,[185] it is safe to assume that they, along with Erich Fromm's analysis of the sadomasochistic character, played an important role in Horkheimer's decision to explore the *historical* foundations of the anthropology of the bourgeois epoch in the period immediately following the publication of the *Studies*. As already noted, the main findings of the empirical study on the German working class in 1929, which were presented in an extremely truncated form in *Studies on Authority and Family*, had already been familiar to Horkheimer for some time. Its results were confirmed dramatically by the general lack of working-class resistance to the National Socialist seizure of power in 1933. However, the preliminary results presented in the *Studies* of the other empirical projects must also have led Horkheimer to reflect more deeply on the origins and consequences of the bourgeois character. For one of the foundations of the Institute's analysis of fascism at this time was that the conditions for its success had been established by bourgeois society. These other studies confirmed that the essential mechanisms of bourgeois society, which were identified in the introductory essays of the *Studies* and later in "Egoism...," continued to play a central role in contemporary European societies. The picture that began to emerge from the empirical research and the specialized essays was by

---

[181] See Fromm's overview of the empirical section of the *Studies*, ibid., pp. 231–8.

[182] Ibid., p. 234–5. For a discussion of the Institute's empirical research projects in the 1940s, see *The Dialectical Imagination*, pp. 219–52.

[183] This crisis was exacerbated by the additional burden of supporting refugee scholars who were fleeing to the United States in increasing numbers in the late 1930s. For a brief discussion of the Institute's financial crisis in the late 1930s, as well as a list of just a few of the refugee scholars the Institute supported, see *The Dialectical Imagination*, op. cit., p. 167–8.

[184] The Institute developed proposals for two major research projects around 1940. The first, a major project on "German Economy, Politics, and Culture 1900–33," was turned down by the Rockefeller Foundation in 1941. The Institute was, however, eventually successful in obtaining funding from the American Jewish Committee and Jewish Labor Committee for its second major research project on anti-Semitism. In fact, it initiated several different studies of anti-Semitism that culminated in the massive *Studies in Prejudice*. For an overview of the origins of these two projects, see Wiggershaus, pp. 307–13; Jay, *The Dialectical Imagination*, pp. 219–27; and Thomas Wheatland, *The Frankfurt School in Exile*, op. cit., pp. 191–226.

[185] Horkheimer himself emphasized that they had not yet come to any general conclusions based on the material presented in the second and third sections of the *Studies*, (see p. x of his preface), but even the preliminary results permitted some tentative conclusions.

no means uniform, but the differences are perhaps what make the results most interesting. We cannot, of course, recapitulate all of these findings here, so we will focus instead on a few dominant tendencies that emerge quite clearly and that illuminate Horkheimer's concept of bourgeois anthropology.

The results of the empirical research and the specialized studies give the overall impression that the traditional mechanisms of bourgeois anthropology were still functioning smoothly in almost all of the European countries that were investigated. The preliminary results from France, Switzerland, Holland, and Belgium all pointed to a relatively intact bourgeois family that was succeeding in socializing the next generation according to its ideals. Only in Germany, particularly in the postwar period, was there a marked weakening of the bourgeois family, which had both positive and negative consequences. On the one hand, it provided a remarkable opening of German society, an "explosion of modernity"[186] from which many groups – such as women, Jews, avant-garde artists, socialists, communists, homosexuals – who had been oppressed, marginalized, or excluded during the rigidly bourgeois Wilhelmine period greatly benefited; the outsider had become an insider, as one scholar of Weimar culture would put it later.[187] On the other hand, the disintegration of the bourgeois family also led to a troubling growth of conscious and unconscious authoritarian attitudes that would soon lead to a massive backlash against the diverse innovative and emancipatory tendencies in Weimar culture. The forced abduction of Kaiser Wilhelm II at the end of World War I, which could be interpreted in social-psychological terms as a liberation from the restrictive father, led to a brief resurgence – at least among the most advanced segments of Weimar society – of what Erich Fromm had described as matriarchal values. Such values included the privileging of pleasure and happiness over delayed gratification, compassion, solidarity, freedom from guilt and neurotic anxiety, lack of the need to punish oneself or others, cynical disrespect for authorities, democratic openness, ironic playfulness, privileging of freedom over fate, and intellectual and personal independence.[188] Yet the fact that these tendencies remained restricted to a relatively small minority, and the unconscious foundations of the bourgeois character remained intact among the "silent majority" of the population, would soon be demonstrated by the fraternal counterrevolution in 1933.[189] As will become clear presently, these contradictory tendencies largely

---

[186] To borrow the title of a volume on Weimar culture edited by Gérard Raulet, *Weimar, ou L'explosion de la Modernité* (Paris, 1984).

[187] Peter Gay, *Weimar Culture: The Outsider as Insider* (New York, 1968).

[188] See Erich Fromm, "Die Sozialpsychologische Bedeutung der Mutterrechtstheorie," *ZfS*, vol. 3, pp. 208–21.

[189] For an account of the virulently masculinist ideology and psychological character structures of one particularly influential group, the *Freikorps*, which would decisively influence the fraternal counterrevolution in 1933, see Klaus Theweleit, *Male Fantasies*, vol. 1: *Women, Floods, Bodies, History*, trans. Stephan Conway (Minneapolis, 1987) and vol. 2: *Male Bodies: Psychoanalyzing the White Terror*, trans. Erica Carter (Minneapolis, 1989). For a more general account of the psychoanalytic model used here to illuminate the development and demise of Weimar culture in terms of the symbolic murder of the oppressive father, followed by a period of matriarchal liberation, followed in turn by a fraternal counterrevolution

explained Horkheimer's increasing ambivalence about the disintegration of the bourgeois family.

Surveying the results of the empirical research and specialized essays presented in the *Studies* leaves no question about the exceptional status of Germany among the countries investigated. For example, the *Studies* presented the initial findings of an empirical research project on the status of sexual morality in the postwar period in Germany. The responses to the questionnaires, which were distributed in 1932 to doctors specializing in sexually transmitted diseases, gynecology, and neurotic disturbances, indicated that sexual morality had weakened substantially in the postwar period, particularly among women.[190] Almost all the doctors agreed that marital fidelity had declined significantly in the postwar period. Most of the doctors agreed that sexual morality had become stricter again near the end of the Weimar Republic.[191] The preliminary findings of the empirical research on sexual morality in Germany was reinforced by several of the specialized studies presented in the following section. In a short report on an unpublished study on the treatment of the family in the social policies of the German government before World War I, the author stresses the relative strength and continuity of the French bourgeois family vis-à-vis its German counterpart, which was weakened by rapid industrialization and urbanization.[192] In a much lengthier article on the diverse and sometimes contradictory currents in the German youth movement before, during, and after the war, the author also stresses economic modernization in the decades prior to the war as dramatically changing the position of middle-class women in particular, which led to a transformation of bourgeois sexual morality that was greatly accelerated by the crisis of authority at the end of the war.[193] Finally, in a brief survey of the literature of the Weimar Republic, with a view to themes of authority and family, the author also highlights the essentially antiauthoritarian and antibourgeois character of the dominant literary and dramatic works (especially expressionism) in the postwar period through 1923.[194] The dominant literature of the middle period of the Weimar Republic (1924–9) displays an exhaustion with the rebellious pathos of its predecessors and a desire to return to bourgeois stability and normality. The failure of this attempt was expressed in the pessimism and polarization of the final period (1929–33), which prepared the way for the return to authoritarianism after 1933.[195]

Whereas the results of the empirical research and specialized studies left little doubt that authority and family were in crisis in Germany in the postwar period, the results from the other European countries conveyed a very different picture. The empirical research project on sexual morality in Weimar Germany was supplemented by a report on the same topic in Holland written by Horkheimer's

---

and a return to an even stricter model of patriarchal dominance, see Herbert Marcuse, *Eros and Civilization* (Boston, 1955), pp. 50–70.
[190] Ibid., p. 272.
[191] Ibid.
[192] Ibid., p. 653.
[193] Ibid., p. 698.
[194] Ibid., pp. 729–30.
[195] *Studies*, pp. 733–34.

former psychoanalyst and close friend, Karl Landauer.[196] Landauer concluded that bourgeois sexual morality, the bourgeois family, and its ideals more generally were still strong in Holland.[197] Landauer notes, for example, that over half of the doctors trained in Holland (both men and women) waited until they were married to have sex for the first time, which led to couples marrying earlier. However, anyone younger than thirty also had to have express legal consent from their parents to get married, which reinforced their dependence on their parents.[198] The parents' consent to the marriage also brought with it a tacit obligation to support the young couple financially – often well into their adult lives – which also reinforced the couple's dependence on their parents.[199] In Switzerland, the preliminary results of an empirical study that was being carried out by Paul Lazarsfeld and Käthe Leichter on authority and family among teenagers and young adults also confirmed the undisturbed reproduction of the bourgeois character there. In their summary of the results, the authors write:

The great majority of the youth have pronounced bourgeois ideals.... No less than 60 times was "work" given as the purpose of life.... Personal desires do not extend very far. They are bound by a professional and family life that is stabile and free from worries. Only rarely was a wish for pleasure or joy in life ventured.[200]

An empirical study on authority and family among teenagers and young adults was also being undertaken in France at the time, under the guidance of Paul Hönigsheim. At the time the *Studies* were published, 2,651 questionnaires had already been returned in Paris alone. The preliminary results indicated that the bourgeois family remained strong there. The author of the summary writes:

According to the impression conveyed by the results so far, one is tempted to say that the French family has remained untouched.... Time and again one notices a certain astonishment that one is being asked about something as self-evident as the relationship and relations of authority between parents and children. One is part of the family without thinking about it.... The patriarchal structure of the family remains solid.[201]

A report on an unpublished study of governmental policies toward the family in France and Belgium in the third section of the *Studies* also emphasized the positive effects of these policies in the past decades in maintaining the

[196] Landauer had fled from Frankfurt in March 1933, and after a short stay in Sweden, went to Amsterdam, where he was able to reopen his practice in the fall of 1933. Landauer's report on sexual morality in Holland was based on his clinical experiences there, as well as conversations with Dutch colleagues. For a brief overview of Landauer's life prior to 1933, see Chapter 5, pp. 188–89. For a more detailed chronology of Landauer's entire life, see *Theorie der Affekte*, op. cit, pp. 13–23.

[197] Landauer's observations were made almost exclusively in a middle or upper-middle class milieu, and thus may not represent Dutch society as a whole. Nonetheless, when compared with persons from a similar social milieu in Germany, Landauer's observations still highlighted the striking differences between the two countries. Landauer's notes at the beginning of his remarks that the Dutch middle class had not been decimated financially to the same degree as the German middle class, and this certainly explained the differences to some degree. *Studies*, p. 285.

[198] Ibid., p. 287.

[199] Ibid., p. 286.

[200] Ibid., pp. 410, 411–12.

[201] Ibid., pp. 448–9.

bourgeois family.[202] Although empirical research and specialized studies from other countries – most notably, Great Britain and the United States – were also presented, the results were not sufficient to permit even cautious generalizations.

Despite the preliminary nature of the material presented in the second and third sections of the *Studies*, the differences between Germany and the other European countries emerge clearly enough to warrant further reflection on their relationship to, and possible effects on, Horkheimer's concept of bourgeois anthropology. Many of the findings, particularly in the countries in which the bourgeois family was still strong, anticipated some aspects of Horkheimer's analysis of the bourgeois character in "Egoism...": the tendencies toward self-denial, preoccupation with work and duty, and unconscious acceptance of the authority of the father. However, some of the other findings also clearly led to Horkheimer's increasing ambivalence about the bourgeois family, which is hardly noticeable in "Egoism...." It was tentatively expressed in his introductory essay to the *Studies* and would gain increasing prominence in his later thought. Although very far from ideal, the bourgeois family did at least, when it was functioning properly, provide a space that was relatively autonomous from the thinly veiled *bellum omnium contra omnes* of bourgeois society, and which offered not only the possibility of developing autonomous subjectivity, but also, largely due to the self-sacrifice of the loving mother, a glimpse of the possibility of nonantagonistic human relations in a postcapitalist society. As we have seen, Horkheimer's recognition of the positive aspects of the bourgeois family always occurred against the larger backdrop of its function in reproducing the forms of social domination inherent to bourgeois society as a whole, but he was also increasingly concerned with the fateful repercussions of the liquidation of the bourgeois family within this larger context. This is why the divergent results of the empirical research and specialized studies in Germany were particularly important for Horkheimer. In retrospect, one can see that Horkheimer's model of bourgeois anthropology was just as heavily, if not more heavily influenced by the bourgeois family in crisis in Germany than it was by the more or less properly functioning bourgeois family in the rest of Europe. The results from Germany were contradictory. On the one hand, the dissolution of the bourgeois family had led to greater freedom, particularly for groups that had been oppressed within bourgeois society. On the other hand, the arduous "civilizing process" of internalizing bourgeois norms, which had already been under way for many generations in Europe, could not be undone overnight. The revolution in Germany after World War I remained incomplete, restricted in many senses to the cultural sphere and to outsiders who, despite their "explosive" presence, remained a minority – and one that was often deeply resented. Even more important, property relations in Weimar vis-à-vis Wilhelmine Germany not only had not changed, they had taken a turn for the worse for most segments of the population, particularly the middle and lower-middle classes. The fact that the economic crises, both in the early 1920s and after the

202 Ibid., p. 651.

great crash in 1929, were much more severe in Germany than in Holland, Switzerland, France, and Belgium was probably the most important cause of the crisis of the bourgeois family, even more important than the war. Any savings that most members of the middle and lower-middle class might have maintained through the war years was destroyed by the inflation in the early 1920s. The phenomenon of "cultural lag," which was one of the most important things Horkheimer was trying to explain with his concept of bourgeois anthropology, was particularly noticeable among these social groups.

8

Reflections on Dialectical Logic in the Mid-1930s

Eine Bestimmung der philosophischen Begriffe ist immer zugleich eine Darstellung der menschlichen Gesellschaft in ihrer geschichtlich gegebenen Verfassung.[1]
Max Horkheimer (1938)

In a letter to Erich Fromm on July 20, 1934, Horkheimer mentioned that he was beginning work on a project on dialectical logic.[2] In another, more substantial letter to Fromm nine days later, he went into some detail about his preliminary work on the project.[3] He outlined some of the central problems he planned to address, including the difference between idealist and materialist dialectics, the role of psychology in a critical theory of history, and his critique of the abstract ego of consciousness philosophy. This attempt by Horkheimer to develop a materialist, or dialectical, logic[4] appropriate to current historical conditions remained central to his concerns throughout the 1930s. This project on dialectical logic represented a continuation of his reflections on materialism in the early 1930s; dialectical logic became the most general philosophical concept that linked together and guided Horkheimer's essays in the 1930s. In fact, in a letter to friend in September 1938, Horkheimer stated clearly that he viewed the essays that he had published until then in the *Zeitschrift* as "in truth merely preliminary studies for a larger work on a critical theory of the social sciences."[5] From other letters that Horkheimer sent to friends at this time, it is clear that the work in question here was the "long-planned work on dialectics"[6] that he had intended to write at least since 1934. In September 1938, Horkheimer was traveling through North America, looking for new place to live where he could work on the project uninterrupted. He was frustrated that his activities at the Institute had prevented him from devoting his full attention to it. He had also just received news of the seriousness of the

---

[1] "A determination of philosophical concepts is always at the same time an interpretation of human society in its historically given form." This quote is taken from Horkheimer's own description of his research project on dialectical logic in 1938. See GS 12, pp. 156ff.

[2] GS 15, p. 160. Gunzelin Schmid Noerr writes that Horkheimer had already planned a project on dialectical logic before he left Europe (ibid., p. 162), but includes no references. This letter includes the first explicit reference to the project I have been able to locate.

[3] Ibid., pp. 177–88.

[4] Horkheimer used both terms – materialist and dialectical – to refer to the project.

[5] GS 16, p. 490.

[6] As Horkheimer put it in a letter to Walter Benjamin from September 6, 1938. GS 16, p. 476.

Institute's financial crisis, which provided further impetus to scale back on Institute activities and turn his attention to the project on dialectical logic.[7] In a letter to a friend from September 1938, Horkheimer wrote, "The necessity to find a less expensive place to live has moved us to look for a small house with a garden in the vicinity of New York. There I will finally find the necessary peace and quiet to realize my long-standing plans for a book. Mr. Marcuse should, if possible, move nearby and provide substantial help."[8] Horkheimer had been discussing the project from the beginning with Marcuse, as one of his letters to Fromm in July 1934 makes clear;[9] but by 1938, his relationship with Theodor Adorno had improved considerably, such that he was also considering Adorno as a possible collaborator on the project.[10] In a letter to Adorno in September 1938, Horkheimer told him that "my thoughts are revolving around *our* [work on] dialectics."[11] The context of the remark leaves no doubt that Horkheimer was referring to the project and alluding to the possibility of Adorno becoming his collaborator. In the end, Horkheimer chose neither a house near New York nor Marcuse as his assistant, but rather a house in Los Angeles and Adorno as his coauthor of what would eventually become *Dialectic of Enlightenment*.

However, *Dialectic of Enlightenment* represents only a partial realization of Horkheimer's original plans for a book on dialectical logic. Not only does it depart in significant ways from Horkheimer's original intentions, it was also cowritten by Adorno, whose intellectual trajectory had differed significantly from that of Horkheimer before they began working together at the end of the 1930s. Thus, reconstructing the development of Horkheimer's ideas on dialectical logic in the mid-1930s will not only illuminate the crucial and hitherto unexamined theoretical context of some of his most important essays in the 1930s, it will also shed light on the prehistory of *Dialectic of Enlightenment* and make it possible to differentiate Horkheimer and Adorno's contributions to it. We will explore this latter issue in more detail later.[12] Our primary concern here, however, is to reconstruct Horkheimer's further theoretical development in the 1930s. We have just examined the concept of bourgeois anthropology, which Horkheimer also considered part of the larger project on dialectical logic. However, that concept and the essays in which it was articulated warrant separate treatment from the project on dialectical logic insofar as they move decisively beyond abstract methodological reflections and attempt to flesh out the *content* of Horkheimer's Critical Theory in the 1930s. With the concept of the anthropology of the bourgeois epoch, Horkheimer articulated the findings of his own and the Institute's empirical research at both the historical and the empirical sociological level. His analysis of historical and social phenomena, such as authority, family, and the instrumentalization of aggression was an attempt to demonstrate concretely how the mediating mechanisms of

---

[7] See, for example, Horkheimer's letter to Adorno from September 11, 1938. GS 16, p. 478.

[8] Ibid., p. 472.

[9] GS 15, p. 170

[10] See Excursus II.

[11] GS 16, p. 478, (emphasis mine).

[12] See Excursus II.

bourgeois society function.[13] Horkheimer's reflections on dialectical logic, on the other hand, were not based on any new empirical research – at least not directly. They attempt to identify, at the most general level, the proper role, possibilities, and limitations of theory itself within bourgeois society. Horkheimer justified this approach with reference to Hegel's *Logic* and Marx's *Capital*.[14] Both works begin by reflecting on the most basic and abstract categories – such as being and nothingness or the commodity form – and move from there to progressively more concrete determinations. To assume that what is immediately apparent is at the same time what is most decisive is to remain trapped at the most unreflective level of consciousness – what Hegel criticized as "sense certainty" in the *Phenomenology of Spirit*. As we shall see, Horkheimer does indeed follow the lead of Hegel and Marx in this regard without, however, hypostatizing any of their substantive conclusions.

Horkheimer's reflections on dialectical logic in the 1930s are located primarily in four major essays. In "The Rationalism Debate in Contemporary Philosophy" (1934), Horkheimer focused primarily on the vitalist critique of rationalism and illustrates how dialectical logic incorporates the insights of *Lebensphilosophie* without rejecting reason *tout court*. In "On the Problem of Truth" (1935), he attempted to develop a dialectical concept of truth that is binding without being ahistorical; one which, in other words, succumbs neither to metaphysical absolutism nor nominalist relativism. In "The Latest Attack on Metaphysics" (1937), Horkheimer sharply criticized the "logical empiricism" of the Vienna School and their rigid defense of the traditional sciences and mathematical logic as the absolute boundaries of legitimate human knowledge. Horkheimer argued that dialectical logic should indeed move beyond those boundaries, and can do so in a way that leads not to irrationalism or metaphysics, but to a less impoverished and affirmative notion of human knowledge. Horkheimer viewed "Traditional and Critical Theory" (1937) as a companion piece to his polemical essay on logical empiricism, which would provide an answer to the logical empiricists' inevitable demand that he elaborate his positive alternative in greater detail.[15] Horkheimer did just this, in a brilliant reconceptualization of the theoretical foundations of Marx's work, which stressed the crucial role of theory as an active and essential moment in the reproduction of the social totality. Although not directly related to his dialectical logic project, Horkheimer's appreciative critique of Henri Bergson, in his 1934 essay "Bergson's Metaphysics of Time," also illustrated some of his larger concerns at this time, as we shall see in our examination of his critique of *Lebensphilosophie*. Despite the differing topics and strategic intentions of these five essays, Horkheimer used each of them to illustrate and develop his

---

[13] This is also the reason why Horkheimer stressed in his introduction to the *Studies on Authority and Family* that the concepts of authority and family do not deserve to be placed at the center of a Critical Theory of society; one must reflect upon the mediating mechanisms of a particular society at a more abstract level in order properly to understand the function of more concrete forms such as family and authority. It is precisely these more abstract mechanisms that Horkheimer wanted to grasp in his dialectical logic.

[14] See, for example, "On the Problem of Truth," pp. 190f and 204f.

[15] See Horkheimer's letter to Katharina von Hirsch from May 4, 1937. GS 16, p. 139.

ideas on dialectical logic. Thus, rather than examining each essay one by one, we shall focus on the reflections on dialectical logic that inform all of them in different ways. Like Hegel and Marx, Horkheimer developed his ideas on dialectical logic in these essays in a manner that is at once historical and systematic. In what follows, we will approach Horkheimer's dialectical logic from an intellectual historical standpoint, while at the same time pointing to its crucial systematic moments. Beginning with Horkheimer's characterization and critique of traditional theory, we will first examine how Horkheimer returns to one of the oldest and most important themes in his Critical Theory, namely the critique of "Cartesian-empirical consciousness philosophy." Next, we will turn to the dichotomy of positivism and metaphysics. Horkheimer identified this dichotomy as one of the defining characteristics of philosophy as a whole in the bourgeois epoch, but he also argued that it finds its most profound expression in Kant's work. Dialectical logic found its first genuine expression in the work of Hegel, who moves beyond consciousness philosophy but is unable to free himself completely from the antinomies of positivism and metaphysics. Marx was the first to break decisively with the metaphysical assumptions that still informed Hegel's philosophy; thus, Horkheimer developed his own ideas on dialectical logic in direct dialogue with Marx. Because we have already examined many of the earlier forms of these arguments, we shall attempt, whenever possible, simply to identify what is new in Horkheimer's essays from the mid-1930s and what he still deemed important for his long-term project on dialectical logic.

THE CRITIQUE OF CARTESIAN-EMPIRICAL CONSCIOUSNESS PHILOSOPHY

As we have seen, Horkheimer's critique of consciousness philosophy was the defining moment in his break with the idiosyncratic neo-Kantianism of his academic mentor Hans Cornelius, and served as a crucial point of departure for the development of his own Critical Theory in the late 1920s.[16] Thus, it should come as no surprise that the critique of consciousness philosophy also served as the point of departure for his project on dialectical logic in the 1930s. In several of his essays from this time Horkheimer picked up the diverse threads of his earlier criticisms of consciousness philosophy and weaved them into a new, more succinct, but also more sweeping critique. The most important new elements that appeared in the 1930s were Horkheimer's unambiguous identification of both of the dominant traditions of early modern philosophy – rationalism and empiricism – with consciousness philosophy. In his lectures on the history of philosophy in the late 1920s, Horkheimer had privileged the empiricist tradition over the rationalist tradition, insofar as the former preserved a vital link to present conditions and the practical implications of knowledge and thus also the historical core of truth. In his essays from the 1930s, in contrast, Horkheimer argued that rationalism and empiricism both rest on the same traditional logical assumptions that characterized consciousness philosophy as

---

[16] See Chapter 3, pp. 85ff.

a whole. In the 1920s, Horkheimer had also recognized the limits of the empirical tradition and had already insisted that empirically based knowledge always
be located within a larger, historically based theory of society as a whole; nonetheless, his more critical reassessment of empiricism in the 1930s marked an
important change of emphasis in his thought. We have already identified some
of the historical reasons for this shift.[17] It is no coincidence that the debate
about Horkheimer's alleged positivist tendencies has focused on his writings
from the mid- and late 1920s. Yet even in his scathing critique of logical empiricism in 1937, Horkheimer was careful to emphasize that it had a completely
different and much less progressive historical function than classical empiricism. Furthermore, he continued to defend the importance of empirical social
and historical research and the integration of the traditional sciences more
generally as necessary components of Critical Theory.

In his essay "The Rationalism Debate in Contemporary Philosophy,"
Horkheimer introduced the concept of "Cartesian-empirical consciousness
philosophy" to explain and criticize the shared traditional logical assumptions
of rationalism and empiricism.[18] The two most important of these assumptions
were a reified and absolute concept of the ego and a unified, static, and dualistic concept of knowledge. We have already examined Horkheimer's critique of
the former in our discussion of German Idealism.[19] The key new argumentative
move that Horkheimer made in the 1930s is to apply this critique to the underlying logical assumptions of rationalism and empiricism. He insisted that "the
philosophy of consciousness – Cartesian rationalism and English empiricism ...
bears an idealist character."[20] Horkheimer made this point in "The Rationalism
Debate..." in the following way:

In these controversies of modern philosophy, the closed individual consciousness is set
on a par with human existence. According to the rationalist tendency, all problems
were resolved when the individual had gained a clear and concrete concept of itself;
according to the empiricist, the matter depends more on bringing order to the panoply
of given experiences. In both cases, truth is supposed to emerge from the introspection
of the rational individual. Action is judged essentially in terms of the degree to which
it is the correct consequence of this truth.... Practical execution appears ... as a mere
consequence of reflection. The well-being of each individual ... depends therefore upon
the adequate functioning of his or her intellectual apparatus.[21]

After Horkheimer had identified the hypostatized *ego cogito* as a crucial logical
prerequisite of both rationalism and empiricism, he was then able to criticize
consciousness philosophy as idealistic and contrast it to his own materialist
position. Horkheimer presented this argument most clearly in some lengthy

---

[17] See Chapter 6, pp. 232–33.
[18] Max Horkheimer, *Between Philosophy and Social Science*, op. cit., p. 220 (translation
amended).
[19] See Chapter 3, pp. 87ff. and 113ff.
[20] *Between Philosophy and Social Science*, p. 222.
[21] Ibid., pp. 219–20. See also Horkheimer's discussion of the abstract ego as a fundamental principle of bourgeois thought in "Traditional and Critical Theory," in Max Horkheimer, *Critical
Theory: Selected Essays*, op. cit., pp. 210ff.

reflections on dialectical logic in one of the aforementioned letters to Erich Fromm. He writes:

Currently all my interest is focused … on the conceptual foundations of dialectical logic…. I have been preoccupied primarily with the difference between the idealist and materialist dialectic. A particularly important aspect of this difference is the role of the ego…. When the materialist turns his attention to the ego, he poses questions that can only be answered scientifically [*wissenschaftlich*], particularly those relating to the social determinants at a given historical moment. The idealist, on the other hand, rejects this additional complication of the inquiry and attempts to determine the ego more or less speculatively. The transformations, which the ego undergoes, are viewed as *necessary steps of knowledge*. In this way individual insights can be integrated into a theory of the ego as independent and uninfluenced by external factors, and knowledge gains the sacred meaning that it possesses in idealism…. The idealist is constantly guided in this thought process by the ideal of attaining a standpoint that is no longer particular and he measures individual insights according to a state, in which human consciousness is *no longer conditioned*, insofar as his knowledge – not necessarily quantitatively, but in terms of what is essential – grasps "the totality." Thus idealist philosophy and thought in general is dominated, right down to the smallest steps of its arguments, by an illusion: the spurious concept of an absolute ego…. The materialist, on the other hand, negates particular insights by consciously placing them in relation to the given historical situation, which must be *practically* overcome.[22]

Horkheimer's description here and in the earlier quote of isolated egos determined by the stage at which they happen to be on a path toward absolute knowledge corresponds almost exactly to Leibniz's metaphysical doctrines of monads. According to Leibniz, each monad contains the knowledge of the entire universe within itself, at varying levels of consciousness, but it has no windows and is related to other monads only arbitrarily. Thus, it is not surprising that Horkheimer returned to this metaphor, which had played an important role in his early writings,[23] in his essays in the 1930s to describe what he considered one of the fundamental characteristics of traditional logic, namely the reified *ego cogito*. According to Horkheimer, the "forceful [*gewaltsame*] isolation of human beings from one another peculiar to the current period" was the socio-historical equivalent of the reification of the abstract ego in traditional logic.[24]

The second important traditional logical assumption that underlies both rationalism and empiricism, according to Horkheimer, is their unitary, static, and dualistic concept of knowledge. Horkheimer made this argument in one way or another in all four of the essays with which we are concerned here. In "The Rationalism Debate…," Horkheimer maintained that rationalism "presupposes a constant relationship between concept and reality, independent

---

[22] GS 16, pp. 179–80 (emphasis mine).

[23] See the discussion of Leibniz in Chapter 3, pp. 100–1 and of Horkheimer's aphorism "Monadology" in *Dämmerung*, in Chapter 4, pp. 160–61.

[24] *Between Philosophy and Social Science*, p. 262. For an example of Horkheimer's use of this metaphor in his essays from the 1930s, see, for example, "Traditional and Critical Theory," p. 202 or "The Rationalism Debate in Contemporary Philosophy," pp. 218–9.

of human praxis," and that among its empiricist critics these "assumptions of Cartesian philosophy remain untouched."[25] Horkheimer continued:

In both philosophical approaches, truth consists in judgments whose concepts are related to individual sense data as the general is to the particular. According to the empiricists, these concepts arise from the sensuous material and are derived by a process of progressive omission of substantive differences – that is, through abstraction. According to the rationalists … they are fundamental unities inherent in reason…. Knowledge is independent of forces external to or fundamentally different from consciousness. Its relation to the object, its task, the limits of its capacity, indeed its most important contents may be determined or at least classified once and for all.[26]

In "The Latest Attack on Metaphysics," Horkheimer went out of his way to demonstrate that empiricism in particular presupposes a concept of knowledge that is ultimately static. Horkheimer made this argument so carefully because the empiricists had always prided themselves on their openness to new scientific findings and their willingness to modify their principles accordingly.[27] Yet despite their rejection of the universal concepts and innate ideas of the rationalists, the empiricists retained an underlying faith in the unity of scientific knowledge, and viewed new research simply as filling in the details of a system whose structure and parameters have already been set and will not be fundamentally altered in the future. In "On the Problem of Truth," Horkheimer made this same point by citing a passage from Kant's *Logic*, in which he describes the process of knowledge accumulation metaphorically as a map whose blank areas are gradually filled in through new explorations, but whose core structure and basic parameters remain the same. For Kant, as for his rationalist predecessors and their empiricist critics, "Traditional logic has nothing to do with the alteration of the 'map' and the construction of new systems of classification."[28] This assumption was articulated explicitly in the twentieth century by the logical empiricists, who argued that experimental physics and modern mathematical logic are the absolute foundation of all rigorous human knowledge.[29] The logical empiricists believed in the ultimate unity of scientific knowledge and also that this unity can be summed up in a limited number of protocol sentences. The logical consequence of this belief, however, was to reduce the epistemological subject to a completely passive entity, who can know but can never fundamentally alter the structure of the world. Horkheimer showed how empiricism in the early modern period implicitly contained many of these same assumptions, but that it relativized them either by retaining a marginal role for the epistemological subject as an organizer of sensual impressions (Locke) or by denying the possibility of ever attaining absolute scientific certainty (Hume). In "Traditional and Critical Theory," Horkheimer characterized the dominant ideal of traditional theory – which

---

[25] "Rationalism Debate…," pp. 217–18.
[26] Ibid., pp. 218–19.
[27] "The Latest Attack on Metaphysics," in Max Horkheimer, *Critical Theory: Selected Essays*, op. cit., pp. 145ff.
[28] "On the Problem of Truth," in *Between Philosophy and Social Science*, op. cit., p. 208.
[29] Ibid., p. 140.

included both classical rationalism and empiricism – as "a unitary system of science which ... will be all-powerful.... The determinative, ordering, unifying function is the sole foundation for all else, and towards it all human effort is directed."[30] In short, consciousness philosophy rests on a concept of knowledge that presupposes uniformity, precludes qualitative change, and forecloses any self-reflexive relationship to history or human praxis.

SCIENCE AND METAPHYSICS: THE ANTINOMIES OF PHILOSOPHY IN THE BOURGEOIS EPOCH

Horkheimer developed his critique of consciousness philosophy in the 1930s with a view to the common underlying assumptions of classical rationalism and empiricism, but then extended his arguments all the way up to contemporary philosophical schools such as logical empiricism. Similarly, he held up Kant's philosophy as the most profound expression of the dichotomy between science and metaphysics, but he considered this dichotomy as characteristic of philosophy as a whole within the bourgeois epoch. As was also the case with his critique of consciousness philosophy, Horkheimer's emphasis on the dichotomy between science and metaphysics had played a crucial role in his earlier work, most notably in his lectures on the history of philosophy in the late nineteenth and early twentieth centuries.[31] Horkheimer portrayed the development of philosophy during this time as a movement from an apotheosis of science and a concomitant rejection of metaphysics in the mid-nineteenth century to widespread skepticism about the traditional sciences and a sweeping return of metaphysics, which peaked in Germany in the 1920s. Horkheimer linked this development to the crises of bourgeois society during this time and, in particular, to its increasingly obvious inability to realize the universal claims with which it had legitimated its rise to power. In his essays in the 1930s, in contrast, Horkheimer showed how this battle between science and metaphysics had characterized bourgeois philosophy as a whole, indeed, how it existed in a more or less mediated way side by side within the work of its most important representatives. By expanding and, to a certain extent, dehistoricizing his analysis in this way, Horkheimer showed how this dichotomy is one of the most fundamental organizing assumptions of traditional logic: closely related, but not identical to the dualist concept of bourgeois knowledge discussed earlier. In what follows, we will briefly examine Horkheimer's assessment of this dichotomy in Kant's philosophy, and then we will see how he criticized its reappearance in *Lebensphilosophie* and logical empiricism.

One of the distinguishing features of modern, mechanical science was its elimination of final causes, of teleological principles, that Aristotle had still considered one of the four basic forms of causation in his *Physics*. In his dissertation and *Habilitationsschrift*, Horkheimer closely examined Kant's attempt to reconcile modern science's mechanical view of the physical world with various forms of teleology, as they appeared in organic entities, works of art, and,

---

[30] "Traditional and Critical Theory," op. cit., p. 198.
[31] See Chapter 3, pp. 124ff.

most importantly, human reason and freedom. Horkheimer came to the conclusion that despite his remarkable efforts, Kant never succeeded in this task,
which remained central to his concerns until the very end of his life.[32] Although
Horkheimer would reassess Kant's philosophy more positively after 1925 –
particularly his doctrine of the primacy of practical reason – he never abandoned his conviction that Kant's philosophy was driven at a very deep level by
the desire to *rescue* metaphysics.[33] Metaphysical principles, such as God, the
immortal soul, and the immutable kingdom of moral ends, reappeared in Kant's
practical philosophy and existed in uneasy tension with mechanical, scientific
principles of pure reason that govern our perception of the physical world.
In his essay "On the Problem of Truth," Horkheimer returned to this dichotomy between science and metaphysics in Kant's philosophy within the context
of a discussion of the philosophical concept of truth in the bourgeois epoch.
In order to demonstrate his main point – that the concept of truth in bourgeois philosophy fluctuates between relativism and absolutism – Horkheimer
showed how these two tendencies are both clearly expressed and exist side by
side in Kant's philosophy. He showed, on the one hand, how Kant preserved
the validity of modern science, while at the same time eliminating its claim to
absolute truth by illustrating the subjective nature of its most basic categories and its inability to grasp the noumenal realm of "things-in-themselves."
Thus, as Horkheimer wrote, "In regard to knowledge of the world, [Kant] is
no less a skeptical relativist than the 'mystical' and 'dreaming' idealists whom
he combats."[34] On the other hand, he also showed how Kant reasserts the validity of absolute principles, not only in the *Critique of Practical Reason*, but
also in the *Critique of Pure Reason*, which, as Horkheimer wrote, "depends on
the assumption that pure concepts and judgments exist 'a priori' in the consciousness, and that metaphysics not only has always existed but will of right
exist for all eternity."[35] Thus, Kant's philosophy is characterized by "analysis
carried through to the end and skeptical distrust of all theory, on the one hand,
and readiness to believe naively in detached fixed principles, on the other."
These competing and uneasily coexisting tendencies "appear in its most highly
developed form in Kant's philosophy," and Horkheimer also argued that they
are "characteristic of the bourgeois mind" as a whole.[36] He made this claim
in discussions of both *Lebensphilosophie* and logical empiricism in his essays
in the 1930s.

Horkheimer's essay "Bergson's Metaphysics of Time" focused in detail on the
dichotomy of science and metaphysics in the work of Henri Bergson, the most
important representative of *Lebensphilosophie* in France. Horkheimer showed
how this dichotomy reappears at the very center of Bergson's philosophy,
namely in his attempts to develop a nonscientific concept of time. Unlike some
of his vitalist successors, Bergson did not reject science out of hand, but he did

---

[32] See Chapter 2, pp. 73ff.
[33] See Chapter 3, p. 112.
[34] "On the Problem of Truth," p. 179.
[35] Ibid., p. 180.
[36] Ibid.

sharply limit the realm of its validity. For Bergson, as for Heidegger later, science is based on a concept of time that is derived from abstract conceptions of space.[37] Yet this notion of time fails to do justice to the unstructured and spontaneous nature of real human experience, according to Bergson. With his notion of time as *durée*, Bergson tried to create a more adequate, alternative conception. Horkheimer noted that Bergson's effort to limit the validity of science and to preserve a "higher" truth unique to human experience placed him much closer to Kant than he suspects,[38] and he devoted the remainder of the essay to demonstrating that Bergson's notion of time as *durée* is indeed metaphysical. Horkheimer argued, for example, that Bergson's concept of time may not be eternal, but it is unlimited, and his belief in our ability to immerse ourselves in and become one with the inexhaustible stream of human experience ultimately obfuscates the finitude of human existence. Horkheimer made a similar objection to Bergson's description of time as mere "change," because it fails to capture the essential consequence of time for living beings of coming into and out of existence. In both cases, Bergson's notion of *durée* denies the reality of human mortality and, like other metaphysical and religious beliefs, provides false consolation for past and present suffering. Horkheimer also objected to Bergson's description of *durée* as unified and indivisible. These qualities also serve an ideological function, according to him, insofar as they obscure the deeply divided nature of contemporary society.[39] Finally, Horkheimer also noted that Bergson's notion of time as *durée* – like Heidegger's notion of time as historicity – leaves no place for the methods of traditional, empirically based historiography and thus undermines the role of the critical historian in the struggle for a better society, or even in simply preserving the memory of past injustice. For even if these wrongs can never be rectified, the historian can at least prevent them from being completely forgotten. Thus, Horkheimer concluded, "Even if this appeal could not become a productive force for a better society, the function of remembering alone places the profession of the historian above that of the metaphysician."[40]

Whereas the vitalists' attacks on science served an important metaphysical function, according to Horkheimer, insofar as they provided compensation and consolation by positing unity and meaning where it did not exist, the logical empiricists attacked all forms of knowledge that were not grounded in sense perception or mathematical logic as metaphysical apparitions. However, Horkheimer argued in "The Latest Attack on Metaphysics" that their attempt to absolutize modern science and traditional logic also led them back to metaphysics in the end. In other words, their attempt to

---

[37] "Bergsons Metaphysik der Zeit," GS 3, p. 229. For an English translation, see "Bergson's Metaphysics of Time," trans. Peter Thomas, *Radical Philosophy*, no. 131 (May/June 2005), pp. 9–19. Unlike Horkheimer, who, despite his criticisms, recognized the importance of Bergson's philosophical achievements, Heidegger refused to give him any credit, seeing him as just another example of the dominant understanding of time in "Western metaphysics" from Aristotle through the present. See *Being and Time*, op. cit., pp. 39, 49, and 500–1.

[38] "Bergsons Metaphysik der Zeit," p. 231.

[39] Ibid., p. 239.

[40] Ibid., p. 248.

radicalize the antimetaphysical impulse of the Enlightenment led them to turn the Enlightenment itself into a myth.[41] Horkheimer began the essay with an explicit discussion of the dichotomy of science and metaphysics, which – he stressed once again – has characterized bourgeois society from the very beginning. Science and technology have without doubt progressed – from the slingshot to the atom bomb, as Adorno once mordantly remarked – but insofar as they rest upon and are guided by traditional logical assumptions, they fail to address the true forces driving their development and implementation.[42] Because blatant social injustice and periodic social catastrophes continue to exist side by side with scientific progress, metaphysics is still necessary to legitimate the existing social order and to compensate those whose sacrifices make its continued existence possible. Horkheimer writes:

Scientific knowledge is formally recognized to be correct; at the same time, metaphysical views are retained. With science alone, mirroring as it does the chaotic reality in nature and society, the dissatisfied masses and thinking individuals would be left in a dangerous and desperate state. It was impossible to get by, either at the personal, psychological or at the social level, without a unifying ideology.... Metaphysical illusions and higher mathematics both form constituent elements of this [bourgeois] mentality. Philosophy is merely the domain in which a systematic effort was made to reconcile the two in some manner.[43]

For Horkheimer, in other words, logical empiricism is firmly rooted within the epochal dichotomy between science and metaphysics, just as is *Lebensphilosophie*, even if the two of them exist at opposite ends of its spectrum. Whereas *Lebensphilosophie* had drawn sharp limits on the validity of the traditional sciences, logical empiricism asserts their absolute validity. Logical empiricism distinguishes itself from earlier forms of empiricism and positivism by consciously linking the traditional sciences to mathematical logic. Thus, as far as Horkheimer is concerned, it shares all the weaknesses of earlier forms of positivism, which we have already examined,[44] such as its elimination of the active, self-reflexive subject of knowledge, its rejection of the distinction between essence and appearance, and its abstract negation of universals. With the addition of modern mathematical logic as a further prerequisite of valid knowledge, its scope becomes even narrower, and its abstract and ahistorical assumptions more apparent. Horkheimer shows, for example, how the logical empiricists believe that all knowledge can be reduced to a single, unified

---

[41] We have already seen that the antimetaphysical impulses of the historical Enlightenment (see Chapter 3, pp. 101ff.) and also the antimetaphysical impulses of Horkheimer's concept of materialism in the early 1930s (see Chapter 6, pp. 227ff.), which drew heavily upon the historical Enlightenment, did not by any means lead to the same conclusions as the logical empiricists.

[42] For examination of the ways in which Herbert Marcuse develops these ideas in his later work, see John Abromeit, "Left Heideggerianism or Phenomenological Marxism? Reconsidering Herbert Marcuse's Critical Theory of Technology," *Constellations*, vol. 17, no. 1 (March, 2010), pp. 87–106.

[43] "The Latest Attack on Metaphysics," (translation amended) pp. 134–5.

[44] See, for example, Horkheimer's discussion of nineteenth-century positivism in Chapter 3 (pp. 127ff.), his discussion of Lenin's *Materialism and Empiriocriticism* in Chapter 4 (pp. 150ff.), and his discussion of the relationship of his own concept of materialism to positivism in Chapter 6, pp. 235–36.

language, namely the language of mathematical physics.[45] Furthermore, even the most sophisticated of modern physicists have been unable to get by without metaphysical supplements to their work, as Horkheimer illustrates with a discussion of Max Planck.[46]

HEGEL AND THE BEGINNINGS OF DIALECTICAL LOGIC

Just as Horkheimer's renewed studies of Nietzsche in the early 1930s had informed his concept of bourgeois anthropology, so Horkheimer returned to Hegel's writings in the mid-1930s in his efforts to develop a dialectical logic.[47] To be more precise, Hegel was even more important for the latter project than

---

[45] "The Latest Attack on Metaphysics" marked a shift not only in Horkheimer's attitude toward the empirical tradition – as noted earlier – but also toward language. In his earlier work, Horkheimer did reflect explicitly on the implications of language for his own Critical Theory; in fact, in accord with his greater proximity at the time to the empirical tradition, Horkheimer pointed to Francis Bacon's famous analysis of the different idols that posed a threat to the pursuit of scientific truth, and identified language as the one that presented the greatest temptation to intellectuals in particular. Horkheimer stated, "The next ones are the 'idola fori,' the idols of the marketplace, which are the illusions that result from language, from the conventions of words. In this regard, Bacon ... could provide some of our most modern philosophers with useful warnings. One thinks here of a certain phenomenological method of attaining 'new' insights through the dissection and so-called interpretation of meaning of words without any relation to reality. For Bacon all words are vehicles of knowledge, but also a danger. ... Trying to understand something with mere chains of thought that are derived from this or that concept, belongs to the scholastic approach, which Bacon fights so energetically and ridicules everywhere as word-wisdom. According to him, knowledge must always be gained through experience, that is, in relation to material things; chains of thought, which develop out of control – even if in a logically rigorous manner – are always unreliable and suspect. ... The danger of remaining in the realm of mere words, fighting over words, getting stuck in the abstract realm of words, is the danger of thinking in general, but especially the danger of the philosopher." GS 9, pp. 87–8. In contrast to Adorno, who was exposed to and fascinated by Walter Benjamin's theory of language already in the 1920s, Horkheimer's views on language seemed to be determined largely by his concerns about the "idola fori" expressed here. One could say that Horkheimer's understanding of language was also expressed in the remarkable clarity of his style, and his extraordinary gift of expressing philosophical ideas, but this would capture only one of its dimensions. Like most of the leading authors of the French Enlightenment, whom he admired, his writing had a strong rhetorical dimension from the very beginning. This was clearly expressed not only in his early novellas and plays, but also in *Dämmerung*, which relied time and again on anecdotes, fables, thought experiments, and other rhetorical devices to make his points. In any case, it was only after his serious engagement with the logical empiricists in the mid-1930s and his disgust with their "barbaric relationship to language" (GS 4, p. 154; "The Latest Attack...," p. 179) that he began to reflect on language in a more sustained and substantial manner. For a good overview of Horkheimer's views on language in the ensuing period, see Gunzelin Schmid Noerr, "Wahrheit, Macht und die Sprache der Philosophie: Zu Horkheimers sprachphilosophischen Reflexionen in seinen nachgelassenen Schriften 1939 bis 1946," in *Max Horkheimer Heute: Werk und Wirkung*, eds. A. Schmidt and N. Altzwicker (Frankfurt, 1986), pp. 349–70. See also Hermann Schweppenhäuser, "Sprachbegriff und sprachliche Darstellung bei Horkheimer und Adorno," in the same volume, pp. 328–48.

[46] "The Latest Attack on Metaphysics," pp. 135–6.

[47] See, for example, Horkheimer's letter to Walter Benjamin from December 3, 1937. Horkheimer mentions here that he has organized an internal seminar at the Institute on Hegel's *Logic*. GS 16, p. 307.

Nietzsche was for the former; whereas Nietzsche's work provided an important confirmation of many of the insights Horkheimer had already won through his study of psychoanalysis, Hegel was the first modern philosopher to develop a dialectical logic, and Horkheimer's own efforts in this direction built directly on the strengths and attempted to move beyond the weaknesses of Hegel's project. Horkheimer states clearly that "materialism is schooled on Hegel's *Logic*,"[48] by which he means not only Marx, but also his own efforts to develop a concept of materialism adequate to the twentieth century. Horkheimer's essays in the 1930s were based, more or less explicitly, on an intellectual historical interpretation of the development of dialectical logic, in which Hegel played a decisive role.[49] After examining the traditional logical assumptions of the rationalists, empiricists, and Kant, Horkheimer illustrates how Hegel overcame the weakness of Cartesian-empiricist consciousness philosophy without, however, being able to emancipate himself from the dichotomy of science and metaphysics that had been so profoundly expressed in Kant's philosophy. Next, Horkheimer shows how Feuerbach and Marx laid the foundations for a materialist critique of the metaphysical remnants of Hegel's philosophy; he highlights in particular those aspects of Marx's work that are still relevant for a dialectical logic appropriate to current historical conditions. The importance of Hegel for Horkheimer's efforts to develop a dialectical logic is also reflected in his critiques of *Lebensphilosophie* and logical empiricism. He accused both of these philosophical schools of falling *behind* the historical level of knowledge attained by Hegel: the former for failing to *preserve* the traditional sciences, the latter for refusing to recognize that knowledge can and must also move *beyond* them. With his dialectic of understanding [*Verstand*] and reason [*Vernunft*], Hegel had already done both, even though his model remained flawed in the end. Thus, in what follows, we will first examine the positive, pathbreaking aspects of Hegel's dialectical logic, then, in our final step, turn to its limitations in order to see how Horkheimer attempted to overcome them with the help of Feuerbach and, more importantly, Marx.

We have already seen, in our examination of Horkheimer's lectures on German Idealism in the 1920s, how Hegel moved beyond Kant and Fichte, from subjective to objective idealism. In their reliance on the abstract ego as the foundation of their philosophy, they had remained, as Horkheimer explicitly argued, firmly entrenched within the tradition of "Cartesian-empirical consciousness philosophy." Thus, it is not necessary to recapitulate Horkheimer's arguments about how Hegel's dialectical logic moved beyond this first decisive component of consciousness philosophy because they remained largely the same in the 1930s.[50] But before moving on to Hegel's critique of the second decisive component of consciousness philosophy – its dualistic and static concept of knowledge – let us quickly examine the ways in which Hegel's dialectical logic preserves the concrete individual, because this was a point that Horkheimer

---

[48] "The Rationalism Debate in Contemporary Philosophy," p. 234 (translation amended).

[49] This interpretation is articulated most clearly in "On the Rationalism Debate..." and "On the Problem of Truth," but it informs the other essays we are examining here as well.

[50] See Chapter 3, pp. 87–8 and 111ff.

emphasized much more after the triumph of National Socialism in Germany in 1933. Horkheimer takes up this issue explicitly in "The Rationalism Debate…" in the context of his larger discussion of the vitalist attack on rationalism. Like Marcuse in his essay "The Struggle Against Liberalism in the Totalitarian View of the State," which was also published in the *Zeitschrift für Sozialforschung* in 1934,[51] Horkheimer addressed attacks on liberalism by various irrationalist and *völkische* tendencies that had helped prepare the way for the Nationalist Socialist victory in 1933. Marcuse and Horkheimer were both at pains to distinguish the dialectical critique of liberalism from these irrationalist attacks.[52] One of the most important differences, according to Horkheimer, was the preservation of the interests of the concrete individual, as opposed to their mere abstract negation. In the course of his argument, Horkheimer refers to Hegel's *Philosophy of Right* to make this point. He writes:

Irrationalism denies the right to individual self-preservation and sees the whole as the meaning and aim of all human activity, as if the interest in the whole were mediated by unconditional subordination rather than by the interests of the individuals for themselves and their kind…. As long as the whole is not constantly judged against the standard of human happiness, the notion of the "common good" is just as dogmatic as that of self-interest. Without the fulfillment of the Hegelian dictum that the "end of the state is the universal interest as such and the substance of this interest is the preservation therein of particular interests," the demand of total surrender to the interests of the state remains mere dogmatism.[53]

Like Marcuse, Horkheimer recognized that Hegel's philosophy also contained a competing tendency, which did in fact subordinate the individual to the abstract social totality, but he linked this tendency to the metaphysical aspects of Hegel's idealism.[54]

We identified the second decisive feature of "Cartesian-empirical consciousness philosophy" as its static, dualistic, and unitary concept of knowledge. At the risk of being overly schematic, one could say that Hegel's *Logic* is neither static nor dualistic, but does remain unitary, according to Horkheimer. Let us examine the first two characteristics before turning to the third, which will lead into our discussion of the metaphysical aspects of Hegel's philosophy. The traditional sciences and traditional logic, upon which consciousness philosophy rests, are static because they always subsume new particulars under preexisting systems of classification. Their concepts are developed from abstracting

---

[51] For the English translation by Jeremy J. Shapiro, see Herbert Marcuse, *Negations*, op. cit., pp. 3–42.

[52] In his 1941 study, *Reason and Revolution: Hegel and the Rise of Social Theory*, Marcuse would provide an entire historical genealogy of Critical Theory in order to distinguish its dialectical critique of liberalism from the irrationalist attack of the fascists and their theoretical bedfellows. It was Marcuse's first book in English, for he wanted to dispel the myths widespread in the Anglo-American world then – and, one must unfortunately say, now as well – that Hegel was a theoretical precursor of the authoritarian state.

[53] "The Rationalism Debate…," pp. 248–9 (translation amended).

[54] For Horkheimer's critique of Hegel's concept of the state, see "The Present Situation of Social Philosophy…," pp. 4–5. For Marcuse's critique of the affirmative aspects of Hegel's idealism, see "On Hedonism" in *Negations*, op. cit., pp. 159–200.

from the particular, from breaking it down into components and classifying it based on the correlation of one or more of these parts with other particulars within the same general category. This is a *mechanical* process, insofar as the particular is dissected into component parts that are treated as if they existed independently from the totality of the particular of which they are a part. Furthermore, the particular is analyzed as a static entity, one which does not develop in time. Thus, the vital relations that exist between not only the various components of the particular, but also the various forms of the particular at different stages in time, are lost from view in traditional logical analysis. Horkheimer illustrates this point in "The Rationalism Debate..." and "Bergson's Metaphysics of Time"; for in their attack of rationalism, Bergson and the other vitalists relied on many of the same arguments that Hegel had used against traditional logic. However, as was the case with the individual, Horkheimer was also intent on showing how Hegel's critique of traditional logic differed from the vitalist attack on rationalism; the former represented a *determinate* and the latter merely an *abstract* negation of the traditional sciences and logic. Horkheimer stressed, in particular, Hegel's preservation of the traditional sciences and logic as a *necessary*, if by no means sufficient, condition of philosophically rigorous knowledge. Just as Hegel had criticized Schelling in the preface of the *Phenomenology of Spirit* for rejecting discursive knowledge in the name of the pseudo-profundity of intellectual intuition – thereby leading philosophy into the night in which all cows are black – so Horkheimer criticized *Lebensphilosophie* for stressing only the limitations and the destructive character of traditional concept formation and for failing to recognize the positive contribution to knowledge made by the traditional sciences. The following description of Bergson holds true for Horkheimer's interpretation of *Lebensphilosophie* as a whole: "All of Bergson's views about the concept correspond to the pre-Hegelian state of logic, otherwise he would not have been able to view and dismiss thinking as the purely mechanical activity of constructing rigid conceptual structures."[55] Horkheimer also objected to the vitalists' all-too-facile dismissal of empirical research. In short, with regard to both traditional concept formation and empirical research, Horkheimer accused *Lebensphilosophie* of a "Versagen im Positiven."[56] They failed, in other words, to complete the logical and empirical work that would have made possible a rigorous critique of traditional science and instrumental reason as well as the social totality in which they are embedded.

Horkheimer praised Hegel not only for preserving traditional science and logic, but also for moving beyond them, for criticizing their static character and placing them within the larger, dynamic, and self-reflexive process of reason. Horkheimer makes this point most clearly in his critique of logical empiricism.

---

[55] "Bergsons Metaphysik der Zeit," GS 3, p. 244. For Hegel's critique of Schelling and other romantics of lesser stature, which reads as though it were written about Bergson, and even more for the irrationalist epigones of *Lebensphilosophie*, see *Phenomenology of Spirit*, trans. A.V. Miller (Oxford, New York, Toronto and Melbourne, 1977), p. 6.

[56] "Failure in the realm of the positive," "The Rationalism Debate in Contemporary Philosophy," p. 238.

Just as Horkheimer took recourse to Hegel to distinguish his own critique of traditional science and logic from *Lebensphilosophie*, in "The Latest Attack on Metaphysics," he also used Hegel to demonstrate how his own critique of metaphysics differed from that of the logical empiricists; for their critique seemed, at first glance, to be similar to his own or even to Hegel's critique of Schelling. However, as we just saw, the logical empiricists refused to recognize as legitimate any knowledge that extends beyond the limits of the empirical sciences and mathematical logic. Horkheimer used Hegel to undermine both of these two pillars of their closed system. He pointed first to Hegel's critique of sense-certainty in the *Phenomenology* as revealing the limits of a purely empirical approach to science.[57] What appears to be the most concrete and certain in the immediate sense perceptions of the here and now turns out, on deeper reflection, to be the most abstract and unmediated form of knowledge that exists. Hegel demonstrated how empirical findings were always not only subjectively, but also socially and historically mediated. The logical empiricists' refusal to reflect on these conditions, was, according to Horkheimer, tantamount to placing science in the service of whatever forces happened to be reigning at the time and reducing science and knowledge in general to a bourgeois profession.[58] Hegel moved beyond this position by defending the right of reason to reflect on and determine why scientific research was conducted in the first place and in whose service its results were placed.[59]

Horkheimer also drew on Hegel to criticize the logical empiricists' fetishization of mathematical logic. He stressed the point that traditional logic had always claimed to grasp the most fundamental principles of man and the universe; the modern, mathematical logic of the logical empiricists still asserts the universality of its own principles, but it does so in complete separation from the empirical and historical world.[60] The principles of mathematical logic are applied after the fact to empirical material provided by the traditional sciences and have no substantial content of their own. Thus, mathematical logic has a passive relationship to the empirical sciences and always remains within the boundaries of its categories and organizational principles, whatever they happen to be at that time.[61] The purely formalistic character of mathematical logic also becomes apparent, according to Horkheimer, when the universality of its principles is called into question by other systems of logic, such as "the material logic of Aristotle and Hegel, which it so bitterly attacks."[62] In contrast to mathematical logic, material logic understands that raising a claim to universality necessitates moving beyond "timeless truths," which, on closer inspections, reveal themselves to be empty tautologies. The way in which Horkheimer grounds this claim also explains why Hegel's or his own dialectical logic is not static. Horkheimer discusses this difficult problem in most detail in his essay "On the Problem of the

---

[57] "The Latest Attack on Metaphysics," p. 157.
[58] Ibid., pp. 165–6.
[59] Ibid., p. 162.
[60] Ibid., p. 167.
[61] Ibid., p. 169.
[62] Ibid., p. 172.

Truth." Horkheimer argues there that the dichotomy between science and meta-physics has a correlate within bourgeois philosophy with respect to the concept of truth: claims to absolute truth on the one hand, and skeptical relativism on the other. We have just seen how both of these dichotomies are expressed in Kant's philosophy. Horkheimer sees Hegel's philosophy as the first substantial attempt to overcome these dichotomies. He writes:

In developing the dialectical method, bourgeois thought itself has made the most ambitious attempt to transcend this antinomy. Here the goal of philosophy no longer appears, as in Kant, to be merely the system of the subjective factors of cognition; per-ceived truth is no longer so empty that in practice one must take refuge in the solidity of faith. While the concrete content is perceived as conditional and dependent and every "final" truth is just as decisively "negated" as in Kant, it does not for Hegel simply fall through the sieve in the sifting out of pure knowledge. Recognition of the conditional character of every type of isolated view and rejection of its absolute claim to truth does not destroy this conditional knowledge; rather it is incorporated into the system of truth at any given time as a conditional, one-sided, and isolated view. Through noth-ing but this continuous delimitation and correction of partial truths, the process itself evolves its proper content as knowledge of limited insights in their limits and connec-tion.... Since the dialectical method does not rest with showing that a thing is condi-tioned but takes the conditioned thing seriously, it escapes the relativistic formalism of the Kantian philosophy.[63]

Thus, Hegel was the first modern philosopher truly to set the "steifen Karrengaul des bürgerlichen Verstandes"[64] (Marx) in motion – to link the static categories and systems of classification of traditional science and logic inseparably to the larger dynamic of history and society.

In so doing, Hegel also overcame the *dualistic* nature of traditional science and logic. By introducing the concept of *substance* and reducing Descartes' *res cogitans* and *res extensa* to mere *modi*, or expressions of this underlying sub-stance, Spinoza had, to be sure, already overcome the most important articu-lation of philosophical dualism in the early modern period, but his concept of substance remained trapped within the rigid geometric forms of his *Ethics*. In the preface to the *Phenomenology of Spirit*, Hegel declared famously that this static substance must be reconceptualized as a dynamic, self-reflexive subject. Horkheimer builds on this important insight of Hegel's, but also moves beyond it decisively. First, he follows Marx in arguing that this subject is not a spiritual entity, mediated primarily by the movement of the concept, but is instead the material life process of society as whole, which consists of concrete individu-als whose interaction is mediated primarily, at least in the bourgeois epoch, by abstract labor. Second, Horkheimer also stresses the blind nature of the type of collective subjectivity that characterizes modern capitalist society, most clearly in "Traditional and Critical Theory":

The individual sees himself as passive and dependent, but society, though made up of individuals, is an active subject, even if a nonconscious one and, to that extent, a subject

---

[63] "On the Problem of Truth," pp. 183–4.
[64] "The stiff cart-horse of bourgeois understanding." *Marx-Engels Werke*, vol. 13 (Berlin: Dietz, 1961), p. 473.

only in an improper sense.... In the bourgeois economic mode the activity of society is blind and concrete, that of individuals abstract and conscious.[65]

Horkheimer does, in other words, preserve Hegel's notion of subjectivity as the most basic category of his dialectical logic. Yet its idealist determination, as the progression of absolute spirit's consciousness of its freedom, is transformed into the material life process of society, which proceeds blindly under the reified social relations of modern capitalism.[66] But before turning to Horkheimer's critical appropriation of Marx for his project on dialectical logic, let us complete our discussion of Hegel by examining the affirmative aspects of his philosophy that Horkheimer explicitly rejected. We have just seen how Horkheimer praised Hegel as the founder of modern dialectical logic, as the first to overcome the abstract ego as well as the static and dualistic concept of knowledge underlying Cartesian-empirical consciousness philosophy. Horkheimer's reliance on Hegel to criticize *Lebensphilosophie* and logical empiricism revealed just how deeply he respected his dialectical logic. Nevertheless, Horkheimer was also convinced that Hegel was not able to move beyond the dichotomy of science and metaphysics that characterized bourgeois philosophy as a whole.

We have just seen how Hegel preserved traditional science; in fact, he saw his philosophy as a whole as a higher form of science. The title page of the original edition of the *Phenomenology of Spirit* clearly marks it as the first part of a "System of Science" ("System der Wissenschaft"), which he would complete later with his *Logic*. Hegel originally intended to call the *Phenomenology* the "Science of the Experience of Consciousness" ("Wissenschaft der Erfahrung des Bewusstseins").[67] Yet despite Hegel's high estimation of science, his philosophy retained a pronounced metaphysical dimension. Horkheimer's critique of the metaphysical dimensions of Hegel's philosophy is at the same time a critique of his dialectical logic, insofar as "logic" designates the most fundamental category in Hegel's thought. In his own efforts to develop a dialectical logic in the 1930s, Horkheimer follows Hegel in this respect; his "dialectical" or "materialist logic" was also an attempt to determine self-reflexively the most important categories – at both the concrete and abstract levels[68] – of a Critical Theory appropriate to the advanced capitalist societies in the early twentieth century. In any case, Horkheimer points to several different metaphysical aspects of Hegel's philosophy. Although Hegel was able to overcome the abstract ego as well as the static and dualistic concept of knowledge underlying consciousness philosophy, his dialectical categories remain – despite their dynamic character – as unitary and closed as any of his metaphysical

---

[65] "Traditional and Critical Theory," p. 200.

[66] On the "material life process of society" as the most basic category of Horkheimer's Critical Theory, see also Chapter 7, p. 250.

[67] For the original title page and title of the *Phenomenology*, see *Phänomenologie des Geistes* (Frankfurt, 1970), pp. 9 and 596, respectively.

[68] So, as Horkheimer stresses in his letters, his project on dialectical logic concerned and included not only abstract categories such as science, truth and praxis, which he addressed in the essays we have been discussing here, but also concrete categories, such as authority and family. See footnote 13 above.

predecessors. Horkheimer makes this point in "The Rationalism Debate..." in the following way:

> In Hegel's thought ... there is in truth only one great process that contains in itself all concepts as its moments, and the philosopher can grasp and represent this process ... once and for all. The individual stages of this representation are thus considered to be eternal relations not just in logic but in the philosophy of nature and spirit as well. All relationships in the completed system are conceived as immutable.... Whoever wishes, at any given time, to grasp the real meaning of any category will have to construct the same image of being, driven by the inner logic of the object ... [which] contains *in nuce* the entire system. The complete theory itself is, in Hegel, no longer drawn into history; it yields an all-comprehending thought, the product of which is no longer abstract and transient. The dialectic is closed.[69]

Hegel's thought is metaphysical, in other words, because the course that the dialectic will take is predetermined from the very beginning; it proceeds the way it does with necessity. Thus, in the final analysis, history is subordinated to the preordained teleology of absolute spirit. So even if this plan must realize itself historically, as Hegel argues, it must also exist prior to, or outside of, history itself. Yet Horkheimer defines modern metaphysics not just in terms of its ahistorical character, but also in relation to its ideological function, what he refers to as *Verklärung*. This crucial concept is difficult to translate, but it essentially means, as we have already seen, positing meaning where none exists and thus providing "spiritual" compensation for real suffering and justifying both the past and present *Weltlauf*.[70] In his essay "On the Problem of Truth," Horkheimer criticizes Hegel's philosophy for being metaphysical in this way. He writes:

> The doctrine of an absolute self-contained truth has the same purpose of harmonizing in a higher spiritual region the "oppositions and contradictions" not resolved in the world. Especially in his later lectures and writings, he stresses that "the sphere of truth, freedom and ... satisfaction" is to be found not in the mechanism of reality but in the spiritual spheres of art, religion and philosophy. He opposes this peace and satisfaction in thought not only to skeptical despair but to the active attempt to overcome the incompleteness of existing conditions "in some other way." ... Hence, Hegel's belief that his thought comprehended the essential characteristics of all being ... represented the conceptual eternalization of the earthly relationships on which it was based. Dialectic takes on a compensatory [*Verklärende*] function.[71]

By locating the ultimate source of his dialectic in a transcendent sphere and by insisting that its development is fixed from the beginning, Hegel reveals his allegiance to a concept of truth that is metaphysical and absolute. In his essay "On the Problem of Truth," Horkheimer's main argument is to illustrate how this absolute, ahistorical concept of truth has coexisted with its opposite, pure relativism, throughout the history of philosophy – and often side by side within the work of individual philosophers – during the bourgeois epoch. Horkheimer

---

[69] "The Rationalism Debate...," p. 239.
[70] "Course of the world." See "Die Tugend und der Weltlauf," *Phänomenologie des Geistes*, op. cit., pp. 283–91.
[71] "On the Problem of Truth," pp. 186–7 (translation amended).

also identifies and criticizes this relativist tendency within Hegel's work; examining it more closely will serve at the same time as a transition to Horkheimer's critical appropriation of Marx's materialist dialectic.

The relativist tendencies in Hegel's thought are closely related to the metaphysical tendencies, according to Horkheimer, insofar as the latter sanction both the course of history and existing social and political conditions. For even though Hegel views conflict as the driving force of history and he believes that history is a progressive realization of freedom and rationality, his teleological assumptions force him to recognize the legitimacy of whatever has triumphed in the past or present. Because the course of history is predetermined, the conceptual work of the philosopher is not determined by the desire to determine which forces have the potential to further the cause of human freedom and rationality in the present, but simply to explain how things have become the way they are. As Hegel famously put it, the owl of Minerva only takes flight at dusk; in other words, the role of the philosopher is reduced to *interpreting* the world rather than using his knowledge to *intervene* and *change* it. Anticipating an argument he would develop in greater detail in his 1938 essay "Montaigne and the Function of Skepticism," Horkheimer describes these relativist tendencies in Hegel's philosophy in the following way:

The attempt to afford justification to every idea and every historical person and to assign the heroes of past revolutions their place in the pantheon of history next to the victorious generals of the counterrevolution, this ostensibly free-floating objectivity ... has acquired validity in the Hegelian system along with the idealist pathos of absolute knowledge. It is self-evident that tolerance toward all views that belong to the past ... is no less relativistic than negativist skepticism.... Since the recognition of the truth of particular ideas disappears in favor of demonstrating what has conditioned them or showing how they correspond with historical unities, this impartial relativism reveals itself as the friend of what exists at any given time. The dogmatism concealed within it is the affirmation of the powers that be.[72]

Horkheimer's critique of the relativistic tendencies in Hegel's philosophy closely parallels his critique of Karl Mannheim's sociology of knowledge.[73] He also accuses Hegel of assuming a free-floating, passive attitude toward history and society, and of placing himself in the position of an omniscient and objective observer, above the fray of real historical conflict. The important question of how Horkheimer proposes to extricate himself from this position, how he legitimates the epistemological validity of his own claims, has concerned many commentators on Horkheimer's work. For, as we have seen, Horkheimer rejected early on Lenin's and Lukács's arguments about the exclusive rights of the proletariat to epistemological universalism. For Horkheimer, those who actively and systematically pursue truth in the form of a Critical Theory of society as whole are neither "firmly rooted" in the standpoint of the proletariat, nor are they "free-floating" in the sense of Mannheim or Hegel. To be sure, Horkheimer does arrogate to "intellectuals" a privileged position in the pursuit and articulation of theoretical truth in the contemporary historical

[72] Ibid., pp. 188–9 (translation amended).
[73] See Chapter 4, pp. 143ff.

period. However, unlike Lenin or Lukàcs, Horkheimer does not, as we shall see, grant intellectuals any *absolute* claims to truth. Untangling these complex and controversial issues leads us to the very heart of Horkheimer's dialectical logic in the 1930s, which proceeds from Hegel, by way of Feuerbach, to Marx and to Horkheimer's own reformulation of Marx's Critical Theory.

HORKHEIMER'S REFORMULATION OF MARX'S CRITICAL THEORY

In contrast to the logical empiricists, Horkheimer did not believe that universal logical categories could be developed in isolation from history, by which he meant not only social history, but also the history of philosophy. Thus, in his own efforts in the 1930s to work out the most important categories of a dialectical logic appropriate to the twentieth century, Horkheimer reconstructed the development of dialectical thought in modern philosophy and determined his concepts in relation to this tradition. As important as Hegel was for Horkheimer's efforts, his philosophy did not represent the final word. We have just examined what Horkheimer considered Hegel's shortcomings. He believed that Marx had overcome most, if not all of them. Horkheimer also believed that no other philosopher or social theorist since Marx had superseded him in any significant way. Freud had, to be sure, developed psychological concepts that were necessary to understand not only twentieth-century societies, but also crucial historical developments throughout the entire modern epoch. However, as became increasingly apparent in his dispute with Erich Fromm near the end of the 1930s, Horkheimer was convinced that psychoanalysis could not be used to understand objective, socio-historical tendencies. It remained an auxiliary science, and claiming otherwise was tantamount to falling back into consciousness philosophy. Horkheimer's work on dialectical logic in the 1930s can and must be seen as an attempt to reformulate some of Marx's key categories in light of changed historical circumstances. In some cases, Horkheimer insisted on the unchanged validity of Marx's concepts; in others, he suggested simply a change of emphasis; and in a few respects, he supplemented Marx's theory with qualitatively new elements. Thus, in what follows we will discuss not only Horkheimer's interpretation of the ways in which Marx moved beyond Hegel, but also the ways in which he developed his own categories in direct dialogue with Marx. After briefly examining the main points of Marx's critique of Hegel, we will examine Horkheimer's appropriation of Marx. We have already seen how and why Horkheimer insisted that Marx's critique of political economy be supplemented with the insights of Freudian psychoanalysis. We have also examined the reasons for and the concrete consequences of Horkheimer's emphasis on the importance of the traditional sciences and empirical research for a Critical Theory of twentieth-century society. Thus, we will not examine the former at all, and will touch only briefly upon the latter. We will, however, return to another key aspect of Horkheimer's Critical Theory, which played a central role – perhaps *the* central role – in his reflections on dialectical logic: his critique of metaphysical and/or progressivist philosophies of history. We shall see how Horkheimer's rejection of any attempt to posit an underlying meaning or predetermined course of history, his insistence on the open-ended character of history, opens the door to some of the most challenging problems of dialectical logic, such as the problem of truth and the relationship between Critical Theory and praxis.

Horkheimer portrays the historical transition from Hegel to Marx – via Feuerbach – most clearly and succinctly in "The Rationalism Debate in the Contemporary Philosophy." He refers there to Feuerbach's critique of Hegel's concept of absolute spirit realizing itself teleologically in history as an inverted, idealistic expression of the history of humanity. Like Marx, Horkheimer both praises Feuerbach, for bringing absolute spirit back down to earth and grounding it in the desires and needs of humanity, and criticizes him, for failing to move beyond an *abstract* concept of humanity. Horkheimer compares Feuerbach's concept of humanity with Dilthey's positing of a unified cultural substrate as the foundation of different historical epochs. As we have seen, Horkheimer remained highly critical of any premature attempt to conceal the contradictions of modern capitalist societies with unitary cultural categories. Horkheimer's arguments here make apparent once again the abiding influence of Marx's *German Ideology* on his thought. Whereas Herbert Marcuse was deeply impressed by the anthropological arguments Marx set forth in his *Paris Manuscripts*,[74] Marx's emphasis in *The German Ideology*– against Feuerbach – on the concrete individual and the deeply divided nature of "humanity" made a more lasting impression on Horkheimer. In his appropriation of psychoanalysis, Horkheimer also insisted that the concrete individual, not any abstract notion of the masses or collective unconscious, should be the focal point of theoretical reflection. Similarly, in his reflections on dialectical logic in the 1930s, Horkheimer did not, of course, abandon his critique of consciousness philosophy. He continued to insist on the preponderance of the "material life process of society," but he also never forgot that this process is constantly mediated by concrete individuals. Thus it comes as no surprise when, in "The Rationalism Debate...," Horkheimer outlines Marx's critique of Feuerbach in the *German Ideology* in terms that reflected some of his own most basic theoretical assumptions. He writes:

Dialectical materialism ... understands the subject of thought not as itself another abstraction such as the essence of "humanity," but rather as human beings of a definite historical epoch. Moreover, these human beings are not hypostatized as isolated units, closed off from one another and from the world; their entire being and thus also their consciousness depend upon their natural endowments every bit as much as upon the overall social relations that have taken shape in their time. According to materialism, therefore, the theory of the social life process is, on the one hand, the most comprehensive mental construction to which analytic research in all areas contributes; on the other hand, this theory is necessarily aimed at the intellectual and material situation, and the impulses deriving from it, that are characteristic of different social classes.[75]

---

[74] See Marcuse's lengthy review essay of the *Paris Manuscripts*, which had just been published in their entirety for the first time in 1932, "New Sources on the Foundation of Historical Materialism," in *Herbert Marcuse: Heideggerian Marxism*, J. Abromeit and R. Wolin (eds.) (University of Nebraska Press, 2005). On the important anthropological dimension of Marcuse's thought, see Stephan Bundschuh, *"Und weil der Mensch ein Mensch ist..." Anthropologische Aspekte der Sozialphilosophie Herbert Marcuses* (Lüneberg, 1998).

[75] "The Rationalism Debate...," (translation amended) p. 240.

However, Horkheimer's Critical Theory also moved beyond the *German Ideology* to encompass Marx's mature critique of political economy. Once Horkheimer had revealed that he viewed not absolute spirit or humanity, but rather the antagonistic social totality of modern capitalist society as the proper point of departure for his dialectical logic, it is but a small step to his claim that Marx had developed, in his mature critique of political economy, the most adequate concepts for understanding this type of society.

Horkheimer makes this claim most clearly in his essay "On the Problem of the Truth" in a discussion of the logical presuppositions of Marx's work. After outlining some of the most general presuppositions of dialectical thinking, which correspond roughly with Hegel's *Logic*, but which also suffer from its weaknesses, insofar as they remain "relatively constant and thus also extremely vacuous," Horkheimer moves to a more concrete level of analysis, and presents his argument that Marx's critique of political economy remains the most important theoretical elaboration of the present historical epoch: "The critique of political economy comprehends the present form of society," as he laconically puts it.[76] Yet Horkheimer is extremely careful not to claim any transcendental or ahistorical validity for Marx's concepts. He insists that their explanatory power lies in their ability to explain the reified social relations peculiar to capitalist societies, the historically unique form of "necessity," or the "second nature" that accompanies them. The strict logical form of Marx's critique of political economy, which develops from the most abstract determination of the commodity, to the more concrete forms of wage labor, profit, rent, and so forth, reflect reified social relations in capitalism, according to Horkheimer. He writes:

This attempt to carry the theory through to the end in the closed form of an inherently necessary succession of ideas has an objective significance. The theoretical necessity mirrors the real compulsiveness with which the production and reproduction of human life goes on in this epoch, the autonomy which the economic forces have acquired in respect to humanity, the dependence of all social groups on the self-regulation of the economic apparatus.[77]

Horkheimer insists that this necessity will continue until social labor is consciously organized to serve the interests of all. Until then, the law of value will continue to dominate all aspects of life, and some version of Marx's categories will remain appropriate for understanding society. Horkheimer illustrates this point by linking Marx's critique of political economy with his own critique of the "possessive individualism" characteristic of the bourgeois epoch.[78] He writes:

As long as the life of society flows not from cooperative work but from the destructive competition of individuals whose relationship is essentially conducted through the exchange of commodities, the ego, possession, the mine and not-mine play a fundamental role in experience, in speech and thought, in all cultural expressions, characterizing and dominating all particulars in a decisive way.[79]

[76] "On the Problem of Truth," p. 205.
[77] Ibid.
[78] On the similarities between Horkheimer's analysis of the anthropology of the bourgeois epoch and C.B. MacPherson's theory of possessive individualism, see Chapter 7, p. 263, footnote 60.
[79] "On the Problem of Truth," p. 206.

In other words, Horkheimer thinks Marx's analysis of modern capitalism was essentially correct, but because Marx's categories are critical and dialectical, because they point beyond themselves to a qualitatively different society, they can by no means be hypostatized as eternal laws. Marx made rigorous truth claims with regard to capitalist society, but his whole project was posited on the possibility of creating a society in which his categories would no longer be true. Horkheimer expresses this critical, dialectical character of Marx's concepts in the following way:

> It would ... be wrong to think that events in a future society could be deduced according to the same principles and with the same necessity as the lines of development of the present one. The meaning of the categories will change along with the structure of the society from which they are drawn and in whose description they play a role.[80]

The obvious question that arises next is how to get from here to there. By placing so much emphasis on the reified social relations of modern capitalism, what possibilities has Horkheimer left open for bringing about a more emancipated society? How, in particular, did Horkheimer address these problems at a time when many of Marx's central predictions, such as the increasing immiseration and growth of the proletariat and its revolutionary potential, seemed to have been proven wrong? Furthermore, how can a Critical Theory, which rests on the premise that a more just and humane society is possible, ground its claims to truth?

We can begin to answer these questions by looking more closely at how *exactly* Horkheimer appropriated Marx's theory in his own efforts to develop a dialectical logic in the 1930s. Horkheimer's insistence on the continuing relevance of Marx's theory did not translate into a dogmatic or rigid adherence to any of its particular aspects. Despite his emphasis in the passages on the logical necessity of Marx's categories, which reflect reified social relations in bourgeois society, Horkheimer rejected the notion that capitalism or Marx's Critical Theory of capitalism were completely closed systems. We have already examined Horkheimer's efforts to integrate psychoanalysis into his Critical Theory and his argument that Marxist theory, if it ignores psychoanalysis, runs the risk of degenerating into a dogmatic philosophy of history.[81] We have also seen how Horkheimer stressed the crucial importance for Critical Theory to integrate the findings of the traditional sciences and to conduct empirical social research in order, once again, to avoid the danger of theoretical ossification. Horkheimer viewed Marx's theory as exemplary in this regard. In fact, he argues explicitly in "On the Problem of Truth" that Marx followed Hegel in preserving the traditional sciences, but departed from him by avoiding a metaphysical philosophy of history. Whereas Horkheimer had discussed the differences between traditional and Critical Theory in Hegel's work in terms of understanding [*Verstand*] and (dialectical) reason [*Vernunft*], he discussed this same distinction in Marx's work in terms of research [*Forschung*] and presentation [*Darstellung*].[82] For Hegel, "understanding stops short at concepts

---

[80] Ibid., p. 205.
[81] See Chapter 7, p. 255.
[82] On Horkheimer's appropriation of Marx's method of *Forschung* and *Darstellung*, see also Helmut Dubiel, *Theory and Politics*, op. cit., esp. pp. 151–4. For a critique of Dubiel's

in their fixed determinateness and difference from one another; dialectic presents them in their transition and dissolution."[83] Horkheimer shows how Marx achieves precisely this transition from understanding to dialectic in *Capital*, through his appropriation and critical reformulation of classical political economy. He writes:

In *Capital*, Marx introduces the basic concepts of classical English political economy – value, price, labor time, etc. – in accordance with their precise definitions. All the most progressive definitions drawn from scientific practice at that time are employed. Nevertheless, these categories acquire new functions in the presentation [*Darstellung*]. They contribute to a theoretical whole, the character of which contradicts the static views in connection with which they came into being, in particular their uncritical use in isolation. Materialist economics as a whole stands opposed to the classical system, yet individual concepts are taken over.[84]

Thus, like Hegel, Marx preserves traditional science; his entire project is formulated as a critique of political economy, and without its findings, *Capital* would not have been possible. Also like Hegel, Marx went beyond the traditional sciences with his critical synthesis, but unlike him, he did not fall back into a closed philosophy of history. For this reason, Horkheimer refers to Marx's method as "the open-ended dialectic."[85] Yet how can Horkheimer reconcile this open-endedness with the aforementioned strict logical character of Marx's theory?

Whereas Horkheimer went beyond Marx by integrating psychoanalytic categories into his Critical Theory, and remained true to his theory with his emphasis on the integration of the traditional sciences and empirical social and historical research, his critique of progressivist philosophies of history addressed an issue about which Marx himself had been ambiguous. On the one hand, Marx believed that capitalism contained certain inherent tendencies which would, if not bring about automatically, at least make the conditions highly favorable for the transition to a socialist society. On the other hand, Marx never completely eliminated the subjective dimension of history. Even though history proceeded "behind the backs" of its human subjects in capitalist societies, according to Marx, it was not predetermined by any transcendent force, as it was for Hegel. Although capital became the dominant subject of world history during the bourgeois epoch, its origins were strictly human: the alienated labor power of workers, which assumed an objective form and dominated those who had been forced to alienate it in the first place in order to survive. As we have seen, Marx captured this negative dialectic with his concept of commodity fetishism. As in his reinterpretation of commodity fetishism in *Dämmerung*,[86] Horkheimer also stresses both sides of the

interpretation, which argues that his application of Marx's categories to Horkheimer's organization of research at the Institute is too mechanical, see Herbert Marcuse et al., "Theory and Politics: A Discussion" *Telos*, no. 38 (winter 1978–9), p. 128.
[83] Quoted by Horkheimer, Ibid., p. 210.
[84] Ibid., p. 209.
[85] Ibid., p. 210.
[86] See Chapter 4, pp. 159–60.

dialectic in his essays in the 1930s: not only the compulsive character of social relations and, ultimately, the course of history itself in the bourgeois epoch, but also the subjective, human origins of the abstract domination of capital, which safeguards the possibility of reining in its power at some time in the future. We have just seen how, in his discussion of the logical foundations of Marx's critique of political economy, Horkheimer stressed the objective, compulsive moment of social relations in capitalism. Yet in his essay "Traditional and Critical Theory," Horkheimer shifted his emphasis back to the subjective dimensions of the negative dialectic of bourgeois society, the moment that Marx's also captured with his concept of *praxis*. Contrary to many misinterpretations of this concept, Marx recognized both the objective socio-historical conditions and the essential theoretical prerequisites of praxis, without losing sight of its equally essential subjective and active moments.[87] Horkheimer did the same with his concept of Critical Theory. He did not, to be sure, confound Critical Theory with Marx's concept of praxis, but he did see Critical Theory as a human activity that preserves and prefigures the possibility of praxis at a time when it seemed foreclosed. Horkheimer's determination of Critical, as opposed to traditional theory, represented in many respects the culmination of his preliminary work on dialectical logic in the 1930s.[88]

In "Traditional and Critical Theory," Horkheimer attempts explicitly to clarify the seeming contradiction between the logical necessity of Marx's categories and the essential moment of subjective freedom in his theory by discussing the concept of necessity itself. He demonstrates that traditional and Critical Theory operate with two qualitatively different concepts of necessity. For the former, causation and necessity are mechanical; they proceed without the intervention of any conscious subjectivity. Horkheimer mentions several examples from the natural sciences to illustrate his point. When studying his object, the natural scientist assumes the role of an external observer. He has no effect on the object he studies, he simply records the laws governing its movement or development. But Critical Theory must not remain content to study the laws governing this or that isolated object; it must, like Hegelian reason [*Vernunft*], or Marxian presentation [*Darstellung*], place these isolated entities in relation to a larger totality, which, according to Horkheimer, is the material life process of society as a whole. Critical Theory "has society itself as its object."[89] As we have seen, Horkheimer follows Hegel in insisting that a dialectical logic move beyond not only Cartesian dualism, which posits the subject as an external

---

[87] On Marx's concept of praxis, see Alfred Schmidt, "Praxis," in *Kritische Theorie, Humanismus, Aufklärung* (Stuttgart, 1981), pp. 110–64, and "Weltkonstitution als Historische Praxis," in *Der Begriff der Natur in der Lehre von Marx* (Frankfurt, 1993), pp. 113–24.

[88] After writing "Traditional and Critical Theory" in 1937, Horkheimer turned his attention to other projects. He continued to organize discussions at the Institute on problems related to dialectical logic (see, for example, the protocols from these discussions published in GS 12, pp. 436–525), but it was not until he moved to Los Angeles with Theodor Adorno in early 1941 that he could begin to work on the project again in a sustained way. The project never came to fruition as Horkheimer had originally planned, but many of the ideas Horkheimer had developed were expressed in *Dialectic of Enlightenment*.

[89] "Traditional and Critical Theory," p. 206.

and passive observer of objects over which is has no control, but also Spinozist monism, which treats the underlying substance of Descartes' *res extensa* and *res cogito* as a static, ahistorical entity. The foundations of dialectical logic and Critical Theory are not substance, but subject. This subject is not a transcendent, metaphysical entity, such as absolute spirit, but rather humanity. Yet within the bourgeois epoch, humanity remains deeply divided, so the subject remains largely blind, its principle form of mediation the law of value, not consensual human will. Hence, the object of Critical Theory can still be described to a certain extent in terms of natural causation, in terms of mechanistic necessity. However, even when Critical Theory describes society in this way, it still preserves an awareness of the subjective origins of reified social conditions and thus also the potential for overcoming them. Horkheimer writes:

Construing the course of history as the necessary product of an economic mechanism simultaneously contains both a protest against this order of things … and the idea of a state of affairs in which man's actions no longer flow from a mechanism but from his own decision. The judgment passed on the necessity inherent in the previous course of events implies here a struggle to change it from a blind to a meaningful necessity.… The concept of necessity in Critical Theory is itself a critical concept; it presupposes freedom, even if a not yet existing freedom.[90]

Horkheimer's arguments here represent an important shift in emphasis in his thought from the early 1930s. At that time, he stressed the importance of viewing bourgeois society as a mechanistic process, dominating by a quasi-natural – in the sense of "second nature" – form of causation. He criticized the dominant tendency in Germany at the time to consider sociology solely as a human science and to reject any similarities it had with the natural sciences.[91] After his emigration to the United States and his confrontation with the logical empiricists and behavioral approaches in psychology and sociology, Horkheimer began to place more emphasis on the active, potentially free, and potentially self-reflexive *subjective* dimensions not only of society, but also of dialectical logic and Critical Theory.[92] This shift in emphasis is apparent, for example, when he refers to Critical Theory as a mode of *conduct* [*ein Verhalten*] or when he reintroduces in his discussion of dialectical logic the concept of *action* [*Handeln*].[93]

---

[90] Ibid., pp. 229–30 (translation amended).

[91] See, for example, Horkheimer's defense of Ernst Mach against Lenin, discussed in Chapter 4, pp. 153–55. At this time, Horkheimer praised Mach's method as an example of the refusal of enlightened reason to capitulate before metaphysics, insofar as he insisted on the unity of theoretical and practical reason, of the natural and human sciences, insofar as both involve determining tendencies and making predictions. Horkheimer argued at this time that Mach's approach held more potential for critical social theory than the various attempts to ground sociology as a human science in Germany in the 1920s. In "Traditional and Critical Theory," on the other hand, Horkheimer argues that identifying laws or tendencies and making predictions is indeed a common characteristic of all traditional theory, but that these laws and tendencies must also be seen self-reflexively, within the larger context of the material life process of society. If this crucial subjective moment is neglected, than stressing the unity of pure and practical reason, on the natural and the human sciences, becomes dogmatic.

[92] For Horkheimer's critique of behaviorism, see "The Latest Attack on Metaphysics," pp. 152ff.

[93] See, for example, "Traditional and Critical Theory," pp. 231–2; "On the Problem of Truth," p. 191; and "The Latest Attack on Metaphysics," pp. 152–4.

Because the material life process of society itself remains the ultimate object of Critical Theory, it attains both a crucial moment of self-reflexivity and also an awareness of its own limitations that set it apart from traditional theory. Critical Theory recognizes its own *active* role in reproducing society as a whole. It makes no pretension to exist outside or above the material life process of society in the manner of Hegel's absolute spirit or Mannheim's free-floating intellectuals. In contrast to traditional theory, in which "the objective occurrence is independent of the theory" and "the observer cannot effect change in the object," Horkheimer refers to Critical Theory as "transformative activity" and "consciously critical conduct" that "belongs to the development of society."[94] Horkheimer argues that the inability of traditional theorists to recognize the unity of theory and praxis prevents them not only from understanding transformative moments in the past – for example, when theory influences the course of revolutionary social movements – but also their own role in realizing or hindering the development of latent, but objective possibilities of creating a more just and humane society in the present. Horkheimer even points to a difference in emphasis on this point between his own conceptualization of Critical Theory and the dialectical methodologies of Hegel and Marx. Echoing his earlier critique of Mannheim, Horkheimer insists that the crucial historical dimension of Critical Theory lies not in uncovering mere correspondences between objective socio-historical structures and theoretical ideas, but in its "conscious relation to historical praxis."[95] On the one hand, the immediate object or content of Critical Theory cannot be separated from history; it is determined by contemporary social struggles, by Critical Theory's "interest in the elimination of social injustice."[96] On the other hand, Horkheimer also stresses that the most basic concepts of Critical Theory do not change radically with each new historical development. Critical Theory must be obstinate enough to recognize the persistence of long-term determinants of social injustice, which Horkheimer identifies with the concepts of modern capitalism and the anthropology of the bourgeois epoch, while at the same being supple enough to recognize the transformation of more immediate categories *within* the bourgeois epoch. As an example of the latter, Horkheimer discusses the transformation of the independent owner-entrepreneur in the liberal capitalism of the nineteenth century, into a nonowning, independent manager on the one hand, and dependent, stock-holding owners on the other hand, in the monopoly capitalism of the twentieth century.[97] Despite the relative constancy of Critical Theory's most basic categories, they still retain their dialectical character insofar as they point toward their own negation; they aim for a qualitatively different society in which they would no longer be valid.

Horkheimer's insistence that Critical Theory play an active role in transforming society, that it take sides in contemporary political struggles, does not, however, translate into a subordination of theory to praxis or, at the opposite

---

[94] "Traditional and Critical Theory," pp. 229 and 232, respectively.
[95] Ibid., p. 234.
[96] Ibid., p. 242.
[97] Ibid., pp. 234–5.

extreme, a belief that theory alone should determine the course of society or historical development. Critical Theory is not "free-floating," as Mannheim would have it, but neither is it firmly rooted, in the sense that it is nothing more than a reflection of the immediate concerns of the proletariat.[98] One of the most important ways in which Horkheimer reacted to the apparent falsification of Marx's claim about the revolutionary role of the proletariat was to sever any *immediate* identification of theory with the praxis of the proletariat. Because the proletariat has already repeatedly demonstrated its susceptibility to acting against its own best interests, it could no longer be assumed, as Lukács had argued in *History and Class Consciousness*, that the standpoint of the proletariat was *ipso facto* a universalist standpoint, or that, in other words, the immediate interests of the proletariat were identical to the interests of society as whole.[99] Horkheimer's stress on the relative independence of Critical Theory and the importance of it being willing to *criticize* working-class politics, if necessary, went hand in hand with his greater emphasis on the subjective moment in theory discussed earlier. In the postscript to his essay on "Traditional and Critical Theory," and in the companion piece to the essay written by Herbert Marcuse called "Philosophy and Critical Theory," Horkheimer and Marcuse both stress the importance of maintaining the relative autonomy of philosophy and the imagination vis-à-vis the immediate concerns of the working class. Yet it would also be a mistake to interpret this shift in emphasis as a "rephilosophization" of Critical Theory, as some commentators have.[100] As Olaf Asbach has demonstrated convincingly, Horkheimer's new emphasis on the importance of philosophy and the imagination did not alter the fundamentally materialist assumptions of his Critical Theory.[101] Among these assumptions are Critical Theory's recognition of its own limitations, a recognition that it is one important means of realizing a more just and humane society in which individuals' needs are met and their opportunities for happiness greater than in antagonistic bourgeois society. Theory is never an end in itself and it cannot fulfill the "messianic function" of grasping the totality.[102] As important as Horkheimer considered Critical Theory for augmenting the possibility of conscious social change, he never succumbed to the delusion of the omnipotence of thought. In the late 1930s, Horkheimer still believed, as he had put it earlier in *Dämmerung*, that the transition to a socialist society would be brought about by people schooled in Critical Theory, or not at all; but he's also aware that Critical Theory is ultimately driven by the interests of concrete individuals in a better life, not by its own perfect knowledge of the social totality or privileged insight into a utopian blueprint of a better society. Horkheimer stresses time

---

[98] Ibid., pp. 223–4.

[99] Moishe Postone's attempt to separate Marx's categories from the historically specific forms of the labor movement in industrial capitalism could be interpreted as developing Horkheimer's argument here. See *Time, Labor and Social Domination*, op. cit., pp. 21–42.

[100] See Helmut Dubiel, *Theory and Politics*, op. cit., p. 106.

[101] Olaf Asbach, *Kritische Gesellschaftstheorie und Historische Praxis: Entwicklung der Kritischen Theorie bei Max Horkheimer 1930–1942/43* (Frankfurt and New York: Peter Lang, 1997), pp. 173ff.

[102] "Traditional and Critical Theory," p. 223.

and again that *knowledge* of the totality is impossible, while at the same insisting that Critical Theory must also remain cognizant of the decisive influence of the social totality on all aspects of its analysis. In any case, Critical Theory never achieves ahistorical validity; it can never separate itself completely from the most important concrete historical tasks in the present.

How then does Critical Theory ground it claims to truth? Despite its pessimistic analysis of the antagonistic tendencies driving bourgeois society, for Critical Theory, history remains radically "open-ended." Its future course depends on the contingent actions of concrete individuals. Critical Theory makes no promises about the future, but its analyses highlight the potential of moving beyond the antagonistic tendencies of modern capitalism. In this respect, the most important truth claims of Critical Theory are not only historical to the very core, they also differ in their logical structure from the truth claims of traditional theory. We have just seen how the dialectical logic of Hegel and Marx moves beyond the formal logic of traditional theory, but it is worth looking once more at the specific implications of dialectical logic for Horkheimer's concept of truth. In "Traditional and Critical Theory," Horkheimer refers to Critical Theory "in its totality" as "the unfolding of a single existential judgment."[103] This concept has been the source of some confusion, even consternation in the secondary literature on Horkheimer.[104] Some commentators, such as Martin Jay, have raised the question: How does Horkheimer ground the legitimacy and validity of such a seemingly sweeping "existential judgment"? To answer this question, let us first examine Horkheimer's own description of the "existential judgment" that forms the (historical) core of his Critical Theory. Horkheimer writes:

To put it in broad terms, the theory says that the basic form of the historically given commodity economy on which modern history rests contains in itself the internal and external contradictions of the modern era; it generates these contradictions over and over again in an increasingly heightened form; and after a period of progress, development of human powers, and emancipation of the individual, after an enormous extension of human control over nature, it finally hinders further development and drives humanity into a new barbarism.[105]

This is the basic dialectic of bourgeois society, whose various manifestations Horkheimer had been analyzing since his break with consciousness philosophy in 1925. The "existential" character of the judgment pronounced on bourgeois society here lies in the fact that it does not have to be the final word in human development. Just as Marx's critical concepts not only describe and analyze – but also point beyond – capitalist society, so Horkheimer's Critical Theory refuses to accept bourgeois society at its own word, as the natural and eternal consummation of history. Horkheimer makes this point explicitly in a short discussion of the status of his concept of an "existential judgment" vis-à-vis

---

[103] Ibid., p. 227.

[104] As Martin Jay points out, one commentator even took the term as a sign that Horkheimer's Critical Theory was a variant of existentialism. See Martin Jay, *Marxism and Totality: The Adventures of a Concept from Lukács to Habermas* (Berkeley and Los Angeles, 1984), p. 210.

[105] "Traditional and Critical Theory," p. 227 (translation amended).

other forms of judgment, such as categorical, hypothetical, and disjunctive. Categorical judgments are, according to him, characteristic of precapitalist societies: "This is the way it is and man can do nothing about it." Hypothetical and disjunctive judgments are characteristic of bourgeois society: "Under certain circumstances this effect can take place; it is either thus or so." Yet Critical Theory follows dialectical logic in maintaining the possibility of qualitative change: "It need not be so; man can change reality, and the necessary conditions for such change already exist."[106]

In any case, Horkheimer did not still believe in the "inevitability of capitalism's collapse" at this time only to abandon this belief later in *Dialectic of Enlightenment*.[107] Probably due in large part to his early exposure to Schopenhauer, Horkheimer had always been critical of philosophies of history that posited a rational, underlying plan, be it positive or negative. As we have seen, this critique of metaphysical philosophies of history ran throughout Horkheimer's work, and was crucial for his project on dialectical logic in the 1930s. Because history is radically open-ended, Critical Theory has a chance to influence its future course for the better, but there are no guarantees. Critical Theory is not omnipotent, but the "single existential judgment" upon which it rests is not a groundless, unmediated, and utopian wish either. Horkheimer stresses that

the individual steps within the theory are, at least in intention, as rigorous as the deductions in a specialized scientific theory; each is an element in the constitution of that comprehensive existential judgment. Particular parts of the theory can be changed into general or specific hypothetical judgments and applied after the fashion of traditional theory.[108]

However, in contrast to the hypothetical judgments of traditional theory, the existential judgment that underlies and informs all the categories of Critical Theory, preserves the consciousness of the historical character of bourgeois society and the possibility of creating a more humane alternative. The question remains, however, how Horkheimer can ground such existential judgments, particularly when they seemed at least in part to have been refuted by historical events.

Horkheimer addresses this problem explicitly in a discussion of the concept of corroboration [*Bewährung*] in his essay "On the Problem of Truth." Horkheimer develops his arguments by differentiating Critical Theory from the pragmatist conception of corroboration. Like Critical Theory, the pragmatists reject transcendental or absolute validity claims. For them, truth is also linked to history and society insofar as it must prove its efficacy under present conditions. What is true for the pragmatists is what works, what is effective and efficient, and/or what "enhances life."[109] Because our primary concern here is to clarify Horkheimer's own concept of truth, we will not pursue the question of whether Horkheimer's interpretation does justice to the pragmatists'

[106] Ibid.
[107] As Martin Jay argues in *Marxism and Totality*, p. 210.
[108] "Traditional and Critical Theory," p. 227.
[109] "On the Problem of Truth," p. 197.

epistemological position. Horkheimer did indeed realize that pragmatism was, precisely on this crucial issue, quite close to Critical Theory. This is the reason why it was so important for him to clarify the differences between pragmatism and Critical Theory. Horkheimer's most important criticism of the pragmatists was that they lacked a theory of society as a whole. Because of this crucial deficit, their concepts retained a formalistic and affirmative character. Horkheimer sees structural similarities between American pragmatism and the various positivist schools of thought in Europe in the mid-nineteenth century, insofar as both presuppose a necessary correlation between the progress of science and the development of a more humane society. The breakdown of this belief in Europe, beginning already after the economic crisis of 1873, that is, the steady decline in legitimacy of science vis-à-vis philosophy, which Horkheimer described in his lectures in the 1920s, seemed to have left the basic underlying confidence of pragmatism unscathed. For unlike later continental philosophers who operated with a pragmatic concept of science, such as Bergson, the pragmatists felt no need to supplement their belief in science with any metaphysical affirmations of a "deeper," nonscientific realm. This satisfaction with science alone reflected what appeared to Horkheimer as a rather unreflective "limitless trust in the world as it is."[110] The pragmatists had not yet attained the level of self-reflexivity implied by a theory of society as a whole. Horkheimer writes:

The epistemological doctrine that the truth promotes life, or rather that all thought that "pays" must also be true, contains a harmonistic illusion if this theory of cognition does not belong to a whole in which the tendencies working toward a better, life-promoting situation really find expression. Separated from a particular theory of society as a whole, every theory of cognition remains formalistic and abstract. Not only expressions like *life* and *promotion*, but also terms seemingly specific to cognitive theory such as *verification, confirmation, corroboration*, etc. remain vague and indefinite, despite the most scrupulous definition … if they do not stand in relation to real history and receive their definition by being part of a comprehensive theoretical unity.[111]

But is Horkheimer begging the question here, or worse yet, advancing a circular form of argumentation whose claims to validity rest on an entity – society as a whole – whose concrete characteristics, even existence, he does not demonstrate?[112]

To be sure, there is a long nominalist tradition, particularly strong in the Anglo-American intellectual tradition, which defends the view, pithily expressed in more recent times by Margaret Thatcher, that there is no such thing as society, only individuals. Whereas Horkheimer is also generally skeptical about unified theoretical categories, and insists on the concrete individual as one of

[110] Ibid., p. 196.
[111] Ibid., p. 197.
[112] For later discussions of the concept of "society" in the tradition of Critical Theory that remain very similar to Horkheimer's original determination, see "Gesellschaft" in *Frankfurter Beigträge zur Soziologie*, vol. 4 (Frankfurt, 1956), pp. 22–39. See also Alex Demirovic, *Modelle Kritischer Gesellschaftstheorie: Traditionen und Perspektiven der Kritischen Theorie* (Stuttgart, 2003), pp. 17–22.

the cornerstones of any Critical Theoretical analysis, he also demands that the individual always be seen in relation to the concrete form of the material life process of society at any given time. Horkheimer views Critical Theory as one moment of social *praxis*; in other words, as one moment in the reproduction of society as a whole. However, as we have seen, Horkheimer considers the substance of modern capitalist societies to be a blind form of subjectivity. Society as a whole develops, according to him, according to the uncoordinated and unplanned, competitive activities of individual producers, each of whom is guided by the imperative to maximize personal gain. Thus, society as a whole remains antagonistic and constantly contains the potential for crisis, even the reversion to barbarism. The foremost task of Critical Theory, according to Horkheimer, is to preserve the consciousness of this dynamic underlying capitalist societies. Almost all of Horkheimer's work can be seen as an attempt to document the existence of these tendencies at various stages in the development of bourgeois society: from his lectures in the late 1920s, in which he interpreted the history of modern philosophy as the mediated expression of the uneven development of bourgeois society in modern Europe; to his aphorisms in *Dämmerung*, in which he presented micrological interpretations of the divergent ways members of different social strata experience seemingly universal aspects of human existence within bourgeois society; to his analysis of the anthropology of the bourgeois epoch, in which he traces the historical development of character structures resulting from the "passive and active adjustment" of individuals' drives to the imperatives of bourgeois society. Horkheimer accuses the pragmatists of having an impoverished concept of praxis, because their notion of falsification or corroboration of truth claims is not linked to a Critical Theory of society as a whole, which in the modern capitalist era is bourgeois society. Thus, in accordance with other types of traditional theory, it tests truth claims solely in regard to their efficacy, efficiency, usefulness, and/ or ability to "enhance life" within whatever isolated section of bourgeois society they happen to be examining at the time. Because it does not relate these truth claims to a larger theory of society as a whole, it runs the risk, on the one hand, of collapsing the distinction between truth and success, and the risk, on the other hand, of prematurely dismissing objectively possible ways of eliminating injustice and suffering, simply because their realization has been hindered until now. Horkheimer writes:

The truth is a moment of correct praxis. But whoever identifies it directly with success passes over history and makes himself an apologist for the reality dominant at any given time.... While it is the duty of everyone who acts responsibly to learn from setbacks in practice, these can nevertheless not destroy the confirmed basic structure of the theory, in terms of which alone they can be understood as setbacks. According to pragmatism, the corroboration of ideas and their truth merge. According to materialism, corroboration, the demonstration that ideas and objective reality correspond, is itself a historical occurrence that can be obstructed and interrupted.[113]

[113] "On the Problem of Truth," p. 200.

More directly and passionately, Horkheimer asks himself what the possible implications of the pragmatists' views might be:

Cannot the crudest superstition, the most miserable perversion of the truth about world, society, justice, religion, and history grip whole peoples and perfectly corroborate the views of its originator and his followers? On the other hand, does the defeat of the forces of freedom signify the disproof of their theory?[114]

Horkheimer's reflections here on corroboration clearly reflect the increasingly desperate and isolated situation he found himself in as a socialist intellectual in the mid-1930s. In fact, Horkheimer's reflections on dialectical logic as a whole represent an attempt to reassess the validity, or lack thereof, of Marx's theoretical project at a time when it seemed, in many ways, to have been disproved.[115]

Let us conclude with some final reflections on Horkheimer's concept of praxis. Horkheimer does indeed view Critical Theory as one moment in the larger "praxis" of the reproduction of society as a whole, but this does not, as we have seen, lead him to subordinate theory to praxis in any way. Horkheimer states clearly, "In regard to the identity of theory and practice, however, their difference is not to be forgotten."[116] Just as Marx's concept of praxis is often falsely interpreted as a justification for voluntarist positions, so Horkheimer's emphatic separation of Critical Theory from the immediate political concerns in the 1930s is often read as a retreat into a young Hegelian position. Yet as we have seen, Horkheimer's separation of theory from immediate political practice takes place within the larger context of the praxis of society as a whole. By preserving a historically and sociologically founded Critical Theory of this society, an awareness that "the whole is the untrue" – as Adorno would put it a few years later – was perhaps one of Horkheimer's most important contributions to socialist theory in the twentieth century. Even if his insistence in "Traditional and Critical Theory" that the "truth" has become in the present the possession

---

[114] Ibid., p. 198.

[115] Gerd-Walter Küsters emphatically makes a similar point in his study, *Der Kritikbegriff der Kritischen Theorie Max Horkheimers: Historisch-Systematische Untersuchung zur Theoriegeschichte* (Frankfurt and New York, 1980), pp. 39ff. He argues that the crisis of Marxism in the 1930s led Horkheimer away from Marx's concept of Critical Theory as a critique of reality, to a concept of Critical Theory as reflection upon its own epistemological foundations. In relation to Horkheimer's project on dialectical logic, Küsters' arguments make sense. Horkheimer did realize that Critical Theory in the Marxist tradition must constantly reflect on its own conditions in light of historical experience. Yet these efforts to maintain the self-reflexivity of Critical Theory did not – contra Küsters – preclude an attempt to develop a Critical Theory of the "reality" of modern capitalism and its contemporary manifestations. As we have seen in Chapter 7, pp. 286ff. Horkheimer's concept of bourgeois anthropology represented a decisive step beyond mere methodological reflections. Even his project on dialectical logic was not conceived as an epistemological project in the traditional sense, i.e. as an attempt to establish the conditions of knowledge in an ahistorical manner. The whole point of dialectical logic was to develop categories that were adequate to current social and historical conditions. Nonetheless, Küsters is correct to emphasize the link between the crisis of Marxism and the crisis of science more generally in the 1930s as perhaps the most important motivation for Horkheimer's reflections on dialectical logic during this time.

[116] "On the Problem of Truth," p. 200.

of a few isolated individuals and groups – among which he of course included himself – sounds dangerously elitist to us today, the subsequent reception of Horkheimer's and his Institute colleagues' work, more than justifies his theoretical obstinacy. Horkheimer would, of course, distance himself in the postwar period from the essays he wrote in the 1930s, and it would run contrary to the one of the most basic principles of dialectical logic and Critical Theory to attempt to apply his insights in an unmediated way to the present. Nonetheless, Horkheimer's defense of Critical Theory as a form of praxis, one that does not need to bow to immediate political concerns, certainly remains one of his most important, and neglected legacies.

Excursus I

The Theoretical Foundations of Horkheimer's Split with Erich Fromm in the Late 1930s

Fromm's Critique of Freud's Drive Theory

Having established the basic concepts and methods that characterized Horkheimer's model of Critical Theory through approximately 1938, we are now in a position to identify the causes and consequences of the rather dramatic shift in his thought that occurred in the subsequent years. At the risk of being overly schematic, one could say that the three most important factors in this shift were Horkheimer's break with Fromm, his increasingly close working relationship with Theodor Adorno, and his general acceptance of Friedrich Pollock's argument about the emergence in the 1930s of a new form of "state capitalism." This brief excursus will examine the theoretical causes and consequences of Horkheimer's break with Fromm. The following, lengthier excursus will address Horkheimer's shifting relationship with Adorno in the 1930s. After setting the stage with these two excursuses, we will be able to add the final piece of the puzzle of Horkheimer's shift, namely the new concept of "state capitalism."

In this study so far, a significant amount of space has been devoted to reconstructing the early theoretical development of Erich Fromm. This careful examination of the early Fromm is justified insofar as Horkheimer's own early theoretical development cannot be understood apart from Fromm's influence. Already in the late 1920s, Horkheimer had sought to secure Fromm's loyalty by offering him a lifetime membership in the Institute and an opportunity to conduct a major research project on the attitudes of the German salaried employees and workers. What strikes the close observer of the development of Critical Theory in the late 1920s and early 1930s are the remarkable similarities and complementarity of the work of Fromm and Horkheimer. It is not an exaggeration to say, as Rolf Wiggershaus does, that Fromm was Horkheimer's most important theoretical interlocutor during this time.[1] Although Horkheimer was always the senior partner in the relationship,[2] Fromm's psychoanalytic training and his abiding interest in applying psychoanalytic categories to social and historical problems put him in a position not only to collaborate with Horkheimer, but also genuinely to contribute to the advancement of Critical Theory. As we have seen in earlier chapters, Horkheimer and Fromm were both

---

[1] *Die Frankfurter Schule*, p. 304.

[2] See, for example, Erich Klein-Landskron, "Max Horkheimer und Erich Fromm," *Erich Fromm und die Frankfurter Schule*, eds. Michael Kessler und Rainer Funk (Tübingen: Francke, 1992), S. 161–80.

interested in a selective and critical appropriation of psychoanalytic categories, which would be placed within a larger Marxist theory of history and society. Both were interested, in particular, in using Freud's early drive theory and his notions of introversion, repression, and compensation to revise and bring up to date Marx's theory of ideology. The collaboration between Horkheimer and Fromm reached a high point in 1935, when Fromm completed his introductory essay for the Institute's collective *Studies on Authority and Family*, which was published at the beginning of 1936. Fromm's essay presented a *psychoanalytic* analysis of the sadomasochistic character, whose origins and development Horkheimer would subsequently seek to explain *historically* in his 1936 essay, "Egoism and Freedom Movements." At this point, there was still an extensive unity in Horkheimer and Fromm's theoretical interests and approaches.

Yet at this same time, Fromm began to move away from orthodox Freudianism. The beginnings of this process were already apparent in his 1935 essay, "The Social Determinants of Psychoanalytic Theory," in which he castigated Freud for various unquestioned bourgeois assumptions that allegedly guided his theory – such as a negative view of political radicalism and his insistence that the analyst maintain a distant and neutral rather than an empathetic attitude toward his patients.[3] The theoretical foundations for Fromm's new position were fully articulated for the first time in a lengthy essay he wrote in the fall and winter of 1936–7. Fromm never published this "fundamental essay" – as he referred to it – but it did become the subject of an internal discussion and debate that would have far-reaching consequences for Fromm and the Institute. Fromm's unmistakable move away from orthodox Freudianism in this and other essays during this time, in combination with a number of biographical factors, culminated in a complete break with the Institute in 1939. In light of the depth of Fromm's involvement with Horkheimer and the Institute, it comes as little surprise that this break was a drawn-out and difficult affair. Because the story of Fromm's departure from the Institute has been recounted elsewhere by several able commentators, there is no need to recapitulate it here.[4] In the following brief excursus, I would like instead to provide a reassessment of one crucial aspect of this story, namely the theoretical split that emerged between Horkheimer and Fromm during this time, which centered on Fromm's critique of Freud's drive theory. Such a reassessment is warranted here for two main reasons. First, Fromm's "fundamental essay" was first discovered and published in 1992, thereby making available a key source to which earlier commentators did not have access.[5] Second, the fact that Horkheimer was not willing to follow Fromm on this issue sheds much light on the basic premises

---

[3] *International Forum of Psychoanalysis*, vol. 9, no. 3–4, trans. E. Falzeder and C. Schwarzacher (October 2000) S. 149–65.

[4] Jay, *The Dialectical Imagination*, pp. 88–106; Wiggershaus, *Die Frankfurter Schule*, pp. 298–307. For Fromm's own retrospective views on the subject, see also "Ein Memorandum in Eigener Sache," *Erich Fromm und die Frankfurter Schule*, op. cit., pp. 249–56.

[5] For a brief overview of how the text was discovered, its main arguments, and the controversies it provoked in the Institute, see Rainer Funk's "Foreword" in Erich Fromm, *Gesellschaft und Seele: Beiträge zur Sozialpsychologie und zur psychologischen Praxis*, ed. Rainer Funk (Weinheim: Beltz, 1992), pp. 13–21.

of his own Critical Theory. In what follows, I will first demonstrate how and why Fromm abandoned Freud's drive theory; second, how Fromm's new position represented an immanent critique of his own early work; and, finally, how this critique pushed him further away from Horkheimer's early model of Critical Theory.

As we have seen, in his early work Fromm relied heavily on Freud's early drive theory, with its distinction between self-preservation and libidinal drives and its emphasis on the much greater variability in the possibility of satisfying, or at least partially satisfying, the latter.[6] This remarkable plasticity of the libidinal drives – theorized for the first time by Freud[7] – made it possible for Fromm to provide more precise explanations for a wide variety of *social* phenomena, particularly those involving real sacrifice and imaginary or symbolic compensation. However, in a dramatic departure from his early work, in his 1936–7 "fundamental essay" Fromm abandons Freud's distinction between self-preservation and libidinal drives and replaces it with a distinction between "naturally given physiological drives" and "psychic impulses that develop historically and in the social process."[8] Fromm's use of the term "drives" [*Triebe*] to refer to biological and allegedly ahistorical needs, and his use of the term "impulses" to refer to needs that have been shaped by social and historical factors, already mark the departure from his earlier position. In his "fundamental essay," Fromm develops this new distinction between biological drives and socio-historical impulses on the basis of a parallel distinction between the two basic tendencies at work in Freud's theory of subjectivity. On the one hand, in his mature theory Freud explains the formation of subjectivity in terms of "object relations" or, in other words, the social relations that shape the child's personality during its formative years and, to a lesser degree, in later years as well. On the other hand, Freud explains subjectivity as the more or less successful result of a physiologically predetermined process of bringing biological partial instincts (the oral and anal erogenous zones) under the control of genital supremacy. Fromm claims that these two different explanations for the formation of subjectivity have almost always been confounded in the psychoanalytic literature.[9] He argues, first, that they should be distinguished sharply from each other and, second, that only the former, social tendency is really convincing and worth developing theoretically. The latter, biological tendency eliminates the historically mediated character of human behavior and reduces it to the merely instinctual behavior of animals.

---

[6] For example, in *The Dogma of Christ*, Fromm wrote: "The sex drives up to a certain and not insignificant point, permit a gratification in fantasies and with one's own body; they are therefore much more independent of external reality than are the ego drives. ... This flexibility and versatility within the sexual drives are the basis for the extraordinary variability of the psychic structure and therein lies also the basis for the possibility that individual experiences can so definitely and markedly affect the libido structure." Op. cit., p. 8.

[7] See, for example, his essay on "Repression," op. cit, or his discussion of the "perversions" in the *Introductory Lectures on Psychoanalysis*, trans. J. Strachey (New York: Norton, 1966), pp. 303–19.

[8] "Determiniertheit," p. 59.

[9] Ibid., p. 27.

Fromm's insistence on a clear distinction between historical impulses and biological drives was, in other words, motivated by his desire to overcome what he perceived as the untenable biological dimensions of psychoanalysis. To illustrate this point, Fromm returns to the concept of character structure, which had played such a crucial role in his and Horkheimer's early Critical Theory, and which would continue to play an important role in both his work and the work of other Institute members after their break with Fromm. Fromm introduces a concept of "social character,"[10] which is defined in antithesis to the allegedly biological aspects of Freud's theory of character structure. Fromm objects, in particular, to Freud's attempt to explain character structure as a direct result of the success or failure of a physiologically predetermined process of psychosexual development. Insofar as Freud adheres to this model and discounts the importance of environmental factors in the formation of character traits, he remains beholden, according to Fromm, to an outdated model of nineteenth-century instinct theory. Fromm writes:

In regard to his theory of the psychic impulses as direct derivatives of pregenital sexuality, Freud is an instinct theorist.... Instinct theorists tend to ground human psychology in animal psychology and to overlook the fact that, just as man has created a second nature in his tools, so a second nature in psychological terms has also emerged inside him, namely, the psychological impulses and attitudes that are specific to man and are neither hereditary and bodily based instincts nor their direct derivatives.... But emphasizing the psychological commonality of humans and animals in this way caused one to overlook the decisive differences between man and animals and the fact that humans have developed qualities that cannot be found in the animal kingdom. This is not an objection to the evolutionary insight that humans have developed from animals, but instead only to a mechanical theory of evolution, which overlooks that the quantity of changes has transformed itself into new qualities that are specific to man.[11]

It is worth noting and emphasizing here that Fromm equates Freud's drive theory primarily with his theory of the partial drives, pregenital sexuality, and psychosexual development, which he criticizes as a "mechanical theory of evolution." We will return to this important point momentarily, but let us first examine some of the other evidence Fromm's provides to support his case against Freud's drive theory.

The main example Fromm provides in this essay of the pitfalls of Freud's drive theory is the anal character.[12] As Fromm reads him, Freud would have to explain the existence of strong "anal" character traits primarily as a direct result of events that took place in an individual's infancy during the anal phase of psychosexual development – such as a stronger than normal tendency to retain one's feces. Fromm rejects this explanation because it traces the existence of character traits back to individual and biological sources and ignores

---

[10] This concept would remain at the heart of Fromm's subsequent work; indeed, he considered it his "most important contribution to the field of social psychology." Quoted by Martin Jay, *The Dialectical Imagination*, p. 99.

[11] "Determiniertheit," pp. 54–6.

[12] Ibid., pp. 60–76.

the fact that social conditions are much more important sources of character formation. Fromm argues:

A genetic theory of the formation of personality types should not be focused on the erogenous zones, but instead on typical constellations that give rise to specific character structures. Insofar as we are interested in character traits that transcend specific individual differences, such constellations are social. We find that what Freud described as the anal character is in fact in its most pronounced form the average character of the European petty bourgeois. Thus, from the genetic point of view, a personality type such as the "petty bourgeois" character appears to be a possible, genetically oriented personality formation and, in any case, to be more correct scientifically than the "anal" character.[13]

In addition to buttressing his case against Freud's drive theory, Fromm's argument here for a *social* explanation of the anal character also represented an attempt to move beyond the relatively crude methodology of the empirical study of German workers, which he was revising for publication at this time. As we have seen, in that study Freud's theory of psychosexual development was appropriated rather mechanically to classify workers' unconscious political attitudes. A revolutionary attitude was equated with the genital character type, whereas "ambivalent" and "reactionary" political attitudes were equated with fixation at a pregenital level. Yet Fromm's argument also pointed beyond the recently published *Studies on Authority and Family* insofar as Fromm was less willing than Horkheimer to grant relative autonomy to the family in the process of character formation. As Fromm put it:

The family [is] not the "cause" of character formation, but is instead the mechanism for transmitting socially determined traits to the individual. In other words, the family is the psychological agent of society.... The way in which children are raised cannot be understood as the ultimate explanatory principle.[14]

In short, with his break from Freudian drive theory – as he interpreted it – Fromm wanted to establish the absolute primacy of the social in the process of character formation; neither biological factors, nor early individual experiences, nor the family could rival the historically specific *social* factors involved in Fromm's theory of subjectivity.

At first glance, it seems that Horkheimer would have had little to object to in Fromm's newfound emphasis on social factors in the formation of character structures. Horkheimer had, after all, always insisted on the primacy of objective factors in his Critical Theory and had even criticized Fromm for attempting to apply psychological categories in an unmediated way to history and society. However, Horkheimer did object to Fromm's critique of Freud's drive theory; in fact, his objections can be seen as the most important cause leading to Fromm's departure from the Institute in 1939. Three issues must be examined in order to understand why Fromm's position was not acceptable to Horkheimer and the other members of the Institute. First, Fromm's reinterpretation of Freud jettisoned certain aspects of his drive theory that

---

[13] Ibid., pp. 75–6.
[14] Ibid., pp. 49–50.

Horkheimer considered essential. Although Horkheimer agreed with many of Fromm's criticisms of Freud's biological assumptions and his teleological theory of psychosexual development, he held firm to another crucial aspect of Freud's theory, namely the plasticity of libidinal drives. Second, Fromm's rejection of the uniquely malleable character of libidinal drives undermined some of the key assumptions of his earlier essays – such as the link between repression and surplus aggression – which had become an integral part of Horkheimer's Critical Theory. Finally, Fromm's new position led him to an existentialist philosophical anthropology, which was antithetical to some of Horkheimer's most basic assumptions.

Fromm identified "drive theory" with Freud's theory of the partial instincts and his theory of psychosexual development. Fromm objected, in particular, to explaining character structures as a *direct* result – in the form of a sublimation or reaction formation – of this physiologically predetermined process of individual development.[15] Horkheimer agreed with Fromm insofar as Freud identified the mature, genital character with bourgeois man. Both Horkheimer and Fromm were interested in historicizing bourgeois man, not naturalizing him as the ahistorical model of psychological maturity. Horkheimer's "Egoism and Freedom Movements" was originally supposed to be called "On Bourgeois Man," and Fromm's *Escape from Freedom* was also begun – with Horkheimer's full approval – as a study of the bourgeois character structure. Like Marx, Horkheimer and Fromm both viewed the dominant bourgeois character structure as a product of modern capitalist society, and both believed the negative aspects of the bourgeois character – such as cruelty, coldness, indifference, and asceticism – could be overcome or at least ameliorated in a postcapitalist society.

Horkheimer's main interest in Freud was his ability to explain the mechanisms of sacrifice, spiritualization, and compensation. To better explain such phenomena and to supplement Marx's theory of ideology, Horkheimer drew on psychoanalytic concepts such as repression and introversion, which rested on Freud's theory of libidinal drives and, in particular, his innovative notion of the plasticity of the libido. This notion of the ability of libidinal drives to attach themselves to just about any object (concrete or imaginary; and to find satisfaction in such cathected objects) was present in latent form from the very beginning of psychoanalysis – that is, Freud and Breuer's first studies of hysterics such as Anna O. and Elizabeth von R.[16] The notion of conversion hysteria, which had figured so prominently in the birth of psychoanalysis as a discipline, rested on the notion that the energy contained in certain affects or desires that had been censored by the individual's conscience – that is, internalized social and moral norms – would not simply disappear, but would remain in

---

[15] Ibid., pp. 61–5. Fromm's argument is here directed against Freud's short essay, "Anal Eroticism and Character Structure," in which he argues that character traits can be understood as a sublimation or reaction formation to the stages of pregenital psychosexual development. *The Complete Psychological Works of Sigmund Freud*, vol. 9, trans. and ed. James Strachey (London: Hogarth, 1974), p. 175.

[16] *Studies in Hysteria, The Complete Psychological Works of Sigmund Freud*, op. cit., vol. 20.

the unconscious, proliferate, and eventually manifest themselves in some indirect way, such as a physical symptom or compulsive behavior. Even if Freud and Breuer were still relying on the trauma theory of the neuroses in their *Studies of Hysteria*, an explicitly sexual model of neuroses that rested on the notion of the plasticity of the libidinal drives would move to the center of Freud's theory in the late 1890s.[17] This dynamic sexual theory of the etiology of neuroses was intended to provide a richer and more nuanced explanation of the "normal" development of sexuality than was possible with the "psychophysiological" model that had guided Freud's (and Josef Breuer's) early explorations of neuroses.[18] During the next two decades, as Freud expanded the scope of psychoanalysis from the etiology of neuroses and their therapeutic treatment to a theory of the "normal" mind and "normal" sexuality, he would begin to rely increasingly on evolutionary models, especially after the publication of *Totem and Taboo* in 1913. Freud would outline the implications of his new evolutionary assumptions for his theory of psychosexual development in the introductory lectures on psychoanalysis he delivered at the University of Vienna between 1915 and 1917.[19] He would not fully develop this evolutionary theory of psychosexual development until 1923, with his introduction of the concept of the "phallic phase."[20] In other words, the evolutionary theory of psychosexual development was a relatively late addition to Freud's theory. This theory was supposed to provide a more precise explanation of the etiology of neuroses based on fixations and regression to early stages in the psychosexual process of development. Yet the basic assumptions of the earlier model, including the plasticity of libidinal drives, remained central to Freud's thinking.

However, Freud's evolutionary theory of psychosexual development also marked the point in which his thinking reflected most clearly the dominant prejudices of his time. As is well known, Freud prided himself on continuing Darwin's legacy by demonstrating that the ego was not even master in his own house.[21] Yet the rather mechanical evolutionary assumptions that became increasingly prominent in his theory of psychosexual development placed him closer to Herbert Spencer and the Social Darwinists than to Darwin himself. Whereas Darwin had stressed fortuitous factors in the process of natural selection and rejected any notion of preordained linear development – thus making it impossible to see humanity as the telos of nature – a wide variety of would-be inheritors of his ideas cast the caution aside with which Darwin

---

[17] Freud's adoption of a new theory of the neuroses, which rested on the dynamic character of libidinal drives, was the main reason why he split with Breuer, who, like Adler and Fromm later, refused to attribute as much explanatory power to sexuality as Freud did. See Frank Sulloway, *Freud, Biologist of the Mind: Beyond the Psychoanalytic Legend* (Cambridge, MA and London: Harvard University Press, 1992), pp. 70–100; and Peter Gay, *Freud: A Life for our Time* (New York: Doubleday, 1988), pp. 67–9.

[18] Sulloway, *Freud, Biologist of the Mind*, pp. 171–237.

[19] See especially Freud's lectures on "The Sexual Life of Human Beings" and "Some Thoughts on Development and Regression – Aetiology," in *Introductory Lectures on Psychoanalysis*, trans. James Strachey (New York: Norton, 1966), pp. 303–19 and 339–57.

[20] In the essay, "The Infantile Genital Organization," *Standard Edition*, vol. 19, pp. 141ff.

[21] *Introductory Lectures on Psychoanalysis*, p. 353.

had discussed evolution and the possibility of applying his findings to human social life. They transformed his ideas into a linear model of teleological development, which had a huge impact on a wide variety of fields. The fact that, in political discourse alone, the evolutionary model was used to justify racism and imperialism,[22] but also to anchor many socialists' belief that the "iron laws of history" were leading inevitably to a more just and rational society, indicates just how influential evolutionary models were in European thought around the turn of the century.

Perhaps it comes as no surprise, then, that Freud's evolutionary assumptions soon became one of the most controversial aspects of his theory. In his criticisms of Freud on this point, Fromm was in agreement not only with Horkheimer, but also with Theodor Adorno and Herbert Marcuse. In his 1955 essay, "On the Relationship between Sociology and Psychology," Adorno takes Anna Freud to task for positing a linear model of psychological development that culminates in the disillusioned instrumental rationality of bourgeois man and denigrates as "immature" all forms of utopian or critical thought that do not conform to its narrow standards.[23] Adorno leveled similar criticisms against Freud himself in *Minima Moralia*.[24] Adorno's criticisms here of Freud and neo-Freudian revisionism echo his lifelong efforts to develop a nonbourgeois concept of maturity.[25] Similarly, in *Eros and Civilization*, Marcuse argues that in a postcapitalist society, some form of "progressive regression" would be possible; with the dissolution of the anthropology of the bourgeois epoch, new forms of emancipated subjectivity would become possible.[26] Yet beyond the Frankfurt School theorists, Freud's evolutionary assumptions have been criticized perhaps most sharply by feminists and queer theorists. If read as a transhistorical, normative account of feminine psychosexual development, Freud's views on women are anachronistic indeed. However, if read as a description of how femininity is forcefully constructed under historically specific conditions of social domination, as certain feminists have suggested, Freud's work becomes a powerful indictment of patriarchal society.[27] Similarly, although Freud's views on homosexuality in particular, and so-called "perverse" sexuality in general, were certainly advanced for his time, his basic assumption that these diverse

---

[22] See, for example, Richard Hofstadter, *Social Darwinism in American Thought* (Boston: Beacon, 1955), pp. 170–200; George Mosse, *Toward the Final Solution: A History of European Racism* (New York: Howard Fertig, 1978), pp. 77–94; and Thomas McCarthy's more recent study, *Race, Empire and the Idea of Human Development* (Cambridge, UK: Cambridge University Press, 2009), pp. 69–95.

[23] Adorno, *Schriften*, vol. 8, pp. 75–81.

[24] *Minima Moralia*, op. cit., pp. 60–6.

[25] For an insightful examination of Adorno's critique of bourgeois subjectivity, see Joel Whitebook, "Weighty Objects: On Adorno's Kant-Freud Interpretation," *The Cambridge Companion to Adorno*, ed. Tom Huhn (Cambridge, UK and New York: Cambridge University Press), pp. 51–73. Whitebook argues that Adorno never succeeded in coming up with an alternative to bourgeois subjectivity, but that such an alternative – which would avoid the pitfalls of contemporary postmodern and neovitalist rejection of subjectivity as inherently oppressive – could be found by reconceptualizing Freud's theory of sublimation.

[26] *Eros and Civilization*, op. cit., pp. 198ff.

[27] See, for example, Juliet Mitchel, *Psychoanalysis and Feminism* (New York: Vintage, 1974).

manifestations of sexuality all represent some form of arrested development vis-à-vis genitally focused, heterosexual "maturity" also seems like a relic of a bygone Victorian age.

For many commentators, Freud's evolutionary assumptions have seemed so problematic that they have rejected psychoanalysis as a whole. In both his "fundamental essay" and in his later work, Fromm insisted that he was not breaking with psychoanalysis, but Horkheimer and Adorno did not agree. For example, in a letter to Leo Lowenthal in October 1942, Horkheimer characterized his own attitude toward Freud's drive theory and Fromm's revision of it in the following way:

> Psychology without libido is in a way no psychology and Freud was great enough to get away from psychology in its own framework.... Where this is needed, we have to refer orthodoxically [sic] to Freud's earlier writings. The set of concepts connected with the *Todestriebe* [death drive] are anthropological categories (in the German sense of the word). Even where we do not agree with Freud's interpretation and use of them, we find their objective intention is deeply right and that they betray Freud's great flair for the situation.... Freud objectively absented himself from psychoanalysis, where Fromm and Horney get back to a commonsense psychology and even psychologize culture and society.[28]

Although Horkheimer's statement here effaces important differences that continued to exist between Fromm and other revisionists such as Horney and Harry Stack Sullivan, his statement that there is no such thing as psychology without libido does go right to the heart of his difference with Fromm. What I am trying to suggest here is that this statement can best be understood as Horkheimer's objection to Fromm's failure to distinguish between the evolutionary aspects of psychoanalysis, which were not fully developed until 1913–15, and the more fundamental notions of repression and the plasticity of libidinal drives.[29] The former notion was present from the very inception of psychoanalysis, and Freud had introduced the latter by 1897 at the latest. By identifying Freud's drive theory with the evolutionary model, Fromm also – wittingly or unwittingly – casts aside the theoretical presuppositions that had guided psychoanalysis prior to the introduction of a mechanical evolutionary model.

---

[28] GS, vol. 17, p. 367.

[29] Frank Sulloway argues that many of these evolutionary assumptions were smuggled into Freud's theory already at the end of the nineteenth century through his abandonment of the seduction theory and his creative transformation of Wilhelm's Fliess's concept of the id: *Freud, Biologist of the Mind*, op. cit., p. 237. Although there is certainly a degree of truth in his claims, Freud did not systematically apply an evolutionary model to psychosexual development until after the publication of *Totem and Taboo* (1913). His discussion of the development of the libido, regression, and fixation in the "Introductory Lectures on Psychoanalysis" (1916–17) presents a much more fully elaborated evolutionary model than one finds, for example, in his *Three Essays on the Theory of Sexuality* (1905). See, for example, Jean Laplanche and J.B. Pontalis's discussion of Freud's concepts of "libidinal stages," "phallic stage," and "regression" in *The Language of Psychoanalysis*, trans. D. Nicholsen-Smith (New York and London: Norton, 1973), pp. 236–8, 309–11 and 386–8. Most important for my argument here is simply the claim that that Freud's evolutionary model of psychosexual development is not identical with his theory of libidinal drives, as Fromm's argument presupposes. Calling the former into question does not necessarily entail rejecting the latter.

One can see how Fromm jettisoned the plasticity of the libidinal drives and the theory of repression by comparing the "fundamental essay" and some of his subsequent work to the essays he wrote prior to 1936. As we have already seen, the distinction between self-preservation and libidinal drives was crucial to Fromm's early work. His new distinction between biological drives and psychological "impulses" essentially takes libidinal drives out of the historical and social spheres and thereby undermines them as the foundation not only of character structures, but also of a whole range of other phenomena, which have far-reaching social implications, such as the instrumentalization of aggression, the role of fantasies in maintaining social domination, and other forms of compensation.[30] The question arises of the extent to which concepts such as repression, introversion, compensation, and even the unconscious are possible once libido theory has been eliminated. In his later work, Fromm decouples his analysis from libidinal instincts and their repression and links it instead to a vague concept of the "expansiveness of life." He argues:

The amount of destructiveness to be found in individuals is proportionate to the amount to which expansiveness of life is curtailed. By this we do not refer to individual frustrations of this or that instinctive desire but to the thwarting of the whole of life, the blockage of spontaneity of the growth and expression of man's sensuous, emotional and intellectual capacities. Life has an inner dynamism of its own; it tends to grow, to be expressed, to be lived. It seems that if this tendency is thwarted the energy directed toward life undergoes a process of decomposition and changes into energies directed toward destruction.[31]

Fromm struggles rather inchoately here to reformulate his earlier ideas about repression and its link to aggression without mentioning Freud's concept of libido. Yet for Freud, what was unique about libidinal energy was that it was malleable, and when repressed, it would not simply disappear, but would take on different forms. One wonders if Fromm's notion of the "expansiveness of life" possesses this same character. Does it have this same ability to assume different forms when they are "thwarted"? Can it also be (partially) satisfied with different objects, thereby facilitating the process of ideological compensation? Repression in the technical sense for Freud is a very specific process that is inextricably bound up with the unique character of *libidinal* drives. When Fromm effaces the distinction between libidinal drives and self-preservation drives by speaking of both as physiological needs that are outside of the historical process, is he not undermining the foundation that made repression and compensation possible in the first place? If this argument is correct, then Fromm's move away from drive theory did indeed undermine the theoretical foundations of his earlier work, which had been so fruitful for Horkheimer. With these points in mind, Horkheimer's deep reservations about the specific way in which Fromm abandoned Freud's drive theory become more understandable.

---

[30] On the role of racial fantasies in maintaining white supremacy, see the following two psychoanalytically informed studies: Joel Kovel, *White Racism: A Psychohistory* (New York: Vintage, 1971) and David Roediger, *The Wages of Whiteness: Race and the Making of the American Working Class* (New York and London: Verso, 1991), especially pp. 115–32.

[31] *Escape from Freedom*, pp. 183–4.

One of the most important consequences of Fromm's critique of Freud's drive theory was his new emphasis on the primacy of socialization over psychosexual development in the formation of character structures, or what he now – fittingly – called "social character." Fromm had, in other words, moved away from a Freudian model of subjectivity based on a never completely resolvable conflict between drives and social norms toward a model in which interpersonal relations in both the person's childhood and later in life shaped the person's character and actions. As he made clear in his discussion of the theoretical underpinnings of his new understanding of social character in subsequent works, such as *Escape from Freedom* and *Man for Himself*, Fromm had moved closer to the theory of interpersonal relations as it had been developed by Karen Horney and Harry Stack Sullivan.[32] Whereas "Freud had believed that the sexual drive was the source of energy of the character ... the progress of psychoanalytic theory," by which Fromm means primarily Horney and Sullivan, "led ... to a new concept which was based, not on the idea of a primarily isolated individual, but on the relationship of man to others, to nature and to himself. It was assumed that this very *relationship* governs and regulates the energy manifest in the passionate strivings of man."[33] It would take us too far afield to explore Fromm's important theoretical and personal relations with Horney and Sullivan in the 1930s and 1940s.[34] For our purposes here, it is simply important to note that Horkheimer and Adorno both sharply criticized Horney and Sullivan's model of "interpersonal relations" for removing the theoretical core of psychoanalysis, namely Freud's insistence on the nonidentity of society and individual and the impossibility of their complete reconciliation. By emphasizing the absolute primacy of society and socialization over individuals' pursuit of gratification, revisionists like Horney and Sullivan did – according to Adorno – express the objective tendencies of monopoly and state capitalism. Yet their own statements were not intended to be historically self-reflexive in this way; they believed they were establishing psychological truths with much broader validity. Thus, Horkheimer and Adorno accused them of unwittingly providing a theoretical justification for a state of affairs that deserved to be criticized and changed.[35] Freud's recourse to biological categories located the individuals' right to the pursuit of happiness at a level that could never be completely subsumed by society. Methodologically speaking, revisionism effaced the difference between psychology and sociology, reducing the former to a mere function of the latter.[36]

[32] Ibid., pp. 10–13; *Man for Himself* (Holt, Rinehart and Winston, 1947), pp. 57–61.
[33] *Man for Himself*, p. 57.
[34] Beginning in the mid-1930s, Fromm had moved closer to Horney and Sullivan not only theoretically, but also personally. In the 1930s, Fromm became involved romantically with Horney and they traveled together frequently and spent as much time together as possible. Through Horney, Fromm became acquainted with Sullivan, who invited to him to join and lecture at his organization, the Washington School of Psychiatry. Fromm remained a member until the end of his life.
[35] Theodor Adorno, "Die revidierte Psychoanalyse," *Soziologische Schriften*, vol. 1, op. cit., pp. 20–41.
[36] Adorno, "Zum Verhältnis von Soziologie und Psychologie."

Although Horkheimer and Adorno's criticisms of Horney and Sullivan certainly had Fromm as an implicit target, they and perhaps Fromm himself, were too quick to identify his ideas with those of Horney and Sullivan.[37] Fromm himself did not want to fall into a theory of total socialization or social relativism. Fromm criticized Durkheim and his school for precisely this reason.[38] Fromm tried to maintain a productive tension between individual and society, he just did so in a different way than Horkheimer and Adorno. Once he had abandoned the tension between libidinal drives and social norms that had guided his early work, Fromm turned to an existentialist philosophical anthropology to maintain the nonidentity of individual and society. As he put it in *Escape from Freedom*:

While it is true that man is molded by the necessities of the economic and social structure of society, he is not infinitely adaptable. Not only are there certain physiological needs that imperatively call for satisfaction, but there are also certain psychological qualities inherent in man that need to be satisfied and that result in certain reactions if they are frustrated. What are these qualities? The most important seems to be the tendency to grow, to develop and realize potentialities which man has developed in the course of history.... This general tendency to grow ... results in such specific tendencies as the desire for freedom and the hatred against oppression, since freedom is the fundamental condition for any growth.... We also have reason to assume that ... the striving for justice and truth is an inherent trend of human nature, although it can be repressed and perverted like the striving for freedom.[39]

In addition to attributing such positive characteristics to human nature as the desire for freedom, justice, and truth, Fromm also posited other negative needs, such as the desire to avoid loneliness, as just as fundamental psychologically as any "physiological" or "sexual" drive.[40] So, although Horkheimer and Adorno's criticisms of Fromm as a revisionist who fell into a theory of total socialization may not have been justified, Fromm's insistence that "psychology must be based on an anthropologico-philosophical concept of human existence"[41] still represented a sharp divergence from Horkheimer's model of Critical Theory both before and after Fromm's departure from the Institute. One of the most consistent features of Horkheimer's early work was his criticism of any transhistorical notions of character or human nature, and in his work in the 1940s Horkheimer continued adamantly to deny the existence of any innate human qualities.[42] As we have seen, for Horkheimer, the tradition of philosophical anthropology could only be appropriated critically by placing it on a historical foundation and transforming it into the study of the character structures of specific individuals and groups in a particular epoch. Horkheimer remained a

---

[37] As Rolf Wiggershaus also points out, *Die Frankfurter Schule*, p. 303.
[38] Out in Erich Fromm, *Escape from Freedom* (New York: Henry Holt, 1994).
[39] Ibid., pp. 287–8.
[40] Ibid., p. 19.
[41] *Man for Himself*, p. 45.
[42] See his "Remarks on Philosophical Anthropology" and our discussion of it in Chapter 7, pp. 249ff.

historical materialist in his refusal to posit any qualities beyond self-preservation and libidinal drives that transcend any given epoch. Furthermore, Horkheimer remained interested primarily in the current bourgeois capitalist epoch and the character structures it produced, not any sweeping theory of religion or human nature.

Excursus II

Divergence, Estrangement, and Gradual Rapprochement

The Evolution of Max Horkheimer and Theodor Adorno's Theoretical Relationship in the 1930s

This study so far has attempted patiently to reconstruct the major concepts and stages in the development of Horkheimer's Critical Theory through the late 1930s. Retracing the steps that Adorno followed on his path to Horkheimer and eventually to *Dialectic of Enlightenment* would require an equally patient reconstruction of his work in the late 1920s and early 1930s – a task that is obviously beyond the scope of this work. Thankfully, scholarship on Adorno is much further advanced than on Horkheimer, so this task has already been attempted by several competent commentators.[1] Here, I would like only to provide an overview of some of the key stages in the development of Adorno's work and his relationship with Horkheimer, which will make it possible to understand the shift that occurred in the latter's work in the late 1930s. To speak of a rapprochement between Horkheimer and Adorno in the 1930s may come as a surprise to those unfamiliar with the prehistory of their friendship. Unlike Horkheimer and Pollock, whose remarkable early friendship and symbiotic working relationship – one recalls their nicknames for one another: Horkheimer was the *ministre de l'intériuer* and Pollock the *ministre de l'extérieur* – had made them virtually inseparable since the age of fifteen, Horkheimer did not develop a serious friendship and working relationship with Adorno until much later. The secondary literature on Critical Theory has yet to fully examine the important differences that existed between Horkheimer and Adorno in the late 1920s and early 1930s.[2] In what follows, I want to demonstrate in particular how and why Horkheimer and Adorno parted ways theoretically in the late 1920s and early 1930s; how this divergence led to a brief period of estrangement in 1933–4; how Adorno's debate with Benjamin, a renewed study of Hegel, and his positive reception of Horkheimer's work in the mid-1930s brought them back together; and how, finally, Horkheimer gradually overcame some of his reservations about Adorno's work and began to move closer to him theoretically. Despite this gradual rapprochement in the mid-1930s, important theoretical differences remained between them; it was

---

[1] Susan Buck-Morss, *The Origins of Negative Dialectics*, op. cit. See also Detlev Claussen, *One Last Genius*, trans. Rodney Livingstone (Cambridge MA: Harvard University Press, 2008) and Stefan Müller-Doohm, *Adorno: A Biography*, trans. Rodney Livingstone (Cambridge UK and Malden MA: Polity, 2005).

[2] Susan Buck-Morss's *The Origins of Negative Dialectics* is the exception, but she tells the story solely from Adorno's point of view. No one has yet fully examined the reservations Horkheimer had about Adorno's work in the 1930s.

not until after Adorno's arrival in New York in 1938 and a period of intense collaboration with him that Horkheimer abandoned many of the key assumptions of his early Critical Theory and moved closer to Adorno, thereby setting the stage for *Dialectic of Enlightenment*. It is crucial to identify the causes of the estrangement between Horkheimer and Adorno and to reconstruct the long and sometimes difficult rapprochement in order to demonstrate that the two authors of *Dialectic of Enlightenment* came to that work from very different paths and that this work ultimately represented a more significant break with Horkheimer's early Critical Theory than it did with Adorno's thought in the 1930s. We will return to *Dialectic of Enlightenment* in the epilogue.

DIVERGENCE AND ESTRANGEMENT

As we have seen, Hans Cornelius played a crucial role in helping Horkheimer establish himself among the faculty of philosophy in Frankfurt. Cornelius also served as Adorno's primary academic mentor. Whereas Horkheimer also had a close personal relationship with Cornelius and remained cordial with him even after he had abandoned his philosophical system in 1925, Adorno had no such personal relationship with Cornelius and was not granted as much respect as Horkheimer. When Adorno decided to submit his *Habilitationsschrift* on "The Concept of the Unconscious in the Transcendental Theory of the Soul,"[3] which would have opened the door for an academic career, Cornelius advised him to retract it. He told Adorno he could not accept it because Adorno had simply paraphrased his own work and failed to produce an original argument.[4] Horkheimer was working as Cornelius's assistant at this time and although he had originally encouraged Adorno to write the dissertation, he also had reservations about Adorno's attempt to reconcile psychoanalysis with Cornelius's transcendental philosophy.[5] This disappointing incident provided Adorno with the impetus he needed to emancipate himself from the strictures of contemporary German academic philosophy, which had always been secondary to his main intellectual and artistic interests. As the Adorno biographer Stefan Müller-Doohm puts it, "It was the only and the last time that Adorno ever made a compromise with his intellectual work."[6] We have seen how Horkheimer's break with Cornelius's consciousness philosophy also provided him with the impetus for the development of a Critical Theory of contemporary society grounded in a self-reflexive theory of the history and anthropology of the "bourgeois epoch." Whereas Horkheimer moved beyond consciousness philosophy through a materialist interpretation of the history of modern philosophy and an engagement with contemporary social theory, empirical social research, and psychoanalysis, Adorno established his own theoretical position at this time primarily through an appropriation of Walter Benjamin's early works, especially his essay on Goethe's *Elective Affinities* and his study *The Origins of German Tragic Drama*.

---

[3] See the discussion of this work in Chapter 5, pp. 197–201.

[4] Müller-Doohm, *Adorno: Eine Biographie*, p. 161.

[5] Jay, *Dialectical Imagination*, p. 87. For a discussion of the reasons why the dissertation did not appeal to Horkheimer, see Chapter 5, pp. 199–200.

[6] Müller-Doohm, p. 157.

Benjamin had submitted *The Origins of German Tragic Drama* as a *Habilitationsschrift* to the University of Frankfurt in 1925, where it was rejected by Hans Cornelius and a professor of German literature, Franz Schultz.[7] Thus Adorno, who was becoming increasingly close to Benjamin both personally and theoretically during this time, already had reason to question Cornelius's judgment. Even though Horkheimer had broken with Cornelius theoretically, he was still working as his assistant at this time and may well have voted against Adorno's *Habilitationsschrift* had he not retracted it.[8] Because he had retracted it, Adorno still had the possibility of submitting a second *Habilitationsschrift*, which he did in 1931. By this time, Cornelius had retired and been replaced by Paul Tillich who, along with Horkheimer, now had the responsibility to judge Adorno's study, *Kierkegaard: Construction of the Aesthetic*. We will undertake a more detailed examination of Adorno's Kierkegaard work in the next section. For our purposes here, it is simply important to note that it presupposed throughout – as Siegfried Kracauer noted in his review of the work[9] – the negative philosophy of history that had informed Benjamin's essay on Goethe's *Elective Affinities* and his study of German tragic drama. Adorno also subscribed fully to the *theological* dimensions of Benjamin's early work.[10] These theological assumptions reemerged in Adorno's study of Kierkegaard in his insistence on the existence of an "absolutely concealed"[11] possibility of redemption, which always escaped the active self-assertion of the forms of transcendental subjectivity that underlay modern science or idealist philosophy, but revealed itself indirectly to the patient scrutiny of the melancholic subject. Adorno's method of discovering unintentional truth in marginal passages of Kierkegaard's work and his commitments to Benjamin's theological assumptions are conveyed clearly in the following passage:

It is perhaps not by accident that the metaphor chooses Hebrew letters, the signs of a language that theologically makes the claim to being the true language. Theological

---

[7] See Momme Brodersen, *Walter Benjamin: A Biography*, trans. Malcolm R. Green and Ingrida Ligers (London and New York: Verso, 1996), pp. 146–50.

[8] As Müller-Doohm suggests, p. 161.

[9] "Der enthüllte Kierkegaard," Siegfried Kracauer, *Schriften*, vol. 5.3 (Suhrkamp: Frankfurt a.M., 1990), p. 266.

[10] Benjamin's attempt in the prologue of *The Origins of German Tragic Drama* to develop an antisubjectivist theory of knowledge, which had made such a deep impression on Adorno, had grown directly out of his earlier reflections on language. As Richard Wolin puts it, "Benjamin's theological philosophy of language can be said to provide the *telos* of his notion of redemptive criticism." Richard Wolin, *Walter Benjamin: An Aesthetic of Redemption* (Berkeley, Los Angeles and London: University of California Press, 1994), p. 37. Benjamin followed the tradition of Jewish mysticism (Kabbala) in positing the existence of an original language, in which there was a perfect correspondence between signifiers and signified that, in turn, allowed consummate comprehension of a pre-lapsarian, harmonious world. However, with man's fall from grace, this original language disintegrated, scattering meaning and comprehension into an infinite number of fragments that could never be completely reconstructed. Nonetheless, a weak redemptive power still resided in each of these fragments and if interpreted carefully would point negatively and indirectly to the utopian potential of the original lost language.

[11] Theodor Adorno, *Kierkegaard: Konstruktion des Ästhetischen* (Frankfurt: Suhrkamp, 1966), p. 49.

truth, however ... is guaranteed precisely by its encipherment and distortedness; the "collapse" of fundamental human relations reveals itself as the history of truth itself. This is shown, totally against Kierkegaard's own intention and therefore all the more convincingly, in a passage of an essay on Marie Beaumarchais; script appears as a model of despair, only to transform itself, gently, into a model of hope.[12]

Yet it was precisely this theological dimension of Adorno's study to which Horkheimer objected most strenuously. In his evaluation of the Kierkegaard study, Horkheimer had unreserved praised for Adorno's critique of interiority and more cautious praise for his efforts to rescue the aesthetic as a form of objective knowledge. He also noted that Adorno "possesses an overview of the problems of philosophy and their history matched by only a few mature scholars" and that he also has an "excellent knowledge not only of contemporary philosophy, but also the entire cultural situation of the present."[13] Yet Horkheimer also emphasized the fundamental differences between his own philosophical intentions and that of Adorno. He wrote:

The direction of the philosophical interests as well as the method of thought and the linguistic formulation of this *Habilitationsschrift* are not related to my own philosophical aims. If Wiesengrund [Adorno] believes he has rescued hope and reconciliation in Kierkegaard's thought, in so doing he has expressed a fundamental theological conviction, which points to a philosophical intention that is radically different from my own and this intention is palpable in every sentence.[14]

Here one finds perhaps the clearest expression of Horkheimer's estimation of the deep theoretical differences that existed between him and Adorno at this time. Despite these differences, Horkheimer did not hesitate to approve the Kierkegaard book as a qualification for Adorno's *Habilitation*.

Three months after the approval of his *Habilitation* by Tillich and Horkheimer in February 1931, Adorno completed the final step in becoming an official member of the faculty of the Frankfurt philosophy department by delivering his inaugural address, which bore the title "The Actuality of Philosophy."[15] Adorno's presentation took place just a few months after Horkheimer's inaugural address as the director of the Institute for Social Research.[16] Adorno's ongoing commitment to Benjamin's ideas was readily apparent in his address, but it was also clearly intended as a response to Horkheimer's remarks a few months before. Adorno takes up, in particular, the relationship between philosophy and the sciences (*die Einzelwissenschaften*)[17] that had been so central to Horkheimer's remarks. In order to understand the

[12] Ibid., p. 224.
[13] Max Horkheimer, "Bemerkung in Sachen der Habilitation Dr. Wiesengrund," Archiv des Dekanats der Philosophischen Fakultät der J.W. Goethe Universität, Frankfurt a.M. (Section 134, Number 4), p. 5. Unless noted otherwise, all translations are my own.
[14] Ibid., p. 7.
[15] Reference to English translation. Although translated as "actuality," the German *Aktualität* here means contemporary relevance, not "reality."
[16] Horkheimer's address, "The Present Situation of Social Philosophy and the Tasks of an Institute for Social Research," was delivered on January 25, 1931.
[17] Science is intended in a broad sense of "*Wissenschaft*," i.e. not just the natural sciences, but also the social sciences and, indeed, any of the established, systematic scholarly disciplines, including psychology and history.

important differences in their views of this relationship, it is important to note that Horkheimer's and Adorno's arguments were motivated by different diagnoses of the most pressing philosophical problems of the time. Horkheimer's remarks were – as we have seen[18] – driven to a large extent by his concern that the philosophically rigorous and justified criticisms of positivism, which phenomenologists and vitalists had articulated at the end of the nineteenth century, had since degenerated into a sweeping and more popular antirationalist discourse that threatened to undermine completely the role of science in philosophy in general and in social philosophy in particular.[19] Against this backdrop, Horkheimer argued that contemporary social philosophy is not possible without the sciences and must strive to integrate their most advanced findings and methods, while at the same time placing them within a larger self-reflexive theory of history and society. He views the task of the Institute as "organiz[ing] investigations stimulated by contemporary philosophical problems in which philosophers, sociologists, economists, historians and psychologists are brought together in permanent collaboration," and "to pursue their larger philosophical questions on the basis of the most precise scientific methods."[20] Without a "continuous, dialectical penetration and development of philosophical theory and specialized scientific praxis,"[21] these tasks are doomed to fail. Although Horkheimer never defended empirical methodology in an uncritical manner, his vision of Critical Theory at this time still assigned a central and essential role to the sciences. The empirical study of the German working class, which had already begun, and the extensive space that would be devoted in the Institute's journal to reviews of literature from a wide variety of scientific fields are just two examples of the ways Horkheimer was already translating these arguments into action.

In "The Actuality of Philosophy," Adorno characterized the relationship between philosophy and the sciences very differently than had Horkheimer. Unlike Horkheimer, Adorno still deemed the positivists' attempts to establish mathematical and natural scientific methods as the sole arbiters of knowledge and experience as a more serious threat than the alleged excesses of any philosophical critiques of positivism. He writes:

The sciences, particularly the logical and mathematical sciences, have set about the liquidation of philosophy with an earnestness which hardly ever existed before. This earnestness is so significant because the separate sciences [*Einzelwissenschaften*], including mathematical and natural sciences, have long since rid themselves of the naturalistic conceptual apparatus that, in the nineteenth century, made them inferior to idealist theories of knowledge and they have totally annexed the contents of a critical theory of knowledge [*Erkenntniskritik*].[22]

---

[18] See Chapter 3, pp. 132–40.

[19] For a more detailed exposition of this argument see John Abromeit, "The Vicissitudes of the Politics of 'Life': Herbert Marcuse and Max Horkheimer's Reception of Phenomenology and Vitalism in Weimar Germany" at https://scholarworks.iu.edu/dspace/handle/2022/440.

[20] "The Present Situation of Social Philosophy and the Tasks of an Institute for Social Research," op. cit., p. 9.

[21] Ibid., p. 9.

[22] "The Actuality of Philosophy," trans. Benjamin Snow, in *The Adorno Reader*, ed. Brian O'Conner (Blackwell: Oxford UK and Malden, MA, 2000), p. 29 (translation amended).

In response to this threat, Adorno criticizes what he sees as the "fundamental category of all empiricism,"[23] namely the notion of some unmediated, sensually perceptible "given," and he offers a robust defense of the epistemological primacy of philosophy over science. Following Hegel's argument against sense-certainty in the opening pages of the *Phenomenology of Spirit*, Adorno argues that the superiority of philosophy's claim to knowledge over that of the sciences rests precisely on this self-reflexive recognition of the mediated character of all objects of knowledge, even the seemingly most "self-evident." He writes:

> Philosophy distinguishes itself from science not by a higher level of generality ... nor through the abstraction of its categories nor through the nature of its materials. The central difference lies far more in that the separate sciences [*Einzelwissenschaften*] accept their findings, at least their final and deepest findings, as indestructible and static, whereas philosophy perceives the first findings which it lights upon as a sign that needs unriddling. Plainly put: the idea of science is research; that of philosophy is interpretation [*Deutung*].[24]

Adorno's defense here of a model of research and *interpretation* provides an interesting contrast to Horkheimer's defense of Marx's model of research and *presentation*. Whereas presentation for Marx and Horkheimer involved placing the empirical research material into a larger, self-reflexive theory of the current historical epoch, interpretation was to answer the questions posed by the sciences through the "construction of figures, or images out of the isolated elements of reality."[25] Adorno's reference to Benjamin's *Trauerspiel* book at this key juncture in his argument leaves no doubt about the source of his concept of interpretation. His further explication of the concept continues in a Benjaminian vein when he insists that placing interpretation at the center of philosophy in this manner would transform it into an *ars inveniendi*, whose primary organ would not be conceptual mediation, but an exact imagination [*Phantasie*] "which abides strictly within the material that the sciences present to it and reaches beyond them only in the smallest aspects of their arrangement."[26] Following Benjamin's concept of allegory, Adorno insists that interpretation is possible "only through a juxtaposition of the smallest elements."[27] In marked contrast to his later criticisms of Benjamin's "Arcades Exposé," in which he chastises Benjamin for simply juxtaposing the plethora of material he had gathered and not providing mediation "through the *total social process*,"[28] here Adorno still insists that "philosophy must learn to renounce the question of totality."[29]

Soon after delivering his inaugural address, Adorno began participating more actively in the philosophy department, offering lectures and seminars

---

[23] Ibid., p. 30.
[24] Ibid., pp. 30–1.
[25] "The Actuality of Philosophy," p. 32.
[26] Ibid., p. 37.
[27] Ibid., p. 32.
[28] Letter from Adorno to Benjamin from November 10, 1938 in: *Theodor W. Adorno and Walter Benjamin: The Complete Correspondence 1928–1940*, ed. Henri Lonitz (Cambridge, MA: Harvard University Press, 1999), p. 283 (emphasis his own).
[29] "The Actuality of Philosophy," p. 32.

of his own and partaking in a discussion of one of Horkheimer's lecture
courses. In the winter semester of 1931–2, Adorno offered a lecture course on
"Problems in Aesthetics," in which he presented his own ideas on aesthetics
through a critique of Johannes Vokelt's largely forgotten 1905 treatise, *System
of Aesthetics*. As Rolf Tiedemann notes in his introduction to the notes that
have been preserved from these lectures, they demonstrate that Benjamin was
"Adorno's most important teacher" at this time, and that the central categories
used in the lectures, such as "image" and "semblance," "have more to do with
[Benjamin's] essay on the *Elective Affinities* and with *The Origins of German
Tragic Drama* than with Vokelt's *System of Aesthetics*."[30] Adorno argues in the
lectures that the historical content of artistic works can be deciphered only
through careful immersion in the works themselves, never by reducing them
to a mere "symbol" or representation of broader historical tendencies.[31] This
antihistoricist argument would remain at the center of his controversy with
Horkheimer in the coming years. Adorno had invited Benjamin to speak in this
course;[32] his unwillingness to accept the invitation was probably motivated by
a reluctance to set foot in the department that had rejected his *Trauerspiel* book
as a qualification for *Habilitation* just a few years earlier. So Adorno's decision
to offer a entire seminar on the *Trauerspiel* book during the summer semester
of 1932 was not only a sign of his theoretical debts to Benjamin, but also an
explicit affront to the department that had thwarted the academic career of
his highly esteemed friend.[33] Although Cornelius had retired by this time, his
former assistant, Max Horkheimer, was still offering courses. In fact, Adorno
also participated during the winter semester of 1931–2 in a discussion of a
series of lectures Horkheimer was giving on the topics of "science and crisis"
and the "difference between idealism and materialism." Notes preserved from
these discussions demonstrate an important theoretical difference between
Horkheimer and Adorno regarding the status of the concept of the "given" –
which had been so crucial for Adorno's inaugural address – and the importance
more generally of the role of empirical evidence in confirming or disproving
scientific theories. Horkheimer insisted here that sense impressions and empirical evidence must be preserved among the epistemological presuppositions of
a Critical Theory of society, but that this presupposition does not imply that the
world is *constituted* by sensual "givens."[34] For his part, Adorno points to the
inevitably subjective character of any sensual given and its determination by
the particular social context in which it is located.[35] Horkheimer and Adorno
agree that sense impressions and "facts" are always socially and historically
mediated, but Horkheimer's greater emphasis in this dispute on the importance

---

[30] Theodor W. Adorno, "Aufzeichnungen zur Ästhetik Vorlesung von 1931/32," *Frankfurter
Adorno Blätter*, vol. 1, ed. Rolf Tiedemann (Munich, Text + Kritik, 1992), p. 36.

[31] Ibid., p. 37.

[32] Müller-Doohm, p. 224.

[33] Some notes from Adorno's seminar on Benjamin's *Trauerspiel* book have been preserved and
published in: *Frankfurter Adorno Blätter*, vol. 4, ed. Rolf Tiedemann (Munich: Text + Kritik,
1995), pp. 52–77.

[34] GS, vol. 12, p. 371.

[35] Ibid., p. 370.

of some form of empirical verification of philosophical theory demonstrates once again their divergent conceptions of Critical Theory at this time. Whereas Horkheimer was making a concerted effort to work out the proper place of the sciences, Adorno believed that only autonomous art and theology could provide access to the transcendent truths and redemptive power required to ground a genuinely critical theory of science and society.

The negative theological assumptions guiding Adorno's Critical Theory at this time were placed on display once again in a lecture he delivered to the Frankfurt Kant Society in July of 1932 entitled "The Idea of Natural History." Adorno describes the main purpose of the lecture as "overcoming [*aufheben*] the standard antithesis between nature and history."[36] To understand his argument, it is crucial to note that Adorno's idiosyncratic concept of nature, as he points out, "has nothing at all to do with the concept of nature used in the mathematical natural sciences" and more closely resembles the traditional concept of myth. Adorno refers to nature and myth as spheres dominated by blind necessity, fate, identity, and repetition of the same. History, in contrast, is the sphere in which this blind necessity is broken and in which the qualitatively new makes its appearance. With his concept of natural history, Adorno attempts to grasp the deleterious ways in which nature (myth) and history have mutually determined one another and have thus prevented mankind from emerging from the never-ending cycle of catastrophes that have characterized its natural (pre-)history thus far. Adorno develops this concept through a Benjaminian-inspired critique of the concept of "second nature" from Georg Lukács's *Theory of the Novel*. In that work, Lukács famously characterized the modern capitalist era as one of "transcendental homelessness," in which meaning no longer inhered in the social totality. He came to this conclusion by way of a comparative analysis – inspired by Hegel's historicization of aesthetic categories – of the modern novel and the Greek epic. According to Lukács, the epic form was the expression of a society in which meaning was still present in the social totality, whereas the psychological form of the modern novel was an ultimately hopeless attempt to reconstitute and represent meaning subjectively – meaning that it no longer existed objectively. Lukács pointed to the antisubjectivist and antirationalist epic novels of Tolstoy and Dostoyevsky as the most promising attempts to overcome this aporia – at least at the aesthetic level. In short, Lukács's argument in *Theory of the Novel* anticipated his discussion of reification a few years later in *History and Class Consciousness* insofar as he was already convinced at this time that the best efforts of modern, Western, rational civilization to overcome myth had instead created a new and more sinister form of blind necessity at the social level.[37] This "second nature" gave the lie to the triumphalist self-understanding of modern society – articulated most clearly in nineteenth-century positivism – of having overcome myth once and for all.

---

[36] Theodor Adorno, *Gesammelte Schriften*, ed. Rolf Tiedemann (Frankfurt: Suhrkamp, 1997), p. 345.

[37] As many commentators on Lukács have pointed out, his concepts of second nature and reification represented a reinterpretation of Max Weber's analyses of bureaucracy and the "iron cage" in light of Marx's analysis of commodity fetishism. See, for example, Habermas, *Theory of Communicative Action*, vol. 1, section IV, "From Lukács to Adorno: Rationalization as Reification."

Although sympathetic to Lukács's pessimistic diagnosis of modern, Western society and his efforts to revive Hegel's historicization of aesthetic categories, Adorno had two main objections to his concept of second nature, which both drew upon Benjamin's early work. First, Adorno objected to the backward-looking, romantic implications of Lukács's argument, which portrayed Greek myth as a non-self-reflexive expression of a meaningful social totality. As an early formulation of the argument in *Dialectic of Enlightenment* – that myth is already a form of enlightenment – Adorno's concept of natural history was intended to call into question the widespread belief that myths were the expression of a simpler, less mediated, and more meaningful form of society. Adorno writes:

The foundation, the mythic-archaic, the supposedly substantial and enduring mythic, is in no way a static foundation. Rather, there is an element of the historically dynamic, whose form is dialectical, in all great myths as well as in the mythical images that our consciousness still carries. The mythic fundamental elements are in themselves contradictory and move in a contradictory manner ...[38]

Adorno's critique of the early Lukács here is indebted to Benjamin insofar as it calls into question any facile distinction between myth and modernity. Far from being an integrated totality, ancient Greek society was already rent with social contradictions, and already produced modern forms of idealist consciousness that express a desire to dominate internal and external nature.[39] In *Dialectic of Enlightenment*, Adorno would describe Odysseus as a prototype of modern bourgeois subjectivity; in "The Idea of Natural History," he points to Plato's idealism as evidence that the drive to dominate internal and external nature did not emerge for the first time in modern capitalist society. He argues that Plato's philosophy

is already the expression of a level of consciousness in which consciousness has lost its natural substance as immediacy.... consciousness has already succumbed to the temptation of idealism: spirit, banned from the world, alienated from history, becomes absolute at the cost of life.[40]

Adorno invokes an argument here that he had already developed in his Kierkegaard book: Natural history is the expression of an attempt by the mind

---

[38] Adorno, *Schriften*, op. cit., p. 363; "The Idea of Natural History," trans. Robert Hullot-Kentor, *Telos*, no. 60 (1984), p. 123.

[39] While in Oxford, Adorno became acquainted with Sir Cecil Maurice Bowra, a classicist who was involved during this time in a debate about the social factors that shaped Homeric epic. Bowra was an outspoken critic of the then popular argument that Homeric epic was a form of popular poetry ("*Volksdichtung*") that was still grounded in myth and directly expressed the "spirit of the people." Classicists at this time frequently pointed to musical epics that had survived in the Balkans as contemporary corollaries of Homeric epic. Bowra sought to dispel the "mythic" character of Homeric epic through a more nuanced, sociological analysis of its production and reception. Adorno's enthusiasm for Bowra's work led to the publication of his "Sociological Remarks on the Origins of Greek Poetry" in the *Zeitschrift* in 1936. Bowra's arguments anticipate and support Adorno's interpretation of Odysseus as a "proto-bourgeois" figure in *Dialectic of Enlightenment*.

[40] Adorno, *Schriften*, vol. 1, op. cit., pp. 363–4; "The Idea of Natural History," op. cit., p. 123.

to completely control nature, or even to posit itself as the creator of it. Yet this attempt to dominate nature leads to the creation of a second nature, which reproduces the blind necessity of first nature in even more destructive social forms.

The second way in which Adorno criticized Lukács with the help of Benjamin lies in his concept of interpretation. For Lukács, the degeneration of social relations and institutions into a reified form of "second nature," or what he refers to more expressively as a "charnal-house of decayed interiorities,"[41] gives reality the quality of an impenetrable riddle. Meaning is completely lost, and its return can only be conceived in terms of an eschatological break with the present. Although no less compromising in its depiction of modern society as a living hell, Benjamin's concept of allegory at least opens up the possibility of mediation in its insistence on the continued existence of meaning in the fragments of a disintegrating social totality and the redemptive potential of rescuing this meaning through philosophical interpretation of these fragments. As Adorno puts it, "Benjamin marks the decisive turning-point in the formulation of the problem of natural history in that he brought the resurrection of second nature out of infinite distance into infinite closeness and made it an object of philosophical interpretation."[42] Attempting to clarify his position once more in reference to Lukács's notion of the "charnal-house," Adorno writes:

For Lukács it is something simply puzzling; for Benjamin it becomes a cipher to be read. For radical natural-historical thought, however, everything existing transforms itself into ruins and fragments, into just such a charnal-house where signification [*Bedeutung*] is discovered, in which nature and history interweave and the philosophy of history is assigned the task of their intentional interpretation.[43]

Adorno goes on to argue that the meaning to be revealed through this process of patiently deciphering fragments is historical. One can see here an early version of Adorno's later argument that works of art are a philosophical-historical "sundial;"[44] their innermost structure not only expresses, but also *protests* against, historically specific relations of social domination, and at the same time points beyond them. Yet this expression and protest – the "truth content" of the work – can only be grasped through patient immersion in, and philosophical interpretation of, the work. Crucial to Adorno's argument here is a protest against any form of historicism that would reduce the work of art to a merely passive representation of underlying historical tendencies, thereby robbing it of its autonomy and its ability to prefigure a society that has escaped the baleful dynamic of natural history. Adorno's argument rests on the implicit claim that self-reflexive historical knowledge can best be attained precisely through this process of interpretation of fragments – in which aesthetic fragments are privileged as the most revealing objects of interpretation – and not through any other methods of historical investigation, such as traditional or even Marxist methods of historical research.

[41] Ibid., p. 357; "Schädelstätte vormoderter Innerlichkeiten," p. 118 (translation amended).
[42] Ibid., p. 357; p. 119.
[43] Ibid., p. 360; p. 121 (translation amended).
[44] Theodor Adorno, "Versuch, das Endspiel zu verstehen," *Gesammelte Schriften*, op. cit., vol. 11, p. 314.

In "The Idea of Natural History," Adorno's distrust of historicism is apparent in his critique of the concept of the epoch, which he associates primarily with Dilthey, but which would also seem to be an essential concept for traditional and even Marxist methods of historical research. Adorno rejects

the attempt to isolate a group of historical elements and to hypostatize them ontologically, because they putatively encompass the totality as the meaning or fundamental structure of an epoch – as, for example, Dilthey did. Dilthey's attempt at an historical ontology ran aground because he did not engage facticity with sufficient seriousness; he remained in the sphere of intellectual history and in the fashion of vague categories of styles of thought entirely failed to grasp reality.[45]

Adorno's critique of the concept of the epoch here is inspired, once again, by Benjamin and, in particular, by his deep distrust of historical period concepts in aesthetics, which reduce works of art to mere examples of larger genres ("tragedy") or periods ("romanticism") and thereby obscure their particularity and truth content.[46] Adorno would invoke this antihistoricist argument time and again in the coming years in his correspondence with Horkheimer. Normally, he would invoke it to criticize Leo Lowenthal's essays on the sociology of literature or Herbert Marcuse's putatively "intellectual historical" interpretations of modern philosophers and philosophical movements. Yet his objections – wittingly or unwittingly – also went to the core of an important difference between his own method and that of Horkheimer. In his 1936 preface to the *Studies on Authority and Family*, Horkheimer would explicitly defend periodization and the concept of an epoch as essential not only to traditional historical research, but also to a self-reflexive Critical Theory of society.[47] One of the main tasks facing historians and Critical Theorists is to divide the past into more or less discrete periods that mark qualitative shifts in the historical development of society. Although Horkheimer was critical of Dilthey's notion that these periods should be defined primarily in cultural terms and were more or less homogenous, he did insist, like Marx, that modern capitalism represented something qualitatively new vis-à-vis the Middle Ages and classical antiquity. Furthermore, the model of historical materialist interpretation, which underlay not only Horkheimer's, but also Lowenthal's and Marcuse's work during this time, was based on the assumption that modern art and philosophy could not be understood outside the context of the uneven development of bourgeois society. The hostility to historicism, which Adorno had appropriated from Benjamin,[48] not only made him suspicious of the basic historical framework of Lowenthal's, Marcuse's, and Horkheimer's work at this time; it also led him to downplay distinctions between ancient and modern

[45] Adorno, *Schriften*, vol. 1, op. cit., p. 361. "The Idea of Natural History," op. cit., pp. 121–2 (translation amended).

[46] For a brief overview of Benjamin's critique of historicism in aesthetics, see Wolin, *Walter Benjamin: An Aesthetic of Redemption*, op. cit., pp. 79–84.

[47] Max Horkheimer, *Critical Theory: Selected Essays*, op. cit., pp. 47–53.

[48] For a discussion of the Benjaminian roots of Adorno's concept of natural history, which attempts to demonstrate that, for Adorno, "history had no meaning in itself, but only in reference to the present, and then only as a critical concept which demystified the present," see Susan Buck-Morss, *The Origin of Negative Dialectics*, op. cit., pp. 43–62. This quote is on page 168 of the same study.

societies as well as myth and modern bourgeois rationality, which were essential for Horkheimer's Critical Theory – at least until the end of the 1930s.

We have seen how, as Adorno moved much closer to Walter Benjamin in the late 1920s and early 1930s, important theoretical differences emerged between him and Max Horkheimer – in regard to their attitudes towards the sciences, their theories of knowledge and of history. Despite these differences, Horkheimer and Adorno did remain in contact throughout this time, they continued to engage seriously with one another's work, and they still clearly held each other in high esteem. For example, in the fall of 1929, well after Adorno's first *Habilitationsschrift* had been rejected by Cornelius, Benjamin and Adorno met with Horkheimer and Pollock in their shared home in Königstein, a suburb just north of Frankfurt, for a series of lengthy discussions.[49] It was during these discussions when Benjamin first introduced his plans for the Arcades Project. Despite his statement in his evaluation of Adorno's second *Habilitationsschrift* in 1931, that the theological presuppositions of Adorno's thought were "radically different" from his own Critical Theory, Horkheimer had many positive things to say not only about Adorno's study of Kierkegaard, but also about his qualifications to become a full member of the Frankfurt Philosophy faculty. We have also seen that Adorno participated actively in discussions with Lowenthal and others of the lectures Horkheimer was giving at this time. Finally, after Horkheimer became the director of the Institute for Social Research in 1931, Adorno was invited to contribute an essay on "The Social Situation of Music" to the first volume of the Institute's journal, which he did.[50] Despite these clear indications of mutual respect and a nascent friendship between Horkheimer and Adorno, unlike Fromm, Lowenthal, or Marcuse, Adorno was not invited to become a member of the Institute for Social Research at this time. When the Institute was forced into exile in 1933, not only was Adorno not invited to join the other members of the Institute in Geneva or New York, he completely lost touch with Horkheimer until the fall of 1934. Adorno would not publish another book review or essay in the Institute's journal until 1936. The fact that Adorno lost touch with Horkheimer and the other members of the Institute at this crucial juncture can only be described as an estrangement and can only be explained in terms of the reservations Horkheimer and Adorno had about each other's theoretical presuppositions – although Horkheimer's skepticism about key aspects of Adorno's work probably played a more important role in this estrangement, not least because Horkheimer's position as the director of the Institute gave him the power to include or exclude Adorno from the Institute's work. In what follows, I would like to describe briefly how, beginning in the fall of 1934, Horkheimer and Adorno began to overcome this estrangement and to lay the foundations for collaborative work in the late 1930s and early 1940s that would culminate in *Dialectic of Enlightenment*.

---

[49] On the "Königstein discussions" and the importance accorded to them by both Adorno and Benjamin, see Buck-Morss, *The Origin of Negative Dialectics*, op. cit., p. 22.

[50] Theodor Wiesengrund-Adorno, "Zur gesellschaftlichen Lage der Musik," *Zeitschrift für Sozialforschung*, vol. 1 (Leipzig: C.L. Hirschfeld, 1932), pp. 103–24.

RAPPROCHEMENT

The rapprochement that took place between Horkheimer and Adorno between 1934 and 1938 occurred at both the personal and the theoretical levels. In fact, the former was complete before the latter. By the fall of 1935, Horkheimer and Adorno had moved beyond the mutual recriminations surrounding the events of 1933, which had led to their brief estrangement.[51] Horkheimer blamed Adorno for not contacting the Institute after 1933 and for preferring an academic career to working with the Institute.[52] Adorno countered that he had always wanted to work more closely with the Institute and would have considered joining Horkheimer and the others in New York, had he only been invited.[53] Through a lengthy correspondence in the following months and years Horkheimer and Adorno gradually reestablished a solid working relationship and friendship. In December 1935, Horkheimer met with Adorno in Paris during a trip to Europe. The following February, Horkheimer invited Adorno to become an official member of the Institute as soon as he had completed his Ph.D. in Oxford.[54] In the second half of June 1937, Adorno spent two weeks in New York and immersed himself in the work of the Institute and theoretical discussions with Horkheimer.[55] On September 8 of the same year, Adorno married his long-time partner, Gretel Karplus, in London with Horkheimer and his wife in attendance as witnesses. In short, the *personal* estrangement between Horkheimer and Adorno remained relatively short lived. Yet important *theoretical* differences remained between Horkheimer and Adorno through 1938 and beyond. As late as January 1938, just prior to Adorno's emigration to New York, Adorno could still describe himself as a "wounded doe," because Horkheimer was still refusing to publish two essays on which he had been laboring for the past two years: one on Husserl and the other on Karl Mannheim.[56] Clearly, Horkheimer still had important theoretical reservations about Adorno's work at this time.

In the following section, we will return to the crucial theoretical differences that remained between Horkheimer and Adorno through 1938, but let us first examine the ways in which Horkheimer and Adorno moved closer to one

---

[51] In May 1935, Adorno had a chance to discuss with Friedrich Pollock, who was in Europe, the disagreements he and Horkheimer had had about his not being invited to join the other members of the Institute in 1933. Adorno stated in a letter to Horkheimer in May 1935 that he had an opportunity to "clear up a series of misunderstandings," and he and Pollock "now viewed this issue as definitively *liquidated.*" Theodor Adorno and Max Horkheimer, *Briefwechsel, vol. 1 (1927–1937),* ed. by Christoph Gödde and Henri Lonitz (Frankfurt: Suhrkamp, 2003), pp. 62 and 64 (Adorno's emphasis). When Horkheimer came to Europe the following December, he met with Adorno in Paris. The tone of their letters before and after this visit makes it clear that they had established cordial personal relations by this time, even though important theoretical differences remained between them. See ibid., pp. 91–109.

[52] GS, vol. 15, p. 252–3.

[53] Ibid., p. 259–62.

[54] *Adorno-Horkheimer, Briefwechsel,* p. 122.

[55] In a letter to Horkheimer sent soon after returning to London from New York, Adorno said of his recent visit: "I have hardly ever, and certainly not since the outbreak of totalitarianism [*des Totalen*], been as happy as I was during these weeks." Ibid., vol. 1, p. 374.

[56] Ibid., vol. 2, p. 19.

another during this time. One can identify three main factors that abetted the theoretical rapprochement between them: Adorno's increasing disillusionment with Walter Benjamin, his renewed interest in Hegel, and his positive reception of Horkheimer's essays during the mid-1930s. There were two main issues that pushed Adorno away from Benjamin's and his own earlier work and closer to Horkheimer's position. First, Adorno reassessed the theological themes in his work without abandoning them. The utopian content of the concept of theology in his writings in the early 1930s was transferred to an idiosyncratic concept of metaphysics that was more secular and more historically grounded. Second, the methodological focus on metaphors, images, and names as ciphers of redemption, which he had appropriated from Benjamin's early writings, shifted toward a more purely philosophical approach: what Adorno called "immanent critique." In addition to his deemphasis of theology and his shift toward "immanent critique," two other factors played an important role in pushing Adorno away from Benjamin and bringing him closer to Horkheimer during the mid-1930s, namely a "renewed and fruitful study of Hegel" and his positive reception of Horkheimer's work during this time. Although Adorno's critique of Hegel's philosophy of history and his privileging of identity over nonidentity remained central to his thought, traces of his renewed engagement with Hegel and the significant influence it had on his thought are not difficult to find. As we shall see, Adorno's enthusiastic reception of Horkheimer's collection of aphorisms, *Dämmerung*, and his essays "Egoism and Freedom Movements" and "The Latest Attack on Metaphysics" also left a significant imprint on Adorno's work during this time.

Adorno's Shift Away from Benjamin

Adorno moved closer to Horkheimer in the mid-1930s through a reevaluation of the meaning and role of theology and metaphysics in his work. These two terms cannot, of course, be used interchangeably, but the meaning they possessed in Adorno's philosophical lexicon did overlap in important ways. Both terms were placeholders for a claim to an emphatic concept of truth that transcended the truth claims of science and any knowledge based solely on what was empirically given. A nuanced delineation of the ways in which these two concepts differed in Adorno's usage would take us too far afield. However, one can say provisionally that in Adorno's work in the early 1930s theology had an emphatically utopian connotation, particularly insofar as it preserved – as it did for Benjamin – the possibility not only of a nonantagonistic, or "reconciled," human society, but also the transformation and redemption of past suffering. The latter moment of the concept, the redemption of past suffering, receded in favor of the former emphasis on reconciliation as Adorno moved away from Benjamin, who continued to defend the "weak redemptive power" of the present vis-à-vis past generations, and closer to Horkheimer, who explicitly criticized this aspect of Benjamin's theory.[57] The

---

[57] For Benjamin's defense of the "weak redemptive power" of the present generation, see his "Theses on the Philosophy of History," *Illuminations*, op. cit., p. 254. For Horkheimer's critique of this aspect of Benjamin's theory, see Chapter 6, p. 231.

concept of metaphysics, which initially had a stronger epistemological content for Adorno, was marshaled in his work beginning in the mid-1930s to counter the widespread positivist tendency to reduce truth claims to what could be established through empirical-scientific and mathematical-logical methods alone. A good example of Adorno's defense of the truth content of metaphysics can be found in the first chapter of the study of Husserl that he was work-ing on at this time.[58] In it, Adorno writes: "How is a science of metaphysics possible? This question demarcates not only the subject of Kant's critique of reason as a theory of knowledge, it also captures the impulse of modern phil-osophy as a whole."[59] Whereas philosophers in the modern rationalist and idealist traditions, such as Spinoza, Leibniz, Kant, and Hegel tried to reconcile the claims of science and metaphysics while preserving the ultimate primacy of the latter, the uncompromising liquidation of metaphysics, which was first advanced by Bacon and the scientific revolution, and which gained momen-tum in the Enlightenment, came to dominate philosophy in the nineteenth and early twentieth centuries. Far from viewing this development as teleological "progress," Adorno argued that the destruction of metaphysics could also lead to the destruction of philosophy itself. He writes:

The transformation of philosophy into science, even as ... a first one that either grounds the sciences or stands above and crowns them, is not a salutary process of matura-tion, in which thought gradually sheds its childlike rudiments, its subjective wishes and projections; on the contrary, it undermines at the same time the very concept of philosophy.[60]

In short, Adorno still viewed metaphysics at this time primarily as a place-holder for an emphatic concept of truth that transcended the increasingly nar-row epistemological boundaries of modern scientific thought and positivism.

As Adorno's work developed, the decidedly – if always negative – utopian moment in his thought, which was initially contained in his concept of theology, was transferred to his concept of metaphysics. This telling shift, which began already in the 1930s, is perhaps nowhere more evident than in the afterword to the new edition of Adorno's study of Kierkegaard, which was published in 1966. In this short afterword, Adorno mentions how his view of certain philosophical problems had changed since the publication of the original edi-tion in 1933, which included the statement that he "would no longer defend metaphysical intentions in such an affirmative way."[61] In truth, what Adorno means here is that he would no longer defend *theological* intentions in such an

---

[58] *Zur Metakritik der Erkenntnistheorie: Studien über Husserl und die phänomenologischen Antinomien*. The title of the English translation, *Against Epistemology*, is misleading insofar as Adorno explicitly defends a certain type of epistemology in the text. In fact, Adorno dis-tinguishes critical, self-reflexive approaches to Marxist theory from the crude dogmatism of Dialectical Materialism (i.e. "DiaMat") precisely in the retention of epistemological reflection as a crucial moment that entered into historical materialism through Marx's determinate negation of German Idealism. As we have seen in Horkheimer's critique of Lenin in Chapter 4, Adorno was in agreement with Horkheimer on this issue.

[59] *Metakritik*, p. 48.

[60] Ibid., pp. 48–9.

[61] *Kierkegaard*, p. 321.

affirmative way, because it was, in fact, theological, not metaphysical intentions that he had defended in that study. As we have already seen, it was these (negative) theological intentions that had proven most objectionable to Horkheimer in his evaluation of Adorno's study of Kierkegaard. Adorno's attitude toward the theological underpinnings of Benjamin's early work and his own current work at this time comes through clearly in letters he wrote to Benjamin in 1934 and 1935. As other commentators have shown, Adorno was concerned that Benjamin's friendship with Brecht at this time was leading him away from the theological assumptions that guided his early work into a crude and reductionist form of materialism.[62] Toward the end of 1934, Adorno was waiting for the arrival of an essay on Kafka that Benjamin was near completing. Adorno hoped that this essay would dispel some of his concerns about Benjamin's newfound affinity with Brecht. In a letter from December 5, 1934, Adorno expressed his regret that "a good ten years ago now" Benjamin was "far less reticent about expressing theological … propositions."[63] After receiving the essay the following week, Adorno was relieved to see that the theological moment still seemed to occupy a decisive place in Benjamin's thought. His response to Benjamin's essay demonstrates that Adorno enthusiastically endorsed this theological moment and that he saw it as the foundation for future collaborative work between the two of them. He wrote:

[In] my own earliest attempt to interpret Kafka … I claimed he represents a photograph of our earthly life from the perspective of a redeemed life … no further words seem necessary to demonstrate our agreement … And this also … touches upon one's position with regard to "theology." Since I always insisted on such a position, before entering into your Arcades [Project], it seems to me doubly important that the image of theology, into which I would gladly see our thoughts fuse, is none other than the very one which sustains your thoughts here – it could be called an "inverse" theology. This position, directed against natural and supernatural interpretation alike, first formulated here as it is with total precision, strikes me as utterly identical with my own – indeed my Kierkegaard study was concerned with nothing else. [64]

At this point, the utopian dimensions of Adorno's thought were still firmly grounded in a concept of negative theology and had not been transferred to a more secular notion of metaphysics.

The next major exchange between Adorno and Benjamin came in the wake of the "Arcades Exposé" (also know by its provisional title "Paris, Capital of the 19th Century"), which Benjamin sent to Adorno a few months later. Adorno's response to this essay was much less enthusiastic than his response to the Kafka essay, in large part because the theological moment seemed to have been eclipsed by a more "historical-sociological" approach. Adorno's remarks to Benjamin make clear not only the ongoing importance of Benjamin's early theological model for his own thought, but also his conviction that this model was what separated their work from that of the Institute for Social Research.

---

[62] Buck-Morss, *The Origins of Negative Dialectics*, pp. 140–43. Wolin, *An Aesthetic of Redemption*, pp. 173–83.

[63] *Benjamin-Adorno Correspondence*, p. 61.

[64] Ibid., pp. 66–7 (translation modified).

Adorno essentially accuses Benjamin of abandoning his deepest theoretical (i.e. theological) convictions in order to win the Institute's support for the Arcades Project.[65] In a letter from May 20th, 1935, Adorno writes:

I am well aware that the Institute ... will find it hard to accept anything other such a historical-sociological work. But you will hardly take it amiss if I openly confess to regarding the "Arcades" not as a historical-sociological investigation but rather as *prima philosophia* in your own particular sense. We certainly have no need to quarrel with one another concerning the decisive significance of the material character of the work, and there is no one who understands better than I do precisely how the interpretation of the piece must be sought in this material character alone. But there is also no one less tempted than I am to try to forego its interpretation and total articulation in the medium of concepts ... for you have already justified certain uninterpreted preliminary materials ... precisely with reference to the final interpretation to be supplied in the "Arcades." ... But there is absolutely no question for me that such a theory can only find its own dialectic in the polarity between social and theological categories, and that because of this, as well as through the interpretive procedure involved, it is in principle remote from the a priori approach of a work destined for the Institute – just as my book on Kierkegaard was – and indeed, a thousand times more so.[66]

[65] Adorno did not realize that Benjamin had already been trying for some time – of his own volition – to give his work a more historical and sociological dimension in order to allay *his own* concerns about the difficulties of grounding his earlier, more theological approach. In response to Adorno's criticisms of his 1935 essay "The Work of Art in the Age of Mechanical Reproduction" and Adorno's entreaties that he return to his earlier, theological approach, Benjamin insists that he has moved beyond the "rhapsodic naiveté" of his earlier work. At that time, Benjamin still intended to give the Arcades Project the subtitle, "A Dialectical Fairy-Tale," which for him "no longer passes muster now." He continues, "This subtitle suggests the rhapsodic character of the presentation as I then conceived it ... But this epoch [of my thought] was also one of a quite unconcerned and archaic form of philosophizing naively caught up in nature. It was my conversations with you ..., Asja [Lacis], Felizitas [Gretel Karplus], and Horkheimer which brought that epoch to an end. There would henceforth be no more rhapsodic naiveté." *Benjamin-Adorno Correspondence*, op. cit., pp. 88–9. Benjamin would make many of the same points three years later in response to Adorno's criticisms of his essay on Baudelaire: "If I refused there, in the name of my own productive interests, to pursue an esoteric intellectual path for myself and to pass on to other matters beyond the interests of dialectical materialism and the Institute, there was more at stake than solidarity with the Institute or simple fidelity to dialectical materialism, namely, a solidarity with experiences which we have all shared during the last fifteen years. Here, too, it is therefore a question of my most personal interests as a writer. I will not deny that these may occasionally do some violence to my original interests. ... I believe that speculation can only begin its inevitably audacious flight with some prospect of success if, instead of donning the waxen wings of esotericism, it seeks its source of strength in construction alone. It is the needs of construction which dictated that the second part of my book should consist primarily of philological material. What is involved here is less a case of 'ascetic discipline' than a methodological precaution." Ibid., p. 291.

[66] *Benjamin-Adorno Correspondence*, pp. 83–4. Interestingly, in a separate letter written to Benjamin from approximately the same time, Gretel Karplus expressed a very similar sentiment regarding the differences between the theoretical approaches of Benjamin and the Institute. She wrote, "I am amazed that Fritz [Pollock] has taken an interest in your sketches; are you really thinking then of contributing work to the journal? I would certainly regard this an enormous danger, for the parameters are relatively narrow ones, and you will never be able to write what your true friends have been waiting for all these years, the great philosophical work which exists entirely for its own sake, which has made no concessions." Quoted by Benjamin in a letter to Adorno, *Benjamin-Adorno Correspondence*, p. 88. It is also interesting to note that the term

Here again we can see that Adorno was still fully committed to the philosophical and theological model that Benjamin had outlined in his earlier work and that Adorno had emulated in his study of Kierkegaard – a model that contained a decided skepticism about the possibility of articulating emphatic notions of truth purely "in the medium of concepts."

While in Oxford in the mid-1930s, Adorno was carrying on an active correspondence with both Benjamin and Horkheimer. Following these two correspondences during this time makes it clear how Adorno moved gradually away from Benjamin and toward Horkheimer without, however, abandoning many of the "Benjaminian" assumptions that guided his thought, or without ever fully accepting many of the basic presuppositions of Horkheimer's model of Critical Theory. In a letter to Horkheimer from February 25th, 1935, Adorno spoke openly of his own "theological intentions" and tried to convince Horkheimer that these intentions, "as uncomfortable as they may be for you," fully converged with his own theoretical intentions, at least in their consequences.[67] Just a few months later – and only a few weeks after he had written the earlier-quoted passage to Benjamin – Adorno seemed to have altered his position somewhat on the question of metaphysics, which was bound up very closely with the question of theology. In a letter to Horkheimer on June 8th, 1935, in which he was discussing Benjamin's "Arcades Exposé," Adorno explained to Horkheimer his high estimation of Benjamin's project but also his fear that the project would not be acceptable to the Institute, because "in my honest opinion, this book was, like my own book on Kierkegaard, too burdened with metaphysics to fit within the program of the Institute." He went on to explain that, after examining Benjamin's recent exposé, he had changed his mind and now believed that Benjamin's project had "completely lost the character of metaphysical improvisation that it once had." He continued, "I don't even want to claim that this is, in the end, a positive development (this is a question that we still need to discuss); in any case, it is positive in terms of its utilization within the program of the Institute, to which it now *conforms*."[68] Adorno's hesitance to fully endorse the sociological-historical shift in Benjamin's work and his insistence that he and Horkheimer still needed to discuss this issue, demonstrates that he had not simply abandoned his own theological premises. Nonetheless, his willingness to criticize his own Kierkegaard book – in a manner that anticipated the aforementioned criticisms that he would make of the book later – do indicate the beginnings of a shift in his thought.[69] This shift

prima philosophia, which has a thoroughly positive connotation in Adorno's remarks here, would soon acquire a completely different, much more critical meaning in Adorno's philosophical lexicon. For example, in a letter to Alfred Sohn-Rethel in November, 1936, Adorno stated, "it seems to Horkheimer and certainly to me that one of the most important goals of a materialist dialectic is to liquidate the idea of a *prima philosophia*." *Theodor W. Adorno und Alfred Sohn-Rethel Briefwechsel, 1936–1969* ed. Christoph Gödde (Munich: Edition Text + Kritik, 1991), p. 11. The term is used in a thoroughly critical way throughout Adorno's study of Husserl.

[67] GS, vol. 15, p. 328.

[68] Ibid., p. 361 (Adorno's emphasis). The original of the last subordinate clause is "dem sie sich *einfügt*," which intentionally expresses Adorno's ambivalence about the newfound "conformity" of Benjamin's project to the Institute's program.

[69] Although it would take us too far afield to trace the further development of this shift in Adorno's later thought, one can say – as I have already suggested – that the utopian content of Adorno's

will become more apparent in conjunction with the following examination of the shift in Adorno's methodology during this time.

The best way to present this shift in Adorno's methodology during the mid-1930s is through a brief comparison of his studies of Kierkegaard and Husserl. A first version of the former was completed in 1931 and accepted by the Frankfurt philosophy faculty as Adorno's *Habilitation*, whereas a second, thoroughly revised edition was published in January 1933. The influence of Benjamin's early work on Adorno is not diminished in any way in the second version, to which I will be referring in what follows. Adorno worked continuously on his Husserl study during his exile in Oxford (1934–7). He was intending to submit it to the philosophy faculty there to obtain a Ph.D. At this time, Adorno had completed three chapters of the study. They were included in lightly revised form in the final version of the book, which he published in 1956 as *Metakritik der Erkenntnistheorie: Studien über Husserl und die phänomenologischen Antinomien*.[70] Adorno wrote an additional chapter and a new introduction for the first edition of the book. So, in what follows, I will refer (with a few exceptions) to the three chapters that were written in the mid-1930s.

The methodological shift that occurred during this time in Adorno's thought appears more clearly against the backdrop of the more profound continuities that existed between his studies of Kierkegaard and Husserl. He argued that both Kierkegaard and Husserl remained trapped within the basic categories of idealism, despite their sustained efforts to move beyond it. Although both philosophers believed these attempts to overcome idealism had been successful and their work had almost without exception been interpreted in this way, Adorno's meticulous examination of their writings was intended to prove just the opposite: that despite their best intentions, they had not only failed to escape idealism, they had in many respects fallen behind its most profound insights. In a second, crucial step, Adorno argued that this failure expressed in both cases a deeper historical truth. Adorno

concept of theology was transferred to his concept of metaphysics and was given an increasingly secular, even materialist form in his later work. The theological impulse did not by any means completely disappear from Adorno's later thought, as the final aphorism in *Minima Moralia* would make clear, in which Adorno writes, "The only philosophy which can be responsibly practiced in face of despair is the attempt to contemplate all things as they would present themselves from the standpoint of redemption" (op. cit., p. 247). Yet Adorno would also argue in his later work that "metaphysical" intentions such as this could only be preserved in a thoroughly secular form. As he would write later in *Negative Dialectics*, "The course of history forces metaphysics toward materialism, which was traditionally its direct opposite" (op. cit., p. 358). Adorno would continue to defend the seemingly paradoxical concept of "metaphysical experience" until the end of his life, but his model for such experience was not transcendent or theological, but anamnestic: Proust's recollections of "fulfilled moments" – the association here with Benjamin's concept of "fulfilled time" in not coincidental – of his childhood provided Adorno with a model of such experience. See, for example, Theodor W. Adorno, *Metaphysics: Concepts and Problems*, trans. Edmund Jephcott (Stanford University Press, 2000), pp. 137f.

70 Theodor Adorno, *Against Epistemology: A Metacritique. Studies in Husserl and the Phenomenological Antinomies*, trans. Willis Domingo, (Cambridge, MA: MIT Press, 1983). The title of the translation is misleading, because one of Adorno's main aims in the book is to *preserve* epistemological reflection (as an open-ended relationship between subject and object) as a crucial moment in a larger dialectical and materialist theory of knowledge and society.

viewed both Kierkegaard and Husserl's philosophy as belated symptoms of the disintegration of idealism, a process that expressed the deeper, underlying disintegration of bourgeois society. For example, Adorno argued that both men's philosophies registered the decline of the bourgeois ideal of autonomous subjectivity: Kierkegaard's existential emphasis on the absolute primacy of the individual and his retreat into interiority represented a desperate, if ultimately unsuccessful attempt to escape the increasing meaninglessness of individuals' lives and their powerlessness in the face of overwhelming objective forces. Much of Kierkegaard's polemical ire was directed against Hegel's celebration of these objective forces as "rational" and "necessary," yet his defense of the "spiritual" and religious realms of existence as the highest, as well as his insistence that an irrational "leap of faith" was ultimately the only path to redemption, ended up reasserting the same domination of nature and blind historical dynamic that characterized both Hegel's philosophy and modern bourgeois society. Similarly, Husserl's sustained critique of psychologism represented a profound insight into the historical decline of the autonomous subject, but his insistence on consciousness as a "sphere of being of absolute origins"[71] and his replacement of an experientially open-ended subject-object dialectic with a static, rationalist methodology (in *Logical Investigations*) or a concept of the "intuition of essences" (in *Ideen*) based on the unmediated givens of individual consciousness, also culminated, according to Adorno, in a reassertion of the same primacy of abstract, subjective categories characteristic of idealism. One could, in other words, read Adorno's argument here with regard to both Kierkegaard and Husserl as a reformulation of Lukács's discussion of the "Antinomies of bourgeois philosophy" in *History and Class Consciousness*, insofar as both Kierkegaard's and Husserl's philosophies express a deeper underlying contradiction in bourgeois society that they are, however, unable to overcome due to the "epistemological limits of bourgeois philosophy." The failure of their efforts to overcome these limits expresses a deeper historical truth about bourgeois society itself. In contrast to Lukács, and also Horkheimer, as we will see, Adorno insists that this historical truth can only be revealed through a micrological immersion in the texts of the philosophers. Only through a painstaking interpretation of the particular does the more general historical truth become apparent. Although not inductive in the strict sense, the methodological assumption guiding the studies of Kierkegaard and Husserl is that the social and historical truth content of a work can be revealed only if one reasons from the particular to the general, and never the other way around. As Adorno would put it in his study of Husserl, "the truth is not in history ... history is in the truth."[72]

Yet if one looks beyond these important similarities between Adorno's two most substantial works in the 1930s, a subtle, yet important methodological shift becomes apparent. An important clue to this shift can be found in a letter Adorno wrote to Benjamin on November 6, 1934. Adorno describes

---

[71] Edmund Husserl, *Ideen zu einer reinen Phänomenologie und phänomenologischen Philosophie: Allgemeine Einführung in die reine Phänomenologie* (Tübingen: Niemeyer, 1980), p. 107.

[72] *Metakritik*, p. 141.

his project on Husserl, which was still in the early stages at this point, in the following way:

> My original idea was to attempt a kind of retranslation of an eminently "philosophical" language back into a language of images; whether I shall be successful in that here and now unfortunately no longer depends simply on me; but I shall certainly not fail to demonstrate the immanent contradictions of such a formal ontology and its grounding.[73]

This quote demonstrates that Adorno had originally intended to approach the Husserl project with the same methodological premises that had guided his Kierkegaard book, in which Benjamin's "language of images" had figured so prominently. It also makes clear that Adorno was no longer certain if he would adhere to this methodological approach in his study of Husserl and that he was seriously considering another approach, namely an analysis of the "immanent contradictions" in Husserl's "formal ontology." It was, in fact, the latter – not the former – approach that Adorno would ultimately adopt in the Husserl study. Yet how exactly did the two differ? Adorno's methodology in the Kierkegaard study could be described as unapologetically aesthetic, if one follows Adorno and Benjamin's insistence that aesthetic categories are at the same time categories of knowledge; even more, that aesthetic categories could provide the key to solving riddles – to use the language of Adorno's inaugural address – that remained inscrutable using the methods of traditional sciences or the concepts of bourgeois philosophy. Reversing Hegel's argument in the introduction to his lectures on aesthetics – that in the modern, bourgeois epoch philosophical concepts had supplanted religion and art as the best means of grasping the deepest human problems and needs[74] – Adorno argued in the beginning of the Kierkegaard book against Hegel's and Kierkegaard's denigration of art and aesthetics as "lower" forms of knowledge and experience vis-à-vis philosophy and authentic religion, respectively. Adorno wrote, "Under the influence of German Romanticism, Kierkegaard's writings prepare the transition of this intention from philosophical systematics – which he critically breaks through – to an artistic praxis of which he was not yet capable."[75] The intention Adorno refers to here is the preservation of self-reflexivity, which Adorno sees as being transferred historically in the nineteenth century from philosophical idealism to aesthetic reflection and artistic practice. Yet Kierkegaard's denigration of the aesthetic in his writings proves that he is not "equal" to the task of attaining full self-reflexivity. Adorno does not hesitate to claim his own adequacy to the task; armed with Benjamin's aesthetic-epistemological categories, Adorno sets out to demonstrate how Kierkegaard's writings remained – despite his own authorial intentions – beholden to the mythical character of idealist philosophy and thus betrayed the fundamental contradictions of bourgeois society.

True to the epistemological-critical program outlined in the prologue to Benjamin's *Trauerspiel* book, Adorno devoted much of his efforts to the

---

[73] *Benjamin-Adorno Correspondence*, p. 55.

[74] See Hegel's "Introduction," to his *Aesthetics: Lectures on Fine Art*, trans. T.M. Knox (Oxford and New York: Clarendon Press, 1988–1998).

[75] *Kierkegaard: Construction of the Aesthetic*, trans. Robert Hullot-Kentor (Minneapolis: University of Minnesota Press, 1989), p. 8.

interpretation of seemingly marginal elements, especially the images, meta-phors, and names to be found in Kierkegaard's writings.[76] It was these images, metaphors, and names that provided the key, according to Adorno, to the unin-tentional truth content of his philosophy.[77] Adorno alerts his reader to the methodological procedure in the first chapter:

Kierkegaard's aesthetic figures are strictly illustrations of his philosophical categories, which they exemplify in primitive simplicity before they have been adequately articu-lated conceptually.... The great intention of allegory conceals itself in their coloration and reduces itself to a smaller scale in their bourgeois miniature format.[78]

In other words, the metaphors and images one finds in Kierkegaard's writings provide a more reliable path to uncovering the objective truth content of his work – what Adorno refers to here as the "grand intention of the allegorical"[79] – than his explicit philosophical arguments, which are "not adequately articu-lated." Examples of this procedure can be found throughout the remainder of Adorno's study. In the second chapter, Adorno focuses on the frequently reoccur-ring image of the domestic interior in Kierkegaard's writings to demonstrate the severe limitations and phantasmagorical character of his existential concept of subjectivity. Pointing in a seemingly arbitrary way to Kierkegaard's use of the metaphor of a mirror to describe his own self-understanding as a writer, Adorno argues that this typical accoutrement of nineteenth-century bourgeois domes-ticity is in fact a symbol of the "imprisonment of mere spirit within itself,"[80] just as the recurring image of the interior points to a purely passive form of subjectivity of one who is thoroughly isolated from larger social processes. Yet this isolation by no means shields the individual from the deleterious effects of the social totality. In the next chapter, Adorno argues that the central motif of melancholy in Kierkegaard's writing is "not merely metaphorical,"[81] but instead is an expression of the "historical spirit [*Geist*] in its natural depth and therefore, in the images of its corporality, the central allegory."[82] Adorno reads

[76] As Siegfried Kracauer put it in his review of Adorno's study, "He submits the metaphors [*Bilder*] that Kierkegaard uses to a process of interrogation, like that of a private detective who refuses to believe the alibi he's been given and instead reconstructs the truth out of minute clues that the perpetrator has overlooked." Siegfried Kracauer, *Gesammelte Schriften*, vol. 5, section 3 (Suhrkamp: Frankfurt, 1990), p. 267 (translation mine). In his review of *Kierkegaard*, Walter Benjamin also praised Adorno's interpretative method: "Nowhere does Adorno's insight go deeper than where he ignores the stereotypes of Kierkegaard's philosophy and where he looks instead for the key to Kierkegaard's thought in its apparently insignificant relics, in its images, similes and alle-gories." Walter Benjamin, "Kierkegaard," *Selected Writings*, vol. 2, 1927–1934, eds. M. Jennings, H. Eiland and G. Smith (Cambridge MA: Harvard University Press, 2005) p. 704.

[77] On the key concept of "unintentional truth" in Adorno's writings at this time, see Buck-Morss, *The Origin of Negative Dialectics*, pp. 77–81.

[78] *Kierkegaard: Construction of the Aesthetic*, op. cit., p. 6 (translation amended).

[79] In his *Trauerspiel* book, Benjamin interpreted these baroque plays as the expression of a quasi-transcendental, allegorical subject, which determined the general conditions of meaning – and lack thereof – during this historical period. Adorno follows Benjamin here in this argument. Whether Adorno was justified in applying the categories from the seventeenth century in an unme-diated way to Kierkegaard's nineteenth-century work is a question that would be worth pursuing.

[80] *Kierkegaard: Construction of the Aesthetic*, p. 42.

[81] Ibid., p. 61.

[82] Ibid., p. 62 (translation amended).

Kierkegaard's preoccupation with melancholy as an expression of the repressive social conditions that exist within bourgeois society, which necessitate the subordination of individuals' impulses to the abstract imperatives of capital and the commodity form – imperatives that are expressed in idealist philosophy in the form of the dominance of an abstract "morality" over inclinations, or absolute "spirit" or "mind" over the body. Adorno points out that whenever Kierkegaard attempts to describe the positive ideal of pure spirit, he almost always uses bodily metaphors.[83] This return of the repressed in his language expresses the deeper dynamic of a society in which man's historical attempt to emancipate himself from the blind forces of nature and myth have overshot their goal and led to the creation of a second nature and a mythical form of rationality every bit as blind and potentially destructive as its archaic predecessors.

Although traces of Adorno's methodology in the Kierkegaard book were still evident in his study of Husserl, overall, his approach had changed substantially. His aesthetically motivated focus on images, metaphors, and names as ciphers of theologically grounded truth gave way to an intense engagement with Husserl's philosophical arguments themselves. Whereas Adorno had essentially bypassed Kierkegaard's philosophical arguments as no longer adequate to changed historical conditions, he took Husserl's arguments much more seriously in an attempt to expose their immanent contradictions. Adorno now argued that by carefully immersing oneself in these arguments themselves and exposing their unexamined assumptions and contradictions, one could demonstrate that Husserl's attempt to overcome idealism had failed no less than had Kierkegaard's. Once this failure had been rigorously demonstrated and the underlying social and historical content of Husserl's categories had been revealed, the superiority of dialectical and materialist over phenomenological theories of knowledge would be evident. As Adorno put it in the introduction to the study: "Instead of disputing individual epistemological issues, the micrological procedure used here is intended to stringently demonstrate how such questions lead beyond themselves and, finally, beyond the entire sphere of epistemology."[84] One sees here that Adorno's emphasis on the epistemological primacy of the particular – in his ongoing allegiance to a "micrological" approach – remains unbroken. Yet the nature of that particular object, which provides access to deeper social and historical truths, has changed from images, metaphors, and names to conceptual arguments. This shift betrays a greater willingness to accept conceptual argumentation as a legitimate form of philosophy; as long as concepts are self-reflexive, they are as legitimate as a more purely aesthetic approach, which relies on "constellations" and "juxtaposition of the smallest elements."[85] Let us briefly examine two of the central contradictions Adorno identifies in Husserl's philosophy in order to see his new methodological approach in action: his critique of Husserl's "logical absolutism" and his concept of the "intuition of essences."

---

[83] Ibid., pp. 51–3.
[84] *Metakritik*, p. 10.
[85] "The Actuality of Philosophy," op. cit., p. 336.

Adorno praises Husserl's famous critique of psychologism, that is, his insistence that logical categories cannot be deduced from the empirical givens of individual consciousness. Husserl's insistence in his *Logical Investigations* on the limitations of any theory of knowledge that takes the concrete individual as its point of departure expressed a genuine insight into the decline of the individual in a postliberal bourgeois society. Yet Husserl's stringent critique of psychologism led him – at least in his early work – to eliminate the subjective moment of knowledge altogether and to fall back into a precritical, pre-Kantian rationalism that dogmatically asserted the objective character of logical categories.[86] Adorno accuses Husserl of defending a "naïve realism of logic,"[87] because he "denies the dependence of logical laws upon any kind of external reality." For him logic "does not express a relationship between consciousness and something objective [*Gegenständliche*], it is instead granted the status of being *sui generis*."[88] However, for Adorno – as for Durkheim, whom Adorno explicitly mentions here[89] – logical categories do not exist outside history in some ideal realm of pure forms; they are grounded in social relations, which under capitalism are antagonistic.[90] He argues, in particular, that logical categories in bourgeois society are modeled on legal norms, which in turn are designed to maintain existing property relations.[91] According to Adorno, in other words, Husserl's arguments fell back into a precritical, non-self-reflexive defense of logic, which – like the idealist philosophy he was trying to overcome – remained cut off and indifferent to the objects it was intended to grasp, subsuming them under its static and abstract categories, rather than preserving an open-ended dialectic between consciousness and object.[92] Husserl's critique of psychologism was intended to wrest the categories of logic from a narrowly scientific grounding of knowledge – an intention with which Adorno was in full agreement. Yet for Adorno, "the self-criticism

---

[86] For an insightful discussion of Adorno's critique of Husserl's logical absolutism, see Brian O'Connor, *Adorno's Negative Dialectic: Philosophy and the Possibility of Critical Rationality* (London and Cambridge, MA: MIT Press, 2004), pp. 129–48.

[87] *Metakritik*, p. 62.

[88] Ibid., p. 77.

[89] Ibid., p. 83. For Durkheim's grounding of logical categories in society, see his *Elementary Forms of Religious Life*.

[90] Durkheim would not, of course, have agreed with Adorno's insistence on the fundamentally contradictory character of modern capitalist society. His work can be seen as a series of attempts to reveal the more fundamental forces of social cohesion – from the division of labor in his early work to traditional or civic religion in his late work – which could be mobilized against social disintegration and class conflict.

[91] See his letter to Horkheimer from December 5, 1935, in which he describes the argument of the Husserl book. *Adorno-Horkheimer Briefwechsel*, vol. 1, p. 101.

[92] Adorno had not yet developed the concept of the "preponderance of the object," which would figure prominently in *Negative Dialectics*. At this point, the epistemological balance between subject and object was more or less equal and not yet tipped in favor of the object. This greater emphasis on the subject, which one also finds in other writings from this period, such as the introduction of *Minima Moralia*, also marks a departure from his early, Benjaminian, antisubjectivist writings and testifies to the influence of Hegel on this thought during this time.

of logic has as its consequence dialectics,"[93] not a dogmatic reassertion of the absolute objectivity of logical categories. Adorno deciphered the social content of Husserl's philosophical arguments here in the following way: "The power [*Gewalt*] of logical absolutism over the psychological grounding of logic derives from the objectivity of social processes, to which the individual is forced to submit but which at the same time remain opaque to him."[94]

Whereas Husserl made very few epistemological concessions to subjectivity in his *Logical Investigations*, the subjective mediation of knowledge reappeared in his 1913 study, *Ideen zu einer reinen Phänomenologie*,[95] with the concept of the "intuition of essences" [*Wesensschau*]. Husserl argued there that thinking was distinguished from perception through *intentionality*; thinking was always a thinking *of* something. Husserl made a further distinction – one that he had explicitly denied in the *Logical Investigations* – between intentional acts of thinking that were directed at abstract, general objects, such as logical concepts, and concrete particular objects, which are now purported to have an "essence" of their own, independent of the abstract logical categories.[96] With this argument Husserl believed he had moved beyond a Kantian understanding of individual (phenomenal) objects in which the raw data of empirical impressions was organized by, and ultimately subordinated to, the universal categories of transcendental subjectivity. By focusing on the intentional act of thinking, the abstract categories of cognition could be "bracketed" and the particular "essence" of individual objects revealed. One can easily see how Husserl's intense effort here to do justice to the particularity of individual objects would have appealed to Adorno, who does in fact state that Husserl's intentions (no pun intended) were good.[97] Yet following the quote from Hegel, with which Adorno opens this chapter of his study,[98] the seemingly concrete essence of the particular object turns out to be mediated in ways that Husserl believes – wrongly – he can simply "bracket" out. Husserl's insistence on the absolute singularity of the "meaning" [*Sinn*] of the intentional act – as the

---

[93] *Metakritik*, p. 81.

[94] Ibid., p. 83.

[95] *Ideas: General Introduction to Pure Phenomenology*, trans. R. Boyce Gibson (New York: Humanities Press, 1969).

[96] Ibid., p. 98.

[97] Adorno's praise for Husserl in this regard highlights his own abiding commitment to the epistemological primacy of the particular. He writes, "[Husserl] ist darauf aufmerksam geworden, dass das einem Sachverhalt Wesentliche, das der Spezies Zukommende, sein 'Spezifisches' nicht erreicht wird von seinem Artbegriff ... Darin harmoniert er mit den Impulsen anderer, sonst sehr von ihm abweichender akademischer Philosophen seiner Generation wie Dilthey, Simmel und Rickert, deren jeder auf seine Weise auf das sich besann, was bereits die Kantische *Kritik der Urteilskraft* motiviert hatte und mittlerweile zur Banalität wurde: dass die kausal-mechanische und klassifikatorische Erklärung nicht ins Zentrum des Gegenstandes dringt, dass sie das Beste vergisst. ... Auch ihm gewährt vielfach ein einziges Konkretes, insistent betrachtet und aufgeschlossen, tiefere und verbindlichere Einsicht in weiter ausgreifende Zusammenhänge als ein Verfahren, das vom Individuellen nur soviel duldet, wie unter allgemeine Begriffe sich subsumieren lässt." Ibid., p. 102.

[98] "Was ich nur meine, ist mein, gehört mir als diesem besonderen Individuum; wenn aber die Sprache nur Allgemeines ausdrückt, so kann ich nicht sagen was ich nur meine." Ibid., p. 96.

guarantee of its particularity – reduces that act to an absolute, unmediated given. Yet this immediacy is false according to Adorno:

Just as no experience [*Erlebnis*] is "singular," but instead points necessarily, through its intertwinement with the totality of the individual's consciousness, beyond itself, so there are not any absolute meanings. Every single meaning … contains, by the power of thought, an element of universality and is more than merely itself.[99]

Here again, Adorno argues that Husserl's effort to move beyond idealism causes him, in fact, to fall behind it. Whereas for Kant our knowledge of particular objects was composed of a synthesis of the active, subjective categories of cognition and the passive impressions of the senses, Husserl's notion of the "intuition of essences" falls back into a purely passive model of subjectivity that intuits the "essences" of equally lifeless objects. The putative concreteness of the particular is gained by removing it from the larger social and historical context, not unlike still-life photography.[100] According to Adorno, the pseudo-concreteness, passivity, and static character of phenomenology represent a marked decline vis-à-vis the philosophical level attained by Kant and Hegel, a decline that, in turn, marks a deeper disintegration of bourgeois society: "With phenomenology bourgeois thought undergoes its final transformation into dissociated, fragmentary determinations, posited one next to the other, and resigns itself to the mere reproduction of what is."[101] Finally, it is worth noting that, in contrast to the Kierkegaard study, one will search in vain for any reference to theology in Adorno's study of Husserl.[102] The undiminished critical and utopian intentions of Adorno's argument are no longer grounded in a prelapsarian theory of language, but rather in the real potential for overcoming the antagonisms of bourgeois society, which are revealed through the procedure of immanent critique.

Adorno's "Renewed and Fruitful Study of Hegel"

The significance of Hegel for Adorno's theoretical development in the 1930s has been a matter of speculation in the literature on Adorno. For example, Marcos Nobre writes, "It is undeniable that the intellectual exchange between Horkheimer and Adorno increased significantly during the period 1935–8 and

---

[99] Ibid., pp. 99–100.

[100] Adorno describes the uncanny affinities between phenomenological intuition of essences and photography in the following way: "[Phenomenology] claims to take possession of reality intact, by isolating its objects and fixing them with the Medusa's glance of a sudden 'ray of vision,' as if they were set up and exhibited in the studio before the photographic lens. Like the photographer of old, the phenomenologist wraps himself up in the black veil of his *epoche*, implores the objects to hold still and in this way is able to create images passively and without the spontaneity of the cognizing subject. … Just as in photography the *camera obscura* and the recorded pictorial object belong together, so in phenomenology do the immanence of consciousness and naïve realism." Ibid., p. 199. *Against Epistemology*, p. 196 (translation amended).

[101] Ibid., pp. 214–5. *Against Epistemology*, op. cit., p. 211 (translation amended).

[102] Which is not to say that this theological motif disappeared altogether. See footnote 71.

that this exchange intensified even more after Adorno's emigration to the U.S. in 1938. But it is difficult ... to say if this substantial intellectual exchange led to a true Hegelianization of Adorno's thought."[103] A close examination of Adorno's writings and correspondence from this time leaves no question that Hegel did acquire more importance for Adorno during this time, even though Adorno never abandoned his fundamental criticisms of Hegel's philosophy – especially of his philosophy of history and identity logic. Hegel in particular, and dialectics in general, already played a crucial role in the Kierkegaard study. One finds numerous passages in which Adorno defends Hegel against Kierkegaard's unrelenting attacks against him, and argues that Kierkegaard's critique ultimately falls behind Hegel's insights. Nonetheless, Adorno's explicit program here was a "liquidation of idealism" that stressed the fundamental flaws of conceptual knowledge as articulated in Hegel's philosophy. As we have already seen, Adorno's turn to Benjamin and to aesthetics as a more profound source of knowledge than philosophical concepts reversed Hegel's judgment of art and aesthetics as epistemologically anachronistic vis-à-vis philosophy. For Adorno, Benjamin's concepts of allegory, dialectical images, and constellations represented a "qualitatively different logical form" than that "underlying the moments of a universal conceptual structure."[104] According to Adorno, "exact imagination[105] which proceeded through a method of "arrangement of the smallest details"[106] in new constellations, was superior to scientific reason and abstract conceptual mediation. We have just seen how Adorno's methodology shifted at this time away from this reliance on constellations and fragments toward a model of what he called "immanent critique." These two methods overlapped in certain key ways and cannot be seen as mutually exclusive, yet crucial differences between them did exist: most important, perhaps, the Benjaminian reliance on images, metaphors, and names as placeholders of theological truth versus the Hegelian attempt to reveal contradictions in the arguments themselves as expressions of deeper social and historical contradictions.

More explicit evidence of Hegel's increasing importance for Adorno can be found in his correspondence and writings during this time. For example, in a letter to Benjamin on September 6, 1936, Adorno reported that he had recently "undertaken a renewed and extremely fruitful study of Hegel."[107] As his debate with Benjamin continued to unfold during this time, Adorno found himself increasingly defending conceptual mediation against Benjamin's continued reliance – most notably in his Arcades Project – on arranging materials in unmediated constellations and leaving it up to the reader to draw his own conclusions. The famous passage from Adorno's letter to Benjamin on November 10, 1938, which contains his critical response to the first draft of Benjamin's essay,

[103] Marcos Nobre, *A Dialética Negativa de Theodor W. Adorno: A Ontologia do Estado Falso* (Sao Paulo: Iluminuras, 1998), p. 98.

[104] "Die Idee der Naturgeschichte," Adorno, *Schriften*, vol. 1, op. cit., p. 359.

[105] "Die Aktualität der Philosophie," ibid., p. 341.

[106] Ibid., p. 336.

[107] *Benjamin-Adorno Correspondence*, p. 147.

"The Paris of the Second Empire in Baudelaire," provides ample evidence of this tendency. Adorno writes:

I see a close connection between the points at which your essay falls behind its own a priori, and its relationship to dialectical materialism – and here in particular I speak not only for myself but equally for Max [Horkheimer], with whom I have had an exhaustive discussion of this question. Let me express myself in as simple and Hegelian a manner as possible. Unless I am very much mistaken, your dialectic lacks one thing: mediation.... Materialist determination of cultural traits is only possible if it is mediated through the total social process.... The "mediation" which I miss and find obscured by materialistic-historiographic invocation, is nothing other than the theory which your study omits. The omission of the theory affects your empirical evidence itself. On the one hand, it lends it a deceptively epic character, and on the other it deprives the phenomena, which are experienced only subjectively, of their real historico-philosophical weight. To express it another way: the theological motif of calling things by their names tends to turn into a wide-eyed presentation of mere facts. If one wished to put it very drastically, one could say that your study is located at the crossroads of magic and positivism. That spot is bewitched.[108]

Although Adorno's criticisms here were directed primarily against what he perceived as a mechanically materialistic approach that Benjamin had assimilated from Brecht, his objections also applied more generally to Benjamin's abstention from conceptual mediation. As Susan Buck-Morss notes, in his essay on Hugo von Hoffmansthal and Stefan George, which Adorno published in a volume in honor of Benjamin shortly after his suicide, he reiterated these same criticisms. She writes:

As Adorno described the fundamental weaknesses of George's approach, implied was his criticism of Benjamin, unmistakable now that their correspondence has been published. Adorno interpreted George's poetic attitude toward sensory attitudes in the same critical terms he had used against Benjamin's (and also Husserl's) philosophical one, claiming that the objects remained "opaque" because they experienced in their given form as "still life" by a "blind intuition without concept."[109]

That a positive reevaluation of the role of conceptual mediation occurred in Adorno's thought in the mid-1930s and that this reevaluation was due in no small part to Adorno's "renewed and extremely fruitful study of Hegel" seems clear.

Despite this reevaluation, Adorno continued to sharply criticize the identitarian foundations of Hegel's concepts. His new position – which he would continue to refine until the end of his life[110] – is articulated clearly in the first chapter of his study of Husserl. Departing from his earlier argument that philosophy must rely on "qualitatively different logical forms" derived from aesthetic experience, Adorno now insisted that philosophy does not distinguish itself from science "through a higher principle or set of instruments," but

---

[108] Ibid., pp. 282–3.
[109] *The Origin of Negative Dialectics*, p. 174.
[110] As Adorno put it in *Negative Dialectics*: "Utopia in regard to knowledge would be to reveal that which is not conceptual with concepts, without reducing the former to the latter." Op. cit., p. 21.

instead "through the use which it makes of its means, especially the conceptual ones, which as such resemble those of the sciences."[111] In other words, Adorno no longer seeks a qualitatively different means of knowledge; he seeks instead to make traditional scientific and philosophical concepts *self-reflexive*. With regard to Hegel, who came closer than any other Western philosopher to fulfilling this task, Adorno focused on eliminating the affirmative, identitarian foundations of his concepts in order to restore their critical, negative character. This project placed Adorno very close indeed to Horkheimer's project of dialectical logic in the late 1930s and became the theoretical core of their collaborative work at this time. Hegel's influence is also apparent in Adorno's more strictly aesthetic writings during this time and, in particular, in his pathbreaking analysis of Schoenberg, the core argument of which is already apparent in his 1938 essay "On the Fetish Character of Music and the Regression of Listening." Rather than trying to show how marginal aspects of Schoenberg's music reveal unintentional truth, Adorno demonstrates how its self-consciously rational *form* and its striving for aesthetic autonomy enabled it to resist, and provide cognitive insight into, the powerful tendency toward the commodification of music and the more general conditions of social domination and reification. At a time when Benjamin's long-standing reservations against aesthetic autonomy had become even more pronounced,[112] Adorno was rethinking the dialectical and historical relationship between form and content upon which Hegel's aesthetics was based. Thus, when the essay on Schoenberg, which was written in the late 1930s, was finally published, it comes as no surprise that Adorno introduced the essay and the volume as a whole with epigrams from Hegel's aesthetics, which stressed the critical, cognitive function of art.[113] One final example of Adorno's new relationship with Hegel can be found in the introduction to *Minima Moralia*, in which Adorno states that he perfected his own method by studying Hegel's method.[114] At the same time, Adorno's undiminished critique of Hegel's affirmative philosophy of history, identity logic, and his subordination of the particular and individual to dominant social and historical tendencies, testified to the persistence of a distinctly "Benjaminian" moment in his thought. In short, one can certainly agree with Robert Hullot-Kentor's statement that "The Hegelian dialectic, passed through Benjamin's idea of allegory, became in Adorno's work the form for the interpretation of all culture,"[115] if one adds that the Benjaminian star in the complex constellation of Adorno's thought was eclipsed to a certain degree in the mid-1930s by the Hegelian star, and that this movement was both a cause and consequence of his increasing proximity to Max Horkheimer.

---

[111] *Metakritik*, p. 52.

[112] For example, in his essay, "The Work of Art in the Age of Mechanical Production," which Adorno criticized for its abstract negation of aesthetic autonomy. See Wolin, *An Aesthetic of Redemption*, pp. 183ff.

[113] Adorno, *Philosophy of New Music*, trans. R. Hullot-Kentor (Minneapolis: University of Minnesota Press, 2006).

[114] Adorno, *Minima Moralia*, trans. E.F.N. Jephcott (London: Verso, 1978), p. 16.

[115] Robert Hullot-Kentor, "Critique of the Organic," translator's foreword to: Theodor W. Adorno, *Kierkegaard: Construction of the Aesthetic*, op. cit., p. xix-xx.

Adorno's Positive Reception of Horkheimer's Essays in the Mid-1930s

If Adorno's debate with Benjamin and his renewed study of Hegel functioned as an indirect impetus for his rapprochement with Horkheimer, his reception of Horkheimer's own writings during this same time brought them together in a more direct manner. Most important in this regard was Horkheimer's collection of aphorisms, *Dämmerung*, and his essays "Egoism and Freedom Movements" and "The Latest Attack on Metaphysics." Adorno's first mention of *Dämmerung* came in a letter to Horkheimer on November 2, 1934, in which he writes that the book made a deep and extremely favorable impression upon him and that he would give it his "Blankounterschrift."[116] In another letter to Horkheimer on February 25, 1935, Adorno mentions that he has been working on his own collection of aphorisms directly inspired by Heinrich Regius, that is, the pseudonym under which Horkheimer had published *Dämmerung*. Adorno writes:

In a couple of months I would like to send you a second manuscript in progress, which you won't be able to accuse of ambiguous language and which Heinrich Regius, if I know him at all, won't deny his approval. It concerns a small book of aphorisms, which ties in directly to Regius, but addresses throughout the situation in established fascism. The title: The Good Comrade.[117]

In addition to demonstrating Adorno's concern that Horkheimer still considered his work too esoteric at this time – a concern we will address in more detail in the next section – this passage demonstrates that *Minima Moralia* was originally inspired by *Dämmerung*. When the work finally appeared ten years later, it was dedicated to Horkheimer on his fiftieth birthday. The name of the aphorism Adorno mentioned was changed in the final version to "The *bad* [*böse*] comrade," but Adorno indicates clearly that this particular aphorism was written in 1935.[118] To a degree matched by few of Adorno's writings, this aphorism provides insight into personal experiences that helped shape Adorno's uncompromisingly demanding and defiantly nonconformist intellectual sensibilities. With the scathing, scarcely sublimated passion characteristic of *Dämmerung*, Adorno shows how certain traumatic experiences in his childhood anticipated the triumph of fascism in Germany. Adorno writes:

As a conqueror dispatches envoys to the remotest provinces, Fascism had sent its advance guard there long before they marched in: my schoolfellows.... The five patriots who set upon a single schoolfellow, thrashed him and, when he complained to the teacher, defamed him as a traitor to the class – are they not the same as those who tortured prisoners to refute claims by foreigners that prisoners were tortured? They whose hallooing knew no end when the top boy blundered – did they not stand grinning and sheepish round the Jewish detainee, poking fun at his maladroit attempt to hang himself? They who could not put together a correct sentence but found mine all too long – did they not

---

[116] That is, he would endorse it fully and without reservation. *Adorno-Horkheimer Briefwechsel*, op. cit., p. 25.

[117] Ibid., p. 57.

[118] *Minima Moralia*, trans. Edmund Jephcott (London: Verson, 1974), p. 193. The original title, "Der gute Kamerad," alluded to a song with the same name that was made popular by the Nazis.

abolish German literature and replace it by their "writ" [*Schrifttum*]? ... Now that they, officials and recruits, have stepped visibly out of my dream and dispossessed me of my past life and my language, I no longer need to dream of them. In Fascism the nightmare of childhood has come true.[119]

Horkheimer had already said of Adorno's *Kierkegaard* that, even though it "still bore the traces of an idealist way of thinking," he had already recognized in it Adorno's "great contempt"[120] for the status quo. Clearly, Horkheimer's *Dämmerung* inspired Adorno to come down slightly from the esoteric heights of the Kierkegaard book and express this contempt more forcefully and directly. Yet the aphoristic form of *Dämmerung* must also have demonstrated to Adorno that Horkheimer's insistence on conceptual rigor, systematic research, and empirical evidence did not preclude a deep suspicion of philosophical system building. To demonstrate this point, Horkheimer – if not Adorno – may well have quoted his esteemed *philosophes*, who stressed the importance of *l'esprit systematique* while at the same time rejecting *l'esprit du système*.

Adorno's response to Horkheimer's essay "Egoism and Freedom Movements" was every bit as enthusiastic as his response to *Dämmerung*. In a letter to Horkheimer on June 29, 1936, Adorno reported that the essay "captivated and moved me to the innermost," and that "the only 'bourgeois' reaction, which I can hold up against it, is envy that I didn't write it myself."[121] In terms of the content of the essay, Adorno highlighted his agreement with Horkheimer's "stance against revolutionaries, who adopt bourgeois morality in a positive way."[122] Adorno drew upon Horkheimer's analysis in "Egoism" of the socio-historical and social-psychological roots of bourgeois morality – and bourgeois sadism – in a study of Richard Wagner that he wrote in late 1937 and early 1938, shortly before his emigration to the United States.[123] Adorno showed how the sadomasochistic character traits analyzed by Horkheimer found expression in Wagner's life and music, which both reflected the larger trajectory of the German bourgeoisie in the nineteenth century: from the romantic rebellion of the *Vormärz* period, to obsequious accommodation to the conservative-monarchical power structure during the *Kaiserreich*.[124]

---

[119] Ibid., pp. 192–3.

[120] To borrow an expression from Nietzsche, who believed that "grosse Verachtung" was the best response one could have to contemporary society and the dominant "herd mentality." See, for example, *Thus Spake Zarathustra*, in *The Portable Nietzsche*, ed. and trans. Walter Kaufmann (London and New York: Penguin, 1968), p. 149. Horkheimer speaks in this letter of Adorno's "mit Hass geschärfter Blick auf das Bestehende." Yet a "view of the status quo sharpened by hate," sounds rather different in translation and perhaps fails to capture Horkheimer's intention or Adorno's sensibilities.

[121] *Adorno-Horkheimer, Briefwechsel*, vol. 1, p. 174.

[122] Ibid. Walter Benjamin also drew upon "Egoism and Freedom Movements" to develop a critique of the "German Jacobinism" of the Social Democratic publicist, historian, and collector Eduard Fuchs. See his essay, "Eduard Fuchs: Der Sammler und der Historiker," *Zeitschrift für Sozialforschung*, vol. 6, no. 2 (1937).

[123] As was the case with the *Philosophy of Modern Music*, Adorno delayed the publication of *In Search of Wagner* until after the war. Theodor Adorno, *In Search of Wagner*, trans. Rodney Livingstone (London: New Left Books, 1981).

[124] On the historical transformation of the German bourgeoisie in the mid-nineteenth century, see Theodor Hamerow, *Restoration, Revolution, Reaction: Economics and Politics in Germany*

In 1848, Wagner had participated in a political uprising in Dresden with Bakunin. His youthful romantic rebelliousness also found expression in his first opera that was ever performed, *Das Liebesverbot* (*The Prohibition on Love*), which Wagner described as a "bold celebration of 'free sensuality.'"[125] The work flopped, no less miserably than the revolution of 1848 in Germany, and Wagner, as so many other members of the middle class of his generation, began to reconcile the "folly" of his youthful "idealism" and to seek accommodation with the forces of reaction. Wagner's next opera, *Rienzi*, which was a big success and would launch his subsequent career, depicts the same "liberation movement" that Horkheimer had examined in "Egoism and Freedom Movements," namely, that of Cola di Rienzi in fourteenth-century Rome. In Wagner's rendition of this historical episode, discipline, virtue, and ascetic morality triumph over "base" desire. Adorno states, "the Roman insurrection is directed against the libertine style of life and not against the class enemy ... From the very outset Rienzi's revolution aims at integration."[126] Adorno goes on to show how, in Wagner's other operas, this eagerness to accommodate oneself to the ruling powers through assimilation to the repressive status quo also explains Wagner's anti-Semitism. Adorno writes:

If as victim Wagner asks for sympathy and so goes over to the rulers, he is nevertheless inclined to despise other victims.... all the rejects of Wagner's works are caricatures of Jews. They stir up the oldest sources of the German hatred of Jews ... the comedy of their suffering not only give[s] pleasure to whoever inflicts it; it also stifles any questions about its justification and tacitly presents itself as the ultimate authority.[127]

Although Adorno's analysis of Wagner's anti-Semitism went beyond Horkheimer's (and Fromm's) categories of the sadomasochistic character structure in ways that anticipated the more varied "Theses on anti-Semitism" in *Dialectic of Enlightenment*,[128] "Egoism and Freedom Movements" did provide

---

1815–1871 (Princeton: Princeton University Press, 1958). On the "re-feudalization" of the German bourgeoisie during the *Kaiserreich*, see Hans-Ulrich Wehler, *The German Empire, 1871–1918*, trans. Kim Traynor (Providence RI: Berg, 1993).

[125] *In Search of Wagner*, p. 11.

[126] Ibid., p. 13.

[127] Ibid., pp. 19, 21, 23.

[128] For example, Adorno also explains Wagner's anti-Semitism in terms of a concretistic form of thinking that he shared with the "other representatives of what Marx called the German Socialism of 1848. ... If in the social process of life 'ossified relationships' form a second nature, then it is this second nature at which Wagner gazes transfixed, mistaking it for the first. From the outset – in 1850 – anti-Semitism is expressed in the categories of nature, above all, those of immediacy and the people, and he already contrasts these categories with 'liberalism.'" Ibid., pp. 23 and 26. Adorno's argument here anticipates, in particular, the third thesis on anti-Semitism in *Dialectic of Enlightenment*, in which he and Horkheimer demonstrate how "bourgeois anti-Semitism," to which the working class is also highly susceptible, equates Jews with the sphere of circulation and "parasitic," as opposed to "productive," capital. The bourgeois celebration of labor as the source of all value, and productivity as the justification for its overthrow of the "decadent" aristocracy, passes seamlessly into a pseudo-socialist worldview, which criticizes capitalism from the standpoint of labor, rather than aiming for the abolition of the historically specific form of labor in capitalism. Rather than recognizing the "concealment of domination in production" as the source of the problem, representatives of the sphere of circulation "in

him with decisive insights into both Wagner's music and the socially determined character structure of the German bourgeoisie in the nineteenth century.

The other essay of Horkheimer's that contributed most to his rapprochement with Adorno during this period was "The Latest Attack on Metaphysics," a scathing critique of logical positivism that was written in late 1936 and early 1937.[129] Adorno's most substantial response to the essay came in a letter to Horkheimer on March 23, 1937, in which he stated: "I read your essay on positivism with the greatest of joy and approval; ... apart from "Egoism and Freedom Movements," I know hardly another essay of yours that I would endorse so unconditionally as this one."[130] As we have already seen, this essay marked a significant shift in Horkheimer's own position. Prior to his emigration to the United States, Horkheimer had been more concerned about irrationalist critiques of science than the positivists' attempts to impose strict scientific limits on philosophy. After becoming more familiar with philosophical discussions in the land of his exile, Horkheimer's concern that the influence of Carnap, Reichenbach, and Neurath – whose work he considered inferior to others close to the school, such as Russell, Wittgenstein, and Moore – was "spreading so rapidly" that a renewed critique of logical positivism had become pressing once again.[131] This shift must have delighted Adorno, who had always been skeptical of Horkheimer's greater sympathy to the tradition of philosophical empiricism. Horkheimer's renewed[132] critique of positivism brought him and Adorno closer together on this key issue; their criticism of positivism would become even sharper – and closer to Adorno's earlier position – in the late 1930s and early 1940s. At this time, Horkheimer's critique still adhered to the larger model of a dialectic of bourgeois society. He still insisted that the empiricist attack on metaphysics had played an essentially progressive role in the early modern period, and only with the historical triumph of the bourgeoisie did it become increasingly affirmative.[133] The single objection to the essay, which Adorno expresses in his letter to Horkheimer, reveals the persistence of this methodological difference between them. Adorno writes, "I have a real objection to just one passage. It's the one that speaks of the impossibility of an immanent overcoming of logical positivism."[134] In contrast to Horkheimer's

which the Jews were historically imprisoned for all too long" are held responsible. *Dialectic of Enlightenment*, op. cit., pp. 141–4. For a more recent analysis of anti-Semitism that builds on and expands these insights, see Moishe Postone, "The Holocaust and the Trajectory of the Twentieth Century," *Catastrophe and Meaning: The Holocaust and the Twentieth Century*, eds. Moishe Postone and Eric Santner (Chicago and London: The University of Chicago Press, 2003), pp. 81–114.

[129] See discussion in Chapter 8, pp. 306–12.

[130] *Adorno-Horkheimer, Briefwechsel*, p. 322.

[131] Ibid., p. 254.

[132] It is worth repeating that Horkheimer was never an uncritical defender of positivism or empiricism, as some commentators, such as Michiel Korthals and Hauke Brunkhorst, have argued. See my critique of Korthals and Brunkhorst in Chapter 3, footnote 163.

[133] See, for example, his letter to Adorno on December 8, 1936, in which Horkheimer says that the essay will demonstrate the "transformation of the function of nominalism since Bacon and Hobbes." *Adorno-Horkheimer, Briefwechsel*, p. 254.

[134] *Adorno-Horkheimer, Briefwechsel*, p. 323.

putatively more "historicist" critique of logical positivism, Adorno insists on an "immanent" critique, which would involve a detailed demonstration of the contradictions in their own arguments, such as he was undertaking at the time in his critique of Husserl. In the following section we will examine this ongoing tension between Horkheimer and Adorno in more detail.

PERSISTENT DIFFERENCES BETWEEN HORKHEIMER AND ADORNO

Although Adorno's methodological shift from a focus on images, metaphors, and names as the placeholders of unintentional truth to a demonstration of the immanent contradictions of an author's work did push him closer to Horkheimer, Adorno's ongoing insistence on the epistemological primacy of the particular and his critique of historicism remained a source of sharp disagreement between the two of them. This disagreement is most evident in Adorno's insistence on the fundamental shortcomings of what he described as a materialist version of "intellectual history" [*Geistesgeschichte*] – a method he attributed to Herbert Marcuse in particular. Because some version of this method continued to guide his own work at this time, Horkheimer rightfully sensed that Adorno's criticisms were implicitly or explicitly directed at him as well. The difference between them emerges clearly in a letter to Horkheimer from May 26, 1936, in which Adorno expresses deep reservations about Marcuse's essay "The Concept of Essence," which had just appeared in the fifth volume of the *Zeitschrift*.[135] Adorno writes:

> It is not enough to demonstrate the material basis of this or that structure of idealist thinking and thus to construct in a certain way a materialist intellectual history; instead, the problem can only be solved by engaging with the technical arguments and working through the idealist theses *immanently*, and by developing the materialist theory rigorously out of a critique of the idealist mistakes, in the strictest sense.[136]

More than a year later, when Horkheimer was still refusing to publish Adorno's essay on Husserl, Adorno returned once again to Marcuse's essay "The Concept of Essence" to try to convince Horkheimer of the superiority of immanent critique. He writes:

> It seems to me that, compared to his [Marcuse's], my essay represents such a significant advance ... that I can't really understand why it should fall under the table, while his appears.... The difference seems to me to be that Marcuse's viewpoint remains in principle intellectual historical and relates social to intellectual historical tendencies from the outside, whereas I have, in any case, set the questions themselves in motion as ones of true and false and in so doing have seriously undertaken a critique of idealism.... According to his view, it seems as if the hour-hand of philosophy moves in accord with the hidden mechanism of society and critical interpretation must be satisfied with demonstrating the concordance of the hand and the mechanism, without ever posing the question of whether or not the clock is running correctly.[137]

---

[135] Herbert Marcuse, "On the Concept of Essence," trans. Jeremy J. Shapiro, *Negations*, op. cit., pp. 43–87.

[136] *Adorno-Horkheimer, Briefwechsel*, p. 148.

[137] Ibid., pp. 456–7.

Adorno may or may not have realized that Marcuse's method in this essay – and others from this time as well[138] – was based on Horkheimer's own model of a dialectic of bourgeois society. Just as Horkheimer in his essay on positivism had examined the "functional transformation of nominalism" as an expression of this historical transformation of bourgeois society, so Marcuse traced the changing function of the concept of essence – from critical transcendence in early modern rationalist philosophy to ideological justification of the status quo in late liberal (Husserl's "intuition of essences," for example) and fascist thought. So it comes as perhaps little surprise that Marcuse and Lowenthal's work continued to appear in the Institute's journal at this time, while Horkheimer was much more hesitant to publish Adorno's Husserl essay. Let us take a closer look at Horkheimer's critique of that essay, by way of a brief examination of their debate about Alfred Sohn-Rethel's work.

Horkheimer's continuing objections in the mid-1930s to the methodological presuppositions of Adorno's theory and to his Husserl essay, in particular, emerge clearly in a debate he had with Adorno at this time about the work of Alfred Sohn-Rethel. Insofar as Adorno strongly identified with Sohn-Rethel at this time, Horkheimer's deep reservations about Sohn-Rethel's work illuminate the differences that still existed between him and Adorno. After emigrating to England in 1936, Sohn-Rethel introduced Adorno to his theoretical work, which centered on an attempt to demonstrate that idealist categories of knowledge, such as Kant's transcendental categories of subjectivity, had emerged historically from the division of mental and physical labor, and that this division had, in turn, emerged on the basis of a commodity-producing, money-mediated society. Sohn-Rethel saw his work as addressing an essential problem Marx had neglected; he believed the critique of political economy needed to be supplemented by a materialist critique of idealist *epistemology*.[139] Adorno was immediately taken with Sohn-Rethel's project and saw profound similarities to his own project on Husserl, as the following passage from a letter he wrote to Leo Lowenthal in December 1936 amply demonstrates:

With regard to the question of potential co-workers [for the Institute] ... I would think first of all of Sohn-Rethel, who is going to visit me here in the next few days. I have his exposé and an accompanying letter.... The letter proved that our intentions are similar to an extent I would not have thought possible. All of you ... should read his manuscript.... For Marcuse it will be particularly interesting, because it contains an exact answer to the question that has become controversial between us, [namely] that of an immanent sublation [*Aufhebung*] of idealism: just like my book, only from a completely different point of departure. He comes to the same conclusions as me: that in the depths

---

[138] For example, in "The Affirmative Character of Culture," which was published in the next volume of the *Zeitschrift*, Marcuse drew once again on Horkheimer's model to demonstrate the transformations in the function of culture in the bourgeois epoch. See, *Negations*, op. cit., pp. 88–133.

[139] See, for example, the introduction to Sohn-Rethel's *Geistige und Körperliche Arbeit: Zur Theorie der gesellschaftlichen Synthesis*, which was finally published in 1970. Sohn-Rethel continued to work on it in the following decades, but his core insight and arguments remained the same. An English translation is also available: *Intellectual and Manual Labor: A Critique of Epistemology* (London: Macmillan, 1978).

of validity [*Geltung*], the genesis [of the idealist epistemological categories] can be found in "praxis" or, as I put it in my Husserl book: truth is not in history, history is in the truth.[140]

For the next two years, Adorno would attempt persistently and energetically to convince Horkheimer that the Institute should support Sohn-Rethel financially and even consider making him an official member. In his letters to Horkheimer, Adorno would continue to stress the deep affinities between Sohn-Rethel's work and his own project on Husserl. He emphasized, in particular, his agreement with Sohn-Rethel's attempt to "deduce logical categories from exploitation,"[141] and his argument that the "system-character of idealism is an expression of the context of guilt [*Schuldzusammenhang*] (i.e. the context of exploitation) of bourgeois society."[142] The similarities to Adorno's critique of Husserl's "logical absolutism" and his notion of the "intuition of essences" were indeed striking. However, it is crucial for our purposes here to stress that, according to Adorno and Sohn-Rethel's argument, the decisive aspects of bourgeois society – such as a division between intellectual and manual labor, commodity production, and a money-mediated economy – from which the abstract character of idealist philosophical categories could be deduced, already existed in classical antiquity.[143]

However, this aspect of Sohn-Rethel's argument, which downplayed the historical specificity of bourgeois society, as well as many other aspects of his thought seemed deeply problematic to Horkheimer. Despite Adorno's repeated entreaties on Sohn-Rethel's behalf, Horkheimer remained highly critical of him during this time. As we shall see momentarily, many of the objections Horkheimer raised against Sohn-Rethel would reappear in his criticism of the essay on Husserl. Horkheimer's criticisms of Sohn-Rethel testify to crucial theoretical differences between him and Adorno, which do not begin to disappear until the major shift occurred in Horkheimer's thought in 1939–40. Horkheimer criticized, in particular, the lack of clarity and critical élan in Sohn-Rethel's writing, his failure to demonstrate the historical specificity of his arguments, and his premature efforts to overcome idealism. For example, in response to an early draft of Sohn-Rethel's project, Horkheimer writes,

[140] *Adorno-Horkheimer, Briefwechsel*, p. 523–4. See also Adorno's letter to Sohn-Rethel on November 17, 1936, in which he states that Sohn-Rethel's work "was the greatest intellectual epiphany I've experience in philosophy since my encounter with Benjamin's work. ... This epiphany registered the greatness and power of its conception, but also the depth of agreement, which went incomparably further than you would suspect and that I suspected myself." *Sohn-Rethel-Adorno Briefwechsel*, op cit., p. 32.

[141] *Adorno-Horkheimer, Briefwechsel*, p. 278.

[142] Ibid., p. 357.

[143] As Sohn-Rethel put it in the introduction to *Intellectual and Manual Labor*, "The distinctive claim, that will be defended in the present study, is that the forms of abstraction characteristic of the social-synthetic function of money, manifest themselves separately and, when this occurs, they reveal themselves as the fundamental organizational principles of the functions of knowledge of the type of thought that becomes necessary in commodity producing, that is, money-mediated societies. They are the principles of knowledge, which form the conceptual basis of both ancient philosophy and the modern natural sciences." p. 17.

Insofar as we can find anything correct in his work, it is theoretical views that have been common to us for a long time, expounded in a vain academic and bombastic language.... The worst thing is the way in which Marxist theory is presented there.... The characteristic irony and the critical function of the Marxian categories are nowhere to be found; indeed, there aren't even any consequences drawn from their specific economic content.... I know that all of that can, if necessary, be understood; but as soon as one has understood *a peu près*, one notices that the author has taken familiar insights and transfigured them idealistically, rather than sharpening them.[144]

More important for our purposes here than his objections to Sohn-Rethel's language was Horkheimer's insistence on more historical mediation in his work. He challenges Adorno to reread Sohn-Rethel's work and ask himself the question "what is the relation of this entire work to historical reality and what has the author understood of it"? Echoing central ideas from his own early work, Horkheimer argues that instead of speaking of "particular people in particular periods," Sohn-Rethel speaks in a much more general and meaningless way of the "form of the being [*Sein*] of things, the existence [*Dasein*] of things, of "man" as such."[145] Finally, Horkheimer also sees Sohn-Rethel's attempt – as Adorno put it – to "liquidate" idealism, as a failure. His failure to adequately ground his arguments socially or historically and his lack of conceptual clarity reminded Horkheimer of "those parts of Schelling's identity philosophy to which Hegel was referring when he spoke of the night in which all cows are grey."[146] Horkheimer does not dispute that Sohn-Rethel was on the right path with his attempt to demonstrate the link between abstract epistemological and logical categories and exploitation; but he also insisted that "Sohn-Rethel uses the concept of exploitation in a purely formal way" and that "it would be a mistake to believe that idealism could be overcome simply by replacing idealist with materialist terminology."[147]

Considering the profound similarities that Adorno himself believed existed between his Husserl book and Sohn-Rethel's project of a materialist critique of idealist epistemology, it should come as little surprise that Horkheimer made some of the same objections to Adorno's essay on Husserl that he had leveled against Sohn-Rethel. Horkheimer's unyielding refusal to publish this essay in the *Zeitschrift* was particularly discouraging to Adorno, because it was based on his main theoretical project at this time. Of the essay itself, Adorno wrote to Horkheimer in July 1937 that "I'm not exaggerating when I say that I have never worked on anything with such great investment; I consider it in all seriousness as my first philosophical work, at least the first with which I am more or less satisfied."[148] Horkheimer was aware of Adorno's investment in this project and that he was eagerly waiting and hoping for a positive response. However, at this point at least, Horkheimer – and Marcuse, who also read the essay – could give his wholehearted approval only to Adorno's underlying aims, not to

---

[144] *Adorno-Horkheimer, Briefwechsel*, p. 252.
[145] Ibid., p. 251.
[146] Ibid., p. 249.
[147] Ibid., p. 268.
[148] Ibid., p. 388.

the method by which he set out to achieve them.[149] In his lengthy and detailed response to Adorno's essay from October 13, 1937, Horkheimer outlined a number of objections. He faulted Adorno for not presenting Husserl's work in a way that would separate what was essential from what was inessential, show how Husserl's position shifted over time, or place it within a larger social and historical context. Instead, Adorno moved directly to specific, technical arguments in his work, whose understanding presupposed a depth of knowledge of Husserl's work that, as Horkheimer frankly admitted, frequently made the text incomprehensible to even him and Marcuse, who had both studied with and written extensively on Husserl. In its present form, Horkheimer considered the text too esoteric for the Institute's journal, which insisted not only upon theoretical rigor, but also political relevance.[150] Horkheimer complained, in particular, that Adorno's discussion of the ideological aspects of Husserl's work, which would be "especially important for an essay in the *Zeitschrift*, disappears behind subtle discussions of the phenomenological material."[151] Adorno's method rested on the assumption that the social and historical content of Husserl's work could be revealed only through a micrological immersion in the arguments themselves. However, Horkheimer found Adorno's attempt to illuminate general social and historical tendencies through a strictly immanent, micrological approach almost entirely unsuccessful. Although he noted that "while reading I myself sensed everywhere the positive and negative relations that you establish between Husserl's philosophy and the current historical situation," he also complained that "for anyone not belonging to a very narrow circle [of specialists] this would be completely impossible."[152] Horkheimer argues that Adorno has failed to ground conceptually the social and historical – and with it, the ideological – function of Husserl's philosophy. For example, he describes Adorno's "analogy between idealist epistemology and the act of exchange" as a "mere association."[153]

According to Horkheimer, Adorno's methodological asceticism, his insistence on a strictly immanent approach, and his refusal to use any external, transcendent arguments or evidence fails not only because he cannot adequately grasp the general from within the strict confines of the particular; Horkheimer also tries to show how Adorno was unable to maintain his own strict standards. Even though he has immersed himself in Husserl's arguments and terminology, his rejection of them in the end would not fail to be perceived by Husserl and his followers as a departure from the "phenomenological method of observation [*Einstellung*]" and the illegitimate application of a transcendent standard. For example, Horkheimer writes:

You claim that Husserl has merely deduced categorial intuition [*kategoriale Anschauung*] and that there is not any descriptive matters of fact upon which it could be based.

[149] Ibid., p. 423.
[150] Horkheimer has often been accused of editing the *Zeitschrift* in a way that was overly cautious politically, yet in this case one sees clearly that political considerations were still central to his concerns and that he wanted to distinguish the journal sharply from its purely theoretical or academic counterparts.
[151] *Adorno-Horkheimer, Briefwechsel.*, p. 425.
[152] Ibid.
[153] Ibid.

With the phenomenological school this claim would certainly be adamantly disputed and I don't see in your essay any way of resolving this dispute immanently.... None of your attempts to demonstrate the impossibility of categorial intuition is really convincing.[154]

Even more problematic for Horkheimer than the shortcomings of Adorno's immanent method was his larger claim that he had, through his critique of Husserl, also accomplished a "liquidation of idealism." Horkheimer notes the similarities here between Adorno's arguments and "the program of an anti-idealist philosophy, like the one Sohn-Rethel is pursuing,"[155] but insists that these arguments are too ambitious. Horkheimer states that Adorno "links the huge question of the refutation of idealism too tightly to Husserl's philosophy and a critique of it. In so doing you place demands on both Husserl and your own arguments which they cannot meet."[156] Even if Adorno had been successful in demonstrating that Husserl's philosophy was riddled with contradictions, this would not, according to Horkheimer, be tantamount to a liquidation of idealism.

Horkheimer's objection to Adorno here is informed by a materialist critique of idealism that differs from Adorno and Sohn-Rethel's. Horkheimer's understanding of materialism and his methodological critique of idealism emphasize *history*, whereas Adorno and Sohn-Rethel focus more on *epistemology*.[157] Horkheimer argues that "Husserl's philosophy is the attempt to secure the continued existence of bourgeois idealism by robbing it of all its constructive power and its utopian function."[158] Horkheimer's understanding of idealism fits squarely within his larger model of a dialectic of bourgeois society.[159] So, for him, idealism was a mediated expression of the historical ascendance of the bourgeoisie. It expressed, in particular, the sharp clash of the emancipatory ideals of the European bourgeoisie with the fragmented, backward, and repressive political conditions in German-speaking Europe. Husserl's philosophy, on the other hand, was linked closely to a German bourgeoisie that had long since relinquished any emancipatory ideals and had instead accommodated itself with the monarchical-conservative status quo. For Horkheimer, in other words, there was an essential difference between Husserl's philosophy and idealism insofar as the latter still contained an important emancipatory moment. The historical difference between the early and late nineteenth century and the transformation of the German bourgeoisie that occurred during this time was crucial to Horkheimer's argument. Adorno's interpretation of idealism, on the other hand, bore a greater affinity to Sohn-Rethel's insistence on the essential continuity of the categories of bourgeois thought from classical antiquity to the present, or to Benjamin's insistence on the mythical character of modern idealist reason. If Hegel and Husserl's epistemological assumptions are essentially

---

[154] Ibid., pp. 426–7.

[155] Ibid., p. 429.

[156] Ibid.

[157] Our examination of Horkheimer's critique of Lenin's metaphysical materialism has already demonstrated the thoroughly historical presuppositions of the concept of materialism in his early critical theory. See Chapter 4, pp. 150–56.

[158] *Adorno-Horkheimer, Briefwechsel*, p. 428.

[159] See Chapter 3, pp. 115–18.

the same – as Adorno was at pains to demonstrate – then the refutation of the one *would* entail the refutation of the other. Like Sohn-Rethel, Adorno did not hesitate to extend this same "liquidation of idealism" all the way back to classical antiquity.[160] For example, in a discussion of "Egoism and Freedom Movements" in a letter to Horkheimer from May 26, 1936, Adorno states that "my work is making it increasingly clear to me just how little in principle bourgeois thinking has ever changed and how all the much ballyhooed difference of standpoints is merely an illusion."[161] Adorno then suggested that this "philosophical historical insight" would probably place his own work in close proximity to a the social and historical insights Horkheimer presented in an essay like "Egoism." Although Horkheimer seems to approve of Adorno's comments, his response makes clear that the conflict that would emerge over the Husserl essay was already latent at this time. Horkheimer described his aim in the "Egoism" essay to explain current political and social tendencies by "bringing them into much closer relation with the *history of the bourgeoisie* than our friends usually do."[162] Other examples of Adorno's willingness to place much more emphasis on the epistemological continuities than the historical differences of bourgeois thought can be found his description of Wagner's Rienzi as the "last Roman tribune and the first bourgeois terrorist"[163] or, of course, his reading in *Dialectic of Enlightenment* of Odysseus as an early representative of bourgeois instrumental reason.[164] This last example shows how Horkheimer – as coauthor of *Dialectic of Enlightenment* – would soon abandon the more historically nuanced understanding he had at this time of the emancipatory content of early modern philosophy in general and the French Enlightenment and German idealism in particular, and would instead adopt a more sweeping and pessimistic understanding of bourgeois reason as a whole as an instrument for the domination of internal and external nature.

Before turning to a brief examination of the ways in which Horkheimer moved closer to Adorno's theoretical position in the mid-1930s, let us cast a quick glance on one final, important difference that remained between the two of them through the end of the 1930s: their ongoing disagreement about the proper role of the sciences in a Critical Theory of society. In his inaugural address in 1931, Adorno had argued that philosophy should be guided by

[160] Just as Sohn-Rethel assumed that the epistemological assumptions of classical idealism and modern science were the same and could both be traced back to the dominance of the commodity form.

[161] *Adorno-Horkheimer, Briefwechsel*, p. 147.

[162] Ibid., p. 156 (emphasis mine).

[163] *In Search of Wagner*, p. 12. Adorno's use of the term "terrorist" here should be understood as part of a larger critique of bourgeois morality and Jacobinism, which had first been articulated by Hegel, who famously showed how moral purity, as articulated theoretically by Rousseau and Kant and put into praxis by Robespierre, could quickly degenerate into terror. Horkheimer built on and expanded – primarily through psychoanalytic categories – Hegel's insights in "Egoism and Freedom Movements," which, as we saw earlier, informed Adorno's analysis of Wagner.

[164] Recent scholarship has dispelled any doubts there were that Adorno was the primary author of this chapter of *Dialectic of Enlightenment*. See the editor's afterword to GS, vol. 5, pp. 427–30.

an "exact imagination" that "remains strictly in the material provided to it by sciences and reaches beyond this material solely in the smallest configurations of its arrangement."[165] The fact that Adorno would not draw on scientific materials nearly at all in his subsequent work in the 1930s, makes one wonder if Adorno's gesture to the sciences here was simply intended to please Horkheimer, who had placed such great importance on them in his own inaugural address as director of the Institute a few months earlier. The material upon which Adorno focused his attention in his contemporary study of Kierkegaard and his subsequent studies of Husserl, jazz, Wagner, and other topics was either philosophical or aesthetic. Adorno's work in the 1930s never relied in any significant way on any research produced in any of the other academic disciplines. Even after his methodological shift to immanent critique in the Husserl study, one could argue that Adorno's continuing emphasis on the epistemological primacy of the particular remained heavily indebted to a methodology based on aesthetic experience. Adorno continued to defend the epistemological primacy of art over the sciences, as the following comments that Adorno wrote to Horkheimer in May 1937 on Marcuse's essay on "The Affirmative Character of Culture" make clear: "It seems to me that art has an entire dimension – the decisive one – which he [Marcuse] completely overlooks, namely that of *knowledge* in the sense of precisely that which bourgeois science cannot attain."[166] In the early and mid-1930s, Horkheimer strived to realize his program for a "continuous, dialectical penetration and development of philosophical theory and specialized scientific praxis" through the Institute's empirical research projects, its interdisciplinary structure, and the extensive section of book reviews in the *Zeitschrift*, which were by no means limited to philosophy and aesthetics, but were also considered empirical and theoretical works in the fields of psychology, sociology, history, political science, and economics. As we have seen, Horkheimer's attitude toward the sciences became more pessimistic in the mid-1930s through his confrontation with logical positivism, which he believed tended unwittingly toward a "pre-established harmony between the specialized disciplines and barbarism."[167] Yet the Institute continued to propose and support empirical research projects in the late 1930s, and the *Zeitschrift* continued to review works from a wide variety of disciplines. When Adorno finally joined the Institute in early 1938, Horkheimer had arranged for him to work on the empirically oriented Princeton Radio Research Project led by their colleague and fellow émigré, Paul Lazarsfeld, who was already on his way to becoming a leading figure of empirical social research in the United States.[168] Horkheimer probably hoped that Adorno's involvement in that project would make him more willing to accept empirical social research as an integral aspect of Critical Theory. However, the disappointing results of Adorno's collaboration with

---

[165] Adorno, *Schriften*, vol. 1, op. cit., p. 343.

[166] *Adorno-Horkheimer, Briefwechsel*, p. 355 (emphasis Adorno's).

[167] Ibid., p. 196.

[168] For an insightful examination of Adorno and Lazarsfeld's relationship and the very telling similarities and differences in their trajectories, see Detlev Claussen, *Theodor Adorno: One Last Genius*, trans. Rodney Livingstone (Cambridge, MA and London: Harvard University Press, 2008), pp. 176–88.

Lazarsfeld are well known.[169] Furthermore, the Institute was initially refused funding for several other research projects they developed at the end of the decade, which increased Horkheimer's suspicion that the sciences in the United States were completely subordinated to the most powerful interests.[170] In short, whereas Horkheimer began to have doubts about the sciences in the mid-1930s, it was not until the end of the decade that he began to adopt – at least temporarily– Adorno's much more skeptical position.[171]

Although Horkheimer remained skeptical in the mid-1930s of Adorno's more strictly philosophical writings, and Adorno's efforts to displace Marcuse as the "house philosopher" of the Institute would not succeed until the end of the decade,[172] Horkheimer's enthusiasm for Adorno's writings on music remained high. Adorno had already published a piece on "The Social Situation of Music" in the first volume of the *Zeitschrift*, and his first essay to appear after his rapprochement with Horkheimer was the essay "On Jazz," which he wrote under the pseudonym of Hektor Rottweiler. Soon after the essay appeared, one of the "house economists" of the Institute, the orthodox Marxist Henryk Grossman, sharply criticized the essay. In a letter to Horkheimer from October 1936, Grossman wrote: "To be completely honest, the essay by Rottweiler (whom I don't know) seems a complete failure to me: too many uninteresting technical details, which are supported by hardly any sociological analysis."[173] In his response, Horkheimer revealed to Grossmann that Adorno had written the essay

[169] For the most recent examination of Adorno's ill-fated excursion into American radio research, see David Jenemann, *Adorno in America* (London and Minneapolis: University of Minnesota Press, 2007). It would not be until the late 1940s, as he completed his work on *The Authoritarian Personality*, that Adorno would develop a greater appreciation for the role of empirical social research in a Critical Theory of society.

[170] I am referring here to the initial draft of the research project on anti-Semitism and the project of "Cultural Aspects of National Socialism." For a discussion of these projects and the reasons they failed (at least initially – the anti-Semitism project would eventually be funded by the American Jewish Committee), see Thomas Wheatland, *The Frankfurt School in Exile* (Minneapolis and London: University of Minnesota Press, 2009), pp. 87–8, 219–42. For Horkheimer's increasingly pessimistic assessment of scientific research in the United States, see GS, vol. 17, pp. 76 and 82.

[171] In the preface to *Dialectic of Enlightenment*, Horkheimer and Adorno write, "While we had noted for many years that, in the operations of modern science, the major discoveries are paid for with an increasing decline of theoretical education, we nevertheless believed that we could follow those operations to the extent of limiting our work primarily to a critique or a continuation of specialist theories. Our work was to adhere, at least thematically, to the traditional disciplines: sociology, psychology and epistemology. The fragments we have collected here show, however, that we had to abandon that trust." Op. cit., p. xiv. Yet as Gunzelin Schmid Noerr points out, this rejection of the sciences did not reflect the fact that Horkheimer and Adorno continued to pursue empirical research projects during this time, nor the fact that empirical social research and interdisciplinary research more generally would become a hallmark of the Institute's work in postwar Germany. "Editorischer Anhang," GS, vol. 5, p. 448.

[172] Jürgen Habermas describes Marcuse as the "house philosopher" of the Institute in the 1930s, because he was responsible for writing essays on reviews (which he did in great number) for the *Zeitschrift* during this time. See Habermas's essay "The Different Rhythms of Philosophy and Politics," in Herbert Marcuse, *Towards a Critical Theory of Society*, ed. D. Kellner (London and New York: Routledge, 2001), pp. 231–8.

[173] GS, vol. 15, p. 641.

and that he considered it "very valuable."[174] Shortly thereafter, Horkheimer expressed his high estimation of the essay in a letter to Adorno:

The jazz essay seems particularly excellent to me. Your strict analysis of this seemingly unimportant phenomena makes visible the entire society and its contradictions.... In this issue of the journal your essay also fulfills the function of preventing the mistaken impression that our method can only be applied to so-called great problems and sweeping periods of history. The essay also demonstrated through its own execution that the correct formulation of the problem has nothing to do with what is considered most important and urgent by the sciences.[175]

Horkheimer's increasing disillusionment with the sciences and his growing acceptance of Adorno's alternative methodological approach is readily apparent here. The next essay Adorno would publish in the *Zeitschrift*, "The Fetish Character of Music and the Regression of Listening," also implemented a micrological analysis of dominant trends in the production and consumption of music to illustrate larger social tendencies. Soon after this essay appeared, Hans Mayer, a less orthodox, yet still Marxist-oriented literary critic who was loosely affiliated with the Institute, penned a thirty-five page critique of Adorno's essay, which contained some of the same objections that Grossmann had expressed to the essay on jazz. Horkheimer's response to Mayer in March 1939 is a strong indication of just how much closer he had moved toward Adorno's position by this time and is thus worth quoting at some length. Horkheimer writes:

The "sociological manner of viewing things" belongs to an academic apparatus whose end we do not regret.... The particular work of music should not be considered as an example of a type of style, establish[ed] through any kind of sociological interpretation, but rather as an object of analysis. It cannot be understood as the sum of technical, plus biographical, plus historical, plus sociological, plus economic explanations. The social content of Beethoven's music cannot be revealed through the sociology of the German society at that time.... Of your theoretical objections [to Adorno's essay], the most important is that the fetish chapter of *Capital* and the antithesis of use-value and exchange-value have been taken arbitrarily out of context and turned into a static musico-sociological schema, which neglects the other essential motives of Marx's analysis, especially his theory of circulation. With regard to the Marxist approach, right now we would only like to say that we do indeed believe that the analysis of the commodity form is not just one among many other equally valid aspects of his theory (which would turn him into a pluralist sociologist), but that instead the category of the commodity is the one that illuminates the entire society like a spotlight.... This aspect of Marx's theory is in its innermost details identical with the critique of reification and I don't think it would be difficult to demonstrate that capital is dominated in even its most minute economic aspects by the theory of reification. One can attain this insight without an intellectual historical appeal to the passages you mentioned from Feuerbach and Hegel, with which we are also familiar.[176]

Horkheimer's unreserved adoption of Adorno's language and categories here is striking. The affinity is certainly due in part to the fact that – as Gunzelin

---

[174] Ibid., p. 660.
[175] GS, vol. 15, p. 691.
[176] GS, vol. 16, pp. 576–7.

Schmid Noerr points out – Horkheimer, Adorno, and other members of the Institute had arranged several formal discussions of Mayer's critique, and that Horkheimer's remarks to Mayer were based on a fourteen-page response to his critique that Adorno himself had written.[177] Nevertheless, Horkheimer did write and sign the letter.

The distance that Horkheimer had traveled from some of the key assumptions of his early Critical Theory can be seen by comparing the remarks in this letter on the concept of reification with some of his earlier remarks. There has a been a strong tendency in the secondary literature to subsume Horkheimer and Adorno's work under a more general concept of "Western Marxism," which takes as its point of departure Lukács's methodological emphasis on the concept of totality, the commodity form, and reification. Although a more detailed examination of the concepts of totality and the commodity form would also reveal important differences between Horkheimer and Lukács in the 1930s, such an examination lies beyond the purview of this work. It is not difficult, however, to demonstrate that the concept of reification, which was one of Lukács's decisive contributions to the revitalization of Marxist theoretical discussions in the 1920s, played a marginal role, at best, in Horkheimer's early Critical Theory. In fact, in the discussions of Horkheimer's lectures on science and crisis from the early 1930s, which we examined earlier, Horkheimer stated clearly his reservations about the concept of reification.[178] Furthermore, one will search for it in vain in Horkheimer's writings in the 1930s. To be sure, Horkheimer discusses commodity fetishism and the manner in which human relationships assume the character of relations between things in a capitalist society.[179] Yet for Horkheimer during this time, reification and the commodity form were not – as they were for Adorno, who integrated Lukács's arguments into his theory to a much greater extent than Horkheimer –[180] the Archimedean point, from which society as a whole could be illuminated "as if by a spotlight." Horkheimer's early Critical Theory relied much more heavily on a nuanced understanding of the history and anthropology of the bourgeois society, which was open to the research and methodologies of other sciences in general and psychoanalysis in particular in a way that differed fundamentally from Lukács's approach. Hence, it would be a mistake to view Horkheimer's Critical Theory as a variation on the larger Lukácsian-determined "Western Marxism." One of the main aims of this study as a whole has been to demonstrate that Horkheimer's path to Critical Theory was independent of that of Lukács and Adorno. Yet the letter to Mayer indicates that many of the fundamental differences that still separated Horkheimer and Adorno in the

177 GS, p. 581.
178 In the protocol of this discussion, Horkheimer is reported to have said that he was "generally opposed to the concept of reification." GS, vol. 12, p. 368.
179 See, for example, the discussion of *Dämmerung,* earlier (Chapter 4, pp. 159ff.), or Horkheimer's "Introduction" to the Studies in Authority and Family, in Max Horkheimer, *Critical Theory: Selected Essays,* op. cit., p. 80.
180 Later, Adorno would also distance himself somewhat from the concept of reification, which had become fashionable at the time, as a result of the existentialist critique of alienation. See *Negative Dialektik,* op. cit., pp. 190–1.

mid-1930s had disappeared by 1939. These differences would become even less noticeable in *Dialectic of Enlightenment*.[181] So it comes, perhaps, as little surprise that in that same letter Horkheimer – who had just a few years earlier had defended his own methodological insistence on a nuanced understanding of the *history of the bourgeoisie* – now echoed Adorno's early claims that "in a certain sense not much has changed at all during the entire bourgeois phase."[182] Horkheimer's remarks here reflect a dehistoricization of his theoretical position, whose progress we will follow more closely in the following, concluding chapter.

---

[181] As Gunzelin Schmid Noerr puts it, "While *Dialectic of Enlightenment* can be placed with nearly seamless continuity within the larger trajectory of Adorno's work as whole, for Horkheimer it represents the most extreme [*exponiertesten*] expression of a phase of his theoretical development, which is clearly distinguishable from his work in the 1930s." "Editor's Afterword," GS, vol. 5, p. 430.

[182] GS, vol. 16, p. 577.

9

State Capitalism – The End of Horkheimer's
Early Critical Theory

In February of 1941, Horkheimer completed "The End of Reason." It would be his final contribution to the Institute's journal, which he had edited for the past eleven years. Yet "The End of Reason" represented the culmination of Horkheimer's previous theoretical efforts not only in a literal sense; he also viewed the essay as the first coherent articulation of the project on dialectical logic that had occupied him for the past several years, and that would remain the primary focus of his and Adorno's efforts in the coming years. In a letter to Leo Lowenthal from February 11, 1942, Horkheimer says the following about "The End of Reason": "I have worked on these thirty pages with Teddy during the last weeks and I dare say that this is a piece of work which gives an idea of what I intend to do in the future. I have worked so closely together with Teddy that I even consider to publish [sic] it in connection with him."[1] A few months earlier, in a letter to Herbert Marcuse, Horkheimer had also described "The End of Reason" as "a conclusion, in a certain way, of my earlier work."[2] To clarify the status of "The End of Reason" as a qualitative shift in Horkheimer's thought and at the same time to conclude this examination of Horkheimer's early Critical Theory, we are left with two interrelated sets of questions. First, how did the transition to the theoretical positions articulated in that essay occur? What motivated Horkheimer to adopt these new positions? Second, how did they differ from his earlier work? Are the differences great enough to justify speaking of a "qualitative shift" in his work? In what follows we will attempt to answer these questions through a brief analysis of the four most important essays Horkheimer wrote during the years 1938–1941: "Montaigne and the Function of Skepticism," "The Jews and Europe," "Authoritarian State," and "The End of Reason." The chapter will be divided into three parts. In the first part, we will see how Horkheimer's essay on Montaigne is still firmly grounded in the basic assumptions upon which his early Critical Theory was based – what we have called here the "dialectic of bourgeois society" – while at the same time anticipating the imminent shift in his thought in certain key ways. In the second part, we will examine "The Jews and Europe" and "Authoritarian State" as key transitional essays in which Horkheimer sets forth for the first time his new understanding of contemporary society as "state capitalist," and his new interpretation of modern history as possessing

[1] GS, vol. 17, p. 266.
[2] Ibid., p. 234.

powerful inherent tendencies that lead to state capitalism. Horkheimer's adoption of the state capitalist argument – an earlier and different version of which had already been developed by Friedrich Pollock – was the primary cause of the shift in his thought during this time. Once Horkheimer had worked out his new position, many of Adorno's arguments, which he had viewed skeptically until then, began to seem more appealing. In "The End of Reason," to which we will turn in the third and final section, Horkheimer definitively crossed the threshold that separated him from his early Critical Theory and laid the foundations for the next phase of his theoretical work, which would find its fullest expression in *Dialectic of Enlightenment* and *Eclipse of Reason*. The fact that Horkheimer also viewed "The End of Reason" as "the first 'official' result" of his cooperation with Adorno was not a coincidence either.[3] A line of direct continuity exists between "The End of Reason" and *Dialectic of Enlightenment*. In fact, one could easily view *Dialectic of Enlightenment* as an attempt to flesh out and provide case studies of the core arguments that are presented in "The End of Reason."

In terms of the content of these four essays, we will focus on two sets of related issues. First, what did Horkheimer see as the essential characteristics of state capitalism and how did he explain its triumph historically? Second, what effects did the adoption of the state capitalism argument have on his theory? We shall see that the state capitalism thesis led to a significant broadening, but at the same time an even more significant flattening out, or de-differentiation, of Horkheimer's thought. Horkheimer's abandonment of the model of a dialectic of bourgeois society led to the disappearance of key distinctions that had structured his earlier thought at both the diachronic and synchronic levels. From the standpoint of state capitalism and its concomitant logic of instrumental reason, differences between thinkers and concepts in different periods disappear, as do differences between opposing thinkers in the same period. Particularly noteworthy in this regard is Horkheimer's abandonment of the defense – which he had made as late as the essay on "Montaigne" – of the critical content of early modern philosophical ideals as an expression of the revolutionary aspirations of the bourgeoisie. Horkheimer now views the genuine function of these ideals as essentially identical with those of their most outspoken opponents, such as the legitimist counterrevolutionary Joseph de Maistre. Even Marx's critique of political economy now seemed compromised to Horkheimer, insofar as it, too, rested upon an immanent critique of bourgeois society, that is, a critique from the standpoint of its own unrealized ideals.[4] Because bourgeois ideals of any kind, from any period, could no longer provide a standpoint of critique, and because state capitalism had allegedly overcome the inherent contradictions of its liberal predecessor, while at the same time preserving relations of domination, Horkheimer had to find a new basis for

---

[3] As Horkheimer stated in a letter to Paul Tillich on February 11, 1942. Ibid., p. 271.

[4] As Horkheimer put it in a letter to Adorno in September 1941: "We have already entered a phase in which the confrontation with the bourgeois ideal no longer suffices. Even the critique of political economy ... is for the same reason questionable. It, too, is clandestinely oriented toward the ideas of power, order, planning and administration." Ibid., p. 172.

his Critical Theory. Adorno's more uncompromisingly negative and more sweeping critique of Western reason as a whole as a form self-preservation, whose domination of internal and external nature ultimately defeated its own purpose, seemed to provide the only alternative to abandoning Critical Theory and succumbing to utter despair. It is also worth mentioning that Horkheimer and Adorno first received a copy of Benjamin's "Theses on the Philosophy of History" at this time. These "Theses," which represented a return by Benjamin to some of the theological motifs that had guided his early work and had so heavily influenced Adorno, also played a role in shaping Horkheimer and Adorno's work in the early 1940s. We will return in the epilogue to these considerations of the relationship of *Dialectic of Enlightenment* to Benjamin and to Horkheimer's essays during this time and earlier. One final example of the important shift that occurs in Horkheimer's thought during this time, which we will examine in the present chapter, is his reevaluation of the period of liberal capitalism. As late as "The Jews and Europe," Horkheimer's attitude toward liberal capitalism was overwhelmingly critical; he sharply chastised those – especially among the exile community – who romanticized liberal capitalism now that it had been destroyed. However, in "The End of Reason," a much more positive picture emerges of liberal capitalism as a brief interlude in the much larger history of centralized domination. Horkheimer now sees the small and medium-sized property owners and entrepreneurs of nineteenth-century liberal capitalism, rather than the prerevolutionary bourgeoisie, as the true social bearers of autonomous reason and critical judgment. Here again, Horkheimer articulates arguments in "The End of Reason" that would remain central to his later thought.

"MONTAIGNE AND THE FUNCTION OF SKEPTICISM": THE BEGINNING OF THE END OF HORKHEIMER'S EARLY CRITICAL THEORY

Horkheimer's discussion in "Montaigne and the Function of Skepticism" of the ways in which the character structures of the ascendant bourgeoisie and the desperate lower classes were shaped by the forces of early modern capitalism represents a clear continuation of his earlier work. Although not as detailed and penetrating as his treatment of the same problem in "Egoism and Freedom Movements," Horkheimer is still vitally concerned in "Montaigne" with what he calls the "genesis of the bourgeois mass individual,"[5] in both its historical and social-psychological dimensions. In "Montaigne," Horkheimer focuses primarily on the role of the Reformation in the creation of a qualitatively new character structure among the lower classes. He writes:

Mediated by their [the leaders of the Reformation] fanaticism, the bourgeois mass individual emerges. He grows out of the childish condition of medieval man by way of the inversion of material desires, the subjugation of sensual impulses to a relentlessly driving ego, and the psychic incorporation of economic and political pressure as duty. Such

---

[5] "Montaigne and the Function of Skepticism," *Between Philosophy and Social Science*, op. cit., p. 282 (translation amended).

individuals adapt themselves to the nascent bourgeois order – but with rancor and a strong faith, with jealousy and guilt feelings, with sexual envy and misanthropy.... They need the ruse of an inscrutable god in order to adapt, for their existence contravenes natural needs and any idea of justice.[6]

Horkheimer's reliance on psychoanalytic concepts to grasp this historical process is even more evident in the following passage:

The notion of a holy commandment or a duty, which at that time constrained the Protestants to the repression or sublimation – or at least the postponement – of their material impulses, has no direct connection with a rational society. Indeed, the function of the Reformers consisted in the introversion of the desires of the masses, the diversion of demands of the dominated away from the rulers and toward their own inner nature.[7]

However, Horkheimer is not only concerned with the lower classes in "Montaigne"; he also describes the formation of bourgeois character structures. Horkheimer's argument could easily be mistaken for Max Weber's thesis from the *Protestant Ethic and the Spirit of Capitalism*, if it were not for his reliance on psychoanalytic and Marxist concepts. He writes:

The bourgeois virtues rest on the postponement of material impulses behind the more enduring interests of the abstract ego. Economic gain is pursued not for the enjoyment it yields but rather for the sake of further gain, and with each new success this striving asserts itself anew as its own true aim. The individual becomes the agent of capital.[8]

As he had in "Egoism and Freedom Movements," Horkheimer describes and analyzes here the development during the early modern period of a qualitatively new "bourgeois" character structure, which takes hold among both the middle and the lower classes, but which has a different function for each of them. For the former, the new character traits develop through an active process of self-assertion and coincide with their own interests, whereas for the latter, they are imposed by force and are not identical with their interests – at least not their immediate interests. This contradiction between material interests and the newly imposed duties can be resolved only by making it unconscious and providing ideal compensation for those who more or less successfully internalize the new social and moral norms. Such compensation includes promises of a better afterlife, the imagined love of the leader, or the "freedom" to shun or persecute with a good conscience those who do not or simply appear not to have internalized these norms.

Although his forays into historical social psychology are noteworthy, Horkheimer's primary purpose in "Montaigne" was to describe the rebirth and transformation of skepticism. Despite its ancient origins, Horkheimer argued that modern skepticism, as first fully articulated by Montaigne, expressed clearly some of the essential features of bourgeois thought as a whole. Modern skepticism's rejection of monolithic systems of belief and its defense of tolerance as

---

[6] "Montaigne...," p. 282 (translation amended).
[7] Ibid., p. 283.
[8] Ibid., pp. 286–7.

both a political and intellectual virtue presupposed an advanced urban culture, such as had already developed in European cities by the sixteenth century – Montaigne himself was the mayor of Bordeaux from 1581–5. In reaction to the horrors and fanaticism of the religious wars of the sixteenth century, Montaigne's skepticism counseled a retreat into a realm of moderate self-interest. Reason had a proper, if limited, role to play in the spheres of commerce and politics – to maintain the proper functioning of the state and the economy. However, if reason claimed the right to establish absolute truths or to call the status quo into question, it was rejected as overstepping its bounds. Skepticism recognized only probability, not certainty in the sphere of knowledge. Contrary to the claims of later critics such as Kant and Hegel, modern skepticism was not a subversive or destructive doctrine. Its defense of moderation and tolerance were essentially conservative. In a manner similar to Luther's "Doctrine of the Two Kingdoms," mind [*Geist*] was granted absolute freedom in the private spheres and the ideal realm of culture as long as it followed the rules in the public political and economic spheres. As Horkheimer put it, "the mind [*Geist*] is bad only as critical theory and practice; to the extent that it falls in line and subordinates itself – as custom, bourgeois efficiency, practical understanding and cultural works – it is tolerated in Protestantism as well as in skepticism."[9] Despite the basically affirmative consequences of skepticism, Horkheimer argues that its defense of tolerance and moderation played a progressive role in the early modern period. The skeptical defense of neutrality helped create a space in which the dogmatic claims of the church and the absolutist state were no longer unquestionable and thus contributed to undermining their authority and paving the way for the triumph of bourgeois society.

Yet once the bourgeoisie had succeeded in replacing feudal political and economic institutions with its own, the content and function of its skeptical ideals changed. Horkheimer's argument here about the transformation of bourgeois philosophical ideals in the nineteenth century is familiar and demonstrates once again the essential continuity of "Montaigne" with the central idea of Horkheimer's early Critical Theory, namely the *dialectic of bourgeois society*. Here, as in his other early lectures and essays, Horkheimer's argument is based on a *historically-specific* and *socially grounded* account of the transformation of the content and function of ideas in modern Europe. He argues that skepticism has lost the critical function it had had during Montaigne's time, and has instead been incorporated into the ideological defense of a form of society that has become anachronistic in its perpetuation of unnecessary suffering and domination, and in its degeneration into new forms of totalitarian collectivism. Horkheimer writes:

Skepticism is a pathological form of intellectual independence; it is immune to truth as well as to untruth.... Like dead religiosity, the churches, and hierarchy, a moribund skepticism – the closing off of human beings toward one another, their retreat into their own empty individuality – belongs to an intellectual disposition in contradiction with the current level of development of human powers.[10]

⁹ Ibid., p. 276.
¹⁰ Ibid., pp. 307–8.

Horkheimer argues that the progressive aspects of Montaigne's skepticism are best preserved today by Critical Theory, which he describes here as a form of "active humanism":

Active humanism as it arises from historical developments themselves now plays the role that once fell to the skeptical philosophers and Reformers.... The humanism of the past consisted in the critique of the hierarchical feudal order, which had become a fetter on the development of humanity. The humanism of the present consists in the critique of the forms of life under which humanity is now being destroyed, and in the effort to transform them in a rational manner.[11]

Horkheimer's insistence that Critical Theory still make an effort to actively create a more rational society testifies to the as yet unbroken ideals that guided his early work. However, at a time when the Moscow show trials left little doubt about possibility for positive reform in the Soviet Union and when the Western democracies were demonstrating a disturbing willingness to recognize and appease the fascist governments of Germany, Italy, and Spain, the increasingly pessimistic tone of Horkheimer's remarks should come as no surprise. In fact, Horkheimer's letters at this time make it clear that the "neutrality" of the Western countries toward fascism seemed particularly symptomatic of the current world-historical situation.[12] This dubious neutrality certainly motivated Horkheimer's interest in the transformation of modern skepticism. At this time, Horkheimer also firmly believed that fascism would continue to be tolerated by the Western democracies – that the interests of the bourgeoisie in maintaining order in their own respective countries would prevent a war between them and Germany and Italy – a belief that was soon proven false and that, as we shall soon see, sheds light on the shortcomings of Horkheimer's increasingly pessimistic views.[13]

So, although "Montaigne and the Function of Skepticism" did represent a continuation of Horkheimer's early Critical Theory in the ways we have just seen, it also anticipated his imminent pessimistic turn in at least two important ways. First, Horkheimer was becoming more pessimistic about the entire tradition of modern Western rationality, and he was beginning to see it in

[11] Ibid., p. 308 (translation amended).

[12] Horkheimer viewed Neville Chamberlain's appeasement politics as the most blatant example of the willingness of the ruling groups in the West to tolerate and work with Hitler. Horkheimer was so dismayed by Chamberlain's policies that he made plans and began to gather material to write a satirical novel about him. Horkheimer envisioned a *Bildungsroman* set in heaven after Chamberlain's death that would "describe the path from the state of consciousness of an English conservative of the ruling clique to complete Enlightenment," and would confirm Chamberlain's fears that "God had democratic or even socialist sympathies" (p. 332). Horkheimer never finished this project. See "Entwurf eines Romans über Neville Chamberlain," GS 12, pp. 329–41.

[13] For example, in a letter from October 7, 1938, Horkheimer wrote, "When judging the political situation since 1933 one must assume that the current German government, since coming to power, fulfills not only a German but also a European function, whose significance the Western powers can not long overlook. The overthrow of the German government could have consequences that neither an English nor a French government could accept. ... I am convinced that, in regard to Central and Western Europe, we can count on a quite long period of peace." GS 16, p. 496. As late as September 11, 1939, Horkheimer still believed that general war was unlikely. See his letter to Juliete Favez, GS 16, p. 628.

increasingly monolithic terms. Second, the argument about state capitalism, which would figure so prominently in the subsequent shift in his thinking, was also anticipated in "Montaigne." Let us briefly examine the first point before returning to the second.

Horkheimer's interpretation of skepticism in "Montaigne" was driven in large part by an effort to identify the negative characteristics of Western rationality, which had been present from the very beginning of the modern period. In his earlier work, Horkheimer had placed much more emphasis on the emancipatory content of early modern philosophy, insofar as it expressed the ideals of bourgeois society, which – true to his Marxist understanding of history – were emancipatory vis-à-vis feudal society, and which were a necessary condition for the establishment of a future socialist society. In "Montaigne," Horkheimer begins to place just as much emphasis, if not more, on the irrational and repressive aspects of bourgeois rationality, which he now argues were present from the very beginning. The distinction between a tendentially more critical, progressive, and substantive concept of reason in early modern philosophy and a tendentially more affirmative, formalistic, and subjective concept of reason in late modern philosophy begins to disappear in "Montaigne." Horkheimer writes:

Important characteristics of the bourgeois spirit [*Geist*] are expressed in Montaigne's ideas.... The tendency to subordinate the truth to power did not first emerge with fascism; irrationalism, just as deeply rooted in the economic situation of the bourgeoisie as the emancipatory traits, pervades the entire history of the modern era and limits its concept of reason.[14]

This tendency toward a more sweeping critique of modern reason as a whole was already apparent in Horkheimer's 1937 essay, "Traditional and Critical Theory." In contrast to his lectures from the late 1920s on the history of modern philosophy, in which he made a clear distinction between a more critical and historically specific empiricist tradition on the one hand, and a more affirmative, transhistorical rationalist tradition on the other, in "Traditional and Critical Theory," Horkheimer stressed the basic equivalence of empiricism and rationalism as two forms of "traditional" theory. These differences in historical periodization and between different thinkers and philosophical schools gradually receded in Horkheimer's thinking in favor of a conceptualization of the entirety of modern philosophy in terms of "subjective" reason. As the following passage makes clear, this tendency gained strength in "Montaigne":

As subjectivism, skepticism constitutes an essential characteristic of all modern philosophy.... Skepticism is the quintessence of nominalism. It lies hidden in all those tendencies at the advent of the modern era that ran counter to Aristotelian scholasticism. For the subjectivization of knowledge, about which the most antagonistic systems concur, is a skeptical function.... In truth, thought comprehends only itself and that which it brings forth. Knowledge is by no means the reflection of an object.... In this respect, Descartes, Hume and Kant belong to the same school.[15]

---

[14] Ibid., p. 278 (translation amended).
[15] Ibid., pp. 278–9 (translation amended).

Horkheimer's notion here of a "subjectivization of knowledge" anticipates the concepts of "subjective reason" in *Eclipse of Reason* and "instrumental reason" in *Dialectic of Enlightenment*. These works could be seen as the culmination of Horkheimer's increasingly sweeping critique of Western rationality. In fact, the critique in *Dialectic of Enlightenment* was even more sweeping and tendentially dehistoricized, insofar as the essence of instrumental, "bourgeois" rationality – the domination of external and internal nature – was seen as being present already in classical antiquity. In *Eclipse of Reason*, in contrast, Horkheimer's argument rested on a distinction between subjective and objective reason – the former characteristic of modern capitalist societies, the latter of classical antiquity.

In addition to his increasingly pessimistic and dehistoricized notion of Western rationality, several clear references to state capitalism exist in "Montaigne," which anticipate the subsequent shift in Horkheimer's thought. On the one hand, Horkheimer still referred to socio-economic conditions in the most advanced countries primarily as "monopoly capitalism" rather than "state capitalism." Also, Horkheimer's approach in "Montaigne" to the state still followed the basic schema of a dialectic of bourgeois society: Despite all of its repressive measures, the role of the state in the early modern period was progressive overall, insofar as it protected the nascent bourgeois economy, permitting it to mature to the point where the absolutist state could be reduced to the liberal "night-watchman state." Yet just as Horkheimer was becoming more pessimistic about the emancipatory content of modern Western forms of rationality, so he was also becoming increasingly critical of *all* forms of state intervention in the present. He writes:

At that time, the role of the state consisted in the (admittedly antagonistic) protection of a burgeoning trade and commerce. In the present, the state tends to act as the organ of the strongest capitalist groups, even where reformist governments seek to make of it a guardian of the economically weaker groups. Its most characteristic form is the *Führerstaat*, in which the consolidation of the industrial and political bureaucracies is realized.[16]

Horkheimer's reference to the fascist *Führerstaat* as the "most characteristic form" of capitalism in the present and his claim that the similarities outweighed the differences between fascist regimes and reformist governments in the West, anticipate Horkheimer's arguments in "The Jews and Europe" and "The Authoritarian State" that liberal capitalism develops naturally and almost necessarily into monopoly capitalism and then into authoritarian state capitalism. Furthermore, in "Montaigne" Horkheimer also sets forth, for the first time, arguments about the destruction in the present of various forms of social mediation, which were grounded in the sphere of circulation under liberal capitalism. Horkheimer stresses, in particular, the subordination of money and finance to the state. He writes:

Money, the universal equivalent … sheds the ephemeral character of independence. It has always mediated and expressed social relations. This becomes openly manifest

---

[16] Ibid., pp. 289–90 (translation amended).

today. The national group that has good apparatuses of production and repression, and which develops on this basis a rigid military and social organization, becomes increasingly independent of money – or, rather, presses it into its service. Domestic finance is formally taken in hand by capital and its state.[17]

Horkheimer also cites Franz Neumann's 1937 essay, "The Change in the Function of Law in Modern Society," to demonstrate that the decline of liberal capitalism and the disappearance of the sphere of circulation has also undermined the neutrality of the law and the independence of the judiciary, and led to more direct forms of social domination by the most powerful state and economic groups. Let us take a closer look now at how Horkheimer fleshes out these arguments about state capitalism.

THE TRANSITIONAL PERIOD: "THE JEWS AND EUROPE" AND "AUTHORITARIAN STATE"

Friedrich Pollock's study *Experiments in Planning in the Soviet Union, 1917–27*[18] testified to the keen interest he and Horkheimer had in the late 1920s and early 1930s in the possibility of overcoming the anarchic nature of the capitalist form of production through conscious economic planning. The stock market crash of 1929 and the ensuing worldwide depression – which the planned Soviet economy withstood much better than the liberal democracies in the West – reinforced Horkheimer and Pollock's belief that planning was a necessary, perhaps even sufficient condition for overcoming capitalism. In his work in the early and mid-1930s, Horkheimer repeatedly stressed the abstract nature of social domination within modern capitalist societies. In contrast to the slavery of classical antiquity or the serfdom of the Middle Ages, class domination in bourgeois society was no longer based directly on inherited power relations. Marx's and Horkheimer's concept of class is historically specific insofar as this form of social domination is dependent on ownership of the means of production, and is mediated by the production of commodities and the never-ending compulsion to accumulate value. The law of value asserts itself "behind the backs" not only of the proletariat, but also the bourgeoisie, who are reduced to "personifications of economic categories."[19] Unlike an aristocrat, whose economic fortunes can never affect his inherited status, a bourgeois who fails successfully to obey the law of value is in danger of falling down into the working class. In *Dämmerung*, in particular, Horkheimer demonstrates how the hyper-dynamic capitalist form of production manifests itself in the form of an *abstract* compulsion that shapes all aspects of life in modern, bourgeois society.

However, as Karl Polanyi and others have shown,[20] the 1930s witnessed a worldwide departure from the laissez-faire economic principles that had

---

[17] Ibid., p. 299.
[18] See the discussion in Chapter 4, pp. 182–84.
[19] Marx, *Das Kapital*, vol. 1 (Berlin, 1955), p. 8.
[20] Karl Polanyi, *The Great Transformation: The Political and Economic Origins of Our Time* (Boston: Beacon, 2001).

guided nineteenth-century capitalism. Although attempts were made in the 1920s – even in the Soviet Union, with its "New Economic Plan" – to return to the gold standard and the principle of free markets, the stock market crash and the Great Depression seemed to leave no doubt that there could be no return to liberal capitalism. The implementation of the first five year plan in the Soviet Union, the rise of fascism in Germany and its consolidation in Italy, and the adoption of Keynesian economic policies in the Western liberal democracies marked the beginning of a new period in the development of global capitalism, which was characterized by more extensive state intervention in the economy. Horkheimer's recognition and interpretation of this global tendency was the most important cause of the dramatic shift that occurred in his thought in the late 1930s and early 1940s. Horkheimer's first efforts to theorize the new tendency toward state-centric forms of capitalism and their social, political, and cultural consequences can be found in his essays "The Jews and Europe," which he finished in September 1939, and "Authoritarian State," which he wrote in early 1940.[21] In what follows, I will draw on both of these essays to demonstrate, first, how Horkheimer interpreted the rise of "state capitalism" historically. Next, we will examine how he distinguished its three main contemporary embodiments, namely the "integral statism" of the Soviet Union, the "reformism" of the Western democracies, and the fascism of Italy and Germany, which he refers to as a "mixed form." Finally, we will pose and attempt to answer the question of why he considered the similarities between the three different forms of authoritarian statism to be more important than their differences.

In "The Jews and Europe" and "Authoritarian State," Horkheimer argues that global capitalism had entered a qualitatively new period of development. One must note, however, that Horkheimer distinguishes between periods of development *within* capitalism on the one hand, and capitalism itself as a distinct historical epoch on the other hand. His designation of the new period as "state capitalist," indicates that he did not believe that a new *epoch* had begun. We will return in the following section to the problems that arose for Horkheimer in his attempt to determine why state capitalism was still *capitalist*. However, the following passage from "Authoritarian State" demonstrates clearly some of the main characteristics of state capitalism, and why Horkheimer viewed it as a qualitatively new *period* within the history of modern capitalism:

State capitalism does away with the market and hypostatizes the crisis for the duration of eternal Germany. Its "economic inevitability" signifies a step forward, a breathing spell for the rulers. Unemployment becomes organized. Only the already well-established section of the bourgeoisie is still really interested in the market. Big industrialists

---

[21] As is apparent from examining the early drafts of "Authoritarian State," the original title Horkheimer chose for the essay was "State Capitalism." See MHA IX.13, documents 1–7. I have not been able to discover the reasons why Horkheimer decided to change the title. At the beginning of the essay, Horkheimer states that "State capitalism is the authoritarian state of the present" (p. 96), which implies that the concept of "state capitalism" was more historically specific than the concept of the "authoritarian state." Horkheimer's decision to use the latter concept as the title for the essay, may have reflected the dehistoricizing tendency in this thought at this time. In any case, the following discussion should make clear the ways in which Horkheimer did and did not consider the new "authoritarian state" to be "capitalist."

today denounce liberalism only when state administration remains too liberal for them, not completely under their control. The modern planned economy can feed the masses better and be better fed by them than by the vestiges of the market. A period with its own social structure has dispensed with the free market, and demonstrates its own particular tendencies nationally and internationally.[22]

Central to Horkheimer's determination of state capitalism is the elimination of the market and the other abstract mediating institutions characteristic of liberal capitalism, such as the rule of formal law and the relative independence of money from state control. Horkheimer also characterizes the transition from liberal to monopoly capitalism in terms of the decline of small and medium-sized entrepreneurs who owned their own firms, and their replacement by large corporations owned by shareholders and run by a board of directors. During the phase of liberal capitalism, small and medium-sized firms were competing primarily with each other within the domestic market; their success or failure depended largely on their understanding of and ability to react to the changing conditions of this market. With the rise of large, joint-stock companies and the tendency toward monopoly capitalism at the end of the nineteenth century, these owner-entrepreneurs of small and medium-sized firms – such as Horkheimer and Pollock's fathers – were increasingly replaced by boards of directors of large corporations who were forced to compete on the international market. Their success in international markets could be enhanced through cooperating and forming larger conglomerates or fixing prices, rather than competing with other domestic producers. As the government became increasingly involved in coordinating and regulating such processes of domestic production, as well as coordinating and regulating the relations between large trade unions and employers associations, monopoly capitalism assumed an increasingly statist form.

Horkheimer viewed this tendency toward the elimination of the domestic market – and, with it, the entire sphere of circulation – as the primary coordinator of economic activity, and its tendential replacement by state planning, as the dominant, universal tendency of the age. Most important for our purposes here, Horkheimer came to see state capitalism as developing *logically* and *necessarily* out of earlier liberal capitalist forms. In fact, Horkheimer states this new insight in sweeping and dramatic terms when he says, "the self-movement of the concept of the commodity leads to the concept of state capitalism, just as for Hegel sense certainty leads to absolute knowledge."[23] At the beginning of the same essay, Horkheimer includes a long quote from Engels that is also intended to demonstrate the "necessity" with which liberal capitalism develops into monopoly and then statist forms.[24] Engels and other prominent figures in the Second International, such as Eduard Bernstein and Rudolf Hilferding viewed this "necessary" process of development positively, because they believed it would eventually lead to socialism. Once the state assumed control of capitalist production, the workers' movement would simply have to

---

[22] "The Authoritarian State," in *The Essential Frankfurt School Reader*, op. cit., p. 97.
[23] "The Authoritarian State," p. 108.
[24] Ibid., p. 96.

take control of the state to effect the transition to socialism. Horkheimer followed Engels and Hilferding in positing a logical and necessary development of liberal capitalism into monopoly and state capitalism, but differed from them crucially in his refusal to accept that state capitalism would continue to develop "naturally" into socialism. In fact, the opposite now seemed to be the case. Horkheimer believed that state capitalism had succeeded in containing the destructive dynamic that had characterized liberal capitalism and had thereby eliminated one of the root causes of conflict and potential dissatisfaction. Horkheimer argued that "the economy no longer has an independent dynamic. It has lost its power to the economically powerful."[25] Like his old friend Friedrich Pollock, who had been developing a theory of state capitalism over the course of the 1930s, which he would present in two essays in the final volumes of the *Zeitschrift*, Horkheimer believed that state capitalism represented a new *primacy of the political over the economic*.[26] As a result, social domination could no longer be conceived primarily in abstract terms using the categories Marx had developed in his critique of political economy; instead, domination had become direct and concrete once again, as it had been before the triumph of the capitalist market:[27] hence Horkheimer's introduction of the concept of *power*.[28] Abstract forms of social domination reveal themselves as specific to the period of liberal capitalism, which Horkheimer now viewed as a "one hundred year intermezzo."[29] More ominously, because the economic dynamic of capitalism had been brought under control, there was no reason why state capitalism could not last forever. As Horkheimer put it, "economically, fascism as a world system could exist indefinitely."[30]

Although Horkheimer sees the tendency toward state capitalism as universal, he does distinguish between three different types of "authoritarian statism": Bolshevism, to which he also refers as "integral statism" or "state socialism"; reformism, by which he refers to the Western democracies and their efforts to introduce elements of a planned economy; and, finally, fascism, which he views as a "mixed form," standing between state socialism and the incipient welfare regimes in the West. Horkheimer's remarks about the differences between these three different types of "state capitalism" or "authoritarian statism,"[31] are fairly limited, so it would be false suggest he had worked out a detailed typology. Our ultimate purpose in examining the differences he does mention is to demonstrate why he believed the tendencies they did share were, in fact, more important. However, it would, of course, be wrong to suggest that

---

[25] GS 4, p. 316.

[26] Friedrich Pollock, "State Capitalism" and "Is National Socialism a New Order?" *Studies in Philosophy and Social Sciences*, vol. 9 (New York: Institute for Social Research, 1941), pp. 200–25 and 440–55.

[27] Horkheimer illustrates this point by stating that "in the *Führerstaat*, those who shall live and those who shall die, are specifically designated." GS, vol. 4, p. 325.

[28] Horkheimer writes, "Striving for profit culminates today in what it has always been: in striving for social power." Ibid., p. 314.

[29] Ibid., p. 315.

[30] Ibid., p. 316.

[31] For the slight differences in Horkheimer's use of these two terms, see footnote 21.

he viewed the differences as completely inconsequential.[32] Horkheimer refers to the "state socialism" of the Soviet Union as the "most consequential form of the authoritarian state" insofar as it had completely abolished private ownership in the means of production. The "state socialism" of the Bolsheviks was also the first to establish itself historically and thus provided both a positive and a negative model for the Western capitalist countries, which were struggling with their "inefficient" market economies and parliaments. The success of the Soviet regime in increasing production at a pace "matched only by the transition from mercantilism to liberalism,"[33] and its relative immunity to the stock market crash and the Great Depression, made it clear to ruling groups in the West that they too would have to impose greater state control. Horkheimer emphasizes that "the authoritarian state is repressive in all its forms," and that "the emancipatory constitution of society" is prevented under state capitalism, in particular, by an "absolutism of ministries" whose authority is enforced by police who penetrate every aspect of life "down to its smallest cells."[34] Yet Horkheimer also argues that the potential for the creation of genuine, emancipatory society is greater in the state socialist countries than in the reformist or fascist versions of state capitalism. He argues that state socialism "stands on the border of something better,"[35] and that if "tendencies toward integral statism develop in other parts of Europe, there is a chance that they will not degenerate once again into bureaucratic domination this time."[36] Demonstrating that the liberal-democratic deficit, which was already apparent in his lectures on the history of philosophy from late 1920s,[37] had by no means been attenuated by his sharp critique of Soviet state socialism, Horkheimer repeated his conviction that political constitutions and democratic rights have been essentially an "instrument of domination," and that "in a new society they will not have any more weight than traffic rules and transportation schedules do in the existing society."[38] Unlike his colleague Franz Neumann, who viewed the Weimar constitution as a significant step toward the realization of genuine socialism,[39] or his friend Friedrich Pollock, who believed in the possibility of a democratic form of state capitalism that would also be a significant step toward socialism,[40] Horkheimer was not yet willing at this time to entertain

---

[32] Horkheimer states, for example, that "for individuals it is of course decisive, which form is finally established. For the unemployed, retirees, businessmen, intellectuals it is a matter of life or death whether reformism, Bolshevism or fascism triumphs." "The Authoritarian State," p. 101.

[33] Ibid.

[34] Ibid., p. 102.

[35] Ibid., p. 104 (translation amended).

[36] Ibid., p. 102.

[37] See the discussion in Chapter 4, pp. 174–75.

[38] GS, 5, p. 304. See also "Die Juden und Europa," GS 4, p. 324.

[39] See, for example, his essays "The Social Significance of the Basic Laws in the Weimar Constitution" and "On the Preconditions and Legal Concept of an Economic Constitution," in Otto Kirchheimer and Franz Neumann, *Social Democracy and the Rule of Law*, ed. Keith Tribe, trans. Leena Turner and Keith Tribe (London: Allen & Unwin, 1987), pp. 27–65.

[40] Friedrich Pollock, "State Capitalism," *Studies in Philosophy and Social Science*, vol. 9 (New York: Institute for Social Research, 1941), pp. 221–5.

the possibility – and much less the necessity – of preserving the best aspects of the liberal-democratic political tradition in a socialist society of the future and insisting on them as a means of getting from here to there.

The other two main types of "state capitalism," namely "reformism" and "fascism," had more in common with each other than with Soviet state socialism, according to Horkheimer. In both reformism and fascism, one could observe the universal tendency toward the development of independent bureaucracies and the subordination of the economy to political control. Horkheimer stresses, in particular, the role of large trade unions in keeping workers' demands well within the framework of the established system. The leadership of these large unions, and of the socialist mass parties as well, developed into bureaucracies that shared the employers' interests in managing the workers and making sure that radical democratic and revolutionary impulses were eliminated or marginalized. In both reformism and fascism, surplus value production is tendentially brought under state control but not eliminated. In contrast to state socialism, in both reformism and fascism several different bureaucratic groups continue to compete with each other for a share of this value. In the following years, Horkheimer would develop a theory of "rackets" to explain this persistence of corrupt competition among different power blocks within state capitalist societies.[41] Whereas Horkheimer sided with Pollock against Franz Neumann in the question of the primacy of the political over economic factors in state capitalism,[42] he agreed with Neumann that fascism in general and National Socialism in particular were not completely monolithic societies, as the following passage indicates: "Within the totalitarian states this tension is so large that Germany could dissolve overnight into a chaos of gangster struggles."[43] Soviet state socialism was more monolithic than reformist or fascist state capitalism, insofar as the Communist party had succeeded in eliminating or completely subordinating the other competing power blocks, such as the state bureaucracy, the military, and large industry.[44] Due to the persistent tensions within fascist societies, an ideology of the *Volksgemeinschaft* was introduced to create social cohesion. In Germany, this ideology hearkened back to the "ideas of 1914," according to Horkheimer, although this time the enemy was defined in more concrete racial terms, in accord with the new, more direct forms of social domination characteristic of state capitalism.[45] The success of the ideology was mixed, according to Horkheimer. Mobilization of the masses of unemployed and state-sponsored work programs were particularly effective

[41] For an overview of Horkheimer's theory of "rackets," see Kai Lindemann, "Der Racketbegriff als Gesellschaftskritik. Die Grundform der Herrschaft bei Horkheimer," *Zeitschrift für Kritische Theorie*, vol. 11 (Lüneburg: zu Klampen, 2000), pp. 63–81.

[42] For an overview of the debate between Neumann and Pollock on the concept of "state capitalism," see Jay, *The Dialectical Imagination*, pp. 163–5.

[43] GS 4, p. 319.

[44] In contrast to National Socialist Germany, in which – as Franz Neumann argued already in *Behemoth* – the National Socialist Party, the state bureaucracy, the military, and large industry continued to struggle with one another for influence through the 1930s and beyond.

[45] For a more recent interpretation of National Socialist ideology, which stresses the importance of the "ideas of 1914," see Peter Fritzsche, *Germans into Nazis* (Cambridge MA: Harvard University Press, 1998).

in winning people over to National Socialism, although Horkheimer argued that their loyalty remained largely pragmatic and not ideological. As long as National Socialism could continue to "deliver the goods," people would follow along. Horkheimer did not believe that fanatical anti-Semitism was the primary motivating factor for most Germans.

Of the three types of state capitalism, Horkheimer's discussion of the reformist version of the Western liberal democracies was least developed. In fact, Horkheimer's arguments tell us more about the weaknesses of his version of the state capitalism thesis than they do about "reformism" itself. The main argument Horkheimer makes about "reformism" is that it cannot possibly last: It did not work in Weimar and it will not last long in the other Western capitalist countries either. In "The Jews and Europe" in particular, Horkheimer argues that liberal capitalism contained a powerful internal logic that drove its transformation into monopoly and then state capitalism. Horkheimer makes it clear that he sees fascism as by far the most likely outcome of this "natural" process of development. Horkheimer refers to fascism as the form of capitalism most adequate to the present and simply as the "truth of modern society."[46] He scolds those who now romanticize liberal capitalism in light of the fascist victory, for they fail to acknowledge that its liberal-democratic political principles were a mere façade behind which much more powerful economic and social-psychological forces existed that pushed well-nigh inexorably toward the current forms of authoritarian statism. Horkheimer argues that anyone who wants to discuss the origins of fascism must be willing to address these deeper forces, which have now emerged from behind their liberal-democratic veneer.[47] He is sharply critical of those who romanticize the Weimar Republic which, in retrospect, appeals more to intellectuals than to workers. The main lesson Horkheimer draws from the failure of the Weimar Republic is that similar efforts to reform capitalism are doomed to fail. Horkheimer argues:

> The statesmen who still believe it is possible to subject liberalism to humanitarian direction, misapprehend its essential character.... Their efforts are nonsensical: they want to subordinate the social stratum [*Schicht*], whose particular interests inherently contradict general interests, to the general good.[48]

Horkheimer also still believed at this point that war between the fascist and reformist branches of the new state capitalism was highly unlikely, because the shared interests of European elites in oppressing their own underlying populations was greater than any real or principled conflicts between them.[49] This argument, which Horkheimer also made repeatedly in letters during this time, reflects his pessimistic conviction that it was only a matter of time before the

---

[46] Ibid., p. 309 and 323.

[47] As he states, "the totalitarian order is nothing other than its predecessor, which has lost its inhibitions." Ibid., p. 309.

[48] Ibid., p. 311.

[49] See footnote 13.

last remnants political liberalism were liquidated and the reformist countries became fully authoritarian themselves.[50]

Although Horkheimer did acknowledge certain important differences between the Soviet, fascist, and reformist versions of the authoritarian state, he considered much more important the overriding, universal tendencies toward bureaucratic control and the subsumption of the economic antagonisms and the independent dynamic of liberal capitalism to conscious political control. Horkheimer's argument that liberal capitalism had a strong inherent tendency to develop into state capitalism was intended as a sharp criticism of the forms of revisionist socialism that came to dominate the Second International and that continued to play an important role in Social Democratic parties in Europe through the 1920s.[51] Simplifying somewhat, one could say that Horkheimer's newfound arguments about state capitalism reversed the arguments of the revisionists that capitalism had a natural tendency to develop into an emancipatory form of socialism. As powerful as the tendency toward state capitalism now seemed to be, Horkheimer refused to hypostatize it. He had always been critical of evolutionary theories, whether they were positive or negative. So even his argument about the necessary development of liberal capitalism into monopoly and state capitalism did not assume the form a negative philosophy of history in the strong sense. Horkheimer continued to insist that state capitalism was not necessarily the end of history. However, he struggled mightily to justify this conviction. In his early Critical Theory, Horkheimer had always argued that the abstract dynamic of liberal capitalism was a function of the historically specific form of production. In other words, he did not view the "logical" dynamic of capitalism as part of a larger evolutionary theory of history, but instead as a historically specific characteristic that would be overcome in a postcapitalist society.[52] Horkheimer could still extend this argument to state capitalism to explain how a dynamic society pushed logically toward its own transformation into a static one. Yet once this static phase had been reached, without the abolition of social domination, Horkheimer was forced to provide a new explanation for the possibility of overcoming state capitalism. If liberal capitalism was in fact nothing more than a "hundred year intermezzo" in a larger history of capitalism, if the abstract forms of social domination

---

[50] In *Three New Deals: Reflections of Roosevelt's America, Mussolini's Italy, and Hitler's Germany, 1933–1939*, trans. Jefferson Chase (New York: Metropolitan Books, 2006), Wolfgang Schivelbusch emphasizes the many similarities and parallels that existed in the 1930s between the democratic United States on the one hand, and fascist German and Italy. Schivelbusch's study helps explain why Horkheimer viewed the similarities between Western democracies and nondemocratic forms of "state capitalism" in Germany and the Soviet Union as more important than their differences and why Horkheimer was so pessimistic about the future of democracy in the West.

[51] Horkheimer's critique here paralleled Benjamin's critique in his "Theses on the Philosophy of History" of evolutionary assumptions underlying the German Social Democratic Party's understanding of history. See *Illuminations*, op. cit., pp. 258–9.

[52] Moishe Postone has worked out this argument in more detail. See *Time, Labor and Social Domination*, op. cit., p. 277–85, 307–84.

that characterized it were also transitory, and if these forms were replaced by bureaucratic relations of power, then the root of capitalist domination could not be sought in the specific features of the liberal period of capitalism. The difference between social domination in capitalism and in other societies began to seem less clear.

At first, Horkheimer continued to try to find a historically specific answer to the question of how even state capitalism continued to possess an internal contradiction that could lead to its overcoming. He argued:

With state capitalism those in power can strengthen their position even more. State capitalism is, to be sure, an antagonistic, transient phenomenon. The law of its collapse is readily visible: it is based on the limitation of productivity due to the existence of bureaucracies.[53]

Yet this solution to the problem of the possibility of overcoming state capitalism quickly proved unsatisfactory to Horkheimer. The main reason he had criticized the revisionists was for their naïve faith in progress and their belief that the unfolding of the forces of production would lead automatically to the elimination of social domination. So, redefining the inherent contradiction in capitalism from one between the forces and relations of production to one between the forces of production and the bureaucracies that now controlled them could hardly be convincing. The other option open to Horkheimer at this time would have been to develop a historically and socially specific explanation for the triumph of fascism and Stalinism, which could also have addressed the possibility of these forms of authoritarian statism developing in the West. However, because Horkheimer had become convinced that fascism and the degeneration of the Soviet Union into totalitarianism could only be explained as two different versions of a much deeper and more powerful universal historical tendency that would also soon overwhelm the Western capitalist democracies, he did not pursue this route. It would have required much more attention to, and more emphasis on, the factors that *separated* the Soviet Union, fascism, and "reformism" than Horkheimer was willing to concede.[54] Therefore, Horkheimer turned instead to a much broader and less historically specific solution, namely a critique of Western reason of whole. This option seemed plausible insofar as the history of Western society and Western philosophy began to seem increasingly monolithic when viewed from the standpoint of the state capitalism argument.

"THE END OF REASON" AS THE END OF HORKHEIMER'S EARLY CRITICAL THEORY

During this same time, Horkheimer was beginning to work more intensely with Theodor Adorno, so it is probably not a coincidence that Adorno's arguments, which Horkheimer had criticized as recently as 1938 for their lack of historical specificity, began to seem more plausible to him. Although he had

[53] GS 5, p. 309.
[54] Here again Wolfgang Schivelbusch's study, *Three New Deals*, sheds much light on Horkheimer's position in the 1930s. See footnote 50.

already essentially adopted the state capitalism argument in "The Jews and Europe" and "Authoritarian State," these two essays remained within the paradigm of Horkheimer's early Critical Theory insofar as they rested on historical forms of argumentation. In those two essays, Horkheimer marshals a wide array of facts primarily from eighteenth-, nineteenth-, and twentieth-century European history to demonstrate how and why state capitalism has developed. With the transition to "The End of Reason" – which, as noted, Horkheimer considered the first fruit of his theoretical collaboration with Adorno – the form of argumentation changed. The argument and aims set forth in this essay represent a significant broadening of Horkheimer's early Critical Theory insofar as he is now concerned with Western reason as a whole. Yet they also represent a significant loss of historical specificity vis-à-vis his earlier work, insofar as the differences between different forms of reason both within modernity and between modern and premodern societies, essentially disappear. Key arguments that Adorno had appropriated from Benjamin's early work, such as his negative philosophy of history, his critique of the domination of nature, and his philosophy of language, were much more compatible with Horkheimer's new approach. Horkheimer and Adorno's acquisition during this time of Benjamin's "Theses on the Philosophy of History," which represented a return of Benjamin to the themes of his earlier work in certain key respects, also reinforced these tendencies in Horkheimer's thought. In the Epilogue, we will have more to say about the Benjaminian spirit of *Dialectic of Enlightenment*. First, to bring this final chapter to a conclusion, let us briefly examine how Horkheimer articulated his new position in "The End of Reason."

Horkheimer's belief that the various forms of "state capitalism" were manifestations and variations of an underlying universal process forced him to rethink some of the most basic assumptions that had guided his early Critical Theory. Although some of the consequences of this reassessment were already apparent in "The Jews and Europe" and "Authoritarian State," the full ramifications did not become apparent until he finished "The End of Reason" in February 1942. Helmut Dubiel has described the shift in Horkheimer's work in the late 1930s and early 1940s as a "rephilosophization of Critical Theory."[55] "The End of Reason" fits Dubiel's description insofar as it focuses on reason, the central concept of the Western philosophical tradition, rather than some more concrete social or historical phenomenon such as state capitalism or the role of the family in perpetuating authoritarian character structures. The essay falls short of a complete rephilosophization insofar as Horkheimer still insists that social relations determine the particular form reason assumes. Yet Horkheimer dehistoricizes these social relations, reducing them to an amorphous notion of class that has supposedly remained unchanged from classical antiquity to the present. Andrew Arato has described the shift in Horkheimer's thought during this time as one "from the critique of political economy to the critique of instrumental reason."[56] "The End of Reason" also fits Arato's

[55] Helmut Dubiel, *Theory and Politics*, op. cit., p. 106.

[56] Andrew Arato, "Introduction: Political Sociology and Critique of Politics," *The Essential Frankfurt School Reader*, op. cit., p. 11.

description insofar as Western reason as a whole is now defined in terms of instrumental reason and insofar as Marx's critique of political economy implied a historically specific critique of "*bourgeois* reason" within the context of modern capitalist relations of production, which Horkheimer now sees as only one manifestation of a much broader phenomenon. The definition of Western reason as a whole in terms of instrumental reason rests on the assumption that reason has, from the threshold of Western civilization to the present, primarily served the function of self-preservation and the domination of internal and external nature. Horkheimer's argument here represents a significant flattening out, or de-differentiation, of his earlier understanding of Western philosophy, both synchronically and diachronically. Essential distinctions between the function of reason in the early and late modern period and in premodern and modern capitalist societies disappear in the face of the basic continuity of instrumental reason. Distinctions between radically different thinkers in the same period – such as De Maistre and Robespierre – no longer seem as important either as their commonalities. The critical function of the Enlightenment in general and the French Enlightenment in particular, which was so crucial to Horkheimer's earlier thought, also disappears. Far from escaping the dominant tendency toward instrumental reason, the Enlightenment is now seen as one of its main manifestations. Finally, in "The End of Reason" Horkheimer also reevaluates the period of liberal capitalism in much more positive terms than he had used to describe it as late as 1939 in "The Jews and Europe."

In the introduction to *Dialectic of Enlightenment*, Horkheimer and Adorno reveal that they had set out to answer a question no less fundamental than that of why humanity had relapsed into a new kind of barbarism.[57] This sweeping perspective guiding their inquiries in the 1940s was already apparent in the opening lines of "The End of the Reason," where Horkheimer writes, "The fundamental concepts of Western civilization are in a process of rapid decay.... The question of how far these concepts are at all valid clamors more than ever for an answer. The decisive concept among them was that of reason, and philosophy knew of no higher principle."[58] So, already in this essay, Horkheimer's subject of analysis had shifted to something no less lofty than the concept of Western reason as a whole. Horkheimer had now taken a step beyond the arguments he had presented in "The Jews and Europe" and "Authoritarian State." In those essays, he had identified the new forms of state capitalism in general and fascism in particular as the "natural" result of powerful tendencies inherent in laissez-faire, liberal capitalism. The triumph of fascism was, in other words, indicative of a universal tendency that threatened to transform the entire world in its fearsome image. Refusing nonetheless to simply accept this

---

[57] *Dialectic of Enlightenment*, trans. Edmund Jephcott, op. cit., p. xiv.

[58] "The End of Reason," *Studies in Philosophy and Social Science*, vol. 9, op. cit., p. 366. My citations of this essay will also be based on the German version, which appeared in a volume dedicated to the memory of Walter Benjamin. This volume was published by the Institute in a very small edition. The German version of the essay has also been published in GS 5, pp. 320–50.

tendency as irresistible fate, Horkheimer strained to identify its sources, hoping desperately that it might still somehow be reversed. Because state capitalism had apparently succeeded in bringing the contradictions of liberal capitalism under control, one could no longer base a critique of state capitalism on the potentially emancipatory unfolding of a contradiction between the forces and relations of production. The critique of state capitalism and the explanation of the universal tendencies that had created it must be located at more fundamental level. For Horkheimer, this level was the very concept of reason itself. If, as Marx had said, the anatomy of the human provided a clue to understanding the anatomy of the ape, so fascism now seemed, to Horkheimer and Adorno, to provide the key to understanding a fatal flaw in the most basic concept that guided Western civilization from its birth. As Horkheimer put it in "The End of Reason," "The new order of Fascism is Reason revealing itself as unreason."[59] If the debilitating limitations of Western reason itself could be identified, perhaps they could be overcome.[60]

What was it then, that fascism revealed about the unreason of Western reason? Horkheimer's answer is revealed in the title of the German version of the essay: "Reason and Self-Preservation."[61] Western reason has, in reality, always been instrumental reason. Its principles failed to transcend "total self-assertion." Yet once self-assertion has become total, it turns against the self, thereby defeating its own purpose. Echoing an argument Adorno first made in his study of Kierkegaard, Horkheimer now identifies Western reason with sacrifice. One asserts and preserves oneself by sacrificing oneself for socially imposed aims. What is rational is what is beneficial to society as a whole. Society is, in fact, held together by individuals pursuing their own self-interest. Whereas Hegel identified this form of social cohesion as unique to modern bourgeois society,[62] Horkheimer now argues that it has existed much longer. He writes:

The individual has to do violence to himself and learn that the life of the whole is the necessary precondition of his own. Reason has to master rebellious feelings and instincts, the inhibition of which is supposed to make human cooperation possible. Inhibitions originally imposed from without have to become part and parcel of the individual's own consciousness – this principle already prevailed in the ancient world.[63]

---

[59] Ibid., p. 387.

[60] The move away from the historical specificity of Horkheimer's early Critical Theory to a critique of Western rationality as a whole placed Horkheimer in much closer proximity to Heidegger's equally sweeping critique of Western metaphysics – even though essential differences remained between them. It would take us too far afield to explore these similarities and differences, but it is worth noting that more recent attempts to emphasize the commonalities of Critical Theory and Heidegger have focused on Adorno or on *Dialectic of Enlightenment*, not Horkheimer's early Critical Theory. See, for example, Alexander Garcia-Düttman, *The Memory of Thought: An Essay on Heidegger and Adorno*, trans. Nicholas Walker (London and New York: Continuum, 2002) and *Adorno and Heidegger: Philosophical Questions*, eds. Iain Macdonald and Krzysztof Ziarek (Stanford University Press, 2008).

[61] "Vernunft und Selbstbehauptung," GS 5, pp. 320–50.

[62] *Philosophy of Right*, op. cit., pp. 124 and 133.

[63] "The End of Reason," p. 369–70.

However, fascism reveals that this determination of reason as self-preservation is irrational, insofar as the self is not really preserved but is instead sacrificed to the social totality. As Horkheimer puts it:

To men in the bourgeois era individual life was of infinite importance because death meant absolute catastrophe.... Fascism shatters this fundamental principle. It strikes down that which is tottering, the individual, by teaching him to fear something worse than death. Fear reaches farther than the identity of his consciousness. The individual must abandon the ego and carry on somehow without it.[64]

Western reason demanded self-sacrifice and the domination of internal nature in order to make oneself useful to society as a whole. However, it also entailed the domination of external nature and other humans. Horkheimer describes the fundamentally instrumental relation of Western reason to nature in the following way:

Cognition thus becomes that which registers the objects and proceeds to interpret the quantified expressions of them. The less human beings think of reality in qualitative terms, the more susceptible reality becomes to manipulation. Its objects are neither understood nor respected.[65]

With regard to the domination of other humans, Horkheimer stresses – as he had earlier in "Egoism and Freedom Movements" – the different motivations and effects of self-preservation among different social classes. The self-preservation of the upper classes demanded manipulation and domination of the lower classes. Horkheimer had now reached the point where he viewed bourgeois ideals such as a liberty, equality, and fraternity as *nothing more* than instruments used in this cynical struggle for self-preservation.

We have already seen how the categories of Horkheimer's Critical Theory became increasingly dehistoricized as a result of his newfound belief in the universal tendencies toward state capitalism. Once Horkheimer had identified the limitations of Western reason as a whole as the key to understanding these tendencies, these tendencies toward synchronic and diachronic de-differentiation became more pronounced in his thought. The differences between premodern and modern thinkers, as well as the differences between contemporary representatives of opposed schools of thought, all disappear to reveal a monolithic notion of reason as an instrument for suppressing internal and external nature in the name of preserving a self that does not really exist. In the following passage, Horkheimer highlights the epistemological dimensions of instrumental reason, which one finds in thinkers as diverse as Aristotle, Locke, and Kant:

Thought becomes what it was designated to be during the Aristotelian beginnings of empirical science, namely, an "organon." As a consequence of Locke and Kant, thought no longer conceives the objects as they really are, but contents itself with ordering and classifying supposedly pure data.[66]

[64] Ibid., p. 384.
[65] Ibid., p. 371.
[66] Ibid., pp. 370–1.

As noted, Horkheimer continues to insist that social domination is the true source of the limitations of Western reason. Yet social domination is no longer understood in a historically specific sense. It is reduced to transhistorical categories, such as "property" and "class." The following passage demonstrates Horkheimer's new understanding of the former category:

Already during the heroic era the individual destroyed his life for the interests and symbols of the collectivity that guaranteed it. From the clan to the state, the group represented property. Property was the institution that conveyed to the individual ... the idea that something of his existence might remain after death. At the origin of organized society, property endured while generations passed away. The monadic individual survived by bequeathing it. Through the legacy, the individual perpetuated himself even after his death, but he did not contradict the principle of self-preservation if he sacrificed his life to the state whose laws guaranteed this legacy. Sacrifice thus took its place as a rational institution.[67]

Whereas for Marx and the early Horkheimer, the significance of private property was specific to modern capitalist society as ownership of the means of production, which mediated between the historically specific classes of the bourgeoisie and proletariat, here property and class are seen as a historical constant.

Horkheimer does qualify his arguments here to a certain degree by emphasizing – as he had in "Egoism and Freedom Movements" and "Montaigne and the Function of Skepticism" – the crucial role of the Reformation in extending instrumental reason to a much broader section of the population. He writes:

The masses turned to religion, but their doing so did not affect the basic rationality of self-preservation.... Protestantism promoted the spread of that cold rationality which is so characteristic of the modern individual. It was iconoclastic and did away with the false worship of things, but by allying itself with the rising economic system it made men dependent upon the world of things even to a higher degree than before. Where formerly they worked for the sake of salvation, they were now induced to work for work's sake, profit for profit's sake, power for power's sake.... There was no other path from the medieval workshop to the assembly line than through the introversion of external compulsion into the compulsion of conscience.[68]

As in his early Critical Theory, Horkheimer does link the forced introversion of instrumental rationality among the "masses" to the rise of modern capitalism; yet the causality of his argument is different. Franz Borkenau and Henryk Grossmann carried out a debate on the origins of modern mechanical, instrumental reason in the pages of the first volumes of the *Zeitschrift*.[69] Even though they disagreed about when to date the origins of modern capitalism, they concurred that the mechanical, instrumental reason should be seen as its product. Although Horkheimer was more sympathetic to Grossmann's arguments, he would have agreed with the larger point both were trying to make, namely that

---

[67] Ibid., pp. 372–3.

[68] Ibid., pp. 373–4.

[69] Franz Borkenau, "Zur Soziologie des mechanistischen Weltbildes," *Zeitschrift für Sozialforschung*, vol. 1, pp. 311–35; Henryk Grossmann, "Die gesellschaftlichen Grundlagen der mechanistischen Philosophie und die Manufaktur," *Zeitschrift für Sozialforschung*, vol. 4, pp.161–229.

reason attained a historically specific, "instrumental" form in modern societies as a result of the rise of a new form of production. Yet in "The End of Reason," the causation is reversed. According to Horkheimer's new argument, instrumental reason was already fully developed in classical antiquity. The rise of capitalism does not give rise to instrumental reason; instead, capitalism is the logical result of its unfolding and simply leads to the diffusion of instrumental reason throughout society as a whole.

The differences in the concept of Western rationality are eclipsed in Horkheimer's work at this time not only with regard to history, but also among philosophers and political leaders or theorists who opposed one another during the same period. To demonstrate the essential underlying uniformity of instrumental reason, Horkheimer chooses the dramatic example of the French Revolutionaries and their counterrevolutionary opponents. One of the most articulate representatives of the latter camp, Joseph de Maistre, argued that "the primary need of man is that his growing reason ... be lost in the national reason so that it may change his individual existence into another, common, existence ... What is patriotism? It is that national reason of which I speak; it is the abnegation of the individual."[70] Horkheimer points out that the historian of the French Revolution, Albert Mathiez – whom he describes as "the apologist of Robespierre" – defined reason in a very similar way: "It admits of no contradiction, it requires oaths, it is made obligatory by prison, exile or the scaffold."[71] Horkheimer concludes that

> the basic unity of the period obliterates differences of opinion. The enthusiasm of the counter-revolution and of popular leaders not only joined in a common faith in the executioner but also in the conviction that reason may at any time justify renouncing thought.... Among all the parties of bourgeois revolution and counter-revolution, the nominalistically purged concept of reason – the principle of self-preservation – is used to justify its own opposite, namely sacrifice.[72]

The continuity of this argument with Adorno's efforts in his study of Kierkegaard – to demonstrate the mythical character of modern reason, which like a primitive ritual has its real basis in sacrifice – is just as clear as its distance from Horkheimer's own earlier work.[73] As we have seen, Horkheimer had previously insisted on the fundamental differences that existed between the British, French, and German Enlightenment, and he had interpreted this differences as a mediated expression of the different levels of development of bourgeois society in the different national contexts. Horkheimer had defended the French Enlightenment as the only one genuinely worthy of the name, because

[70] "The End of Reason," p. 369.
[71] Ibid.
[72] "Vernunft und Selbsterhaltung," GS, vol. 5, pp. 325 and 329.
[73] See "Reason and Sacrifice," in *Kierkegaard: Construction of the Aesthetic*, op. cit., pp. 106–22. It comes as no surprise that Horkheimer cites positively at the beginning of "The End of Reason" Walter Benjamin's *The Origins of German Tragic Drama*, i.e. one of the main sources of Adorno's earlier theological convictions, which Horkheimer once described as "radically different" from his own theoretical intentions. "Vernunft und Selbsterhaltung," p. 322.

of its explicitly critical and emancipatory content.[74] In 1933, in the face of the National Socialist seizure of power, he had argued:

> Today it is claimed that the bourgeois ideals of freedom, equality and justice have proven to be bad; but not the ideals of the bourgeoisie, rather conditions that do not correspond to them, have demonstrated their indefensibility. The leading ideas of the Enlightenment and the French Revolution are more valid than ever.[75]

The distance Horkheimer had traveled since this time is clear. The Enlightenment ideals that once seemed like the best defense against the Nazi moloch, were now themselves implicated in a much larger process, of which fascism was the symptom and terminal end point.

In addition to the new focus on the limitations of Western rationality as a whole, and the accompanying diachronic and synchronic de-differentiation of his categories, the positive reevaluation of the period of liberal capitalism in "The End of Reason" also marks the beginning of a new phase in Horkheimer's Critical Theory. This reevaluation marks a significant departure from the position he had articulated as recently as "The Jews and Europe," in which he sharply criticized those who romanticized the liberal phase of capitalism now that it had been destroyed. In that essay, Horkheimer had insisted that there was no going back to liberal capitalism, and such a return would be pointless anyway, because the inherent tendencies of liberal capitalism had themselves given birth to fascism. Horkheimer's position in "The End of Reason" is quite different and much more consistent with his later thought, in which a highly idealized notion of liberal capitalism became the source of the few redeeming qualities of modern society. The model of a *dialectic of bourgeois society*, which had informed his early Critical Theory, rested on the assumption that the ideals articulated by the bourgeoisie in their ascent to power provided the foundation for a Critical Theory of society – at least insofar as those ideals were developed and applied to concrete social relations, as Marx had done in his immanent critique of political economy and bourgeois society. According to this model, the triumph of liberal capitalism in the nineteenth century represented the phase in which the emancipatory ideals of the bourgeoisie were abandoned and no longer taken seriously. With the bourgeoisie firmly in power, its revolutionary ideals were transformed into an abstract, spiritualized form and were not applied to material relations.[76] After the shift in Horkheimer's Critical Theory in the late 1930s and early 1940s, he viewed these ideals as illusory at best, and fully complicit in the larger unfolding of instrumental reason at worst. Furthermore, he viewed the triumph of liberal capitalism and the flourishing of a relatively large number of small and medium-sized entrepreneurs, who competed with one another and succeeded or failed based on their own ability to understand and judge the shifting relations of the market, as the social precondition of a form of autonomous reason and critical judgment that goes beyond

---

[74] See Chapter 3, pp. 103ff.
[75] "Materialismus und Moral," GS, vol. 3, p. 137.
[76] See Chapter 7, pp. 279–81.

mere instrumental reason. We have already seen how Horkheimer understood the historical transformation of liberal capitalism into monopoly and state capitalism. Let us briefly examine his description of the social, cultural, and intellectual consequences of this transformation, which will also make clear why liberal capitalism suddenly appeared in a much more positive light.

Horkheimer argues that the destruction of liberal capitalism eliminated all of the mediating mechanisms that had, on the one hand, lent social domination its abstract character, but had, on the other hand, also provided a relatively autonomous sphere of existence in which relatively autonomous forms of culture and intellectual life could flourish. Horkheimer would have agreed with Hegel's description in the *Philosophy of Right* of post-dual-revolution[77] European societies as consisting of three relatively autonomous spheres – the family, civil society, and the state – which each followed its own independent logic while at the same existing together as a larger totality. The passage from this form of liberal capitalism to monopoly and state capitalism destroyed the boundaries that existed between the family, civil society, and the state. The social totality itself had been de-differentiated and reduced to a single logic of authoritarian control. Horkheimer now argues that the best aspects of liberal culture, such as autonomous reason and critical judgment, independent artistic production, a private sphere of family life that remained separate from the both the economy and the state, and even the very concept of individuality itself, were all made possible by these mediating mechanisms. The decline of small and medium-sized entrepreneurs and the tendential elimination of the market and price mechanisms as the primary means of circulating and regulating the production of goods threatened to destroy them. In "The End of Reason," Horkheimer focuses, in particular, on the decline of the autonomy of the individual and the family, which go hand in hand. He writes:

With the disappearance of independent economic subjects, the subject as such disappears. It is no longer a synthetic unit; it has become senseless for it to preserve itself for some distant future or to plan for its heirs. In the present period the individual has opportunities only on short term. Once secure property has vanished as the goal of acquisition, the intrinsic connection between the experiences of the individual disappears.... Today the individual ego has been absorbed by the pseudo-ego of totalitarian planning.[78]

Horkheimer goes on to show how the dissolution of the individual under monopoly and state capitalism is closely linked to the destruction of the independence of the family. From the Institute's *Studies on Authority and Family*, Horkheimer had already learned that economic crises lead to crises in the family which, in turn, give rise to authoritarian personality types. Yet in the *Studies*, the traditional, bourgeois patriarchal family was still seen as an ambivalent phenomenon; it reinforced dominant power relations as much as it created a "haven in a heartless world" in which strong egos and independent judgment could develop.[79]

---

[77] Here I am following Eric Hobsbawm's use of the term "dual revolution" to refer to the French and Industrial Revolutions. See his *The Age of Revolution: 1789–1848*. (New York, 1962).

[78] "The End of Reason," p. 377.

[79] Erich Fromm was already at this time more critical of the bourgeois *pater familias* and his departure from the Institute certainly contributed to Horkheimer's shift on this position.

By "The End of Reason," this ambivalence had been eclipsed by a more positive account of the traditional bourgeois family, which Horkheimer would continue to defend until the end of his life. Horkheimer now interprets the decline of paternal authority in purely negative terms. He writes:

During the heyday of the family the father represented the authority of society to the child, and puberty was inevitable conflict between these two. Today, however, the child stands face to face with society at once, and the conflict is decided even before it arises. The world is so possessed by the power of what is and the efforts of adjustment to it, that the adolescent's rebellion, which once fought the father because his practices contradicted his own ideology, can no longer crop up.... Since Freud, the relation between father and son has been reversed.... The child, not the father, stands for reality. The awe which the Hitler youth enjoys from his parents is but the pointed political expression of a universal state of affairs. [80]

Although I have purposefully avoided any psychological interpretations of Horkheimer's work throughout this study, his argument about the decline of liberal capitalism, paternal authority, and autonomous subjectivity parallel the events of his own life so closely that it seems irresponsible to categorically exclude such interpretations in this particular case. Horkheimer's and Pollock's fathers were, after all, ideal typical representatives of middle-sized entrepreneurs who had ridden the wave of German industrialization and economic boom in the Wilhelmine period to great success. In his youth, Horkheimer's disgust with bourgeois society expressed itself in a strong rebellion against his father and his desire that he succeed him as the director of his textile factory. Horkheimer's affair with and later marriage to Rosa Riekher, who was his father's secretary (and a gentile), was another example of Horkheimer's rebellion against his father. The dominant image of the nineteenth-century bourgeois entrepreneur in Horkheimer's writings in the 1930s as a representative of a social group that had abandoned its erstwhile emancipatory ideals and was content to restrict the validity of these ideals solely to the cultural and spiritual realms, was still largely in accord with the negative view of bourgeois society from his youth. By the early 1940s, however, a very different image of the middle-sized entrepreneur as the social foundation of all the best aspects of bourgeois culture had emerged. The revolutionary ideals of the early modern period, which Horkheimer had once praised, were now seen as being fully complicit in the much larger narrative of the unfolding of instrumental reason. This shift can be seen as, among other things, a reconciliation with Horkheimer's own father. In his later interviews, Horkheimer would himself repeatedly stress just how important the process of rebellion and reconciliation were in his own life. Without wanting to reduce Horkheimer's argument here about the systematic effects of state capitalism to nothing more than a psychological reconciliation with his own father – which would be absurd – one can nonetheless see how Horkheimer's own life experiences informed his claims. Although Adorno was sympathetic to the argument about a state capitalism to a certain extent, he was less amenable to the pessimistic description of the decline of paternal authority, which also permits one to associate this particular set of claims with Horkheimer.

---

[80] "The End of Reason," pp. 381–2.

Before concluding this chapter, let us take a brief look at one particularly sophisticated attempt to interpret the dramatic shift that occurred in Horkheimer's Critical Theory around 1940. In his essay (cowritten with Barbara Brick), "Critical Theory and Political Economy" and his book *Time, Labor and Social Domination*, Moishe Postone focuses on the shift that occurs in Horkheimer's thought between 1937 and 1940 by comparing his essays "Traditional and Critical Theory" and "Authoritarian State." Postone's characterization of this shift agrees in most respects with my own. In his analysis of "Authoritarian State," he too identifies a loss of historical specificity in Horkheimer's thought. He points, for example, to Horkheimer's new reliance on the nonidentity of the concept and the object as the foundation for his critique of instrumental reason as a failure to develop a genuinely self-reflexive and immanent critique of modern capitalist or contemporary state capitalist society. He plausibly emphasizes the link between Horkheimer's new, sweeping concept of instrumental reason and an equally sweeping concept of labor conceived of as the domination of nature. He identifies the much stronger concept of necessity that emerges in Horkheimer's work at this time, in the form of a negative philosophy of history which posits a well-nigh ineluctable tendency of dynamic, liberal capitalism to transform itself into a static, state capitalism. Finally, and perhaps most importantly for Postone, Horkheimer's understanding of state capitalism as a static, noncontradictory social formation, in which the independent dynamic of capital has been subdued to a new primacy of politics, led him to an abandonment of Marx's basic concepts, which he allegedly now viewed as only applicable to the liberal phase of capitalism. This characterization of Horkheimer's new position is accurate, but Postone's explanation for *why* the shift in his thought occurred seems more problematic. Postone argues that this "pessimistic turn" in Horkheimer's thought can be explained based on faulty "traditionalist Marxist" assumptions that had been present in his work from the beginning.[81] Postone argues, in particular, that even Horkheimer's early Critical Theory was based on a "historically indeterminate concept of labor;[82] that it was only epistemologically, but not truly historically or socially, self-reflexive;[83] that it was based on a problematic evolutionary theory of history;[84] that it did not adequately incorporate Marx's critiques of Ricardo and Hegel;[85] and that it was based on an affirmative concept of totality that assumed that the given relations of production prevented the underlying forces of production from developing fully and being organized rationally, but that failed to examine the composition of those forces themselves as the true

[81] He writes, "Horkheimer's traditional Marxist point of departure meant from the very beginning, then, that adequacy of the concept to actuality was implicitly affirmative – but of only one dimension of the totality. Critique was grounded outside of the categories, in the concept of 'labor.' When 'labor' no longer seemed to be the principle of emancipation, given the repressive results of the abolition of the market and private property, the previous weakness of the theory emerged manifestly as a dilemma." *Time, Labor and Social Domination*, p. 116.

[82] Ibid., p. 113.

[83] Ibid., p. 108.

[84] Moishe Postone, "Critical Theory and Political Economy," *On Max Horkheimer: New Perspectives*, op. cit., p. 248.

[85] Ibid., p. 241.

source of capitalist social domination.[86] Let us examine Postone's arguments here one by one.

Postone defines "traditional Marxism" as a critique of capitalism from the standpoint of a transhistorical concept of labor as the "metabolic interaction" of humans and nature. Such critiques fail to grasp the dual nature of labor under capitalism and fail to see that Marx's theory is a critique of the historically specific role that abstract, commodity-producing labor assumes as a quasi-objective form of social mediation.[87] We have already seen how the interpretation of Marx and critique of capitalism in Horkheimer's early Critical Theory decisively moves beyond such a critique from the standpoint of labor.[88] However, to supplement this argument, it is worth reiterating the critique of philosophical anthropology that was so crucial to Horkheimer's early Critical Theory. A transhistorical concept of labor would entail such a static philosophical anthropology, which Horkheimer rejected. Unlike Marcuse, who tried to develop such an anthropological critique based on the discussion of species being in the *Paris Manuscripts*,[89] Horkheimer rejected any such attempt to posit a transhistorical determination of "human nature" or "human labor." He describes in "Egoism and Freedom Movements" and "Montaigne and the Function of Skepticism" the ways in which the new forms of labor and labor discipline introduced at the dawn of the new capitalist epoch, led to the formation of new character structures among both the upper and lower classes. In addition, Horkheimer never identified – as Lukács did in *History and Class Consciousness* – the "standpoint of the proletariat" as the epistemological Archimedean point of Critical Theory. As we have seen, already in his 1927 critique of Lenin's *Materialism and Empiriocriticism*, Horkheimer argued that Critical Theory was not "firmly rooted" in the "standpoint of the proletariat."[90] Thus, his elaboration of this same argument in "Traditional and Critical Theory" underscored Horkheimer's long-standing criticism of a critique of capitalism solely from "the standpoint of labor."[91]

Postone's claim that Horkheimer's early Critical Theory was only epistemologically rather than historically or socially self-reflexive and that it was therefore only "apparently dialectical" also seems unfounded.[92] We have already seen how Horkheimer's Critical Theory developed as a critique of consciousness philosophy and an insistence that philosophy in particular and theory in general cannot be understood outside of the social and historical context in which they are located. Throughout his early Critical Theory, this context was a historically specific notion of a dialectic of bourgeois society. We have also seen how Horkheimer's early thought cannot be interpreted as an attempt to establish abstract methodological guidelines for a formalistic

[86] Ibid., p. 234.

[87] *Time, Labor and Social Domination*, pp. 43–83.

[88] Chapter 4, pp. 177–78.

[89] Stephan Bundschuh, "*Und weil der Mensch ein Mensch ist...*" *Anthropologische Aspekte der Sozialphilosophie Herbert Marcuses*, (Lüneburg: zu Klampen, 1998).

[90] Chapter 4, pp. 150ff.

[91] On this point, see also Chapter 8, p. 329.

[92] *Time, Labor and Social Domination*, p. 116.

Critical Theory. Horkheimer's early Critical Theory was an attempt to determine the historically specific forms of social mediation that existed in modern bourgeois, capitalist society – from concrete forms, such as authority and family, to the most abstract forms of philosophy and metaphysics. As we have seen, Horkheimer's concepts were explicitly dialectical, in the sense that they aimed not simply to grasp these forms descriptively, but at the same to time to critique and point beyond them. Horkheimer viewed Critical Theory not as a passive reflection, but as a form of action or conduct that could potentially affect the way in which society developed. In his early Critical Theory, Horkheimer developed an original formulation of the active role of knowledge in reproducing the social totality, which built on Marx's materialist critique of idealist epistemology.

We have also seen how Horkheimer was, from his first encounters with Schopenhauer onward, deeply skeptical of evolutionary theories of history. He criticized Hegel, Dilthey, and Mannheim for tacitly or overtly defending such theories, which foreclose the fundamental openness of history and restrict human freedom by positing a preordained path of development. On this point, Horkheimer's interpretation of the evolutionary theories as a historically specific expression of the underlying dynamic of capitalism itself, seems – as I pointed out earlier – very close to Postone's own position.[93] Regarding the fourth point, that Horkheimer failed adequately to incorporate Marx's critiques of Ricardo and Hegel, one can also point to many counterexamples in his early work, such as the following passage:

In *Capital*, Marx introduces the basic concepts of classical English political economy – value, price, labor time, etc. – in accordance with their precise definitions. All the most progressive definitions drawn from scientific practice at that time are employed. Nevertheless, these categories acquire new functions in the presentation [*Darstellung*]. They contribute to a theoretical whole, the character of which contradicts the static views in connection with which they came into being, in particular their uncritical use in isolation. Materialist economics as a whole stands opposed to the classical system, yet individual concepts are taken over.[94]

For Horkheimer, the crucial difference between Marx and the classical political economists was the dialectical nature of his concepts, which grasp their object as historically specific and subject to transformation, not as eternal laws of nature. Marx's concepts consciously aim for a society in which they would no longer be valid. We have already examined Horkheimer's nuanced interpretation and appropriation of Marx's critique of Hegel, but because Postone identifies Hegel primarily with an evolutionary philosophy of history, it is perhaps worth reiterating Horkheimer's interpretation of Marx's Critical Theory as an "open-ended dialectic," which he contrasted to Hegel's metaphysical philosophy of history. Finally, Postone also claims that Horkheimer subscribed to a positive concept of totality in his early Critical Theory, which implied that the forces of production needed simply to be rationally organized and

---

[93] See footnote 52.
[94] *Time, Labor and Social Domination*, p. 209.

not fundamentally transformed. This argument, as Martin Jay has also pointed out,[95] overlooks the crucial differences that existed between Horkheimer's critical and more circumscribed understanding of the concept of totality and Lukács's argument in *History and Class Consciousness* that the concept of "totality" is what separates Marx's theory from all bourgeois theory. The argument Postone attributes to Horkheimer seems much closer, in fact, to Lukács's efforts to theorize the proletariat as the subject-object of history, whose interests are identical with the interests of humanity as a whole. Overcoming the fragmentation imposed on the proletariat under capitalism would make possible a rational organization of the social totality.[96] However, our discussion of Horkheimer's project on dialectical logic and his insistence that Marx's categories point beyond the "bourgeois epoch" make it clear that Horkheimer would not have disagreed with the following interpretation by Postone of Marx and the concept of the totality: "Marx's assertion that capital, and not the proletariat or the species, is the total Subject clearly implies that the historical negation of capitalism would not involve the *realization*, but the *abolition* of the totality."[97]

Postone's argument that Horkheimer relied on a positive concept of totality fails to do justice to the fact that Horkheimer followed a different path to Critical Theory than Lukács. Horkheimer's early Critical Theory does not fit neatly into a larger narrative of Western Marxism that begins with Lukács and his concept of totality. Such an interpretation works much better for Adorno's writings in the 1930s than Horkheimer's. Despite his Benjaminian-inspired criticisms of Lukács – which we examined earlier – Adorno's heavy reliance on the concept of reification placed his Critical Theory in the 1930s much closer Lukács. Horkheimer was critical of this concept in the early 1930s and did not begin defending it until after he started working more closely with Adorno.[98] Similarly, it is mistake to read positions that Horkheimer developed in collaboration with Adorno in the late 1930s and early 1940s back onto his early Critical Theory. Despite the shifts that occurred in Adorno's thought in the 1930s, the continuities between his Critical Theory in the 1930s and *Dialectic of Enlightenment* were much greater than Horkheimer's. Postone's claim that the continuities between Horkheimer's early Critical Theory and *Dialectic of Enlightenment* were more important than the differences projects back onto his early Critical Theory positions that he developed only later and downplays the crucial differences that existed in the 1930s between Horkheimer on the one hand, and Lukács and Adorno on the other. The concept of instrumental

[95] Jay writes, "Horkheimer and his colleagues had no illusions about the impending normative totalization of the world by the proletariat celebrated in *History and Class Consciousness*." *Marxism and Totality*, op. cit., p. 208.

[96] In his critique of Horkheimer, Postone links Horkheimer's early Critical Theory to the "one-sided" and "one-dimensional" strains of Western Marxism that emanate from Lukács's appropriation of Weber's critique of occidental rationality. Postone points, in particular, to Lukács's concept of "reification" as a symptom of the shortcomings of this tradition. *Time, Labor and Social Domination*, pp. 115–6. However, as we have seen, Horkheimer was critical of Lukács's concept of reification and did not begin defending it until he started working more closely with Adorno in the late 1930s. See Excursus II, pp. 392–93.

[97] *Time, Labor and Social Domination*, p. 79.

[98] See Excursus II, pp. 392–93.

reason as the domination of nature, which had remained essentially unchanged from classical antiquity to the present, was already present in Adorno's Critical Theory in the 1930s. As I have attempted to demonstrate here, the same cannot be said for Horkheimer. After adopting the state capitalism thesis, Horkheimer fundamentally rethought some of his most basic assumptions.

To be sure, Horkheimer's early Critical Theory does demonstrate some of the elements of "traditional Marxism" as defined by Postone. Like Pollock, Horkheimer was very interested in the idea of a planned economy and at times may have believed that planning – or, in other words, a rational form of distribution – alone was a sufficient condition for overcoming capitalism, and thereby failed to grasp the contradiction of capitalism at the more fundamental level of production. Nonetheless, it would also be a mistake to overemphasize the importance of Pollock's economic ideas to Horkheimer's Critical Theory in the 1930s. Horkheimer was by far the more dialectical thinker of the two. Pollock always admitted and Horkheimer also recognized that Pollock had strong positivistic tendencies. In the end, the effort the dissociate Horkheimer's Critical Theory in the 1930s from Pollock, Adorno, and Lukács is also intended to demonstrate the important "nontraditional" aspects of Horkheimer's Critical Theory in the 1930s, including his emphasis on historical specificity, his well-developed notion of dialectical concepts, and his critique of evolutionary philosophies of history. To be sure, Postone has worked out the dual nature of labor, and the role abstract labor plays in capitalist societies as a quasi-objective form of social mediation, much more clearly than Horkheimer ever did. Yet the much needed critique of traditional Marxism, to which Postone has contributed so much, would benefit more from recovering the nontraditional aspects of Horkheimer's aforementioned early Critical Theory than overlooking the important differences that existed between him and Pollock, Lukács, and Adorno.

Epilogue

Toward a Historicization of *Dialectic of Enlightenment* and a Reconsideration of Horkheimer's Early Critical Theory

If we are to believe the epigraph from Hegel's *Phenomenology of Spirit*, which stands at the beginning of this study, the presentation and critique of ideas are inextricably intertwined insofar as both involve the inherently negative "effort of conceptualization."[1] My presentation of the transformation of Horkheimer's Critical Theory in the preceding chapter was carried out very much in this critical spirit. This study of Horkheimer has led me to the conclusion that Horkheimer's and the Institute's work from the late 1920s and 1930s could serve as a more promising point of departure for contemporary efforts to renew Critical Theory than his writings after 1940. In what follows, I would like briefly to present some additional reasons and evidence for this conclusion. Any attempt to make such an argument must, of course, reckon with the formidable *Dialectic of Enlightenment*. Although I have attempted throughout this study to adhere methodologically to Hegel's insistence that critique can proceed only on the basis of conceptual presentation, I would like to propose a shortcut here – one that, hopefully, will not compromise my main conclusion. Rather than reconstructing the main arguments of *Dialectic of Enlightenment*, the following critical remarks will rely instead on two of the main arguments from the preceding chapter: First, that the most important reason for the transformation of Horkheimer's thought around 1940 was his adoption of a modified version of Friedrich Pollock's "state capitalism" thesis; and second, that this transformation reached a preliminary culmination in "The End of Reason." With this essay, Horkheimer crossed a threshold into a qualitatively new phase in the development of his thought. It laid the foundations for his two most substantial theoretical works of this period: *Dialectic of Enlightenment* and *Eclipse of Reason.*[2] Insofar as *Dialectic of Enlightenment* rests on the arguments presented in "The End of Reason" and on the "state capitalism" thesis in particular, the criticisms presented in Chapter 9 of the latter text can also be applied to the former.[3] Chapter 9 should have made

---

[1] For a good introduction to the concept of negation in Hegel's philosophy, see Herbert Marcuse's preface, "A Note on the Dialectic," to the 1960 edition of *Reason and Revolution: Hegel and the Rise of Social Theory* (Boston: Beacon, 1960).

[2] For another attempt to periodize Horkheimer's life and work, which comes to similar conclusions as my own, see Alfred Schmidt, "Max Horkheimer's Intellectual Physiognomy," *On Max Horkheimer: New Perspectives*, op. cit., pp. 25–48.

[3] Many other commentators have pointed out the important ways in which *Dialectic of Enlightenment* rested on Pollock's "state capitalism" thesis. See, for example, Manfred Gangl,

clear that the shift from a historically specific, self-reflexive theory of capitalism to a tendentially transhistorical critique of power and the domination of nature, which plays such a crucial role in *Dialectic of Enlightenment*, is already present in "The End of Reason." Nonetheless, let me identify the limits of my critique right away by stating the obvious: The arguments presented in "The End of Reason" by no means exhaust *Dialectic of Enlightenment*. There are many aspects of *Dialectic of Enlightenment* that move well beyond "The End of Reason" and that are still relevant to contemporary theoretical discussions – such as the critique of the culture industry and the multidimensional analysis of anti-Semitism. So my *plaidoyer* here for a critical historicization of *Dialectic of Enlightenment* will be limited to those aspects of the text – which are, nonetheless, substantial – anticipated by "The End of Reason."

From the standpoint of the "state capitalism" thesis, it appeared to Horkheimer that history had come to a standstill. He could find no reason to doubt why some form of the "authoritarian state" would not maintain itself in perpetuity. His newfound conviction that state capitalism had triumphed in the present also led Horkheimer to reinterpret the past. As we have seen, his thought underwent a process of synchronic de-differentiation around 1940 that pushed him much closer to the position he had rejected in his debates with Theodor Adorno in the late 1930s, namely that bourgeois thought had always been the same.[4] This tendency was reinforced when, in June of 1941, Horkheimer and Adorno first received a complete copy of Benjamin's "Theses on the Philosophy of History." As Susan Buck-Morss has argued, Benjamin's theses represented a return to the theological motifs that had guided his early thought, but which he had abandoned in his more explicitly political essays from the 1930s.[5] As we have seen, Adorno had objected to Benjamin's abandonment of these themes, which had been crucial for his own study of Kierkegaard and his early conception of "natural history." With the shift toward immanent critique in his study of Husserl, Adorno had also moved away from Benjamin's early work to a certain degree; nonetheless, he must have seen the "Theses on the Philosophy of History" as evidence that Benjamin had returned to the theological themes of his earlier work, as Adorno had urged him to do in the mid-1930s. In any case, there can be no doubt that the "Theses on the Philosophy of History" exercised a strong influence on *Dialectic of Enlightenment*. Horkheimer and Adorno received the "Theses" during the time when they were laying the foundations for that work. Several commentators have described the elective affinities between *Dialectic of Enlightenment* and Benjamin's theses.[6]

"Staatskapitalismus und *Dialektik der Aufklärung*," *Jenseits instrumenteller Vernunft: Kritische Studien zur* Dialektik der Aufklärung, eds. Manfred Gangl and Gerard Raulet (Frankfurt, Berlin, Bern, New York, Paris, Vienna: Peter Lang, 1998), pp. 158–86; and Willem van Reijen and Jan Bransen, "Das Verschwinden der Klassengeschichte in der *Dialektik der Aufklärung*: Ein Kommentar zu den Textvarianten der Buchausgabe von 1947 gegenüber der Erstveröffentlichung von 1944," GS, vol. 5, pp. 453–7.

[4] See Excursus II, p. 393.

[5] *The Origins of Negative Dialectics*, op. cit., p. 168.

[6] See, for example, Richard Wolin, *Walter Benjamin: An Aesthetics of Redemption*, op. cit., pp. 265–72.

In a letter to Horkheimer not long after receiving the "Theses," Adorno himself wrote: "This work, more than any other of Benjamin's, reveals his proximity to our own intentions, especially the conception of history as a permanent catastrophe, the critique of progress and the domination of nature, and the interpretation of culture."[7] Most important for our purposes here is the influence the "Theses" exercised on the philosophy of history underlying *Dialectic of Enlightenment*. There is little question that this philosophy represented a return to the antihistoricist notion of "natural history" that Adorno had articulated earlier in the shadow of Benjamin. The influence of the "Theses" was not limited to Adorno either. Not long after learning of Benjamin's tragic and untimely death, Horkheimer and Adorno decided to publish a small volume dedicated to his memory. The two essays of Horkheimer's, which most clearly marked the transition away from his early Critical Theory and toward *Dialectic of Enlightenment*, "Authoritarian State" and "The End of Reason," both appeared in the volume. Both essays demonstrate remarkable similarities to Benjamin's "Theses."[8] In short, the influence of Benjamin's "Theses on the Philosophy of History" on *Dialectic of Enlightenment* reinforced the tendencies toward the dehistoricization of Horkheimer's early Critical Theory.

Many commentators have criticized the transhistorical notion of instrumental reason as the domination of internal and external nature that is so crucial for *Dialectic of Enlightenment*.[9] I concur with most of the criticisms, and I have examined the pitfalls of such antihistoricism here in the second excursus and in Chapter 9. Insofar as it rests on a transhistorical notion of the domination of nature and not a nuanced theory of the development of modern bourgeois society – such as one finds in Horkheimer's writings in the late 1920s and 1930s – *Dialectic of Enlightenment* fails to satisfy one of the necessary conditions of dialectical thinking: historical mediation. However, let us briefly consider one possible objection to this interpretation. Perhaps it would be a mistake to criticize *Dialectic of Enlightenment* for the transhistorical character of some of its central concepts because Horkheimer and Adorno were really only concerned with history, as Benjamin put it in his "Theses," as " it flashes up at a moment of danger," that is, only insofar as it can critically illuminate the present.[10] Such an interpretation is indeed plausible, but it by no means obviates the necessity for historicization. As Horkheimer points out in his interpretation of Hegel, genuinely critical historicization does not simply deny the truth of an idea; instead, it insists that its truth is relative and bound to a particular moment.[11] Historicization in this sense seeks not only to negate,

[7] GS, vol. 17, p. 60.

[8] For a discussion of the ways in which Horkheimer's arguments in these two essays moved much closer to some of Benjamin's key positions, see Susan Buck-Morss, *The Origins of Negative Dialectics*, pp. 171–4.

[9] Moishe Postone, "Critical Theory and Political Economy," op. cit.; Gerd-Walter Küsters, *Der Kritikbegriff in der Kritischen Theorie Max Horkheimers*, op. cit.; Manfred Gangl, *Politische Ökonomie und Kritische Theorie: Ein Beitrag zur theoretischen Entwicklung der Frankfurter Schule* (Frankfurt: Campus, 1987).

[10] Walter Benjamin, "Theses on the Philosophy of History," *Illuminations*, op. cit., p. 255.

[11] See Chapter 8, p. 317.

but also to preserve, those aspects of an idea or work that were true at the time. Yet it also has the task of determining which aspects of an idea or work are still relevant and which no longer speak to us in the present. The uncompromising negativity of *Dialectic of Enlightenment* was without question a remarkable and thoroughly appropriate expression of the catastrophic historical events that were unfolding at that time. As Adorno would write later:

After Auschwitz, our feelings resist any claim of the positivity of existence as sanctimonious, as wronging the victims; they balk at extracting any kind of meaning, however tenuous, out of the victims' fate. And these feelings contain an objective moment of truth after events that give the lie to the construction of immanent meaning which emanates from affirmatively posited transcendence.[12]

The fact that Auschwitz was possible in modern Western society constitutes the undeniable truth content of the uncompromising negativity of *Dialectic of Enlightenment*. Adorno's provocative argument – that the social, psychological, and historical conditions that had made Auschwitz possible continued to exist after the war, and that, therefore, other historical catastrophes of similar magnitude were still possible – must be taken seriously.[13] One of the most important legacies of Horkheimer and Adorno's work is their identification and analysis of the powerful subjective and objective tendencies toward authoritarianism that exist and are constantly reproduced in modern capitalist societies. Yet the question of whether the view of modern society from the perspective of Auschwitz is the only possible one must also be posed. An understanding of history that sees fascism as the telos or the "truth of modern society"[14] must also lead to serious distortions. We have already seen how Horkheimer's predictions regarding the course of the war and the postwar world, which were based on such an understanding of history, were proven wrong. The Western powers did fight against fascism, and neither fascism nor authoritarian state socialism have in the meantime engulfed the rest of the globe.

Such considerations have led Jürgen Habermas and other serious interpreters of Critical Theory to question the theory of modern society underlying *Dialectic of Enlightenment*. Habermas writes:

Dialectic of Enlightenment does not do justice to the rational content of cultural modernity that was captured in bourgeois ideals (and also instrumentalized along with them).... Horkheimer and Adorno ... commence their critique of enlightenment at such a depth that the project of enlightenment itself is endangered.... The suspicion of ideology ... is turned not only against the irrational function of bourgeois ideals, but against the rational potential of bourgeois culture itself ... what is unexplained throughout in their certain lack of concern in dealing with the (to put it in the form of slogan) achievements of Occidental rationalism.[15]

---

[12] *Negative Dialektik*, p. 354. *Negative Dialectics*, trans. E.B. Ashton (New York: Continuum, 1973), p. 361 (translation modified).

[13] See Theodor Adorno, "Education after Auschwitz" *Critical Models: Interventions and Catchwords*, op. cit. pp. 191–204.

[14] GS, vol. 4, p. 309.

[15] *The Philosophical Discourse of Modernity*, pp. 113, 114, 119, and 121, respectively.

As is well known, Habermas has attempted in his own theory to preserve and elaborate the "rational content of modernity" that he believed Horkheimer and Adorno had neglected in *Dialectic of Enlightenment*. The fact that Horkheimer and Adorno's most dire fears about the postwar world did not come true and that they themselves began more emphatically to defend the "rational potential of bourgeois ideals" that were incorporated – albeit partially and imperfectly – in the constitutions of the Western democracies testifies to an important moment of truth in Habermas's criticisms of *Dialectic of Enlightenment*.[16] Yet even if one accepts Habermas's criticisms, it is important to keep in mind that the two main objections he makes to *Dialectic of Enlightenment* do not apply to the model of Critical Theory one finds in Horkheimer's early work. As I have been at pains to demonstrate in this work, Horkheimer's early Critical Theory did defend the "rational potential of bourgeois ideals" and did not succumb to a "negative philosophy of history." Horkheimer's model of a "dialectic of bourgeois society" was not deterministic, nor was it based on the assumption – as was *Dialectic of Enlightenment* – that bourgeois ideals were fundamentally corrupt; it demonstrated the historically specific barriers that had developed within bourgeois society to the realization of these ideals and the active role that Critical Theory could play in overcoming these barriers. Habermas's adoption of the model of a "dialectic of bourgeois society" in his early study, *The Structural Transformation of the Public Sphere: An Enquiry into a Category of Bourgeois Society*, testifies to the compatibility of Horkheimer's early Critical Theory with his efforts to overcome the limitations of *Dialectic of Enlightenment*. Habermas's main argument, that the critical and revolutionary role played by the public sphere in the early modern period was increasingly undermined as the bourgeoisie consolidated its hegemony in the nineteenth century, fits squarely into Horkheimer's interpretation of modern European society.

In his efforts to recover and reintegrate the best aspects of the liberal-democratic political tradition, Habermas has done much to address a deficit that existed not only in *Dialectic of Enlightenment*, but also in Horkheimer's early thought. Yet as John McCormick has recently shown, soon after completing his study of the public sphere, Habermas abandoned the model of a "dialectic of bourgeois society" and developed a new theory of modernity as the differentiation of value spheres, which was more indebted to Weber, Parsons, and Luhmann than to Horkheimer's early work.[17] Rather than focusing on the crucial historical shift within the bourgeois epoch, Habermas's new theory is grounded on a sweeping distinction between modern and premodern societies, which represents a loss

[16] For one example of Adorno's defense of the liberal-democratic constitution of the Federal Republic of Germany, see John Abromeit, "The Limits of Praxis: The Social-Psychological Foundations of Theodor Adorno's and Herbert Marcuse's Interpretations of the 1960s Protest Movements," in *Changing the World, Changing Oneself: Political Protest and Collective Identities in West Germany and the U.S. in the 1960s and 1970s*, eds. B. Davis, W. Mausbach, M. Klimke and C. MacDougall (New York and Oxford: Berghahn, 2010), pp. 26–7.

[17] John McCormick, Weber, *Habermas and the Transformations of the European State: Constitutional, Social and Supranational Democracy* (Cambridge UK and New York: Cambridge University Press, 2007).

of historical specificity vis-à-vis Horkheimer's early work. Despite his claims that *The Theory of Communicative Action* represents an attempt to continue the model of Critical Theory developed by the Institute for Social Research in the 1930s,[18] Habermas has explicitly broken with the Hegelian, Marxist, and Freudian foundations of Horkheimer's early work. Habermas's new model, which draws instead on the Kantian and pragmatist philosophical traditions and the tradition of evolutionary psychology, relies primarily on *normative*, not historical or social-psychological, forms of argumentation. However one evaluates the merits and demerits of Habermas's massive theoretical project, it should now be clear that his criticisms of *Dialectic of Enlightenment* do not apply to Horkheimer's early Critical Theory. I would like to suggest that Horkheimer's early Critical Theory can provide those interested in the tradition of the Frankfurt School with an alternative to both *Dialectic of Enlightenment* and to Habermas's later work. Habermas deserves credit for addressing the liberal-democratic political deficit in Horkheimer and Adorno's early work, but a Critical Theory adequate to the twenty-first century cannot afford to jettison the legacies of Marx and Freud, as Habermas has done. A new model of Critical Theory would need to preserve the traditions of historical materialism and psychoanalysis along with the best aspects of the liberal-democratic political tradition.[19] However, an elaboration of these claims will have to wait until a future study; let us return to our main argument: the need for a critical historicization of *Dialectic of Enlightenment* and a reconsideration of Horkheimer's early Critical Theory.

In Chapter 9 we saw that Horkheimer's shift to a theoretical position that anticipated *Dialectic of Enlightenment* was motivated primarily by his acceptance of a modified version of Friedrich Pollock's "state capitalism" thesis.[20] Horkheimer believed that the contradictory dynamic of capitalism had been brought under control for the foreseeable future by the different versions of authoritarian state capitalism. Due to this new "primacy of the political," the categories of Marx's critique of political economy were allegedly no longer relevant, insofar as they had described a society that was dominated by an abstract process of the self-valorization of capital that was ultimately beyond anyone's control. However, as Moishe Postone has convincingly argued, Horkheimer and Pollock's model of "state capitalism" reflected social and historical conditions that were specific to the mid-twentieth century.[21] Horkheimer and Pollock outlined the new forms of state-centric capitalism that emerged around the globe in the wake of the definitive collapse of the liberal world order in the late

---

[18] Jürgen Habermas, *Theorie des kommunikative Handelns*, vol. 2, (Frankfurt a.M.: Suhrkamp, 1981), pp. 554ff. See also "Introduction," *Max Horkheimer: Between Philosophy and Social Science*, op. cit., p. 12.

[19] Under "best aspects" one could include, minimally, the division of powers, the rule of law, and the preservation and expansion of subjective rights. These rights need not include unlimited property rights, but they would not only preserve basic civil rights (including the right "to be different without fear" as Adorno once put it), but also create new social rights, such as the right to adequate housing, health care, and education.

[20] See footnote 3.

[21] Moishe Postone and Barbara Brick, "Critical Theory and Political Economy," op. cit., p. 246.

1920s.[22] At the time, Horkheimer could find no reason to doubt that the various forms of state-centric capitalism could maintain themselves indefinitely. The fact that they persisted only a few decades and that the independent dynamic of capital reasserted itself with a vengeance during the era of neo-liberal globalization casts serious doubt on his assumption that the underlying contradictions of bourgeois society had in fact been overcome.[23] Toward the end of his life, Adorno also recognized that the seeming disappearance of the contradictory dynamic of capitalism was in fact an epiphenomenon that would not persist much longer.[24] If we return to the interpretation of *Dialectic of Enlightenment* discussed earlier – that it was in fact intended primarily as an interpretation of the present – it now appears as an expression of a historical period that was much shorter lived than Horkheimer and Adorno originally believed. In retrospect we can see that state capitalism did not, in fact, signal the end of the bourgeois epoch, as Horkheimer and Adorno believed in the 1940s.[25] The most recent global economic crisis and the persistence of authoritarian social-psychological tendencies diagnosed by Horkheimer and Fromm in the 1930s provide further evidence that we are still living in the "bourgeois epoch."[26] Thus, Horkheimer's early model of Critical Theory, which still rested on a critical appropriation of Marx's categories and an analysis of the "anthropology of the bourgeois epoch," should still speak to us in important ways.

There is no compelling reason to single out *Dialectic of Enlightenment* as the principal work of the "first-generation of the Frankfurt School." Such a construct implies a uniformity both among and between the "generations" that has never really existed. This study has attempted to demonstrate that Horkheimer (with the help of Erich Fromm) developed a model of Critical Theory in the 1930s that was distinct from *Dialectic of Enlightenment*. The model of a "dialectic of bourgeois society," which underlies Horkheimer's early work, is just as important in the tradition of Critical Theory – and has more contemporary relevance – than the later model of a "dialectic of Enlightenment." Not only does Horkheimer's early Critical Theory provide a more nuanced interpretation of the historical Enlightenment, which resists its reduction to a mere episode in the larger unfolding of instrumental reason; but the greater

---

[22] Karl Polanyi, *The Great Transformation*, op. cit.

[23] It is generally agreed that these state-centric forms of capitalism came to an end in the West in the 1970s with the rise of new "post-Fordist" forms of increasingly globalized "flexible accumulation," and in the East with the final collapse in 1989 of the Soviet Union, which was unable to adapt its centralized economy to the changed conditions. See David Harvey, *The Condition of Postmodernity: An Enquiry into the Origins of Cultural Change* (Cambridge, MA: Blackwell, 1990) and *A Brief History of Neo-Liberalism* (New York: Oxford University Press, 2005).

[24] Theodor Adorno, "Spätkapitalismus oder Industriegesellschaft?" *Soziologische Schriften*, vol. 1, op. cit., pp. 354–70.

[25] See footnote 23.

[26] On the continuing relevance of Horkheimer and Fromm's social-psychological categories in the postwar period, see John Abromeit, "The Limits of Praxis: The Social-Psychological Foundations of Herbert Marcuse and Theodor Adorno's Interpretations of the 1960s Protest Movements," *Changing the World, Changing Oneself: Political Protest and Collective Identities in the 1960s/70s West Germany and U.S.*, eds. B. Davis, W. Mausbach, M. Klimke, and C. MacDougall (Oxford and New York: Berghahn Books, 2010).

openness of Horkheimer's early Critical Theory to research in other disciplines and to empirical social research also speaks to us more today. Rather simply dismissing the "bourgeois" sciences as fatally flawed, as he and Adorno did in *Dialectic of Enlightenment*, in his early work Horkheimer followed the examples set by Hegel and Marx, with their distinctions between understanding and reason, and research and presentation, respectively. In the 1930s, the Institute drew freely on research conducted in many disciplines, while at the same time incorporating it into a larger, self-reflexive theory of history and society, which refused to simply accept the current academic division of labor as an unquestionable fact. Such a model bodes well for those who want to avoid a sterile theoretical purism on the one hand, and an unreflective fetishism of the facts on the other. Such a model should appeal not just to Critical Theorists, but to anyone who shares Horkheimer's belief that the ultimate aim of the pursuit of knowledge is not the establishment of timeless truths, but rather the improvement of the lives of finite human beings.

Selected Bibliography

Horkheimer's Works

A comprehensive bibliography of Horkheimer's published works (including translations) can be found in volume 19 of his *Gesammelte Schriften*. Volume 18 of
the *Gesammelte Schriften* includes a comprehensive index of Horkheimer's
correspondence.

In German:

Gesammelte Schriften. 19 Volumes. Edited by Alfred Schmidt and Gunzelin Schmid
  Noerr. Frankfurt a.M.: Fischer Verlag, 1985–1996.

In English:

A Life in Letters: Selected Correspondence. Trans. and Ed. Manfred R. and Evelyn
  Jacobsen. Lincoln and London: University of Nebraska Press, 2007.

"Bergson's Metaphysics of Time." Trans. Peter Thomas. *Radical Philosophy*. No. 131
  (May–June, 2005): 9–19.

Between Philosophy and Social Science: Selected Early Writings. Trans. G. Frederick
  Hunter, Matthew S. Kramer, and John Torpey. Cambridge, MA: MIT Press, 1993.

Critical Theory: Selected Essays. Trans. Matthew J. O'Connell. New York: Continuum,
  1992.

Critique of Instrumental Reason: Lectures and Essays since the End of World War II.
  Trans. Matthew J. O'Connell. New York: Continuum, 1996.

Dawn and Decline: Notes 1926–1931 and 1950–1969. Trans. Michael Shaw.
  New York: Seabury, 1978.

Eclipse of Reason. New York: Continuum, 1974. Max Horkheimer and Theodor
  W. Adorno. *Dialectic of Enlightenment: Philosophical Fragments*. Trans. Edmund
  Jephcott. Ed. Gunzelin Schmid Noerr. Stanford: Stanford University Press, 2002.

Other Key Works Cited

Adorno, Theodor. *Gesammelte Schriften*. 20 Volumes. Ed. Rolf Tiedemann. Frankfurt
  a.M.: Suhrkamp, 1997.

"The Actuality of Philosophy." Trans. Benjamin Snow. *The Adorno Reader*. Ed. Brian
  O'Conner. Oxford, UK and Malden, MA: Blackwell: 2000.

*Against Epistemology: A Metacritique. Studies in Husserl and the Phenomenological
  Antinomies*. Trans. Willis Domingo. Cambridge, MA: MIT Press, 1983.

"The Idea of Natural History." Trans. Robert Hullot-Kentor. *Telos*. No. 60 (Summer,
  1984).

Kierkegaard: Construction of the Aesthetic. Trans. Robert Hullot-Kentor. Minneapolis:
  University of Minnesota Press, 1989.

Minima Moralia. Trans. Edmund Jephcott. New York and London: Verso, 1974.

Negative Dialectics. Trans. E.B. Ashton. New York: Continuum, 1973.

Asbach, Olaf. *Von der Erkenntnistheorie zur Kritischen Theorie des Gesellschaft: Eine Untersuchung zur Vor- und Entstehungsgeschichte der Kritischen Theorie Max Horkheimers 1920–27.* Opladen, Germany: Leske und Budrich, 1997.

Kritische Gesellschaftstheorie und historische Praxis : Entwicklungen der Kritischen Theorie bei Max Horkheimer 1930–1942/43. Frankfurt a.M., Berlin, Bern, New York, Paris, and Vienna: Lang, 1997.

Benjamin, Walter. *Illuminations*. Trans. Harry Zohn. Ed. Hannah Arendt. New York: Schocken, 1968.

Buck-Morss, Susan. *The Origins of Negative Dialectics: Theodor Adorno, Walter Benjamin and the Frankfurt Institute.* New York: Free Press, 1977.

Claussen, Detlev. *Theodor Adorno: One Last Genius.* Trans. Rodney Livingstone. Cambridge MA: Harvard University Press, 2008.

Dubiel, Helmut. *Theory and Politics: Studies in the Development of Critical Theory.* Trans. Benjamin Gregg. Cambridge, MA: MIT Press, 1985.

The Essential Frankfurt School Reader. Eds. Andrew Arato and Eike Gebhardt. New York: Continuum, 1982.

Fromm, Erich. *The Dogma of Christ: And Other Essays on Religion, Psychology, and Culture.* Trans. James Luther Adams. New York: Holt, Rinehart and Winston, 1963.

The Working Class in Weimar Germany: A Psychological and Sociological Study. Ed. Wolfgang Bonß. Trans. B. Weinberger. Warwickshire, UK: Berg, 1984.

Habermas, Jürgen. *The Philosophical Discourse of Modernity.* Trans. Frederick G. Lawrence. Cambridge, MA: MIT Press, 1987.

The Structural Transformation of the Public Sphere: An Inquiry into a Category of Bourgeois Society. Trans. Thomas Burger. Cambridge, MA: MIT Press, 1989.

Theory of Communicative Action. vol. 1. *Reason and the Rationalization of Society.* Trans. Thomas McCarthy. Boston: Beacon, 1984.

Theory of Communicative Action. vol. 2. *Lifeworld and System: A Critique of Functionalist Reason.* Trans. Thomas McCarthy. Boston: Beacon, 1987.

Herbert Marcuse *Negations: Essays in Critical Theory.* Trans. Jeremy J. Shapiro. Boston: Beacon, 1988.

Jay, Martin. *The Dialectical Imagination: A History of the Frankfurt School and the Institute of Social Research, 1923–1950.* Boston, Toronto, and London: Little, Brown and Company, 1973.

Küsters, Gerd-Walters. *Der Kritikbegriff in der Kritischen Theorie Max Horkheimers.* Frankfurt and New York: Campus, 1980.

Löwenthal, Leo. *An Unmastered Past: The Autobiographical Reflections of Leo Lowenthal.* Ed. Martin Jay. Berkeley, Los Angeles and London: University of California Press, 1987.

Lukács, Georg. *History and Class Consciousness.* Trans. Rodney Livingstone. Cambridge, MA: MIT Press, 2002.

The Theory of the Novel. Trans. Anna Bostock. Cambridge, MA: MIT Press, 1971.

On Max Horkheimer: New Perspectives. Eds. Seyla Benhabib, Wolfgang Bonß, and John McCole. Cambridge MA: MIT Press, 1993.

Migdal, Ulrike. *Die Frühgeschichte des Frankfurter Instituts für Sozialforschung.* Frankfurt and New York: Campus, 1981.

Müller-Doohm, Stefan. *Adorno: A Biography.* Trans. Rodney Livingstone. Cambridge, UK and Malden, MA: Polity Press, 2005.

Postone, Moishe. *Time, Labor and Social Domination: A Reinterpretation of Marx's Critical Theory.* Cambridge, UK: Cambridge University Press, 1993.

Sichel, Kim. *Germaine Krull: Photographer of Modernity*. Cambridge, MA: MIT Press, 1999.

Stirk, Peter. *Max Horkheimer: A New Interpretation*. Hemel Hempstead: Harvester Wheatsheaf, 1992.

Studien über Autorität und Familie: Forschungsberichte aus dem Institut für Sozialforschung. Ed. Max Horkheimer. Paris: Felix Alcan, 1936.

Theodor Adorno and Walter Benjamin: The Complete Correspondence, 1928–1940. Trans. Nicholas Walker. Ed. Henri Lonitz. Cambridge, MA: Harvard University Press, 1999.

Wiggershaus, Rolf. *The Frankfurt School: Its History, Theories and Political Significance*. Trans. Michael Robertson. Cambridge, MA: MIT Press, 1994.

Wolin, Richard. *Walter Benjamin: An Aesthetic of Redemption*. Berkeley and Los Angeles: University of California Press, 1994.

Index

Positivism, 23, 57, 66–7, 81, 92, 111, 120, 125–9, 131–2, 137, 139, 141, 143, 228, 232–3, 235–6, 259, 268, 304, 311, 353, 356, 363, 376, 381, 383, 389

Postone, Moishe, 2, 177, 217, 329, 381, 409, 420–4, 427, 430

Pragmatism, 13, 232, 332–3

Praxis, 42, 66, 151, 155, 180, 241, 307–8, 318, 322, 326, 328, 333–4, 353, 369, 384, 388–9

Psychoanalysis, 11, 17, 52, 81, 85, 142, 158, 185, 187, 189–96, 198–204, 206–8, 210–12, 216, 219, 226, 252, 255, 274–6, 279, 313, 321–2, 324, 339, 341, 344, 346, 350, 392, 430

Rationalism, 11, 71, 95, 98–103, 105, 112, 115, 117, 143, 197–8, 200, 232, 267, 303–6, 308, 314–15, 372, 400, 428

Reformation, 11, 244, 261, 266, 272–3

Reich, Wilhelm, 201, 286

Reichmann, Frieda (Fromm-), 185, 187, 189, 192–5, 201, 203, 213

Reik, Theodor, 205, 207, 252

Renaissance, 10, 69, 90–3, 97, 120, 239, 244

Ressentiment, 169, 206, 281

Riekher, Rosa, 16, 21, 31–2, 40–2, 44, 48, 50, 53–4, 58, 60, 68–9, 165, 181, 191

Rienzo, Cola di (also spelled "Rienzi"), 261, 263, 265, 270–1, 288, 380, 388

Robespierre, Maximilien, 263–4, 270–1, 288, 388

Rousseau, Jean-Jacques, 15, 106, 169, 174, 264, 271, 278, 388

Ryazanov, David, 182

Sadism, 278–9, 288, 379

Savonarola, Girolamo, 263, 270–1, 273, 288

Scheler, Max, 91, 121, 132, 136–7, 218, 235, 249

Schelling, Friedrich Wilhelm Joseph, 23, 57, 113–14, 117, 136, 315–16, 385

Schmid Noerr, Gunzelin, 2, 23, 25–7, 62, 90, 120–1, 142, 145, 152, 157, 185, 192, 290, 301, 312, 390, 392–3

Schmidt, Alfred, 2, 28, 47, 139, 152, 155, 165, 170, 196, 326, 425

Schopenhauer, Arthur, 24–5, 27–8, 46–8, 52–3, 60, 79, 131, 134, 148–9, 160, 165, 196–7,

230, 242, 281, 331, 422; *Aphorismen zur Lebensweisheit* (The Wisdom of Life), 24; *The World as Will and Representation*, 60, 165

Sensualism, 106, 110, 233–5

Skepticism, 7, 15, 37, 54, 73, 110–12, 116, 130, 175, 233–6, 308, 320, 360, 366, 398–400

Smith, Adam, 108–9

Social Democratic Party (SPD), 37, 41, 43, 56, 179, 182, 204, 212, 223, 254, 280, 379, 409

Social totality, 82, 123, 129–30, 138, 156, 158, 163, 239–40, 303, 314–15, 323, 329, 356–8, 370, 414, 418, 422–3

Sohn-Rethel, Alfred, 366, 383–5, 387–8

Soviet Union, 41, 61, 150, 178, 180–3, 399, 402–3, 406, 409–10, 431

Spengler, Oswald, 135–6

Spinoza, Baruch, 94–6, 98–100, 115, 154, 317, 363

Stalin, Joseph, 180–2, 410

State capitalism, 15, 17–18, 227, 336, 346, 395, 400–5, 407–12, 414, 418–20, 424–6, 430

Stirk, Peter, 2, 7, 70, 90, 242, 257, 265, 268

Studies on Authority and Family (see "Institute for Social Research")

Theology, 101–2, 272, 356, 362–4, 366–7, 374

Tillich, Paul, 143, 197, 351–2

Toller, Ernst, 41, 43–4, 51

Utilitarianism, 233, 237

Vitalism (see "Lebensphilosophie")

Voltaire, 48, 99, 102, 104, 106, 108, 158, 169, 230; *Candide*, 48, 230

Weber, Alfred 145, 186, 203, 213

Wesensschau, (see "Intuition of Essences")

Weil, Felix, 16, 55–6, 61–2, 64, 182, 188

Wiggershaus, Rolf, 1–2, 62–3, 143, 183, 186, 192, 259, 282, 288, 293–5, 336–7, 347

Wolff, Christian, 76, 98, 111, 115, 198

Zeitschrift für Sozialforchung, (see "Institute for Social Research")

Zetkin, Clara, 55–6

Zionism, 20, 188, 203

Made in the USA
Middletown, DE
27 July 2018